The Gun Digest® Book Of

Trap & Skeet Shooting

4TH Edition

by
Chris Christian
and
Rick Sapp

©2004 KP Books

Published by

Gun Digest® Books

An imprint of F+W Publications
700 East State Street • Iola, WI 54990-0001
715-445-2214 • 888-457-2873
www.gundigestbooks.com

Our toll-free number to place an order or obtain
a free catalog is (800) 258-0929.

Library of Congress Control Number: 2002107613

ISBN-13: 978-0-87349-428-1
ISBN-10: 0-87349-428-8

Designed by Kara Grundman
Edited by Dan Shideler

Printed in the United States of America

ABOUT THE AUTHORS

Co-author Chris Christian is an award-winning free-lance outdoor writer whose work has appeared in virtually every major outdoor magazine in the country. His editorial credits include publications as diverse as the *Palatka Daily News, Florida Sportsman, Gun World*, and *Thickets Hunting and Fishing Guide*.

After a decade-long hitch in the U.S. Navy during the Vietnam era, Christian settled on the banks of Florida's St. John's River, where he embarked on a new career as a hunting and fishing guide. He occupied his few empty hours by penning articles for various sporting publications, an avocation which quickly blossomed into a full-time gig.

An enthusiastic shotgunner, Christian is a former AA Class skeet shooter who prefers to stay well-rounded in all games instead of specializing in just one. He divides his time between Trap, Bunker Trap, International Skeet, 5-Stand, and American Skeet – all of which he considers practice for his favorite shooting game: Sporting Clays.

Chris Christian

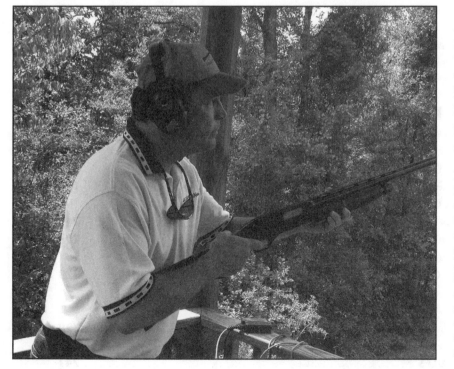

Rick Sapp

One of the best-rounded figures in outdoor sports literature, **co-author Rick Sapp** has been blessed with the opportunity to shoot, hunt and fish across the United States. He has taken trophy bears with a bow and arrow, pulled walleye through holes in the ice of frozen Minnesota lakes, "tossed his cookies" over the side of fishing boats on the Gulf of Mexico, and missed spectacularly easy shots on skeet station #7.

Growing up on an island off the coast of Florida, Rick loved nothing better than tying a BB gun on the handle bars of his bicycle and pedaling to remote and romantic hammocks, sand dunes and swamps, to stalk bears, re-create Civil War battles or even fight alongside Superman and Roy Rogers. A veteran of the shooting, hunting, and outdoor trades industry, Sapp has a breadth of interests and expertise that is equaled by few and exceeded by none. Today, Rick's driving passion is to understand and write about the spirit of the shooting sports and the outdoor adventure.

TABLE OF CONTENTS

INTRODUCTION

Hallelujah! People are finally discovering that smoking a clay target isn't just something to do with your shotgun when bird seasons are closed. It's a lot of fun in its own right, and it's a sport the entire family can enjoy in a congenial, safe, and environmentally friendly manner. It's not as though clay targets are some sort of endangered species. They're made of pitch and resin and if we run short of them, we'll just make more!

We won't be so presumptuous as to claim that this book will make you a champion at any shotgun game. Reaching that level of expertise requires the keen reflexes, visual acuity and hand/eye coordination–plus plenty of practice–that are hallmarks of any successful athlete.

Some people have it and some people don't. However, if you are a novice or intermediate shooter, we are firmly convinced that you will find in these pages the information you need to improve your game. And it wouldn't surprise us if some expert shooters find a nugget or two in this volume to help them get that all-important "one more bird" – often the difference between the winner and the runner-up.

This book is organized into well-defined chapters covering Trap, Skeet, and Sporting Clays separately. This is an organizational device only. We certainly don't intend to suggest that these games are radically different from one another, or to imply that the techniques that apply to one do not apply to another. Nothing could be further from the truth.

Truth be told, an aerial target is an aerial target. Regardless of its distance, angle, speed, and direction, the shooter must have the gun properly positioned on his shoulder, must have his body properly oriented toward the target, and must keep the gun moving when he triggers the shot. Other major assets are a properly-fitted shotgun, the correct choke for the job, and quality loads that will get the job done. Poor equipment selection will hurt your scores; good equipment will improve them. You'll find a lot of discussion about these factors in this book, and understanding their importance will prove a benefit to you as you participate in any shotgun sport.

There has always been friendly disagreement among shooters over the various differences in skill levels required to achieve success in the array of shotgun games. Naturally, the most difficult game usually happens to be the one the individual at the podium shoots best!

Having shot all the games discussed in this book, some more successfully than others, we have our own opinions on this subject and cheerfully pour the following gasoline onto the fire:

The easiest game to learn initially is 16-Yard ATA Trap. You don't have to think – you just point the gun at the trap house and react to whatever target comes out.

The easiest game to master is American-style Skeet. It may look complicated at first, but once you learn the required position and lead for each target it becomes the easiest game in which to run 25 straight.

The most physically challenging game is International Skeet. The extreme low gun position and speed of the targets will test your coordination to the limit. It makes the other games look easy.

When it comes to the game that's the most fun, it's got to be a toss-up between Sporting Clays, Doubles Trap, and Bunker Trap. All three are fast-paced and offer challenges that are all their own.

The game requiring the greatest overall skill level? We'd have to say FITASC/Sporting Clays. No two courses are alike, and shooters have to adjust quickly to tremendously varied target presentations, each possibly requiring the shooter to change not only his load but his choke, stance, and shooting technique as well. The best way to learn all these challenging games is to shoot Trap and Skeet from a low gun position. You'll see all of these targets on the sporting fields!

We are very fortunate to be living in The Golden Age of shooting games. Never, and we mean never, has their been such a wide range of shotguns, loads, and accessories all specifically designed for us clay-busters. Regardless of whether your shooting budget is limited to the family cookie jar or you've just won the Powerball lottery, you'll find that you can afford serviceable, high-quality equipment that will help you get to the top of your personal game.

But the bottom line will always be this: an aerial target is an aerial target, no matter which game you're shooting at the moment. Open this book, and start mastering them all!

The Authors

ACKNOWLEDGMENTS

No book of this size and scope is produced solely on the efforts of one person. This one is no exception, and we enjoyed help from a number of folks who deserve special recognition and our very sincere thanks.

To Skeet masters Keith Otero, Roy Dear, and Mary Beverly; Sporting Clays champions Bill Whitehurst and Bonnie McLaurin; and Trap experts Jim Pettingill and Mark & Lisa Sever, we offer our sincere thanks for the knowledge you shared.

A special thank-you to shotgun coach Lloyd Woodhouse of the United States Shooting Team for his invaluable insights into the more subtle aspects of successful clay target shooting.

To Jack Baier of Turkey Run Sporting Clays course and Wayne Pearce of the Gator Skeet & Trap Club for graciously giving us free run of their facilities. A special thanks to our friends at the Palatka Skeet Club and to skeet shooter Bob Lee for his invaluable photographic assistance.

To those industry experts who so willingly gave of their time and expertise, we offer a very sincere thanks. Without them, this book would not have been possible.

And, finally, a special salute to Staff Sergeant Joseph J. Johnson of the Public Affairs Office of the United States Army Marksmanship Units.

THE ART OF WINGSHOOTING

Reducing an aerial target to a puff of dust, or a ball of feathers, has been called a combination of art and science. That is about as succinct a definition of wingshooting as I have ever heard. It applies whether the target is made of pitch and resin, or feathers and bone.

The classic aspects of wingshooting will be addressed in later chapters. As we go along, we will discuss the "tools of the trade": the newest shotguns, effective loads, proper barrel and stock work, chokes, patterns and the other invaluable aids that play such a large role in wingshooting success.

For now, however, the artistic side of wingshooting is worthy of consideration on its own. If you have ever watched a master wingshooter break aerial targets with a consistent combination of fluid grace and blazing speed, I think you will agree that it is true artistry. Nevertheless, it may surprise you to learn that no two shooters execute that artistry in precisely the same way. The reason is that it is extremely rare to be able to shoot directly at a moving target with a stationary gun and hit it. Simply put, one must deliver the shot charge to the place where the target will be when the shot charge arrives. That requires the gun to be moving at the moment the shot is triggered and most often it will be pointed somewhere other than directly at the target!

In that respect, connecting with an aerial target is no different from an NFL quarterback tossing a deep pass to a sprinting receiver going deep. The quarterback certainly cannot throw the ball directly at the target because it would land far behind. Instead, he must place it at a point where the receiver and the ball will meet. The Brett Favres of the world have learned to accomplish that feat (usually) without requiring that their receiver break stride. The journeymen of the game also get the job done, although not quite as impressively and perhaps not in the same manner. The same is true of wingshooting.

The Basics of Lead

A number of shooting techniques result in the shot charge and target arriving at the same place at the same time. Each requires the shooter to comprehend a slightly different relationship between his muzzle and the target. Nevertheless, even shooters using the same technique occasionally have different explanations for the relationship they see at the instant they trigger the shot.

Market hunter Fred Kimble shot thousands of ducks during the 1800s, but it is said that he could not consistently explain lead on a flying bird. Still, Kimble is considered by some shotgun historians to have been one of the greatest shots of all time. Kimble said that the most common lead he used on ducks crossing at 40 yards was one bird length. At 60 yards, his lead increased to two bird lengths. That is not much lead!

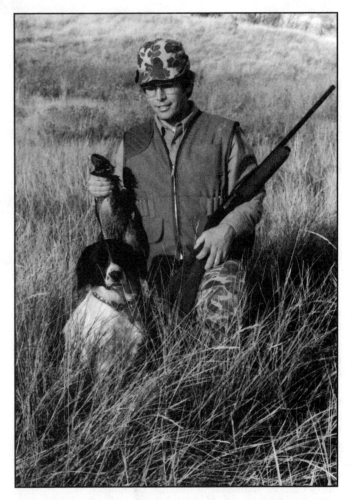

Author Rick Sapp began his wingshooting career with a Remington 1100 semi-auto and a friend's Springer spaniel named Katy in the pheasant fields of Minnesota and South Dakota. "With a good dog, even a blind man will hit a bird every now and then," Rick says. (Photo courtesy Don Friberg)

The average mallard measures about 24 inches in length. If the average speed of a flying mallard is about 35 miles per hour and the target range is 40 yards, the lead required would be about 6 ½ feet if the shot charge velocity is 1235 feet per second. Yet, curiously enough, Kimble saw no more than 24 inches of lead.

According to my computer, Kimble could not have killed any ducks. Yet, he is considered to have been one of the finest wingshots who ever lived. How did he do it? This is the

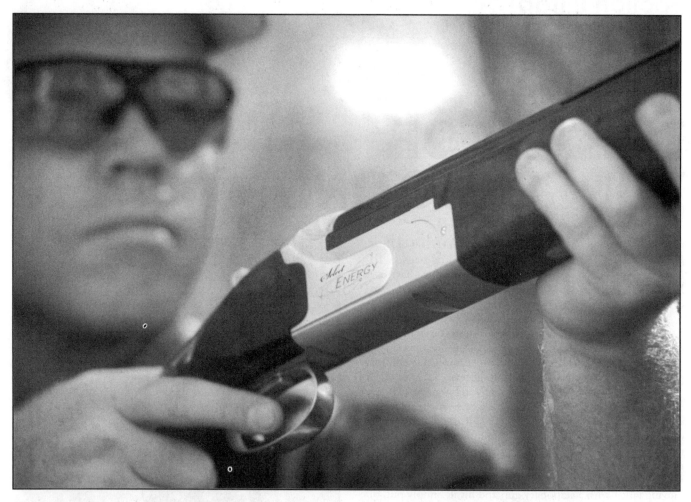

The hallmark of most successful competitors is the ability to focus. This means different things to different people, but it is "compartmentalizing" the brain. Focus on THIS shot. Put the lost bird at the last station completely aside, along with the annoying shooter standing too close to your back and the slightly bent frame of your shooting glasses. Look at – contemplate – one thing: breaking THIS bird. (Photo courtesy Winchester)

point where the individual artistry and ability of a wingshooter surface.

There are several useful shooting techniques that will put you on a bird. Computer figures can be given for the "sustained lead" method, sometimes called the "maintained lead" by our British friends. As we will see later, this is the only shooting system in which precise leads can be computed and remain true for all shooters. With the leads he said he observed, Kimble could not have used this system. Instead, he had to have used one of the "fast-swing/swing-through" techniques.

The "swing-through" shooter begins with the gun mounted <u>behind</u> the moving target and swings the muzzle through it. He triggers the shot when he reaches a distance in front of the target that his previous experience and subconscious mental computer tells him is correct for "lead," the amount of forward allowance that will put his shot charge effectively on the target. Using this technique, the gun is moving faster than the target and there is a delay between thought and action. That microsecond delay involves the body's muscles and the mechanical action of the shotgun. By the time both of these elements are overcome and the primer ignites the shell, the gun has continued to swing past the target and the true lead is actually greater than you perceive. Although Kimble may only have seen two feet of lead on a 40-yard crossing target, his shooting style actually gave him more than that.

You can test how the "swing-through" method works for yourself. Pound a stake into the ground and back up 30 to 40 yards. Now, swing your shotgun from left to right through the stake. Trigger a shot when your eyes tell you the gun muzzle is dead-on the stake. You will not hit it. Your shot will land past the stake in the direction you are swinging.

Repeat this exercise and vary the speed of your swing. You will soon realize that the faster you swing, the farther beyond the stake the shot charge lands.

The more quickly your mind perceives the relationship between your muzzle and the target (or "reads the bird picture") and the more consistently you react to it, the more consistent the impact point of the shot charge will be.

This is why no two shooters can be taught in exactly the same manner. A slight difference in swing speed or a minor variation in visual acuity or reflexes will cause shooters using the same "fast-swing/swing-through" technique to steadfastly maintain that they use two completely different amounts of lead on identical targets.

Every individual's basic biomechanics and the way we learn to use our muscles are different, so it is virtually impossible to clone a shooter. Teaching that there is only one correct way to shoot an aerial target is to deny that individuals are just that: individuals.

To become a good shooter, each person must first be

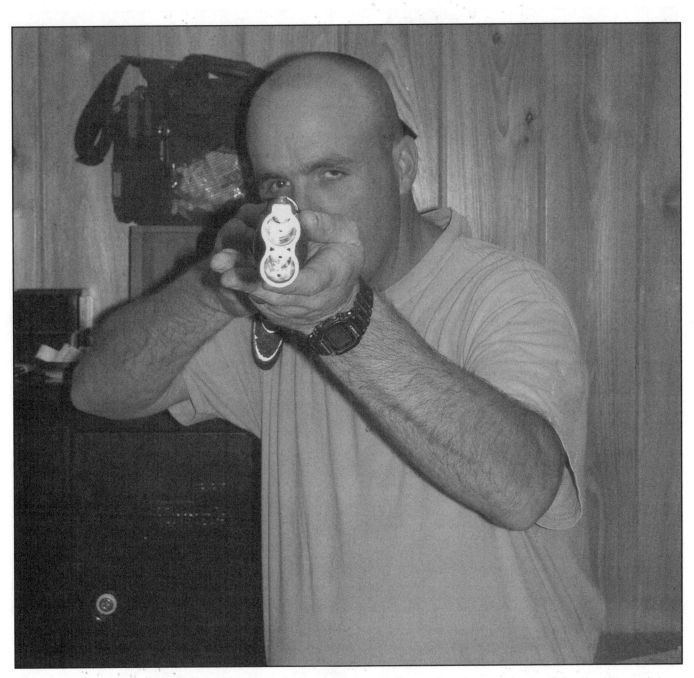

For the ideal gun hold position, your eye should consistently look along the flat surface down the center of the rib when you bring your gun to position. This is something you can practice at home in front of a mirror.

grounded in the fundamentals. After that, the shooter is free to develop his or her "personal style." Some shooters are perfectly comfortable with an extremely fast swing on close-range (under 20 yards) targets. They swing so quickly that they will say they see no lead at all; they shoot when the muzzle connects with the bird. Double that distance and some shooters change their shooting style to more of a "sustained lead" or a "pull-away" technique. Why do they abandon the fast swing just because target distance increases? The answer probably is that they are not comfortable trying to quickly perceive the two to three feet of forward allowance they require. They find that at distant birds a more controlled shooting technique is not only comfortable, but also effective for them. For other shooters, the reverse might very well be true.

Stance Is Important

Knowledgeable shooters will attempt to learn as many of the various shooting techniques as they can and then will determine which works best for them under varying shooting conditions. One of the fundamentals of any shooting equation, however, is achieving a proper shooting stance.

Your stance provides a platform for your gun and allows you to place the load on the target. That is really all it does, yet this simplification is sometimes overlooked when new shooters are excited about busting birds.

Consider that a rifleman attempting to place a single bullet within a five-inch circle at 200 yards from a standing position requires a rigid platform to execute a precise shot. Anything he can do to minimize body movement and sight wobble will

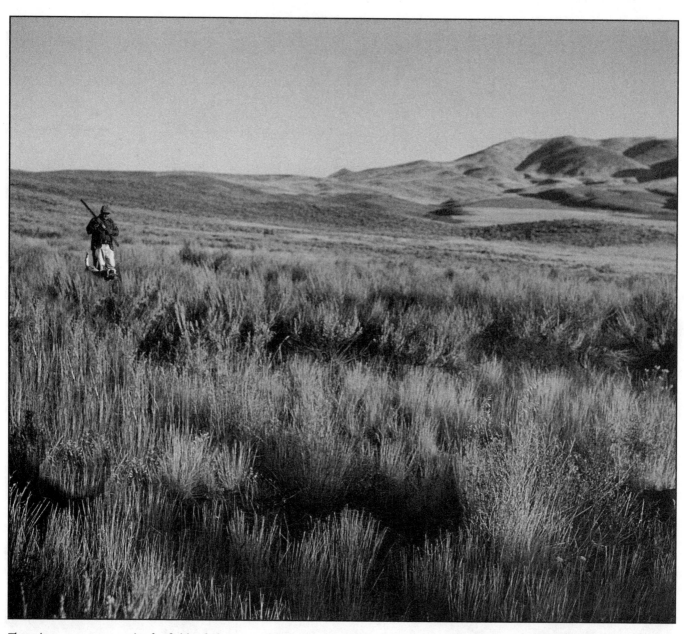

There is no greater practice for fields of pheasants than trap or sporting clays. The basics of shooting on the line and in the field are the same. You will, of course, need to put them into practice faster and with more unexpected angles in the rolling hills of South Dakota.

be beneficial. Shooting a rifle calls for weight to be evenly distributed, with perhaps a slight emphasis on the rear foot. The shooter's arms holding the gun must be brought close to the central body mass, and the leading hand should be in direct alignment with the body's long axis for best support. The entire objective is to "freeze" the gun long enough to align the sights with the center of the target and the shot to be triggered.

A shotgunner has very different requirements. The shot must be triggered from a fluidly moving gun and the body must be relaxed enough to swing the gun through a considerable arc. A rifleman who moves his gun a fraction of an inch an inch will miss his mark, yet a shotgunner who is, for example, taking a high house station four target in international skeet may need to swing as much as 90 degrees to hit a bird at 20 yards!

Obviously, the stance that works for the rifleman will not work for the shotgunner. Binding themselves into too rigid a stance is one of the biggest mistakes new shooters make.

The shotgunner needs to be able to execute a wide range of movement in both the horizontal and vertical planes, because he or she may have to swing quickly on rising, falling or even sharply angled targets. Such fluid movement is best accomplished with greater weight (and hence, balance) on the forward foot. Some shooters prefer a weight distribution in the neighborhood of 60:40 between the front and the back foot; others like even more weight forward. Hips need to be free to pivot and they are what actually drive the body into the shot. Flex in the knees is desirable, but too much may contribute to erratic gun movement.

A rifleman's stance is rigid. A wingshooter's stance must be one of controlled aggression, a coiled spring ready to release upon command.

The stance that works best for a six-foot 200-pound male may not be the best for a shorter or stouter male or for a female shooter. Shooters must establish a stance or body position that

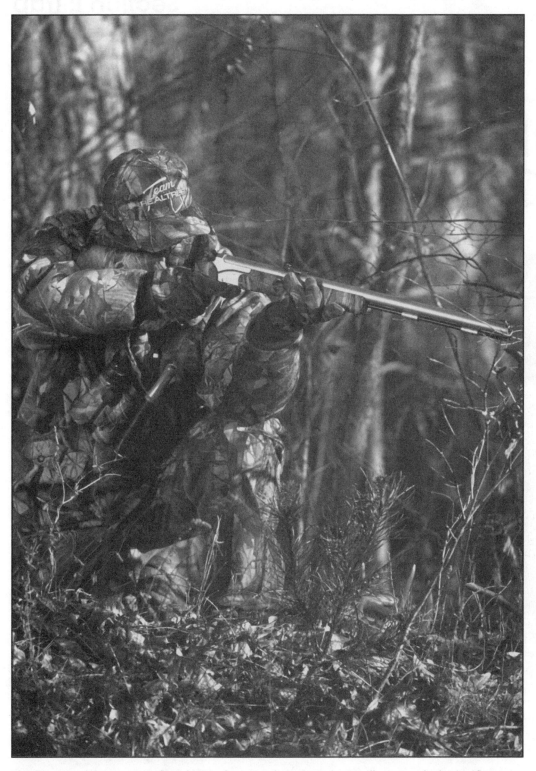

may be identical! As I have said, shooters cannot be cloned. What is true and good and right for one shotgunner may not be for another.

Sometimes shotgunners alter their stance for different shooting situations. In games shot with a pre-mounted gun (doubles trap, bunker trap and handicap trap), some shooters put a little more flex in their knees and a bit more crouch in their body than when they are shooting from an unmounted position. The reason for changing stance is that these are all rising targets, so increased flex in the knees provides a little more power to drive the gun through the target with a fast-swing technique.

Change to sporting clays, international skeet, 5-stand or other games and a low or unmounted gun works better for many. With a low gun, your upper body assumes a more upright position with slightly straighter knees. The most important aspect of stance in low gun games is that the gun be mounted smoothly and consistently every time. The more flex and body crouch the shooter has, the more his critical shoulder pocket shifts as he moves his body to the target. Keeping the body upright and relying on increased hip pivoting achieve a more consistent gun mount.

To become an accomplished wingshooter, you need to understand and practice the fundamentals of stance and gun control.

This big game hunter camouflaged in Realtree Hardwoods Green HD illustrates the basic rifleman's stance – arms close to the body, rigid, centered in support. Effective shotgun shooting requires almost the opposite, emphasizing fluid movement, weight forward, knees flexed and arms bent at 90 degree angles – a coiled spring. The stance has been called "controlled aggression."

lets them do two things: move and swing the gun in a relaxed, controlled manner and yet maintain a stable center of gravity.

When the shotgunner finally finds "his stance," he will detect a noticeable difference in the way he assumes the basic position before calling for a target. Nevertheless, the resulting scores

You will need to pay attention to lead on each shooting station on still and windy days. Then, it is simply a matter of seeing a lot of targets flying at different speeds and different angles. If you are conscientious, your mental computer will soon learn to execute the swing and lead, and pigeons will begin to break as if you had been shooting all your life.

THE OLDEST SHOTGUNNING GAME

Trap machines need occasional servicing and frequent loading. It is a side of the game that shooters rarely see or understand unless they are more than a little curious. Throwing American Trap at a club near you, a LaPorte 185 TA holds 10 columns of 40 birds each or 400 total clays. Recocking time is 1.8 seconds and trajectory can be adjusted without tools. Throwing distance is between 22 and 110 yards.

The game of trap shooting has been around for centuries. One of the earliest printed mentions of the game was in 1793 in an English publication known as *Sporting Magazine*. The article stated that the sport was "...well established recreation." One would assume that it was primarily an English sport at that time. The targets, live pigeons, were held in a box or "trap" as it later came to be called. The birds were released via a string that lifted the lid when the shooter "called for the bird." The first known records of an organized version of trap in the United States may be those contained in the 1831 records of

the Sportsman's Club of Cincinnati, Ohio.

Trap continued to be shot with pigeons into the 20th century although the use of live birds has fallen into disfavor with the public. In 1866, Charles Portlock of Boston, Massachusetts, introduced a glass ball to American target shooters. His balls met with limited success because the levers used to propel them were incompatible with the fragile glass globes, and many balls shattered when they were launched.

Glass ball shooting began to decline when, in about 1880, George Ligowsky invented the first clay pigeon and a machine

The woman with the gun is at least pointing in the right direction, but her stance ensures that she will miss more targets than she hits, even from the 16-yard position. Errors: Vertical stance. Feet together. Left hand too far out on the gun. With a little coaching, she can overcome all of these errors.

to throw it effectively. This was a significant step for shotgun games because the new, disc-shaped clay pigeon simulated the flight of a live bird, whereas the older glass balls were simply lobbed into the air.

Ligowsky's pigeons were actually made of clay and baked in an oven. They were apparently quite hard and it took a precise shot to break one. Today's clay targets are made primarily of pitch and are easier to break.

Trap Shooting Today

Today, the Amateur Trapshooting Association (ATA) regulates trap shooting in America. A complete copy of their rules is included in the end pages of this book.

A trap field consists of a single launcher located in a trap house and partially buried in the ground. Five shooting positions are situated 16 yards behind the trap house and spaced three yards apart. The "16-yard" event, the most common trap game, is shot from these five positions.

From each of the 16-yard positions a lane, marked in yardage increments, leads backward to a point 27 yards behind the trap house. "Handicap trap" is shot from these various yardage markers.

The trap machine launches clay disks at unknown angles for each station. Clays fly within 17.14 degrees of the right or left of the trap center, which is aligned directly with shooting position three. These oscillating traps have built-in interrupters that stagger the flight patterns and prevent the shooter from "reading the trap" or guessing the angle of flight before he or

she shoots. Thus, the shooter is never precisely certain where the bird will fly. The only guarantee is that it will be within a defined zone for each of the five stations.

Standard clay targets are used, and they may be any of a number of colors or color patterns. The pre-set trajectory puts birds between eight and 10 feet above the ground at 10 feet in front of the trap and propels them to a distance between 49 and 51 yards from the trap house.

The two-foot vertical range spread is allowed under ATA rules and compensates for different wind and weather conditions. Most trap ranges set the bird height to about 10 feet under conditions of no wind or a gentle breeze. Should a strong wind blow directly into the trap house, the target trajectory will be set lower to retard rapid climb of the bird and allow it to travel the minimum 49-yard distance. A head wind can make the target climb rapidly. A tail wind, on the other hand, prevents the target from climbing and under these conditions range personnel usually set the target launch to the full 10-foot height to keep a clay in the air long enough to make the required 49-yard distance.

Occasionally, wind shift during a match prevents targets from flying within the prescribed height range and falling within the required distance. In this case, a competitor is well within his rights to ask the referee to stop the match and reset the machine.

The most popular trap event is "16-yard" shooting. Shooters compete within a class system based on their previous scores or known ability to assure that they contend with competitors

Table 2-1. Yard Trap: Classification by Established Average Or Known Ability

Classification	Singles	Doubles
SIX CLASSES		
AAA	98% and over	96% and over
AA	96.25% and under 98%	92% and under 96%
A	94.75% and under 96.25%	89% and under 92%
B	93% and under 94.75%	86% and under 89%
C	90% and under 93%	82% and under 86%
D	Under 90%	Under 82%
FIVE CLASSES		
AA	97% and over	93% and over
A	94% and under 97%	89% and under 93%
B	91% and under 94%	85% and under 89%
C	88% and under 91 %	78% and under 85%
D	Under 88%	Under 78%
FOUR CLASSES		
A	95% and over	90% and over
B	92% and under 95%	85% and under 90%
C	89% and under 92%	78% and under 85%
D	Under 89%	Under 78%
THREE CLASSES		
A	95% and over	89% and over
B	91% and under 95%	83% and under 89%
C	Under 91%	Under 83%

Table 2-2. Trap: Special Competition Categories for Men and Women*

Category	Age
Sub-Junior	Less than 15
Junior	15 to less than 18
Veteran	65 years and older
Senior Veteran	70 years and older

*Women are identified in ATA rules as "ladies."

who have similar skill levels. Previous scores generally require a shooter to have engaged about 500 registered targets, and the percentage of those targets broken will be his or her average. A 16-yard event may have as many as six classes, but if shooter turnout is light, the ATA provides for reducing that number to five, four, or even three classes. See the Table 2-1 for the breakdown. ATA rules also establish competition categories based on the age of the shooter, as shown in Table 2-2.

ATA rules state that no shotgun with a larger bore than 12-gauge may be used. This allows competitors to shoot any of the smaller gauges although few do so because the decreased shot charge is too great a handicap for serious competition. If you are shooting for fun, though, there is nothing wrong with using a smaller gauge. Chris Christian has shot many a round of trap with both the 28-gauge and the 410-bore. "It's fun and

frustrating," he says, "but still a lot of fun!"

Formerly, a three-dram, 1⅛ -oz. 12-ga. load containing premium black #7½ shot was called a "trap load." The new ATA rules are consistent with the 1⅛-oz. 12-ga. load of #7½ (maximum) shot and still ban nickel- and copper-coated shot while allowing lead, steel, bismuth, or "other composite non-toxic shot materials."

Today, with versatile powders, the ATA regulates shells by velocity rather than by dram. You cannot shoot registered birds with 12-ga. loads that exceed 1,290 fps; with 20-ga. loads that exceed 1,325 fps; or with 28-ga. loads that exceed 1,350 fps.

Many shooters today use lighter 12-gauge loads to reduce recoil, reserving the maximum loads for handicap rounds and the second shot in a doubles match.

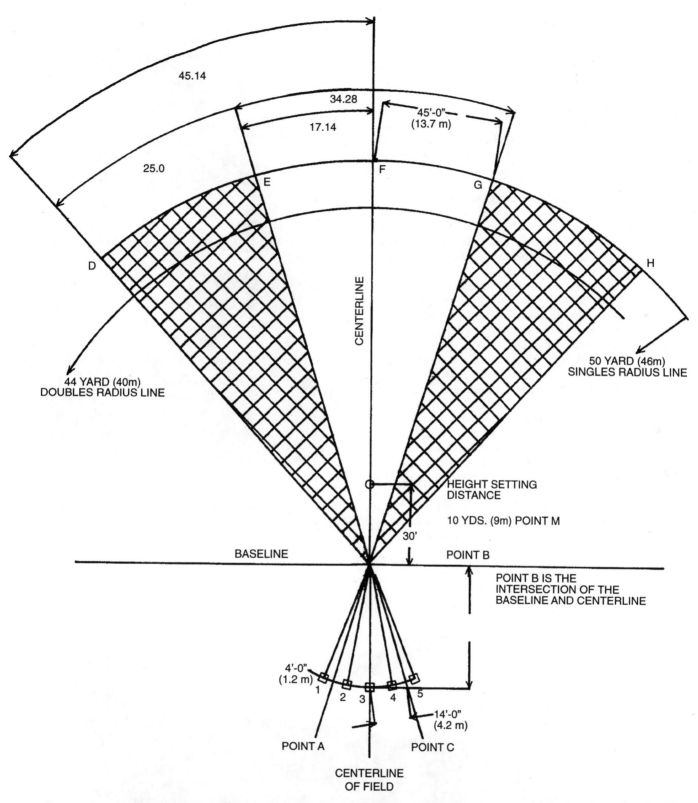

The "Approach" to a trap field positions the trap house and five stations plus the layout of an approach for handicap shooting. The "Field" shows schematically where the traps will fly within regulation parameters. Newcomers to the game should study this diagram so that they are familiar with the options before they call for their first bird.

Etiquette and Procedures

A single round of trap consists of 25 shots and a trap squad may contain up to five shooters.

Each shooter will take one of the five positions or stations and the shooter on station one is the first to shoot. Once he has fired, the shooter on station two may then call for a bird and the other shooters calling for birds in turn. This rotation is repeated until each shooter has fired five rounds from his station.

At that time, the trap puller/scorer calls "Change," followed by a quick rundown of the number of birds each contestant hit at that station: "Change...1-3, 2-4, 3-5, 4-2, 5-1." This means, "It is time for shooters to move to the next station. The shooter at station number one broke three birds. The shooter on station two broke four birds. Station number three ran it clean (broke all five). Station four only hit two birds and the shooter on station five needs help because he only managed to hit one."

Shooters then move to the next station in a clockwise manner, station one moving to station two and the shooter on number five rotating to station one. When everyone has reached his new position, the shooter who began the round at station one (and who is now at station two) begins again. This person is the first shooter at each new station.

Guns may not be loaded until every shooter is at his or her station and the leadoff shooter has called for his first bird. Knowledgeable shooters load their gun with only one round at a time and only when the shooter two positions ahead of them calls for a bird. When moving between stations, the gun must be unloaded and the action open.

It is common for the scorer to call missed birds as the competitors shoot, shouting the word "Lost" to denote a miss. In order to score a hit, the shooter must only knock a visible piece off the target. This sometimes creates differences of opinion between the scorer and the shooter.

The scorer is invariably right, at least if he is experienced. He is in position to do nothing but watch the bird as it leaves the house and is unencumbered by the pressures and decisions facing someone with a loaded gun in hand. Still, scorers are human and they do make occasional mistakes. If a shooter believes the bird broke, it is appropriate to say so. If one or more of his squad mates agrees, a scorer will often change his call.

Trap is fast-paced. In fact, of all the shotgun games, a round of 16-yard trap is usually completed most quickly, in about 12 to 15 minutes.

Trap shooters become accustomed to a quick-paced rhythm, and a shooter who is slow or who continually questions the scorer's calls will disrupt it. Such shooters are not viewed favorably by their squad mates.

It will not take you too long to realize the value of a shooting vest that holds live shells and hulls. The breathable Bob Allen mesh vest will give you a long, lightly padded gun pad and large lower pockets.

Besides your gun, shells and hearing protection, you MUST have ballistic eye protection to shoot competitively in trap, skeet, sporting clays and other shotgun games where busting clay pigeons is the objective. These shooting glasses are from Olympic Optical.

If you move toward the shooting line without hearing protection, someone will notice and remind you ... or you should hope they will. With your ear positioned just inches from the exploding shell, the noise is louder than the space shuttle at take-off.

Courteous trap shooters make every effort to fall into the shooting rhythm of the squad. It is important that, when you take your position, you are ready to shoot. You should have all of the shells and any other accessories you need in your pockets.

This rhythm is important to many veteran shooters. Often, they will make every effort to shoot on squads composed of others with whom they have shot with in the past and who provide the right rhythm.

Finding and keeping a squad rhythm is not solely for convenience. A herky-jerky squad can disrupt a shooter's concentration and lower his score. Conversely, a smoothly functioning squad that "hits the zone" can elevate a shooter's score. Trap is one of the few shooting games in which fellow shooters can exert a positive or negative influence on another's performance without any conscious effort.

New trap shooters should be attentive to shooting rhythm. The idea of rhythm on the field is one reason trap shooters have gained a reputation for being somewhat aloof and keeping their opinions to themselves. Whether this is true across-the-board is arguable; however a trap squad will not usually display the laid-back, gregarious attitude that you often see among skeet or sporting clays shooters. This quality of aloofness should not be considered hostility. It is simply an element of the concentration required to shoot well.

For this same reason, you will not hear much conversation among squad members during a shoot. Unless it is only a fun shoot, squad members will not freely offer advice and shooting pointers while the round is in progress. The best trap squads are focused, business-like and move quickly. That is the nature of the game. New trap shooters would do well to keep this in mind and emulate it because it will have a positive effect on their scores and their progress as a competitor.

Shooting Accessories

You need very few accessories to step up to position one on a trap field. Eye protection is extremely important on any shooting venue and should always be worn. Many ranges require it. Ear protection helps prevent permanent hearing loss and reduces recoil fatigue. Quality hearing protectors go a long way toward helping you avoid a flinch.

Shooting vests and shell pouches are convenient. At some point in your shooting career, you will want to obtain them. Vests and pouches are not essential for trap, however, because there is not much movement on the field. You have ample time to pick up the box of shells at your feet and haul it to the next station; more than enough time to reach down and grab a shell from it when you are ready to load. If you are saving your empty hulls to reload, though, you will need something to put them in and an inexpensive belt pouch works well. Trap is not a complex game. It is fast-paced and great fun.

(For a complete run-down on all the accessory possibilities, please read the "Accessories" chapter in Section IV.)

THE FUNDAMENTALS OF TRAP

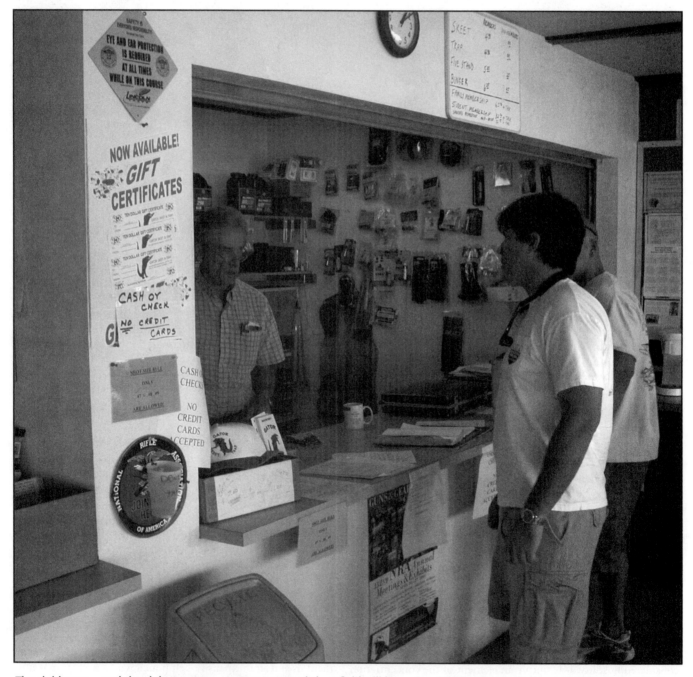

The clubhouse – and the club manager – at any trap and skeet field will be an invaluable source of information for the newcomer. Here, you can find a local coach or instructor in shooting and perhaps in reloading, used guns for sale, the latest magazines, empty shells for reloading, accessories and ammo for sale.

When calling for a bird, the trap shooter has two positions. With the gun mounted, he can follow a "high gun" or a "low gun" technique, depending not on whether the gun is mounted on the shoulder, but how high above the trap house a shooter points the gun before the target emerges.

Shooting trap is not a thinking activity: it is a feeling activity. In the movie *Star Wars*, the old Jedi knight Obi-Wan Kenobi tutors young Luke Skywalker to "use the force" or to trust his instincts, his "inner eye." At the risk of offending some veteran trapshooters, shooting trap effectively is like "using the force." Targets fly out of the hidden launcher so quickly that there is little time to think, to calculate lead. The best shooters eventually become instinctive.

Trap shooting is deceptively easy. Moving from initial exposure, which can be a frustrating experience, to an ATA "AAA"

classification (breaking 98 percent or better in singles and 96 percent or better in doubles) certainly requires a lot of hand-eye coordination, but pointing the gun and pulling the trigger eventually become instinctive. Thinking about the shot quickly becomes over-analysis, and it can ruin a perfectly good game. Instead, one reacts through a round or, like the old Jedi, learns to trust one's instincts.

In effect, trap is not much different from someone suddenly tossing a ball at your face. You do not do a lot of thinking about the ball. Your hands automatically come up to intercept

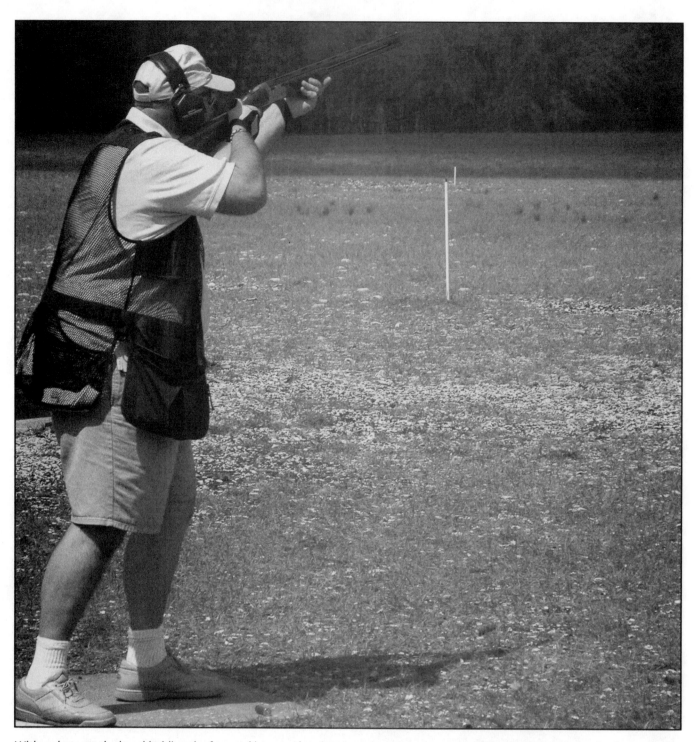

With a shotgun, the hand holding the fore-end is more than just a support. It is the steering wheel, driving the gun in the vertical and horizontal planes. This shooter's stance puts his weight well forward, but his left hand appears to be positioned beneath the shotgun. This flaw in gun hold would limit his range of smooth movement.

it. If you have good reactions and your body is in proper position, you will catch the ball. If not, you may deflect it or, if you are really slow or clumsy, take one in the eye.

That pretty well sums up trap. The only point of difference between the baseball analogy and actual shots on the field is that instead of intercepting an incoming baseball with your hands, you are intercepting an outgoing clay target with a shot charge. In both cases, that task is best accomplished if you have assumed the proper body position (or stance) to allow your reflexes to take over.

What follows in this chapter is a systematic plan for getting started in trap. Much of the advice on basic body position and gun handling will also apply to the other clay target games described in this book.

Proper Gun Hold

We have already mentioned that unlike a rifle, which must be held steady to hit a target, your shotgun must move. If the charge has a chance of intercepting the target, the gun must flow to and through it as the shot is triggered. One of the most frequent causes of missed clay targets at any game is stopping the movement of the gun when the shot is fired. This is called "anticipation," and it always results in the shot string flying behind the bird. Some new shooters encourage missing by holding the gun incorrectly.

Your shotgun touches your body at four different places: both hands, your cheek and in the shoulder pocket. It must make contact in a consistent manner every time the gun is shouldered or the point of impact of the shot charge will change. In addition, the gun position must be comfortable enough to allow you to move the gun smoothly in any direction, horizontally or vertically. A tightly gripped, locked-in gun mount might be fine for a rifleman, but it is a disaster for a shotgunner.

Grip and stance are basic. However, it is the authors' experience that consistent gun mounting is the greatest problem for new shooters, especially those who have rifle-shooting experience. These shooters often incorrectly assume that gun mount and body position should not offer them any freedom of movement. In this matter, they are simply wrong.

With a shotgun, your leading hand, the one holding the fore-end of the gun, is more than just a gun support. Think of it like the steering wheel of an automobile because that is what the leading hand does: it drives the gun in the vertical and horizontal planes. If your hand is improperly positioned on the fore-end, you will lose some of that control.

Placing your hand too far back toward the receiver offers good biomechanical advantage for moving the gun up and down, but very little for moving it side to side. Too far forward is the reverse difficulty: it robs power to move the gun up and down quickly.

Top shooting coaches recommend that your leading hand should be placed on the fore-end at a point that allows your elbow to form a 90- to 100-degree angle between your forearm and upper arm. Your leading arm should then form a 45-degree angle with the side of the gun. This 45-degree angle is the best compromise for both vertical and horizontal movement. A greater angle than 45 degrees inhibits vertical movement while less restricts horizontal movement. Trap shooters need unrestricted movement in both planes.

Since shooters are built differently, this should simply be considered a starting point from which the shooter can discover his best stance. Nevertheless, many top shooters have found that a slightly different fore-end hold works best for them.

The arm angle of your trigger hand is another matter. If your elbow is too low, it can reduce the shoulder pocket area into which your gun butt needs to lock. This may cause the gun butt to shift position as it recoils. If your elbow is too high, it will create a large shoulder pocket, but a high arm position strains the muscles of your shoulder and arm. Most shooters find that the best arm position for them lies somewhere between these extremes.

Another variable affecting scores is the position of your head. Simply put, your head should be erect. When mounting the gun, bring the gun to the face instead of the other way around. Consistent head positioning goes a long way to ensuring that your shot string will fly in the same manner every time you pull the trigger.

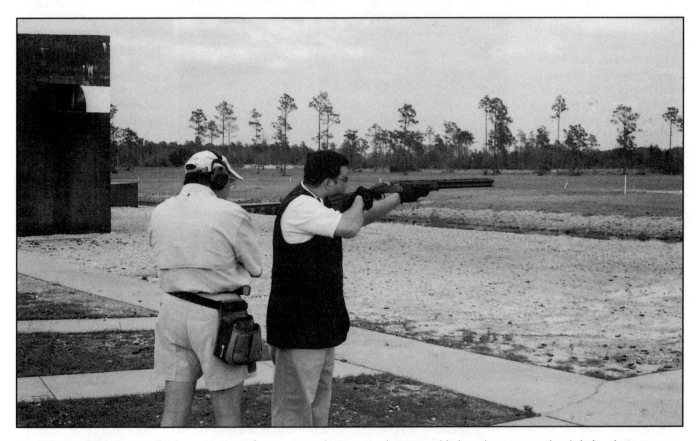

Getting some basic instruction is a wise move for new trap shooters, and most world-class shooters say that it helps them to occasionally have another professional critique their game. Coaches understand the subtleties of body position and proper gun hold and can save new shooters much time in discovering the importance of these factors on their own. A coach can often help experienced shooters climb out of a slump much more rapidly than if they relied on their own intuition.

Stance and Weight Distribution

Regardless of his or her build, a shotgunner may constructively think of the body as if it were built like a tank. Everything below the hips is the chassis that provides support; everything above the hips is the turret that pivots to swing the gun. A correct stance allows this to happen.

The feet should be spread a comfortable nine to 15 inches apart. Too wide a stance inhibits upper body movement because it makes the shooter less balanced. Too narrow a stance can similarly disrupt a shooter's balance. Weight distribution should favor the leading leg (the left leg for right-handers) with about a 60:40 or even a 65:35 ratio between the front and back leg. Some shooters favor keeping the back leg straight with a bit of flex in the leading knee. Others shoot with both knees slightly bent. Although you will see world class shooters stand in the most unusual positions imaginable, it is advisable to avoid any exaggerated crouch, at least while you are learning.

Those who prefer a more deliberate shooting style often stand relatively upright. Fast and instinctive shooters typically want their knees slightly flexed, and they use the stored energy in their legs to help drive the upper body and achieve the gun speed needed for this style of shooting.

Natural Point of Aim

Natural point of aim is the position in which the gun is pointing when a shooter brings his gun to the firing position with no further body movement. When the shot is fired and the gun recoils, it will return to this position.

The concept of a natural point of aim is equally important for riflemen, pistol shooters and shotgunners. Once it is discovered, the shooter has the best natural body position for the selected target and the widest area of body movement available to move to either side of the target.

Finding your natural point of aim for any given target is easy. First, take your normal shooting position and focus on the aiming spot. Now, bring the gun to the firing position and close your eyes. Raise the gun to the recoil position and then lower it back to the original position. Now, open your eyes.

If the gun is back on target, you are at your natural point of aim. Chances are it will be to one side or the other. Correct

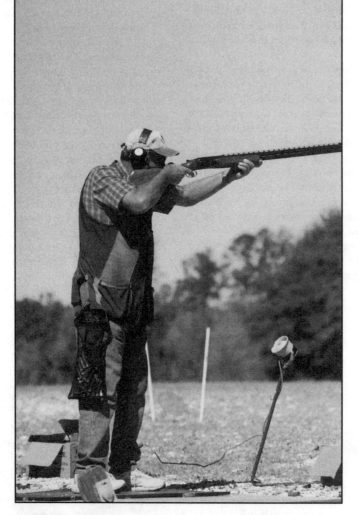

This experienced shooter shows good form throughout with the more vertical stance preferred by many sustained lead marksmen. Note the slight bend forward, as if leaning into the bird.

this by moving your leading foot in the direction you want the gun barrel to move, while shifting your back foot as necessary to maintain your basic stance. Adjustments to natural point of aim are always made with the feet, never with the upper body. Your upper body remains set while the feet are moved to position the gun where you want it to aim. The procedure is the same whether you are shooting a rifle, pistol or shotgun.

Understanding your natural point of aim is critical for a shotgunner because it will determine your swing arc. If your arc is not sufficient to drive through the target, you will lose the bird.

One Eye or Two?

Human vision operates on the binocular principle. Focused on a single object, your two eyes work in concert to establish depth perception. For most people, one eye – the master eye – will be more dominant and will sharply define the target, while the "off eye" provides the second opinion needed for depth perception. (We will discuss how and why you should determine your master eye in a later chapter.)

Expert shotgun shooters take advantage of the binocular principle and shoot with both eyes open. The master eye looks along the rib while the off eye looks past the barrel, confirming the estimation of depth or distance. With practice, this is easy in skeet and sporting clays. In fact, many shooters estimate distance, speed and shot angle without a conscious thought because this is the only real way to track extreme angle targets.

This process is a little tougher for trap shooters because they will naturally sight down the barrel as they wait for the bird. Because targets are primarily moving away from the shooter, they can be picked up easily with just one eye. Sometimes your off eye will close as you sight down the shotgun rib on a trap field, even if you have no trouble keeping both eyes open at skeet or sporting clays. Even experienced trap shooters sometimes have to remind themselves consciously to keep both eyes open. This usually happens after they miss two targets in a row!

If you do not shoot trap with both eyes open, you tend to concentrate too much on the rib and bead of the gun and not enough on the target. You are forced to quickly acquire the target as it comes out of the house and determine its exact course.

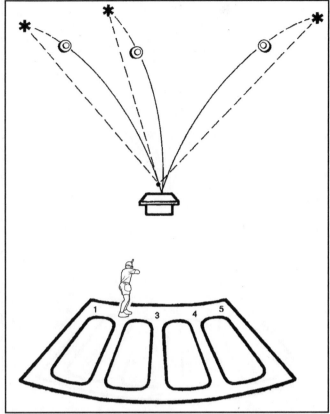

Station One: Target array on station one requires that right-handed shooters fudge their natural point of aim to the left in order to have the swing room required for the extreme left-hand target.

Station Two: Moving one station to the right shrinks the target angles and allows shooters to shift their body position more towards the trap house center.

If you do not, the bird gets a long head start and this throws off your timing. With both eyes open, you can maintain the proper rib picture, and quickly acquire the bird.

One of the most important things any shotgunner can do to improve his score shooting any clay target game is to make "both eyes open" a consistent part of the mental checklist he runs through before calling for a bird.

Muzzle Position

In trap, when you call for a target, you have to start with the gun muzzle in some position. Contrary to the opinions of some experts, there is no single correct position that every shooter should emulate. Actually, there are two techniques that can be effective, "high gun" and "low gun." These terms refer to how high above the trap house a shooter points the gun before the target emerges, not whether the gun butt is on or off the shoulder.

All ATA trap targets emerge from a point near the center of the trap house and on a rising angle. High gun shooters prefer to position the muzzle about four feet above the house and let the bird rise upward and through the barrel. If a shooter is using both eyes, he can pick up the bird quite well with this system, since the off eye will "look through" or past the barrel and will have no problem acquiring the bird. A shooter who uses only one eye will have real problems with a high gun muzzle position.

Most high gun shooters favor high-shooting guns, those that pattern from six to 18 inches above the bead. Combined with a

high gun hold and binocular vision, this will let a shooter find the target and break it quickly with a relatively small degree of gun movement. High gun shooters tend to focus their eyes farther from the trap house – about 15 to 17 yards – and break the birds a bit farther onto the field. This is what I call a "deliberate" shooting style, almost rifle shooting with a shotgun.

A high gun hold is probably the most popular technique among veteran shooters. However, it may not be the best way for new shooters to develop their skills.

Many coaches believe that new shooters gain skill more quickly if they start with a low gun hold. In this case, the muzzle points at the back edge of the trap house or slightly below it.

There are three reasons why a low gun hold may help a novice shooter develop skills faster:

First, with the gun pointed at the top of the house, the bird will always emerge over the muzzle, with both bird and muzzle within the shooter's vision. For those who cannot shoot with both eyes open, this low hold is one of the few ways they can achieve success in trap. Instant target acquisition combined with a clear muzzle picture makes maintaining a proper sight picture easy. Using the low gun technique, your eyes focus where the bird will first appear. This helps you acquire the bird quickly, which is necessary for a low gun hold to be effective.

Second, a low gun technique requires the shooter to do the most important thing every great shotgunner must learn: swing the gun! The bird will emerge as an orange streak flying past the gun muzzle so a shooter cannot be lazy going after it. The

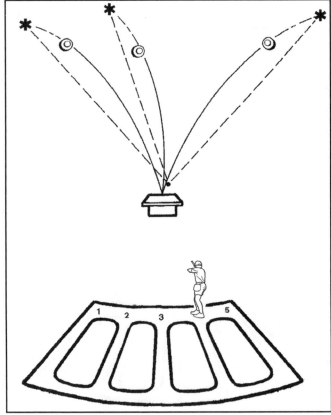

Station Three: Here the shooter sees even-angled targets on either side of center, which requires that he be prepared to react quickly in either direction.

Station Four: Right-handed shooters begin to have problems when they reach station four, because of the restricted swing range to their right side. They will have to fudge their natural body position to the right if they intend to hit many extreme right-angled targets.

shooter will have to swing quickly to catch it. This awareness builds the shooting speed needed for the shooter to get onto the bird while it is still climbing at high speed and still unaffected by the wind. It is a more consistent target and the shooter does not have to make changes in his sight picture to accommodate environmental extremes. You drill 'em and kill 'em the same way every time. This is the "fast-swing" technique in action. It has one additional benefit: lead is substantially reduced because of the speed of your swing!

The target requiring the greatest lead in trap is the extreme 22-degree angled shot on stations one and five. Some deliberate shooters say they use anywhere from 18 inches to three feet of lead on these targets and break them at about 35 to 39 yards. Shooting the low gun hold and the fast swing, author Chris Christian says he seriously doubts if he sees a lead greater than two target lengths, about eight inches. "I break those targets at about 30 yards," he says, "where I have a dense, yet optimum pattern from an Improved Cylinder or Light Modified choke with either #8 or #8½ loads. On the more gently-angled shots, I shoot at the leading edge of the bird. Lead is not something I spend much time thinking about. I just swing, pull the trigger and smile!"

The final advantage to a low gun hold is that because of the speed of the swing directly through the bird and the closer break range, you can shoot trap with the low gun technique using a standard field-stocked, flat-shooting gun.

For all of these reasons, the low gun technique is better for a new shooter than the more rigid, deliberate high gun technique. Once a shooter begins with the low gun position and learns the basics, it is not hard to change to a high-shooting gun and the higher hold, should he choose to do so.

Station Shooting Positions

The last thing a new trap shooter needs to learn is where to put his natural point of aim for each station. This varies depending upon whether the shooter is right- or left-handed, using a deliberate or fast swing, shooting with one or two eyes open, and uses a high gun or low gun position. Here are the options by station.

Station One

The toughest target on this station is the extreme left angle. All shooters have to move their natural point of aim to the left to have the swing-room to hit it. For right-hand shooters this means establishing their natural point of aim near the left corner of the trap house. Lefties may have to go a bit outside the house since they will not have as much swing to the left as a right-hander.

Low gun, fast-swing shooters will then shift the gun back to the rear center of the trap house, just below the edge. Regardless of which angle the target takes, it will come out right over the muzzle. This center-back trap house hold will be the same

Station Five: This is the toughest station for right-handed shooters. The extreme right-angled target can get away from a shooter if he does not fudge his body position to it. The left-hand targets do not require a lot of swing arc because they appear to the shooter more as straight-aways. Set up for the greater angled target and you will improve your score on this station.

for a low hold, fast-swing shooter on all five stations.

High gun shooters should place the muzzle at a point above the left-hand corner of the house, although there are some, generally those with Bunker trap experience, who will also use a high-center-back hold for all houses. We will explain why when we get to the chapter on International trap.

Station Two

At position two, the angles decrease. Move your natural point of aim back toward the center of the house: about two-thirds

of the way to center house from the left edge for right-handed shooters, and a little farther left for lefties. High gun shooters position their gun above the house, midway between the center and the left edge.

Station Three

The angles are even at this center position and most right-handed shooters tend to take a natural point of aim about six inches right of center house while lefties point about six inches to the left. This gives each some built-in fudge toward their weak swing side. High gun shooters shift the gun about the same distance to the side of center to prevent a straightaway target from hiding under the barrel.

Station Four

Position four is a mirror image of station two. Right-handed shooters begin fudging their natural point of aim to the right, almost to the edge of the trap house, to accommodate their restricted right-side swing. Lefties remain a bit closer to center trap. The high hold is midway between center and right trap house edge.

Station Five

This is the mirror image of station one. For right-hand shooters it is one of the toughest shots in trap. It is best to take a natural point of aim about a foot or so past the right edge of the trap house. Lefties should aim close to the edge of the house.

If right-hand shooters do not consider that difficult left-to-right angle and turn their body position with it, they will lose this bird. On station number one, lefties have to do the same thing with the extreme left-angle bird.

Trap Reading

The last matter that needs addressing is a phenomenon called "reading the trap." Some shooters think they can figure out what target angle is coming next and be ready for it. Experts will tell you that you cannot, at least not often. Anticipating targets is a good way to get caught with your pants down and lose a target. Trying to anticipate target angle is a bad habit and will eventually cause you to shoot lower scores.

Once you have the right body position – those detailed here will serve as starting points – trap becomes an easy game to learn. When the target appears, you simply react. Try not to think. Try not to outsmart the target launch. Just drill the bird in front. What makes trap a challenging game to master is the need to force the body to make the correct reaction each time a target appears.

Trap is the only clay target game where pump-action shotguns like this Remington 870 Classic Trap single barrel are still competitive. Of course, shooting a pump gun year-round for competition and for hunting helps the shooter learn to handle the recoil and work the action without greatly disturbing his swing and shot picture.

SHOOTING HANDICAP TRAP

During the early days of trap, all shooters competed on an equal footing. As with any competitive event, however, it soon became apparent that all contestants were not created equal. It was not long before the same names began appearing at the top of the leader board, match after match. Since trap has always been more financially oriented than other clay target games, this was not good for attendance at meets. Why would a shooter with only modest skills or someone whose skills were still growing pay an entry fee when he or she knew they were going to lose it all?

Match organizers realized that if only five or six shooters had a realistic chance of winning, that was about as big as a match was going to be after all the other shooters figured out who these individuals were! A handicap event was match organizers' way of encouraging more than a half-dozen shooters to show up.

Handicap trap is a singles event shot in the same manner as the standard ATA "16 Yard" match: in the same order, at the same targets and on the same field. The difference is that individual competitors are moved back from the 16-yard front line based on their individual scores and averages. The minimum move is to 19 yards for new lady and new sub-junior (less than 16 years old) shooters or 20 yards for men: the maximum is to 27 yards. Increments are measured in half-yards, but shot in whole yards. Thus, a shooter might be assigned a 23-½-yard handicap and then shoot from the 23-yard line. The resulting score will compete directly against those shot by all other competitors, no matter what their handicap yardage.

The purpose is to put all shooters on an equal footing by assigning each of them an individual handicap based on their ability. A similar handicapping procedure is followed for golf and other games. Like many handicap systems, though, trap's handicapping effort has not always worked perfectly.

In the last few years, it has become apparent that shooters whose skill has earned them a spot on the 27-yard handicap line are still the ones to beat … even with an 11-yard disadvantage! It is extremely rare for instance for a 23-yard shooter to beat a 27-yard shooter – despite the four-yard difference in target distance. The 27-yard shooters are still superior, their skill and reflexes making them the ones to beat. The 27-yard shooters also win because they understand the critical differences between the game as it is shot from the 16-yard line, and that played from the handicap ranges. There are serious differences, both obvious and subtle!

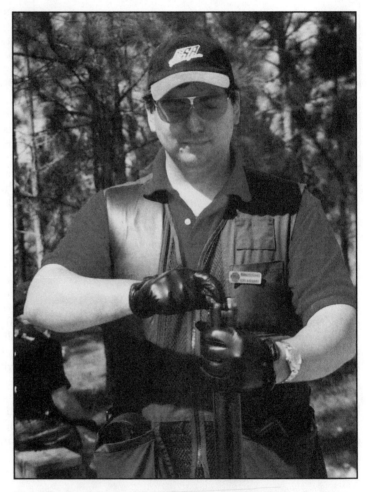

The difference between 16- and 27-yard positions is the distance to the target. An Improved Cylinder choke is usually adequate when it is combined with a 1⅛-ounce load of #8½ shot. Slower shooters may need a tighter choke than this, however.

Loads and Chokes

The most obvious difference shooting between the 16- and 27-yard positions is of course the distance to the target. A quick 16-yard shooter will break his birds about 30 yards from his shooting position. This is a comfortable range for pattern control. An Improved Cylinder choke is adequate when it is combined with a 1⅛-ounce load of #8½ shot. That shot size

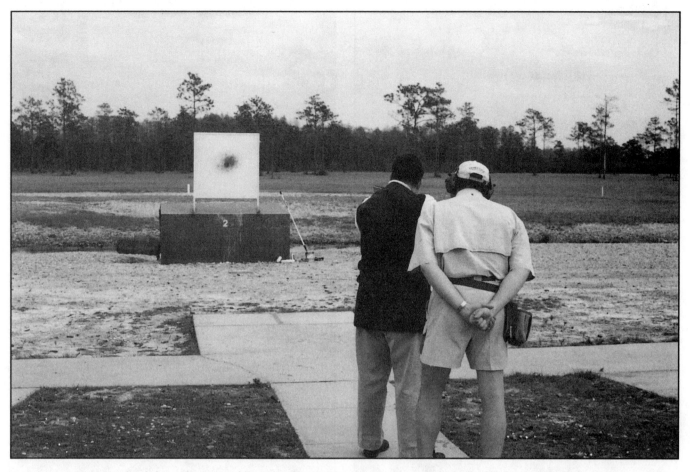

As you earn your way back from the 16-yard line, the shooting becomes progressively more difficult. Curiously, however, veterans of trap tournaments testify that shooters whose skill has earned them a spot on the 27-yard handicap line are still the ones to beat, even with an 11-yard disadvantage! As they become progressively accustomed to greater distances, good shooters adjust quickly, especially with a little coaching.

has enough target-breaking power and provides almost as many pellets in the load as a 1⅛-ounce #9 skeet load. Because #8½ shot fills out an Improved Cylinder pattern very well, it gives the shooter more than enough pattern density and a margin for error, too.

Slower 16-yard shooters often rely on a Light Modified (also called Skeet #2) or Modified choke and the same load with #8 • shot. They find this combination works well in the 33- to 37-yard range at which these leisurely shooters usually break their birds.

Start moving shooters back from the 16-yard line however and the game changes. You can forget using #8½ shot in any load at any range past 33 to 35 yards; at longer distances, that shot size is not heavy enough to consistently break birds and you will lose some targets that heavier shot pellets would break. Shooting at greater range means you must now choose #8s and tighten your choke to maintain effective pattern density. The down side is that even fast shooters lose some of the margin for error if you are shooting much beyond the 20-yard handicap line. Slower shooters at the same range find they break their targets at about 40 yards and that requires a denser pattern than a Light Modified or Modified choke will produce. They must increase their choke to decrease the distribution of shot in the pattern.

When you earn your way back to the 27-yard line, breaking birds consistently really gets tough! Quick shooters have a target break point somewhere between 40 and 50 yards and for

leisurely gunners that point is out farther than 50 yards. You still have only 1⅛ ounces of shot to do the job even with maximum loads.

The demands on load and choke at this range are severe. For some time, everyone assumed that no 27-yard shooter could break 100 straight targets because the loads would not be up to the task! That did not remain the case for long, as shot quality and wad development rose to the task.

What handicap distance demonstrates, however, is that the game requires much more precision the farther one is removed from the comfort of the 16-yard line. Shot size must increase to maintain target-breaking power, but that results in a decrease in pattern density over smaller shot. Therefore pattern density must be maintained by using tighter chokes that throw smaller patterns, because the larger the shot size the fewer pellets there are in a given load to make up the pattern. The margin for error goes right into the toilet.

"Any small error at 27 yards is a miss," Florida shooter Lisa Sever says. Lisa earned her 27-yard handicap while she was still in college. "One minute mistake is all it takes to drop out of the top echelon of competition. At the 16-yard line, you can recover and get at least a piece of the bird. Not at the 27-yard line. You must have much more polish in your swing and point."

Shooting from the farther handicap ranges, as Lisa does, requires some serious changes in equipment and mental attitude from that required for 16-yard shooting.

Two gunners at a 5-stand event illustrate that there is no one "correct" approach to successfully busting clay. The shooter on the left, shooting a crossing pattern, has an aggressive and stable stance with some weight forward. The shooter on the right, who was in the same squad at the running rabbit station, has a more vertical stance and seems to lean forward at the waist.

The most notable change is in the firearm used. The majority of top handicap shooters prefer a single-barrel gun with a long sighting radius. This is why we see the graceful 32- and 34-inch-barreled guns so often on the trap line. The longer barrel, yet slightly lighter muzzle weight inherent in such guns (compared to a double gun), provides a more precise aim and greater muzzle control than what can be achieved with the over-and-under that dominate the doubles game. Many top-quality trap guns are offered as a two-barrel set with both a single barrel and over-and-under barrels fitted to the same receiver.

You can bet that the single-barrel will be choked tighter than a banker's heart. While Modified and Improved Modified chokes are commonly seen on the 16-yard line (with slightly more open chokes being popular in doubles), Full (.035-inch constriction) and even Extra-Full (.040-inch+) are the rule from 27 yards.

Some shooters do quite well with relatively flat-shooting guns, but many top handicap shooters want a high-shooting gun. This allows the shooter to stay under the bird for a more precise target picture than that achieved with a "flat" gun that must be swung up and through the bird to cover it. A higher shooting gun also helps compensate for a shot charge that will be losing velocity and actually be starting to drop in its trajectory as the 40-yard-plus mark is reached.

Shot size normally is confined to #7½, although some shooters try to stretch #8 shot in an attempt to maintain a dense pattern. Loads run the gamut from light to full three-dram equivalent, depending on the shooter's preference and confidence level.

Even with the proper equipment, handicap shooters must develop a good mental approach to their handicap. One of the first things they do is beat "the illusion." A target at the 16-yard line appears to be moving fast, so the shooter realizes he must move quickly to catch it. The target seems to leap from the trap and rapidly move out of the shooter's field of view because of his closer proximity. The illusion of speed makes the shooter go after it. Move back the 11-yard difference to the 27-yard line and the picture or the image changes. The shooter's field

One problem with learning to shoot handicap trap is that the space/time continuum seems to fall slightly out of round. There is a visual illusion, based on an 11-yard difference, that the shooter has more time to get on the bird. Wrong. If you wait too long, you are toast in this game!

est increase in lead on the angled targets. The mental aspect of beating the illusion of more time yet not getting in a big hurry is important in dealing with handicap targets."

The late shooting great Frank Little offered some additional advice for those who want to become great handicap shooters. Frank's philosophy was that all 16-yard trap should be considered little more than practice for the 27-yard line. He advocated using the same tight, full choke #7½ load at the 16-yard line that you would at the 27-yard line. His reasoning was simple and straightforward: with that choke and load, any target that does not become a small puff of black smoke at 16 yards was not pointed well enough to have been hit at 27 yards. If you can hit 16-yard targets with that combination, 27-yard birds will be much easier. That is getting very precise indeed!

of view around the field is noticeably much wider. The 27-yard bird emerges into this wider field of view looking smaller, of course, but it also appears to be moving more slowly! It does not seem to require the immediate "now" movement to catch it. If you buy into "the illusion" that you have time to get onto the bird at 27 yards, you will miss more than you hit.

The Handicap Illusion

This visual illusion, based solely on an 11-yard difference, gives the shooter the impression that he has all the time in the world to get on the target. Actually, because of the narrower arc of swing, there is much less physical gun movement required at the 27-yard line than at the 16-yard mark.

That is the illusion. Although gun movement is certainly reduced, the gun must be moved as quickly – or more quickly – than it would be when shooting from the 16-yard line if the target is to be hit within any reasonable break range.

A slow shooter on the 27-yard line is in for a difficult round. Of course, those who have shot their way back to trap's toughest position are well aware of that and any tendency toward laggardly shooting behavior would have been put behind them long before.

"You have to get to that 27-yard target just as quickly as you would at 16 yards," Lisa Sever has said. "The appearance of more time is just an illusion, but it fools a lot of newer handicap shooters. For me, one of the keys to handicap shooting is to realize that I do not have the time that the visual appearance of the target tells me I do, but to also realize that I can't anticipate the target or rush it. I have to make myself wait until I can acquire and read the target before I make my move, then move smoothly and precisely – and without hesitation – to the bird. There is no real change in body or foot position and only the slight-

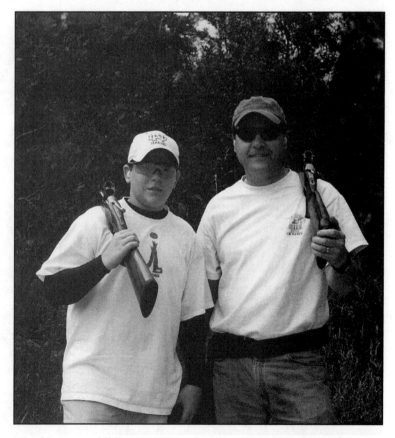

Watching your children grow up to become responsible and proficient with the shotgun is one of the great pleasures offered by shooting sports like trap, skeet and sporting clays. Jim Willard and his son Gradon shot together at a recent sporting clays event.

DEALING WITH DOUBLES

Doubles trap was introduced to the tournament format in about 1911 to spice up the game. It is safe to say it has succeeded quite admirably at that goal.

As the name implies, doubles trap consists of two birds released simultaneously on two separate flight paths: one bird is set to fly at the extreme 22-degree angle to the right while the other is set for the same angle to the left. Since both birds are launched from the same trap, their velocity is slightly less than that of a singles target from the same machine because the added weight of the extra bird robs a couple of feet per second of speed from the throwing arm.

The doubles game is shot from the 16-yard line in a standard

Having missed his first shot, this weekend trap shooter swings his semi-auto and misses low and behind the now distant second bird. (Both birds are visible slightly above the trees.) If this shooter had taken instruction in stance, gun hold and point of aim, he would quickly find that this is an easy shot for a left-hander from the 16-yard line.

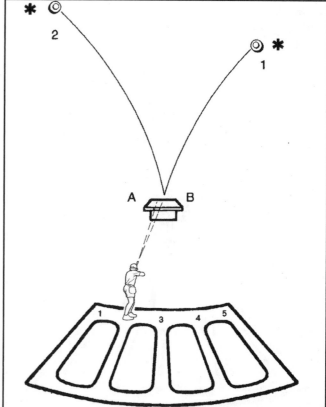

Station One: Line "A" shows proper natural point of aim to left-hand corner of the front of the house for a right-handed shooter (left-handers will want to move further left). Line "B" shows the gun hold moved back to the center of the trap house. Target #1 now becomes a straightaway that can be taken quickly with the shooter having enough swing room to catch and drive through target #2.

Station Two: Right-handers shift their natural point of aim back to a point half way between the corner and the center of the house. Target #1 is a very slight-angled target that most fast-swing shooters will break by shooting at the leading side of the bird. Target #2 requires less lead here than it did from station one.

five-shooter squad. A full round consists of 25 pairs (50 birds). Shooters fire at five pairs from each station. Thirteen pairs are presented on the first walk through the stations. This is followed by a short break and then the remaining twelve pairs are presented on the next walk-through.

At each station, the shooter loads two shells, firing one shell at each target. The on-the-field official moves the shooters through the five stations, making certain that the proper shooting order is maintained.

Many shooters consider doubles trap the toughest ATA trap game and it is not quite as popular as singles or handicap trap. One reason it is not extremely popular is that doubles requires shooters to have a gun capable of firing two rounds and some shooters refuse to put down their single-barrel guns. Another reason, however, is the intimidation factor: many trap shooters have trouble dealing with two targets in the air simultaneously. A lot of that, of course, is mental.

I recently watched a shooter who was a competent skeet and sporting clays gunner step up in a squad of veteran ATA trap shooters for the very first round of doubles trap he had ever fired. This shooter did not even own a trap gun, so he used his sporting clays gun and slipped in Skeet 2 and Improved Modified tubes. Treating the targets just like sporting clays birds, he broke 40 out of 50 the first time he ever shot the game! The trap shooters on the squad, who knew he had never shot the

game before, were surprised at how well he picked up this supposedly difficult game. The shooter himself was not surprised. He said he "… didn't think it was all that difficult." He was not intimidated by seeing two targets in the air at the same time because in sporting clays he sees that all the time!

Simultaneous targets are common in skeet and sporting clays. In fact, skeet shooters regularly deal with two targets that are not only traveling slightly faster than doubles trap birds, but also are flying in opposite directions! They find nothing out of the ordinary about seeing two targets at once and do not allow that to intimidate them.

I think some trap shooters who fail to perform as well in doubles as they do in the singles and handicap games have talked themselves into being intimated by seeing two targets in the air. Doubles is not that tough of a game.

Remember that the targets not only fly a bit slower in doubles, but they are locked into one flight path. In sharp contrast to singles trap games, where the bird may take one of a number of different flight paths and the shooter must identify the flight angle very quickly, in doubles the shooter always knows precisely where to look for the birds. The angle will not vary throughout the round. The angle to the shooter will change as he moves from station to station, but it will always be the same for that station.

This means the shooter can set up for a very quick shot on

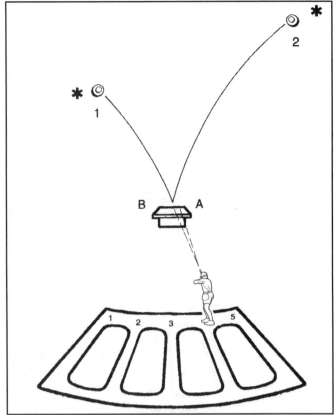

Station Three: Equal angle on both targets means the natural point of aim is brought six inches to the right of traphouse center with the gun hold shifted to traphouse center. Target #1 is taken quickly and target #2 requires shooting at the leading edge. Left-handed shooters will want to take target #2 first, since they will have a greater swing arc to the right side.

Station Four: This is the reverse of station two. A right-handed shooter will want a point of aim midway between the house center and right-hand front edge, and a gun hold at traphouse center. The left-hand bird is taken first here.

whichever bird he desires to shoot first and then swing right over for the second. Any shooter who has had experience at skeet doubles will find this familiar.

Doubles Strategies

Here is a station-by-station look at how some of the best shooters approach this game:

Station One

The right-hand bird is virtually a straightaway shot while the left-hand bird is an extreme right-to-left quartering shot. The most effective sequence is to set up the initial gun hold dead-on the straightaway. Take it just as fast as possible and then swing quickly over to the outgoing angled target.

The reason for taking the straightaway bird first is simple: it takes less gun movement and as soon as the gun fires the shooter can give all his attention to the tougher, angling bird. If the angling bird is shot first, the shooter is left with a long and possibly falling, straightaway shot that is easy to swing past and miss. In fact, if the straightaway is taken as the second bird, the shooter will actually have to stop his swing and aim deliberately at the bird. That is bad form with a smoothbore. For this reason, veteran doubles shooters advise that the straightest-flying bird always ought to be shot first.

Right-handed shooters will not find this particularly diffi-

cult from station one because they can swing more easily to the left than to the right. If a shooter takes his natural point of aim about six inches to the left of the center of the trap house and then moves the gun back to dead center, he should then have all the body movement the shots require. Left-handed shooters may have to fudge more to the left.

Station Two

The angle on the left bird is now decreased, while the right-hand bird gains a slight amount of angle to the right. It is no longer a true straightaway. Still, it is the straighter target and should be taken first. It will require shooting at the leading edge of the bird, but the lead is not much for a fast-swinging shooter. Right-handed shooters can position their natural point of aim at the center of the trap house, and most shooters will then have plenty of swing room left for the angled bird. Left-handed shooters may still have to fudge that position a bit to the left of the center of the trap house.

Station Three

This is the toughest shot in the doubles game and it intimidates a lot of shooters. Neither bird is more straightaway than the other, and both leave the trap house diverging at a 45-degree angle. Here is where the known course of the target can really pay off.

Station Five: This is one of the toughest shots for a right-handed shooter. He will want to take a point of aim to the right-front edge of the house, or maybe even a few feet outside, in order to have the swing room for the right-hand bird. Gun hold is on center of the house. The left side bird is broken quickly as a dead straightaway target. Left-handed shooters will not need as much fudging to the right side of the trap house.

One of the birds has to be shot first, of course, and many right-handed shooters find they will do better by taking the right-hand bird first, actually fudging their natural point of aim toward it. Their greater left-side swing arc will still give them plenty of time to take the left bird with the second shot. Neither bird will have a great degree of angle to its flight path and little lead is required. Knowing the exact flight path, the shooter can jump his first bird very quickly. Left-handed shooters often do better taking the left bird first.

None of this however is carved in stone. Some shooters find that reversing the above procedure pays off because they do better on long shots that have only a slight quartering angle on them. The shooter must experiment and see what works best for him.

Station Four

We have now come to the reverse of station two. The left-hand bird becomes the more straightaway and should be taken first. Left-handed shooters can usually set up right on the center of the trap house, but right-handed shooters will likely have to shift their natural point of aim about six inches right of center to have the swing-room needed for the second bird.

Station Five

This becomes the mirror image of station one with the left-hand bird being a true straightaway and the right bird flying at an extreme angle. Right-handed shooters often have problems with this station because they fail to shift their natural point of aim far enough to the right to allow them to keep their cheek on the stock for the right-hand bird. I often shift my natural point of aim all the way to the right-hand corner of the trap house just for that reason. You do not need perfect body position on the first bird because it has no flight angle, but the second bird will get away if you run out of swing room. Left-handers often have this same problem on station one.

When a shooter sets up for shots in the above manner, gun movement for all shots becomes consistent. In essence, you square a corner with the gun: straight up on a vertical line for the first bird and straight across (with just a slight upward angle) for the second bird. There is no confusion, and with a little practice, you will find your gun goes to the second bird automatically, just like in skeet doubles.

The faster you can shoot the first target the better off you are, because you will be able to catch the second bird at a consistent spot on its flight path where it is still rising. Having a consistent second target is important because you do not have time to aim! Your must swing through the shot and fire quickly and if you catch the bird at a consistent spot, you will have an easy time breaking it consistently.

Shooting the first target quickly is easy in this game because you know exactly where it will appear. Some top shooters who opt for high-shooting guns have refined their initial gun hold on the first target so well that they can break it with almost no gun movement! It becomes much like a skeet low house seven, in that respect.

One problem shooters often have with the first target is that they are thinking about the second one. They try to rush the first bird and often subconsciously start swinging the gun toward the second bird before they trigger the shot on the first. That kind of mistake will lose that first bird every time! One way to avoid this problem is to shoot a practice round of doubles, but only load a shell in the first barrel. Once you realize you cannot possibly get the second bird because there is no shell for it, the natural tendency is to make sure you get the first. Then swing the gun through the second bird and trigger your imaginary shot.

It sounds simple and unorthodox, but the exercise is designed to program your subconscious to make certain you get the first bird. For shooters who consistently have trouble with the first bird, this is a good way to get that on-board computer properly programmed. It does not do any good to hit every second bird if you miss all the first shots; your score is still only 25x50. You get the same score if you hit all the first birds and miss all the second shots. In either case, 25x50 is not a great score. It helps if you can whack both birds in a pair.

Some very good singles shooters often have trouble with the second bird. They fail to realize that the swing they must use to get from the first to the second bird is faster than the same swing they would use to take that bird as a single. If they use the same bird picture, they may well be shooting in front of that bird. A shooter who is consistently missing the second bird should not automatically assume he is behind it. Often, the reverse is actually true.

Loads and Chokes

Loads and chokes for doubles trap are strictly a matter of personal choice, but it is my experience that many shooters are over-choked for the first bird. Modified is commonly consid-

Unless you only want to shoot half of the doubles game, your mono trap gun is useless. Lay aside your single barrel Charles Daly Empire AE-MC Mono Trap with the adjustable comb and pick up your double barrel Charles Daly Superior II Trap VR-MC. Two different chokes are an asset in doubles, but shooters can also choose a Modified or Light Modified tube and a quick-opening load of #9s for the first shot, and a tighter-patterning load of #8s for the second shot.

ered to be the best choice for 16-Yard singles, and many shooters select it for their first shot on doubles. However, you have to consider that because you know exactly where that first bird will be and because you are making a conscious effort to shoot it quickly, you may be taking that target significantly closer to the gun than you would in 16 Yard singles.

When I shoot doubles, I doubt seriously if the first bird gets any farther than 27 yards from the muzzle before I fire. That is almost in the range of a Skeet 1 choke and a load of #9s! In fact, I know several shooters who use just that combination for their first shot. My first choice for the first barrel is a 1⅛-ounce Federal #8½ trap load from an Improved Cylinder choke. There is plenty of target-breaking power in that combination out to about 35 yards and I am not going to let the first target get that far away. The larger pattern, however, will get me some extra birds if I am having a "sloppy" day. If I am shooting one-ounce loads (either #8½ or #8s), I tighten down to a Skeet 2 choke, but that is as tight as I will go on the first barrel in doubles.

A Modified choke and #8 shot is much more powerful than one needs for the first target in doubles. The tighter pattern can cost you a slightly mis-pointed bird that a more open pattern would catch.

The second bird is an entirely different story.

The second target will generally be farther out than would be the case in singles. I normally use a Skeet 2 choke for singles with a load of either #8½ or #8s, because I am a fast shooter. That is not enough performance for a second bird in doubles, even though I am trying to get there quickly. In doubles, I shift to an Improved Modified choke with a full 1⅛-ounce three-dram load of #8s. For the second bird, most shooters find they need at least one choke tighter than they would in singles.

If you are shooting doubles with a single-barreled repeater having only one choke option, consider a Modified choke with a 1⅛-ounce #9 Skeet load for the first shot. This load will open up a bit faster than larger shot sizes, giving what amounts to an Improved Cylinder pattern. You will have enough power to break targets to a bit beyond 30 yards. Go with a three-dram 1⅛-ounce trap load for the second shot. If you reload, consider using softer chilled shot for those #9s to open the pattern for the first shot Then, stick to premium hard shot for the second load.

Doubles trap may be a bit more challenging than other trap games, but in my opinion it is a lot more fun. I have also found it to be excellent practice for sporting clays because you will see many of those kinds of shots on the sporting fields. It is a game well worth playing, especially if you want to learn other games.

Doubles trap may be the only time you will ever see #9 shot on the line. Quick shooters can get on the first bird in plenty of time for the smaller shot to be effective, and the increased pattern density from the larger number of pellets allows more open chokes, and a little more room for error. A tighter choke and heavier shot are definitely required for the second bird.

INTERNATIONAL TRAP

Members of the international competitive shooting community seldom embrace the shooting games that we enjoy in the US. They seem to regard the American versions as rigid, somewhat stuffy, and so easy that top shooters can regularly shoot perfect scores. When we look at our trap game and compare it to the international version, even the staunchest patriot has to agree with them.

The result is that competitive shooting events held under the banner of the International Shooting Union or UIT (*Union International de Tir*, the governing body for international shooting sports) have been modified to increase the level of difficulty and make them far more challenging. That is certainly true for the international version of trap, or as it is sometimes called, "bunker trap" or even "trench trap."

Trap Machines

The difference in the international and standard U. S. game starts with the machines used to throw the targets. American-style or ATA trap, as it will be referred to from this point, uses a single clay bird machine that is set to vary the target spread. The machine is placed at ground level and throws targets within a 34.28-degree arc. The speed of each ATA target is about 41 mph.

International trap uses 15 separate machines, all placed below ground level. Each launcher is adjusted to throw at a specific angle. There are five shooting stations, as in ATA trap, and three machines are allocated for each station. For example, a shooter on station three will take targets only from trap launchers seven, eight, and nine. The left-hand trap (the number sev-

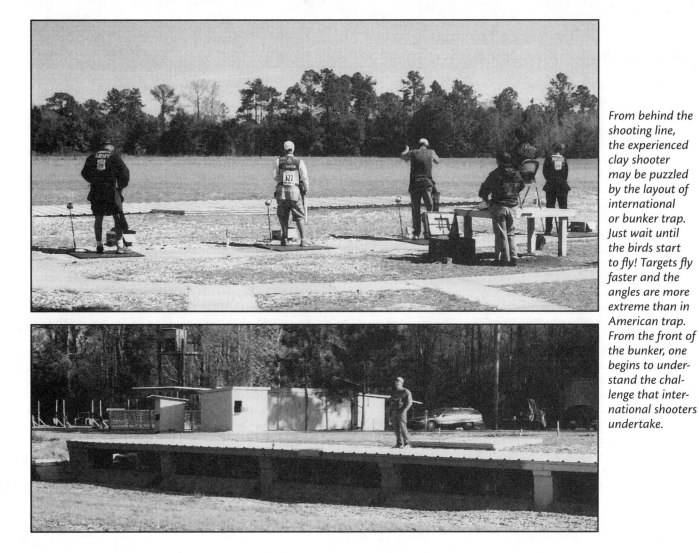

From behind the shooting line, the experienced clay shooter may be puzzled by the layout of international or bunker trap. Just wait until the birds start to fly! Targets fly faster and the angles are more extreme than in American trap. From the front of the bunker, one begins to understand the challenge that international shooters undertake.

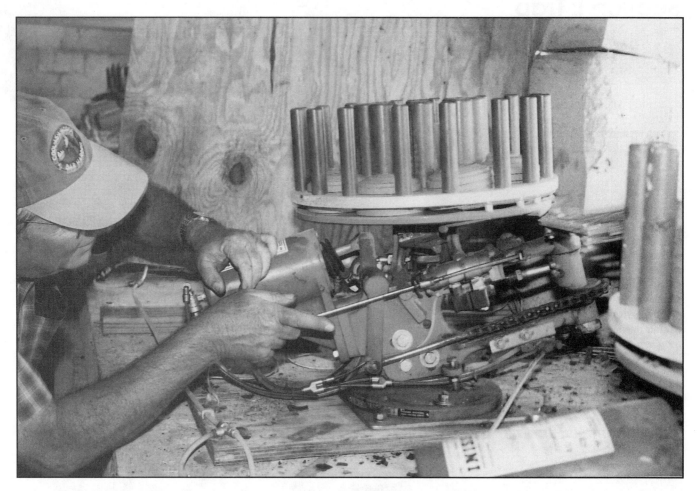

Gainesville, Florida's Jim Pettengill makes adjustments to fine tune one of the 15 trap machines inside the bunker.

en trap) will throw birds at an angle to the right, and the right-hand trap (number nine) throws them to the left. Instead of the maximum ATA angle of 17.14 degrees from center, the International angle can be as much as 45 degrees for a total arc of 90 degrees. The center trap throws a straightaway bird.

The elevation of the targets is also more varied and can be extreme. ATA targets are fixed to throw at a single elevation, about 30 degrees. International targets may be launched anywhere within a window of 3.0 to 3.5 meters above ground at a point measured 10 meters in front of the trap house. Targets from a trap set to the lowest elevation may travel 70 yards and never rise more than one meter off the ground. The next target thrown may skyrocket almost straight up!

The same variation also exists in target speed. A low target that travels 70 meters may reach a speed of 60 mph and fly directly away from the shooter. That is one of the fastest clay targets that you will ever see. A target thrown at a more vertical angle, one that covers only 60 to 65 meters will be significantly slower.

The conclusion is that international targets travel farther, faster and at angles twice as extreme as anything seen on a regulation ATA trap field. Allowed international loads make things more difficult also. The 12-gauge is standard and the maximum allowable shot charge is 24 grams, or about ⅞-ounce. ATA shooters are allowed to use up to 1⅛ ounces of shot.

A round of international trap consists of the same 25 targets as ATA, but international shooters get a break here. They are al-

lowed to fire twice at any target and it scores just as dead if it is hit with the first or second shot.

In ATA trap, a shooter fires five rounds per station and rotates to the next station. Not so in the international game. A shooter fires one round and then rotates immediately to the next station. It is a game of constant movement with the shooter making five complete passes down the line. During the course of the round, the shooter receives two targets from the right-hand trap machine, two from the left, and one from the center at each numbered station. Birds are thrown in random order and the shooter does not know what is coming next. Some shooters however, try to remember what has been thrown (much like a blackjack player counting cards). They feel this gives them a slight advantage near the end of the round when they may know (or think they know) what target remains to be thrown from a specific station. Of course, if they make a mistake and are waiting intently for a target that has already been thrown, they are probably going to miss.

Over/unders dominate the international game. Most shooters favor a choke in the .018- to .022-inch constriction range (about Modified) for the first barrel and often use the same #8½ shot size favored by international skeet shooters. A fast shooter will generally get onto a target with the first barrel at a range of 25 to 30 yards and #8½ pellets have plenty of target-breaking power at that range. Given the increase in pellet count in the load and the more open choke, the gun will throw a wider pattern. The second barrel, however, will be choked down to

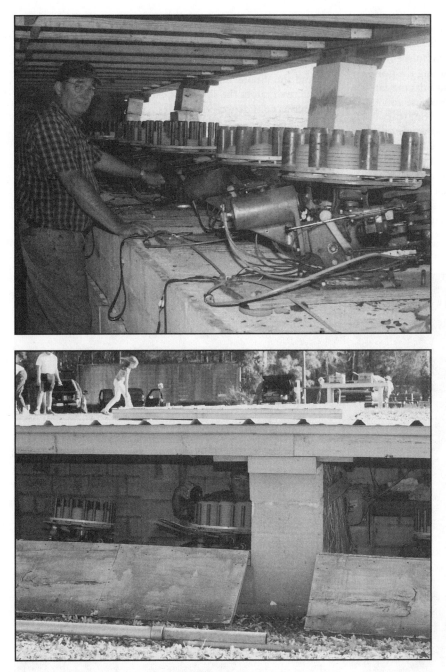

The view inside the international bunker and from the outside looking in. The variety of possible targets that can be thrown makes anticipating the exact angle and speed extremely difficult.

targets will always come up from under the gun. In the international game, you cannot do that, because a low target will run right underneath your barrel and be completely blocked from your vision. You may not even see the target until it is way out in the field and about ready to hit the ground."

The philosophy of holding a lower gun is, as we will see later, the same as that used in sporting clays to prevent the barrel from blocking one's visual acquisition of the bird. Woodhouse recommends shooters adjust in the following manner.

"There are five marks on the front of the trap house, facing the shooter," he explains. "Each mark locates the center trap for that particular station. It also marks the point at which the targets from the right- and left-hand traps will cross on the field. This is a physical mark, and most successful shooters will hold their muzzle right on that mark to make sure that the target always comes out above the gun."

The extreme angles that can be thrown also require that shooters adjust their foot position or natural point of aim as well.

"Most shooters will have a wider swing range to the off side (swinging to the left for a right-hander) and still be able to stay with the gun, meaning keeping their cheek firmly on the stock and their head down. A long swing to the strong side (right swing for a right-hander) will often cause the gun and shooter to separate," states Woodhouse. "For this reason I recommend that the natural point of aim be moved slightly to the strong side. I would suggest that a right-handed shooter take a natural point of aim six inches to the right of the house mark and then swing the gun back to the mark when calling for the target. The reverse would be true for a left-handed shooter. This helps increase the swing range to the strong side to accommodate the severe angles in international trap."

Second Shots

Another factor that American shooters find both fascinating and at times disconcerting is the second shot that is allowed should their first shot miss. The second shot is, unbeliev-ably, a difficult habit to accept for ATA trap shooters. When the shot is fired in that game, whether the bird is hit or missed, well-taught shooters will dismount their gun. This becomes an automatic, subconscious response and it can be difficult to change. The second shot in international trap must be a sub-conscious response, in and of itself, and that has to be learned through practice, too.

Many international shooters train to force their second shot, even if the first hits. This way the second shot becomes as automatic as the first. Here is how Coach Woodhouse suggests this be done: "I encourage shooters to fire both barrels, even if the first barrel scores," he explains, "but only under certain conditions."

the Full range (.028- to .032-inch) and stuffed with a #7½-size load in the event the shooter misses with the first barrel because the bird must then be broken at a greater range.

Changes in Technique

The international version of trap is a good bit more challeng-ing than the ATA version and it requires a change in technique to shoot well. Few people understand the differences (and the changes required) as well as Lloyd Woodhouse, longtime coach of our US Olympic shotgun team.

"The first change an ATA shooter will need to make," Wood-house notes, "is in his initial gun hold. The ATA version allows you to hold at a higher point over the trap house because those

Woodhouse says that if you get into the habit of breaking the target with the first shot, and not shooting the second (because there is no reason to), then you become complacent. "You start coming out of the gun," he says, "pulling the gun away from your cheek after the first shot. If you miss the target with the first barrel, then you are doomed because you are coming off the gun and the target will get away from you.

"However, just triggering the second shot after you break the target with the first one is no good either because it conditions your subconscious to shoot at nothing. You don't have a target. I tell my shooters to do one of two things. If you hit the target with the first barrel, then pick a piece of that broken target and follow it with your eyes and gun until it hits the ground. If you are in a good position and feel very confident that you can break that piece of target, then shoot it. If not, and you don't feel confident, then just follow it down."

Either way, Woodhouse feels the shooter is now alert, "with" his gun and still following targets in the target zone. "If you ever require a second shot," he says, "this becomes a perfect rehearsal for those times, because it makes you keep the gun alive and the shooter stays ready to shoot. Lastly, breaking a little piece of target the size of a quarter at 40-plus yards is a tremendous confidence-booster. It's a very positive thing for the shooter."

Double Trap

If international trap sounds like a tough game, there is an even tougher version called "Double Trap." This game is now incorporated into international competition for both men and women.

Double trap uses the same 15-trap layout as the singles game, but only the three trap launchers on station three (numbers seven, eight and nine) are used. As competitors rotate be-

Shooting bunker trap is one thing. Competing in international venues is a different experience. Egalitarian Americans tend to be surprised and amused by the European tradition of dressing up for a day of shooting. The shooter the photo is Terry Wieland, an American, who has written extensively about fine shotguns. (Photo courtesy AYA)

Double trap requires a slight change in tactics compared to those used in standard, International trap. Since all targets come out of the trap house at a rising angle, a shooter can use the high gun hold favored by ATA shooters. Unlike in sporting clays, most coaches advise their students to take the trailing bird first and then swing through to the leading target.

The final or "C Scheme" uses traps seven and nine, with a setting of five degrees left and right, respectively, and at a three-meter height.

The speed of double trap targets is the same, regardless of the scheme.

A round of double trap consists of 25 pairs, or 50 targets. In competition, this is repeated three times for 150 birds, which is followed by a 25 pair shoot-off round for the top shooters.

"Although this game is relatively new," says Coach Woodhouse, "it is here to stay in international competition."

Double Trap Tactics

Double trap requires a slight change in tactics compared to those used in standard international trap.

Since all targets come out of the trap house at a rising angle, a shooter can use the higher gun hold favored by ATA shooters. Because the speeds are slower and the angles and target order are known to competitors, the first

International (Bunker) Trap Classification

Classification	Singles	Doubles
Master AA	93.00 percent and up	90.00 percent and up
A	87.00 – 92.99 percent	80.00 - 89.99 percent
B	80.00 - 86.99 percent	70.00 - 79.99 percent
C	73.00 - 79.99 percent	below 73.00 percent
D	Below 73.00 percent	Below 60 percent

tween stations, the angle at which they are shown the targets from the center machines will change the nature of their shots.

Three basic setups, or schemes, can be used in this game. Each uses only two of the three traps, with a pair of birds launched simultaneously.

The "A Scheme" uses trap launchers seven and eight. Trap seven is fixed at an angle five degrees to the left of dead center with station three and at a height of 3.5 meters at a point measured 10 meters in front of the trap house. Trap eight is set at zero degrees (a dead straightaway from station three) at a three-meter height. Both targets travel 50 meters, which means their speeds are slower than international trap. They more resemble ATA target speed and their speeds are constant throughout the round.

The "B Scheme" uses traps eight and nine. The number eight trap is a dead straightaway at a 3.5-meter height, while the number nine trap is set at a three-meter height and five degrees to the right.

bird can be jumped on quickly. Most shooters opt for a relatively open Modified choke with the #8½-shot international load for the first barrel. The second barrel will be choked tighter with a #7½-shot load.

"In all schemes," Woodhouse explains, "the targets will appear essentially as leading and trailing birds. Just as in sporting clays, I advise my shooters to take the trailing target first and then swing through to the leading target. This avoids the shooter standing there with a 'dead gun,' or having to make complicated changes in gun direction and speed."

Although that sounds uncomplicated and straightforward, double trap is not easy. In fact, if you compare the score percentages that are used to rank shotgun competitors into various classes for the different games, you will see that a shooter can miss a lot more double trap targets and still be a Master (AA) class shooter than at any other game. This is what makes double trap so challenging.

TOP TRAP GUNS

Like virtually all clay target games, trap began as an attempt to duplicate field shots on actual game birds. To an extent, the current game does that just fine. However, it only applies to flushing birds moving quickly away from the gunner and rising as they do so. Birds having that flight pattern include occasional pheasant, quail, sharp-tail grouse and chukar partridge, among others. The fact that trap targets are launched at a speed far higher than any game bird can achieve on the flush actually makes modern trap an optical illusion. Real birds rise in flight, but they do not do it very quickly.

What a trapshooter gets when he calls for a bird is a target that appears to be moving away from him, either as a straightaway or at a quartering angle, yet is actually rising quickly.

This means that shooters need a gun that will place the shot charge above the actual point of hold to compensate for the sharp climb of the target. If the gun shoots "flat," as we would want for skeet, sporting clays, or perhaps a hunting gun, then a shooter must actually cover the target with the muzzle of the gun, swinging right up through the target and blocking it out. Since that causes a shooter to lose sight of the target at the critical moment he triggers the shot, a flat-shooting gun becomes a factor that will decrease the shooter's score.

As a result, guns that win in trap are those that place the center of their pattern well above the point of aim. In some cases, depending on the shooter, that might be as little as three inches at 40 yards. Other shooters favor a much higher shooting gun and I have seen some that have a built-in elevation of over 18 inches at that range.

That can be achieved simply by installing a different rib on the barrel. I had an extra 28-inch barrel for my Franchi Pres-

Shotguns can be purchased for a few hundred dollars or for more than a hundred thousand dollars. The difference in any company's basic gun and its top-of-the-line is often in the accents and specialized touches: gold inlays, custom engraving and the grade of walnut selected for the stock and forearm. (Photo courtesy Rizzini)

The characteristic elevated, ventilated trap rib built in to most high quality trap guns is obvious on this Bruce Bowen Custom Trap. It may be ordered with your choice of point of impact: 100, 80, 70 or 60 percent.

tige fitted a number of years ago and it elevates the pattern nine inches above my point of hold at 40 yards. I did not need to alter the stock. By switching back to the 26-inch barrel with its flat rib, I can use the gun for trap, sporting clays and skeet. Some shooters get the gun to shoot high by having the barrel bent slightly upwards. This is not obvious to the naked eye, but this elevates the pattern.

The most common way to produce a high-shooting gun is to raise the comb height. This effectively raises your eye, which functions as the rear sight, and the gun will then shoot higher. This can be done with either a detachable cheekpiece or with a high-combed stock. Most guns marketed as trap guns will have a drop at comb of 1⅜ inches, instead of the 1½ inches that is almost standard for field-grade guns.

Another factor that determines an effective trap gun is its handling quality. Stand behind a skeet shooter addressing a mid-field crossing shot and you will see him swing his gun through a degree of lateral movement that will cover a range of up to 15 yards as he tracks and breaks the target. Stand behind a trap shooter, and you will see that even the most extreme bird angle will not cause him to move the gun more than about two feet from his starting position. That movement must be very quick and forceful and must drive right through the target. That driving motion has proven to be best accomplished with a longer, heavier gun that tends to stay moving once it gets started. The most effective trap guns are those with barrels in excess of 30 inches in length and with a weight of 8½ to 9½ pounds.

Trap shooters also favor tighter chokes than those pursuing skeet and sporting clays. A fast trap shooter, shooting from the 16-yard line, might get onto a target when the bird is at a range of 25 yards. More likely, it will be 30. If he or she is a little slower, the bird could be 35 to 40 yards away from him. A Modified choke is considered to be a relatively open choke for trap, although I feel it is about the best choice for the 16 Yard game if the shooter is using quality, hard-shot loads. The handicap and doubles games are best played with Improved Modified or Full choke.

A shooter engaging targets from the 27-yard handicap line is looking at shots of 40 to 50 yards and many will opt for Extra-Full choking.

If a shooter plays the doubles game or international trap, he needs a gun capable of firing two shots. If he just shoots 16 Yard and handicap singles, a single-barrel gun works fine. Those who play all the trap games sometimes use a two-barrel set: an over/under receiver that is fitted with a single barrel and a set of double barrels.

The ardent trap shooter ends up with a gun that has a very limited application for any other shooting game or actual fieldwork. Long, heavy, and tightly choked, the trap gun is a specialized tool for a specialized game. If you want to win this game, you will need one.

Today's Trap Guns

Although the top trap-shooting outfits tend to be specialized on the long and heavy side, you do not need a specialized trap gun if you just want to go out and shoot for fun. An aerial target is an aerial target. It flies: you shoot it. That can be done quite nicely with any shotgun, although it does get a little tough with the 410 and 28-gauge! I routinely shoot trap with my 28-inch-barreled 12-gauge Ruger Red Label, just to keep in practice for the outgoing targets that I often see in sporting clays. All I do is slip in a Modified or Light Modified tube instead of the Skeet I and Improved Cylinder tubes that normally occupy the gun when shooting skeet or clays. I make certain that I have loaded up with #8s instead of #9s and I am ready to have some fun. With this flat-shooting gun I cannot float the bird above the bead and have to make certain that I swing up and through the target, but that is what I would have to do on outgoing sporting clays targets anyway. I could never win the Grand American with this gun, but I carry a 90 percent average with it. Since I do not shoot trap on a serious competitive basis, this approach makes a lot more sense to me than investing anywhere from $1,000 to $25,000 for a specialized gun that is not particularly suited for anything but trap.

If you want to take your Mossberg, Winchester or Remington hunting pump gun out to the trap range, do it! For that matter, try trap with any make or model shotgun you happen to own. If it has only a fixed Improved Cylinder choke, do not worry about that either. Use a 1⅛-ounce 12-gauge trap load. If you miss the bird, do not blame the gun and choke! If you decide that you want to be a serious trap competitor, then you can consider a specialized trap gun, but you do not need it to start.

If you are ready for a specialized trap gun, here is a look at the best ones currently available. Unless otherwise noted, all are chambered for 12-gauge shells, and all prices cited reflect manufacturer's suggested retail price.

Entry-Level to Intermediate

EAA (www.eaacorp.com)

European American Armory says that if you want a pretty gun, one that costs so much that it virtually requires you to carry it in a fancy case, you should "buy the competition's gun."

EAA imports the Baikal IZH-18 Max single barrel shotgun from Russia. This inexpensive gun is available in 12 and 20 gauge and .410. "If you have to have a fancy, expensive gun," the company says, "buy one from the other guys."

The venerable Remington 1100 in the Classic Trap version with Monte Carlo Stock and five-round magazine capacity for 2¾-inch shells.

John Bernkrant calls the Baikal IZH18 Sporting ($299) an ideal trap gun for the beginner. It features a single, chrome-lined hammer-forged ported barrel (29½-inches in 12-gauge and 28½ inches in 20-gauge) with a raised vent rib and two sight beads. The Monte Carlo-style walnut stock has cast off, hand cut checkering and a pistol grip. The overall weight is a little light at about 6½ pounds. This gun features a selectable ejector/extractor system, a cocking/de-cocking system and comes with three screw-in chokes.

Remington (www.remington.com)

With a reputation as the shotgun manufacturer whose products every shooter can afford to buy and at some time does buy, Remington recommends only two of its numerous smoothbores for trap shooting. The Model 1100 Trap uses the basic gas gun design for the 1100-series that has made it extremely popular in the field and among casual trap, skeet and sporting clays shooters. In its Classic Trap mode, this 12-gauge holds four shells in the magazine and one in the chamber. Its 30-inch barrel is topped with a light contour vent rib with twin sight beads and comes with Mid Handicap (.034) and Long Handicap (.041) Rem-Chokes. The overall length is 50½ inches and length of pull is listed as 14½ inches with a 1⁷⁄₁₆-inch drop at comb and two-inch drop at heel. The 1100 weighs 8¼ pounds and the high gloss wood stock is graded semi-fancy American walnut. The trigger is gold plated.

For shooters who want their trap experience to replicate their field experience, Remington recommends its "historically significant slide-action" Model 870 Classic Trap pump-action shotgun. The 870's dimensions are practically identical to the 1100, except that its weight is listed as four ounces less.

Browning (www.browning.com)

Browning seems to offer everything you could possibly want in a shotgun, from down-and-dirty hunters like the $668 BPS 12-gauge pump in Mossy Oak Shadow Grass for waterfowl to the fully engraved Citori 525 Golden Clays that lists for $4,429 in its 28-gauge and .410 models.

Browning introduced the single barrel $1,290.00 BT-99 trap gun in 1969. Since then, Browning claims, its 2¾-inch chambered smoothbore has earned an "enviable reputation" on the range. Available with either 32- or 34-inch barrels, with a high-step ¹¹⁄₃₂-inch-wide floating rib, these guns are back-bored and fitted for the Browning Invector-Plus choke tube system with Full choke tubes supplied. With the 34-inch barrel, the 51-inch BT-99 weighs 8 pounds, 5 ounces. The stock configuration is conventional, with a length of pull of 14⅜ inches; drop at comb 1⁷⁄₁₆ (conventional) and a drop at heel of 1⅝ inches. Length of pull is 14⅜ inches. For an extra $248, you can purchase the BT-99 with an adjustable comb.

For 2004, a BT-99 has been redesigned in a lighter, smaller package that Browning says is ideal "for smaller-framed shooters." The BT-99 Micro is available with a 32- (7 pounds, 13 ounces) or a 30-inch barrel. Although other dimensions remain the same as the standard BT-99, the length of pull has been shortened to 13¾ inches.

Virtually any gun that carries the name Citori will be a fine, reliable shooter and many will perform flawlessly – at least up to and perhaps beyond the shooter's abilities – on the trap field.

The $2,209 Citori XT Trap 12-gauge is specifically advertised for trap. It is available with 30- or 32-inch (8½-pounds) back-bored barrels and is respectively 47 or 49 inches in length. Barrel porting improves pattern density and reduces muzzle rise and felt recoil. The XT over/under is chambered for 2¾-inch shells. Drop at comb is 1⁹⁄₁₆-inch; drop at heel is two inches. The tapered, high post rib is ¼- to ⅜-inches wide. The handsome XT Trap has a silver nitride receiver with gold accents while the stock and forearm have a glossy finish. Browning's Triple Trigger system allows you to adjust the Citori's 14⅜-inch length of pull and switch between three gold-plated trigger shoes: wide checkered, narrow smooth and wide, smooth canted. For an extra $266, you can purchase this gun with an adjustable comb featuring ⅝-inch height adjustment and a right-hand palm swell. Includes highly polished Full, Improved Modified and Modified interchangeable, stainless steel Invector-Plus choke tubes.

The new, $2,648 Citori XS Special has an engraved silver nitride receiver and satin-finished forearm and adjustable comb. This 12-gauge comes with five black-oxide-finished, stain-

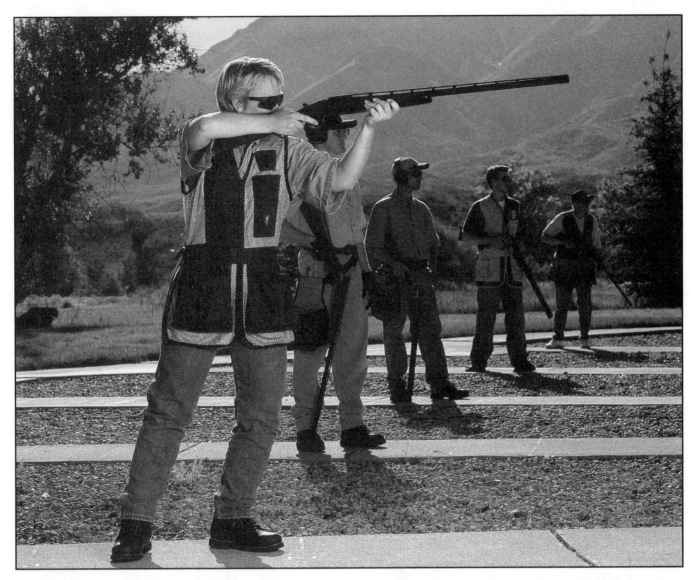

Young people on the shooting line banging away with Browning's BT-99 Micro. The conventional stock, beavertail fore-arm and high-post rib are ideal for small frame shooters.

Browning's Citori XT Trap with optional adjustable comb features a silver nitride receiver with gold accents; a ported, vented barrel; high post rib and right-hand palm swell.

less steel Midas chokes which extend beyond the barrel for easier installation and removal: Modified, Light Modified, Improved Cylinder, Cylinder and Skeet. The floating rib is tapered from eight to 11 mm and topped with a HiViz Pro-Comp sight and mid-length bead. The XS Special is chambered for 2¾-inch shells and is available with 32- or 30-inch ported barrels in weights of 8 pounds, 12-ounce and 8 pounds, 9 ounces respectively. The 1⅞-inch drop at comb and drop at heel dimension is adjustable. Length of pull is 14⅜ inches. The walnut stock is carved with a comfortable right-hand palm swell and the versatile gold-plated Triple Trigger system.

Winchester/US Repeating Arms (www.winchester-guns.com)

The $2,030 Winchester Select Energy Trap over/under 12-gauge is new for 2004. Its Monte Carlo stock and forearm feature distinctive oval checkering pattern. The comb can be raised to virtually any shooting position and moved for cast on or off in seconds. The Select Energy features a wide runway rib, mid-bead sight and TruGlo Tru-Beat front fiber optic aiming point. The barrels are ported to tame second-shot recoil, have vented side ribs and are available in back-bored 30- or 32-inch lengths. Chambered for 2¾-inch shells, three Invector-Plus chokes are

Winchester's Select Energy Trap comes with a standard or an adjustable comb. Barrels are factory ported and vented top and side. With 30- or 32-inch barrels, an adjustable trigger shoe and contrasting chrome receiver finish, this is a handsome gun.

The Master Trap 12-gauge over/under from FAIR has an 11 mm vented rib mounted on chrome-lined barrels. In the de Luxe version, this gun is also available in 20-gauge.

Beretta has been making guns since 1526. Its 682 Gold E is chambered for 2¾- or 3-inch shells. Overall weight is 8.8 pounds.

included: Extra Full, Full and Improved Modified.

The overall length of the Winchester Select Energy Trap with a 32-inch barrel is 49¾ inches. Length of pull is 14⅝ inches; nominal drop at comb is a little deep at 1¾ inches; nominal drop at heel is 2¼ inches. This gun weighs 7⅞ pounds. You can cut $159 off the suggested retail price if you purchase the gun with a non-adjustable comb.

F.A.I.R.

Here is another shotgun from Brescia, Italy. In business since 1971, F.A.I.R. manufactures a family of competent trap over/unders – Master de Luxe, Master, SRL 802 and Jubilee 702 – that are available, depending on the specific model, in 12- or 20-gauge. The 29- or 30-inch barrels have ventilated upper and side ribs. The top rib is 11 mm on 12-gauge guns and 9 mm on 20-gauge. They are topped with an interchangeable bright dot sights. Guns come with a gold-plated single trigger, standard pistol-grip-style walnut stock and forend. A rubber, ventilated recoil pad is standard.

Beretta (www.berettausa.com)

One of the oldest gun makers in the world, if not the old-est, Beretta dates its origins to at least 1526. The Italian company is well represented in both U.S. and international competition. Beretta says that in the Olympic games since 1956, its shooters have won nine gold medals, seven silver medals and nine bronze medals. Couple this with 147 world championship

medals in trap, double trap and skeet since 1978 and Beretta qualifies as a force to be reckoned with in smoothbores.

The new three-inch-chambered DT10 Trident 12-gauge has been designed in configurations to shoot any clay game, according to Beretta. At about $9,557, the DT10 Trap Combo is the top-of-the-line offering. Barrels from 30- to 34-inches are available and the DT10 comes with five interchangeable chokes. The gun is sold in a padded, hard-sided case and features an adjustable, gold-plated trigger, field-removable trigger group, palm swell and adjustable stock. The stock and forend are select grade, gloss finished checkered walnut. Drop at comb is 1½-inches; drop at heel is 2.28 inches on the straight comb and 1½ inches on a gun with a Monte Carlo stock. The progressive step rib is ⅜-inch by 5⁄16-inch and includes a white front bead and steel mid-bead. Weighing in at 8.8 pounds, the DT10 can be special ordered with left-hand cast, including a left-hand palm swell and trigger shoe.

A step down from the DT10, the 12-gauge 682 Gold E Trap with an adjustable stock carries a suggested retail price of $3,933. Throw in the combo top single barrel and the price rockets to $5,003.00. Beretta says this gun's Optima-Bore barrel has a "long forcing cone and overbored internal bore diameter." Barrels are available in 30, 32 and 34 inches. Four chokes are included as is a hard-sided case with room for the gun, choke set and spare parts. The gold-plated trigger is adjustable for pull length, and the 682E comes with two trigger shoes. The progressive step rib is ⅜- by ⅜-inch.

The 682 Gold E is chambered for three-inch shells and features a highly select, checkered Monte Carlo walnut stock and forend. The fully adjustable stock is accompanied by a palm swell and can be special ordered with left hand cast, including left hand palm swell and trigger shoe. Drop at comb is 1½ ½-inches and drop at heel is 2.28 inches. The 682E weighs 8.8 pounds. A serious over/under gun for serious shooters, this model is built for versatility and durability, right down to replaceable bearing shoulders on the monobloc and hinge pins.

Beretta's new AL391 Teknys Gold Trap costs in the neighborhood of $1,791. This handsome 12-gauge comes with three choke tubes and your choice of 30- or 32-inch barrels. The AL391 is a semiautomatic, gas-operated gun with self-compensating exhaust valve. The checkered stock and forend are hand-

Typically, the difference between very expensive and economy shotguns is the amount of hand-finishing involved. This Spanish craftsman is burnishing an AYA Coral de Luxe.

The Charles Daly Empire AE-MC Mono Trap is available with or without a fully adjustable comb. It comes with 30- or 32-inch ported barrels with three multi-chokes.

somely oil-finished walnut and the receiver features colored enamel inserts. Drop at comb is 1.34 inches and drop at heel is 2.36 inches. The Gel-Tek recoil pad consists of a soft, yet scratch-resistant and durable polymer shell and an inert, recoil-absorbing silicon gel core that is unaffected by temperature or time.

The AL391 is "accessorized" with a gold-plated trigger that contrasts with the satin nickel-finished receiver and its raised flat rib is ⅜- by ⁵⁄₁₆-inch. The rib is interchangeable from flat to stepped and tapered to parallel. A fluorescent orange TruGlo fiber optic serves as the front aiming point. Fitted into the buttstock is an 8½-ounce recoil reducer. This gun weighs 7.9 pounds.

AYA (www.aya-fineguns.com)

You have heard of this Spanish company as AYA, which stands for Aguirre y Aranzabal. While many of the AYA guns can be special ordered and custom fit, they have a series of over/under shotguns that are fine for trap.

The MD series begins with the entry level MD2. The black action holds a single trigger (selective trigger is optional), and

the gun is available with 28- or 30-inch chrome-lined barrels in fixed or multi choke designs. The stock and forearm are, of course, hand-checkered and oil finished walnut. This 12-gauge features automatic ejectors.

At the high end of the AYA trap line is the MD6S Custom with fabulously engraved silver-nitride sideplates and exhibition-grade walnut stock and forearm. Otherwise, the features of this expensive over/under are essentially the same as its less costly cousin, the MD2.

Charles Daly (www.charlesdaly.com)

The Charles Daly Superior Trap ($1,629) features the distinctive high trap ventilated rib, 10 mm wide from beginning to end. The side rib is ventilated and barrels in lengths of 30 or 32 inches are factory ported.

Empire II over/under shotguns such as the Empire AD-MC Mono Trap have an adjustable comb and an adjustable, gold plated trigger. The cost is $2,999 or $2,059 with a fixed comb. This gun is available as a combination set – 32-inch single barrel and 30-inch over/under – for $3,099 and with the adjustable comb and case for $3,749. The scrollwork on the sil-

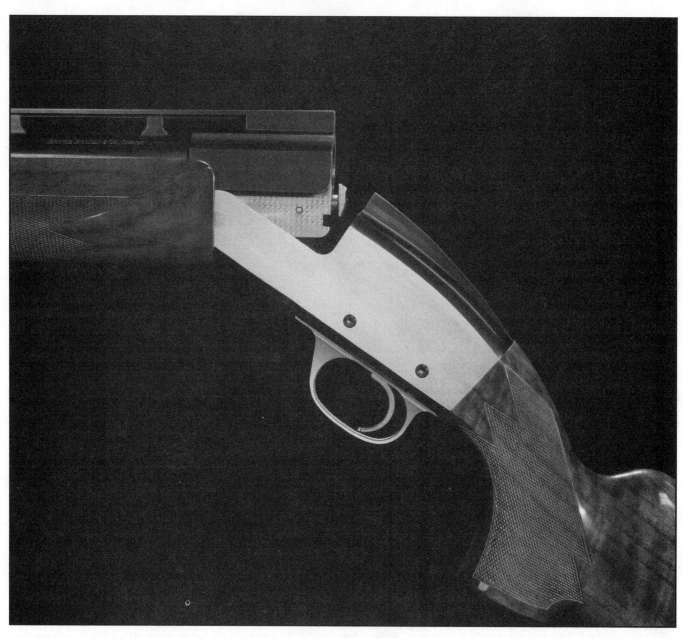

The difference between slamming a door on a cheap car and on an expensive car is the sound of craftsmanship and value. Maybe you cannot define it other than thinking a cheap car sounds "tinny." You can hear and feel that same quality difference when you open an expensive, custom-built single barrel Bruce Bowen Trap Gun.

ver action features delicate scroll engravings and two gold inlaid hunting scenes. Five choke tubes are included and you can choose the European style cheekpiece or the Euro-Swept Bavarian cheekpiece.

Advanced

With the exception of the upper-end Berettas or AYAs, all of the previously discussed shotguns fall into the light-to-moderately-priced class and are essentially mass-produced guns using modern manufacturing techniques that allow parts to be made to exceptionally tight tolerances. When a technician on the assembly line puts a gun together, he or she does so by pulling a part out of a parts bin and installing it. If it fits, and is within specification, it stays. If not, it goes back into the bin and another part is selected. Such modern production methods allow a quality product to be assembled with a minimum of cost-

ly hand fitting and without the need to employ highly trained, expensive assemblers. One might consider these guns to be the Fords and Chevrolets of the smoothbore family, and this description applies to those shotguns you will find listed in the skeet and sporting clays sections as well.

Some shooters are not Ford and Chevy folks, however. They are more comfortable with a Mercedes or a Ferrari, and if you attend almost any competitive shoot, you will find folks who can afford them. They do not mind paying five to 10 times what the Ford cost as long as they feel they are getting a premium product. That same philosophy holds true for shotguns as well, and the next gun makers discussed fall into that class.

In the mid-range are the custom guns like the Bruce Bowen Custom Trap Gun. In Sturgis, South Dakota, perhaps best known for its monster motorcycle rally, Bruce Bowen builds custom single-barrel trap guns. Bruce says he prefers that his

SKB has produced quality firearms in Japan for 150 years but they have been available in the US for only 36 years. You can buy SKB's trap gun as an unsingle or over/under-unsingle combo. Barrels are chrome lined with lengthened forcing cones and stocks are standard or Monte Carlo style, fixed or adjustable. An unsingle, 32-inch barrel with adjustable comb and Monte Carlo stock is listed at $2,398 or $3,089 in the combination version.

customers come to his new 8,000 sq. ft. factory (it has an indoor shooting range) or make an appointment to meet him on the road at a national shoot for a personal measurement before any wood is cut for a stock.

A nine-pound Bruce Bowen & Company Custom (**www.bb-guns.net**) is available with all the options. The elevated, ventilated trap rib may be ordered with your choice of point of impact: 100%, 80%, 70% or 60%. The .740-inch bore 12-gauge barrel is available in 32-, 33-, 34- and 35-inch lengths and comes only in a Full, fixed choke version. Bruce will build your gun with either a standard pull or release trigger, but both are included in the base price of $16,500.

Of course, stocks are custom-built to your interests and measurements. Bowen says he cuts each block of walnut by CNC to the appropriate general dimension and then hand shapes and polishes the stock to the individual needs of the shooter. Straight or Monte Carlo stocks are available from custom English or Turkish walnut. If desired, Bowen will build adjustability into your comb. Engraving is available and can be individually designed and the price negotiated.

Krieghoff, Perazzi, Ljutic and others can be considered – at least by commonly accepted shooter deference – as the Mercedes and Ferraris of the competitive shotgun world. The reason for that, other than their hefty price tag (to $25,000 and sometimes more) is the high degree of hand fitting involved. Unlike mass-production guns with interchangeable parts, these guns consist of parts that are individually hand fitted and hand formed. All critical components such as the sears, the trigger system, lugs and receivers are machined in rough form and then hand fitted and finished by highly skilled craftsmen to produce an individual gun.

Once the basic gun is complete, the same care extends to fitting the gun to the customer. Mass-market guns come with standard stock dimensions, but not these. The customer can determine exactly what stock dimensions are needed in terms of length of pull, pitch, drop at comb and heel, cast, rib height and width. The result is a handcrafted shotgun precisely tailored to the shooter.

Because most of these guns are personally fitted to a particular shooter, you rarely see a new Krieghoff, Perazzi or Ljutic on the shelf at your local gun dealer. Only rarely are these models made with "standard" stock dimensions for off-the-rack sales. On those occasions, the customer will have the option of selecting a buttstock with different dimensions or even an adjust-

able buttstock. Generally, however, when you see one of these guns on a gun dealer's rack, it is a used model and you will not see many of those. Folks who favor these upper-end guns tend to hang onto them for quite awhile! Very expensive guns are generally purchased directly through an authorized distributor or sales representative who assists the customer in ordering the measurements and features he requires. While each of these makers offers a number of different models, the only true difference among them is typically in barrel, rib and stock configurations and of course in the quality of engraving on the receiver. The heart of the gun, the action, will essentially be the same. The various model designations are simply a brief way to describe the different features.

Krieghoff (www.krieghoff.com)

The Krieghoff manufacturing facility is located in Ulm, in southern Germany, with U.S. offices in Ottsville, Pennsylvania. Krieghoff was founded in 1886 and today is known as one of the premier shotgun manufacturers in the world. While the K-80 12-gauge and the new K-20 sub-gauge are the primary guns known in the US, Krieghoff builds many guns only for the European market.

The K-80 was introduced in 1980 and is available today as a single barrel gun, an over/under or in a combo-pack. Krieghoff's theory was to make one receiver work with numerous combinations of barrels and stocks. This way a single high quality, hand engraved receiver could, with the simple attachment of a different barrel and/or stock combination, shoot any competition game or go to the field for pheasants or woodcock. Your receiver could thus handle anything from a 410-bore over/under in the morning and a 34-inch "unsingle" barrel in the afternoon.

The idea worked, which might be expected, what with parts built by hand. Chambered for a 2¾-inch shell, K-80 receivers are engraved in a classic scroll pattern, case hardened and plated in durable satin nickel. They are available in traditional blued, brilliant coin or the classic case-colored finish. Trigger pull is adjustable between 3¼ and 3¾ pounds. The K-80 has a wide, smooth trigger shoe with deeply curved profile for control and comfort. It is adjustable back and forth for best grip length. Release triggers (those that fire when released as opposed to those that fire when pulled) are available in single and double configurations.

In lengths from 30 to 34 inches (30 to 32 inches for over/

Krieghoff shotguns have a well-deserved reputation for fine shooting and utmost reliability. Their K-20 is one of the premier clay shooters in the world.

unders), the distinctive K-80 barrels are not joined by a rib. Thus, Krieghoff says, they heat and cool independently. This reduces weight and wind resistance, Krieghoff advertises, when you swing on a crossing target. Additionally, you can change the impact point of the bottom barrel of an over/under by using different hanger attachments or spacers: nine separately sized hangers are available for fixed choke barrels and six for adjustable choke barrels. This barrel hanging system allows you to choose your pattern ratio for the bottom barrel from a flat-shooting 50-50 to as high as 70-30. For trap, the bottom barrel is customarily set at 70:30.

Although there are no joining ribs between barrels, the K-80 has four different matte-finished, adjustable and interchangeable top ribs and one of them, tapering from 12 mm at breech to eight mm at muzzle, is specifically designed for trap. These top ribs allow you to shoot flat on impact or change to as much as a 90:10 ratio. Barrel ribs have a white pearl front sight and metal center bead.

Krieghoff says its barrels are engineered with a long forcing cone and are over-bored to reduce recoil and produce more uniform patterns. Fixed choke barrels have a Full choke on stop and Improved Modified on bottom. Choke-tubed barrels come with five replaceable chokes from Super Full to Improved Cylinder.

The "unsingle" barrel is fired by the under-barrel firing pin. It sits low in the receiver and this, in theory, results in less muzzle flip and felt recoil. The unsingle barrel point of impact adjusts by hand without tools via two coin-slotted screws and a small wheel.

Five stock designs are available for American trap shooters, three Monte Carlo and two straight, each with equal drop at comb and heel. You can also have a stock custom made,

even take your own chunk of wood to the office. Impervious to moisture, Krieghoff stocks are shaped from European select walnut with ambidextrous palm swells and are finished in satin. Stocks remove easily with a stock wrench. Length of pull is standard at 14⅜ and the K-80 weighs 8¾ pounds. A fitted aluminum case is provided with each gun.

Perazzi (www.perazzi.it)

Brescia, Italy sits at the foothills of the Alps, but at the pinnacle of world shotgun manufacturing. That is not bad for a company with only 100 or so employees that produces only a dozen shotguns a day and is not even 50 years old! Like the Krieghoff, the Perazzi is available with many, many options. This manufacturer builds expensive, world-class guns in single barrel, double barrel and combo sets. Options include adjustable-impact ribs, adjustable stocks and a wide variety of barrel and choke options.

The Krieghoff and the Perazzi are generally considered the pre-eminent shotguns on the international competition circuit and are among the favorites of top-ranked US shooters. One look at the high-quality, lusciously-engraved scenes from the field, from ancient history, or from Greek and Roman mythology will move most U.S. competitors to put on their gloves before handling one of these smoothbores.

As an example of the possibilities, the MX2000RS Combo is a totally adjustable gun. The single barrel comes in 32-, 34- or 35-inch lengths in Full choke or tapped for a variety of choke tubes. The high adjustable rib is tapered from ⁷⁄₁₆-inch to ⁹⁄₃₂-inch. The over/under barrel is available in lengths not commonly found in the US: 29½, 31½ and 34 inches. The over/under comes with fully-ventilated or half-ventilated side ribs. The trigger housing is removable for quick cleaning and the

Perazzi is generally thought of as the pre-eminent shotgun in the world. You can buy an MX8 American 12-gauge trap model with a single barrel or double barrel. Both have ramped, tapered 7⅙ x ⁹⁄₃₂ inch ribs. The basic gun is beautiful and ultimately functional in its "stripped-down" mode, but if you splurge for magnificent custom engraving and gold inlays, the sky is the limit on cost.

SKB's Unsingle barrel is equipped with an aluminum adjustable rib. The point of impact can be adjusted from 50/50 to 90/10 by rotating a small knurled wheel located in the muzzle support block.

trigger is gold plated. The stock and beavertail forend are made from select grade walnut, and the adjustable comb is available in wood or rubber.

If you have to ask how much a Perazzi costs and you simply cannot afford to travel to the factory in Brescia, Italy to have a gun fitted to your personal specifications, you can not afford to own one. According to their 2004 price list, the MX2000RS Combo described above will run about $19,493. Cheap. The MX8 SCO Gold Trap Combo is listed at $60,624 and, yes, some Perazzis do cost more than $100,000!

Ljutic (www.ljuticgun.com).

The only American gunmaker offering a competitive shotgun that has a reputation in the same class as the Krieghoff and Perazzi is Ljutic (pronounced "Lutik"), based in Yakima, Washington. These guns have earned a worldwide following because of their precision and durability. In fact, some Ljutics built in the early 1960s are still in active competition. Ljutik is a family business and founders Al and Nadine, both ATA Hall of Fame competitors, are still active. Everything is machined, nothing stamped or cast, from solid steel billets for "Shotguns to Last a Lifetime."

The Centennial Pro single barrel trap gun is available in alloy steel for $5,695 or stainless steel for $6,695. These hand-made

guns are lightweight and feature a 33-inch screw-in choke barrel. Order an adjustable comb and point of impact and you can expect to pay $8,995 (blued $7,995). The Centennial Pro includes Al Lutjic's patented recoil reduction system that produces 50 percent less felt recoil than most shotguns, according to Ljutic.

The Mono Gun single barrel trap gun is available from Ljutic in six models for $6,495: standard rib, medium rib, medium rib with screw-in chokes, Olympic rib (with or without screw-in chokes) and Deluxe PR03. The medium rib height is about half that of Olympic rib. Expect to pay $7,995 for a stainless version. All models come in American walnut and are offered with custom detailing, with the exception of rollover combs, cheek piece stocks and extreme cast on and off which carry added labor charges. You may also select English walnut and up-grade the standard checkering patterns. Release triggers can be installed on the Mono Gun. Barrels are available in 32-, 34- and 35-inch lengths and Ljutic charges an additional $300 for screw-in choke barrels. Ljutic guns are delivered in a very high-quality Americase guncase.

Whether you choose an off-the-rack mass-produced model or a top-of-the-line custom-fit model, there are plenty of effective trap guns available. If you want to win at trap, you would do well to consider one of the guns discussed above.

TRAP LOADS

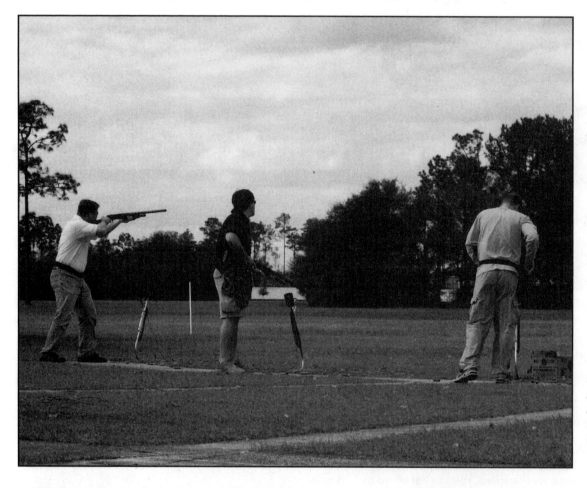

The heaviest load allowable under American Trap Association rules is a 12-gauge, 1⅛ oz. load of #7½ shot at 1,290 fps.

Of all the clay target games, trap is by far the easiest for which to select highly effective loads, whether you purchase factory shells or choose to reload. In fact, there are not more than a few load combinations that most shooters find suitable.

The heaviest load allowable under ATA rules is a 12-gauge, 1,290-fps, 1⅛-ounce load of #7½ shot. This has become such a standard that loads in this combination are invariably referred to as "trap loads" and every ammo manufacturer offers them. These are also some of the most highly refined shotshells in the clay sports game. Any reloader who thinks he can beat the performance of factory trap loads, and stay within the rules, is kidding himself. The best one can hope to do is equal their performance.

These loads have the power to break any target on a trap field – even the 50-yard-plus birds you will see from the 27-yard handicap positions. If a shooter wanted to standardize on one load and one load only for this game, he could not go wrong with this one.

All that power and recoil, however, is not always needed. In fact, a number of shooters have found that switching to lighter loads and, sometimes, smaller shot can help their scores.

Number 8 shot will reliably break any clay target out to about 35 yards. By the time the target gets to 40 yards, the breaking power of a load of #8s starts to get a bit "iffy." Since virtually any shooter on the 16-yard line will break his target inside 35 yards, there is no reason not to use #8 shot for that event, and some very good reasons why you might want to.

According to Winchester, a 1⅛-ounce load of #7½ shot (.095 inch diameter) will contain about 350 individual pellets. The same charge of #8 (.090 inch diameter) will have about 410. Consequently, #8s put approximately 17% more pellets in the pattern. Shooters can take advantage of this by using a slightly more open choke, which will increase the size of the gun's pattern. If you are not scoring as well as you would like at the 16-yard line with a Full-choked gun and a #7½ load, shifting to an Improved Modified or even Modified choke and #8 loads can give you a few more birds. You have a larger usable pattern and the individual pellets still have enough energy to break the target.

Lighter Loads

Another option with #8 shot is to drop to a lighter load. A one-ounce load of #8s will contain about 410 pellets, or just slightly more than a 1⅛ ounce load of 7½s. The lighter shot charge will, if the powder charge is the same, result in slightly less felt recoil, yet will put the same number of pellets in the air. Many savvy shooters shift to one-ounce loads of #8s for 16-yard work simply to reduce the cumulative effects of recoil over an extended match. That can pay dividends by keeping them a bit fresher at the end of the day, and they are not really sacrificing pellet count or pattern size over the heavier 1⅛-ounce #7½ load.

While the three-dram load is fairly standard in trap, many shooters opt for lighter, 2¾-dram loads with the same 1⅛-ounce shot charge. The heavier dram load moves at about 1,235 fps while the 2¾-dram gets about 1,120 to 1,165 fps, depending upon the powder used. It is my opinion that, from the 16-yard line, the slight reduction in velocity makes no difference in a shooter's score, just in the recoil he will absorb. The lighter loads are softer shooting. When moving back to longer handicap distances, however, I do tend to favor the full three-dram, 1⅛, #7½ load.

Another load option is a one-ounce, 2¾-dram load of #8½ shot. This one moves at about 1,180 fps, and one-ounce of #8½ shot carries about 480 pellets. This is as soft a 12-gauge load as you can shoot that still has enough energy to get the job done. In fact, in an 8½- or nine-pound gun, this load will produce less recoil than most seven-pound 20-gauge guns, or 5½- to six-pound 28-gauge guns!

The drawback to this load is that #8½ pellets start to run out of target breaking power at a range of just over 30 yards. However, a quick shooter will break 16-yard targets at under that range. The increased pellet count allows the use of a Modified choke, to increase pattern size, with a significant – and I do mean significant – reduction in felt recoil.

Some of the best scores I have ever shot from the 16-yard line have come with this shell in a Modified-choked gun. How-

ever, you cannot ride the target and take your time. This load works well when you get on the bird quickly! Still, the incredibly soft-shooting qualities of this (or any other 2¾-dram one-ounce package) make it worth the time it takes to experiment with it from the 16-yard line.

I know some shooters who have attempted to use #9 shot with an open choke and shoot quickly. I have yet to see that tactic be successful. Number 9 shot runs out of consistent target-breaking power right around 25 yards, and that is an awfully close range at which to break all your 16-yard targets. Some days it works, some days it does not.

My own trap load selection runs like this: Anything beyond the 20-yard handicap line calls for the full three-dram, 1⅛-ounce load of #7½ shot; inside that, I feel comfortable with the 2¾-dram, 1⅛-ounce loads. At the 16-yard line I have no problem with a one-ounce load of #8 shot, or the same load of #8½s.

The Trap Rule

According to ATA rules, a contestant cannot use:

• Any load with a velocity greater than 1,290 FPS (Feet Per Second) with a maximum shot charge of 1⅛ ounces (31.89 grams), or 1,325 FPS with a maximum shot charge of one ounce (28.30 grams), or 1,350 FPS with a maximum shot charge of ⅞ ounces (24.80 grams), as measured in any individual shotshell. These velocities are maximum and no individual shotshell shall exceed these limits for the designated shot charge. In addition, no load containing more than 1⅛ ounces (31.89 grams) or any shot larger than Number 7½ can be used. Shot charges are maximum and no charge may exceed the charge amount by more than three percent.

• Any shell loaded with black powder.

Remington has more than 20 different load specifications in its Game, Heavy Game and Sport Loads. They feature an all-plastic uni-body hull, Kleenbore priming, Power Piston one-piece wads, chilled shot and specially formulated powders for uniform patterns

Headquartered in Ontario, Kent Cartridge has purchased Activ and Gamebore. Their lead, All-Purpose Diamond Shot is designed for clay shooting and for small, fast game birds like dove and quail.

Factory Ammunition

Here is a look at what some of the major ammunition makers offer in 12-gauge trap loads.

Kent Cartridge (www.kentgamebore.com)

Established just in 1996, Kent Cartridge of Ontario, Canada has already purchased Activ (West Virginia) and Gamebore (England). Kent was founded with the purpose to develop a "non-toxic shotshell to equal or exceed high quality lead shot for waterfowl." Their Tungsten Matrix shot contains, Kent says, the "only true alternative to lead," but it is lead in their Diamond Shot All Purpose line that is designed for clay shooting.

The 12-gauge line of 2¾-inch All Purpose shells offer several combinations of shot size suitable for trap (#7½, #8, #9), ounces of shot (one, 1⅛) and powder dram equivalency (2¾, 3). Velocities (in fps) range from 1,145 (1⅛ ounce, 2¾ drams) to 1,290 (one ounce, 3¼ drams).

PMC (Precision Made Cartridges) (www.pmcammo.com)

Headquartered in Nevada, PMC offers two lines of shotshells for 12-gauge trap shooting. Their 2¾-inch Field & Target Specific shells are rated at 1,230 fps with three drams equivalent of powder and 1⅛ ounces of #7½, #8 or #9 shot. PMC achieves their "High Velocity" loads by reducing the amount of shot from 1⅛ to one ounce and thereby bumping up rated speeds to 1,250 fps.

According to PMC, their DymaFlex one-piece plastic wad flexes and cushions the shot on firing, and its integral shot cup completely encloses and protects the shot from deformation during its trip through the barrel. The result is shot that flies true for better, denser patterns.

Federal Cartridge (www.federalcartridge.com)

Federal has been building shells since 1916 in Anoka, Minnesota. It was purchased by ATK (Alliant Techsystems) in 2001 and today manufactures loads for every size smoothbore: 10, 12, 16, 20, 28 and .410.

In the standard trap sizes – 7½, 8, even 8½ and 9 – Federal has a dozen cartridges in its Premium Gold Medal Target line that are possibilities for trap and three in the Top Gun Target line. Shot speeds range from 1,145 fps to 1,235 fps for a couple of special, long range handicap loads that can reach out from the 27-yard line.

Federal maintains its paper shell offering, perhaps due to continuing demand from reloaders: N119 (24 gm. - 7½), T117 (1⅛ ounce - #7½, #8, #9), T118 (1⅛ ounce - #7½, #8, #9), T171 (1⅛ - #7½, #8), T171 (Low Recoil: 1⅛ - #7½, #8) and T175 (1⅛ ounce - #7½, #8, #9).

Remington (www.remington.com)

Some names seem synonymous with the American shooting heritage and Remington is certainly one of them. Remington's line-up for the shotgun is extensive in its Premier STS (Skeet-Trap-Sporting) and economical Gun Club line.

The Gun Club line has three, 12-gauge 2¾-inch shells (GC12) useful for trap. The GC12L has 2¾ drams equivalent and 1⅛ ounces of #7½, #8 or #9 for 1,145 fps shots. The GC121 is loaded with one ounce of #8 and boosts the velocity of 1,185 fps. Finally, the GC12 is hyped to three drams equivalent of powder in #7½ and #8 for a 1,200 fps shot string. Remington says the Gun Club line allows many shooters to get "acceptable reloading life while stretching their shooting dollar."

The Premier STS line is available for all gauges, but in the 12 you can buy it in standard, low recoil and handicap versions in #7½, #8 and occasionally in #8½ and #9. Rated velocities measured at three feet from the muzzle range from 1,100 fps (STS12LR) which carries a light, 2½dram equivalent, to the Premier STS International (STS12IT) at 1,325 fps with ⅞-ounces of shot (#7½, #8½) and 3¼ dram equivalent. Remington says the STS shell is the "most reloadable shell you can shoot."

Winchester/Olin (www.winchester.com)

This Alton, Illinois company has been building shotshells since 1886. Today, their Double A (AA) high strength and economical Super-Target (TRGT) loads are a standard at any shooting line.

Winchester's AA hard shot target loads were introduced about 40 years ago and the suggested retail price is about $7.90 per box of 25 shells or 32¢ per shot for the more common loads. Shells with the "HS" or high strength designation are superbly reloadable, Winchester says. All of the standard loads are present in the AA line from a 2¾-inch shell as straightforward as the AA127 with 2¾ drams equivalent and 1⅛ ounces of #7½ shot (1,145 fps) to an over-the-limit 1,350 fps load and ⅞ dram equivalent international loads.

In the 1⅛-ounce Super-Target 12-gauge shotshell line, Winchester has designed two value-priced shells in #7½ and #8 shot sizes. The three-dram equivalent shells are rated at 1,200 fps while the 2¾s are rated at 1,145 fps. Super-Target shotshells are designed for the "high-volume, cost-conscious shooter" who does NOT want to reload. Suggested retail price is $5.70 per box or 23¢ per shell.

Eley Hawk (www.eleyhawkltd.com)

Eley is an old manufacturing name in England, but relatively new to the US shooting scene. Eley or Eley Hawk reports that it is capable of producing "well in excess of 10,000 cartridges

Winchester's new Super-Target loads for 12- and 20-gauge guns also have a load of 1⅛-ounce #7½s in steel for ranges with lead restrictions.

Rio's best trap loads have a five percent antimony mixture rather than the standard three percent. This gives them slightly better breaking power because antimony reduces lead's inherent brittleness.

Sport Loads from Remington are economical, multi-purpose loads. They are built with premium Power Piston wads and plastic Uni-body hulls. Loaded with #8 shot – one ounce for the 12-gauge and ⅞ ounce for the 20-gauge – these loads are ideal for skeet, trap and sporting clays as well as field work.

per hour" at their factory in Minworth, Sutton Coldfield, England, and that is certainly more than I will need this year.

Eley has eight lines of clay target cartridges, each designed in a slightly different configuration: Eley First (an entry-level cartridge ideal for the price-conscious shooter), Eley Blues (a low recoil club cartridge), Eley Superb Competition (a fast, low recoil high antimony magnum shot for distance), Eley VIP (ultra-hard professional caliber shot), Eley VIP Sporting (a "fine

fiber wad cartridge" for speed and low recoil) and Eley Competition Trap (for the 20-gauge).

A selection of loads is available in both one- and 1⅛-ounce loads. Eley specifies the wad – plastic or "fibre" – as well as the percent of antimony in each load. The company also notes both "muzzle velocity" and "observed velocity." The 12-gauge Eley Superb Competition chambered for a 2¾-inch shell for instance, has a 1⅛-ounce load of #7, #7½ or #8 shot. The wad is plastic and the "head" measures 16 mm. Not only that, but the lead has five percent antimony and the muzzle velocity is 1,450 fps which makes it too hot for legal trap, but the observed velocity brings that rating down to an acceptable 1,130 fps. Eley says the VIP is designed for "smooth recoil and unrivalled speed."

Fiocchi (www.fiocchiusa.com)

Manufactured in Ozark, Missouri since 1986, and in Italy since 1876, Fiocchi offers a range of hard, uniform shot that is designed with unique one-piece plastic wads.

Fiocchi specifies four 12-gauge, 2¾-inch lead trap loads for "the high volume and discriminating shooter." The 12MS3 holds 3 drams equivalent and one ounce of shot in #7½, #8 and #9 size for 1,250 fps. 12MS118 lowers the powder to 2¾ while raising the shot to 1⅛ with a resultant speed of 1,150 fps.

Two "low recoil trap lads" in #7½ and #8 use high antimony lead. The 2¾-dram equivalent achieves 1,140 fps with 1⅛ ounces of shot while the three-dram achieves 1,185 fps. (Known since ancient times, antimony is used in varying amounts from three to perhaps seven percent to harden and increase the mechanical strength of lead shot.)

Rio Ammunition (www.rioammo.com)

This American subsidiary of a Spanish corporation offers shotshells specifically designated as trap loads. Target Load 28 is a 2¾-inch shell with one ounce of #7 1/2 or #8 lead and 2¾ drams of powder for 1,210 fps at three feet from the muzzle. Its heavier, 1⅛-ounce Load 32 produces 1,150 fps speed, but its Top Trap 32 Load is rated at 1,250 fps for longer-distance handicap shooting. The Top Trap/Sporting rounds are mixed with a five percent antimony alloy rather than the standard three percent.

Trap Reloads

Shooters who prefer to load their own shells will find a wealth of good load recipes in any number of loading manuals. Federal, Winchester and powder manufacturers like Hodgdon, Alliant and IMR (the latter now owned by Hodgdon) offer informative pamphlets on loading data for their components. These days, most of the information can be accessed through their Internet sites. A few observations on trap reloads are in order, however.

It is an accepted and proven fact that, all other factors being equal, the harder the lead shot (higher antimony content) the tighter the load will pattern, the more uniform and evenly-distributed the pattern will be, and the shorter the shot string. This is because hard shot suffers less deformation in the barrel as it is fired. Round, undeformed pellets fly true and maintain a more consistent velocity. Soft pellets (low antimony or chilled shot) do not make it out of the barrel in a perfectly round condition. This causes a number of pellets in the load to veer away from the main pattern, becoming what smoothbore shooters call "fliers." Fliers offer greater resistance to the atmosphere, resulting in their losing velocity faster than the round pellets.

Reloaders remember that if the shells hit the ground, they usually belong to the club.

This causes them to fall behind the main shot charge, which extends the shot string. The farther the shot has to travel to the target, the more the pattern falls apart.

Trap is not a close-range game. Twenty yards is a very short shot and it takes a real expert to get onto a bird that quickly. From the 27-yard handicap line, shots of 50 or more yards are common. Serious trap shooters simply cannot afford fliers, patchy patterns or long shot strings. If you load your own trap shells, use top quality, high-antimony shot. It costs more, but it is the quickest way I know for a shooter to increase his score. If you've never reloaded ultra-hard shot before, get ready for some sticker shock: as of April, 2004, Midway USA of Columbia, Missouri (www.midwayusa.com) was offering seven pounds of bismuth #7½ shot for $92.99 ($13.29/pound) and seven pounds of # 7½ BPI Hevi-Shot at $94.99 ($13.57/pound). In comparison, Widener's Reloading and Shooting Supply of Johnson City, Tennessee (www.wideners.com) was offering an 11-pound bag of #7½ BPI nickel plated lead shot for $24.99

($2.27/pound) and a 25-pound bag of # 7½ Star lead shot for $12.50 ($0.50/pound).

Powder selection for trap loads is rather wide, and a number of powders of different burning rates will work quite well. I tend to avoid quick-burning powders. My experience has been that they tend to provide a slight increase in recoil – more of a sharp rap than the softer push I prefer – and some of them can be rather dirty-burning, leaving lots of powder residue in the gun. Owners of semi-auto gas guns who use these powders may find that they need to clean their bores and receivers more frequently. Powders with a slightly slower burn rate will deliver the same velocities at slightly lower pressures and they're easier on the shoulder, too. You may not notice the difference in recoil immediately, but it will become apparent after a couple of boxes of shells.

Whether you buy 'em or load 'em, contemporary trap loads are simple to select. The key is to try as many as possible and use the one that works best for you.

Chapter Nine

THE EVOLUTION OF SKEET

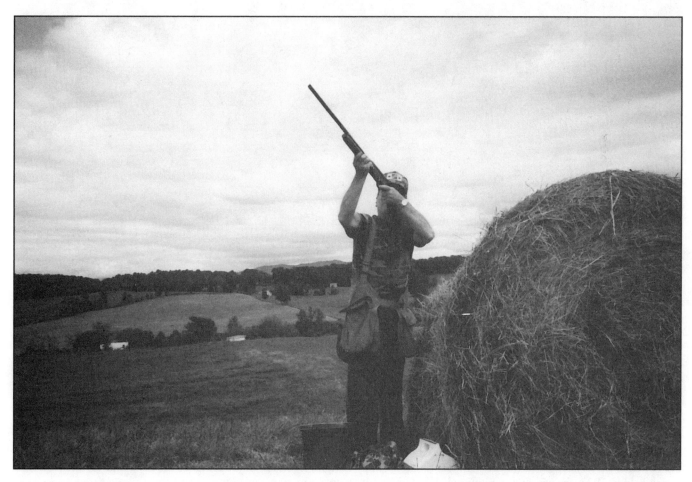

The game of skeet evolved in the US in the twentieth century when wingshooters realized that the practice they were getting did not prepare them for dove, quail, grouse and woodcock. Today, the fast passing shots from low and high traps are a great prepa-ration for darting, diving, fast-moving mourning dove. (Photo courtesy Ed Oehmig)

The clay target game we call skeet got its start shortly after the turn of the century when three avid Massachusetts wing-shooters got tired of missing game birds in the field.

You could probably win a trivia bet on this one: it was C.E. Davies, his son Henry, and shooting buddy William Foster who invented the game that ultimately grew into what we know today as skeet. They realized that the game of trap would not duplicate the angles and flight patterns of all game birds. So they bolted a trap machine to a plank and, by altering their position in relation to the trap and setting it at high and low elevations, they found they could re-create the flight of virtually any bird … and have a heckuva lot of fun in the process!

The original shooting layout was a full circle with a 25-yard radius. The circle was marked off like the face of a clock, with shooting stations located at each hour. The launcher was positioned at 12 o'clock and threw the targets at six o'clock. Two rounds were fired from each of the 12 stations, with the twenty-fifth shot fired from the middle of the field and the target flying right over the shooter's head. This original version of skeet was referred to as "shooting around the clock" and lasted in that form for a couple of years.

The obvious drawback to a 360-degree shot fall zone was overcome in 1923 when Foster, then editor of the bygone *National Sportsman* magazine, conceived the idea of two traps

Skeet is a wonderful game that you can shoot with practically any shotgun.

set within a semi-circle rather than one trap in a full circle. Not only did this allow the game to be played on much less land, but it also earned the gratitude of the spectators and those who drove automobiles to the shoots.

Unfortunately, the new version of the game did not have a name, so Foster sponsored a contest to create one. From more than 10,000 entries, the name "skeet," a derivative of the Scandinavian word for "shoot," was selected. Mrs. Gertrude Hurbutt of Dayton, Montana, submitted the name and won a $100 prize for her effort.

Skeet was originally developed as a bird hunter's game and it even required a low gun position when calling for the bird. It has evolved into a formalized competitive event and winning has gotten to be very tough. In the first national championship match held in 1927, the winning team missed eight targets out of 125. Today, a top-ranked shooter who misses eight targets out of 1,000 should consider taking up golf!

This level of perfection often intimidates new shooters, but it should not. I certainly do not intend to take anything away from those steely-eyed AAA and AA Class shooters who run 100 straight targets and consider it nothing more than a warm-up. They are true masters of the game and their form and timing are practically perfect. To be brutally honest, however, skeet lends itself to that type of performance. Of all the clay target games available today, skeet is by far the easiest. A look at a skeet field will show you why.

Field Layout

A skeet field is laid out in a semi-circle with trap houses located at both ends, at three o'clock and nine o'clock. The left-hand house is called the high house and launches the bird from

a distance of 10 feet above the ground, and at a slight upward angle. The right-hand house is the low house and sends the bird out at a more abrupt upward angle from a position three feet above the ground.

The launchers are locked into a fixed position and throw the bird to the exact same spot every time. When properly regulated, they will launch the bird at about 42 to 45 mph and the bird must travel between 58 and 62 yards through the air, landing at a predetermined spot under "no wind conditions."

Seven shooting stations are set in a semi-circle around the outside of the field. Station one is directly under the high house, with the following stations moved 26 feet, 8 inches to the right of the previous station. The last station, number eight, is located in the center of the field, midway between the two houses.

Ten feet forward of station eight is a white stake called the "Eight Post." Launchers are regulated to send the bird directly over the top of this stake.

The speed and flight path of the bird are fixed. The shooter knows precisely where it will come from, where it will go, how fast it will be traveling and when it will be launched. The shooting positions are fixed and each shooter will see the same speed and angle of the bird for each presentation from that station.

Each shooting position will show the shooter a different angle, but once the shooter learns the proper lead and technique for each of the stations, he has all the information he needs to break every target consistently. After that it is simply a matter of bio-mechanics or, as a former Olympic gold medal winner said, "Making your body work like a machine."

The shooting format for standard skeet is simple. A squad,

Competitive skeet is a four-gauge event. If you want, you can buy four separate guns, perhaps staying in the same family, for instance the imported Charles Daly line, or you could buy a 12-gauge and equip it with aftermarket tubes that allow you to compete in sub-gauge events.

composed of up to five shooters, starts at station one and works around the field to station eight. At stations one, two, six and seven, each shooter is given four targets: a single bird from the high house followed by a single from the low house and finally a pair of doubles where both the high and low house birds are launched simultaneously. When shooting singles, the high house target always comes first. In doubles, the outgoing target (regardless of which house it came from) must be shot first, then the shooter swings back to pick up the incoming bird. At stations three, four and five, the shooter will get only a single target from each house (no doubles), with the high house coming first. At station eight, he will shoot the high house, then the low.

Four Gauges

Competitive skeet is shot as a four-gauge event. In a registered match, where scores are kept for classification purposes, the 12-gauge event will be open to all gauges 12 or smaller, using shot loads not exceeding 1⅛-ounces of shot. The 20-gauge event is open to all guns of 20-gauge or smaller, with a shot charge not to exceed ⅞-ounce. The 28-gauge event can be shot with either the 28 or the .410 and a shot load of not more than ¾-ounce. The .410 event requires the .410 with no more than ½-ounce of shot. Regardless of the gauge actually used, all scores will be recorded under the gauge in which the event is officially scheduled.

The only restriction on shot size is that no shot smaller than #9 (2 mm) may be used. However, some ranges will have individual restrictions on shot size, based upon the size of their shot fall area.

This does not mean that in order to shoot skeet one must have four gauges. You are quite free to enter only a specific gauge event, if you desire, and to shoot non-registered practice rounds with whatever you want.

That doesn't mean that if you are an inexperienced shooter you must go head-to-head with the experts. The skeet classification system is designed to pit shooters against those of similar abilities. In skeet, that system is based on the percentage of registered targets you have broken.

Etiquette and Procedures

A round of skeet consists of 25 shots. However, it is advisable to have an extra half-dozen shells with you, because it is possible to break both birds during a doubles presentation with one shot. In this case, you have to shoot them over again. It is also common to get a broken bird ("no bird") out of a house in doubles and not be able to stop yourself from shooting in time. "No birds" are also re-shot. Therefore, you can use more than

25 shells in a round and nothing is more irritating to those waiting their turn to shoot than to have a shooter run back to his car for more shells.

A skeet squad can be as many as five shooters. The reason for limiting it to five is that most traps do not hold enough birds for any more than that. The sign-up sheet determines your shooting rotation in a squad. It is your responsibility to know which shooter you follow.

On the skeet field, a gun is never loaded until the shooter actually steps onto the three-foot-square shooting pad to take his turn. The rest of the time the gun must be visibly unloaded. With pumps and semi-autos, rack the action open and lock it there; break open double guns. This is only common sense and it not only guarantees that the gun is unable to fire, but it lets everyone else in the squad confirm that at a glance. Skeet shooters are among the friendliest and most gregarious members of the shooting community. I have yet to see an experienced skeet shooter who did not genuinely want to see everybody have a good time and do all he or she could to help inexperienced shooters learn the game. However, nothing will turn this same shooter into a rampaging demon faster than discovering that one of his squad mates is wandering around behind him with a loaded gun.

Skeet shooting is one of the safest participant sports there is. In fact, more people are injured while bowling, playing golf, jogging and swimming than are ever hurt on a skeet field. Strict adherence to the safety rules keeps it that way.

While waiting for your turn to shoot, do not crowd the shooter already on the pad. Be in line and prepared to take your place when the time comes, but the only person who should be within 10 feet of the shooter on the pad is the target puller/referee.

Some skeet ranges have a rule that as soon as a fired shell hits the ground it becomes the property of the range. It is advisable to check to see if that rule is in effect before you start a round. If it is, you must abide by it. Most of these clubs collect those shells and sell them to ammunition reloaders to help offset the cost of operating the field. If there is no such rule, it is perfectly permissible for the shooter to pick up his empties as he leaves the shooting station, as long as it is done expeditiously. The only time on the skeet field that is truly "yours" is the time you are on the pad shooting. Causing delays at other times is infringing on the time another shooter has paid for.

When you step onto the pad to shoot, it is generally accepted that the target puller will release the target at the first sound from you. If you are not prepared for the target, it is a good idea to say nothing. When you call for the bird, do so in a loud enough voice that the puller can clearly hear you. It makes little

Shooting geese from a Kolpin Top Gun blind requires the same shooting skills as one learns on the skeet range: correct gun hold, proper lead and follow-through.

difference what command you give: "Pull," "Yaaah!" "Now!" Whatever you are comfortable with is perfectly acceptable. Just be consistent in the command and you will help yourself by making the puller's job easier. With a smooth functioning squad, a round of skeet should be completed in no more than 20 minutes, often less.

Skeet Accessories

Serious shooters always wear eye protection. In skeet, if it is not a range rule, you should nevertheless consider it mandatory. Many shots in skeet are incoming birds and when the shooter breaks the bird, the pieces can keep coming. A piece of broken clay bird traveling at almost 45 mph can cost you an eye. It is common to get pelted with a few shards during the course of the round, whether from birds you have broken yourself or from birds others have shot; maybe even from the adjacent field. Any shooter not wearing eye protection on a skeet field is taking an unnecessary chance with his vision.

Hearing protection is also an excellent idea. Not only does it protect your hearing, but it will also go a long way toward guarding you from recoil fatigue and flinching brought on by continued exposure to high noise levels. A jumpy, tired shooter will not perform well. Muff-type protectors can be uncomfortable for some, but there are a number of excellent molded plugs designed to fit comfortably inside the ear that do not interfere with bringing the gun to your cheek. Even an inexpensive set of throw-away foam plugs is better than nothing.

You also need some effective way to carry your shells as you move around the field. If you are saving hulls for reloading, you will need a place to put those empties, also. Many shooters favor a shooting vest with large pockets to hold both. These can be purchased with a small amount of padding in the shoulder

These All Sport Glasses from Walker Game Ear have multiple lens options that allow you to change your view of the skeet range with changing light and weather conditions. You must have eye protection. Look for eyewear that is rated for ballistic impact.

Ear protection is a necessary item in your skeet kit. Whatever style you choose, make sure they have the best NRR (noise reduction rating) that you can afford. The electronic styles have a sound suppression circuit that very effectively muffles the blast of a shotgun.

area to help dampen felt recoil. Belt pouches are also available. These have divided compartments that perform quite well and are both inexpensive and comfortable. Either the vest or the belt is preferable to lugging a box of shells around in your hand or trying to stuff 30 12-gauge shells into your Levis.

Gun breakdowns can occur on the range but most are not quickly repairable, so there really is not much point in carrying a tool kit with you.

There is one little item, however, that can help: a shell knocker. It is possible for a fired shell to lodge in the chamber or for a "squib load" (either a reload or a fresh factory round; it happens with both) to leave a wad stuck in the barrel. A cleaning rod will remove either, but cleaning rods are cumbersome to tote. A simple solution is a piece of brass rod about six inches long. If you shoot all four gauges, its diameter should allow it to slip down a .410-bore tube. Dropped down the barrel, it will dislodge most obstructions and it can be carried easily in your back pocket. It is annoying for a squad member to have a jammed chamber or an obstructed barrel when it is his turn to shoot and not have anything handy with which to clear it. Toting a shell knocker will make you a popular squad member.

The governing body for skeet competition in America is the National Skeet Shooting Association (NSSA). You will find a full copy of their current rules printed in this volume.

Skeet is a simple and enjoyable game. Best of all, most shooters will have an easy time finding a skeet range near where they live.

SKEET SIMPLIFIED

Of all the clay target games, skeet is without a doubt the easiest to learn. Unlike trap and sporting clays, where targets may take varying trajectories when released, the path of every skeet target is fixed. Shooters know precisely when the target will be launched, what path it will take and how fast it will be going.

Once the shooter learns the proper body and gun position for each station, along with the required lead, he has all the information required to break every target consistently. This chapter will provide that information, but before that, we will take a moment to review the two most effective shooting techniques: "fast-swing" and "sustained lead."

Lead Techniques

With the **fast-swing technique**, the shooter begins with the gun behind the target. The shooter then swings the barrel quickly through the target at a speed faster than the target is moving. One shotgunner described it as "painting the bird out of the sky with the muzzle." As the muzzle overtakes the target, the shot is triggered when the shooter sees the required amount of lead.

The advantage to the fast-swing technique is that it is the most effective way to handle almost any aerial target, including trap, sporting clays and feathered game. Because the gun must be moving much faster than the target, the shooter has an almost automatic, built-in means of compensating for targets moving at varying speeds: the faster the target is going, the faster the shooter swings the gun to catch it. On the skeet field, a fast-swing shooter has the specific advantage of getting onto the target more quickly than the sustained lead shooter. This is an advantage on windy days when targets sometimes dance to their own tune. The faster you can break it, the better off you are.

The disadvantage, if it can rightly be called such, is that it is impossible to explain precisely what length of lead is required for each station because no two fast-swing shooters will see the same lead. Individual reaction times and swing speeds vary. One shooter may swear he sees only two feet of lead at station four, while the next may claim it takes four feet. Mastering the fast-swing technique requires practice

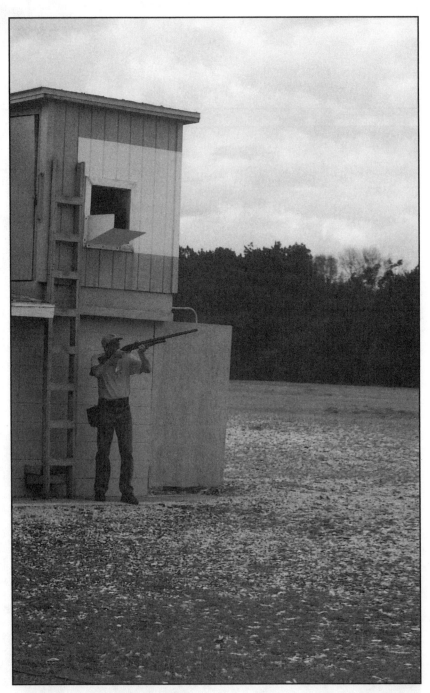

This shooter at station one appears to have his point of aim directed over the center stake or "Eight Post." All skeet targets must fly over the Eight Post and it is the point of aim for all stations except eight. Although his form appears to be a little too vertical and his hand on the gun's forend a little too tight for smooth swing, he is shooting a pump and swing on station one is minimal.

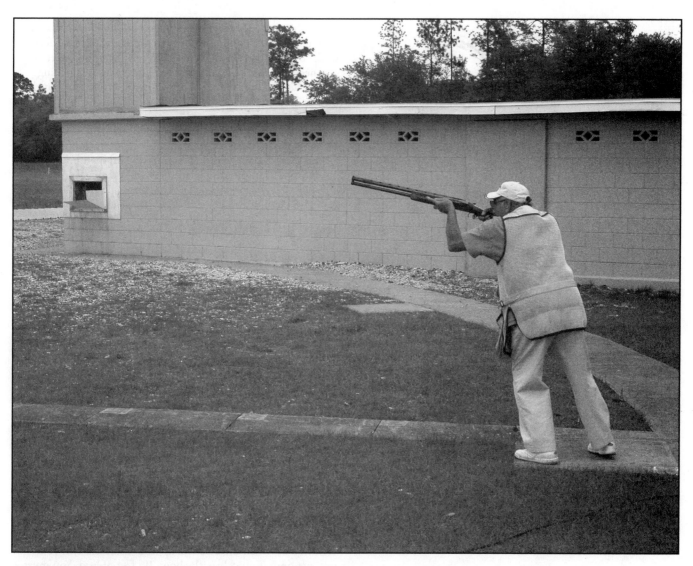

On skeet station five, use about a three-foot lead on both the high and low house. Shooting with good form and stance, this shooter is well prepared.

and repetition in order to program your mental computer. It is however, time well spent because it will make you a better and more versatile shooter. It will also be to your advantage should you take up trap or sporting clays and it will certainly increase your gamebird average in the field.

Sustained lead, on the other hand, requires that the gun muzzle start ahead of the bird and never get behind it. Once ahead, gun and target speed are matched while the shooter seeks a precise lead before triggering the shot.

This works well in skeet because you know every lead in advance. The disadvantage (other than being a poor choice for targets of varying speeds whose precise lead is unknown) is that it requires more time to get onto the target than the fast swing. This does not at all hurt the shooter on the easy, lazy incoming targets and indeed, many fast-swing shooters will revert to the sustained lead technique on them. It can result in shooters' "riding" an outgoing target too long and may cause problems if there is a stout breeze. In doubles, because you have to fast-swing through the second bird, you cannot use this technique.

If skeet is the only shotgunning you do, the sustained lead technique can make you a AAA-ranked shooter. Unfortunately, it sometimes causes problems in other wingshooting areas and then shooters have to go through the traumatic experience of

"unlearning" this technique. That said, all of the leads given in the balance of this chapter dealing with the fundamentals of skeet are sustained leads, since those are the only leads that will be essentially the same for every shooter. For those who wish to learn the more effective fast-swing technique, cut these leads in half as a starting point. You will quickly see if you need to increase or decrease your body rhythm.

A Station-By-Station Look at Skeet

Station One

This station positions the shooter directly under the high house and presents four targets: high and low house singles, and one pair of doubles (one bird from each house).

The high house target is easy but deceptive. It appears to be a straightaway shot, but because it is launched from above the shooter and has a slight upward angle, it is not. You must actually lead this target by shooting underneath it. If you shoot it like a straightaway, you will miss it by going over and behind it every time!

To break this target, take a comfortable shooting position that aligns gun and body on the Eight Post. This advice will hold for virtually every station on the field, because it is advan-

A belted shell pouch and a slip-on shoulder pad are adequate for starters, but as they gain more interest and proficiency in skeet, most shooters will quickly opt for a shooting vest such as this mesh model from Browning.

tageous to have your body set for the best shooting position at the point at which you will actually break the target. Since every target on the field is calibrated (if the trap machines are properly adjusted) to send the bird directly over the Eight Post, it makes sense for this to become your focal point. If the Eight Post is where you set up, you will be in position to break every station, with the possible exceptions of high house two and three, low house five and six, and station eight, which we will explain as we reach them.

Once you are positioned, bring the muzzle up to about a 30-degree angle above horizontal and call for the bird. As soon as the bird appears over the muzzle, swing down and through the bird, triggering the shot when you see a six-inch lead below it. Take this bird as quickly as you can, because if you allow it to get beyond the Eight Post, it starts to drop rapidly and becomes a much tougher shot. "Riding" this bird will occasionally cause you to break the low house bird also with the one shot, when shooting doubles at this station. That results in a "do-over."

If you are having trouble with high house one, increase the gun angle to 45 degrees. This will cause you to swing faster to catch the bird, and it often helps.

Low house one is easy. Again, align your body on the Eight Post and then bring the gun back to a point about four feet to the outside (left) of the house. On any incoming skeet target, never align the gun directly on the trap house opening where the bird will emerge. This will temporarily blot out the bird as it emerges and will interfere with your ability to pick it up quickly.

Once the bird is released, swing smoothly with it; yet do not be in a hurry to break it. Veteran skeet shooters want to break this target (along with low house two and high houses six and seven) in the same place they will break it during doubles. Let the target reach a point about 45 degrees off your left shoulder and take it there. The lead for this target is one foot. If you get into the habit of shooting station one singles in this manner, doubles are easy. You take the high house quickly and when you come back for the low house, you will find it right where you normally break it as a single.

Station Two

Station two presents four targets: high and low house singles and one set of doubles. This station, however, is not as easy as station one.

The high house shot is one of the tougher targets on the field. It is a vicious quartering angle that must be taken quickly and with a lot of lateral body movement. Right-handed shooters have trouble with this station because the body does not swing as well to the right as it does to the left.

Start by positioning on the Eight Post or maybe just a bit to the right of it to give yourself a little more room to uncoil. Pivot the body to bring the gun about two-thirds of the way back to the house. If you come too far back toward the house, you may not catch this target. Put the gun at the same elevation at which the bird will appear. Once the bird comes out, get onto it quickly with about 2½ feet of lead. You must follow through on this shot. Any slowing or stopping of the swing will result in a miss. This is true of any skeet target, but especially so on high house two.

Low house two is much easier. Treat it just like low house one and extend the lead to between 18 and 24 inches. Let the bird fly to a point almost equal with your position. That is where it will be during doubles.

Doubles are the same as at the last station. Get on the outgoing target (high house) quickly, and come back to find the incoming low house right where you normally break it as a single.

If you have a problem with high house two, the answer is to swing faster and shoot quicker. You must be aggressive on this target.

Station Three

During a standard round of skeet, one takes two targets at this station, both singles, one each from the high house (first) and one from the low house. The high house is an outgoing quartering shot similar to high house two, but you have more time and it is an easier shot. Position on the Eight Post or a bit to the right of it and give the bird three feet of lead.

The low house is an "incomer," similar to low house two, but becomes more of a crossing shot due to the distance. Position as with low house two and give this target 3½ feet of lead.

One problem with station three (along with four and five) is wind. If there is a breeze, these targets can do some serious dancing! It pays to develop the habit of getting onto these birds quickly. That will also help you when you shoot doubles and find yourself taking doubles at these stations.

Station Four

As in station three, the shooter is presented with two singles. Both are direct crossing shots and are the longest that you will see on a skeet field. These birds are 21 yards away from the shooter when they cross the Eight Post. The lead for the birds from both houses is four feet.

I prefer to position on the Eight Post for both houses and try to break the pigeons as they cross the post. Some shooters use a different foot position for the high and low houses at this station (as well as three and five), but I do not concur because it causes problems when you shoot these stations in the doubles game. As long as you position your natural point of aim on the Eight Post, you have all the range of movement you require for both singles and doubles.

Until this point, shooters have been seeing new angles and shots at each station. As you move to station five, however, things begin to become familiar.

Station Five

This is nothing more than station three in reverse, with the high house becoming the incomer (and still shot first) and the low house becoming the outgoing target.

Take the high house using the same 3½-foot lead used on low house three. Take the low house with the same three-foot lead as high house three. Positioning on the Eight Post is the same.

The biggest difference is that the low house takes a more abrupt upward angle because of your proximity to it and you must rise with it. Other than that, every bit of practice you take at station three helps you with station five, and vice versa.

Station Six

This is the mirror image of station two. Shoot the high house first. It is a gentle incomer similar to low house two. Body position is the same, as is the 18- to 24-inch lead used on low house two.

Low house six becomes the outgoing target and is a sharp and rapidly rising target. For right-handers, however, it is easier than the "Demon High House Two" because the body uncoils better to the left. Shoot it the same way, using the same body position and 2½-foot lead.

For doubles, shoot the outgoing low house first and take the incoming high house as it draws in to a 45-degree angle to the shooter's right.

Shoot station six the same way you shot station two.

Station Seven

This is the easiest station on the field. Shoot the high house first, but let it get close, and use a one-foot lead.

The low house looks like a dead straightaway and, if you have a little upward angle in your initial gun position, it is. This target can be broken with no gun movement. Position the gun and your body on the Eight Post, elevate the gun barrel to a point about eight feet above it and, if the launcher is regulated properly, the target will "appear" right over your front bead.

Pull the trigger – dead bird.

Doubles at this station are so easy one wonders why they even bother. Take the outgoing house with no gun movement and let the recoil ride the gun up to perfectly pick up the incoming bird.

If you are introducing a new shooter to skeet and you want to build their confidence quickly, take them to station seven first.

Station Eight

Having completed a trip around the outside, it is now time to step inside and face two of the most intimidating targets on the field.

High and low house eight targets are not "gimmes," but they are not nearly as tough as they appear, and you have more time to shoot them than you might think.

The reason these two targets are intimidating is that they are close. In years past, some shooters even used special "spreader" loads to handle them. Once shooters found out how easy these targets were to break, however, the station eight birds lost their intimidation factor.

Take high house eight by positioning gun and body right on the trap house opening, then moving the gun four feet to the right of the trap house. As the bird comes out, swing quickly up and through it, triggering the shot just as the gun muzzle passes the bird and shows just a hint of daylight between bird and muzzle.

Shoot the low house by positioning on the opening and then moving the barrel three feet to the left of the house. When the bird comes at you, swing up and through and break the shot the moment the muzzle blots out the bird.

These targets are that simple.

If you have been counting shells, you know that we have only fired 24 of our 25 shells. Shotgun shells generally are packaged in boxes of 25, of course – so what becomes of that "extra" twenty-fifth shell? That shell is called the "option round," and you can use it to take a second shot at the first target missed during the round. (Even if you hit this "second-chance" target, however, it's still scored as a miss.) If you get to low house eight without a miss, you may fire the unfired option round as a second shot on that station. If you hit it, you've scored 25-straight. (If you have never run 25-straight skeet targets before, performance pressure makes Number 25 the toughest shot on the field. If you make it, it is also the most satisfying.)

Getting to that point, however, takes proper equipment and intelligent practice.

All-Important Practice

The foregoing angles, leads and body positions provide all the information required to break every target on the field consistently. To make use of this information, though, a shooter must see, and break, enough of those targets to build the positive subconscious images needed for success. There are good and bad ways to arrive at that point.

In the opinion of many good skeet shooters, the worst possible way to start is for a new shooter to simply fall in with a squad and start shooting. This is because a new shooter sees new angles and shots at each station. Before he can begin to understand and master them, he is whisked off to the next station where what is new begins all over again. Along the way he or she will get a lot of well-intentioned advice from the other shooters on the squad, yet much of it will be confusing, hard for a novice to understand and sometimes even contradictory. This makes for a poor learning environment.

The most effective way to learn skeet (and the most efficient in terms of time and ammunition spent) is to start with one particular shot and work on it until it is burned into the subconscious. Then, move on to the next shot presentation.

At first, begin working on the easy incoming shots and ig-

Station One, High House: This deceptive target looks like a straightaway, but shooters must actually trigger the shot with the barrel below the target if they are to score.

Station One, Low House: Smart shooters are in no hurry to break this easy shot and allow it to reach the same point where they will shoot it as a double. It is easier to find it when you always look for it in the same place.

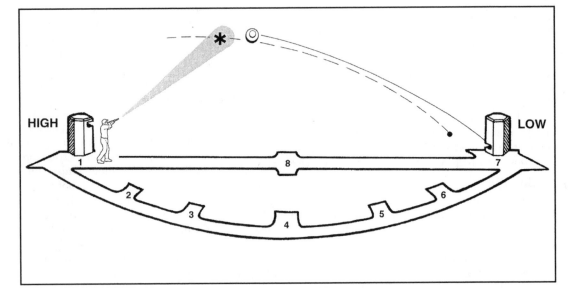

Station Two, High House: A tough shot for right-handed shooters, this requires a lot of lateral body movement, and a shooter must drive forcefully through the target. Get sluggish here and you will miss.

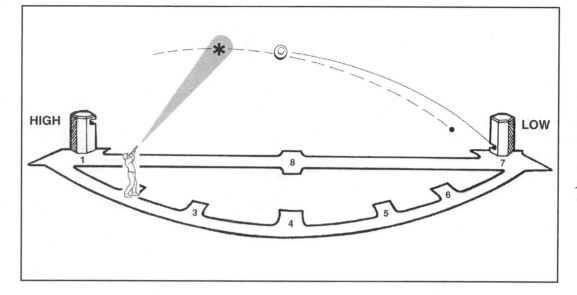

Station Two, Low House: This is very similar to the low house target from station one. Shoot it in the same place with just a slight increase in lead.

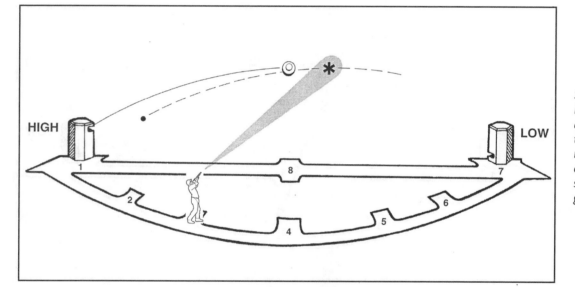

Station Three, High House: An easier angle than station two high house, this requires another foot of lead but gives the shooter more time to get onto the bird.

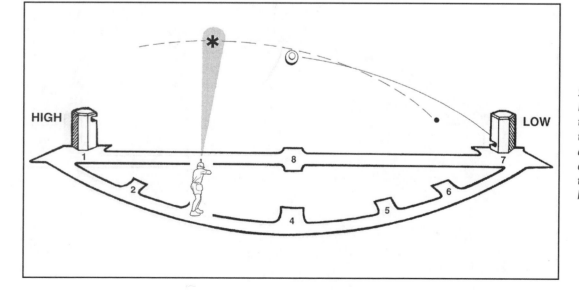

Station Three, Low House: This is one of the easier targets on the field when taken as a single. The shooter has plenty of time to find it and establish the correct lead.

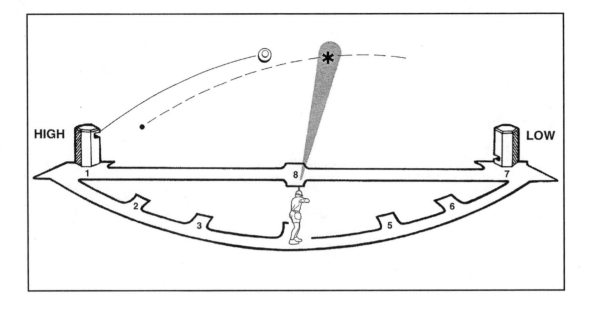

Station Four, High House: This is one of the longest shots you will see on a skeet field and it tricks many sustained lead shooters who do not believe they need a four-foot lead on a 21-yard target. Fast-swing shooters can cut that lead in half.

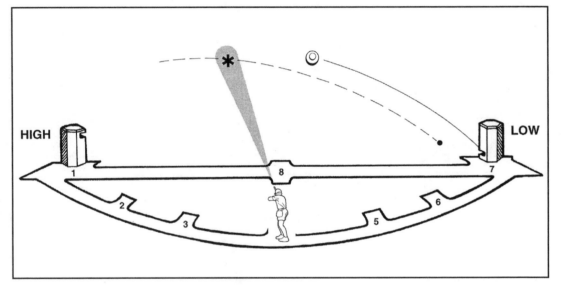

Station Four, Low House: Virtually the same shot as from the high house, but in a different direction. If you break both station four targets near the "Eight Post," you do not have to change foot position.

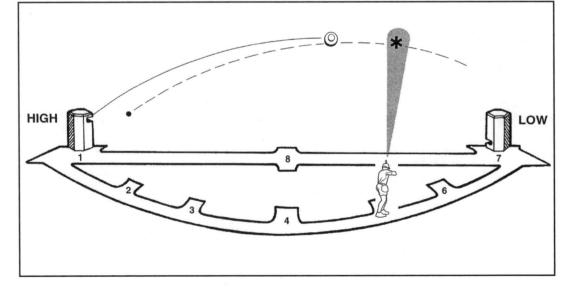

Station Five, High House: This is almost the mirror image of the station three low house. The lead is the same.

Station Five, Low House: Very similar to station three high house except that the target is usually climbing a little more. The leads are the same and the shooter must concentrate on swinging up and through the target.

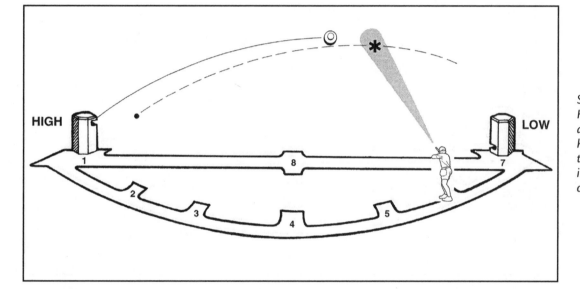

Station Six, High House: This is an easy as the station two low house shot, although the target is often falling slightly, depending on wind direction.

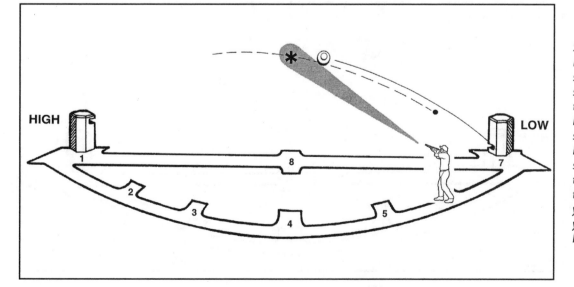

Station Six, Low House: Left-handed shooters have the same problem with this target that right-handers do on the station two high house. You must swing quickly through this target and trigger the shot as soon as you have your lead. If you hesitate, you will lose this bird.

Station Seven, High House: One of the easiest shots on the field, this target should be broken in the same place you will see it as a double.

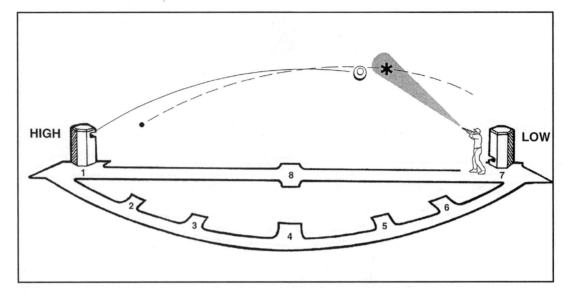

Station Seven, Low House: This is the only target on a skeet field that can consistently be broken with no gun movement. "It's a true 'gimme,'" says co-author Chris Christian.

Station Eight, High House: More intimidating than it looks, shooters should swing fast through this target and trigger the shot as soon as the muzzle reaches the leading edge of the bird.

Station Eight, Low House: The closest shot on a skeet field, with many birds broken only four yards off the muzzle. Fast-swing through the target and trigger the shot as soon as the muzzle blots out the bird.

In any competition, your shooting squad will be important to you. Whether you are personally compatible is less important than whether your shooting rhythm is compatible. It's also important that the squad's shooting etiquette recognizes the need for all shooters to step to the line with plenty of room to swing and a quiet, unhindered moment to focus before pulling the trigger.

nore everything else. This builds a shooter's confidence and demonstrates the symmetrical nature of the game.

Start at station one and work on the low house until you become proficient. This sometimes takes as few as four or five shells. Once you have a solid feel for that target, move to low house two. It is virtually identical, except for the lead, and the positive experience with low house one is a benefit at low house two. Then go to low house three and do it again. Stations five, six and seven require work on the incoming high houses until you have a firm grasp of all these shots.

When you reach this point, move to station four to work on both high and low houses. The leads are identical, and these shots are similar to those you have already learned at stations three and five. This also accustoms you to swinging quickly on fast-moving targets, because until now all shots have been lazy incomers. Station four is the perfect spot to make the shift from deliberately taking incomers to aggressively pursuing outgoing birds.

After that, it is back around to stations three, two and one, and then over to five, six and seven for work on the outgoing targets. Station eight comes next and the final lesson is putting it all together with doubles.

Using this approach, the time required to give a new shooter a solid, working knowledge of the game is reduced from months to weeks. I have seen students expend as few as 10 boxes of shells in practice, then go out, and pop 23 birds the first time they shoot a complete round!

Assuming you find a competent instructor, progressive lessons like this can also prevent the shooter from acquiring bad habits at the start. Bad habits will do some serious damage to a shooter's scores.

Common Errors

To achieve a good score in skeet, which we have said was perhaps the easiest shotgun game, a shooter must still execute the fundamentals properly. Sometimes this does not happen, though. There are three very common ways to miss even the easiest skeet target and they will, on occasion, plague shooters at almost any level of skill.

The most common mistake is lifting the head from the gunstock. Not surprisingly, this seems to be the bane of new shooters as well as those who have taken significant time off from the game. Under these conditions, targets seem to be the size of aspirin tablets moving at about the speed of a Patriot missile and new shooters will often pop their heads off the stock to get "a better look" or simply locate the target. When the head comes off the stock, the shot charge goes high every time.

There is no quick and easy cure for this, other than to continually remind yourself to "Love Thy Wood." Take plenty of care when mounting the gun to ensure a proper cheek weld with the stock. That cheek weld is critical to success wingshooting. Maintaining a cheek weld is a shooting basic that the shooter must continually work on and reinforced.

Stopping the swing is another quick way to blow a target and surprisingly, this often seems to affect mid-level shooters the most. This error can be especially prevalent among shooters who rely completely on the sustained lead technique since it can, at times, encourage indecision and hesitation.

New shooters see targets moving so swiftly that they must swing very quickly to catch them and this forces them to swing through the target. Once a shooter gains some experience, however, two things happen at about the same time: the targets suddenly grow much larger and they slow down. The experienced shooter knows he has plenty of time and becomes more concerned with getting "just the right lead." The gun swings through the target, the correct lead is obtained, analyzed, trimmed up a bit, and then the subconscious says, "We've got it! Pull the trigger."

Then, just as the trigger gets slapped, the gun stops and the shot charge sails harmlessly behind the target.

The best way to avoid this is to think of wingshooting in the same light as many other sports: *one must follow through.* If a golfer stops his swing the moment his club makes contact with the ball, or if a bowler stops his arm movement when he lays the ball down on the alley, or if a tennis player quits the instant his racket strikes the ball, what would the results be? Nothing. Zip. *Nada.* No follow-through equals no good results.

Shotgun shooting is no different. To hit an aerial target, the gun must be moving at the moment the shot is triggered and it must continue to follow right on through the target. If stopping your swing troubles you, try following the broken pieces and mentally take a second shot. If you develop the habit of staying with the broken pieces after the shot, even if for just a fraction of a second, you will not have to worry about stopping your swing.

The last of the common problems is simply not being ready when you call for the bird. Unbelievably, this can often sneak up on experienced shooters without warning.

What happens is this: you have broken that target hundreds, maybe thousands of times; you could do it in your sleep, and with one hand tied behind your back. You never miss that bird. Then, you step on the shooting pad and let your mind drift. Bingo! When the bird comes out, you're unprepared. Your timing is completely off and the bird sails away unscathed.

I watched a terrific shooter lose his concentration at a national championship once and he admitted his gaffe afterward. He stepped to the shooting pad, took a moment to admire an airplane flying overhead, called for the bird and found his mind was still on the airplane. He missed.

Nearly everyone develops a little routine when he steps onto the pad. Some people squiggle around. Some adjust their shooting vest or glasses. I sweep all the little bits of broken target off the pad with my foot. The point is that we all do something. While our small habits may look a little quirky to others, they are actually an important part of our shooting game. These individual quirks are our subconscious minds' way of preparing us to execute the shot. Let the subconscious do its job. If you have a comfortable "pad routine," do not deviate from it or you may short-circuit your own success.

When you are about to conduct a complicated movement that requires a number of coordinated body movements and mental decisions, all happening in about 1.2 seconds, your subconscious mind is the best friend you have. Do not get in its way.

Combine your personal routine with an understanding of proper leads and angles and an effective practice regime that lets your subconscious absorb them, and you will find that skeet can indeed be as simple as it is fun.

Individual Skeet Classification					
Class	12-gauge	20-gauge	28-gauge	.410-bore	Doubles
AAA	98.5% and over	98% and over	97.5% and over	96% and over	97% and over
AA	97.5-98.49%	97-97.99%	96.5-97.49%	94.7-95.99%	95-96.99%
A	96-97.49%	94.5-96.99%	94-96.49%	91-94.69%	91-94.99%
B	93.5-95.99%	91-94.49%	90.5-93.99%	86-90.99%	85-90.99%
C	90 to 93.49%	85.5-90.99%	85.5-90.49%	80-85.99%	80-84.99%
D	85.5-89.99%	under 85.5%	under 85.5%	under 80%	under 80%
E	under 85.5%	n/a	n/a	n/a	n/a

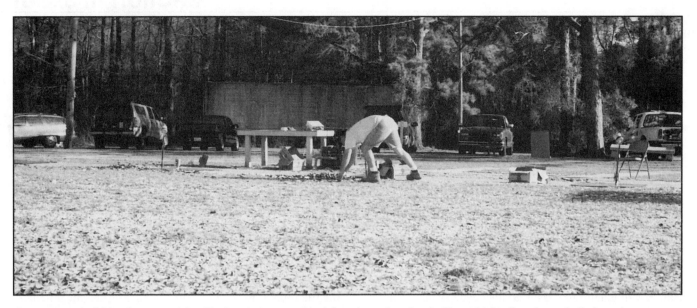

If an empty shell hits the ground, it will often belong to the club or host shooting facility, which offers these shells for sale at two to three cents each to reloaders to help defray operating expenses. Because many avid clay target shooters are reloaders, it may save embarrassment to inquire about a club's rules before you begin filling your shell pouch.

Robert Paxton, All-American

Robert Paxton, owner of Paxton Arms in Dallas, Texas, began shooting skeet competitively when he was 15 years old in 1969. Just two years later, he won the World Championship in his age division. Since then, he has won four additional world titles and has been selected for the Open Men's All-American Team 33 times. He has been elected to the NSSA and Texas Skeet Halls of Fame and is the current chair of the skeet All-American selection committee.

Paxton knows skeet inside and out, but he may be most proud of an event that took place almost 15 years ago. In 1990 and 1991, he set the long run record, breaking 2,173 registered targets without a miss – with a 20-gauge.

When he missed that 2,174th target, he says he simply reloaded and called for his option, which he broke.

"All good things eventually come to an end, don't they," he says without any bitterness at missing the shot from station six. "It was good training. When you miss and the scorer marks a zero, it doesn't help to get upset. You can't make it up like you can in golf, so don't let it affect your shooting."

Paxton opened Paxton Arms in 1978 (www.paxtonarms.com) to sell competition shotguns and accessories. He carries products by Krieghoff, Kohler, Perazzi, Beretta and Briley. "I used to teach professionally, but it got to be too much work," he says, "teaching, shooting and running the store."

Still, he definitely recommends that new shooters work with a coach. "It will take years, literally, off your learning curve, whatever sport you are in," he says. "It's the same with skeet as it is in tennis or golf, I imagine. Many clubs have volunteer coaches who are only interested in building membership and that means helping you be successful and have fun."

Paxton taught the sustained lead technique for breaking targets rather than the swing-through technique. Because of the highly structured nature of skeet – the shooter knows what is coming on every shot and the gun is pre-mounted and pointed – it is easier to learn the proper leads.

"If you learn the leads and the basics of form and handling, and then if you can apply the lessons consistently," he believes, "there is no reason you should not begin breaking 98 percent. It's all mental, you know."

A problem with skeet is that it is so regimented and to reach their greatest potential, shooters eventually have to fight through a wall of boredom or staleness. Paxton taught his students that if you stay with the fundamentals and keep your head in the game, it should not be that hard to shoot thousands of birds without a miss. It is, after all, a simple matter of mechanics.

"To be successful, make a mental checklist," he says. "It is easy to begin daydreaming on the shooting line. It is a dilemma. You want to shoot mechanically, but can't fall asleep. To shoot at a high level requires hard mental work each shot. Visualize the shot and your lead; see the barrel and target; practice your follow-through. You can't miss a single target in competition and win."

In a normal skeet event, you will shoot 100 targets in all four gauges. Friday afternoon, you will shoot 50 doubles, 100 birds. Sunday, the people who have shot perfectly will shoot in a "last man standing" shoot off. The High Overall champion will have shot something like 398 out of 400 – and that is just a good club shoot.

Don't take up skeet with the determination that you are going to make a living at it, Paxton warns. "It isn't a big money sport." Even a big shoot will only award a couple thousand dollars to the Open HOA. "I guess that's because it isn't exciting to watch," he says. "It is exciting to shoot, though. Maybe only the top 10 skeet shooters in the world win enough money to pay all their expenses."

You begin skeet shooting because it is fun. Take a semi-auto, perhaps in a sub-gauge, to the range and bang away to get a sense of the game, he says. Then, if you like it, get some instruction and you are on your way!

SHOOTING SKEET DOUBLES

There was a time when you did not have to survive a shoot-off to win a trophy at a skeet championship, but if you want to take home something for the trophy case today, you must be good at doubles. For that matter, if you are looking for the "High Overall" (HOA) trophy, you will have to shoot doubles anyway, so you may as well prepare.

There are stations in skeet where doubles (two targets launched simultaneously from the high and low house) are shot. This is a normal part of the game, and one that any shooter will learn to handle simply by shooting skeet. When you get to the actual game of doubles, however, you will find that it is slightly different and that you will shoot two different versions of it: regular doubles and shoot-off doubles.

Regular doubles is a scheduled event in any skeet tournament. The program will usually say "25 Pairs" or "50 Pairs." The former indicates a 50-round match, while the latter calls for 100 rounds. Regular doubles is a 12-gauge event, although that does not stop shooters from using smaller gauges. In fact,

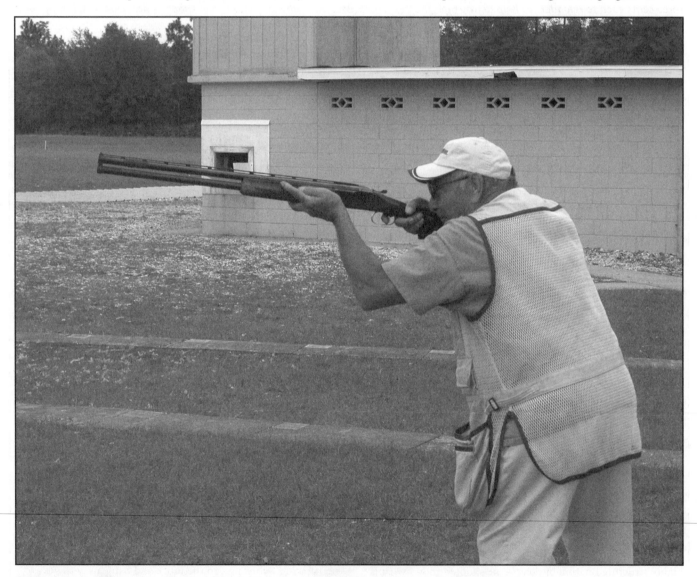

Two targets traveling in opposite directions at high speed make skeet doubles, especially from stations three, four and five, extremely challenging. Any shooter who intends to win should spend extra practice time at these stations because most class skeet match wins are determined in a shoot-off right there.

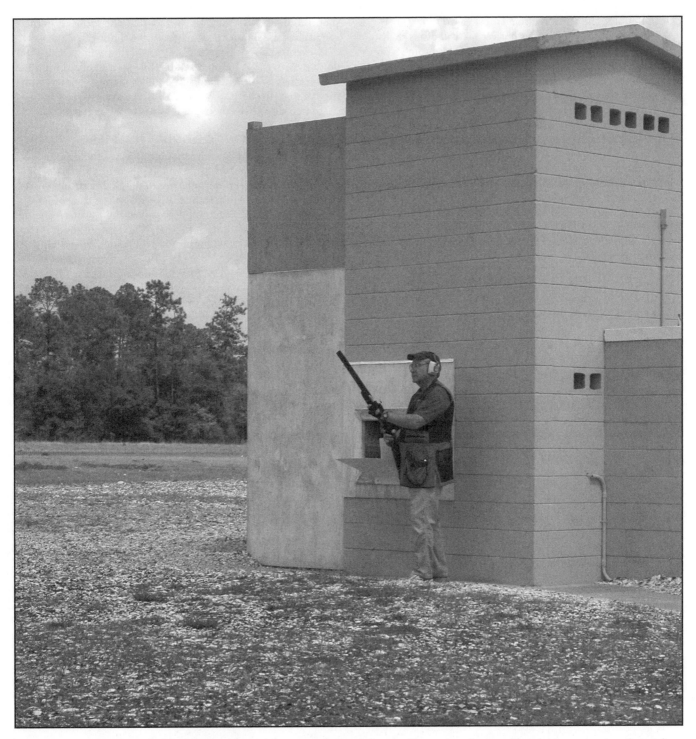

Station 7 may be the easiest of all in skeet for a right- or a left-hand shooter. No purpose is served by altering your shooting style from standard skeet at this station or on stations one, two or six. Shoot them as you always do.

the 20-gauge is the tool of choice among top shooters. Shooting the 20-gauge sharpens their hand-eye coordination and handicaps these shooters in a way that gives them extra pride in their ability to bust birds. As is true of everyone who has achieved proficiency in some public sport, shooting the 20 allows them to show off, too. It is a perfectly natural and reasonable thing to do.

Regular Doubles

Regular doubles proceeds as follows: a shooter starts at station one and is presented with the same pair of doubles seen in standard skeet. He shoots the high house bird first. At this station, he shoots only the one pair. Moving to station two, the shooter sees the same thing: basic skeet doubles, with the high house again shot first. By now, the shooter has fired four shots and moves to station three, where the game changes.

In standard skeet, station three is a pair of singles, one from the high and one from the low house. In doubles, the shooter gets both at once. The high house bird is taken first. At station four the situation repeats.

Station five presents two birds simultaneously, but this time the outgoing bird is taken first. Stations six and seven offer one pair of doubles, the same as a standard skeet round.

At this point, the shooter has not yet fired all of his shells, so he now makes a reverse trip around the field. From station seven, he goes back to six and repeats the doubles presentation there; then he goes back to five and does it again.

When he reaches station four on the return swing, the shooter encounters a major change. The rules require him to take the low house bird first, and this can be one of the toughest shots on the skeet field. The reason is simple. This is the only time the shooter ever shoots the low bird first on station four, and it does terrible things to a person's subconscious computer.

Moving back to three, things get back to normal and the high house is shot first as was station two.

That completes the first half of a doubles round. It requires 24 shells. The second half is identical except that it finishes on station one, instead of station two, in order to get rid of the remaining two shells.

Shoot-Off Doubles

Shoot-off doubles is a condensed version of regular skeet doubles. Here, shooters move between stations three, four and five with the order of the targets the same: high house always first at three, low house always first at five, and alternating between high and low house at four. This will continue until one shooter has not missed and he or she is the champion.

Shoot-off doubles was created when skeet scores began to become so perfect that a standard 100-bird match would see several shooters with a perfect upper level score. It was simply a way to decrease the amount of time it would take to conduct a shoot-off and determine a winner in the event. What makes

shoot-off doubles so tough is the fact that one shoots it in the gauge class the shooter used to get to the shoot-off.

If several shooters tie in the .410 class, they will have to shoot doubles with the .410. Some clubs will run a standard round of doubles first, and then shoot-off doubles for any shooters who survive that. In the 12-, 20- and 28-gauge events, you can expect to go directly to shoot-off doubles in those gauges.

How to Shoot Doubles

Doubles intimidates many shooters, but it shouldn't. In fact, regardless of the doubles game you are shooting, shoot-off or regular, only three stations offer anything different from what you have already seen in standard skeet: stations three, four and five. For that reason, no purpose is served by altering your shooting style for stations one, two, six and seven: shoot them as you always do. You will want to make some changes for three, four and five, however.

At station three, your normal foot position on the three mid-field crossing stations (three, four and five) would have the body aligned to break both birds over the center stake. Some top shooters, when shooting these stations as singles in the regular round, shift foot position for each of the two birds, but I do not recommend that unless you have shot long enough to know it benefits you.

With the body aligned on the Eight Post, you are in position to use your full range of body movement to break each single over the stake. Unfortunately, in doubles, this foot position can hinder you. I have not seen more than a handful of shooters who can shoot fast enough to take both the first bird and the second with their body aligned on the stake. The second (low

Station One Doubles: The high house target is taken first with normal lead and the gun is swung back to break the low house target at an angle of about 45 degrees to the shooter's left.

Station Two Doubles: Shoot the high house target first and break the low house target at the same point it would be taken during singles.

Station Three Doubles: The high house target must be taken quickly in order to get the gun back to the low house target. Shooters often fudge their natural point of aim to the high house side of the field in order to have sufficient swing room for the low house target, which is usually taken beyond its normal position when shot as a single.

Station Four Doubles: This is considered the most difficult station in doubles since the high house is taken first the first time the station is shot and the low house taken first the second time through.

Station Five Doubles: The low house is taken first, and many shooters will shift their natural point of aim to the low house side of the field to increase the swing distance on the second bird. A tail wind will cause the high house bird to hunt the ground quickly, requiring the shooter to speed up his timing.

house bird) is invariably going to get beyond the stake. If you align your body with the stake, you may have trouble picking the target up and catching it.

This is a situation where you know the second bird is going to be tough. Experienced shooters will usually fudge their body position to favor that bird.

It becomes a matter of individual reaction time and shooting style, but every shooter will benefit by shifting his basic station-three-position in the doubles round toward the high house side of the stake. I normally start new shooters with an alignment almost halfway back to the high house and see where we need to fine-tune it from there. This binds the body slightly on the outgoing first bird (high house), but it gives perfect position on the

second. Some shooters can handle the slightly restricted swing on the high house and some cannot. Those who have trouble catching the high house bird may have to start easing their gun position back toward the stake.

You do not have to wait to shoot a doubles round to find out if this is the case with your shooting rhythm. You can practice this while shooting standard skeet. Simply adjust your initial gun position back toward the high house on singles at station three until you find the point at which you are too bound up to take high house three. Once you find what your body's limitations are, you can begin adjusting your gun position to give you the best shot.

The first time we visit station four we encounter a similar situ-

Station Six Doubles: The low house target is taken first and the incoming high house broken at about a 45-degree angle to the shooter's right. This can be a difficult shot for left-handed shooters.

Station Seven Doubles: This is the easiest doubles shot on the field. With proper gun hold position, the low house bird can be taken without moving the gun, and the recoil will lift the gun into the perfect position to pick up the high house target.

ation. Shoot the high house first and the low house can get away from you. I recommend that you make the same readjustment of the body to the high house side of the field.

The second time we see station four it is a different situation. Now the low house is first. If you discount the subconscious re-action to shooting the low house bird first, this is actually not as tough a shot as shooting the high house bird first. The reason is that when you take the high house second, its normally higher trajectory tends to keep it in the air longer than the low bird. Many shooters find they can use a normal "align on the stake" position here and get away with it. Others find that only a slight fudging toward the low house is all they need to get back smoothly on high four for the second shot.

Station four, however, is one skeet station where a heavier second load is a major asset. Regardless of where you catch the second bird at station four, it is going to be one of the longest shots you will ever see on a skeet field. You are pushing the range at which #9 shot will reliably break a target. I favor a 1⅛-ounce 12-gauge load of #8½ shot or a one-ounce load of the same if I am shooting the event with a tubed 20-gauge. The heavier shot pellets will get you an extra bird now and then, and sometimes that is enough to win.

A number of shooters who routinely opt for the 20-gauge in this event use a full one-ounce load of #8½ for all of their doubles shots, simply to remove the possibility of confusing different shot size loads during the pressure of a shoot-off. They know the importance of a heavier load for the second shot on the middle stations and do not want to take the chance of not getting one in the gun. For the same reason, many experienced competitors have a few #8½ loads made up for the 28-gauge and .410 as well. They may not use them in regular skeet, but if they do have a good day in those gauges, they know they will

have to run them in the shoot-off and the heavier loads can come in handy.

Station five is similar to station four on the second swing-through. The high house becomes the second bird and its trajectory favors the shooter. You do not need to fudge as much toward the low house from a basic "align on the Eight Post" position, but some shooters find it does help to edge to the low house side slightly.

This shift in body position is a purely individual matter. There is no single correct foot position for every shooter because body shapes, swing speeds and reflexes are different. You accept the fact that favoring the second bird is a good idea, and then begin experimenting with foot position until you find the one that works best for you.

One way you can definitely help yourself in the doubles game is to change the way you shoot singles in regular skeet. If you have ever watched a top shooter, you will see that he or she takes every mid-field crossing shot as soon as possible. In fact, these competitors try to break them before the clays get to the stake. This is obviously an asset in the doubles game, because the faster you can break the first bird the more time you have for the second and the less you have to fudge your gun position for it.

Fast shooting also becomes an asset on a windy day. It takes a strong wind to affect the flight path of a skeet target before it gets to the stake because it is still under the influence of the launcher's velocity. By the time it gets to the stake, however, the wind catches it, and you may find that terrible things happen. If you shoot doubles in a laid-back, "ride the target forever" mode and the wind comes up, you are going to get murdered. You have to be a little excited and pumped up to shoot good doubles.

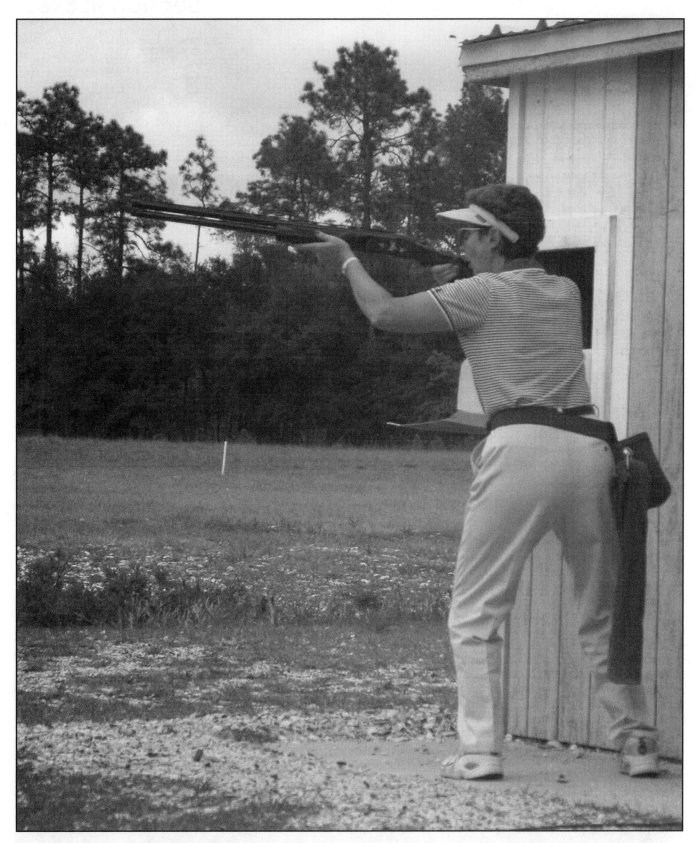

This doubles shooter's aggressive, ready posture with plenty of weight on her forward foot should ensure that she has no trouble swinging through a bird on station seven.

Doubles is a different game, but not radically. It is no more difficult than standard skeet. In fact, classification scores show that over the course of 100 rounds, doubles is only about one bird harder.

Doubles is a game you should master if you hope to advance to the top levels of the shotgun sports. If you are going to win any trophies in skeet today, you will have to do it in a shoot-off, and doubles is the game.

INTERNATIONAL SKEET COMPETITION

International shooters look at our American skeet game as somewhat tame. The international venue requires shooters to Skegin from a low gun position, so do not expect to shoot many 100-straight birds. (Photo courtesy Winchester)

Unlike American skeet, the International game requires that you call for the bird from the low gun position. This may be difficult for people who shoot sporting clays and just need their gun below the armpit. International skeet requires a permanent, contrasting strip on your vest "from the side to the front of the outer shooting garment placed at the top of the shooter's hip line." The stock of the gun must touch this line at the low gun "ready" position.

The game we shoot as "American skeet" has been called, correctly, the easiest of the various clay target games to master. That lack of challenge has not set well with our English and European counterparts, though. As a result, they have modified the game to a slightly different and infinitely more difficult version for international competition. In this chapter, we will review what our shooters face in World Cup and Olympic competition.

International skeet is shot on the same field as the American version. All distances and dimensions are identical, but the target order and the speed are quite different.

Firing Order

On station one, international shooters first take a high house single and then a pair of doubles. As in American skeet, the high house is shot first. There is no single target from the low house, which is one of the easiest shots in skeet. Moving to station two, the shooter repeats the same procedure with a single high house and a pair of doubles.

At station three, the shooter must deal with a single from each house and then a pair of doubles, with the high house target taken first. On station four, the procedure is the same. Station five presents a pair of singles, with the high house target taken first, and then a pair of doubles, with the low house taken first.

Moving to station six, the shooter sees a single from the low house and then a pair of doubles, with the low house taken first. At station seven, the single targets are shot first, followed by one pair of doubles, with the low house shot first.

On station eight, the shooter loads one shell and takes a single from the high house. At that point, the shooter unloads the gun, turns completely around to the low house (turning to the outside of the field in a clockwise direction), loads a single shell and takes the low house single. There is no "option round" as there is in American skeet.

Thus, the international course of fire deletes the easiest shots in American skeet (low houses one, two, seven and high houses six and seven) and replaces them with the toughest shots on the field, which are doubles from three, four and five. In effect, it takes away the "gimmes" and incorporates shoot-off doubles into the basic round. This alone tends to prevent a lot of perfect scores, but wait – it gets even tougher!

Gun Position

International skeet requires shooting from a low gun position, and when they say low they're not kidding! Competitors must have a permanent contrasting strip (about one inch wide and 9¾-inches long) from the side to the front of the outer shooting garment placed at the top of the shooter's hip line. The stock of the gun must touch this line at the low gun "ready" position, and you cannot move the gun from it until the target actually appears. You have the gun butt on your hip when you call for the target and, as in sporting clays, the target release device is equipped with a variable delay of up to three seconds.

Compared to the ready gun position in sporting clays, international skeet is much lower and requires more gun-handling skills.

International rules allow competitors to bring the gun to their shoulder for a brief pre-target sight picture only at stations one and eight. They must then immediately return to the ready position before calling for the target.

Target Speed

International skeet targets are cranked up to a higher speed than their American counterparts: about five mph faster, in fact. This requires that they be more stoutly constructed to take the higher launch velocity and, in addition to being made from harder materials, they have a reinforcing ring on the throwing ring. How tough are they? Lloyd Woodhouse, coach of the U.S. Shooting Team (USST) told me of a picture he has from a competition in Cuba that shows him standing with all of his 195 pounds on one foot atop a target, and the target is just fine!

It is not uncommon to find unbroken targets on an international field, clays that have a few holes punched completely through them. It takes a solid, center-pattern hit to get that all-important "visible piece" in this game.

The last significant differences between the two skeet games are the load and gauge. International skeet is shot almost exclusively with the 12-gauge, while American Skeet uses the 12, 20, 28 and .410. The maximum allowable load for international is

Whatever game you are shooting – trap, skeet, sporting clays or hélice – you will shoot better if you are comfortable. This waterproof Bob Allen Rain Jacket with padded chest protector has a nylon outer shell, taped seams and suede ambidextrous pads.

It is not uncommon to find unbroken targets on an international skeet field, says U.S. Shooting Team coach Lloyd Woodhouse, or clays that have a few holes punched completely through them. It takes a solid, center-pattern hit to get that important "visible piece" in this game.

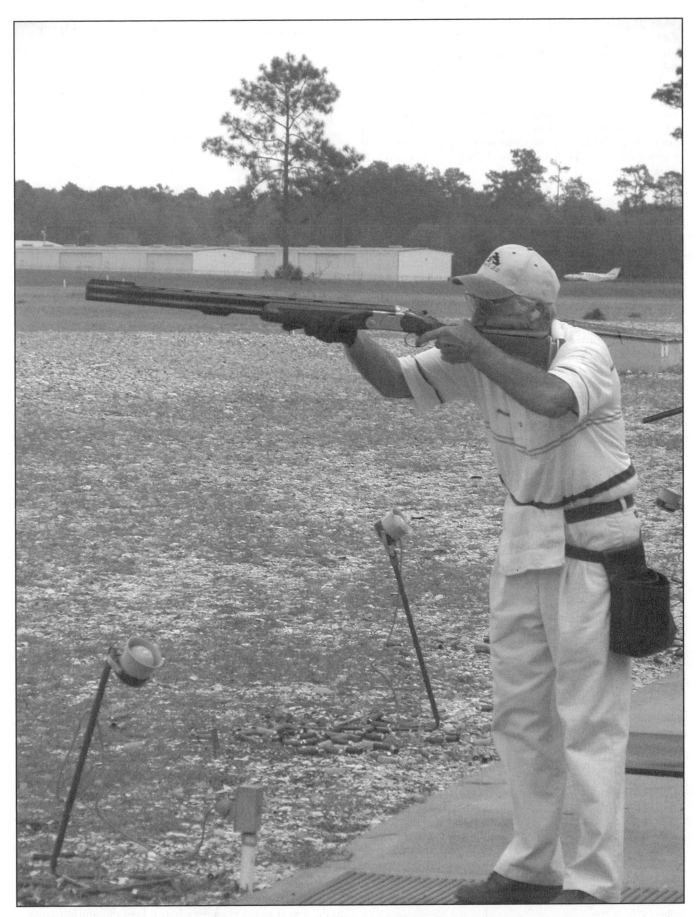

Since international skeet is very fast, developing a fluid gun mount is critical. "We find that a leading-arm elbow position of 45 degrees gives the best compromise for effective movement in all directions," says acclaimed coach Lloyd Woodhouse.

a mere 24 grams (about ⅞-ounce) with a maximum shot size of #7½.

In former years, many USST shooters favored Federal Cartridge international loads in size #8½. A couple of the shooters, however, opted for the #7½ load for the second shot on doubles from stations three, four and five. The #8½ shot incidentally, is an excellent doubles load for American skeet, as well as for many shots in sporting clays. Despite the diminutive shot charge, this load is an awesome performer and it will really crush a target. Recoil is light and its 1,330 fps velocity gets it to the target fast.

Guns and Gear

Guns for international skeet are little different from the 12-gauge guns used for our version of the game. One sees both over/unders and gas-operated semi-autos in competition, although the stackbarrel guns do predominate. The standard skeet constriction of .004- to .005-inch is considered the best bet. The preferred barrel length for the over/unders falls right within the 28- to 32-inch range that we see on skeet fields in this country. One difference is that ported guns may not be used in international competition, but given the gentle recoil of the 24-gram load they are not really much of an asset.

The only significant difference in guns between the American and the international games is the recoil pad. Because of the extreme low ready position, the pad needs to be smoothly radiused at the top to aid in a smoother gun mount. Most shooters also round off the inner edge. This is also common in sporting clays. Some competitors go a bit farther and apply a slick-surfaced PVC or Teflon tape to the sides and sometimes to the top of the pad to remove that sticky "pencil eraser" feel that can cause drag on the shooting vest with some types of rubber pads.

When it comes to selecting a shooting vest, the international style, which has a slick-faced shooting pad extending completely down the gun-mount side, is the overwhelming favorite.

Eye and ear protection is mandatory and, as in American-style skeet, is a superb idea because you can get pelted with an occasional target piece during a round. Some competitors are taking a page from their sporting clays counterparts and opting for electronic ear plugs. These contain an electronic cutoff circuit that shuts out noise levels above a certain decibel level, yet amplifies low-level sounds. Many instructors wear them because it makes their teaching job easier and allows better communication with their shooters. On the international and sporting clays fields, they have one additional valuable advantage: they can amplify sounds enough to let you actually hear most trap machines release the target. To my way of thinking, that is of no small importance!

The variable target delay of up to three seconds can result in a significant change in the timing of a shooter who is used to having the target appear immediately when he calls for it. On an international field, the target may come immediately or it may be delayed long enough to bring on the jitters. With conventional ear plugs the only target acquisition device the shooter has is visual. In the real world, we tend to blend all of our senses into one system. With the amplification powers of electronic ear plugs, we can now use both sight and sound to acquire the target. These can be a real advantage to some shooters and they are now commonly accepted at sporting clays events. This technology will certainly work its way onto the international fields as well.

Shooting Tips for International Skeet

International skeet is far more complex and challenging than the American version. Not surprisingly, it can create problems for shooters used to the tamer American sport.

"The biggest problem for new international shooters is getting the smooth and consistent gun mount down pat," says Lloyd Woodhouse, who taught our Olympic shooters the finer points of scattergunning for more than a decade. "Gun handling is critical in this game and it must become a subconscious learned response. That can take a lot of practice, and a lot of shooting."

Interestingly, Woodhouse and his assistant coaches have developed a training system that works on the principle of starting with the easy shots to build the shooter's confidence and gradually progresses to the more difficult shots. Woodhouse calls it "stage training."

"The theory," Woodhouse has explained, "is to set the stage for success, and this works well to develop gun handling skills. We start a new shooter off with a pair of low house station one single targets. This is a very easy shot and gives the shooter 1.4 to 1.6 seconds to mount the gun. Then we move to station two and shoot low houses again. Once the shooter is comfortable with this, we move to stations six and seven and shoot the incoming high houses. All of these are easy targets that give the shooter the maximum amount of time to mount the gun. This ensures that the shooter experiences success."

On the next stage, Woodhouse continues, his shooters return to station one and start working their way through the stations, taking only the low houses. "As we reach stations four through seven, we gradually decrease the 'time look' at the targets and require the shooter to increase the speed of the gun mount. Nevertheless, we start with the easy targets and build the shooter's confidence before we begin asking more of him or her. There is a significant difference in the time element for gun mounting between a low house one and a low house six."

By slowly decreasing the amount of time the shooter has to consciously think out and execute the gun mount, he notes, USST coaches get the mount so rigidly built that it becomes a subconscious learned response. That lets the shooter keep the conscious mind on important things like acquiring the target and executing a smooth swing and follow-through.

Developing a fluid gun mount is critical in this game, as well as in sporting clays. It is easier if one starts with the proper hand position on the gun. In that respect, regardless of the type of shotgunning one does, the following advice from our former Olympic Team coach is well worth studying:

"Biomechanically," Woodhouse has explained, "if you put the elbow of your leading hand directly below the gun, like a rifleman's stance, you have the greatest leverage for moving the gun up and down, but the weakest leverage for moving the gun from side to side. If you move that elbow out to a 90-degree angle from the gun, you now have the maximum leverage for side movement, but the weakest leverage for up and down movement. We find that an elbow position of 45 degrees gives us the best compromise for effective movement in both directions, and that is where we like to start a shooter. After that, we can fine-tune the position over time."

The same is true for moving the hand forward and back on the forearm, he continues. "If the hand is way out on the forearm, the elbow is almost straight. If you move it back almost to the trigger guard, then the elbow is bent too much. In that position your arm can support a lot of weight. If you move the hand forward and straighten your elbow, then you will not be able to hold as much weight. The farther back your hand is on the forearm, the heavier the muzzle seems and the more it has a tendency to whip. If the hand is moved way out on the forearm you have very positive control over the muzzle, but minimum strength to move it. By starting with the 45-degree elbow position, you automatically adjust the forearm hand to the best compromise position."

Woodhouse adds, "Many American-style skeet shooters not only have the forearm elbow out to almost a 90-degree angle, but stick the trigger hand elbow out the same way also. They can get away with this because from a pre-mounted gun position they really only have to move the gun on a horizontal line unless, of course, the wind is blowing and making the targets rise and fall above and below their normal track. When that happens, the wind eats these shooters up because they don't have the biomechanical leverage to quickly and precisely adjust their elevation."

Another problem many American-style shooters have with international skeet is their initial body position when calling for the target. As in American skeet, the international shooter takes his natural point of aim at the point where he expects to break the target. That will vary with the targets, although the center stake (Eight Post) is a good place to start for singles on stations one through seven. For doubles on stations three, four and five, it does not hurt to fudge that natural point of aim toward the more difficult target, which will be the second bird. The problem arises when the shooter pivots his upper body back to the house for his initial acquisition of the target.

"I have yet to see an American-style skeet shooter who shoots a sustained lead, which is what I teach my shooters, who didn't have to make adjustments in that body position for the international game," says Coach Woodhouse. "Normally, you would adjust your visual acquisition point a little farther out from the house because the targets come out a little quicker. Many American shooters will take an initial gun hold position on a line just about parallel with the face of the house, or a little inside that. We recommend they increase that to about 10 to 20 degrees farther toward the center of the field."

Fast-swing shooters will find that is not always necessary. They can often take their normal position.

The exception to this is station eight. This is one case where increased target speed, combined with low gun position, re-quires the shooter to compensate. Both the high and the low houses send their targets to the boundary stake in about 6/10-second. Shooters must take the target inside that, normally in about 4/10-second. That is not much time to mount the gun, acquire the target and see the lead! Adjusting your foot position can help here.

"One problem right-handed shooters have with station eight," Woodhouse says, "is that they often face too far into the house. Your natural point of aim comes into play big-time here, because these shots are subconscious. There is no real time for thought. If you were to take the distance from the center stake back to the house window and divide it into thirds, two-thirds of the way back to the stake is where most people break those targets. That should be the natural point of aim, that circle of air two-thirds of the way back to the stake. The initial acquisition position should have the upper body pivoted back to a point just outside the house. Many shooters tend to look into these houses, crowding them too much, and it will hurt on these targets."

One area where shooters will not have to make many adjustments is their leads. Despite the targets' increased speed, the leads remain virtually the same. The increased gun speed required to align with the target, whether the shooter uses the sustained lead or the fast-swing technique, will compensate for the increased target speed.

Surprisingly, one of the biggest factors that can adversely affect skilled shooters making the transition from American skeet to international skeet is not physical, but mental.

"One of the most important things a shooter has to condition his mind to accept in this game is that he is not going to shoot many 100 straights," Woodhouse has stated. "In American skeet, if you shoot a 99x100 in a major match, you can go home. There will be shooters who have shot perfect scores and they will settle things in a shoot-off. This is not so in international skeet. You can miss a target and still win the match. Even the best will miss. A shooter must accept that and develop the mental discipline to miss a target and still maintain his focus. That shooter must realize that he or she is still in contention, and get right back down to business. I spend a lot of time working on just that mental aspect with our shooters, and it is very important if you want to win."

While international skeet is not nearly as popular in this country as is our more sedate version, it is much more challenging. This game will truly test your skills.

| International Skeet Classification ||
Class	Average
Master (AA)	95.00% and up
A	87.00 - 94.99%
B	81.00 - 86.99%
C	75.00 - 80.99%
D	below 75.00%

TOP SKEET GUNS

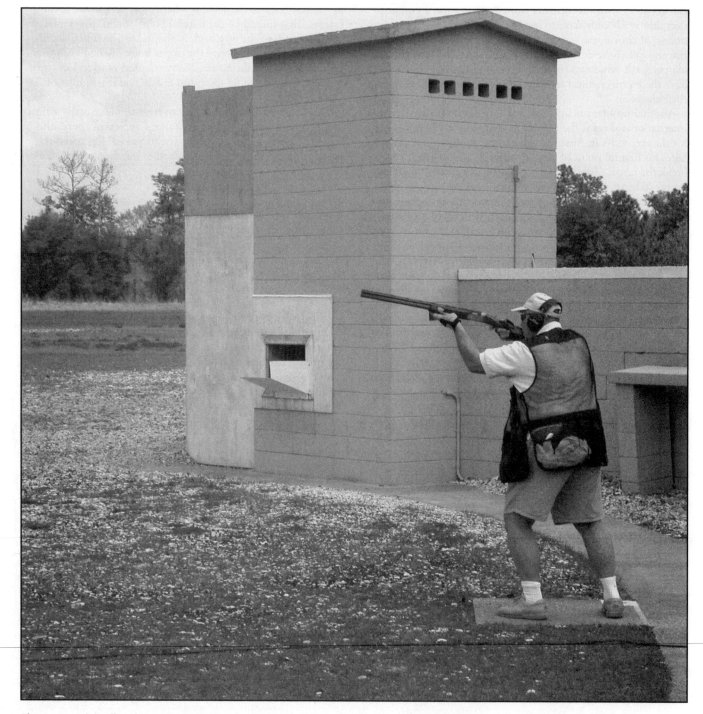

Skeet was originally a hunter's game that began in the U.S. and while it provides excellent practice for fast crossing shots in the field, it now has all the hallmarks of having a full life of its own. Complex, even "rigid" rules. All-American teams. International competitions. And guns designed for quick, steady movement from bird to bird.

Rizzini's new Premier 12-gauge over/under with a 28-inch barrel is an excellent gun for skeet shooting. Barrels are chrome-lined and the rib is vented top and side.

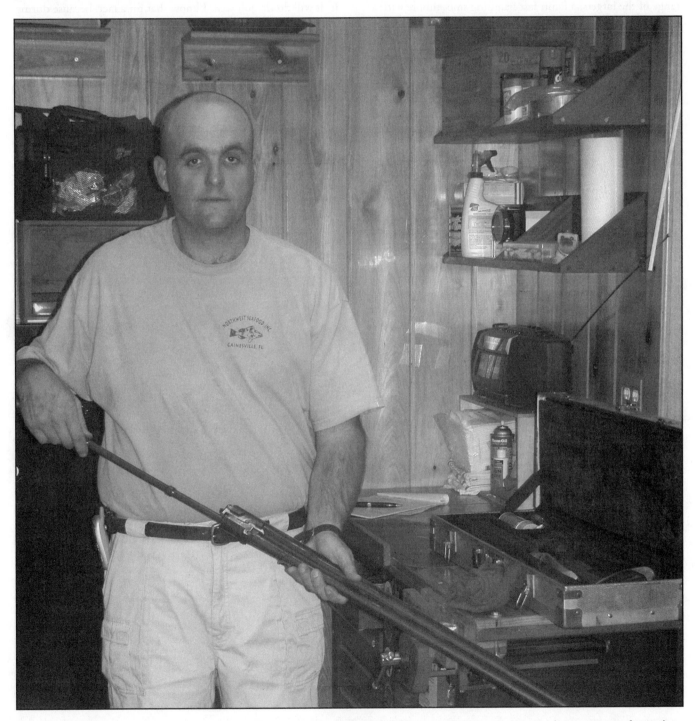

Tubes are a relatively inexpensive alternative to buying multiple guns in different gauges. Contemporary skeet masters often tube a 12-gauge for 20- and 28-ga. and .410 and omit shooting the 12-gauge entirely.

Hunters created skeet as a hunter's game. Since the inventors were northeastern upland bird shooters who occasionally dabbled in ducks, the game reflected that in the quick, close nature of the shots, similar to those one would commonly see when hunting grouse, woodcock and small-pond mallards. In fact, the longest shot you will see on a skeet field is about 27 yards and that length only rarely. The closest shot is less than four yards and most range from that to about 20 yards.

The way the original game was shot, it more closely resembled sporting clays than contemporary skeet. The gun was required to be off the shoulder when the bird was called for – low gun position, as it is called today. Given the nature and range of the targets, a light, fast-handling smoothbore with a wide-open choke was a distinct asset.

In fact, a specific degree of choke, called Skeet 1, was developed for this game. For a 12-gauge, that is a constric-

tion of .004- to .005-inch and is intended to place the entire shot charge within a 30-inch circle at 25 yards. An additional choking, called Skeet 2 (or as it is more commonly called, "Light Modified"), is about .012-.014-inch and was intended to provide a slightly denser pattern for the longer second shot on Skeet doubles. (An over/under choked Skeet 1 and Skeet 2, by the way, is an extremely effective upland bird gun.)

For all practical purposes, however, a standard Improved Cylinder choke (.009-inch constriction in a 12-gauge) will deliver just about the same performance on a skeet field as either of the skeet chokes. If you have a gun that is choked Improved Cylinder and want to shoot some informal skeet, use it. It will do the job well. I know that for a fact, because during my early years in competitive skeet, I shot only a 12-gauge, and it was a gas gun with a single barrel choked Improved Cylinder. I shot my way into 12-gauge AA class with it.

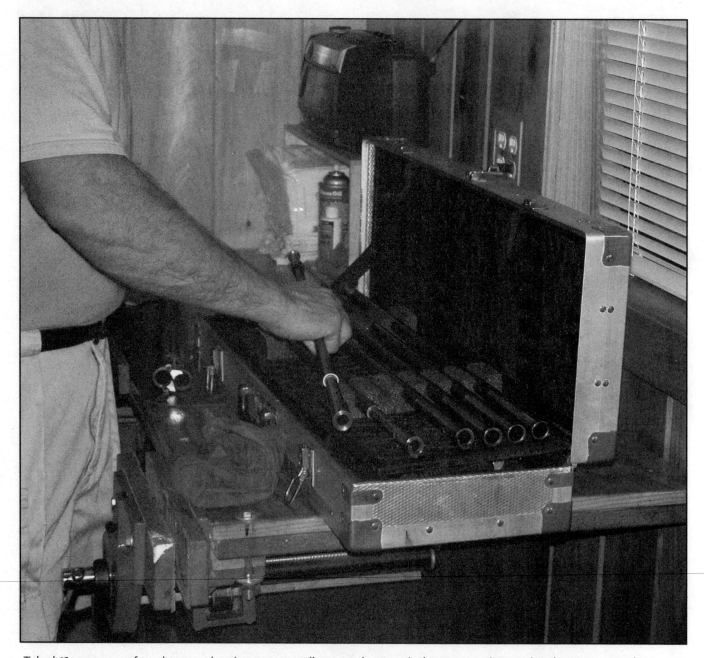

Tubed 12-gauge guns for sub-gauge shooting are an excellent – and economical – way to enjoy varying the gauge ... and the challenge.

Almost any good field gun can run the table in skeet if the shooter is capable. An open-choked gun like the Weatherby Athena III Classic Field in 12- or 20-gauge with a 26- or 28-inch barrel should give you scores to be proud of right away.

Ruger's Red Label over/under is available in 12-, 20- and 28-gauge. You can order this gun with a pistol or straight grip. A .410 tube set is available for the 28-gauge.

The Remington Model 332 over/under puts in regular appearances at the skeet line. Three barrel lengths – 26, 28 and 30 inches – and a narrow, eight mm vent rib make this an extraordinarily versatile gun in the field and for clay shooting.

The Modern Skeet Gun

Today, skeet is shot from a pre-mounted gun, which removes the requirement for serious gun handling ability and the radiused buttpads commonly found on sporting clays guns. This practice has also encouraged the use of longer barrels with more muzzle weight that promote a smoother swing. As recently as five or six years ago, a 26-inch barrel was considered standard for an over/under. Today, 28 inches is about as short as many want to go, and a number of shooters opt for barrels in the 30- to 32-inch range. Interestingly, the shift to longer barrels is a direct result of the knowledge gained on the sporting clays fields.

If you want to use the skeet range as a means to tune up for the fall hunting season, just use an open-choked hunting gun that will deliver two shots. That much still applies. If you want to win a major skeet tournament, however, you are going to have problems.

Skeet has become as ritualized, and stylized, as any clay target game in the world and, as one might suspect, there is a specialized breed of gun that wins.

Competitive skeet is shot as a four-gauge event – 12, 20, 28 and .410. You can shoot in only one of those gauges (I did for a number of years.) but you will be confined to winning (or losing) in that class only. A High Overall (HOA) match winner must shoot all four.

The four-gauge ability can be accomplished in a number of ways. In years past, competitors might simply show up with four different guns, and they might have been a somewhat unusual mix of pumps, semi-autos and double-barrel smoothbores. Others might have selected what could be termed a "matched" four-gun set. Remington offered its excellent Model 1100 semi-auto in that manner for a number of years and even included barrel weights for the smaller gauges that would give all of the guns the same weight and, some said, the same feel. Winchester offered its over/under Model 101 as a four-gun set, and other makers followed suit. However, that approach has fallen out of favor today.

Another method that still enjoys some popularity is an over/under with four separate barrel sets.

Barrel Tubes

Still another approach, which has been used by past champions, is to use a light-recoiling 12-gauge gas-operated semi-auto for the 12-gauge class, and use an over/under with interchangeable sub-gauge tubes (a 20-gauge gun with 28 and .410 tubes) in the remaining classes.

Contemporary masters, however, have a totally new approach. They use a 12-gauge over/under with 20, 28 and .410 tubes, and omit the 12-gauge shell entirely. They have found that a shooter of reasonable skill does not require the full 1⅛-ounce 12-gauge shot charge to break a skeet target. They elect to use the 20-gauge (usually with 1-ounce loads) in the 12-gauge event, shifting to the legal 20-gauge ⅞-ounce load for the 20-gauge event, and then using the 28 and .410 tubes for those events.

What they get with that approach is a three-gauge capability where each gauge has the exact same balance, weight and feel as the others. There is an old adage that goes, "Beware of the man with one gun because he probably knows how to use it." That applies here, and it is true. The only difference in gun feel between the different gauges, when set up in this manner, is the recoil generated by the different gauges.

Sporting clays shooters who shoot in sub-gauge classes often use the same system.

That requires an explanation of sub-gauge insert tubes. Chuck Webb of Briley Manufacturing, probably the largest and most respected maker of these tube sets (approximately $1,350.00 per set), gives *Gun Digest* the following comments:

"Insert tube sets have come to dominate the skeet market in the last dozen years," he states, "and they're popular with sporting clays shooters as well.

"The tubes," he continues, "or, at least the ones we make, are constructed of 6061 aircraft aluminum, with the chambers made from titanium and secured to the barrel via threading. We can make these tubes with a fixed choke but normally supply them with interchangeable stainless steel choke tubes with four choke tubes per gauge. You can certainly order additional tubes. Briley makes one of the widest selections of constrictions in the industry. The interior and exterior aluminum surfaces of the barrel are hard-anodized and, if the tubes are used properly, they will last the life of the gun."

What you have with insert tubes are interchangeable barrels-within-a-barrel, complete with their own extractors and inter-changeable chokes.

Fitting these tubes requires that the gun be sent to Briley. That is required because the tubes are precisely fitted to your barrel. In most cases, the fit is so close that a tube for the top barrel will not go into the bottom barrel of the gun!

While skeet and sporting clays shooters using over/unders are

The Benelli SuperSport 12-gauge with ComforTech synthetic stock is designed to bring felt recoil with any shell to a minimum. Benelli extended CrioChokes help reduce pellet deformation, and the ported barrel is intended to minimize muzzle climb for fast second target acquisition

Browning makes its Citori XS Skeet in 12- and 20-gauge with 28- or 30-inch barrels. It is also available with an adjustable comb.

All Browning Sporting Clays, XT and XS Series Citori shotguns come equipped with the "Triple Trigger" System which allows its shooters to adjust the length of pull and switch between a wide/checkered, a narrow/smooth and a wide/smooth canted trigger shoe.

the biggest customers for these specialized accessories, they can be fitted to any break-action shotgun (side-by-sides and single shots).

According to Webb, Briley long ago tested their tubes with target-sized steel shot and found no problems with their use. If there is a way to damage the tubes, it is when a shooter attempts to insert them into a gun for which they were not fitted. For shooters of even minimal intelligence, that should not be a problem, because the tubes are serial-numbered to the gun.

"If your 20-gauge tubes are inserted into a different 12-gauge shotgun," Webb says, "you might possibly split the tube on firing; there will be no chance of injury to the shooter, however, just damage to the tube. The 28-gauge and .410 tubes (because of the smaller inside diameter and greater amount of metal)

could probably be shot on their own as individual barrels, but the 20-gauge does need the support of the barrel to which it was fitted. That's about the only way you can mess up a tube set."

Sub-gauge tubes will add 10 to 14 ounces of weight to the barrels of the gun, and many shooters find the added muzzle weight an advantage when it comes to executing a smooth swing.

Knowledgeable shooters who know they will "tube" a gun often opt for a model with a weight of around eight pounds. By the time the tubes are installed, this brings the total gun weight to a bit less than nine pounds and makes a comfortable package. If the tubes are added to an already heavy gun, the additional weight might be uncomfortable. A shooting buddy had an older, tubed Remington 3200 (which, although no longer made, is an excellent but heavy gun) and found that he shot it better without tubes in 12-gauge. He found the additional weight fatiguing.

While tubes are the way to go if you want to win, shooters who just want to enjoy the game on an informal basis can get by very nicely with just one gun and gauge. In fact, my advice to that type of shooter would be to stop reading here and turn to the chapter on guns for sporting clays. Any one of those in 12- or 20-gauge would be an ideal choice and also a great performer on the sporting fields and the autumn bird fields.

Skeet's Top Guns

Competitive skeet shooters will also find the sporting clays over/unders to be excellent choices as the basis for a tubed skeet gun set. If a wider range of choices is desired, major manufacturers offer the following in skeet models (all priced cited are manufacturer's suggested retail price):

The Superior II Sport VR-MC 12-gauge semi-auto is built with Turkish walnut buttstock and forend. You can choose from 28- or 30-inch factory-ported barrels. Three chokes are included. The 10 mm ventilated rib has a mid-bead center sight and fluorescent bead front sight.

Tristar imports several models of European semi-autos and over/unders such as this SC 512 in its Valmet series. The 512 is available in three clays-shooting models, any of which would be fine for skeet: 12-gauge Sporting, 12- or 20-gauge Youth/Ladies and 12- or 20-gauge Field. Barrels are backbored and chrome-lined with three-inch chambers.

The most popular Perazzis on the skeet fields are the MX8 and MX2000/8. Each is available with a detachable trigger group, interchangeable or fixed chokes in both barrels and a number of different rib configurations. Essentially, a Perazzi is expensive because it has a reputation for superior shooting and because it is personally fitted to the buyer.

Ithaca (www.ithacagun.com)

So you want to buy a new shotgun with which you can try a little skeet and later take to the field for dove or woodcock, too. And money is tight. There are two schools of thought. If you buy an inexpensive gun, you are sure to be discouraged because it may shoot erratically and the guys with the $25,000 Perazzis will look down on you. Then you are stuck with a cheap gun. The second school of thought is to buy a solid but inexpensive smoothbore and see if you enjoy the shooting games. What do you have to lose? If you hate skeet shooting after you try it, you're not out much money. If you love the game, you can trade up and use the less expensive gun for hunting or as a back-up.

If you decide to give the inexpensive gun route a try, why not look for an Ithaca? These New York guns are completely made in the U.S. and have a good reputation that is identical with your financial conditions. The Model 37 Deluxe pump 12-gauge with three-inch chamber will do about all you want.

Even though the folks with the gas guns and over/unders will probably eat your lunch at the shooting line, you are there to learn – not to expect to beat the guys with the Krieghoffs.

The versatile Ithaca Model 37 has a steel receiver, deluxe grade stock and forend, 26-inch vented rib and brown recoil pad. It comes in several versions and is also available in 16- (2¾ inch) and 20-gauge (3 inch) and weighs between six and seven pounds. Barrels are available in 24-, 26- and 28-inch lengths and three flush mount choke tubes are included. Length of pull is 14 inches, drop at comb 1½ inches and drop at heel 2¼ inches. With bottom loading and shell ejection, this gun is ambidextrous. The manufacturer's suggested retail price begins at $824 and goes to about $1,185.

Ruger (www.ruger.com)

Ruger, "Arms Makers For Responsible Citizens," is located in Southport, Connecticut. Its Red Label over/unders, in 12-, 20- and 28-gauge, are excellent competition-grade guns in the low-

The Krieghoff K-20 20-gauge over/under is built with "all the technical refinements made in the famed K-80, adapted to the smaller receiver," the company says. It can also be fitted with 28-gauge and .410 barrels.

With a 28-inch barrel, the Winchester Model 1300 Sporting/Field is a versatile pump-action shotgun that can really open up to shoot the short range action in skeet. Working the pump however will test if you are fast enough – and accurate enough with all that extra upper body movement while you are aiming and following through.

The Jubilee 702 from FAIR may be ordered from Cabela's in 12- or 20-gauge with 28- or 30-inch barrels.

to-middle price range. If you enjoy shooting the .410, Ruger sells a fitted tube set for its 28-gauge gun.

The Red Label has been around for some time. Its 20-gauge is chambered for 3-inch shells and comes with a choke tube wrench and five chokes: Skeet 1 and 2, Full, Modified and Improved Cylinder. You can order a Red Label with hammer-forged, back bored alloy steel barrel in lengths of 26, 28 or 30 inches. The overall length of the 30-inch gun is 47 inches and its weight is 7¼ pounds. Length of pull is 14⅛ inches.

Red Label stocks are shaped from premium grade American walnut and two styles are offered: pistol grip and straight English-styling. Each gun features a drop at comb of 1½ inches and a drop at heel of 2½ inches. You can also purchase a Red Label with a "Target Grey All-Weather" stock, but this feature is available only in 12-gauge.

Ruger has standardized its pricing for Red Labels. The standard price for a Red Label with walnut stock, stainless steel receiver and blued steel barrels is $1,545. Order an all-weather synthetic stock with low-glare, stainless steel receiver and barrels and you will pay the same thing. Add $180 per gun for factory engraving (pistol-grip style stocks only).

The classic, satin-finished American walnut forend and straight, comb stock have 20-line-per-inch checkering. The overall length of the 332 is 47½ inches with a 30-inch barrel and its weight is eight pounds. Drop at comb is 1⁷⁄₁₆ inches and drop at heel is 1⅛ inches.

The venerable 1100 autoloader in Tournament Skeet edition is available in 12- and 20-gauge versions. The 1100 holds five shells: one in the chamber and four in the magazine. The 26-inch barrels carry a light contour vent rib and both Cylinder and Modified (Skeet) Improved chokes are supplied. The overall length is 47 inches and the 1100 has a 14³⁄₁₆-inch length of pull with a drop at comb of 1½ inches and drop at heel of 2¼ inches. The 1100 weighs eight pounds.

Benelli USA (www.benelliusa.com)

Benelli is a 33-year-old Italian manufacturer with a factory in Urbino. Benelli USA, headquartered in Accokeek, Maryland, is allied with Franchi and Uberti. Best known perhaps for turkey hunting, slug guns and military or police arms,

The three-barrel, multi-gauge SKB skeet set offers a consistent weight, balance and feel. The 20, 28 and .410 barrels are fitted with individual fore-ends, and an airline-approved, fitted aluminum case is included with the set. The stock is available with a fixed or adjustable comb.

Remington (www.remington.com)

Remington's Model 332 over/under was designed as a field gun, but because of its relatively modest price and known durability, it is seen frequently at the skeet line.

Based on a modified box lock action of under-lock design, Remington says the Model 332 "provides an exceptionally low profile for superior 'pointability' that closely resembles a side-by-side without sacrificing strength, safety or ease of loading." The lightly engraved receiver is milled from a solid block of ordnance grade steel.

The satin blued Model 332 12-gauge is chambered for three-inch shells and is available in three high-strength chrome-moly steel barrel lengths: 26, 28 and 30 inches. Remington says its fully brazed side ribs mean a solid barrel-to-monoblock assembly. The eight mm-wide steel vent rib has two beads. Three chokes are included: Improved Cylinder, Modified and Full.

Benelli recommends its 12-gauge SuperSport and Sport II autoloaders as high performance competition shotguns.

You will be able to identify the $1,600 SuperSport on a skeet line because its looks are so unusual. The "ComforTech" stock is carbon fiber with imprint checkering in the pistol grip and a soft gel comb insert that mounts against the shooter's cheek. Benelli says this smooth, cushioned surface eliminates the "neck-snapping impact of comb against cheek." The stock is split diagonally from the heel of the buttstock to a point just behind the pistol grip. Eleven synthetic "recoil-absorbing chevrons" fill the holes in both sides of the stock. According to Benelli, the result of the redesign and materials selection is a lighter weight gun with as much as 48 percent less felt recoil than similar shotguns. In addition, you can adjust the Super-Sport's length of pull (drop and cast) with a "shim kit." Drop at heel is 2¼ inches and drop at comb is 1⅝ inches.

Two gel size pads are routinely available for the SuperSport,

The 12-gauge SKB skeet guns are fitted with a 9.5 mm ventilated, sloped rib. The rib has three center channel grooves bordered by two raised, matted surfaces. The rib for small gauge skeet models is 8.5 mm.

standard (14⅜-inch length of pull) and short (14-inch length of pull). Differently shaped pads are available for left hand and right hand shooters. As part of the "ComforTech" stock system, Benelli says muzzle climb is reduced significantly compared to a hard stock and butt pad, and this puts you back on target faster for a second shot.

SuperSport factory ported barrels are available in 28- and 30-inch lengths. You can carry as many as five shells: four in the magazine and one in the chamber. With the 30-inch barrel, the SuperSport is 51.6 inches long and weighs 7.95 pounds. Each barrel is topped with a high visibility red bar sight on the tapered (10 mm to 8 mm), stepped rib.

Benelli says its hammer-forged barrels are cryogenically treated, frozen to -300 degrees Fahrenheit. This process changes the steel at the molecular level, evening out the grain structure for a smoother bore surface that resists fouling.

The "performance tuned" 85TSS skeet over and under from SKB is available in 18 models: four gauges, fixed or adjustable combs, Monte Carlo or fixed combs and a finger-groove fore-end. The 12-gauge barrels are backbored and chrome-lined with lengthened forcing combs. Automatic ejectors are standard.

Five extended chokes are included. Longer choke tubes allow a more gradual constriction of the shot charge, reducing pattern-destroying pellet deformation.

The $1,430 Sport II is built with a satin walnut stock and fore-grip and can be purchased with 28- or 30-inch barrels. Otherwise, specifications for the Sport II are identical (length of pull, choke tubes provided, etc.) to those of the SuperSport.

Browning (www.browning.com)

Offering one of the largest product lines in the shotgun game, a shooter should have no trouble finding a 12-gauge Browning skeet gun or a gun that can be very nicely tubed for sub-gauge shooting. Models are also offered in all four gauges (12, 20, 28 and .410) that will shoot well enough to win consistently at the skeet line, and all are offered with Browning's Invector choke tube system.

The critical dimension for Browning's Citori XS Skeet are

as follows: length of pull, 14⅜ inches; drop at comb and at heel, 1¾ inches. The XS Skeet is available with either a fixed ($2,363) or an adjustable ($2,629) comb. With a 30-inch barrel tipped with a HiViz Pro-Comp front sight, the XS weighs 7 pounds, 15 ounces.

This 2¾-inch chambered gun, with either a fixed or adjustable comb, can be ordered with a 30- or 28-inch barrel in 12- or 20-gauge editions. All barrels are back-bored barrels with chrome-lined chambers and are ported to reduce recoil and barrel bounce, thus speeding up target acquisition. The silver-nitride receiver is lightly engraved.

The Citori XS Skeet's walnut stock and forend are given a satin finish and its side ribs between the twin barrels are ventilated. The XS Skeet features a primary top high post rib for quick sight alignment. The right-hand model has an exaggerated palm swell and the trigger is gold-plated. The standard XS is not checkered.

Charles Daly (www.charlesdaly.com)

The Superior II Sport ($1,589) over/under has a stylishly designed silver action with gold inlays of clay birds in flight. The action is hot forged from a block of chrome nickel steel, heat-treated and matched to chrome-moly steel barrels. Internally honed, chromed and polished, these factory ported barrels have been tested to perfectly handle any type competition shot, lead or steel. Barrel lengths are 28 or 30 inches long and have a 10 mm wide ventilated rib.

All Superior II shotguns come with a gold-plated single selective trigger and selective automatic ejector. Five interchangeable choke tubes are included.

Mossberg (www.mossberg.com)

For those who want to take their venerable Mossberg hunting shotgun to the skeet range and throw some lead – go right ahead! Pump and gas operated guns from this Connecticut company are not commonly found in competition, but nothing says they can't be. Let the Citori owners look down their noses at your Mossberg while you concentrate on trying to show them how to bust targets.

One of Mossberg's most popular models is the 500. It is available with wood or camouflaged synthetic stock and foregrip. It is a pump-action shotgun that comes in either 12- or 20-gauge or .410 and plenty of choke tubes are available. Barrels are interchangeable – 24-, 26- and 28-inch lengths – and the gun is chambered for three inches. Length of pull is a short 13 ⅞ inches with a drop at comb of 1½ inches and drop at heel of 2⅜ inches. Approximate weight is 7¼ pounds with the 28-inch vent rib barrel. The gun holds six shells. Expect to pay about $316.00 for this gun out of the box.

Beretta (www.berettausa.com)

This Italian gun maker has a richly-deserved reputation in the competition arena and offers several models in its skeet gun line. Frankly, almost any Beretta over/under with a relatively open choke will work as a skeet gun, but several are specifically designated as such.

The 12-gauge DT10 Trident Skeet is a typical Beretta: Beautifully grained and checkered stock and forearm; low-profile monolithic box lock chambered for a 3-inch shell. The comb is adjustable so that you can develop a personal sight picture. Drop at comb is 1⅜ inches; drop at heel is 2⅛ inches; and weight is a comfortable 7 pounds, 15-ounces. This model has a blued and polished receiver and your choice of 28- or 30-inch blued barrels. The single trigger is gold plated and adjustable for length of pull while the trigger assembly can be removed without tools for cleaning or maintenance.

The flat tapered rib is ⅜ x 5⁄16 inches. A white front bead and steel mid-bead give the shooter fast aiming points. The DT10 comes in a hard-sided carry case with five interchangeable choke tubes. Expect to pay $6,866 for this high-grade shotgun.

At $3,933, the 682 Gold E Skeet is less expensive but still offers an adjustable comb so that you can make this gun fit more comfortably and securely against your cheek. This over/under has a low-profile boxlock action, 2¾-inch chambers and ventilated side ribs. The 12-gauge barrels are 28 or 30 inches, your choice. The Gold E Skeet has polished, blued barrels and a handsome, polished aluminum receiver with futuristic engraving.

The 682 Gold E is chambered for three-inch shells and comes with five choke tubes: Improved Modified, Modified, Improved Cylinder and Skeet 1 and 2. Drop at comb is 1½ inches and drop at heel is just over 2⅓ inches. The flat tapered rib is ⅜ x 5⁄16 inches. This fine gun weighs 7½ pounds and comes in a black, hard-sided carrying case. A palm swell is standard and the 682 can be special ordered with left hand cast, palm swell and trigger shoe.

Perazzi (www.perazzi.it)

On the international skeet fields of the world, this high-grade Italian gun maker enjoys THE true world-class reputation. American-style skeet shooters will find that the Perazzi's handling qualities and legendary reliability will benefit them, to put it mildly.

The most popular Perazzis on the skeet fields are the MX8 and MX2000/8. All Perazzi differ slightly in weight and balance, but with the Perazzi line that is simple to change, since all have interchangeable stocks that allow a shooter to precisely custom-fit the gun to himself and to whatever clay target game is pursued. Each gun is available with a detachable trigger group, interchangeable or fixed chokes (in one or both barrels), a number of different rib configurations and barrels in the unusual lengths of 28⅜, 29½ and 31½ inches.

The stock and forend are superior grade walnut. These guns come as a two-barrel set with a lightweight spare barrel fit for gauge reduction tubes. The fixed rib is tapered 7⁄16 x 9⁄32 inches with half ventilated side ribs.

Critical dimensions on the Perazzi line are just about whatever a shooter wants them to be, and overall weight varies with barrel and stock dimension changes. Expect some sticker shock if you are upgrading from a Browning Citori or even a Beretta DT10 Trident. These Perazzi skeet guns can be yours for a cool $10,841 to $12,757, but you do have a choice of 12- or 20-gauge. On the other hand, Perazzi may ask you to come to Italy for a personal fitting. Is that a perk or a problem?

Krieghoff (www.krieghoff.com)

The K-80 series has earned a reputation as one of the top competitive shotguns in the game. A Krieghoff skeet gun will be a top performer on any course. As each skeet shooter deals with the fundamental challenge that is unique to the clay game, namely how to achieve similar gun weight, feel, sight picture and balance in all gauges in order to shoot consistently round after round and event after event, Krieghoff offers a variety of options to suit the particular needs. The weight of any gun combination is approximately 8¾ pounds and essentially varies only with barrel length.

K-80 skeet guns are distinguished primarily by their barrel configuration featuring your choice of ribs, chokes and weight. To that end, K-80 skeet guns come as over/unders or two-barrel sets for the shooter who prefers a "heavyweight" or a "lightweight" concept. Typical skeet configurations are 28- or 30-inch barrel length, fixed chokes or choke tubes, and a choice of eight mm rib (gentle taper) or 12-8 mm tapered flat rib. The barrels have a white pearl front bead and metal center bead.

You can order the K-80 in 12-, 20-, 28-gauge or .410. The gold-plated single triggers are adjustable for trigger length and pull (3¼ to 3¾ pounds). As of March, 2004, the standard grade K-80 Skeet with 28- or 30-inch barrels, case and full-length sub gauge tubes listed at $9,570 from duPont/Krieghoff Guns in Vero Beach, Florida.

Krieghoff pistol grip stocks and forends are cut from select European walnut, hand checkered and finished in satin epoxy. Ambidextrous palm swells are standard and a stock can be removed quickly with a standard stock wrench. All Krieghoffs are delivered in an aluminum carry case.

Kemen USA (www.fieldsportltd.com)

Manufactured in Spain, Kemen has a lot in common with Perazzi and Krieghoff. It is a high-quality name – primarily in Europe – based on a high-quality product that has won international competitions for many years.

The eight-pound Kemen KM-4 ($6,264) has been a mainstay of the Kemen name in the US for many years. This high-end 12-gauge over/under shotgun features a drop-out trigger assembly, various rib options including flat or stepped and a high-grade walnut, Schnabel fore-grip and stock. The stock dimensions with pistol grip and palm swell are custom tailored to a customer's specifications. Length of pull is 14⁹⁄₁₆ inches. The KM-4 has a single, non-selective trigger.

Barrels are 30 inches long with vented side ribs. The top rib is 11x7 flat vented. A set of Briley extended chokes is included.

Kemen shotguns are imported from Spain by Fieldsport in Traverse City, Michigan, and include a hard-sided case. Kemen barrels, forend and trigger parts are interchangeable with Perazzis.

F.A.I.R. (www.fair.it)

As the U.S. is increasingly incorporated into the flourishing European economy, expect to see more Italian guns on the shooting line – guns other than the established Perazzi. The Italian gun-maker FAIR builds a gun in four models specifically for skeet shooting: Master de Luxe, Jubilee 700, Jubilee 702 and SRL 802. These guns may be ordered in 12- or 20-gauge with 28- or 30-inch barrels. Barrels are vented at top and side and are chrome-lined for corrosion resistance. The top rib is 11 mm on the 12-gauge gun and nine mm wide on the 20-gauge. The price of these models varies by the amount and quality of engraving and whether the receiver housing is simply blued like the barrels or is finished in silver.

Although price range in current US dollars is sometimes difficult to establish with guns made outside the US and imported on a limited basis, a slightly used 702 20-gauge with 28-inch barrels in a condition rated "98 percent" by Cabela's was recently selling for $2,495 through the Cabela's website at www.cabelas.com.

SKB (www.skbshotguns.com)

The initials "SKB" were derived from the Samurai family name Sakaba. The vowels were simply dropped out of the name and the company was formed in the Ibaraki province of Japan (north and east of Tokyo on the Pacific coast) in 1855.

The SKB Series 85 has been in the line for years and is still available as a back bored gun. Backboring means that the interior bore of the shotgun is slightly enlarged beyond the normal dimensions. For instance, the SKB 85 over/under is opened or over-bored direct from the factory beyond the SAAMI standard of .729 to .735. Oversize bores allow the wad of a shell to spread slightly thus reducing friction as the wad travels the length of the bore. The benefits are denser and more evenly distributed patterns, and a reduction in felt recoil.

The standard features of the "85" include a low-profile receiver with a box-lock action, manual safety, single selective trigger, automatic ejectors and a matte sighting plane equipped with a nickel center post and white front bead. All skeet style buttstocks, regardless of gauge, are fitted with a radiused butt pad from Pachmayr for a fast, sure mount. The 12-gauge models are performance-tuned, which means that they feature oversized diameter bores, lengthened forcing cones and the Briley competition series tube system. Skeet models are available in the following three grades: 785, 585 Gold, and 585 Standard.

The performance-tuned 85TSS skeet over/under is available in 18 models and the skeet multi-gauge set is available in two models. The three-barrel multi-gauge set delivers consistency in weight, balance and feel.

The 85TSS skeet models feature a new semi-wide, 9.5 mm ventilated sloped target rib with three center-channel grooves with matte-finished outer edges fitted with a nickel center post and Hi-Viz Litepipe competition sight (optical quality, injection-molded plastic). This sighting plane ensures fast target acquisition and proper alignment for a slight, instinctive advantage.

The 20- and 28-gauge and .410 barrels are fitted with individual forends and an 8.5 mm ventilated sloped rib. An airline-approved, fitted aluminum case is included with the three-barrel skeet set to protect your investment.

The 85TSS 12-gauge barrel group is available with "Pigeon Porting" by Mag-Na-Port. This porting process is accomplished by electrical discharge machining (EDM) that ensures smooth incisions of exact dimensions. "Pigeon Porting" reduces perceived recoil by as much as 20 percent and muzzle lift by 60 to 80 percent.

The SKB 85TSS is available in fixed or adjustable comb options. The adjustable comb version has a maximum adjustment range of one-half inch laterally and vertically. Length of pull on the fixed comb is 14⅜ inches. Drop at comb is 1½ inches and drop at heel is 2³⁄₁₆ inches.

A 12-gauge with a 30-inch barrel chambered in 3 inch weighs eight pounds, four ounces with a fixed stock.

Like many specialty shotguns, the cost of an 85TSS varies depending on the options, but expect to pay $2,139 for the 12-gauge with a 30-inch ported barrel and fixed comb. Add $180 for an adjustable comb.

Afterword

While the above-mentioned guns are all suitable for competitive skeet, they are not the only choices available. As we mentioned earlier, all you really need is an open-choked gun that will fire two rounds, and with the wide availability of factory guns fitted with interchangeable choke tubes, it is quite easy to find a quality hunting shotgun that can do informal double duty on the skeet fields.

Though side-by-side doubles are seldom seen on the skeet range in the hands of serious competitive shooters, you will see them toted by a number of bird hunters warming up for the fall season each year. If you happen to own a fine side-by-side like the Merkel Model 200E, or the American Arms Brittany or Gentry models, there is no reason not to spend an afternoon on the skeet field with it. If you do, you will find afternoons in the fall bird fields much more productive.

SKEET LOADS

As is true of trap, skeet does not require a diverse selection of loads. While competitors will be required to obtain loads for four different gauges, the maximum permissible shot weight per gauge is tightly defined and, with the exception of the 12-gauge and one application of the 20-gauge, nothing is to be gained by deviating from that.

The 12-gauge is allowed a maximum of 1⅛ ounces of shot, with the 20-gauge carrying ⅞-ounce, the 28 holding ¾-ounce and the .410 only ½-ounce.

Shooters are allowed some latitude in shot size, but again, the nature of the game pretty well dictates that little is gained by using any shot size other than #9.

Skeet is a close-range game. In fact, the farthest shot a shooter will see on a skeet field is about 27 yards. In standard skeet, this occurs only if the shooter really hesitates on an outgoing target and lets it get so far out that such poor form would likely dictate a miss anyway. In the doubles game, it is possible to see longer shots on the second bird at stations three, four and five than one would see when shooting them as singles. These

birds can often be "shot out of position" and may present longer than normal shots, but they do not approach the range at which trap targets are routinely broken. In contrast, many shots will be quite close – low house eight for example is commonly broken only three yards off the muzzle – and the majority of shots on the remaining stations do not exceed 20 yards.

Since #9 shot will reliably break any target inside 25 yards, it has become the almost universal choice for skeet. With a pellet count of about 585 pellets per ounce (Winchester standard shot size), that gives a 1⅛-ounce 12-gauge load a pellet count of over 650 individual pellets! The 20-gauge packs 510, with the 28-gauge and .410 carrying 435 and 292, respectively.

That means the ¾-ounce #9 load in the 28-gauge is packing a lot more pellets than a full 1⅛-ounce load of #7½s, which carries only 390 of them.

Number 9 shot will do the job, but there are two instances where shifting to #8½ shot can help. The first is on the second shot in the regular doubles game. These targets can get out far enough that they verge on being close to the outer limits of #9

Bird in the air! Skeet was developed by upland bird hunters. At first, the game was shot in a circle, but it became much more popular – and viewer friendly – when it changed to the semi-circular format today. Because of the close-shooting action, #8½ and #9 shot is usually prescribed.

Winchester's AA Super Sport for the 12-gauge is offered in 1⅛-ounce of #9 shot in its #AASC12 load. Shorter barrel, open choke and this load means vaporized skeet clays!

shot's reliable break range. I find that a few #8½ loads in my pocket are confidence boosters, since I know they will consistently break targets five to 10 yards farther than #9 shot. I generally use #9s for standard skeet, and the first bird in doubles, with the #8½ load reserved for the second shot. Other shooters opt for a lighter load of #9s for the first shot and a heavier load of the same size shot for the second, theorizing that the increased pellet count provides multiple hits to add striking energy at those outer range limits. I would not argue with that approach, either. I do know that my doubles scores have improved and become more consistent after switching to the larger shot size for the second shot. I will be the first to admit that it may be strictly psychological. I know the shells will break the target in any legal position, so I am not inclined to hurry or change my rhythm. Maybe #9s would work just as well, but the mental game is every bit as important as the physical game, and if the larger shot makes me feel better, there is no reason I should not use it in that situation. The difference in pellet count between #9 and #8½ is not significant enough to make a serious difference.

The second situation where I favor #8½ shot is in ½-ounce .410 loading. This little rascal needs all the help it can get!

Early in my shooting career, when I was searching for the "magic load," a veteran shooter advised me not to even bother patterning the .410. "It's too frustrating," he stated. After ignoring his advice and running many test patterns, I have to admit he was right.

My experience with the ½-ounce .410 load indicates that consistent patterns are rare. Even the best factory loads will occasionally throw one with a few holes that a bird could slip through, or maybe be struck by only one or two pellets. That may not be enough to give the shooter that all-important "visible piece." My solution to that has been to increase the shot size to provide more striking energy per pellet. By going to #8½ shot for the .410, I decrease overall pellet count from about 290 to around 240, but each individual pellet packs more punch. It takes fewer #8½ pellets to break a bird than it does with #9s. Since I cannot control pattern density, the only thing I can do is get more punch from each individual pellet, and #8½ gives that to me.

That increase in pellet size is not something that will be a night-and-day difference, but it will get me an extra bird or

two, and that is more than enough reason to use it. I tend to think of it like chicken soup for a cold: it can't hurt.

Although shot weights for the 20, 28 and .410 are pretty much carved in stone (nobody in his right mind opts for lighter loads with these), a number of shooters find that lighter 12-gauge loads are a plus. The less recoil you absorb during the day makes you a better shooter at the end of the day. Many shooters find the one-ounce load to be as much shell as is required. Others opt for the security of the full 1⅛-ounce load, but select one of the 2¾-dram "Lite" versions. I know that some shooter use the three-dram, 1⅛-ounce load, but it is rare because it is not needed. In fact, some top shooters do not even bother with the 12-gauge at all: they shoot the 12-gauge event with their 20-gauge. One obvious reason is decreased recoil. Skilled shooters do not need more than ⅞-ounce of #9s to break a skeet target anyway.

Another reason is convenience. Most top shooters today shoot over/unders fitted with sub-gauge tubes. In order for the tubes to fit properly, the barrel must be clean. If a shooter has a good score in the 20, 28 or .410 event in the morning segment of a tournament, he knows he faces the possibility of a shoot-off in the same gauge at the end of the day. If he pulls the tubes and starts running 12-gauge rounds through the gun he will have to scrub the barrel in order to reinsert the appropriate tubes later.

Thus, the 12-gauge has somewhat disappeared from the competition skeet fields, at least in the hands of skilled shooters. Instead, an "illegal" skeet load is becoming perfectly legal – the one-ounce 20-gauge. It is legal to use in a 12-gauge event because even though the shooter may be using a 20-gauge, he is still allowed the 12-gauge maximum shot charge of 1⅛ ounces.

Here's what the ammo makers offer for those who favor factory fodder.

Factory Ammunition

Federal Cartridge (www.federalcartridge.com)

For effective skeet shooting, we are looking for a good load of #9s and perhaps an occasional #8½ in all competitive gauges: 12, 20, 28 and .410. Minnesota's Federal Cartridge makes at least one of each.

In the 12-gauge shell, there is much to choose from in the Premium Gold and Top Gun lines. A standard 2¾ offering such as T116 will give you 1,200 fps with 1⅛-ounce of #9, but to save your shoulder you might want to drop down to a one-ounce load in T113 or T175, both of which are plenty fast for skeet at 1,180 fps. For #8½ shot, look for Federal's T113 (one ounce at 1,180 fps) or T114 (1⅛-ounce at 1,100 fps: an Extra Lite, shoulder-saving load).

Federal has one designated shell for each sub-gauge in Premium Gold. The 2¾ T206 for 20-gauge guns loads ⅞ ounces of #8s or #9s at 1,200 fps. (This shell is also offered in the Top Gun Target line as the new TG20 at 1,210 fps.) The 2¾ T280 for 28-gauge loads ¾ ounce of #8½ or #9 at 1,230 fps. The 2¾ T412 for .410 loads ½ ounce of #8½ or #9 at 1,230 fps.

Winchester (www.winchester.com)

While many of the 12-gauge "Double A" Winchester loads are offered in #9, it does not at this time offer any #9s in its more economical Super-Target line. You can choose the AA SuperSport line even though it is designated for sporting clays shooting, but the hotter powder and speedier shot (1,300 fps minimum) are not assets in skeet shooting. The AAL12 Xtra-

Lite, in either one ounce of #8½ or #9, should be a fine load for all skeet shooting challenges. At 1,180 fps it is plenty fast enough, and it will be easier on the shoulder than the AA12 (1,145 fps), which carries 1⅛-ounce of shot.

Winchester has easy-to-remember designations for its sub-gauge shells, which are all rated at 1,200 fps. The 2¾-inch AA20 for 20-gauge loads a 2½ dram equivalent with ⅞ ounces of #8 or #9. The 2¾-inch AA28 for 28-ga. packs two dram-equivalents of powder with ¾ ounce of #8 or #9. The 2½-inch AA41 for .410 packs the maximum powder charge and ½-ounce of #9s.

According to Winchester, its HS (for High Strength) shells are excellent for reloading.

Remington (www.remington.com)

The Gun Club target loads are Remington's economical line. They offer a couple 2¾-inch loads of #9 shot, one for the 12-gauge (GC12L: 1⅛ ounces, 2¾ dram equivalent: 1,145 fps) and one for the 20-gauge (GC20: ⅞ ounces, 2½ dram equivalent, 1,200 fps).

Because we are concentrating on current offerings in the #8½ and #9 size, Remington offers a variety of shell options in its Premier STS target loads. The folks in Madison, North Carolina, say that these shells are loaded with extra-hard, target-quality shot. Although Remington says its Low Recoil load (STS12LR) for 12-gauge is designed "specifically for the avid skeet shooter," it is not offered in # 8½ or #9. The closest shell is the 2¾-inch STS12L Light Target load in #7½, #8, #8½ and #9 with a full 2¾ drams of powder and 1⅛ ounces of shot rated at 1,145 fps.

In sub-gauges, Remington has several loads for the 20, 28 and .410. The 2¾-inch STS20LR is loaded with 2½ drams and ⅞ ounce of #8 or #9 at 1,135 fps. The 20-gauge STS20H shell has a full ounce of #9 and spins the shot out at 1,200 fps. In 28-gauge shells, look for #8s (STS28SC) or #9s (STS28), each at 1,200 fps with ¾-ounce of shot and 2 drams of powder. For the .410 or 36-gauge, Remington's 1,200 fps offerings are in #8½ or #9 with ½-ounce of lead and the maximum allowable drams of powder.

PMC (Precision Made Cartridges; www.pmcammo.com)

PMC does not currently offer an #8½ shell, but they have plenty of #8 and #9. Their Field & Target Specific loads are offered in their Bronze Line and all skeet gauges are offered.

For 12-gauge guns, PMC's FT128 #8s and FT129 #9s are chronographed at 1,230 fps with 1⅛ ounces and a full, three-ounce dram equivalent. These same shells are offered with only one ounce of lead and an increased shot velocity of 1,250 fps.

If you are shooting a 20-gauge, you have a choice of #7½, #8 and #9 shells at 1,230 fps. All are fully loaded with ⅞ ounces and 2½ drams. The 28-gauge and .410 are equally served at 1,220 fps in #7½, #8 and #9 shot in the PMC FT loads. (In the Gold line, PMC loads up their sub-gauges with shot and powder. For instance, their HV419 for .410 is a 3-inch shell that carries ¹¹⁄₁₆ ounces of #9 shooting at 1,135 fps.)

Kent Cartridge (www.kentgamebore.com)

Kent's 2¾-inch Diamond Shot loads are available in #8 and #9 shot, but only in 12- and 20-gauge loads. Their new 12-gauge shell K122GT32 for #7½, #8 and #9 is loaded with 1⅛ ounce and 2¾ drams of powder. At 1,145 fps, it is plenty for skeet. Dropping down ⅛-ounce in shot to the K122GT28

in all sizes raises velocity to 1,200 fps and perhaps give your shooting shoulder a rest, too.

In the 20-gauge shell, both one-ounce (#6, #7½, #8) and ⅞-ounce (#7½, #8, #9) shells are offered with 2½ drams.

The Gamebore-brand loads are designed strictly for field use in loads #5, #6 and #7, but loads are available for all four skeet gauges.

Rio Ammunition (www.rioammo.com)

Rio Ammunition is an American company headquartered in Houston, Texas, the offspring of a Spanish company that has been producing shotshells since 1896. Today, they say, their shotshells are sold in more than 70 countries.

Rio's 2¾-inch 12-gauge designated skeet loads contain #9 shot. Load 24 has ⅞ ounces, Load 28 has one ounce and Load 32 has 1⅛-ounce. Loads in #8½ are not available, but #8 loads are plentiful. Rio says that their target loads feature a three per-cent antimony alloy while their top target loads have five per-cent.

A 2¾-inch target load is available for smaller gauges as well in #7.5, #8 and #9. The 20-gauge is loaded with ⅞ ounce (1,250 fps), the 28-gauge with ¾ ounce (1,300 fps) and the .410 with ½ ounce (1,200 fps).

Fiocchi of America (www.fiocchiusa.com)

For Fiocchi, let's look at the sub-gauge loads first because they are very specific. The 2¾-inch 20-gauge uses ⅞-ounce of #7½, #8 or #9 high antimony lead while the 28 and .410 come in #8 and #9 only. All three loads achieve 1,200 fps.

In Fiocchi's 12-gauge series, there are literally a dozen load possibilities to choose from. With Fiocchi, as with so many companies, the differences between these loads are relatively small and usually involve variations in the types of powder to give a hotter, faster, or perhaps even a slower-burning load. Again, the differences are so small as to be insignificant except perhaps to a ballistician. Your task is to find a shell that works best in your gun and with your shooting form.

In one-ounce, 2¾ high antimony lead loads, Fiocchi offers four shells that are graduated in velocity from light to heavy: 12TL Target Light (1,150 fps, 2¾ dram: #7½, #8, #8½, #9),

Remington's Premier STS is their "reduced recoil" shell. These clay loads feature the STS mouth design where skive depth is increased to one-half inch. Thus, it travels beyond the hinge point of the crimp and greatly reduces the angle of taper.

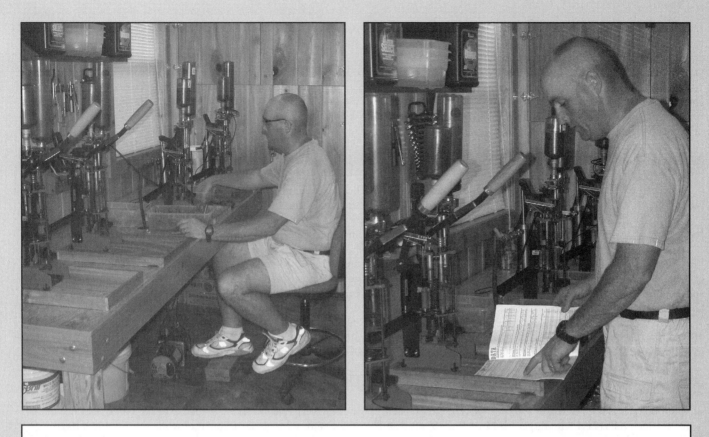

The Reloader

Reloaders can certainly save money by purchasing the equipment and components for sub-gauge shooting. Money-savings has a trade-off however, which is time, effort and an initial cash outlay. Not the least important is learning to follow specific load recipes. After all, if you are not careful, you can get hurt.

These days, corporations that produce reloading products will happily send you a copy of their gauge-powder-shot-hull recipes and many are available on line. Alliant, for instance, has a full catalog for all powders posted on the Internet at www.alliantpowder.com.

Florida's Scott Richardson has been shooting competitively for three years and has won the state championship in his shooting class. He has since converted a room attached to his garage for reloading. About seven feet wide by 20 feet long, he paneled the walls with cypress planking, laid a quarry stone-pattern tile and installed a window air conditioner. The room is

---

12 TH Target Heavy (1,200 fps, 3 dram: #7½, #8, #8½), 12TX Little Rino (1,250 fps, handicap load: #7½, #8, #8½) and 12CRSR Crusher (1,300 fps, maximum load: #7½, #8, #8½, #9). With some minor differences, the same general pattern of velocity progression is available in 1⅛-ounce loads.

Eley (www.wwy.co.uk)

You do not see many Eley cartridge boxes discarded after an American skeet event, but they are more common at high-end sporting clays events. The American skeet has to learn simple metric conversions to use international loads and also must accustom himself (or herself) to the European concern for "head" size in millimeters (mm), type of wad (plastic or fiber) and such interesting measurements as muzzle velocity versus observed velocity. Several European manufacturers, Eley being one of them, provide data on the percentage of antimony in each load selection, something not found in standard American catalogs.

There is not an #8½ in the Eley line-up, but there are plenty of #9s. The 2¾ Eley Superb with 16 mm head and plastic wad has five percent antimony in its 1⅛-ounce loads of #7, #7½

and #8. Muzzle velocity is listed as 1,450 fps while the observed velocity is 1,130 fps.

Eley does not offer 28 or .410 shells, but does have a few selections for 2¾-inch chambered 20-gauge guns in ¾- and ⅞-ounce loads. These #7½, #8 and #9, 3 percent antimony shot loads are actually called the Competition Trap or CT shells.

Reloads

Most serious skeet shooters are reloaders, and the reason is simple: economy. If you do a "best buy" by case-lot of the four different gauges, you will find that the 12, 20 and .410 cost virtually the same, while the 28-gauge generally runs about 20 bucks more. Considering that the .410 carries less than half the shot of the 12-gauge (with the 28-gauge running about 65 percent) and that both use less powder, it is difficult to explain why they should cost as much as or more than a larger 12-gauge shell, but undoubtedly lesser demand, as compared to the 12-gauge loads, has something to do with it.

Skeet shooters who load their own can realize a savings of about fifty to sixty percent on the smaller shells, and around

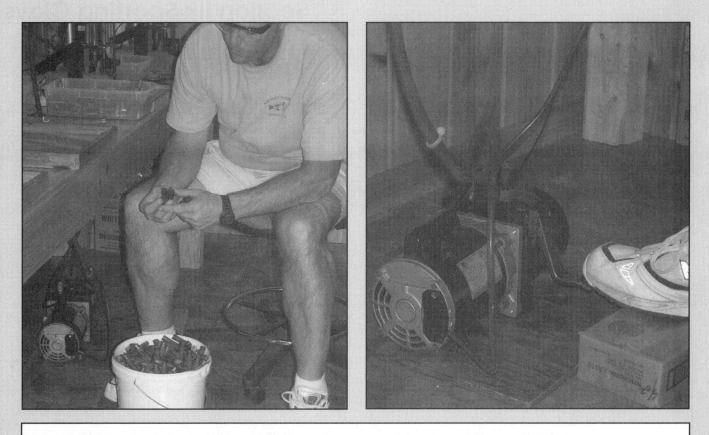

forty percent on the 12- and 20-gauges.

Shot selection for skeet loads is not quite as critical as for trap. I favor hard shot for everything in trap, but do not mind the less expensive chilled shot for the 12- and 20-gauge loads. In fact, novice shooters might actually be helped by softer shot in these two gauges. You have more than enough #9 pellets in even the ⅞ ounce 20-gauge load to break the close-range targets. The drawback is that it is difficult to get the load to open up. Soft shot does that better than hard shot.

Kent's Diamond Shot loads for #8 and #9 are currently available for 12- and 20-gauge.

The 28-gauge is an under-appreciated little jewel. It is such an efficient shell that good hard shot can make it every bit as effective, in skilled hands, as a 1⅛-ounce 12-gauge load. Indeed, a number of shooters find they can carry the same average with both. Not surprisingly, many shooters opt for the 28-gauge as their practice load because it is truly an effective skeet shell. Inside 30 yards, it will break anything the heavier 12- and 20-gauge will, and with softer manners.

With the .410 loading, hard shot becomes mandatory. While I do like the miniscule shell (and even do some bird hunting with it), it needs help and cannot really tolerate soft shot even though many budget-conscious shooters do load it with that. I have a preference for #8½ shot in this shell, but I know that many skeet shooters familiar with the .410 swear by standard #9 loads.

While handling the loading chores for four different gauges may seem like a complex endeavor, it is not: two sizes of shot – two different grades (hard and soft) in size #9 if you prefer – the appropriate wads, and just a couple of different powders are all it takes to give you your best shot.

Chapter Fifteen

"THE MOST FUN YOU CAN HAVE WITH A SHOTGUN"

Sporting clays, or hunter clays as it has sometimes been called, is not the rigidly-programmed, predictable clay target game we find in trap and skeet. Nor is it a game that lends itself to perfection. Even the world's greatest shots miss with surprising regularity and a perfect score in a tournament is virtually unheard of.

This is a game where everybody will miss, laugh about it and go on to the next shot. This is probably why it is well on its way to becoming the most popular shotgun game in the country.

That has not always been the case. In fact, just 20 years ago sporting clays ranges were about as common as good manners at a punk rock concert. In those days, however, the sport was already well established in Europe and it was beginning to make its presence felt on these shores. Today, it is safe to say that the majority of new shotgun ranges being constructed or those under re-construction are either dedicated to sporting clays or incorporate sporting clays into their program.

For shotgunners who are bored with the unvarying fare of

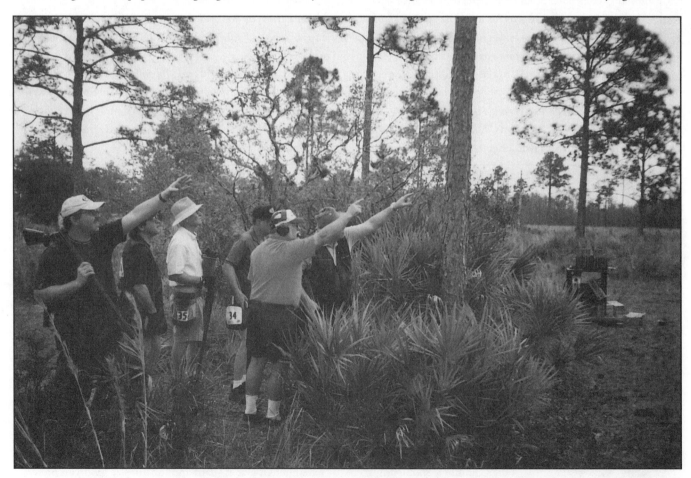

When you advance to a new station on a sporting clays venue, your squad has a right to call for a bird. Be alert, because this is your opportunity to see the flight path and made a decision about the break point before the shooting starts.

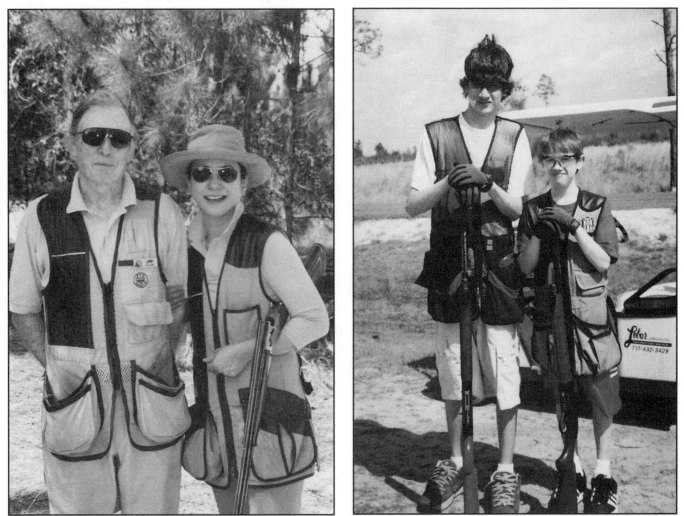

Sporting clays is a relatively new shooting sports phenomenon in the U.S. and its relaxed, egalitarian approach to events has proven popular for all ages, both sexes and young and old. Connecticut's Jim and Anna Marie Collins have discovered the pleasures and challenges of traveling and shooting together as have Pennsylvania brothers Kent (taller) and Kevin Sarciano. Although Kevin (14 years old) just began shooting, Kent has been shooting since he was 10 and was a Sporting Clays All American in 2003.

trap and skeet, the first taste of sporting clays is a smorgasbord! Targets zip by at speeds and angles previously unseen on American ranges. Sometimes it is a single clay leaping from a hidden trap and disappearing behind a conveniently placed tree before the surprised gunner can even react. Just about the time the gunner has that target figured out, the boom of his shotgun sends another target speeding across the field … or two targets may pop up. They might be crossing, climbing, incoming, outgoing, quartering, streaking high overhead or even falling.

Just when the shooter starts to get comfortable with that selection, a sneaky range operator will change the speed or angle on the trap or even move the shooting stand, leaving the hapless gunner to face an entirely new set of challenges.

For many wingshooters, this game is as much fun as you can possibly have with a shotgun.

Sporting Clays Origins

Sporting clays began its popular rise in England just about the same time that skeet was becoming the favored new game in America, in the early 1920s. It would be incorrect to say it was an immediate success. Over the last 25 years or so, it slowly grew into the most popular shooting game in England.

Historians credit Orvis with sponsoring the first sport-

ing clays match in the United States, in 1983. The game had been played here before that, however. Remington Farms, in Maryland, had a version of hunter clays in the late 1960s. The firm imported British course designer Chris Craddock to these shores and, using the hilly, wooded terrain of Remington Farms, he was able to lay out an impressive course.

In 1985, an interested group formed the United States Sporting Clays Association, and in 1989, the National Sporting Clays Association (affiliated with the National Skeet Shooting Association) became the dominant, governing body for this game in the U.S.

How Sporting Clays Works

Sporting clays takes trap and skeet several steps further. While a sporting clays shooter will see some of the same angles that he might on a trap or skeet field, that is about as similar as the three games get. There are significant differences between sporting clays and trap and skeet:

1. Like other games, the shooter calls for the bird. However, in sporting clays the puller may wait up to three seconds before he releases the target. Some launching controls even have a built-in variable delay, similar to international skeet.

All sporting clays shots begin from a low gun position and the proper position can vary depending upon the angle of the shot.

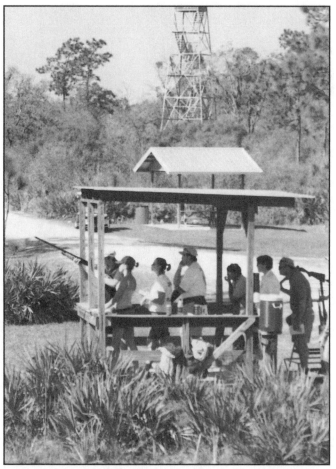

Everyone on the squad plus the puller and scorer want to huddle near the shooter and watch the action. The advantage of shooting second or later is that you can watch the first person in action and get a strong indication of where you want your pattern to kill the bird.

2. When calling for the bird, the shooter must have the gun in a low position, meaning the entire buttstock must be visible below the armpit. (This rule was recently relaxed by the NSCA.) Mount your gun when the birds become visible.

3. Other shotgunning games provide for alibis. If a gun or ammunition malfunction occurs, the rules allow a shooter to re-shoot the target. This is not always the case in sporting clays. Alibis are allowed but are more limited and the rules applying them are stricter.

4. Shotguns of 12-gauge or smaller are allowed. Shooters may use different guns at different stations and guns fitted for multiple barrels with different length barrels and chokes are permitted. Shooters may also change barrels or choke tubes between stations. Sporting clays is occasionally referred to as "golf with a shotgun" and some shooters bring along a full bag of guns.

5. Trap and skeet use one target. In sporting clays, five different targets may be incorporated in a single round:
   A. The standard clay bird;
   B. A slightly smaller (90mm) bird that flies faster;
   C. A 60mm bird (about the size of a tennis ball) that really gets moving;
   D. A battue target, about ¼-inch thick and very flat, that takes some highly unpredictable paths during flight;

and
   E. A thicker, tougher version of the standard clay target used as a ground-bouncing rabbit. This sturdier target takes a harder hit to break.

6. Targets may be presented as singles, true pairs (when both targets are launched simultaneously), following pairs (the second target is launched behind the first, at the puller's discretion and often with a time lag) or as report pairs, where the second target is launched at the sound of the shooter's first shot.

7. If this is not confusing enough, there are also "poison birds," targets of a separate and clearly discernible appearance that may be inserted at random anywhere in the match. A shooter firing on this target is rewarded with a miss. Shooters who refrain from shooting at these targets score an automatic hit. You never know when or where one will pop up except that they are never thrown as true pairs.

Terrain Hazards

As you can imagine, these rules give course designers a tremendous amount of latitude and they are encouraged to use it. It is common for courses to use existing terrain features to place obstructions deliberately in the path of a shooter. For example, some targets may fly through trees or brush and only give the

A target on the ground! Both ends of the running rabbit station. In photo one, the bird is away and visibly bouncing while in photo two, the shooter sees the target and takes aim. This is a target presentation you will never see in trap, skeet, crazy quail or hélice!

shooter a small window of visibility. Alternatively, there may be two or three windows available on a given shot and each will change the basic nature of the shot. It is then up to the shooter to determine which might be to his best advantage.

The use of natural terrain features can also result in targets presented below the shooter as he stands on a hilltop or targets that fly uphill from the shooter. In most cases, shooting cages are required to restrict the shooter's range of movement and require him to break the target within a relatively confined area.

The result of this course latitude means that sporting clays courses, like golf courses, will differ across the county. No two will be the same. If this were not difficult enough, course managers are encouraged to make frequent changes to their target presentations just to keep things interesting. What results is one of the most challenging and enjoyable shotgunning experiences possible.

Sporting Stations

Since courses vary considerably, there is no standard sporting clays range as there is in trap and skeet. Shooters see a wide variety of target presentations, and this has made sporting clays a thinking shooter's game. You cannot react your way around a sporting clays course. You must think your way through it, analyzing each individual station as you come to it. Here are some of the target presentations you are likely to see.

The Rabbit Run

Sporting clays traces its roots to hunting and that flavor lingers. Virtually all of the various sporting clays target presentations represent a situation that will occur in the field. They are invariably named after specific "critter" shots.

Sporting clays courses around the world are often designed to reflect the local hunting traditions as well as a geographical adaptation of the terrain. Many American wingshooters learn from an early age not to shoot rabbits while bird hunting because they may run the risk of hitting one of the bird dog – or worse, teach the dogs bad habits. This is not necessarily the case in Europe. Rabbits are fair game in any "rough" or "walk-up" hunt and thus, the rabbit target has become a staple of many sporting clays courses.

The rabbit is a ground-bouncing target using a sturdier clay. The rabbit launches from a special machine so that its flat edge hits the ground and bounces across it. Sometimes field managers place a piece of carpet at the first contact point the clay makes with the ground to help cushion that initial blow. These targets are not as easy to break as standard clay because of their heavier construction. There is no way to predict precisely what path the target will take after it first hits the ground.

Course managers may create a short, narrow opening for the target to pass through or they may let it sweep across open ground. Sometimes this target launches as a following target or a report target in conjunction with an aerial bird. The rabbit may run partially on the ground and then bounce smoothly into the air. The most common range to shoot this target is 15 to 40 yards.

This is a quick-sweeping shot that demands a strong follow-through and last minute corrections to account for erratic movement. Not surprisingly, this is a tough target, even more so because many American shooters must overcome an ingrained mental block that prevents them from shooting a target on the ground.

Woodcock

This is usually a low overhead or extremely hard crossing throw that gives the shooter only a quick glimpse of the target. Doubles might be thrown here. The range is generally 20 yards and under.

Some ranges may throw these targets from multiple traps located at various positions in front of the shooter. This is quick, fast shooting with a wide-open choke.

Duck Tower

The duck tower is often a 40- to 70-foot tower with as many as five stations laid out around its base. The tower may be behind the shooter with birds going away or quartering away and falling off to the side. There is often one station where the target may be a sharp incoming angle. The targets may be standard, 90 mm or 60 mm, unless you have a truly devious course manager, in which case who knows what you will get. Some managers install an oscillating trap, add a "poison bird," or do something even more radical. Expect to shoot this one anywhere from as close as 20 to more than 60 yards.

The high, fast crossing shot is popular and, depending upon your shooting window, can be fun and easy – or fun and difficult, but in sporting clays, the emphasis is always on safety and fun.

Dove

Doves are similar to ducks in that both are launched from an elevated position. Often, however, they will be incoming angled shots unless the course manager puts out extra shooting stations along the flight path and thus creates overhead crossing targets. The incoming Dove Tower at Cherokee Rose in Griffin, Georgia, has a cage that limits the downward position of the gun. The target house is dead ahead of the shooter and throws what looks like a high house eight skeet shot, except that the birds are almost 15 yards up and traveling as true pairs. It is possible to start behind both birds, swing through them and take the trailing bird first, then continue the swing to get the lead bird. You just have to shoot this fast, and there's not much room for error.

Grouse Bluff

This is the most charitable name you'll hear this difficult ulcer-maker called. It is generally set up as hillside shot with the shooter looking down into a gully. Some stations may have crossing shots and often stick a tree or two along the flight path to make you think about the shot. Others may have a more "away" angle. Some stations combine both by putting in two different shooting platforms that will alter the angle from crossing to outgoing. Regardless, if you see the word "grouse" on a station, expect it to be tough!

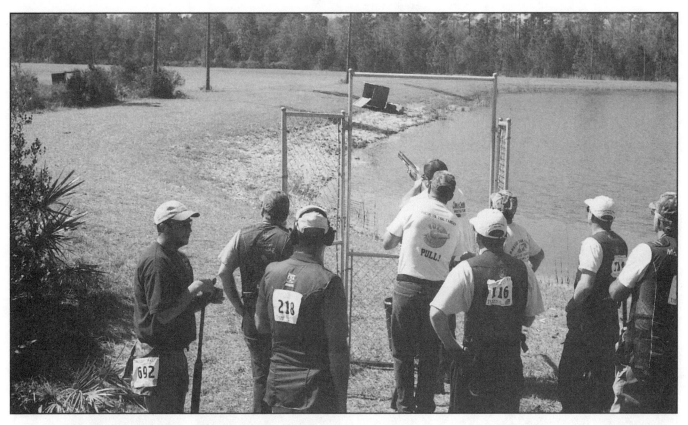

Shots over water are usually wide-open and the tendency is to take your time, but depending on the distance to the target, the spacious shooting situation may cause you to shoot late and behind the bird.

The sharp vertical angle this target took into the trees – a "Rising Ringneck" or perhaps "Rising Sharptail" – only gave the shooter a few seconds to fire for effect.

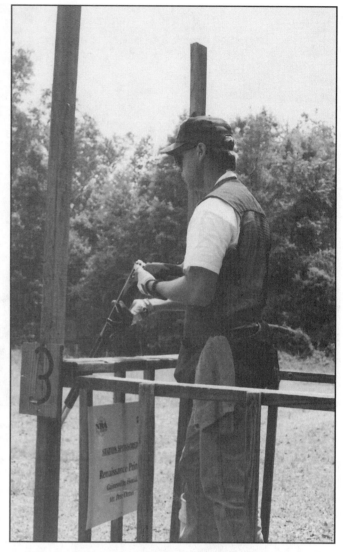

Major sporting clays events always have a few stations that you can shoot just for fun. This station at the TM Ranch near Orlando, Florida featured six presentations over water. Shots were as close as 20 yards and as far as 60 yards!

Guns are loaded only when the shooter steps onto the cage to take his turn. Violating this rule will get you thrown off any course in the U.S – and rightly so.

Blue Bill Pass

This is similar to a low-angle duck tower. The purpose, I suppose, is to simulate a passing shot on a lesser scaup blue-bill duck. They often skim low and fly faster than hell. That is what these targets do. Some shots may have a slight outgoing angle, but many will be hard crossers. If the course manager has a sense of humor, there may be four or five shooting stations scattered along the flight path, each of which changes the angle, distance to the target and the lead. This station may be shot from 20 to 50-plus yards, and the longer shots are some of the toughest.

Duck Boat

Our favorite course designer has been drinking too much again, and this time dragged home an old boat. You get into it to shoot. Sometimes it actually floats in water, other times it lays on a bed of very wobbly truck tires. Just getting a steady shooting position in the boat is tough enough, but hitting the targets, which may be incoming, crossing, or outgoing at 15 to 40 yards, is even tougher.

Springing Teal

This trap is angled skyward and the birds go almost straight up. You will get the full range of presentations here: singles, true pairs, report and following doubles. Do you try to hit them on the climb at relatively short range or wait until they peak out or try to hit them as they fall? If you wait too long you may have a 60-plus-yard shot!

Rising Sharptail

This event often uses the little 60 mm target and throws it away from the shooter at a rising angle. Because of the speed and the small size of the target, this can often call for a Full choke and a high velocity load, even though the birds may be taken inside 40 yards.

Whistling Bobs

This simulates the close range flush of a quail with the target heading quickly away from the shooter and, just like its namesake, heading quickly to cover. This calls for fast shooting with an open choke!

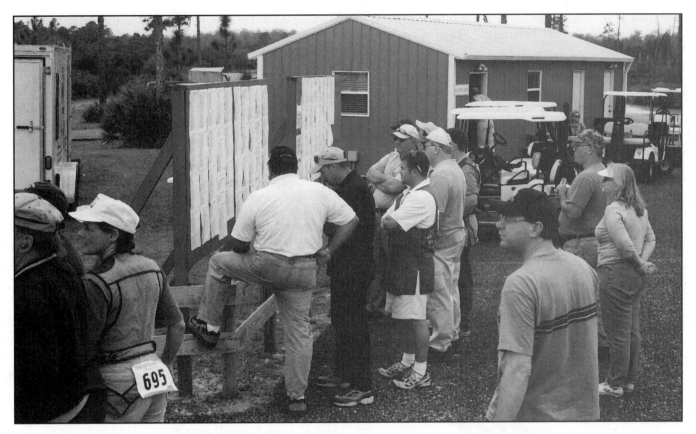

Any big shoot will have a leader board where you can check your placement within your shooting class. There is always a crowd around the regularly updated sheets, but whether knowing where you stand is helpful to you depends on your personal psyche and goals.

Sneaky Snipe

This can be similar to the rising sharptail, except that the targets may not achieve a great deal of height. The window on this station can be quite small, with the target often starting out against a wooded background, zipping across a small patch of open sky, and then back across the background.

Duck Pond

Another crowd-pleasing favorite, this station has three strategically placed traps that can throw incomers, outgoers and settling crossing shots to a shooter on a small stand that juts out into a pond. You do not know what you are going to get when you call for a bird.

Rising Ringnecks

This is a steep-climbing bird, similar to springing teal, but at a shorter range. Often there is another bird, quartering away, that joins the first.

Modified Dove Tower

Sometimes seen as a component of a standard dove tower, this station has targets coming from behind the shooter on a high, going away angle. It looks a lot like a skeet high house, one on steroids.

The foregoing is a basic look at some of the presentations offered on courses around the country, but it certainly is not all-inclusive. Sporting clays is not scripted and veteran shooters do not want it to be. If course design and target presentations ever reach the point where shooters begin to run clean scores, things will change. That is the nature of sporting clays.

Etiquette and Procedures

Sporting clays is a laid-back game and the procedures are similar to skeet. A squad of two to five shooters proceeds through the course with a course guide/puller. The shooting rotation within the squad may be set by the course guide or left up to the shooters. If shooters want to change the rotation of that shooting order, there is nothing in the rules to stop them.

Like skeet, each shooter steps onto the shooting station as his turn comes. The first shooter to take the station has the right to "see" the targets, to call for birds to be thrown without firing, so he and the other members of the squad can actually see what they are up against.

"Seeing targets" is an important step. If you are in a squad where the first shooter ignores this factor, remind him between stations. The first shooter has a responsibility to call for birds to be shown and every shooter on the squad benefits. If he continually forgets, change his rotation and get somebody in the first spot who is more considerate.

When a visible piece is knocked off, targets are scored as a hit. Doubles are treated differently than in skeet or trap. If the shooter manages to break both birds with one shot, he is credited with both and saves a shell.

When shooting doubles or pairs, if the shooter misses the first target he has the right to fire his second shell at it or try to get both targets with the second shell. If the shooter breaks both targets with either the first or the second shell, he gets credit for both.

If a target in the air is broken by pieces of another target, it is treated like a "no bird." When this happens, the shooter receives whatever score he got on the first shot and the doubles are thrown again. The shooter must attempt to hit the first target, but he will already have that scored. It is only the second target that is scored.

Scorers call missed birds as "lost." If the shooter disagrees with the call, he must make his protest before firing another shot. The scorer then must poll the other shooters, or even the spectators, and can change his call based on that input. If he does not change it, his call stands.

In the event a gun is acting up, the shooter can ask the puller/referee for permission to test-fire it. Other than that, every round fired is for score.

As with skeet, it is good etiquette to know your rotation order in the squad; to be ready to step to the shooting pad when your turn comes; and not to crowd the shooter on the pad.

Accessories You Will Need

A good sporting clays course is like a golf course: you'll do a lot of walking. Some ranges have golf carts available, but you will have to tote all your necessary items with you.

A shooting vest is an excellent idea. You will want some place to put the five to fifteen shells you use on each station. You may want divided pockets in the vest to keep #7½, #8 and #9 shot separate. As we will see later, changing loads for different targets can be a big plus. Since sporting clays requires a low gun starting position, you will also want a vest of the international style. Remember that these do not have a distinct shoulder pad to catch on the recoil pad during the mount. Instead, they have a smooth face, often with padding on the shooting side to allow a sloppy gun mount to keep the buttstock where it belongs.

Vests made for sporting clays shooters often have loop-type holders or small pockets to hold extra choke tubes and a tube wrench. You will most likely have to change tubes as well as shot loads during an event. A good sporting clays vest will keep everything where you can find it in a hurry.

A standard round of sporting clays consists of either 50 or 100 birds, and that represents a lot of shotshells to carry. In addition, experienced shooters carry between three and five – or even more – different loads. It is easy to see that stuffing everything in your vest pockets is going to leave you exhausted by the end of the round. That is a lot of weight to wear throughout the round. Instead, get a tote bag to carry your shells, shell knocker, choke tube lube, spare eye and ear protection, maybe a plastic bottle of water, lens cleaning paper and other items you might want or need.

The only time you will have to lug a separate shell bag is between stations. The rest of the time, toss it on the ground and let Mother Earth pack the load. You would be surprised what a difference that can make by the end of the day. Four or five boxes of shotshells weigh a bunch!

If you are shooting a course that does not offer golf cart transportation between stations, consider the shoes you are wearing. There can be a lot of walking involved and toting a shotgun and a lot of shells means you are wandering around, up hill and down, dragging 20 or more pounds! Jogging shoes are a good idea. The smore comfortable your shoes, the better you will feel.

A round of sporting clays takes a lot longer than a round of trap or skeet and there is more physical exertion involved. You might want to carry an energy snack and drink. Dried fruit is great, since its sugar gets to work quickly and does not give you false energy like the refined sugar in candy.

That is a lengthy list, but sporting clays is a complex game. It is a thinking shooter's game, one that will test the versatility of both your equipment and your shooting technique. It is also a heckuva lot of fun and can be addictive!

When you first try sporting clays, you may want a simple and compact plastic case such as the 100-Round Shotshell Case from MTM as you walk from station to station. This case has a removable choke tube holder and space inside for four boxes of shells.

GETTING STARTED

Unlike trap and skeet, sporting clays is not a game that can be learned by rote and shot on reflex. The variation in target speeds, distances, angles, target sizes, and the different multiple target presentations inherent in sporting clays make that impossible.

For example, it is easy to tell a skeet student the best foot position and the proper lead for station four. That target will be the same whether you shoot it in Maine or California. The ATA has rigidly prescribed its speed, flight path and distance. This is anything but the case in sporting clays.

You might find one course's rabbit target a rather simple shot, thrown from a slow-speed manual trap at a modest 15 yards from the gun. The next course may zip a rabbit target from a higher-speed electronic trap at a range of 40 yards! You cannot even use the same choke for the two shots, let alone the same lead. That is what makes sporting clays such a challenge.

The successful sporting shooter does not necessarily "learn" to shoot this game. Instead, he learns a well-rounded selection of shotgun techniques, and then applies the correct technique for the target presentation he is facing on that particular station. Sporting clays is a thinking shooter's game.

Gun Position and Handling

Sporting clays begins with the gun in a low gun position before you call for the bird. In standard sporting clays, the butt must be visible below the shooter's armpit. It cannot be shouldered until the bird actually leaves the trap.

This is one of the most overlooked areas of sporting clays instruction, especially if the shooter has had some experience at trap and skeet where the targets are called for from a mounted gun position. It is also one of the most important aspects of good shooting and the reason should be obvious: unless the gun is mounted to the same position each time, it will not shoot where you are looking each time. If you fail to achieve a consistent mount, your body position, target lead and shooting technique become moot points because you will not be on the bird even if you do all of the other things correctly.

If you doubt the truth in those words, watch what happens to a skeet shooter who has some skill (B Class and above) the first time he tries to shoot a round of skeet from the sporting clays low gun position. His score will drop markedly. Trap shooters will likely fare even worse. Yet, every one of those shots and angles are ones he will have seen many times before. He knows the leads and techniques. It is just a question of mastering gun-handling skills.

You must learn and then practice gun-handling skills. It also helps if your equipment is properly set up.

A well-fitted shotgun is a tremendous asset, which is why experienced sporting clays shooters will go to the time and

trouble to have their guns correctly fitted. It also helps if the heel of the recoil pad is smoothly radiused (that is, rounded) to prevent snagging as the gun comes up. Some shooters also put a slight radius on the inside edge of the recoil pad to further reduce drag. The toe of the pad also gets a smoothing. This aids in a smooth dismount of the gun because, as we will see later, good shooters sometimes dismount the gun between shots on some target pairs.

There are only a million reasons to introduce your youngster to shotgun games, but here are four: the unbreakable bond you will form, the lifetime skills your youth will learn, the opportunity to teach respect for firearms and safety, and the chance to pass on our firearms and shooting sports heritage.

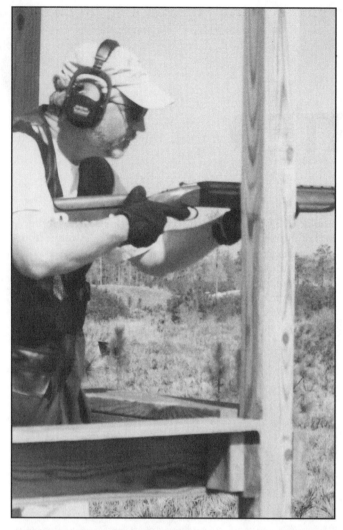

Sporting clays typically begins with the gun in a low gun position before you call for the bird. Usually, the butt must be visible below the shooter's armpit and cannot be shouldered until the bird actually leaves the trap. In practice, most shooters unconsciously fudge a bit.

When selecting a vest or shooting shirt for sporting clays, you will want one with an international-style shoulder pad that extends down the front of the vest. Those made for conventional trap and skeet have a small pad that often catches the gun's recoil pad and makes a mess of the gun mount. The fewer things you have on your vest or gun to snag, the smoother and more consistent your gun mount will be.

Stance also plays a role. Trap and skeet shooters can exhibit some of the most uncomfortable and exaggerated stances one could imagine. Some of the semi-crouch, feet-stuck-together, body-wound-up-like-a-spring stances make a consistent gun mount a real challenge!

A novice should learn to stand up straight with the feet opened to about shoulder width. There should be no exaggerated crouch and one should not lock the knees. Some shooters are more comfortable with their weight spread evenly, while others like just a touch more weight on the leading foot. This provides better balance, a smoother swing and wider swing arc. Novice shooters often tend to take a "rifleman's" stance,

with weight on the back foot. This is not good because it restricts the swing. The only time back foot weight is good form in sporting clays is when a high incoming target must be taken almost directly overhead.

The shooter's grip on the forend of the gun is another overlooked point. You should move your hand around on the forend until you find the point where you can mount and dismount the gun without strain using the forend (leading) hand only. That point is usually a bit farther back than the shooter started with, especially if he has been shooting trap or skeet from a pre-mounted position. This will alter the weight distribution between the shooter's hands and make for a much smoother and more consistent gun mount.

Additionally, there is the matter of an erect head. When mounting the gun, always bring it to the face; never bring the face to the gun! To do so encourages a lot of bobbing and weaving of the head, and since your eye is essentially the rear sight on your shotgun, you can imagine what that does to your score.

Proper gun handling techniques give you a comfortable stance with a maximum range of movement. Your eyes will lock onto the bird and the gun will come up smoothly and consistently without a great deal of conscious thought.

Master the gun mount and you are well on your way to becoming a good sporting clays shooter. Neglect it and you will have more trouble scoring than you need.

One final matter concerns where to position the barrel before you call for the bird. There are only two hard and fast rules: (1) The muzzle should be within your range of vision so that it and the bird can be viewed simultaneously before the mount is begun; (2) The muzzle should never be held above the flight path of the target. If the bird leaves the trap and ducks under the barrel, you will temporarily lose sight of it and your focus on it. You then have to reacquire it, and that wastes time.

This obviously means that there is no single correct gun hold position. A ground-bouncing rabbit requires a lower gun hold than a high, incoming dove. In pairs involving different targets, such as a rabbit and a snipe, the hold should be correct for the first target you will engage.

Body Position

In the skeet section, we discussed the importance of aligning your body to its natural point of aim. For most skeet targets, that will be near the Eight Post, since all targets are directed toward it. The principle of natural point of aim is still valid in sporting clays, but it is tougher to define and it changes with the shot.

Determining body position starts with figuring out where you want to break the target. Every target has an ideal break point on its flight path where it fairly screams, "Kill me!" Not surprisingly, this is called the "kill zone." Given differing abilities and reaction times among different shooters, the best kill zone for each shot may vary among shooters. You have to figure out where it is for you and position your shooting stance to take advantage of it. This, in effect, becomes the sporting clays shooter's Eight Post. It may be nothing more than a small circle of air.

Multiple targets can complicate that, since a perfect position for one target may not be so for the other. Because lifting the feet to shift position while a bird is in the air is virtually guaranteed to cause a miss, you will have to do the same type of fudging that occurs during skeet doubles. Give yourself enough swing room to break the first target and fudge your body position toward the second. This is one reason why an upright, fluid stance is so important in sporting clays.

Equally important is the point to which you pivot your upper body to get your "first look point," the spot on the flight path where you first visually acquire the target. New shooters tend to come back much too far toward the trap. This often causes the bird to get by them, and then they have to really unwind to catch it.

Given the variety of target presentations, there is no hard and fast rule here either. Top shooters prefer to come back to the trap hard enough to put some coil in the body, and this makes them unwind a bit when moving to the bird. This generates gun speed during the mount. If the bird is consistently outrunning you, however, you may have to position yourself even more toward the kill zone.

Exceptions to that are some extremely quick and close crossing shots. Sometimes it can be to the shooter's advantage to take a first look point close to the house because it will make you swing like hell to catch it. At times that is exactly what is needed to break that target! Time and experience will also alter your first look point.

The more proficient you become, the more you can fudge to the kill zone. Depending on the shooting technique you use, your first look point can also be altered.

Shooting Techniques

Sustained lead and fast swing were both explained in the "Skeet Simplified" chapter, and there's not much point in discussing them again here. Both have their uses in sporting clays and they parallel those in skeet. Sustained lead is a good way to handle incoming targets that angle slightly away from the shooter, while the fast swing is generally a superior technique for crossers, out-goers and quartering shots.

The biggest disadvantage to the sustained lead in sporting clays is that it requires you to know the lead. You must have handled that distance and angle successfully in the past and have filed the amount of daylight you see between muzzle and target away in your little on-board computer. Some experienced shooters who have virtually seen every shot can make good use of the sustained lead in a far wider variety of presenta-

tions than most shooters. The technique does not work nearly as well for novices and intermediate shooters in this game as it does in skeet. The problem is that we see new leads and angles on each new course.

Another factor is target speed. The velocity of skeet and trap targets is fixed. Sporting clays use machines that throw at different speeds, and the size and shape of the targets also produce different speeds. All of this complicates the game for a shooter using a relatively unforgiving technique that requires the exact speed, distance, and direction to be known. With the fast swing, the speed of the target will tend to accelerate your gun speed and that in itself can help compensate for varying target speeds.

There are essentially five types of sporting clays shots – coming at you, going away, crossing, straight up and running rabbit (on the ground) – it may well be worth your time to hire a professional coach like NSCA Level 2 Instructor Bob Knopf to help you through the intricacies of adjusting stance, gun hold, lead and even proper fit. (Photo courtesy Bob Knopf)

The authors believe that the fast swing is the bread-and-butter technique for sporting clays. The faster the target is moving, the faster you have to move to nail it. There is, however, another technique that can be extremely useful. The individual who explained it to me called it the "pullaway" and I will use the same explanation, although I'm certain some shooters might poke holes in this definition.

The pullaway came about as a direct result of the low gun position used. It is not effective from a pre-mounted position, nor is it easy to accomplish. It works because of the body's natural tendency to lock eyes upon an aerial target while the upper body uncoils to track it in flight. If one executes the proper gun mount technique, the eyes never leave the target and the gun comes up to look exactly where the eyes are looking. Since the body is moving while you are mounting the gun, gun speed has already been generated. Once the gun is mounted, it is still moving at body speed, which is moving at target speed. At that point, the gun speed is quickly increased and the shot triggered.

In practice, it works like this: take your natural point of aim in the kill zone, pivot the upper body to the first look point, call for the bird and, as it appears, swing with it as the gun comes up. When the gun hits the cheek and shoulder, it is on the bird, not at a point behind it as with the fast swing. As soon as you see the bird picture, the body accelerates the swing and triggers the shot as soon as the lead is recognized. For all

Paired trap machines can make your sporting afternoon a challenge. Doubles can be thrown simultaneously, or in sequence or as report pairs (the second being flung immediately after you shoot the first one).

practical purposes, you trigger the shot within milliseconds of the gun mount.

This particular technique results in two very positive things for the sporting clays shooter. The first is a reduction in lead. The sudden acceleration of the gun, which is essentially moving at target speed, creates a faster swing than possible with other techniques. Going back to the skeet field, from a low gun position you need about four feet of lead to break a station four crossing shot with the sustained lead. With the fast swing, the lead decreases to a bit more than two feet. With the pullaway, it is cut even further, to about what appears to be 18 inches. It is worth remembering that this is a 21-yard direct crossing shot on a 45 mph bird. Some of the closer, slower targets on a sporting clays range can be broken by virtually shooting at the bird. The reduction in lead is primarily why the pullaway technique achieved its popularity.

It is common in sporting clays to have crossing shots in the 40-plus-yard range. If you shoot a sustained lead, you will need more than 10 feet at 40 yards. That is too much for most human brains to compute and hold because you have no real frame of reference. The pullaway cuts those long leads down to something with which we can be more comfortable and consistent.

Another factor enters the picture with sustained leads that are long, and that is which way the target is crossing. A right-handed shooter will have the gun to the right cheek and the right eye looking down the rib. The left eye, assuming the proper "both eyes open" technique, will be looking down the left side of the barrel. If the target is crossing from the left, both eyes can easily see and track it. This provides the binocular vision we humans require for accurate depth perception.

If the target is a right-to-left crosser however, the left eye can be blocked from seeing it by the gun. Holding a precise lead is extremely difficult with only one eye if the lead exceeds more than a couple of feet, and doubly tough if the target is rising.

There are some outstanding sporting clays instructors who recommend that right-handed shooters use the pullaway on all right to left crossing shots (the reverse being true for left-handers) just because of this. They teach the fast swing or sustained lead for targets going the other way.

Regardless of the circumstance, the pullaway can greatly reduce the lead required on a target. Another advantage is the control it gives a shooter over where he breaks his targets.

Because one fires the pullaway almost simultaneously with the mounting of the gun, the only restriction on how quickly you can break the target is how fast you can mount the gun. Conversely, by delaying the mount, you can comfortably break targets at different ranges.

Going back to skeet station four, a standard shot that any shooter can duplicate, you will find that from a low gun position you cannot break the target with a sustained lead in a consistent manner until it has gone 10 to 15 feet past the Eight Post. The fast swing lets you take it on the Post and the pullaway lets you break it 10 to 15 feet in front of the Post. So you can break it anywhere along the flight path you choose just by delaying the gun mount. Some of that control can be had with

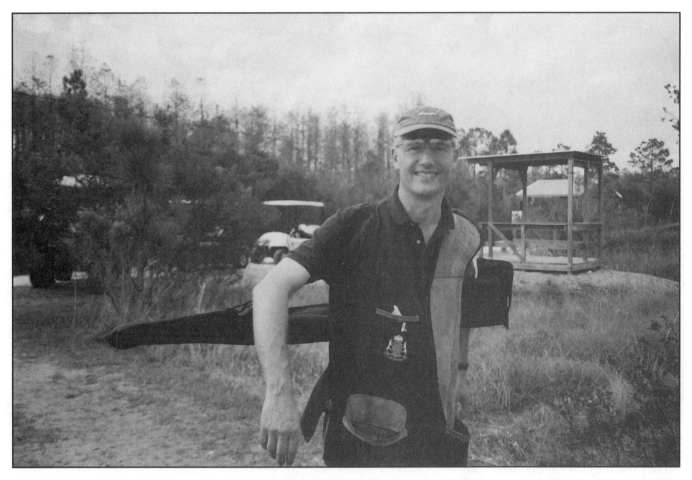

The smart shooter will slip his gun into a soft-sided case between stations and certainly between events. A hot gun will attract dust and the build-up of grime can suddenly cause an unnerving halt in your shooting day. For less than $50, you can buy a fine portable slip case and, given the cost of a quality shotgun, that is cheap insurance.

Many shooters testify that the finest way to ease your children into a shotgun is to start them with a BB gun or a pellet gun such as this Winchester by Daisy.

the fast swing, but the pullaway offers a larger degree of control. When you have to break a bird in a narrow window in trees or brush, or take one bird in a pair very quickly in order to get a reasonable shot on the second, the pullaway is worth its weight in gold. When you have to make a shot quickly, regardless of the speed, distance or angle, the pullaway can be lightning fast.

Multiple Targets

Once a shooter has a handle on the above techniques of gun mount, stance, body position and shooting techniques, he now must consider how to handle the gun on multiple targets.

A single target is just that. Shoot the thing, reload and call for the next presentation. Pairs, however, require some thought about how you will deal with them.

"Following pairs" are one bird launched within three seconds of the shooter's command with a second bird launched at some time within three seconds of that, at the puller's discretion. Shooting from a fluid, low gun position, experienced shooters find the act of mounting the gun itself to be an integral part of the shot-making process. So what do you do after you break the first bird and are waiting on the second? Smart shooters drop the gun from their shoulder! This makes both shots the same. That is also why these shooters radius the toe on their

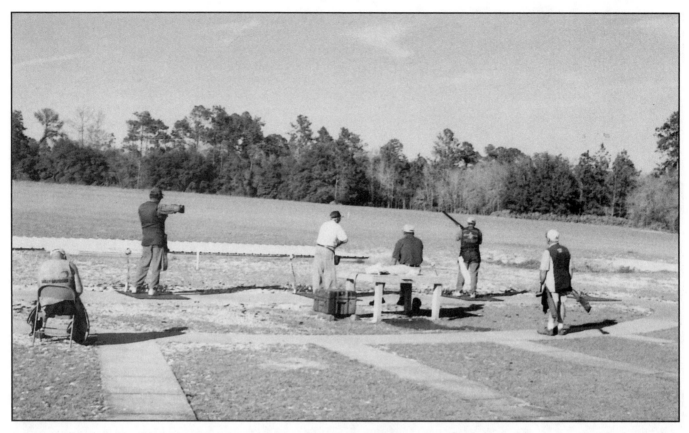

For competition, nothing beats the training in the faster and slightly more difficult international games. Here, shooters are banging away at bunker trap, which throws targets faster and at more diverse and unexpected angles than American skeet and trap. It is excellent practice for a sporting clays course.

recoil pad. It makes the dismount as smooth as the mount. You do not have to drop the gun back to the original starting position. It is easier to just push it slightly away from the shoulder and drop the butt slightly to unlock the cheek.

Once a shooter becomes accustomed to this, he will find it also works on "report pairs," where the second bird is launched at the sound of the shot fired at the first. You do not have as much time, but you do not need it. You are not going back to a rigid low gun position, merely dropping the buttstock. You do not have far to go to remount the gun and with a bit of practice the partial dismount becomes as smooth as the mount.

In both cases, it beats the heck out of smoking the first target with a fluid gun mount and then standing there with a dead gun locked into your shoulder while you try to find, and then re-establish, swing speed on the second target.

"Simultaneous pairs" present a totally different challenge. If they are different targets (Fur & Feathers, for example), some skilled shooters still do a slight dismount after the first bird. If they are true pairs, there are few shooters skilled enough to do it. Most of us cannot, at least not if we want to shoot the second bird in the same county as the first. You have to analyze the flight path of the birds and determine how you can best swing through the first to get the second without slowing the gun.

Sometimes that means taking the trailing bird first and then accelerating to catch the lead bird. It works on some stations. Other times, you may have to take the lead bird first, recover from recoil, and catch the second with a classic skeet shooter's pre-mounted fast swing.

Every now and then, if the Good Lord is smiling on you and the course designer had an off day, you may find one point in the flight of that pair where you can kill both with one shot. This usually happens after they have gotten out a bit. If you happen to miss, well ... you now have an even longer shot on the second bird. This is a gamble, but sometimes it can be worth it. Smart shooters will watch the targets at viewing to see if it is feasible. If you can pull it off, it impresses the heck out of the other shooters.

These gun handling techniques are markedly different from those used in conventional trap or skeet. However, trap and skeet ranges are the best place to learn them. The reasons are time and money.

Most shooters have to travel a good bit farther to find a sporting clays range than a trap or skeet setup. Sporting clays also takes a lot longer to shoot. A round of 50 birds can take a squad most of the afternoon. A round of sporting clays also costs a lot more than trap or skeet. At my skeet club, a member's fee for 25 birds is $2.50 and $5.00 for 50 targets. A 50-bird round of sporting clays will run between $25 and $50, depending on the range.

Cross Training Practice

To learn fluid gun handling and the various shooting techniques, a shooter must see a lot of targets and a variety of angles. It is fast and cheap to do it on a skeet or trap range. It is also valid practice because you will find virtually every angle presented to you in trap or skeet at some point on a sporting clays field.

At most skeet clubs, it is common for a few sporting clays aficionados to open their own field and play their own games.

One thing the authors have discovered is that they focus on the shooting, and when the time comes to drive to a course, we are always looking for ... something. Multi-pocketed bags such as the #D15DL from Boyt help us keep our gear assembled. Boyt, incidentally, calls this their Gun Dog Bag, but it has a padded interior with a hard-sided plastic box for spare parts, choke tubes or your shooting glasses (in their protective case). Heavy-duty olive-drab canvas exterior with top-grain leather trim.

They shoot between the existing stations to look at new angles, and frequently back up 10 or 15 yards from the mid-field stations to practice long crossers.

Sporting clays shooters also practice on trap ranges by starting at the 16-yard line, then moving progressively forward until they are standing right behind the trap house. When you get on a sporting clay field, you will see those same shots represented as quail, pheasants, and rising sharptails. You will have a far better handle on them than you would if your experience with those angles has been limited to a few expensive rounds of sporting clays.

Because you will see more targets in less time, you can hone your gun mounting technique more quickly. There is nothing in anybody's trap or skeet range rules that says you cannot call for a target from a low gun position, so why not take advantage of that to fine-tune your gun handling skills?

For that matter, why not take advantage of cross training to master shots that are giving you fits on the sporting clays fields? Bonnie McLaurin, a world-class female shooter, has remarked, "Shooting sporting clays is a lot like fighting a forest fire. Just when you get a problem solved in one spot, something flares up in another area."

That sort of thing happens all the time. A perfect example is one particular tower shot on a local sporting clays range. It is not a difficult shot. I have been looking at skeet targets like that for years. Essentially, the bird comes off a 20-foot tower to the right and angles out into the field to the left at about 45 degrees. The target is very visible and is normally broken at about 20 yards, slightly to the shooter's right side.

This is a simple shot and one I did not think needed to be rushed, at least not until they threw a true pair with the birds

in trail. Then the smooth rhythm I had been using to take the singles resulted in my second shot being at a 30-yard falling bird. Not my cup of tea!

The singles were easy, but the pairs were killing me. So I decided to speed up my shot rhythm, and promptly screwed everything up! Now they were all eating my lunch.

I solved the problem at a skeet range. I backed up about 10 yards from a point midway between stations two and three to duplicate the angle and distance on the shot and began practicing what could be called a slight variation of the pullaway shot. Upon seeing the bird, I would mount the gun, get spot-on the bird, and immediately accelerate forward. The amount of lead was nothing. I triggered the shot as soon as the acceleration began. It did not take a full box of shells to get the timing right. With pairs, all I had to do was mount on the trailing bird, fire, and swing smoothly through the first.

I invariably run that station now, and it only took 15 minutes on a skeet range to figure out how to do it!

Another station that was giving me fits was also deceptively simple. The trap was located behind and to the right of the shooter. Three singles would come out at angles varying from a moderate quartering angle to a dead straightaway. Pairs launched at the moderate right-to-left angle. The shot was not difficult. The problem was the lack of time because the birds were in the bushes within 25 yards.

I first started shooting this station by screwing my body all the way around to the right to stare right at the trap house. I found I did not have time to catch the birds, though, and was missing some easy singles because of it. I adjusted by moving my first look point farther out into the field and found that caused me to shoot as soon as the gun hit my shoulder – almost spot or snap shooting. This resulted in my shooting behind birds with any angle on them.

That took four boxes of shells shooting from low gun from the 16-yard trap line to correct, and it was quite an interesting experience. I think I broke only eleven birds my first round. I had no problems with the extreme angled shots; I was missing the gentle angles. I discovered that I was rushing the shot and shooting behind the birds. Once I altered my timing to mount the gun slightly behind the bird and then move smoothly and unhurriedly through it, I started popping 22 to 23 per round.

That slight bit of practice and a little change in timing was all it took, and I now run that sporting clays station regularly. I have no idea how long it would have taken me to discover that solution by just shooting that one sporting clays station until I got it right, but four rounds of trap cost less than one round of sporting clays!

Another problem cross training has aided me greatly in is the building of speed on those close, quick, "in your face" targets that many Southeastern sporting clays ranges love to throw. If you measure distance and angle, a lot of these targets are not that tough. But increase the birds' speed, and stick some trees and bushes on the field for them to duck behind periodically, and things get a bit more complicated.

You have to jump these birds quickly. Having learned my clay target style as a sustained-lead American skeet shooter, I just was not getting the job done.

Swearing off the slower American skeet targets for a while

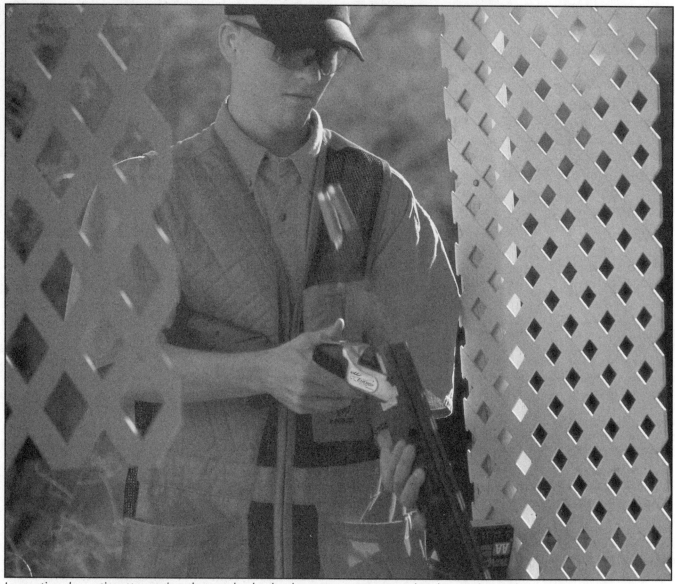

In sporting clays, etiquette requires that you load only when you are up on stand and preparing to shoot. Once you have shot, break open your over/under or leave the semi-auto open before you turn to exit the stand. (Photo courtesy Winchester)

and shifting over to the international skeet range worked wonders on my speed. In fact, if I had to pick one clay target game that would benefit sporting clays shooters the most, that would be it! If you are just out to practice, you do not need to adopt the gun-on-the-hip starting position: use your normal sporting clays low gun position. The faster speed of the international targets will certainly improve your speed.

Combine that with a few rounds of trap, and maybe some selected skeet stations, and you will find lovely things happening to your scores. You can even practice your techniques for following and report pairs simply by telling the puller what you want him to pull.

The only realistic sporting clays practice you cannot get on a trap or skeet range is trailing true pairs or perhaps the bouncing bunny. With this "intensified" training regime, however, the first time you do step onto a sporting clays field you will have a working knowledge of the various techniques you will need.

As you step up to a new station, view the target presentation and then analyze the shots with the following factors in mind.

(1) What is the range at which you will be engaging the targets? This will determine your choke and load selection for that station. (2) If pairs are presented, which bird will you take first? Which shooting technique will be most effective for each? This is not something you should try to figure out after the birds are in the air!

Sometimes you will have no choice in the order. At other times you may have wide latitude, including taking a trailing bird first and driving through to the lead bird or taking the lead bird first and then executing a fast swing on the trailer or maybe even taking both with one shot. Planning how you will shoot is important because it determines your kill zone, and that in turn determines your initial stance and gun hold position. Remember to note the flight path of the first bird you will shoot, and make sure your gun hold is correct for it.

After that, sporting clays is just a matter of properly executing your shot plan. I admit, often that is easier said than done – which is one reason why sporting clays is the most challenging shotgun game around!

CLAYS' TOUGHEST SHOTS

Hitting aerial targets is nothing more than matching their combination of speed, angle and altitude with your gun. That much holds true regardless of the clay target game. Veteran trap or skeet shooters will recognize many of the angles the first time they step onto a sporting clays field, and the reverse is true, too.

What separates sporting clays from other games is that while you may be presented with a familiar target speed, angle and altitude, those features come in the form of targets of widely varying size, weight and construction.

Launch two dissimilar targets from the same trap at the same angle, speed and altitude, and you will get two targets with dissimilar flight characteristics. That is something only seen in sporting clays, because all other games use a single standardized target. Skeet and trap targets exhibit standard and consistent flight characteristics, unless affected by the wind. You can predict their movements.

The bottom line is that the sporting clays station you shot yesterday can be radically different today due to nothing more than a change in the targets loaded in the trap machine.

Another factor that separates sporting clays from other games is the array of target presentations. When you factor in the mix of different targets and combine that with the possibility of seeing those targets as singles, following pairs, report pairs, and even simultaneous (true) pairs, then you can have a tremendously varied shot presentation. That is why the game cannot be learned by rote and shot on reflex. Every station must be thought through – not only the flight path of the targets, but their highly individual flight characteristics as well.

Clay Targets

Standard Target

This is the same target used in trap and skeet. It has a relatively stable flight path. It is 110 mm in diameter, and even casual shooters are familiar with its performance. We will use it as a yardstick to measure the performance of the other clay targets commonly encountered in sporting clays.

Midi Target

This bird has the same configuration as the standard, but at 90 mm is smaller in diameter. It has the same flight characteristics as the standard but can be one of the more frustrating targets on the field.

The targets used in sporting clays come in several sizes and each has its uses: standard and the thinner battue (110 mm in diameter), midi (90 mm), mini (60 mm) and ground-running rabbit.

The reason for this is that determining the distance to the target is very important in figuring lead. The midi target is often mixed in with standards, but because it is smaller, it is deceptive. It can fool a shooter into thinking it is a standard target just at longer range!

Its speed can be deceptive, too. Because it is smaller and lighter, it can leave the trap faster, yet because it is lighter, it will slow down faster than a standard bird. Throw it with a standard target as a pair, as is often the case, and it may be the lead target for the first portion of the flight and then be overtaken by the standard. This can play real hell with a shot plan! The challenge for the shooter is to be able to identify the target as a midi quickly and understand the difference it will display in flight. It can require a different shot plan than when facing two standard targets as a pair.

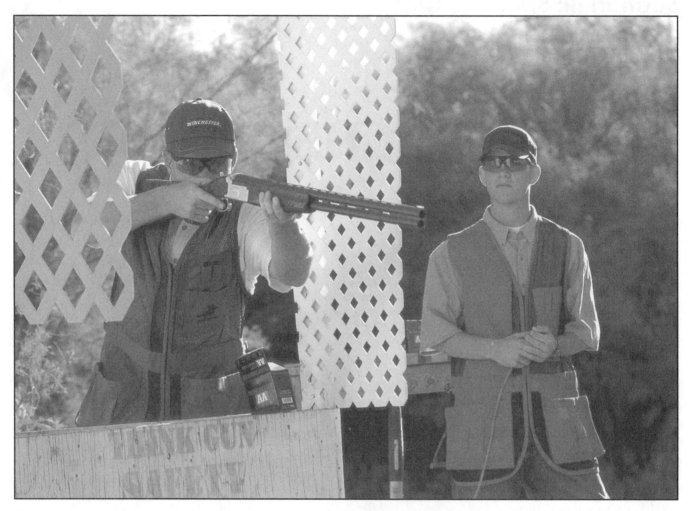

There is only one gun presentation like this in clay shooting – the Running Rabbit. Thrown across the ground, the rabbit will dance and jump and roll unexpectedly and often in a most aggravating manner! (Photo courtesy Winchester)

Mini Targets

This 60 mm saucer is the smallest target normally thrown in sporting clays. Like the midi, it is just a scaled-down version of the standard. Unlike the midi, however, it is seldom misinterpreted. When this one is thrown, there is little doubt. It is like shooting at an aspirin tablet traveling at Mach 1.

The problem with minis is that their light weight really makes them zip out of a trap and their small size can make it difficult to get an accurate fix on the range. Because of their size, they can slip through pattern gaps easily, so they can require a denser shot pattern.

Another item to factor in with minis is that most of the time the target is completely black and they are generally thrown as a part of a pair. The pair might be two minis, or a mini in combination with a midi or a standard. It is easy to lose sight of this target and concentrate on the brighter one. They tend to get out there fast and blend into any vegetation in the background. This means the shooter must concentrate on finding the best visual window and take the target as quickly as possible.

When range operators throw this target in tight, tree-lined quarters it can be extremely difficult to pick up and hit.

Battue Targets

This is a very different target than the three previous ones. It is a 110 mm target, but only ⅜-inch high and with a slight center dome. Its flight characteristics do not resemble any other target. Because of this, it is a very difficult bird to hit, and it demands great discipline from the shooter. Not only will the battue's unusual shape cause it to change attitude in flight, but it will also change profile!

The most common presentation for battues is as pairs, generally as crossing shots; sometimes with a very slight outgoing or incoming angle. As they launch, they present a very slender profile to the shooter: they are edge-on flat! Some shooters call them "flying razor blades" and they can be difficult to hit early in their flight. At a point somewhere around mid-flight, they begin to turn on their edge and present a fuller profile. This is called "development" and the target is now easier to find with a shot pattern. This "development" continues until the shooter sees it as a round disc. Unfortunately, by the time the bird gets that far it is generally beginning to drop quickly and actually picking up a bit of speed again as it falls.

The shooter must wait until enough of the target "develops" to be hit yet not waste too much time. Since range operators normally throw battues as pairs, the second bird is a difficult shot. Farther away and falling, it can be a frustrating target.

Rabbit Target

This standard-sized 110 mm target is always presented as a ground-bouncer rolling on its edge. Since the ground is uneven, the target path may vary considerably. Some "rabbits" may zip across flat, some may bounce high and wild, and oth-

Sporting clays gives you an opportunity to shoot many different types of targets, not just the standard 110 mm that you see in trap and skeet.

ers may do both. No two targets will be perfectly alike in their running path. Because the rabbit target is thrown into the ground, it is made sturdier to avoid breakage. Therefore, it may require a shot charge heavier than its range would indicate in order to be certain of a break. Rabbits may be thrown as the only target on a station or they may come as singles or as following or report pairs. Operators seldom throw these as true pairs. They are often the first target of a "Fur & Feather" presentation, with the second target (usually a standard) as an outgoing or quartering away target in about the same general distance range.

Reading the type of target and understanding what it will do is only part of the process. You also must determine exactly what it is doing in relation to the shooting stand.

Terrain, trees, changes in elevation, and landscaping can paint a deceptive picture of what the target is actually doing. Shadow and light can play tricks on the shooter, too. Good range operators will use all of these to create serious optical illusions. Some targets may look like they are true crossing shots yet fly on a slight incoming or outgoing angle. A target launched downhill may appear to be rising when it is actually falling. One that appears to be rising may actually be losing speed and falling.

An inventive range operator can create more illusions than a magician. If you shoot without thinking through the illusion, you will likely miss.

Developing Shot Plans

Another consideration in sporting clays is having a shot plan for true pairs. Many expert shooters are convinced that if they miss the first target, they should fire at it again instead of shifting to the second bird. This often happens among shooters with a hunting background or with experience in a game like international trap. There are some valid points to that argument.

A shooter firing at a target is already concentrating on that target. It has been acquired, tracked and engaged. If the shot misses, the gun is already traveling with that target and it sometimes takes only a slight correction in point and hold to nail it with a follow-up shot. For some shooters, this is an effective way to salvage at least one bird out of a pair when the first shot misses.

Some shooters are not mentally geared to go after one bird twice, though. Skeet shooters are an excellent example. They shoot doubles as a regular part of the game and only get one shot per bird. Skeet doubles invariably requires that the gun track be radically altered for the second bird. Shoot-off doubles, for example, from stations three, four and five, demand that the gun direction be quickly reversed to acquire a target moving in the opposite direction. It becomes a fluid, learned subconscious response to leave the first target, whether it is hit or not, and immediately go after the second bird.

For shooters with this mindset, it may be well to stick with

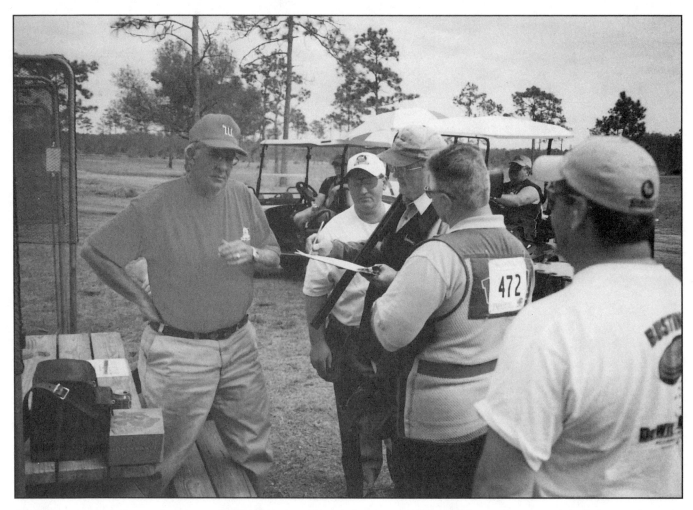

To get the most out of your shooting experience, it helps to have a good squad that can discuss an approach and then evaluate the stations. In a good squad, the learning never stops.

the shot plan to fire one round per bird, regardless of the results. Changing a preconceived plan that has been executed countless times before is very difficult to do in the millisecond available for a decision.

With the above in mind, here are some thoughts on developing shot plans for the more common target presentations seen on sporting clays courses.

Incoming Tower Shot

These stations simulate incoming ducks or doves, and the towers may be as high as 100 feet.

On singles, the best bet is to be patient. Put some weight on your leading food and wait for this target to come to you, but do not be in a hurry to take it. Give the shot time to develop and wait until it approaches a direct overhead shot, then mount the gun only when you are about to shoot. This gives

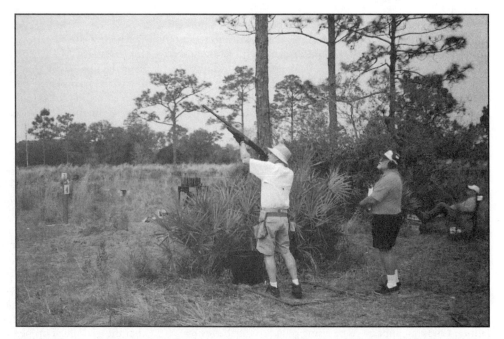

One of the toughest bird presentations in sporting clays is the springing teal. It is thrown fast, almost straight up to a height of 70 feet or so. To shoot it successfully, delay your mount until the target has almost reached its apex, and then mount and shoot it at the momentary pause at the top of its flight.

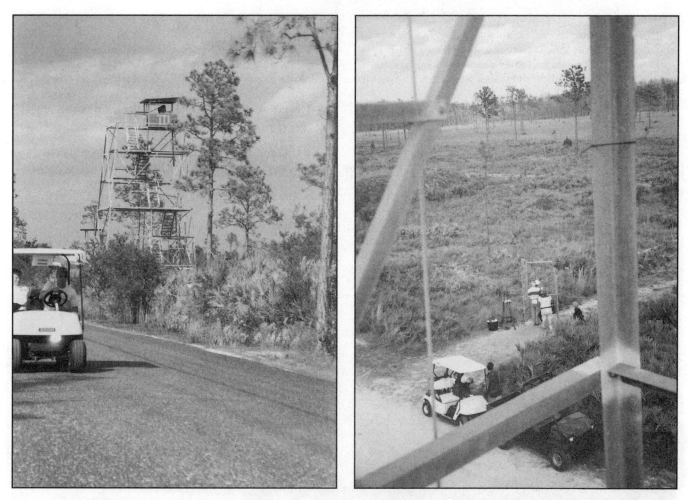

One cruel course designer placed the trap machine on top of a high tower and forced the shooters below to take an outgoing, overhead dropping shot. Photos of the final Seminole Cup at the TM Ranch, Orlando, Florida.

A typical fur and feather presentation is a rabbit followed immediately – or worse, simultaneously – by a crossing shot. If the course designer is imaginative, and many are, the crossing shot will be in the opposite direction as the running rabbit. To make a smooth swing and follow through, you are required to pay close attention to the call-birds and any shooters who may be in line before you.

you the largest possible target surface to shoot at and makes the shot a relatively simple one. The shooter swings through the bird and triggers the shot as soon as the barrel passes the leading edge. A skeet choke and #9 skeet load are usually the best choice, as most of these shots are made within 15 yards of the gun.

Following and report pairs are shot the same way, and the gun should be slightly dismounted between shots. True pairs are a little tougher. If the pairs are taking the same track, consider taking the trailing bird first and then continuing the swing through the first bird. Leads are minimal and the recoil of the gun will help move you from the trailing bird to the leader. That, of course, assumes that the shooting cage gives you enough room to get on the birds quickly and that the birds are traveling within five or six feet of each other. If not, take the leading bird first; leave the gun mounted, and then fast-swing through the second target. Often when a shooter faces an incoming tower shot, he will find his gun angle restricted by the construction of the shooting cage to prevent his shooting the trap machine.

If birds are launched on separate flight paths, take the most direct incoming bird first, and as quickly as you can. This gives you time to acquire the second bird, which will now be an incoming shot with some angle away from the shooter. Some shooters prefer to dismount the gun after the first shot and then remount for the second. Dismounting between shots gives you a better visual acquisition on the second target and, if you have worked on your gun handling skills, the remount and shot will be almost simultaneous. Leads are minimal in either case, since the targets are closing on you. I have never seen this shot presented where a Skeet choke and #9s were not the best bet.

Springing Teal

This target is thrown fast, almost straight up to a height of about 70 feet, and may be traveling slightly toward or away from the shooter. It intimidates many shooters with trap or

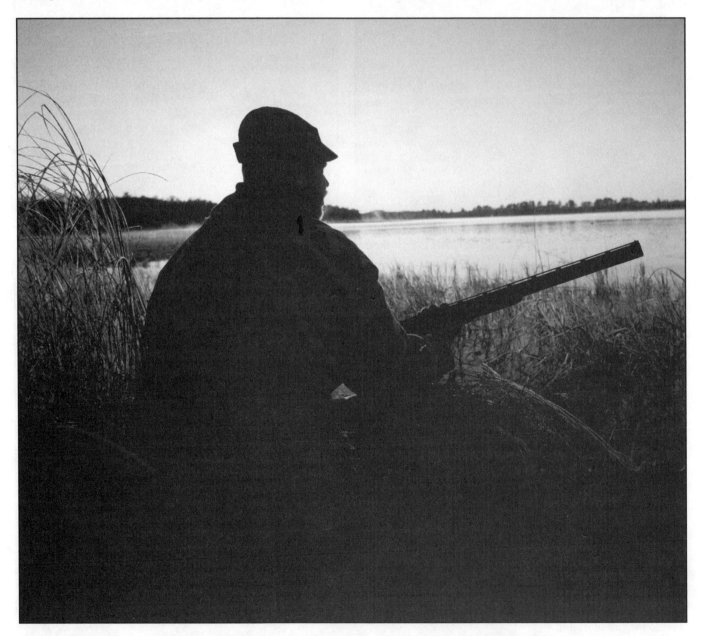

Duck hunters see every type of shot presentation–except perhaps the rabbit–and the only game available to give them the right practice is a challenging sporting clays course. (Photo courtesy Sturm, Ruger)

skeet experience but surprisingly, shooters with little shotgun experience find it easy! The reason is that they wait until the bird gets to the top of its flight, and then they shoot it as a stationary target as the bird hangs there. They forget about lead. That is the way to do it.

To shoot springing teal, your gun hold point should be high, with weight on the front foot. Delay your mount until the target has almost reached its apex. Then mount the gun, perch the bird on top of the bead and take it. When dealing with true pairs, take the target that hits the lower apex of its flight first, and then let the recoil swing you up to the second.

Dealing with this presentation takes some timing. If you are off, hitting the bird at the last portion of its upward flight is the better choice. Once it starts to fall, it becomes a very difficult target.

Outgoing Overhead Dropping Shot

This simulates a dove coming in from overhead and behind, and it confuses some shooters. If you are one of them, go to a skeet range and spend a box of shells shooting the high house one target – albeit one on steroids.

The first checkpoint for this shot is almost directly overhead, with a little weight on the back foot. Shift your weight to the front foot as you acquire the target. The gun muzzle is high. Pick up the target as quickly as you can, mount the gun with the muzzle either spot-on or slightly behind the bird, then swing down and through it. Trigger the shot when you see about six inches of daylight between the muzzle and the bird. Take this shot as quickly as you can because if you do not, it becomes a long-range dropping target. It will then become one of the toughest shots you will ever see! Hit it quick, and it is relatively easy. You can handle this shot well with an open choke and either #9s or #8½ shot.

This presentation is almost never seen as a true pair, but if you encounter it as such, take the trailing target first and drive through to the second, doubling the lead for the second bird. For following or report pairs, dismount the gun between shots and bring the upper body back to the initial first look point.

The Driven Shot

This is very similar to the incoming tower shot, except the birds start at a lower elevation and rise. The procedure, however, is not that different. You still need to swing quickly through the bird and trigger the shot when the muzzle passes it. If there is a difference, it is that the lead is a bit less. If the birds are close, you can nail this presentation as soon as the muzzle blots out the bird. A skeet choke and #9 shot are the best bet. Spreader loads will help if the birds are within 20 yards.

If you face simultaneous pairs in this presentation, you must acquire the targets as quickly as possible and nail the first bird fast. In this case, taking the leading bird first is the best bet. You may not have time to take the trailer and then catch the lead bird. Let the recoil carry your gun to the following bird. Regardless of the pair presentation, this is fast, close shooting. It pays to get pumped up for this one!

Fur & Feather

This gives you a rabbit for the first target, followed (as a report, following, or simultaneous pair) by an aerial target, which is usually a standard. The gun-hold point on this must be for the rabbit, which you should take as quickly as is comfortable. Resist the temptation to rush the first shot to the point where you miss it. Make sure you get the rabbit, and then let the oth-

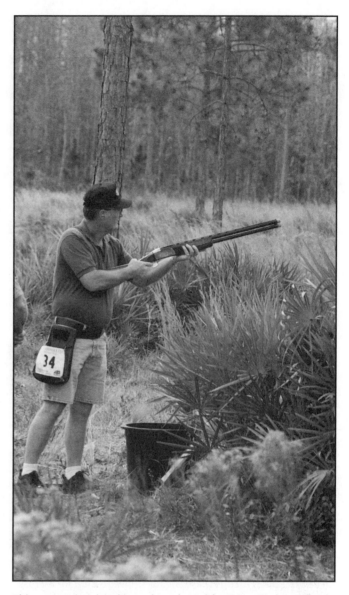

This competitor is taking a breath and focusing on the path of the birds – this was a long going-away shot – with his gun at the low-gun position before calling for the throw.

er target take care of itself. Rushing is the biggest mistake new shooters make on this presentation and it costs them the rabbit. You will not get far if you always miss the first target in a pair.

The best advice for true pairs is, "Kill the first target every time!" The second target will, through practice and repetition, break on its own!

On following and report pairs, dismount the gun after the rabbit. That gives you better visual ability to pick up the aerial bird. This is normally not a difficult shot, being usually a mild quartering-away or a gentle crosser. Open chokes, with #8½ for the rabbit and #9s for the bird, are good choices. Special spreader loads can help, too.

Going Away Shots

You will see these shot profiles quite often. Most of the time there will be some quartering angle on any singles targets and on one bird in a pair. The other bird in a pair will often be a dead straightaway with some rising angle on it.

The range at which these targets may be engaged can vary

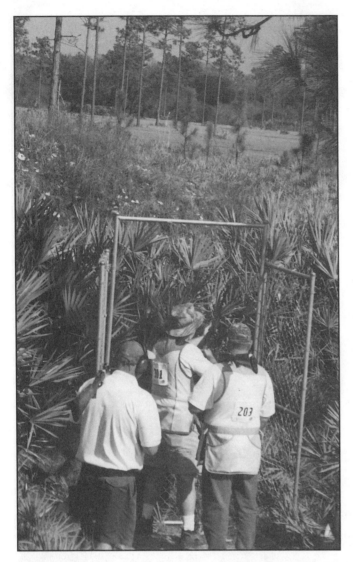

A tightly confined shooting lane over the palmettos and between the pines means these shooters have to plan for a crossing shot.

through a screen of trees or brush. You may get them at more than 40 yards sailing across a relatively open area. Same angle, same target speed – but vastly different techniques are required to break them.

Many hard-crossers in sporting clays will be in the 15- to 25-yard range. These require a lot of lateral body movement, due to the closeness of the launching platform to the shooter. Some of the best possible practice you can get for these is to spend a day on a skeet range working on the outgoing targets from stations two, three, five and six. You have to get the first look position close to the house, and then uncoil rapidly as you swing through the target.

The best shooting technique for these is the fast swing-through. Few shooters can pinpoint the target quickly enough to execute a good pullaway shot.

Leads are often minimal. The faster the target is moving, the faster the gun has to swing to catch it. The faster the gun is moving, the less apparent lead is needed. Targets within 15 yards can often be broken, even by a somewhat lazy-swinging shooter, by shooting as soon as the muzzle meets the bird.

With report and following pairs, a gun dismount between shots is the best bet. On true pairs, swing through and take the trailing target first, and then continue your gun movement to swing through the leading target. It's a good idea to fudge your natural point of aim a bit toward the direction of the second target (leading bird) when dealing with true pairs. You may need the extra swing room, because the second bird is likely to be taken out of the position where you would expect to break it under less strenuous presentations.

This is nothing more than aggressive shooting. You have to go after any close-range crossing target aggressively; if you lay back, you are finished! It is pure reflex and speed of swing. The story is a little different on long crossing shots.

A target that makes you really coil up and unwind at close range gives you a lot more time at longer range, even if it is the same speed and angle. The increased distance between you and the target allows your field of view to become greater and you can acquire the target with less body movement. For many, there seems to be a discrepancy between apparent speed of crossing targets at ranges inside 25 yards and those beyond that. I do not have to move as much to take a station five hard right-angle shot in trap from the 27-yard line as I do from the 16-yard line. The increased distance to the target means less body movement for the shooter and the same holds true here in sporting clays.

Since I have that extra time, I tend to shoot all 30-plus-yard crossing shots with the "pullaway" technique instead of the fast swing. It works for me and gives me an apparent lead on a 40-yard crossing target of about four to five feet, as compared to the more than 10-foot lead I would see with a sustained lead, or the six- to seven-foot lead I would see with a swing-through. There is plenty of time to dismount the gun between shots on following or report pairs and, if you are using the pullaway, you will want to do so.

I would use this procedure for anything except true pairs. There, I would fudge my natural point of aim to the direction the target is traveling, take the trailing bird first with a pullaway, and then swing through the lead bird.

If you face battue targets on this presentation, you may have to fudge your body position even more to the target direction side, since experienced shooters wait longer for these targets to "develop" enough to be consistently broken.

considerably, from 10 to 35-plus yards. Regardless of the range, it is important to have weight on the front foot and pick up the first bird as soon as possible.

The choke and shot size depend upon the range. This is generally Skeet 1 or Improved Cylinder territory, with shot in the #8½ to #8 range: the narrower profile of these targets will give you fewer pellet hits, so larger pellets are a must to bust off a visible piece.

For a second or so on a rising target, there will be a period where it levels out and flies almost straight. That is the time to break it. If you wait too long and the target starts to drop, you have a much tougher shot.

On true pairs, take the straightaway as fast as you can. It may be a dead straightaway or slightly rising. Then move to the quartering bird. It pays to fudge your natural point of aim to the second bird.

Crossing Shots

These can be of the most varied shot presentations you will see in sporting clays. You may get crossers at 12 yards moving

5-STAND: CLAYS WITH A TWIST

Sporting clays is still growing as the hottest shotgun game in America, and it's a rare clay target shooter who has not shot a few rounds.

A traditional sporting clays course takes a lot of land; in fact, it could require as much land as a nine-hole golf course. While the shooting stations themselves do not require that much room, one has to plan for shot fall areas, and #7½ shot (the largest size allowed) can travel almost 340 yards through the air. The areas where it lands cannot, in a very practical sense, be used for anything else. That means a good sporting clays course can eat up a deceptively large amount of property, and property is not cheap or, in some areas, readily available.

Another drawback is that the game is both time- and labor-intensive. As with golf, it takes a fair amount of time to negotiate a course and a squad will require the services of a course guide/puller. If manual traps are used on any station, someone has to be paid to operate them. For all of these reasons, a num-ber of variations of sporting clays have arisen. Let's take a look at some of the better-known of them.

5-Stand Sporting

The brainchild of Scottish-born Raymond Forman, this shotgun game is a computer-driven contest that can be set up on existing trap or skeet fields, even using some of the traps already in place. Five-stand can be run by one operator, and shooters can be cycled through in little more time than it takes to shoot a round of trap or skeet. Nevertheless, this game can offer virtually every shot found on a full-sized sporting clays course. Some of the country's top range operators feel this may be one of the most significant things to happen to sporting since it arrived on these shores.

"The 5-stand game is a real money maker for us," one operator noted. "Our emphasis is on corporate and group enter-tainment. We needed a game that could be shot day or night,

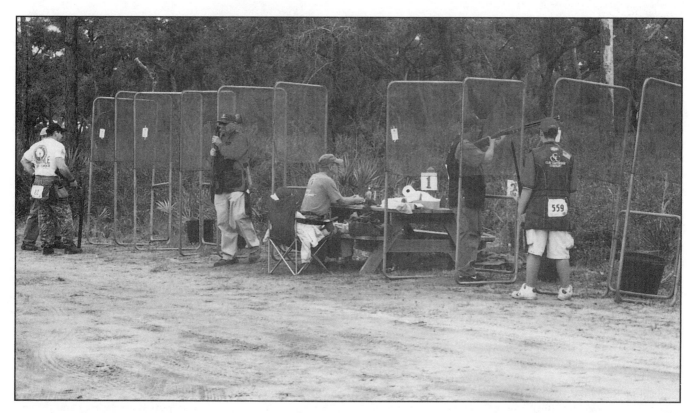

5-Stand sporting clays is a great way to shoot a variety of target presentations in a limited space. Shooters stand side-by-side and rotate to their right after they shoot. Target presentations can be changed quickly, even between squads

Competitors who are not accustomed to the caged feeling and standing in line with their squad members may have some initial difficulty with 5-Stand shooting, but when they begin to focus on the fundamentals, they quickly overcome these obstacles.

rain or shine, 365 days a year. That is not feasible with sporting clays. You cannot afford to cover walkways and shooting stations on a full-sized course and lighting them up for night shooting would take a huge bank of lights."

The new games use so little space that he can both cover the shooting stations and light the field economically. "We do not get weathered out like we do on our full-size sporting course," the course operator said, "so this has become a commercial range operator's dream set-up."

For an idea of just how economically beneficial these games can be, I talked to Skeet Hall of Fame shooter Danny Mitchell, who operates the Wolfe Creek Gun Club near Atlanta, Georgia. Danny reported that on one recent weekend a few years ago his range threw sixteen rounds of trap, 174 rounds of skeet (which required opening six fields, with personnel to run them) and 97 rounds of NSCA 5-stand sporting. One man, on one field, handled all the sporting rounds! That is an enormous reduction in cost.

While the new 5-stand games have logistical and economic advantages for the range operator, do not be lulled into thinking they are just cheap, "fast-food" versions of the real game. They are not. In fact, they can be every bit as challenging as traditional sporting clays or even moreso.

There are a number of versions of the 5-stand game. One is the original Raymond Forman version that is still seen on some ranges. This utilizes the "Birdbrain" computer to operate four to eight trap machines. The machine throws the same five shots for each shooter in random order. Five shots from each of the

five stations make a convenient 25-target round. The shooter does not know what target will emerge when he calls for the bird. The game has three different levels, with three degrees of difficulty. On Level One, the shooter sees all singles. Level Two throws three singles and one simultaneous pair. Level Three presents two true pairs and one single, and it taxes even an experienced shooter's abilities.

Forman's game was never standardized. The last time I shot it was at Cherokee Rose in Griffin, Georgia, and here is what was offered: As you stepped onto the field you were confronted with five shooting stations arrayed in a straight line, each with its own shooting cage. Each shooter started at one station, received five targets, and moved to the next. As you changed stations, the angles changed and the shots varied considerably. On the far left side of the field, trap one launched a rabbit target across the middle of the field and a snipe target that took a similar crossing angle. Farther out from it was a grouse trap that launched a hard-angled shot that, depending where you were on the stations, could be a fast outgoing, quartering target or a long-range crossing shot. Trap three was located just forward and below shooting station three and was a wobble trap that simulated flushing quail on outgoing angles. Trap four, located outside the edge of the field on the right-hand side, was a teal trap throwing high birds that settled into the middle of the field. Inside of that trap, on the right, was trap five, a fast-climbing pheasant. Trap six was located on the roof and threw a high, outgoing dove.

These targets were tough to master with repeat practice.

Many major competitions set up 5-Stand shooting events to vary the routine and shooting opportunities, and to maximize their available space.

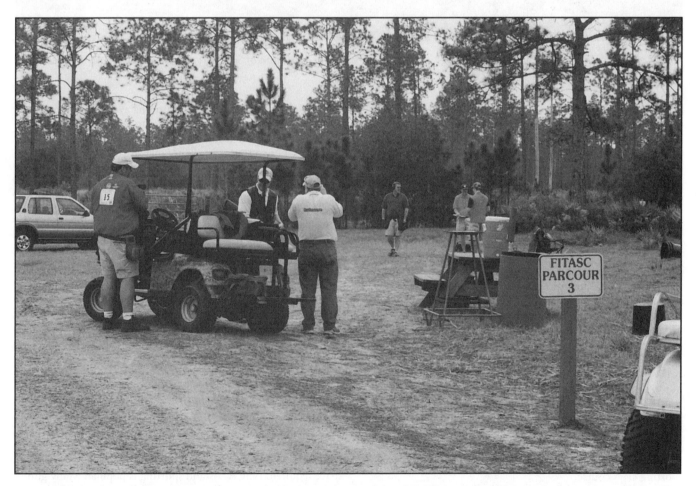

This shooting game centers on the Parcour, French for "layout." In traditional FITASC, a Parcour is a 25-target station with three different shooting positions for each station. In a 100-bird round, shooters visit four different layouts.

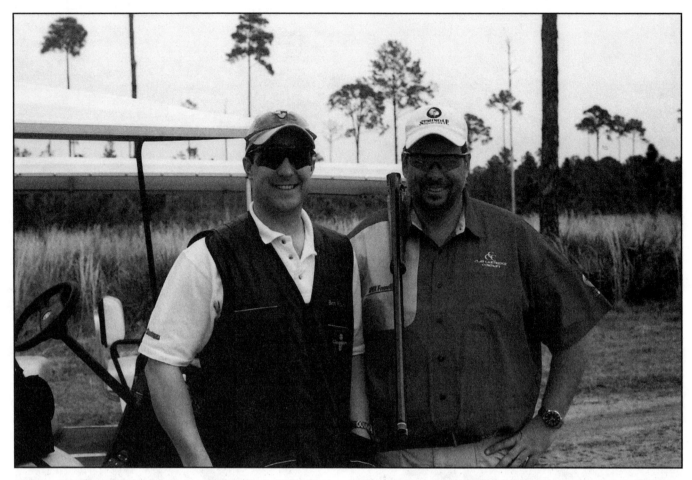

FITASC shooters Will Ferrell (right), representing Camillus Cutlery, and Ben Brunton of Salisbury, England. Ben is a former FITASC World Champion.

What made it tougher was that they were thrown randomly, and you had to change stations every five rounds. The only time you knew which target to expect was when the trap threw a broken "no bird" target. It would then repeat that presentation. 5-stand was one of the first mini-sporting games.

5-Stand Standardized

In 1992, the National Sporting Clays Association (NSCA) purchased the rights and trademark to 5-stand Sporting and made a few changes. The biggest was that the random order of the targets was dispensed with and targets are now thrown in a known order that can be read from a menu posted at each shooting station. They also began a campaign to bring more standardization to the game.

The purpose of some standardization is to establish NSCA 5-stand Sporting as a game that can be shot anywhere in the country. This is important for competition with registered targets. If there is going to be any consistency in sporting clays, at least one version of the game must become standard. That is not to say, however, that it must become rigid.

The criteria for sanctioned NSCA 5-stand Sporting are not tightly drawn. The field must have either six or eight individual traps and, except for one specialty trap, they must be automatic. Hand-set, manual traps can create a safety hazard on the small field, where the same situation would not exist on a larger sporting clays course.

To qualify as a sanctioned course, the following targets must be presented in the array: a tower outgoing bird, an incoming bird, a right-to-left crosser (or quartering away), a left-to-right crosser (or quartering away), a rabbit, and a vertical "teal-type" target. If the range is using eight traps instead of the minimum six, the extra two traps can greatly increase the options in target presentations.

Three levels of difficulty are retained (Level One, singles; Level Two, three singles and a true pair; Level Three, one single and two true pairs), but the order is known and posted on a menu at the shooting station. That order, however, can be changed on a daily basis by changing the number of the trap, the angle of the trap, or even by moving the trap. For example, if a Level One shooter is going to get a single from trap one (all traps are clearly numbered so as to be visible to the shooter on each station), it might be a rabbit today and an outgoing tower tomorrow by simply changing the trap number. It allows a good deal of variation in the basic field.

The field can also be set to play different games just by changing trap angles, although those changes will not be called sanctioned NSCA 5-stand sporting. One can even configure the traps to regular sporting clays rules and have a registered sporting clays match.

Although the NSCA-sanctioned version does have a set of criteria, much versatility is built into the equipment layout, and it can be quickly configured to a variety of other games.

Because of the cost and versatility and the small amount of space required, NSCA 5-stand sporting is popular. Many gun clubs that do not have the room for a full-sized range do have all the space required for this game. A number of ranges have

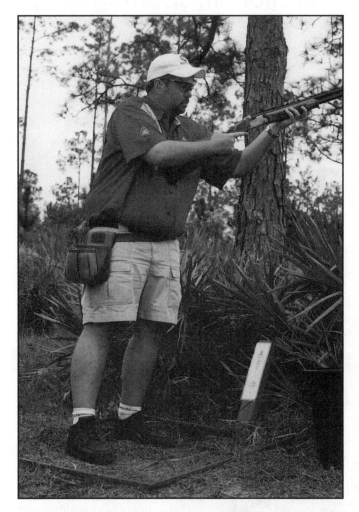

Will Ferrell demonstrates proper low-gun technique, weight forward, hands in proper gun-hold position. The shooter never sees the same shot more than twice on a typical Parcour.

what they refer to as a "5-stand" range, although they often do not meet NSCA standards. These are often quite varied in their target fare and can be a lot of fun to shoot.

Because the targets and angles are known, the NSCA version is perfect for television and spectator coverage.

FITASC

While mini-games are ideal for ranges with limited space, there is another game that is making inroads onto the US sporting scene: FITASC.

FITASC stands for Federation Internationale de Tir aux Armes Sportives de Chasse and it is one of the two world bodies (the other is the International Shooting Union or "UIT") governing international shotgun competition. The FITASC version of sporting clays is to that game what international skeet and trap are to the American versions of those games – more challenging!

This game centers on the Parcour or layout. In traditional FITASC, a Parcour is a 25-target station with three different shooting positions for each station. In a 100-bird round, shooters visit four different Parcour.

There are no shooting cages in this game. There is a shooting pad, about a meter square in size. In the traditional version, targets were thrown in a 360-degree arc around the shooter. For obvious reasons, participating as a spectator was not encour-

aged! The newer version deletes the 360-degree target arc, adds a fourth shooting position to the Parcour, and keeps shooter firing more restricted. Thus, it is more spectator-friendly!

In the Americanized version of sporting clays, each station may have a number of traps but will throw only a few birds per trap. The English version uses fewer traps, but shifts shooters around the layout more and throws more targets from each trap. Many English stations use only two traps but keep things very interesting by presenting many different angles. FITASC falls more in line with this design.

The major difference between FITASC and American sporting clays is the degree of varied presentations a shooter will see as he moves to the different shooting positions on each Parcour. The shooter never sees the same shot more than twice. Generally, the first time it will be a single and, at the second presentation, the same target will be incorporated into a pair of doubles.

By moving shooting positions radically, the angle on the shots can change considerably, and what might be a relatively easy target from one position may be extremely difficult from another. The wide spectrum of target presentations includes greatly varying ranges. It is quite common to have targets as close as 10 yards and as far away as 60 yards from the same shooting position. This poses an interesting problem for the shooter, because once he steps onto the shooting position he cannot change his chokes! All shots must be handled with what is in the gun.

A varied load selection is far more important in FITASC than in standard sporting, and some competitors carry as many as five or more different loads of varying shot sizes, weights and velocities. Since shooters may also shoot twice at any single, it is common for competitors to tote 100 or more rounds for a 25-bird shoot.

Another difference in this game is the gun position when calling for the bird. Traditional sporting and the various 5-stand games require the butt of the shotgun be off the shoulder and visible below the armpit. FITASC competitors are required to have a stripe on their shooting vest that extends 25 cm downward from the top of the shoulder toward the hip. The gun butt must be visible below the bottom of the line. In World Class matches, they measure the vest line!

Like NSCA 5-stand sporting, the trap order in FITASC is known and displayed on a menu at the shooting position. As the squad moves to a new position, the first shooter is allowed to have the targets thrown one time for viewing. Once on the shooting pad, the shooter engages all his singles. Then he or she is followed by the next shooter. When the singles are done, shooters return to the pad for doubles, and the second shooter in line now becomes the first. This rotation continues in order that every member of the six-man squad is required to shoot first for at least one new presentation.

This game requires about the same amount of land as a full-sized sporting course, so it is not growing rapidly. It is growing in individual popularity, however, as many veteran sporting shooters seek new challenges. A number of established sporting clays ranges have incorporated the game on available space.

In the US, the governing body for FITASC is the National Sporting Clays Association.

Though each of these various games is similar enough to sporting clays so that the same equipment and techniques can be used, each is different enough to increase the challenge to the shooter. The fresh look of a game such as 5-stand sporting should ensure its popularity for years to come.

Chapter Nineteen

THERE'S MORE TO LIFE THAN A 12-GAUGE

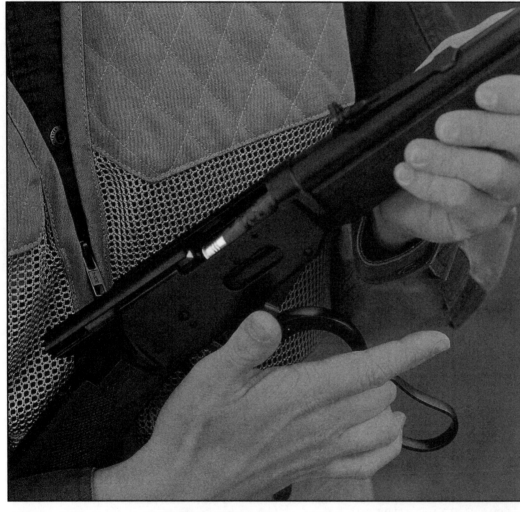

If you begin this chapter with a sense that the 12-gauge is a "Real Man's Gun," a serious gun for competition and hunting and that the other, smaller gauges – 20, 28 and .410 – are just toys or are not serious, well, read on. The difficulty of breaking targets increases arithmatically as you step down in gauge, but you will soon discover that the feel is one of geometrically increasing difficulty! (Photo courtesy Winchester)

Most of what one sees or hears about sporting clays centers around the 12-gauge. That is understandable. It has been the dominant gauge in competition since the sport's inception, and will continue to hold that position. It is certainly not the only bore size seen on the sporting fields, however.

Many people shoot sporting clays strictly for fun and have no real interest in registered competition. As they are discovering, you can have just as much fun with the smaller gauges as you can with the 12-gauge, and each passing year sees more sub-gauges making their way to the sporting courses. This has not gone unnoticed by course managers. In fact, many are now utilizing bits of extra land to set up shorter, less demanding courses that not only allow shooters to use smaller gauges, but serve a second purpose by providing a slightly less challenging course to introduce new shooters to the game.

The interest in sub-gauges has not escaped the notice of the ammo makers, either. In fact, in a move that should clearly demonstrate how strong that interest actually is, several have brought out special sporting clays loads for the 20, 28 and .410 guns.

In fact, there is enough interest in sub-gauge sporting that the NSCA now incorporates sub-gauge classes into registered competition, as has long been done in skeet.

Sub-gauge sporting is not a passing fad or fancy. It is here to stay and is certain to grow in popularity because it adds an extra dimension of challenge. A number of insert tube manufacturers say that sporting clays shooters are now starting to have their 12-gauge guns "tubed" to smaller gauges in the same manner as skeet shooters.

How effective can the little gauges be at this demanding game? To be perfectly honest, the 12-gauge will always be the best choice if breaking the maximum number of targets is your goal. The smaller gauges cannot of course match the load versatility and long-range power of the bigger bore: they just cannot carry the shot to do it. With that obvious statement out of the way, however, it must also be said that the sub-gauges can offer surprising performance when target distances are kept at less than 35 yards. Many of the shorter, sub-gauge courses do that.

Getting the most out of sub-gauges is not quite as easy as with the 12. The load selection, whether you buy them or build your own, is so varied in that gauge that many shooters no longer do much in the way of choke tube changes; they just change their shells to adjust patterns. That approach is less effective in the smaller gauges. Pattern control becomes more important and it is best achieved by balancing both load and choke. If your favorite 20, 28 or .410 is not fitted for interchangeable choke tubes, the biggest favor you can do yourself is to have it done. Hastings, Briley, Seminole, Clearview and others can perform this work. Though I do not use a large selection of choke tubes in the 12-gauge, when I head out with a 28-gauge or .410 I want to be carrying Skeet, Improved Cylinder, Modified and Full tubes. They will be needed.

You will also want to fit the gun to yourself with the same care you would apply to your favorite competition 12-gauge, maybe more. The smaller gauges do not give you much margin for error, so good gun fit is critical.

On the plus side, these additions will make the gun a much better performer in the game fields. In addition, a few rounds of sporting clays before bird season will certainly improve your ability to bust feathers instead of clays!

20-Gauge

Although the 20 qualifies as a sub-gauge, a reasonably skilled shooter is not handicapping himself very much on any targets inside the 35-yard mark. The 20 is plenty under those conditions, and its lower recoil level and lighter weight are often an asset to small-framed shooters.

There is a wealth of top-quality 20-gauge over/unders on the market. Many have been introduced specifically for sporting clays, with back-bored barrels, long choke tubes and barrels in the preferred 28- to 30-inch range.

For maximum recoil control, it would be hard to beat guns like the popular Remington 1100, Beretta Teknys Gold or the Browning Gold. Their gas-operated actions alter the recoil impulse noticeably and produce a soft-shooting smoothbore. Have one of them properly fitted to the individual shooter, add a basic selection of choke tubes and you will have a fine tool for

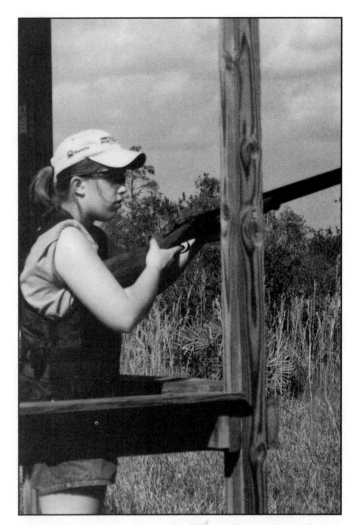

Plenty of women are finding that clay shooting is a level playing field. With the same equipment and training, women have the strength, coordination and intensity to compete toe-to-toe with men. The 20-gauge is an excellent place to start young shooters and as they get used to the bumping their shoulder takes, they may – or may not – want to try the 12-gauge.

sporting clays.

Experienced 12-gauge shooters have learned that care in selecting the right load for the target distance can boost their scores. The same approach is even more important with the sub-gauges.

For ultra-close ranges (10 yards and under), any ⅞-ounce load of #9 shot that opens quickly is an asset. Look for some-

Although it has recently grown its reputation for police and tactical operations weaponry, Benelli's $1,435 Legacy 20-gauge, with its 26-inch barrel appropriately choked, will perform well at skeet and sporting clays. It accepts both 2¾- and 3-inch shells.

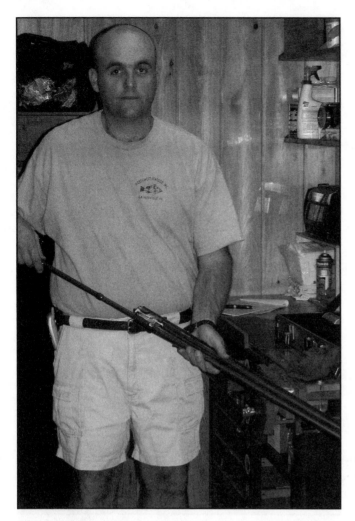

Scott Richardson of Gainesville, Florida shoots a Beretta over/under and for sub-gauge events, slips in his set of Kohler tubes.

one-ounce skeet loads in #9. These are intended for skeet shooters who use the 20 in 12-gauge events and they are an excellent choice for 20-gauge sporting in a factory load for this range. When a company offers this same load with their premium hard target shot in sizes #7½, #8, and #8½ as well, you probably have the best sporting clays lineup for the 20-gauge. It would be hard to think of a more complete load selection.

Beyond 25 yards, we start to see a decrease in the breaking ability of #9 shot. A proven way to increase that power, while maintaining as much pattern density as possible, is to shift to #8½ shot. A one-ounce load in this size becomes my first choice for shots in the 20- to 30-yard range, but it is a combo you will have to load yourself. About as close as you can come to the ideal load is #8 shot in a ⅞-ounce target load. There are some one-ounce field loads in the same shot size. The target loads, by virtue of their harder shot, generally produce better results, despite carrying fewer pellets per shell. Results can also depend on how well your individual barrel handles the full one-ounce load. It is worth taking time to do some test patterning here. A good one-ounce load of quality #8 shot is a consistent target-breaker out to 35 yards. Some very smart shooters handload a one-ounce nickel-plated #8 shot load for over-30-yard shots, and they do marvelous work beyond 35 yards. The ability of nickel shot to maintain tight patterns and short shot strings improves 20-gauge performance at this range.

Beyond 40 yards, the 20-gauge starts to become marginal. Reloaders have the option of going to #7½ nickel shot in either ⅞-ounce or one-ounce loads, depending on which patterns best in their barrel. If your gun has a three-inch chamber, there are magnum versions of acceptable loads available that pack 1⅛ ounces of #7½ nickel. Other long-range alternatives include any of the premium copper-plated, buffered field loads offered by several companies in size #7½.

28-Gauge

Inside 30 yards, this little jewel does not really take a back seat to the bigger gauges. Between 30 and 40 yards, it does need some help (perhaps nickel shot) and beyond 40 yards it does help if a shooter has a sense of humor. That is not a knock on the 28-gauge. It just points out that there is a limit to what you can expect from ¾-ounce of shot, no matter how efficient the shell or how carefully constructed the load.

Moderately priced 28-gauge guns of the clay target persuasion are becoming more common, depending on how you define the term "moderately priced." One of the sweetest-shooting of these is the classic Remington 1100 autoloader (actually the Remington "sporting clays" version, although the difference is strictly in the advertising). Remington has also chambered their 870 pump for the 28, and if you like pumps you will certainly like that one. Browning offers a 28-gauge pump in its

thing like a felt-wad 20-gauge that opens a bit faster than a plastic shotcup. Several products referred to by names like "brush wad" are available in 20-gauge and create excellent short-range loads when stuffed with an ounce of soft #9 shot. Another alternative will be any of the softshot promotional loads. Generally, they are available in size #8 as the smallest 20-gauge offering, but they spread pretty quickly and that is what counts here.

Moving to the 15- to 25-yard range, it is hard to argue with any 20-gauge #9 skeet load. This is exactly the range where they were designed to offer optimum performance. Look for

Ruger builds its Red Label shotguns in 12-, 20- and (pictured) 28-gauge. It also offers a tube insert for the 28 that allows you to shoot .410 shells.

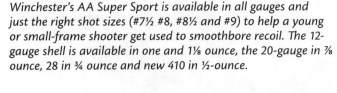

The 9410 is Winchester's lever-action 410. The 2½-inch chambered 9410 was introduced in 2001. It comes equipped with the Invector Choke System and will shoot everything from high performance shotshells to slugs.

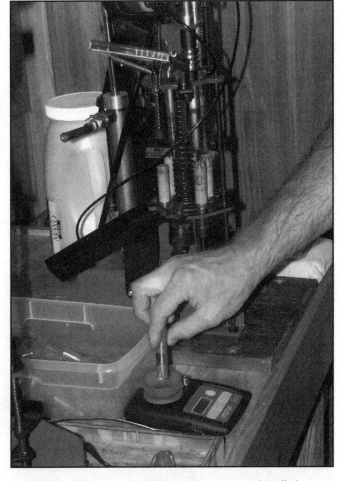

Winchester's AA Super Sport is available in all gauges and just the right shot sizes (#7½ #8, #8½ and #9) to help a young or small-frame shooter get used to smoothbore recoil. The 12-gauge shell is available in one and 1⅛ ounce, the 20-gauge in ⅞ ounce, 28 in ¾ ounce and new 410 in ½-ounce.

Doublechecking your reloading equipment occasionally is an exceptional idea, especially the amount of powder headed for sub-gauge shells.

BPS Hunter line for about $528, and these are quality guns as well.

Moving up in price we find the Browning Citori Gran Lightning for $2,483 and the Ruger Red Label with a straight or pistol grip for $1,540. Beyond these, 28-gauge guns get a bit pricey, yet they are certainly exquisite.

The relative lack of affordable guns is almost matched by the availability and price of ammunition. Because they're a specialty item when compared to the omnipresent 12-gauge, 28-gauge shells run about $20.00 a case more than the 12-gauge. You will also find a rather limited selection of shells. This is one situation where it can really pay to reload. Not only can you save a significant amount of money on your shells, but also you can greatly expand the versatility of this small round.

In the ultra-close-range area, the best choice among factory rounds are the standard ¾-ounce, 1,200 fps, #9 skeet loads offered by everybody that makes a 28-gauge load. A better choice by a wide margin is a softer 28-gauge "brush wad" with ¾-ounce of soft #9 shot. It is strictly the province of handloaders, but inside 15 yards you would think you were shooting a 12-gauge.

From that range out to almost 25 yards, you will be well served with a standard skeet load using good hard shot. The little 28 is an extremely efficient shell and will break under 25-yard targets just as well as a 12- or 20-gauge. In fact, many skeet shooters carry as good an average with the 28 as they do with the 12-gauge.

Beyond 25 yards, out to almost 35 yards, #8½ shot becomes the best choice. In factory shells, this is available from Federal as the ¾-ounce and from Remington, which also offers a 28-gauge sporting load. Kent Cartridge has a 2¾-inch 28-gauge shell with ¾-ounce of shot that is offered in #7½, #8 and #9. Even Rio Ammunition offers a 28-gauge target load in #7½, #8 and #9 rated at 1,300 fps at three feet from the muzzle. For reloaders, shifting to hard target-grade #8 or #8½ shot in your standard skeet load recipe will accomplish the same thing for a little more than half the cost of factory shells.

Pushing the 28-gauge beyond 35 yards is not easy, because you really do not have enough shot to work with. Winchester offers a one-ounce load in sizes #6, #7½ and #8. For factory ammo shooters, whichever load patterns best in your gun is your best option. My solution is to go at least to a 1,200 fps, ¾-ounce handload of #8 of very hard shot, perhaps even nickel.

I have mentioned nickel-plated shot quite a bit, because it simply gives the best pattern performance at extended range in any gauge. It is more expensive than lead shot, but in the case of the 28-gauge it is money well spent. When you factor the cost of nickel shot reloads against the cost of factory rounds, the nickel shot loads are not only cheaper but more effective as well. If you develop an affection for the 28-gauge and you really want to wring the most out of it, becoming a reloader is the way to go.

.410

Whoever designed the 410-caliber (or "36-gauge," as it is often called in Europe) was either extremely drunk or had a wickedly twisted sense of humor. In fact, no one even seems to want to own up to creating it. The best I have been able to find in any reference work is the fact that the shell "just sort of appeared" at some point in history!

The big problem is the extremely small diameter of the hull in relation to the shot column length. This encourages a lot of pellet deformation and long shot strings. Even with a Full choke and hard shot, .410 patterns fall apart by the time they reach 35 yards and they become noticeably patchy as close as 20 yards. This shell also operates at higher pressures than its larger cousins, which aggravates the shot deformation problem even further. Getting consistently smooth and even patterns from a .410 is tough. Nevertheless, there is a certain appeal to this miserable little rascal.

Inexpensive .410 shotguns are common. Even the heaviest loads have recoil levels that could only be described as minuscule and a fair selection of shells can be found virtually anywhere ammunition is sold. A knowledgeable shooter would conclude that if the 28-gauge was as readily available in affordable guns and ammo as the .410, the latter would probably fade from the scene – but they aren't, and so it won't!

Although I am neither a fan of pumps nor a real devotee of the .410, I admit that one of my favorite fun guns is an old and well-worn Mossberg 500 pump. It is light, cute and fun to shoot. A few years ago, Hastings installed interchangeable choke tubes in that gun, and subsequent experiments with loads and chokes were remarkable.

When it comes to spreading a pattern quickly at close range, the .410 has no peer, unless the other guns are loaded with spreader wads. Using the basic skeet choke tube, this gun will produce a circular pattern of about 25 inches at 15 yards with a three-inch #9 shot load. By comparison, a soft-shot 20-gauge field load from a similar choke will create a pattern of about 19 or 20 inches at that range. That .410 pattern will be uniform enough to consistently get the job done. The pattern will go completely to hell by 20 yards, but inside 15 yards it is a clay-busting little fool!

Once the range increases beyond about 15 yards, I am through with the skeet or improved cylinder tubes. The patterns are too patchy with any load. This is where the .009-inch Modified tube makes a big difference. Even though it is technically a Modified choke in the .410, it does the best pattern-

Browning's Little Skeeters mini tube gauge reducers ($50 per pair) fit in the bore of your favorite shotgun and allow you to shoot several gauges of ammunition in a single gun. They are a fraction of the cost of conventional, multi-gauge tubes, Browning says, and will not affect the overall feel or swing of your gun.

ing job from 15 to about 25 yards. In fact, custom gunsmiths in the skeet game have come to the almost universal conclusion that the most effective .410 constriction for skeet shooters is .008-.009-inch. Anytime you can get a half-dozen top gunsmiths to agree on the same thing, consider it a Universal Truth!

With the .009-inch tube in place, I like the 2½-inch #9, ½-ounce skeet load out to just beyond 20 yards, and shift to the same load in good hard #8½ shot for birds out to 30 yards. This is one case where less is better, as these ½-ounce loads will generally deliver better patterns than most three-inch loads. The short shot column and hard, target-grade shot produce less pellet deformation than the longer shot column in the 3-inch load. (Substituting nickel shot for lead can change that, though.) These loads are readily available from the factory in the skeet lines from Remington, Winchester and Federal, with the ½-ounce #8½ loads being found in the .410 sporting clays numbers from Federal (the SC412) and Remington (SP410SC). If a shooter confines his .410 endeavors to ranges under the 30-yard mark, he can get by quite nicely with these three different loads and a pair of choke tubes.

Beyond 30 yards the going gets tough with the .410. Choking the #8½ loads down through a full tube will produce a fairly tight center core pattern at 30-plus-yards, with little margin for error. If you do not point it like a rifle, you are going to miss. Even if you do, you start to run out of power to break targets at about 35 yards. Shifting to hard #8 shot in a ½-ounce load produces a pattern that looks acceptable on paper but just does not seem to work in real life. There is not enough shot in the charge to compensate for the inevitable effects of shot

stringing, which do not show up on a stationary patterning board. Shot stringing produces more than a few holes in actual practice. That often results in gaps in the pattern that cause the bird to be hit with just one or two pellets, and that may not be enough to get that "visible piece." Although #7½ shot works well with larger gauges because it increases the striking power of individual pellets, it does not seem to help here. You just do not have enough pellets in the load to do the job. The pattern density isn't there.

I have spent a lot of time looking for a 35-yard .410 load and will be the first to admit that, even with a full choke tube, I have not found one I like. All the 3-inch factory loads use shot that is just too soft to take the abuse it receives in that long, small-diameter shot column. If you are stuck with factory loads, the best bet is to pick a 3-inch #7½ load and hope you can get a couple of pellets onto the bird. Do not even bother to pattern the loads; it is too frustrating. Shoot for real. Alternate between a Modified and Full tube, and keep track of which performs best for you.

If you reload, you have a better option with 3-inch loads of #8 nickel shot. It is not perfect, but it is the best choice I have found when you have to push the .410 into the 30- to 40-yard range. You will not ever confuse this load with a 12-, 20- or even a 28-gauge load, but it will give you about as much as you can expect from a .410.

It helps to have a sense of humor any time you take a .410 onto a sporting clays range. You are going to need it.

Give the sub-gauge guns a try if you shoot for fun. They will provide that in spades.

Even a small youngster with confidence can handle a .410 and probably a 28-gauge, if the crowd is supportive of his efforts. On a sporting clays course, the .410 is a challenge for even a mature shooter, so a 28 may be the minimum if parents expect a youngster to score enough targets to stay happy, interested and progressing.

THE ALL-AMERICAN

All American sporting clays shooter Bobby Fowler, Jr. of Houston, Texas gives demonstrations, competes actively and teaches shotgunners the fundamentals and mechanics of successful shooting. "When you approach one of the basics carelessly," he says, "you miss."

Bobby Fowler, Jr., who lives in Houston, Texas, was 38 years old when we talked by telephone – and he had already been shooting competitively for half his life. The excitement and zeal for shooting and the intensity that has made this international champion a shooting sports star were still loud and clear in his voice, though.

Bobby's Internet site at www.eliteshooting.com lists his competitive sporting clays victories from 1995, and they are extensive. Terms like Team USA, All American, HOA Champion and FITASC Champion are sprinkled through his resume like grains of salt on your Saturday morning scrambled eggs. More than you want to count. The man knows his game and has a passion for winning, but his biggest thrill these days is passing on his knowledge to other shooters.

"Anymore, I get the biggest kick out of promoting my sponsors and helping my students build their skills," he says. "I guess it's like a daddy being there to help his kids grow up."

According to Bobby, the very best way to move upward in the ranks of sporting clays top shooters is to work hard on the fundamentals. Whether you are a many-time sporting clays All American as he is, or a novice approaching his or her very first competitive event, such basics as stance, gun hold, weight distribution, focus and follow-through are the foundation of success at any level.

What Bobby Teaches versus What Bobby Practices

"I'm an active competitor, but I also travel to give demonstrations and teach the techniques of good shooting," Bobby Fowler says. "There are two levels of instruction. In a typical first-level school, students learn and practice the basics under my direct supervision. The basics are the things every shooter needs to understand and put into practice before he pulls the trigger. I want students to understand stance, gun hold and orientation to the target break point and build them an unforgettable routine, every shot, without fail. When you forget something basic or perform it carelessly, you more often than not fail, so this is what we work on in the lower-level school."

Bobby teaches Double-A shooters as well as introductory classes. These are often men and women who are older than he and have as much shooting experience, but rarely as much course savvy and nowhere near his success. "Double-A and Masters shooters know the fundamentals very well, so we build on them. There are only so many shot presentations you will see in sporting clays – incoming, outgoing, crossing, teal (straight up) and running rabbit (on the ground) – and we learn how to orient or position for each of them so that when the school is over, they can practice effectively."

Bobby teaches his students that sporting clays is as much a mental as a physical or gun handling game. In a sense, he teaches the mental fundamentals.

"There has been a lot written about the mental aspect of competition," he says, "and most of it is true. Mental toughness is the ability to concentrate on a single objective or task to the exclusion of all other thoughts. To become a champion, you have to be focused. You cannot be thinking of the next station, the next joke to tell your squad or the things your spouse asked you to pick up on your way home. If you want to win on a consistent basis, you can only concentrate on putting a shot string exactly where it has to go to bust a bird."

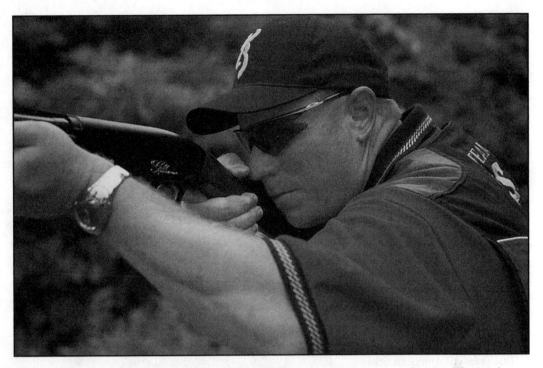

Shooting coach and frequent High Over-All competitor Bobby Fowler, Jr. says the mental game is just as important as the physical game. "I teach people to concentrate on the next shot," he says, "to leave the success or failure at the last station behind them." In this respect, he admits that he does not follow his own advice. "I like to know where I am in the standings," he admits. "It helps motivate me."

Because shooting a good clays course may take several hours, Bobby realizes that the average person cannot keep tightly focused for that long, with as many natural distractions as there are along the way, and not collapse in exhaustion. "Teach yourself to relax between stations," he says. "If you have done well, be happy. If not, laugh about it and recall the fundamentals. Whatever you did 'back there' is done. You can't really take it with you and you can't re-do it. It's over. Look forward. Relaxing some between stations helps you save energy for what you might call a 'burst of concentration' for the next pair of birds."

For Bobby, the mental game involves a stand-up act, a consistent approach to breaking one bird – or two in the case of doubles – at a time. He even has a pre-shot routine: loading.

"I take between eight and ten seconds to load," he says. "I put the shells in and then line them up to the exact same orientation every time. Since shells are round, this may seem silly, but I line up the type on the bottom of the shell casing the same way every shot. What this little ritual does is slow me down. There's no hurry. This helps me establish a methodical pace and it puts me in a familiar place. It reminds me to think of the fundamentals. 'Holding the gun firmly against your cheek. Where are you going to break this target? Remember to follow-through.' I have trained myself to perform this little ritual before every shot. It works for me, so I drill the idea of developing a familiar routine into my students' heads in class."Speaking of routine, Bobby says he gets nervous before every big shoot and has had to adjust. "I expect to be nervous and have learned how to make that loose energy work for me," he says. "I use it to focus, to think positive no matter what else is happening in my life. I translate the butterflies in my stomach into kind of a visioning process." Bobby has learned to ac-

cept his nervous stomach before a shoot, to think of it as his body's way of getting prepared.

Actually, Bobby Fowler, Jr. experiences two nervous episodes: before and during a shoot. Everyone who is shooting seriously and wants to win rather than just show up is tempted to look ahead, he says, especially if they have run a station or two. Use this natural anticipation – which, after all, is just another term for nervousness – to focus on the shot problem you have immediately before you. Never think of such things as how close you might be to winning your division. (This is not easy, but that is why it is called 'discipline.' Everyone's mind wanders, even a trained yogi. This is natural. Accept it and gently guide it back to the station you are on.) During the shoot, many things can cause your mind to drift off – a lost bird or a stuck wad, for instance – but as you build your skills, you will be able to stay focused and channel your anticipation more thoroughly.

In one area, Bobby's routine varies significantly from the advice he gives his students. Unlike many shooters, he keeps score. He keeps up with his position on the leader-board. "I like to know where I am in the standings, know what I have to shoot for," he explains. "For a young shooter or a new shooter of any age, this amounts to pressure they can do without. I don't recommend paying attention to anything other than the shot you are making right now. Let your score surprise you. So, yes, I actually don't practice what I teach on this point."

Notes About Practice

Many AA and Masters shooters break 1,000 targets a week and Bobby has gone through years when he has shot 1,600 in some weeks! "You want to make everything you do automatic," he says. "You want your movements and even your thoughts to become repetitive and totally predictable. So, when you get to the shooting line in something of a machine-like trance and begin breaking everything that is thrown at you, you know you have arrived in the zone. Nothing will get you to this point faster than a shooting coach and hours of practice breaking birds."

These days, Bobby practices three to four times a week with his ported, extended choke 12-gauge Browning 525 over/under and the same Winchester Super Handicap shells that he takes to a clays venue. His selections are three-dram #7½ and #8 loads. "Shot size selection is important," Bobby says. "The smaller the pellet the less energy it carries at distance, but the larger the pattern will be. So, for close shooting I use the #8s, and as the bird gets out to 40 yards or so I switch to #7½s."

This Texas All American believes that after you understand how your gun patterns, choke selection should be a big part of your learning curve and practice as well as your game-day ritual. While drams of powder and shot size control energy delivery, choke controls pattern size. At less than 20 yards, use an open choke. At 20 to 35 yards, he suggests Improved Cylinder or Light Modified. From 30 to 50 yards, the Modified is about right and at 50 yards, switch to Full.

Unlike much advice about practicing with smaller gauges to make your 12-gauge shooting more effective, Bobby says he practices with every gauge. "I compete in sub-gauge events," he says, "but I don't substitute practice with them for practice with the 12-gauge. The guns are different and they feel different. Nevertheless, whatever gauge you are using, if you approach the shot with proper fundamentals, you can be challenged. Watch the target. Stare a hole in it, like a baseball pitcher staring his pitch over the plate and into the catcher's glove. Think of the old Superman serials on television where he had laser-like light rays coming out of his eyes. That's the concentration you want. In a sense then, the gauge you shoot doesn't matter."

Every gauge has its merit, but the fundamentals of shooting a 20 or 28 or even a .410 are not different from a 12-gauge, he says. "You just have to remember that you have a lot less shot available so you have to be smoother in your presentation. A 28 or .410 gives you less room for error. For 12-gauge practice, I

Even in tight shooting spaces like this one, Bobby Fowler teaches that there are only half a dozen shot presentations in sporting clays. One trick to mastering any shot combination, even in tight quarters, is to approach the station with a plan and then to work the plan.

often step back to handicap distances or shoot doubles in other games like skeet and trap. When I get tired of that, I tighten the choke. After a miss or two, the constricted shot string wakes me up."

The Elements of Bobby's Game

Because Bobby typically uses the sustained lead shooting technique, it seems to many observers that his shots are relaxed and unhurried.

This is good, but it is a bit of an illusion, he says. Switch

Bobby Fowler, Jr. shoots the Browning Citori 525 Sporting. The 525 comes with a beautiful silver nitride receiver with intricate scroll engraving and a walnut stock and Schnabel-style forearm. It is available in 12, 20 28 and .410. In the 12- and 20-gauge models, the comb is adjustable. Expect a comfortable right-hand palm swell, gold-plated trigger and five choke tubes.

from sustained lead to the "come from behind and push through" style of shooting and it can seem – because there is much more gun movement – that the shooter is hurrying his or her shot. But this is all a matter of perception caused by a particular style of shooting. However they see and manage lead, effective shooters are smooth and learn good follow-through.

The mental game is extremely important, but it is not complete without a complementary physical game.

Bobby believes in staying in shape and says that physical conditioning, especially when you are shooting sporting clays, is more important than most people realize. "In trap or skeet, unless the day is extremely hot, it is possible to come off the line without much strain. This is not the case in sporting clays. In clays you walk and lug ammo and guns and so on from station to station for what can feel like miles."

Perhaps it helps that Bobby married a fitness instructor, but today he works out at least three times a week.

"I had a really good year in 2000 and then decided to take some time off from exercise," he says. "That phase lasted about a year and a half and during that time, I didn't do as well. I began to feel sluggish after a day of shooting. Now that my wife acts as my fitness instructor, I lift weights and walk the treadmill regularly. When I finish a course these days, I'm not as winded. I still have energy at the end."

The games have become so competitive that Bobby does not know if the average shooter can compete effectively at the highest levels of sporting clays without professional coaching.

"When you are ready to make the move from the level of a good shooter to elite status," he says, "it is important that you train with a professional coach. A professional will pick your shooting game apart and help you put it back together seamlessly. Your coach, should not only be someone who has 'been there and done that,' but someone who is a good communicator as well as a good shooter."

Bobby not only keeps the stock of his Browning 525 Citori firmly in place on his cheek, he is able to teach the fundamentals and beyond, as evinced by students like Cole Storey, an All American First Team member who has worked with Bobby for two years, and Nadim Nasir, a current Second Team All American.

"There is a difference in levels when selecting a coach," he says. "A person who is a good shooter and a reasonably good communicator can work with almost anyone and help him or her shoot better. However, a shooter who is trying to bust the 80 out of 100 mark will have to build a different program from that of, say, an elite shooter who is trying to raise her or his average from 90 to 94. There are a lot of reasonably good coaches out there for the first step. For the second step, do yourself a favor and choose a professional, because if you really listen to their advice and put it into practice, it will occupy hours of your time over months and maybe over years. Sporting clays is not the cheapest game in town, so you want somebody who can help you get it right."

TOP SPORTING CLAYS GUNS

Sporting clays is a game with its roots firmly planted in the hunting fields, so one would assume that any field-grade shotgun would be an acceptable choice. That assumption is correct, but it relies heavily on one's definition of the term "acceptable."

If your reason for shooting sporting clays is to tune up for the fall season, then by all means, use the gun you intend to carry into the field. If you want to learn the capabilities and limitations of your favorite smoothbore – or yourself – there is no better way to do it than by spending a few summer weekends on a sporting clays range. It makes no difference what gauge you shoot or what type action your gun has. If it will spit out two shells, it becomes an acceptable choice.

If your goal is to play the game for the game's sake, however, you might be disappointed with your favorite field gun.

Gun Requirements

Sporting clays is a demanding and varied game. You will see targets, distances, angles and presentations that appear in no other clay target sport. To master this game, if such a thing is possible, you need a gun equal to the challenge. Fortunately,

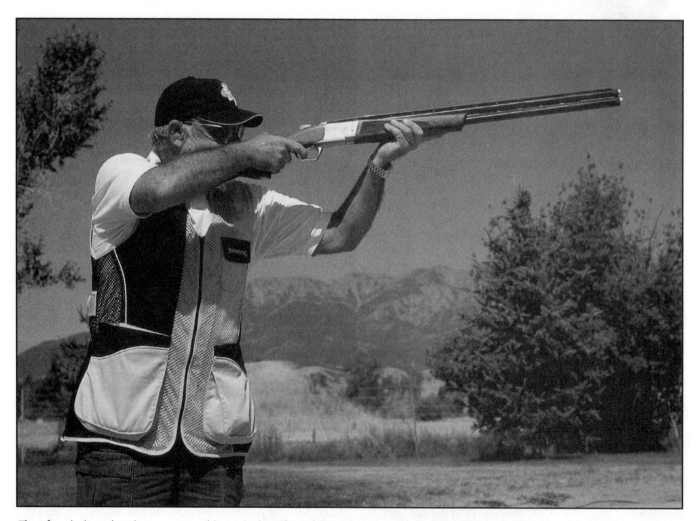

The often-imitated saying among architects is that "form follows function." In the field of shotgun design and especially coupled with the demands of innovative sporting clays courses, this is especially true. (Photo courtesy Browning)

The 12-gauge Ruger Red Label is available with a composite stock, which Ruger calls its "Target Grey All-Weather Red Label Shotgun." This gun is available only with a pistol-grip stock, but you have a selection of 26-, 28- or 30-inch barrels.

the game has been in existence long enough in the U.S. and Europe that top competitors know what combination of factors characterize an effective gun. Here is a butt-to-muzzle look at what the experts think works best and why.

The first concern is mounting the gun quickly to your shoulder, since all sporting clays shots begin with the gun butt clearly visible below the armpit. A recoil pad with sharp edges or a lot of deep serration on the face is going to inhibit fast mounting by catching and dragging on your clothing. If you fumble a gun mount and do not lock it in, you can pretty well kiss these targets goodbye! For this reason, a more rounded pad with a relatively smooth face is a major asset. So too is having the buttstock properly fitted to your individual build. If you cannot snap the gun into a smooth and consistent mount, then everything else becomes uncertain.

Although actual "bird picture" over the barrel is a matter of individual preference, most sporting clays shooters want a relatively flat-shooting gun that has its pattern impacting equally above and below the bead.

The rib and bead arrangement is another matter of personal preference. I know some excellent shooters who do not want any beads on their rib. Their contention is that if the gun is fitted properly, beads are nothing more than a distraction.

Other shooters fare well with a step in the rear of the rib and a single front bead. Some prefer a large bright bead, while others favor something smaller and more subdued. I shoot best with a flat rib and double gold bead arrangement. This may sound like nitpicking, but the picture you see over the sighting plane is a critical part of your subconscious triggering mechanism. When you find the set-up that makes you comfortable, you will shoot better. Changing bead arrangements is a relatively simple matter and worthy of experimentation.

When sporting clays first became popular, shooters opting for over/unders often settled on relatively short barrels of 25 to 26 inches on the theory that the lighter guns, with a more between-the-hands balance, would get on targets faster. Time and experience have shown that not to be the case. Stack-barrel shooters today invariably opt for barrels in the 28- to 32-inch range, and even longer, because the additional weight forward promotes a stronger, smoother swing with less chance of stopping the gun.

I shoot the 30-inch-barreled Ruger Sporting Clays Red Label noticeably better than my standard Red Label with 28-inch tubes. That two inches of barrel may not sound like much, and both guns have the same overall weight, but the longer-barreled gun balances ⅜-inch forward of the hinge pin, while my stan-

Mossberg's 500 pump features ported, interchangeable barrels, vented rib and interchangeable choke tubes developed for "superior patterning using lead, steel and other non-toxic loads."

The Weatherby Orion Super Sporting Clays 12-gauge has a cast-off stock from top to bottom of the butt (three to six mm) to provide a better fit against the shoulder and improved balance and feel. It also features a schnabel forearm and three barrel lengths: 28, 30 and 32 inches.

Here is a 12-gauge semi-auto from Weatherby. The SAS Sporting Clays comes with 28- or 30-inch barrels. It features a walnut stock and ported barrel and includes five extended chokes.

Perazzis have interchangeable buttstocks that can be ordered in a wide range of dimensions for length of pull, drop at comb and heel, cast-on/cast-off or straight comb with sloping field pistol-grip stock or a Monte Carlo stock. This customizing prohibits publishing final suggested retail prices, but with a Perazzi, if you have to ask, perhaps you can't afford it!

Winchester's new Select Energy Sporting is distinguished by the oval checkering pattern on the pistol grip stock and forend. It is sold with 28-, 30- or 32-inch barrels and a TruGlo competition front sight and mid-rib bead.

Skeet and sporting clays allow you to bring your turkey gun to the course and expect to walk away with a respectable score. You will probably not win a tournament, but if you are a good shot, your Mossberg pump will not embarrass you. (Photo courtesy Mossberg)

dard gun balances right at the hinge pin. That small difference is worth a few extra birds per round. Those who favor semi-autos or pumps say they find the 28-inch barrel a bit more effective than 26-inch tubes.

The ability to gain improved pattern control over the widely varying ranges one sees in sporting clays has given rise to a serious interest in custom barrel work designed to enhance shotshell performance. Many of today's sporting clays guns have lengthened forcing cones, back-bored barrels and long chokes. Given the need for a quick follow-up shot, many shooters have found barrel porting to be an aid because it reduces muzzle jump and gets them back on target a bit faster.

Given the need for frequent choke tube changes, many manufacturers produce tubes with knurled ends that protrude from the barrel. This allows them to be quickly changed without a wrench. A very nice touch on any interchangeable tube intended for sporting clays is an identifying system that allows the shooter to determine what tubes are in the gun by simply looking at the muzzle, instead of having to remove the tube to find out. It is a nice convenience. It is not hard to forget what tubes you have in the gun in the heat of competition.

Sporting Clays Guns

Guns with all of the above features were not very common in years past. Today, however, sporting clays is the hottest thing in shooting, and every shotgun maker has models specially designed for this game – and those same "competition" guns make excellent field guns! Here is a look at who is doing what.

Ruger (www.ruger.com)

Neither cheap nor expensive as shotguns go, Ruger's Red Label over/under guns are positioned above those on display at the BoxMarts and below the guns you must have custom fitted. The suggested retail price for one of these Connecticut smoothbores is $1,545, but as with any suggested retail price, you should expect to pay less than that when you negotiate your own purchase.

You can have a Red Label built with a variety of options. All standard gauges are available, 12, 20 and 28, and Ruger builds a .410 tube set for their 28-gauge guns should you really wish to face a sporting challenge. Choose from two types of American walnut stocks and forearms, pistol grip or straight English-style grip. The black, synthetic "All-Weather" stock is available only in pistol-grip styling. Stocks and forearms are lightly checkered for more secure gun hold.

Ruger over/under 12- and 20-gauge guns are chambered for three-inch shells. The 28-gauge is chambered for 2¾-inch. Rugers are shipped with shell ejectors, but these can be deactivated so that you can manually remove or extract the shells. (Reloaders often prefer this option.)

Receivers can be ordered plain or engraved with either a walnut or synthetic stock. If you order a gun with an engraved receiver, expect to pay an additional $180. Plain receivers for walnut stocks have a brushed finish while those for All-Weather models have a dusky, non-glare finish.

Barrels are stainless on guns with All-Weather stocks or hammer-forged, blued steel with walnut stocks. All-Weather barrels on guns with engraved receivers are polished like the receiver. Without engraving, they come with Ruger's dusky Target Grey finish. All-Weather guns have stainless steel components and the exposed stainless steel parts on Target Grey models have a corrosion-resistant, low-glare finish. Available barrel lengths are 26, 28 and 30 inches, except that the 28-gauge cannot be ordered with a 30-inch barrel. A choke tube wrench and five, steel-shot compatible choke tubes are included: two Skeet #1 (one for each barrel), Improved Cylinder, Modified and Full. Barrels are back-bored for softer recoil and more uniform patterns. The dovetail, free-floating rib has a single gold bead aiming point. (The 30-inch barrel for 12-gauges has a second, mid-rib gold bead.)

The Red Label has a 14⅛-inch length of pull with a walnut stock and 14¼-inches with a synthetic stock. The drop at comb is 1½ inches. The drop at heel is 2½ inches with a walnut stock and a quarter-inch longer with a synthetic stock.

The 12-gauge with a 28-inch barrel is 45 inches long and weighs about eight pounds.

Mossberg (www.mossberg.com)

Although this Connecticut company is not known for shotguns for shooting clay targets, their 500 Pump-Action All-Purpose 12- or 20-gauge will do the job. If such a gun accompanies you to the field for turkeys or pheasants or ducks, you ought to take it to a sporting clays venue for a couple rounds before the season opens. You will be surprised at the results.

The 500 All-Purpose in either 12- or 20-gauge comes with either a checkered wood or smooth, black synthetic stock and forearm. These three-inch chambered guns feature interchangeable ported barrels with a ventilated rib with front and mid-point bead sights. Although 24- and 26-inch barrels are available, for sporting clays, the 28-inch blued barrel would almost

The Model 2000 semi-auto 12-gauge from Stoeger is a value-priced gun that, with the appropriate choke in place, will handle most shooting chores on the competition line.

The new Cynergy Sporting 12-gauge from Browning is available with a walnut or a composite stock and forearm. Barrels are back-bored and factory ported. Note the stylized stock, recoil pad and forend.

Browning's Gold Sporting Clays 12-gauge semi-auto has long been a favorite among value-conscious fans of repeaters. It features a 28- or 30-inch ported barrel, front HiViz Tri-Comp sight with mid-bead and comes with three chokes.

Ithaca pump-action shotguns like the New Classic Model 37 which you use for jumping woodcock and ruffed grouse out of heavy cover are fine for most stations in sporting clays, especially with the 28-inch barrel and the three, flush-mount choke tubes included. Ithaca calls this distinctive fore-end a "ringtail" style.

Caesar Guerini is making a move into the U.S. shotgun market with guns like the Magnus Sporting over/under in 12- and 20-gauge. The adjustable trigger moves up to one-half-inch to accommodate hand size and length of pull.

The Franchi Alcione features full pistol-grip styling and a high quality name brand gun for less than $2,000.

Franchi's Alcione 612 Sporting 12-gauge has a reputation for reliability and smooth handling.

Charles Daly 12-gauge over/unders are imported from Italy. Barrels are honed, chromed and polished in 28- or 30-inch lengths.

Beretta's new DT10 Trident L Sporting 12-gauge has rich floral engraving around the receiver beautiful walnut stock and Schnabel grip, gold-plated trigger and your choice of 30- or 32-inch barrels.

The Remington 1100 semi-auto may have been in every shooter's sights at one time. This long-lived gun model has proven itself as a rugged and versatile gun. The good ol' 1100 in the Sporting 28"-barrel flavor features a fiber optic front sight and steel mid-rib bead for fast target acquisition.

SKB says that mastering sporting clays requires a shotgun that provides a responsive fit, is well balanced between the shooter's hands, has a smooth swing, a fast sighting plane and a crisp trigger. Its 85TSS is designed for "fast target acquisition and hard-hitting patterns without producing shooter fatigue."

certainly be your best choice, and the longer barrel gives you a total gun weight of 7½ pounds. Three extended Accu-Choke tubes for lead, steel and other non-toxic loads are included.

The specifications for this 7½-pound $316 shotgun are as follows: length of pull, 13⅞-inches with a walnut stock and 14½-inches with a synthetic stock. The drop at comb is 1½ inches while the drop at heel is 2⅜-inches (walnut stock) and 2⅛-inches (synthetic stock). The overall length with a 28-inch barrel is 47½ inches

Mossberg also sells an All-Purpose .410 that is chambered for a three-inch shell. The 24-inch vented rib is topped with twin beads and has a fixed Full choke. It comes with a wood or synthetic stock and weighs 6¼ pounds. Purchase a new Mossberg shotgun and the company will include a free gun lock.

Weatherby (www.weatherby.com),

Founded in the 1940s, Weatherby is headquartered in California, but its semi-automatic shotguns are Italian-made. They feature self-compensating gas system to reduce felt recoil and an oversized Delta safety button on the rear of the trigger guard for what Weatherby calls "fast, easy access."

The SAS Sporting Clays 12-gauge ($849) is chambered for a 3-inch shell and is available with 28- or 30-inch chrome-lined, back-bored (to .735) barrels. Back boring improves shot patterns, reduces recoil and helps curb shooter fatigue. The factory-ported barrels feature a long forcing cone to help minimize recoil and shot deformation. Barrels have a ventilated top rib with mid-point and front aiming beads.

With a checkered walnut stock and forearm, the sporting clays gas gun weighs between seven and 7¾ pounds depending on the density of the walnut. An included shim spacer system

The SKB 85TSS receiver is produced in two sizes: a standard frame for 12-gauge and smaller for others. It is cut from a forged steel ingot by computerized CNC to precise dimensions marked in thousandths of an inch. The final result is a low profile box lock receiver with a modified "Greener" style crossbolt lock at the top of the receiver.

allows you to fit the stock to your body and style. You can order a gun with more cast on/cast off or drop for a better fit and improved target acquisition.

The Weatherby trigger system drops out for cleaning by punching out two pins in the 7075 T-6 alloy aluminum receiver. It snaps back and locks into position just as easily.

Five of Briley's Integral Multi-Choke system extended steel choke tubes and a choke wrench are standard: Improved Cylinder (.013), Modified (.022), Full (.040), Sporting Clays I (SCI: .007) and II (.016). The tops of the chokes are notched for identification.

Specifications for the Weatherby semi-auto are as follows: 14¼-inch length of pull, drop at comb 1½ inches and drop at

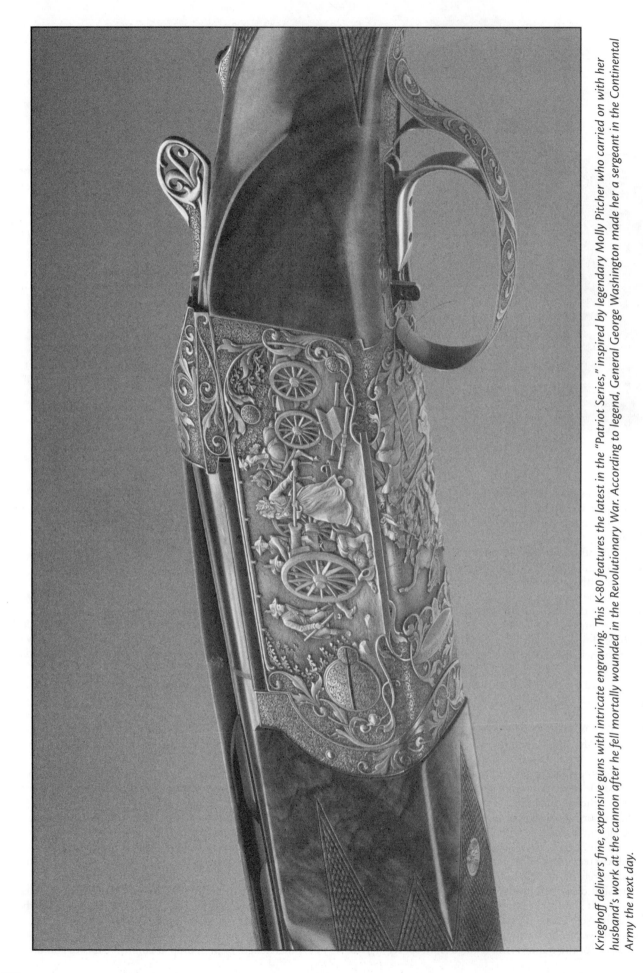

Krieghoff delivers fine, expensive guns with intricate engraving. This K-80 features the latest in the "Patriot Series," inspired by legendary Molly Pitcher who carried on with her husband's work at the cannon after he fell mortally wounded in the Revolutionary War. According to legend, General George Washington made her a sergeant in the Continental Army the next day.

In a similar manner to the area around Brescia, Italy, the Basque country in northern Spain is home to a tradition of custom gun manufacturing. AYA Excelsior over/unders for trap and sporting clays are built there in 12- and 20-gauge. Barrel lengths available are 28-inch, which is standard, or 29 or 30.

heel 2¼ inches. The overall length with a 30-inch barrel is 50 inches. A 12-gauge with 30-inch barrel weighs about eight pounds.

Weatherby also makes a fine over/under 12-gauge for sporting clays. The Orion SSC ($2,059) has a 3-inch chamber, a checkered target-style pistol grip and schnabel fore-end. The walnut stock is satin oil-finished and cast-off three to six mm for a better fit. Receivers are handsomely engraved and fitted with a gold-plated single, selective inertia trigger. Look for a sliding top safety, barrel selector switch and automatic ejectors.

The 28-, 30- or 32-inch ported barrels have lengthened forcing cones and are back-bored to .735 on all 12-gauge guns. A matte-finish, ventilated top 12 mm rib with mid-point and white front aiming beads reduces glare and works with side vents to dissipate barrel heat. Additional multi-barrel sets are available so that you can quickly change gauges and barrel lengths. Interchangeable, stainless steel screw-in Briley Multi-Chokes are included (28- and 30-inch barrels come with Skeet, Improved Cylinder, SCI, SCII and Modified chokes). These chokes are certified for steel shot through Modified.

Specifications for the eight-pound Weatherby (30-inch barrel) over/under are: 14¾ inches length of pull, 1½ inches drop at comb, and 2¼ inches drop at heel. The overall length with a 30-inch barrel is 47 inches.

Perazzi (www.perazzi.it)

Arguably the most respected name in top-end competitive shotguns, Italian gun-maker Perazzi offers what amounts to total custom fitting in their basic over/under sporting clay models (all three in 12- or 20-gauge): the MX8 ($10,841), MX12 ($10,841) and MX2000S ($12,167). The prices quoted are for a gun with minimal engraving and should be considered base cost. Upgrading to SC3 Grade engraving for the MX8, for example, quickly raises the price to $18,394, and moving farther upward in design and execution including gold inlays brings the cost of this gun to $31,275 and it tops out eventually to $100,449!

Barrel lengths are available from 27⁹⁄₁₆ to 34 inches. Interchangeable chokes are optional in one or both barrels. Perazzi choke tube designations are marked on the tube for quick identification. The flat tapered barrel rib and the side ribs are "half-ventilated." The 12-gauge rib measures ⁷⁄₁₆ by ⁹⁄₃₂ while the 20-gauge goes ³⁄₈ by ⁹⁄₃₂.

Critical stock dimensions on a Perazzi are essentially whatever you want them to be, because if you can afford one of these fine but very expensive guns, you can probably afford the trip to Brescia, Italy to have the gun fitted to you personally.

Perazzis have interchangeable buttstocks that can be ordered in a wide range of pull lengths, drop at comb and heel, with cast-on or cast-off, or straight comb with sloping field pistol-grip stock or a Monte Carlo. In effect, you are custom-building the gun when you buy it. Obviously then, the overall length and weight can vary widely with barrel and stock selection. Perazzis are not the kind of gun you buy off the rack at the local firearms emporium, but those who can afford them swear by them. After spending $25,000 (or even much more) on a fine shotgun, you would, too.

Winchester/US Repeating Arms (www.winchester-guns.com)

Winchester's Select Energy Sporting over/under 12-gauge is new for 2004 ($1,871 without adjustable comb and $2,030 with). Its Monte Carlo walnut stock and fore-end feature distinctive oval checkering and have a slight right hand palm swell. The adjustable comb moves from 1¼ to 1¾ inches, thus accommodating virtually any shooting position, including cast-on/cast-off, in seconds.

The Select Energy features a wide, tapering runway rib, mid-rib bead and TruGlo Tru-Bead front fiber optic aiming point. Barrels are ported to tame second-shot recoil, have vented side ribs and are available with back-bored 28-, 30- or 32-inch barrels.

Chambered for 2¾-inch shells, the Select Energy includes a choke wrench and three Invector-Plus choke tubes: Full, Modified and Improved Cylinder.

The overall length of the Select Energy with a 30-inch barrel and fixed comb is 47¾ inches. Length of pull is 14 5/8 inches; drop at comb is 1½ inches; and drop at heel is two inches. This gun weighs 7⅝ pounds.

Winchester's Super X2 semi-automatic comes in two 12-gauge models. Both are chambered for 3-inch shells and come with two easily changed gas pistons for load versatility. Shim spacers are included so that you can adjust drop and cast.

The unusual Signature Red Sporting has a red-dyed hardwood stock and fore-end. The pistol grip hardwood stock and fore-end are appropriately checkered and coated with what Winchester calls an all-weather "Dura-Touch" coating. You can buy this gun with 28- or 30-inch barrels and five choke tubes are included. The 30-inch barrel gives the gun a total length of 51 inches and a length of pull of 14⅜ inches. Drop at comb is 1½ inches and drop at heel is 2⅜ inches. This smoothbore weighs 8¼ pounds and retails for $976.00.

The X2 3-inch Sporting Clays also comes with a standard checkered, satin-finished hardwood stock and forend. Retailing for $959, other dimensions and accessories are the same as the Red Sporting.

You could certainly use the venerable Model 1300 Speed Pump 12-gauge pump-action for sporting clays. It features a TruGlo Tru-Bead front sight with mid-point bead for fast target acquisition and checkered, satin-finished walnut stock and fore-end. The 28-inch barrel comes with five supplied choke tubes and a vented rib barrel. This pump is 3-inch chambered and retails for $439.

Winchester's innovative Model 9410 is a lever-action .410-bore shotgun. I mention it here because it could be perfect for starting someone in sporting clays or perhaps getting a youngster up and running or – yes – even for a challenging afternoon for experienced shooters.

The 9410 comes in several models and three choke tubes (Full, Modified and Improved Cylinder) are included with each, as is a strong, T-style tube wrench. A walnut straight grip stock and forearm are standard on the Traditional 9410. The 20- or 24-inch barrel readily handles all current factory 2½-inch .410 shotgun loads. A modified shallow "V" adjustable rear sight is paired with a fiber optic TruGlo front sight. The total shell capacity is nine or 10 – depending on the loads used – including one in the chamber. Length of pull is 13½ inches while drop at comb is 1⅛ inches and drop at heel is 1⅞ inches. In Traditional styling with three chokes, this 6¾-pound .410 shotgun is offered at a suggested retail price of $645.

Stoeger (www.stoegerindustries.com)

The Model 2000 semiautomatic 12-gauge ($435) from Stoeger has a satin-finished walnut stock and forend. Its chrome-lined 26-, 28- or 30-inch barrels are proofed for steel shot and use a white bar sight on top of a vented rib as an aiming point. Equipped with the 30-inch barrel, it is 51¼-

"Spend a thousand dollars or so on an MP233 Sporting," EAA says, "and place the rest in a savings account and you will have all the gun you need." The Russian-made MP233 over/under 12-gauge has a removable trigger for cleaning, cast-off stock with palm swell and ported, hammer-forged barrels.

The Rizzini Artemis DeLuxe 12-gauge for sporting clays features a pistol-grip stock with palm swell and target fore-end in extra-select walnut. It comes cased in a cloth sleeve. Barrel lengths are 28, 29, 30½, or 32 inches.

inches long and weighs seven pounds, three ounces. It will accept 2¾- and three-inch shells and has a 14½-inch length of pull. The Model 2000 comes with Cylinder, Improved Cylinder, Modified, Improved Modified and Full chokes. Stoeger also sells a slightly lighter synthetic stock model ($420) with either 26- or 28-inch barrels.

Stoeger's Condor Supreme Deluxe ($500) comes in 12- and 20-gauge version with a selective trigger and automatic ejectors. Barrels for the 12-gauge gun come in 26- and 28-inch lengths while the 20-gauge also has a 24-inch barrel. Barrels are topped with a vented rib and red-bar sight. This shotgun comes with Improved Cylinder and Modified screw-in chokes. A 12-gauge with a 28-inch barrel is 44 inches long and weighs 7.8 pounds. All models have a 14½-inch length of pull.

Browning (www.browning.com)

The star of Browning's 2004 shotgun line is its new Cynergy 12-gauge, which has a suggested retail price of $2,690 for the Grade I with walnut stock and forend and just $40 less for the composite. Except that the stock of the composite model is adjustable – an important difference to be sure – these eight-pound over/unders have practically identical specifications: ported, back-bored barrels in 28, 30 or 32 inches with shell ejectors. Each has a tapered top rib of 5/16 to 7/16 inch with a HiViz Pro-Comp front sight and white mid-bead. The chrome-plated chamber holds 2¾-inch shells and the gun has an overall length of 45 to 49 inches depending on the length of the barrel. Critical dimensions include a length of pull of 14¼ inches, a drop at comb of 1⁹/16 inches and a drop at heel of 2⅜ inches. Special features include a low-profile silver nitride receiver with stylistic engraving, interchangeable new Inflex Recoil Pad system in three sizes, and a choke set with Full, Modified and Improved Cylinder tubes.

A mid-range Citori is a step down in price from the new Cynergy, and Browning recommends several Citori over/unders for sporting clays. The new $2,648 Citori XS Special 12-gauge

is available with 30- or 32-inch ported barrels. Top and side ribs are ventilated. The floating top rib tapers from eight to 11 mm and comes with a HiViz Pro-Comp sight and mid bead. Five extended chokes are supplied: Modified, Light Modified, Improved Cylinder, Cylinder and Skeet. The satin finish on the adjustable stock and fore-end plus a silver nitride receiver and gold-plated trigger make this a handsome gun. It is chambered for 2¾-inch shells and weighs about 8½ pounds.

The $4,027 Citori XS Pro-Comp 12-gauge is a true "step up to the line" over/under shotgun. It has ported barrels, an adjustable comb, right hand palm swell, removable tungsten-alloy forearm weight and movable/removable barrel weight. Like the XS, the Browning Triple Trigger system lets you choose three different trigger types. It comes with 28- or 30-inch ported barrels and weighs about nine pounds.

We need to also mention the venerable Citori 525 Sporting over/under because it is available in 12, 20, 28 and .410. You can order the 12- and 20-gauge models with an adjustable comb, and five extended chokes are supplied: Modified, Light Modified, Improved Cylinder, Cylinder and Skeet. The 12- and 20-gauge guns are available with 28-, 30- and 32-inch barrels except for the 28 and .410, which come in 28- and 30-inch lengths. All four gauges have a 14¾-inch length of pull and cost about $2,650. Expect an oiled finish on the walnut stock and forend and a lightly-engraved, silver nitride receiver. The upgraded version of this gun has high-grade walnut and more intricate engraving with gold inlay for a cool $4,236.

In the semiautomatic line, Browning's Gold Sporting Clays guns come only in 12-gauge with 28- or 30-inch ported barrels and three choke tubes: Modified, Improved Cylinder and Skeet. Each includes two interchangeable gas pistons for optimal performance with light or heavy loads. These pistons can be changed in minutes without tools, Browning says. The Gold "Golden Clays" gun has a 14¼-inch length of pull, a silver nitride receiver with handsome engraving, and a price tag of $1,596. At $1,033, the Gold gun is a basic model, while the

As the U.S. is increasingly incorporated into the European (and perhaps the world) economies as an equal partner, you can expect to see more international shotguns banging away at clay birds than just Perazzis or Krieghoffs. FAIR imports the Italian-made LX 600 Sporting in both 12- and 20-gauge models.

Tristar imports its Silver Series 12-gauge over/unders from Spain. The Silver Sporting features an automatic ejector, single selective trigger, channeled broadway vented rib and ported barrel with target bead. Available barrels are 28 or 30 inches.

shorter (13½-inch length of pull) Gold Ladies model is available only with a 28-inch barrel for $966. All three of these guns weigh just a little more than 7 ½ pounds.

Ithaca (www.ithacagun.com)

The folks at Ithaca Gun in New York say you can have fun shooting competition games with a pump, and besides, it is excellent practice for the field. Pump-action guns are not shot in truly serious competition, but you do see them in the friendly rounds when friends get together on the weekend.

Available in 12-, 16- and 20-gauge, the Ithaca Deluxe and Classic series are built with vented rib barrels and three, flush-mount choke tubes. Raybar sights and brown or sunburst recoil pads are standard. English straight or pistol-grip stocks can be selected. Barrels to have extended forcing cones, a nice touch. The Sporting Clays 12-gauge has a three-inch chamber and barrel lengths of 28 and 30 inches. Expect to pay less than the $1,995 suggested retail price.

Caesar Guerini/Guerini USA (www.caesarguerini.com)

Here is another fine Italian shotgun manufacturer from Brescia, the ancestral home of Perazzi, among others. Relatively new to the US scene, Guerini's Summit Sporting and Magnus Sporting over/unders in 12- or 20-gauge are handsome and effective . They feature a lifetime warranty, too. Guerini USA says that each gun is balanced approximately one centimeter in front of the hinge pin for increased stability in the hand.

The Turkish walnut stock and Schnabel-style forearm of the Summit ($2,650) are checkered and oiled to a high luster. The 14¾-inch stock is cut to a pistol grip design with a right-hand palm swell. Guerini says that the included stock wrench allows you to remove the stock without removing the recoil pad.

The Summit's long dual forcing cones are designed to optimize performance in barrels that have a ventilated side rib for rapid cooling and a 10 mm parallel target top rib with

double beads. Each Summit comes with extended, screw-in competition chokes tuned for sporting clays. Look for automatic ejectors with oversized cams. Barrels and chamber are chrome-lined.

The Summit's receiver has a "Tinaloy" double nickel finish and a "classic French Grey" appearance. The gold-plated, single selective trigger is adjustable up to one half inch to accommodate different-sized hands. It is chambered for a 3-inch shell.

The Magnus Sporting ($3,395) has all of the features of the Summit with upgraded wood and sidelock-style receiver instead of a boxlock. The receiver is embellished with fine scroll engraving featuring gold game birds. Each Guerini shotgun comes in a lockable fitted hard case.

Franchi (www.franchiusa.com)

These fine Italian guns began showing up in the U.S. after World War II. Today, Franchi is part of the Benelli USA business family along with Uberti's classic reproductions and Stoeger. Extended, knurled chokes are supplied for the 30-inch ported barrels of Alcione shotguns in Improved Cylinder, Modified and Full. (Improved Modified and Cylinder are also available.) Textured walnut stocks have full pistol-grip styling. Additional common elements of the Alcione over/under and semi-auto include a length of pull of 14¼ inches and front and mid-barrel bead sights. Both of these gun models are supplied with a custom-fitted hard case and cleaning kit.

The Alcione SL Sport 12-gauge over/under ($1,650) weighs 7.7 pounds. It is 47 inches long, has a 2¼-inch drop at heel and 1⅜-inch drop at comb. Sideplates on the receiver are handsomely engraved. It is also available for left hand shooters with cast-on in the buttstock. The safety and gold-plated trigger are mechanical. If you want to compete in sub-gauge events, Franchi sells an interchangeable 20-gauge barrel set.

For fans of semiautomatics, the Alcione 612 Sport 12-gauge ($975.00) is 51 inches long, weighs 7.1 pounds and has a 2½-inch drop at heel with a 1½-inch drop at comb.

Charles Daly (www.charlesdaly.com)

This Pennsylvania firm imports fine 12-gauge over/unders from Italy and semi-automatics and pump-action guns from Turkey. Their Superior II Sport ($1,589) and Empire II Sport ($1,949) have internally-honed, chromed and polished barrels that hold up to plenty of shooting with lead or steel shot. Look for factory porting, a 10 mm ventilated rib with dual front (fiber optic) and mid-point aiming beads and five multi-chokes for the 28- or 30-inch barrels. The receiver of the Superior II features gold clay bird inlays while the Empire II has etched decorative scrollwork, single, selective gold-plated triggers, and walnut stock and forend.

The Charles Daly Superior II Sport 12-gauge ($599) gives you three multi-chokes (Full, Modified, Improved Cylinder) in 28- or 30-inch factory ported interchangeable barrels that are internally honed and polished. A wide, 10 mm ventilated rib has a mid-bead and fluorescent bead front sight. Stock and forearm are Turkish walnut.

Beretta (www.berettausa.com)

You see a lot of Berettas at the sporting clay shooting stands because this fine company offers an excellent selection of fine guns at a variety of price levels.

At the top of the line is the $6,383 Trident Sporting with over/under barrel lengths available in 28-, 30- and 32-inch lengths and the new $7,797 Trident L Sporting with 30- or 32-inch barrels. Both of these eight-pound 12-gauge guns have a high gloss walnut stock and Schnabel forend. Look for a field-removable trigger group with gold-plated single selective adjustable trigger. Rich, floral engraving decorates the receivers, which are chambered for 3-inch shells. Barrels have a raised, flat top rib (3/8 x 5 1/16-inch), and both top and side ribs are vented to promote rapid heat loss. The standard aiming points are a front white dot and mid-rib bead. Drop at comb is 1½-inches and drop at heel is 2⅓-inches. Five chokes are included, as is a fitted hard-sided case.

The beautiful EELL Diamond Pigeon Sporting is available in all gauges for $6,207. After that, Beretta steps down its over/under line gradually, reducing the sticker shock and the elegance of a gun's presentation. Expect to pay $3,485 for the Gold E Sporting 12-gauge and between $2,547 and $4,892 for the Pigeon-grade sporting guns, but in this class, you have a selection of 12, 20, 28 and even .410! The 687 EL Gold Pigeon II Sporting Combo ($5,720) gives you 30-inch barrels in 28-gauge and .410. Beretta's over/under entry-level gun, at least in terms of price (its performance would cause it to be a top-of-the-line gun in some other manufacturer's offerings), is the 686, which retails for $2,008 in 12- or 20-gauge. And at $1,856, the new 686 White Onyx Sporting comes only in 12-gauge but still includes a beautiful walnut stock and forend, five choke tubes and a fitted, hard-sided carry case.

For lovers of semi-autos, the Beretta Teknys Gold Sporting ($1,653) and Urika Gold Sporting ($1,377) will still throw lead accurately while softening the felt recoil of a shot. Both guns feature overbored 12- and 20-gauge barrels with flat, floating ribs. The Teknys comes with a fiber optic TruGlo sight while the Urika has a white front bead. Triggers are gold plated and stocks and forends are select walnut. These guns are built with a 3-inch chamber, and the 12-gauge Teknys models are fitted to accept a special 8½-ounce stock recoil reducer. The Urika stock is designed to accept the recoil reducer as an option.

Remington (www.remington.com)

The only gun in the Remington catalog that specifically carries the "competition" sporting clays label is Remington's versatile semiautomatic Model 1100 Sporting gas gun in 12, 20, 28 and .410. The soft-recoil action of these gas guns cuts down on shoulder fatigue, keeping you fresh and, as Remington says, "gives you an edge over the competition."

Stocks and forearms are semi-fancy American walnut finished with a high gloss. The 12- and 20-gauge guns ($878) have 28-inch barrels. The new 28-gauge and .410 ($901) have 27-inch barrels. All barrels are fitted with light, contour vent-ribs with a white Bradley front bead sight and steel mid bead. The receiver and barrel are blued and highly polished. The trigger is gold-plated.

These semi-autos have a four-shell magazine capacity and come with four extended choke tubes (Skeet, Improved Cylinder, Light Modified and Modified).

The eight-pound 12-gauge measures 49-inches and has a 14 3/16-inch length of pull. The 20, 28 and .410 have 14-inch pulls. The 20 and 28-gauge guns weigh seven pounds and the .410 is 6½ pounds. All have 1½-inch drop at comb and 2½-inch drop at heel.

Remington's satin-blued Model 332 over/under ($1,624) could easily work for sporting clays and undoubtedly many do show up in the box. The 332 is 12-gauge-only with a 3-inch chamber, front and mid-rib aiming beads on a raised, 8 mm vented rib and three high strength chrome-moly steel barrel lengths: 26, 28 and 30 inches. Other features include a handsome walnut stock and fore-end with deep finger grooves and fully brazed side ribs for a solid barrel/mono-block assembly. The 332 comes equipped with Improved Cylinder, Modified and Full chokes and automatic ejectors.

SKB (www.skbshotguns.com)

This century-and-a-half old Japanese manufacturer pretty much covers the waterfront with its new 85TSS over/under, available in 18 models with multi-gauge sets available in eight models.

The 12-gauge 85TSS ($1,949) is chambered for a 3-inch shell and features your choice of barrels: 28, 30 or 32 inch. Barrel length determines the precise weight of the gun at approximately one ounce added weight per inch. The "85" with a 32-inch barrel weighs eight pounds, nine ounces. Each top barrel carries a nickel center post and bright Hi-Viz Comp-Sight. The ventilated step rib is 12 mm wide. Barrels are available with Mag-Na-Port's "Pigeon Porting" as an option (about $200). A system of screw-in chokes is available and three tubes (Skeet 1, Skeet 2 and Modified) are included.

All SKB shotguns have lengthened forcing cones that provide a much more gentle transition for the shot column. The lengthened forcing cone leads to better downrange performance by diminishing pellet deformation and is responsible for a reduction in felt recoil. (The forcing cone is the transition immediately forward of the chamber. Typically, a shotgun has an abrupt diameter change from the chamber into the bore.)

All 12-gauge "85" over/under barrels are backbored. In other words, the interior bore is slightly enlarged. In the 12-gauge, the nominal SAAMI bore diameter is .729. SKB 12-gauge "85" over/unders are oversized to a nominal bore diameter of .735. (Instead of starting with a .729 bore and removing metal to create the larger diameter, SKB manufactures a .735 bore to begin with. SKB claims that this maintains the barrel's strength.) Oversized bores allow the wad to spread, slightly reducing friction as it travels the length of the bore. The benefits are denser and more evenly distributed patterns and a reduction in felt recoil.

The walnut stock of the "85" is available with a fixed or an adjustable comb for an additional $200. The stock and essential dimensions are a 14½-inch length of pull, 1⅝-inch drop at heel and 1⅝-inch drop at comb. A high grade walnut stock costs an additional $400.

Ljutic (www.ljuticguns.com)

Well-known on the trap circuit, the firm's $19,995 LM6 series over/unders with select-grade walnut stocks and fore-grips and custom hand-checkering are still built to individual customer specifications, resulting in a gun with whatever critical stock dimensions you require. Barrels are available in 28- to 32-inch lengths, and interchangeable choke tubes are available.

Total Ljutic gun weight is about 8¾ pounds. Many sporting clays competitors favor such heavy guns, both for their smoother swing and lessened recoil. Multiple barrel sets are offered as an option, raising the price to $26,995. One of Ljutic's more interesting options is in the trigger mechanism. It can be supplied in pull/pull, release/pull, or release/release fashion.

Krieghoff (www.krieghoff.com)

"The challenge of sporting clays," Krieghoff says, "lies in the fact that you start with a dismounted gun and shoot at a nearly infinite variety of targets. Whether you are on an English sporting course or a FITASC parcours, the game requires a fine balance between the well-honed instincts of a good wing shot and the controlled, measured performance of a clay target veteran."

This manufacturer's K-80 Sporting 12-gauge over/under, chambered to accept either 2¾ or 3-inch shells, is available with a host of options and personal adjustments. The single selective trigger is adjustable for length of pull and weight (from 3½ to four pounds). This gun weighs 8¾ pounds and comes with a fitted aluminum case with slots for extra barrels. A standard grade K-80 Sporting with five choke tubes and a hard-sided case costs $8,595 from duPont/Krieghoff in Vero Beach, Florida, as of March, 2004.

Three barrel lengths are available for the K-80: 28-, 30- or 32-inch. Both stacked barrels accept choke tubes, five of which are provided: Skeet, two Improved Cylinder, Modified and Improved Modified. Other choke constrictions are available from Krieghoff. You may choose from two rib configurations, tapered flat (12 to eight mm) or eight mm. Ribs have a white pearl front and metal center bead.

Krieghoff stocks are cut from walnut in multiple standard configurations. The Sporting International stock has 14⅜" length of pull, drop at comb of 1⅝ inches and drop at heel from between 2¼ to 2¾ inches. The fore-arm is schnabel-styled.

You can shoot sporting clays with a K-20 over/under as well. This standard grade 20-gauge weighs in at $8,595. Just for fun, the K-20 with three-barrel set (20-, 28-gauge and .410), with five choke tubes per barrel and a three-barrel case, is priced at a hefty $16,105.

Lanber (www.lanber.net)

A 40-year-old Spanish manufacturer, Lanber offers several 12-gauge over/under smoothbores that are certifiable clay-busters. The Model 2097 comes with 28- or 30-inch barrels and 2¾- or 3-inch chambers. Its pistol-grip stock and Schnabel forearm are cut from polished walnut. The gun is 44½-inches long, has a 14⅜-inch length of pull, a 1⅜-inch drop at comb, and a 2⅛-inch drop at heel. The front sight on the vented rib is a white bead, and the side rib is vented.

Lanber 12-gauges such as the models 2089 and 2098 are available with 28 or 30-inch barrels. The elevated, vented rib is topped with a red bead aiming point, and Lanber opens the spaces between the barrels as much or more than most other manufacturers for rapid heat dissipation. Length of pull is 14.6 inches.

Rizzini USA (www.rizziniusa.com)

As is true of many high quality manufacturers, most Rizzini over/under shotguns can be used successfully on clay targets. Still, Rizzini has been building over/unders for 40 years, and five of its models are specifically designated as sporting clay weapons.

Rizzini's Vertex Sporting, S2000 Sporting, Artemis DeLuxe, S790 EL and Premier Sporting are all 12-gauge smoothbores chambered to accept 2¾-inch and 3-inch shells. Barrels come in the same lengths for these guns (28, 29, 30½ and 32 inches), chokes are fixed or interchangeable, and the top rib is .394-inches wide. The Premier has a 34-inch barrel option. Top and side ribs are ventilated. Drop at comb is 1½ inches while drop at heel is 2⅛ inches. The pistol-grip stock with palm swell and target fore-end in select, hand-checkered walnut are common to each of these guns, as is their 7¾-pound weight. You have a choice of chrome-plated or blued action, and the trigger's length of pull is adjustable. Expect your gun to be fitted with automatic ejectors and to arrive in a hard-sided carrying case.

The Premier Sporting is also available in a 20-gauge model and, while other critical dimensions are the same as above, its weight is about half-a-pound less.

Rizzini is justifiably proud of its optional 360-degree adjustable comb ($280 extra). This comb adjusts up and down, and side to side and allows for the actual pitch of the comb to be adjusted also.

You may wonder how, with so many identical specifications, how these models differ. The difference seems to be in the quality of the wood in the stock and forend and the engraving on and around the receiver. The Vertex ($1,890), Premier Sporting ($2,650, except for the 34-inch barrel Premier which has a parallel comb stock and costs $2,850), S2000 ($3,575), Artemis Deluxe ($5,475) and S790 EL ($6,600) are all equipped with long forcing cones and five extended chokes.

EAA (www.eaacorp.com).

John Bernkrant calls his import business EAA or European American Armory Corporation. Headquartered in Florida, EAA imports a wide variety of shotguns, pistols and rifles. His basic models for sporting clays shooting are the Baikal IZH27 Sporting and the Baikal MP233 Sporting. The EAA philosophy is to import a good, reliable gun: "If you want a label," John says bluntly, "a big name, a wall hanger, a fancy catalog, or a fancy carry case, buy the competition's gun."

The IZH27 over/under ($629) comes in either 12- or 20-gauge with a 3-inch chamber. The 29½-inch factory-ported barrels come with two sight beads and three screw-in chokes:

Improved Cylinder, Modified and Full. Features include a single selective gold-plated trigger, automatic selective ejectors (which may manually be switched to extractors), a vent rib, a walnut cast-off stock with palm swell and pistol grip, walnut forearm and rubber butt pad. In either gauge the 7½-pound IZH27 has a 14½-inch length of pull, 45½-inch overall length, 1½-inch drop at comb and 2½-inch drop at heel. The polished nickel receiver is lightly engraved.

The MP233 12-gauge ($899) is essentially the same gun as its cousin, the IZH27, except that the single selective trigger assembly with coil springs is removable for cleaning and care.

AYA (www.aya-fineguns.com).

Even if you cannot pronounce the Spanish manufacturer Aguirre y Aranzabal you may know these fine shotguns as AYA. In the Basque Country of northern-most Spain, this company has been in business since 1915 with sales – as of April of 2004 – approximating a million guns, mostly side-by-sides. According to the European mindset, the way an instrument looks is as important as how it shoots, and even though the action and mechanics of the low-priced and high-priced guns are the same, the higher price can be many thousands higher because of engraving, specialty woods and gold inlays. Gun-makers ask for an eight-month (or greater) lead-time to craft an AYA to your precise specifications.

AYA says its Coral, Coral de Luxe or Excelsior over/unders are fine for sporting clays, but the Excelsior is an especially handsome gun. AYA says the Excelsior in 12 or 20-gauge has true sidelock, forged steel action. This gun comes with or without automatic ejectors, with double or single (selective or non-selective) triggers and with your choice of 28-, 29- or 30-inch barrels. The pistol-grip stocks and forends are custom built from select walnut. Five chokes are available from Full to Cylinder. The gun weighs about 7 pounds, 11 ounces.

As an example of the cost and specifications of an AYA, an MD-6 over/under 12-gauge with 30-inch barrels, vented top and middle rib with "Rose and Scroll" engraving was being offered for $6,095 from New England Custom Gun Service (www.newenglandcustomgun.com) in March, 2004. This gun weighed 7 pounds 14 ounces and featured a 14⅞-inch length of pull.

Tristar Sporting Arms (www.tristarsportingarms.com)

Tristar imports firearms and accessories from the European community of nations – shotguns, rifles, pistols and replica guns.

Tristar says that ownership of one of their Breda series shotguns from Brescia, Italy "confers prestige on its owner." The Mira Sporting 12-gauge semi-auto ($950) has a high gloss finish on the walnut buttstock and forearm. It comes with five choke tubes, a 30-inch chrome-lined barrel and wide, 10 mm vented rib. Stock spacers to alter the drop and pitch of the stock are provided. The seven-pound Mira Sporting shoots either 2¾ or 3-inch shells.

The new 7½-pound Breda series Pesago Sporting 12-gauge over/under ($3,644) has an adjustable and removable trigger group. The oil finished walnut stock and fore-end are hand-checkered. The blued receiver features a 3-inch chamber, removable trigger group and automatic ejectors. The Pesago's 30-inch barrels are topped with a wide 11 mm rib. Both top and side ribs are vented. Five chokes are standard, as is an ABS fitted case.

Tristar offers several over/unders of upgraded Italian

design. The TR series Royal ($1,319) offers a silver finish with gold engraving on the side of the receiver, three chokes and a semi-fancy, straight-parallel walnut stock. You may buy the 7¾-pound TR-Royal with 28- or 30-inch barrels. Vented top and side rib, automatic ejectors and 2¾-inch chambers. The TR-SC has a silver-finish engraved frame with 3-inch chamber and a vented, 10 mm rib. The TR-L has the same features as the SC, but is dimensionally designed with a 28-inch barrel for female shooters.

The new Valmet 512 SC Sporting 12-gauge over/under ($1,160) is available with 28-, 30- or 32-inch barrels. This gun is backbored and the barrels are chrome-lined. Other features include a 3-inch chamber, ventilated top (11 mm) and side ribs, ejectors, five choke tubes, and a luminous red front sight bead with brass middle bead.

The Spanish-made Silver Series Sporting over/under is specifically designed for heavy duty sporting clays shooting ($899) and is branded by Rizzini. It features automatic ejectors, a single selective trigger, 28- or 30-inch ported barrels and a 2¾-inch chamber. Tristar says this 7½-pound gun is steel shot compatible.

F.A.I.R. (www.fair.it)

There seems to be a "thing" about fine Italian-made shotguns. Following Perazzi's lead, FAIR of Brescia, Italy, has been making inroads into the top levels of U.S. competition.

FAIR offers at least seven over/unders for sporting clays. Depending on the model, they are offered in 12- and 20-gauge: Jubilee 702 (12/20), Jubilee 700 (12/20), Master de Luxe (12/20), SRL 802 (12/20), LX 600 (12), LX 692 (12) and Premier (12). The 28-inch ported barrels are vented at top (11 mm for 12-gauge, nine mm for 20-gauge) and side. The pistol-grip stock and fore-end are hand-checkered walnut. Dimensions vary by model and shooter preference. Interchangeable chokes are available on request.

Diamond Guns (www.diamondguns.com)

Diamond is a division of ADCO Sales, headquartered in Massachusetts. You are probably familiar with the ADCO name from its well-advertised red dot sight. Modestly priced, gold engraved Diamond semi autos are occasionally seen at sporting clays shooting stands now that clays has grown in popularity. At this time, Diamond imports 12- and 20-gauge semi-autos and pumps, but the company says that 28s and .410s are on the way.

A Gold Series Diamond semi-auto costs about $549 at full retail. The stock and fore-end can be ordered in Turkish walnut or black matte polymer. The gun handles 2¾- or 3-inch loads and the chrome-lined, 28-inch barrel comes with three slotted choke tubes and a choke tube wrench.

Century International

Located in Boca Raton, Florida, Century imports Khan shotguns. Over/unders fall under the Arthemis line and the semi-autos are called Centurions. Stocks and forearms are made of Turkish walnut, and the chrome-lined 28-inch barrels are machined from 4140 steel. Arthemis over/unders are available in all four popular gauges with a 10 mm top rib, schnabel forend, single selective trigger and five choke tubes with wrench. The 45-inch, 7⅓-pound 12-gauge over/under with 3-inch chamber, gold inlay and Monte Carlo stock comes in right around $400. A similar Centurion semi-auto will set you back about $279.

SPORTING CLAY LOADS

Sporting clays has been referred to as "golf with a shotgun," and the description is an apt one. No other shotgun game can match the diversity of shots with which you'll be confronted in sporting clays, nor will the speeds and distances at which those targets are encountered be found anywhere else.

For that reason, there is no such thing as the "ideal sporting clays load." When you stop to consider that the shot being addressed at the moment may be broken 10 yards off the gun, and the presentation at the next station could be 50 yards out, it becomes obvious that one load cannot do it all.

The best choice in a 50-yard load could easily be the worst for a 10-yard shot. The longer bird will require heavier shot pellets to maintain striking power, plus a dense pattern and a very short shot string to get the pellets concentrated at the target. At 10 yards, the shooter will be best served with a very fast-opening load, and shot size is unimportant. Even the smallest shot will smoke a clay target at that range, assuming the pattern can find it.

Change that scenario to a 25- or 30-yard shot, and either of the above "ideal" loads would be a poor choice!

Load Selection Is Important

Most sporting clays shooters are well aware of the need to be equipped with a selection of interchangeable choke tubes to handle varying distances. The knowledgeable shooters are also becoming aware that they must give equal thought to the selection of shells they carry. In fact, many experienced shooters feel that a minimum of three different loads – short-, medium- and long-range – is a minimal approach. Most favor five distinctly different loads, varying in shot size, payload weight, velocity and even shot hardness.

For shooters looking to build a versatile shell selection, you can certainly find it represented within the selections offered by the various ammo makers. Often, however, for the reasons we will discuss below, simply buying someone's "sporting clays" load may not give you the best shell for the job. Here is what is available for the various shot problems you will encounter on a good sporting clays course.

Ultra-Short Range

Although extremely close-range shots (under 10 yards) are not as common in sporting clays as they are in skeet, they certainly occur, and the most effective shell is not hard to define. You need one that opens the pattern quickly. A shooter with a 12-inch pattern will have considerably more chance to break a tight target than one with a five-inch pattern. Shot size is not a critical requirement here: any size target pellet will do. Since #9 shot packs the largest pellet count per load, it is the odds-on favorite. This size shot also exhibits the tendency to pattern less tightly than larger, sturdier pellets, making it a doubly good choice.

Sporting clays competition may be the most exciting shotgun sport in the world unless you are a fan of the more expensive European import, hélice. Fortunately for shooters who scalp from their local BoxMart and for those who prefer premium loads, there's a great deal of ammo to choose from.

Remington's Premier STS Target and Premier Nitro Gold Sporting Clay Target Loads are developed specifically for clay shooting and are available in all loads needed to bust birds with consistent success.

Kent Velocity Diamond Shot is available for 12-, 20- and 28-gauge. This is a versatile load for the 12-gauge. #K122SL32-8 uses a spreader wad for 1⅛ ounces of #8 lead.

Remington's Express Extra Long Range Loads are available from 12-gauge to .410 in #7½. The 12- and 20-gauge are also available in #9.

Regardless of the choke in use, and without resorting to custom "spreader" wads, there are three basic ways to increase close-range pattern spread: use soft shot, which tends to deform under firing pressures and produces a lot of out-of-round pellets that become fliers; increase velocity, which results in essentially the same thing if less than ultra-hard shot is used, and will even encourage some pattern spreading with #9 shot,

regardless of its hardness; or opt for shells with fiber wads instead of modem one-piece plastic shotcups. These will also open patterns. Any one of these factors alone can increase pattern size. Combine a couple of them, and it can make a noticeable difference at close range.

One easy way to accomplish this is to stock up on the ubiquitous promotional ("Dove & Quail") loads that dot the BoxMarts at the beginning of each fall season. These generally toss a one-ounce charge of shot, not as hard or as precisely formed as those produced by premium target loads, at velocities around 1,300 fps. Their inability to deliver tight patterns is legendary and that makes them an excellent and inexpensive choice for ultra-close sporting targets. The fact that they carry only a one-ounce charge makes no difference because there are more #9 pellets in a one-ounce load than you need at ultra-close range anyway. All you have to do is get the pattern to open quickly, and these are some of the fastest-opening factory-loaded shells available. Their patterns may be as full of holes as a rusty bucket at 30 yards, but they work very well up close.

Another option would be any of the high velocity (1,300-plus fps) target loads carrying one ounce or less of plain lead shot. Not as effective as Dove & Quail loads, these are a much better bet than premium target loads that are intended to throw dense, uniform patterns.

Practically any of the skeet #9 or #8½ loads will work well for ultra-close shooting, especially with an open choked gun and a shell that it fitted with a brush-style wad that allows the pattern to open immediately.

Close Range

Many shots on a sporting range will fall within 10 to 20 yards, and effective shells for these are easy to find. Select any good #9 skeet load because this is precisely what they were designed to do. Again, those loads that we have talked about in the skeet chapter will be especially useful.

Reloading is a relatively simple task for shotshells. Seat the primer in the base. Pour in the powder. Seat the wad and fill it with shot. Then, crimp the top tight. Follow the directions in your reloading manual and you are ready to shoot.

Medium Range

Twenty to 30 yards probably represents the majority of the shots found on a sporting range and good shells for these are easy to find. Trap loads such as those discussed in the chapter on successful loads for trap shooting are ideal. This is the range at which the #8 loads were designed to operate at their best. On the shorter shots, some feel a one- or 1⅛-ounce load of #8½ shot is hard to beat. They have plenty of target-breaking power to a range approaching 35 yards. On the longer shots, #8 is superior. It will do the job out to about 40 yards. In either case, you benefit from the increased pellet count over loads using #7½. Some ammo makers offer #8 loads with a fiber wad, and they are also effective within this range.

Long Range

You get into handicap trap ranges at 40 to 45 yards, so it only makes sense that a heavy three-dram #7½ trap load would be an excellent choice, and it is. On the shorter side of the range, the 2¾-dram, "Lite" 1⅛-ounce, #7½ loads also work very well. Many manufacturers specify ultra-hard shot in fast cartridges for these ranges. Eley's VIP Sporting or Superb Competition, for instance, with relatively high antimony content, is an excellent choice.

Ultra-Long Range

The 45-plus-yard shots are some of the toughest shots you'll see on a sporting clays range, and not just because distant targets take a good punch to break. They also take a fast load

to catch! While the heavy handicap trap loads in #7½ are still a good bet, some shooters are finding that the International trap loads are a better choice. Although they start with only about ⅞-ounce of #7½ shot, their special shotcups and plated shot pellets give them a very tight-patterning ability at extreme range. Since most of them are moving at 1,300-plus fps, they are also an aid in cutting down the long leads required for those

Whatever loads and chokes you find suitable to your gun and your shooting style, some type of vest or even a bag or box such as this heavy-duty nylon Bob Allen four-box shell carrier will be your new best friend on a long sporting clays course.

extreme distances. In addition, they normally exhibit very short shot strings that get the most out of their smaller shot charge. They are gaining a lot of favor among sporting clays shooters when the targets get "way out there."

When it comes to breaking distant targets, the most effective shells will generally be those with nickel-plated shot. These are noticeably more expensive than shells containing other types of shot, but you will not need many of them in a round. They are well worth the extra cost when you need them.

Lyalvale's High Velocity Competition has not been mentioned but deserves notice. An English shell tested in international competition, these were first introduced in 1986 and have been upgraded virtually every year. The 1⅛-ounce, 2¾-inch shell comes in #7½, #8 and #9 and uses Vectan A1 as a single base, clean burning powder for this low base (⁵⁄₁₆ inch) 1,400 fps speedster.

Reloads and Components

While NSCA rules prohibit reloads at major matches, they allow them to be used at the club level, at the discretion of the club. The individual club rules on reloaded shells will understandably vary, and shooters will certainly want to inquire about them before taking the time to roll their own.

If your club allows them, handloads can allow the sporting shooter to create some specialty loads that you will not find readily available from the major makers. An enthusiastic sporting clays shooter himself, Dave Fackler of Ballistic Products (www.ballisticproducts.com), has come up with a number of interesting wad designs and has found a few more that he imports from Europe. They allow the reloader to craft effective custom loads and, coupled with BPI's Mica Wad Slick ($6.95 for eight ounces) to dust the wad and hull, will get the most out of every handload combination.

For ultra-close-range shots, even the soft-shot promotional loads are not going to give a large pattern inside 10 yards, although they will open up a good deal more than hard-shot target loads. Getting a pattern to open up very quickly, actually scattering the shot, is an advantage here. If you double the diameter of your pattern you do not just double your chances of getting the shot on target – you increase it by a factor of four. That is well worth the time spent making up some special "spreader loads," perhaps with a brush wad without a constricting shotcup.

Creating these specialty loads used to require inserting a separate component, either a cardboard X-spreader, or a spreader post, into a standard wad during the loading process. One can also cut the shot-protecting petals on a standard target wad back to about a quarter of their original length. These methods will still work, but there are easier ways to do it today.

The Ballistic Products 12-gauge G/BP Dispersor X-12 wad ($6.99 for a bag of 200) is a one-piece, easy-to-load wad with an integral X-spreader molded right into the shotcup. As the wad leaves the muzzle, the specially-designed petals fold back and allow the spreader to really get the pattern open quickly.

Another option is the G/BP 12-gauge Brush Wad ($5.79 per bag of 200), which is nothing more than a standard plastic wad without a protective shotcup. This was created to counter the rules some clubs have against wads with an X-spreader. Either of these wads can be loaded with one to 1⅛ ounces of shot, at various velocities. If softer grades of #9 shot are used, these wads will more than double the pattern size of conventional loads. The Dispersor is at its best under 15 yards, while the Brush Wad works well out to 20 yards.

Another option that is particularly useful in the close-range area is the G/BP Piston Skeet wad ($5.99 per bag of 200). This is a conventional one-piece target wad that uses a unique petal arrangement to promote fast-opening patterns in the 10- to 25-yard range. It is very popular with European international skeet shooters for that reason. This can be used with standard American components and makes a great skeet load. It is at its best with harder grades of shot and throws some wide yet uniform patterns from an open-choked gun. When loaded with #8 shot, it becomes a very useful shell for longer shots in the 20- to 30-yard range.

Mid-range shots can be handled quite well with standard trap load recipes, and they will be discussed in our reloading chapter.

Effective extra-long-range loads (45-plus yards) can be difficult to assemble from conventional target components, so a full shotcup is recommended. This style of wad will usually handle shot charges from one to 1⅛ ounces and is designed to produce maximum pattern density at extreme range. When loaded with #7½ nickel shot, it helps build a fine, extra-long-range load and will break 60-yard birds.

While toting a large and varied selection of shotshells may seem like a lot of trouble, it is one of the best ways to take the initiative on any sporting clays course. If you are going to "play golf with a shotgun," it makes sense to have all the clubs in your bag!

All shotgun sportsmen are aware that lead is an environmental contaminant. At this time, steel is rarely used on sporting clays courses and, except in rare instances, not at all in trap and skeet shooting. Still, the occasional sale or closing of a shooting range with tons of lead on and in the ground causes a great deal of debate and discussion among sportsmen, in government and in environmental circles. The use of steel or composites in all shotgun loads and the abandonment of lead may not be that far out on the horizon.

SEMI-AUTOS vs. OVER-UNDERS

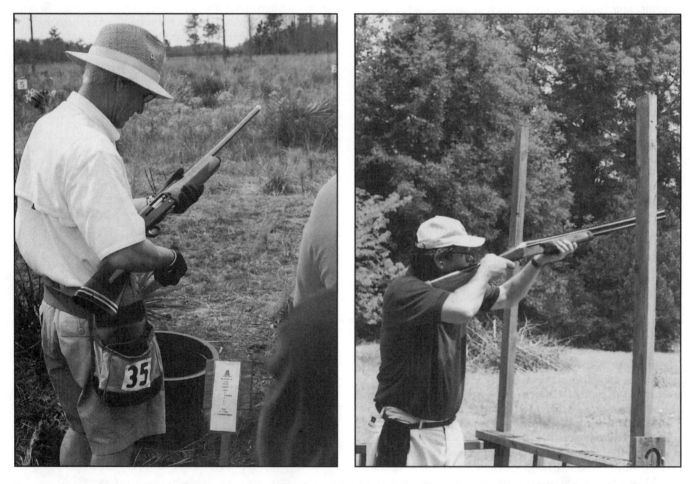

Over/unders such as the Krieghoff K-80 that author Rick Sapp (right) is shooting have the reputation of being better handling smoothbores than most semi-automatics. On the other hand, semi-autos demonstrably transfer less recoil to the shooter.

If your shooting goal is to improve your shooting skill in a duck blind or in the woods for grouse or woodcock, then you should shoot the gun you hunt with for every clay sport. There is no better way to learn what to expect from your gun and any combination of chokes and loads than by actually putting it all to the test in trap, skeet and sporting clays.

If, however, you intend to pursue any of the shotgun games for the fun and the challenge of quality competition, you will very quickly discover that there are only two shotgun types

that will take you into the winner's circle: a gas-operated semi-automatic or an over/under. That is not a knock on pumps or side-by-side doubles, just a simple statement of fact.

To excel, a shooter needs a gun that will reliably fire two shots, while allowing total concentration on the target. Pump guns such as the fine Winchester 1300 Sporting/Field ($439) require the shooter to manually chamber the second round. Some experienced scattergunners can do that with remarkable skill. Exhibition shooter Tom Knapp, who travels for Benelli and Federal Cartridge, has been making a living with fast-action pump guns for years. On the competition range however, even the best shot will score a couple of targets fewer per round with a pump than they would with the gas gun or over/under.

Side-by-side doubles such as a fine Merkel Model 47E ($3,790) can be lively handling smoothbores. They can get off two rounds very reliably. Unfortunately, the broad sighting plane offered by the twin barrels has been proven to give less precise leads on targets traveling on a largely horizontal plane, and that includes most game targets.

That pretty much leaves us with gas guns and over/unders, and the debate over the relative merits of each action type can be a lengthy one. Often that debate will generate far more heat than light. Which is the best choice?

Recoil

The uncomfortable but inescapable fact of recoil is one of the two biggest reasons shooters select a gas-operated semi-auto in preference to an over/under. The gas gun is commonly believed to have less felt recoil. If you are talking about factory guns right out of the box, that statement is probably true.

When a gas-operated semi-auto is fired, a small amount of propellant gas is bled off from the barrel through one or more small holes drilled into the barrel. The gas acts to operate a piston mechanism within the fore-end that mechanically forces the bolt to the rear. An extractor mounted on the bolt grips the rim of the fired shell to pull it out of the chamber as the bolt recoils. When the bolt has drawn the shell back far enough to strike a fixed piece of metal called the ejector, the shell is automatically kicked out of the gun. While all of that is going on, a new shell is released from the tubular magazine onto the shell carrier below the bolt. As the bolt moves forward under spring pressure the carrier rises to position the shell, and the bolt rams it into the chamber for the next shot.

That's a lot of mechanical "stuff" going on at one time.

Actual recoil depends on the weight of the gun and the power of the shell. Obviously, then, an eight-pound 12-gauge firing a 2¾-dram, 1⅛-ounce load will have less recoil than the same gun firing a 3¼-dram, 1¼-ounce shell.

The gas gun does not necessarily reduce the actual reaction from the exploding powder. What it does is retard it and spread it over a longer period. This makes a gas gun feel like it is a softer-kicking gun. You get a shove instead of the sharp rap that would be produced by a fixed-breech gun of the same weight firing the same load.

With that said, I will now point out that my 12-gauge Ruger Red Label over/under delivers less recoil punishment to my

The X-Coil all-weather Recoil Pad from Browning is a lightweight composite that can easily be fitted to your stock when you find your gun's recoil unacceptable. The X-Coil has a radiused heel for fast mounting and a surface texture that prevents slipping when you shoot in the rain.

shoulder than my 12-gauge Franchi Prestige gas gun when firing the same loads. With the Franchi, which is a very soft shooting gas gun, 100 rounds in an afternoon will have me reaching for an aspirin bottle as I leave the range. With the Red Label, I do not need the aspirin. How can this be so?

The reason is the difference between actual recoil (which can be measured in foot pounds of energy) and perceived or "felt" recoil, which is how our bodies react to recoil. The latter is the more important of the two, and is dependent on a number of factors including how well the gun fits the shooter and what cushioning material is present between the shooter and the gun.

Put another way, a heavyweight boxer who delivers a solid left hook to your jaw with his naked hand will injure you and perhaps his own hand severely. If that boxer is wearing a 16-ounce boxing glove, however, he will probably just knock you down and give you a headache. Nevertheless, the actual foot-pounds of energy (kinetic energy = ½ mass x velocity²) in the punch would be the same.

That is the case with my Red Label. It was fitted precisely to

The shotgun sports are essentially divided into two camps: advocates of over/unders and fans of semi-autos. The trick is to find the right fit and balance within your budget and shooting interests. With a little attention to fitting, all other arguments can be overcome or sidestepped.

me by stock fitter Jack West, and has a thick KickEeze recoil pad and his padded comb. The Franchi has a KickEeze pad as well, but no padded comb. The Franchi feels slightly softer on firing, but the Ruger feels better over the long run.

Any shotgun can have its felt recoil reduced noticeably in this manner. If the stock treatment is done to a gas gun, it will probably be a bit softer shooting than an over/under, but both can be made to produce less felt recoil than they did out of the box.

That is why the question of recoil between the two guns, in my mind, only comes into play if we are dealing with unaltered factory guns. In that case, the gas gun wins the recoil war. However, that should not be the reason for selecting one over the other. Each can be made to shoot soft enough so that any shooter can enjoy them.

Balance and Handling

This is one area where over/unders have a perceived advantage. The twin barrels poking out past the fore-end give more forward weight than the single barrel on a gas gun. This promotes a smoother swing, and one that is more difficult to stop once started. As a result, the targets are hit more often because follow-through is more effective.

The balance and handling qualities of any shotgun are determined by the way the weight of the gun is distributed. If there is a bit more muzzle weight, the gun tends to swing more smoothly. If there is more weight in the butt, the gun seems to mount more quickly but can be a little more "whippy" or loose on the swing. Over/unders tend to have a bit more muzzle weight and thus swing a bit more forcefully and positively.

You can, however, alter the balance of a gas gun to give you the same swing characteristics of an over/under.

If you want to add a little more muzzle weight, fill an empty shotshell with shot, crimp it, seal it with duct tape, and stick it in the forward portion of the tubular magazine in place of

the wooden plug that is already there. A 12-gauge shell full of shot will weigh 2½ to 3 ounces. The weight will lie forward of the leading hand and will promote a smoother swing. You can add up to three weights and customize each for your preferred balance.

However, what if you feel the muzzle is too heavy? Stick one or more of the shot-filled shells in the stock bolthole in the buttstock. It is that simple.

You can change the balance and handling qualities of the over/under as well. Just add weight where you need it, and there are many products on the market to make that easy. Meadow Industries "Barrel Buddy" attaches to the underside of the barrel and gives you the option of adding up to eight ounces of weight. It cannot be used with a semi-auto because it prevents the fore-end from sliding off the gun in the normal manner during takedown, but it works well for over/unders. Buttstock weight can always be added via shotshells (fired and shot-filled, not live shells) in the bolthole of the stock.

Few shooters will need to change the balance of their gas guns. Many makers are adding a bit more muzzle weight to semi-autos as they bring out specialized models.

In short, if you do not like the way the gun balances as it comes from the factory, you do not have to accept it. It is so easy to change that the discussion of balance and handling between the two gun types essentially becomes moot.

The One Choke Syndrome

If you shoot a gas gun, you have only one choke available at a time. If you shoot an over/under, you have a choice of two. This is often touted as a major advantage of the stack-barrel. Again, there is some truth in that, but not as much as many might suppose.

There are a number of clay target games where having only one choke is no handicap, such as ATA 16-Yard trap, and handicap trap. Every target is going to be broken within one

One knock on semi-autos is their relative mechanical complexity. If you take this gun apart for cleaning, unless you can do it blindfolded, perhaps you should label and tag the parts! In truth, giving a semi-auto a thorough cleaning is not that difficult, but it requires your complete attention.

For example, you are facing a Fur & Feathers presentation on a sporting clays course. It gives you a rabbit target at about 15 yards and a quartering-away aerial target that is supposed to be broken around 25 yards. The ideal choke for this would be a straight Cylinder choke for the rabbit and an Improved Cylinder for the bird. Or you can shoot them both with the Improved Cylinder or a Skeet 1 choke simply by using a quick-opening load of #9s in the first barrel and a 1⅛-ounce load of hard, target-grade #8s in the second barrel. The first load could be an inexpensive promotional load with soft shot, a spreader reload using one of the Ballistic Products wads designed for that, or perhaps a less expensive shell from the Remington Gun Club line, a GC12L. Quick-opening shells will give you as large a pattern as you are going to get at that range, regardless of the choke tube in the gun. The second load of hard #8s provides plenty of pattern density and individual pellet target-breaking power for the longer shot, even if you shot them from a straight Cylinder choke and for this shot, you might want the higher grade Remington Premier STS12L shot.

relatively narrow range, and one choke is fine. Ditto for the close shooting in American skeet.

The ability to use different chokes is often cited as a reason for the twin-barreled gun's popularity in sporting clays, but it is rare to find a station where the shots vary more than 10 yards in range difference. Regardless of whether they are singles, report pairs, true pairs, following pairs, or simultaneous pairs, once you know the range you can generally find one choke that is right for both birds.

One game where the shot array may present targets at wildly varying ranges from the same station is FITASC (Federation Internationale de Tir aux Armes Sportives de Chasse: one of two international governing bodies for shooting sports). Here, you step into a shooting station with your gun and loads, and must shoot whatever is presented with the chokes you have in the gun. You cannot change them once you step up to shoot. You may get a target at 15 yards and the next may be at 50. Shooting that game, it helps to have the versatility of two choke tubes readily available, but it is possible to make one choke serve multiple tasks.

How does a shooter make one choke do the work of two? Easy. By changing the loads in his or her shells. Many shooters assume that if they want the proper pattern for the range encountered, they must put the proper choke tube in the gun. That is not true. You can vary the pattern performance of your gun by simply changing your shells.

If that sounds confusing, consider this: in clay target games we do not grade the targets. All it takes to score a kill is to knock a visible piece off the target that the scorer can see. A target that is "inkballed" (powdered) counts no more than a target that is merely chipped.

If your load gives you that visible piece, no matter how small it may be, who cares what your actual pattern looks like?

A growing number of shooters are doing more shell changing than choke tube changing, even if they shoot an over/under.

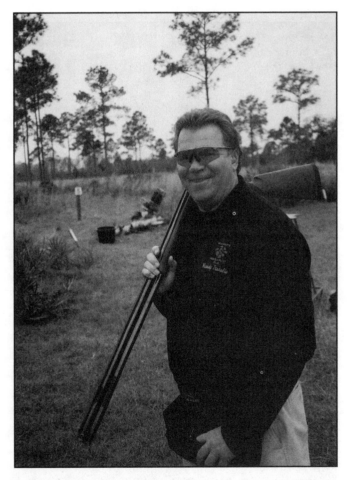

Randy Travalia, owner of the Horse & Hunt Club near Minneapolis, demonstrates another reason that most top shooters prefer an over/under. It's easy to carry!

To take an extreme example, think of a FITASC shot where you might have one bird at a bit under 20 yards and a second at a little over 45. Many would choke Skeet 1 in the first barrel with a load of #9s, and slip a Full choke tube in the second barrel with a load of #7½s. The single choke shooter, however, can accomplish the same thing with a Full or Improved Modified choke (you have to choke for the longer bird) and then effectively open up that barrel to a Skeet 1 choke by using one of the fast-opening loads for the closer bird. The spreader-type loads will usually open a Full choke to about Improved Cylinder and a Modified choke to about Skeet 1.

More subtle modifications can be made by altering the velocity and shot hardness of the loads. Soft shot at high velocity will usually pattern one complete choke wider than the tube you are using. Hard, target-grade shot at moderate velocity will often pattern a Full choke tighter.

Few sporting clays ranges throw shots beyond 30 yards, and a shooter with a single barrel gun can do just as well as a shooter with an over/under. If a farther target is thrown, choke for it, and use a spreader load to open patterns for any closer target.

The usefulness of spreader loads is the reason that a gas gun shooter is not at a disadvantage merely because the gun offers only one choke.

This covers the three most common reasons for making the selection of either an over/under or a semi-automatic gas gun. From my viewpoint, there is little real difference between them – at least so far. Now, let us get down to the real, nitty-gritty differences.

Reliability

The over/under wins here. No argument. In fact, the very best any gas gun shooter can do is to make his or her gun as reliable as an over/under. The reliability factor is very important in all shotgun games.

In some games, if you cannot fire on the target for any reason, you lose it. Other games will give you a certain number of "alibis" and allow targets to be re-shot. Even then, a limit exists and beyond that you lose targets.

A gun malfunction can also be devastating to your confidence and adversely affect your subsequent performance. It is very difficult for the subconscious mind to perform the tasks required to break a target if it is wondering if the gun will go off! A gun malfunction early in the game, or in the key later stages of a match, can cause you to miss subsequent targets even if the malfunction never recurs. A mind is a terrible thing to mess up and a malfunction can do it.

Because of the large number of moving parts and mechanical operations required, a gas gun will never be as reliable as a fixed-breech over/under. That is the biggest single reason why top competitors show a marked preference for the stack-barrel guns. If you can stuff the shell in the gun and close the action, the primer will be struck when the trigger is pulled. If the shell is any good, it will go off. Not so with gas guns. They can be working perfectly and still screw up!

The gas gun requires near-perfect ammunition, and the power level of the shell must be sufficient to operate the action,

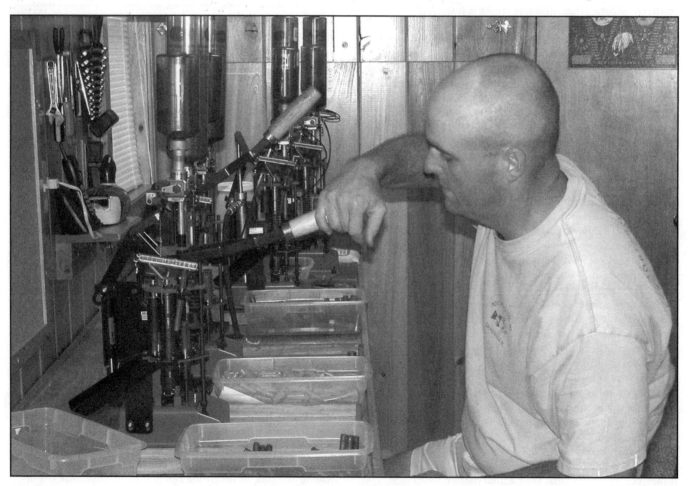

Virtually any shell you can shove into an over/under and have the primer go off will work in those guns, but semi-autos need near-perfect ammo to feed and extract smoothly. Reloaders must take extra care.

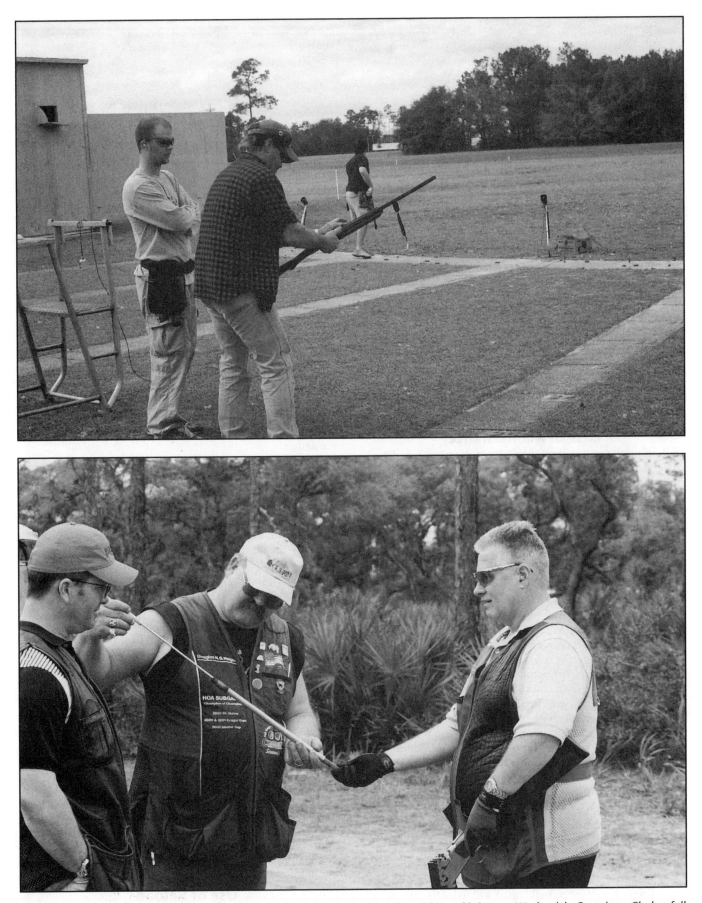

Regardless of the type of gun or the manufacturer, things go wrong. Murphy said it and it is true. Wads stick. Guns jam. Chokes fall in the dirt. Approaching a malfunction with a sense of humor will help you cope and the people around you will rally to your assistance, even if you are in a neck-and-neck shoot-off with them.

One thing all advocates agree on is that a side-by-side, regardless of its quality, does not usually provide the sharp sighting plane needed for competitive clay shooting. This Ruger Gold Label 12-gauge is a high quality side-by-side that is 45 inches long and weighs 6⅓ pounds.

yet not so powerful that it generates too much gas energy. That can cycle the action too fast and result in a failure to feed a second shell. I have light target loads that will run 100 straight on the skeet range in my Ruger Red Label, yet will not cycle the action on my Franchi.

If you reload, you must make certain that every shell is as perfect as a factory load. A hull that is worn, slightly out of round, or has a poor crimp may fail to feed and fire. That shell will operate just fine in an over/under though, if it will just fit into the chamber.

Gas guns must also be kept scrupulously clean if they are to even approach stack-barrel reliability, and that brings us to another factor:

Ease of Maintenance

Cleaning an over/under is simplicity in itself: unhook the fore-end, open the action, dismount the barrels, brush them out and reassemble. A little light lube on the ejector/extractor arms and the barrel hinge, and the gun is ready to kill pheasants or shoot another tournament.

Gas guns are more tedious. The fore-end must be removed, the barrel slid out of the receiver – with care taken not to lose any of the little O-rings found in most gas-operated systems. Then the piston has to come off and all the attendant parts laid out – and we are not done yet. Smart shooters also "drift" out the retaining pins that hold the trigger/shell carrier group in place (You do have a drift punch and small hammer, don't you?) and, for detailed cleaning, remove the bolt.

Now that the gun is disassembled, here are some potential problem areas:

1. Trigger/shell carrier. Flush it out with something like Outer's Crud Cutter and allow it to dry. Spray the assembly lightly with Break-Free or any similar lube before reassembling. The reason this part must be cleaned is that unburned powder flakes can work their way into crevices and tie up the shell carrier. Some powders are notorious for this. When that happens, your gun becomes a single shot. It is a common problem and an area many shooters neglect.
2. Scrub the barrel, naturally, but you're not finished yet. Pay particular attention to the gas ports. They can become clogged with carbon, reduce gas flow, and cause a feed malfunction. You will also need to remove plastic fouling from the chamber. This is left by the outer surface of the shell itself from heat generated upon firing. If allowed to build up, it will seriously impede the gun's ability to feed and extract shells. Standard bore cleaning solvents and brushes do not remove it. I use a bore brush wrapped with 0000 steel wool. Once

you scrub the chamber, leave it slick and dry! Oil in the chamber contributes to both feeding and extracting malfunctions.
3. Follow the manufacturer's instructions for cleaning the gas system. Some have certain lubrication "do's and don'ts." Remember to add some light lube to the action bars and the channels they ride in within the receiver. This is another area where unburned powder can cause the gun to foul.

That will handle routine cleaning. Every 10,000 rounds or so, it is advisable to take the gun to a good gunsmith for a thorough strip down and tank dunk cleaning.

Considering all of this, is it any surprise that most fine shooters who fire 10,000 to 30,000 rounds per year prefer over/unders?

Durability

Another win for the over/under. At the risk of offending a few gas gun makers, the most expensive gas-operated semi-auto made will not even come close to the lifespan of even a moderately priced (but well-made) over/under. No one can predict how many rounds each type gun will handle before it is ready for the scrap heap, but the very top competition gas gun shooters consider replacing them annually and have one or more backup guns on hand.

Ease of Repair

As a rule, the gas gun wins this one. This is especially true if you are shooting a well-known model that has been around for a few years, a gun like the Remington 1100 or the various Winchesters. You can likely find parts and service at your local gunsmith. He knows what small parts routinely break or wear out and keeps them in stock. Since gas guns are all designed for modern mass production with parts interchangeability, replacing parts is easy. When over/unders need repairs, they are more complex. Generally, it is best to send them back to the factory. If the gun is an American-made model with solid repair facilities, turn-around time can be relatively quick, but expect four to six weeks. If you have an expensive European model, repair time can sometimes stretch into many months.

On the plus side, over/unders seldom require minor repairs. When a well-made gun needs fixing it is generally after a lot of shooting, more than many shooters will do in two or three lifetimes!

Use of Reloads

The stack-barrel wins hands down on this one, for reasons that have already been mentioned. Another factor that comes into play, however, is that over/unders are easier on the shells

The cost of two styles of gun that will each accomplish the shooting task for clay games can be small or significant, even within the same product line. The new, moderately priced Beretta 686 White Onyx Sporting lists for about twice that of the corresponding semi-autos. The Xtrema, pictured in Realtree Hardwoods HD and tricked out for turkey hunting, is a similar gun to the Urika Sporting.

and you can generally squeeze a few more reloads per hull from them. Their mechanism does not ram the empties around and then toss them all over the ground. You just simply pluck them from the chambers and stick them in your pocket. That can be especially important if you are shooting on a range whose policy is "When a shell hits the ground, it becomes the property of the club."

Since most serious competitive shooters are reloaders, this has become one of the strong points in the over/unders favor.

Cost

The second biggest reason shooters choose semi-autos over over/unders is that they cost less to acquire than a good quality stackbarrel. The cost difference can be a significant factor for shooters on a budget, and that is something the shooter will have to decide. However, in some cases, that difference can be deceiving.

There are a number of budget-priced over/unders on the market, but they must be made with parts that are not the highest quality possible. In order to obtain an over/under with the quality needed to be a top competitive gun, you are looking at a suggested retail price of at least several thousand dollars. A smart shopper can generally save a few hundred dollars if he looks for the best "street price."

Quality gas guns like the Remington 1100, Browning Gold, Verona 692 Gold ($1,765) and Beretta models have a retail price that is a few hundred dollars less. The "street

price" philosophy also applies to them. (See for instance www.ozarkguns.com.)

If you are thinking of entering serious competition, the total difference in price of $800 to $1,000 may not be worth the increased inconvenience of the gas gun. That price difference is, after all, only about the equivalent of five to seven cases of shotshells. When you are talking about a gun you may want to keep, shoot, and possibly even invest a bit of money in
for custom fitting, that difference becomes a lot smaller. You are only talking about a few months' supply of shells as the price difference on a quality gun you may well pass on to your children.

Over/unders also hold their value. If you decide you want to change guns after 20,000 or so rounds, you will get a much larger percentage of your original purchase price back if the gun you are selling is a well-made over/under that has been cared for properly.

Try selling a gas gun that has gone 20,000 rounds and most knowledgeable shooters will not even look at it.

These last are the real reasons why over/unders dominate competitive clay target games.

This is certainly not meant to denigrate gas guns. With the exception of the reliability factor, they will hold their own with the over/unders when it comes to busting clay targets. Nevertheless, making a decision as to which type of shotgun to buy is more involved than that.

IF THE GUN DON'T FIT. . .

A ported barrel such as this Mossberg 500 pump will reduce "muzzle-jump" and help you get on a second bird faster than if all of the energy were in-line.

Pattern performance is crucial to shooting success, and any smoothbore operator who wants to get the most benefit out of every shot will spend time at the pattern board. (Photo courtesy Mossberg)

We Americans I believe still tend to see ourselves as rough-and-tumble people of the frontier with a close, personal relationship with our guns. Unlike most other places in the world, we hunt in great numbers. Even our electronic entertainment is full of gunfire. We buy guns for home defense. This becomes something of an ego problem when we confront the International versions of shotgun games, which tend to be a good bit more difficult than ours.

As Americans, we may have a tendency to jump to the "bang," the explosion, the result, the quick fix. By the millions, we go to the local BoxMart, buy a shotgun and a license and straightaway go out hunting. Consequently, the average shotgun owner rarely understands or has patience with the idea of fitting the gun to his body, his style, and his eyes. The idea of fitting is perhaps one of the details – such as fine engraving and scrollwork – that does not seem to belong in our western egalitarian environment. In this case, we have a lot to learn from "old Europe."

When we see a seven-foot college basketball player next to a retired five-foot computer programmer in a shoe store or an auto showroom, we naturally understand that they are buying shoes or vehicles built to different styles and patterns. One size does not fit all. The basketball player needs a sport utility vehicle with plenty of room for his long legs and size 13 feet. The computer programmer can get by very happily with an economical sub-compact. Why then is it a difficult concept that these two individuals would require differently fitted guns to consistently hit their target? One size gun does not fit all either.

Manufacturers are not concerned about the basketball player's personal dimensions any more than those of the computer programmer. They build to standardized patterns, patterns that are "generally acceptable" to the public as a whole. Browning and Beretta do not know who has a 35-inch sleeve or who has a 29-inch. They cannot know who wears thick glasses and who has high, bony cheekbones. Except for the most expensive or custom-produced guns – an Italian Perazzi or even an American Ljutic, for example – the average manufacturer cannot have every purchaser wait in line for individual measurements and stock modifications before he purchases a gun.

Many shooters have, through trial and error, learned to adapt to these one-size-fits-all guns, figuring out how to crawl their body around on the stock to get everything lined up perfectly … or at least lined up most of the time. They have also learned that they shoot better with some makes of guns than with others. This is because manufacturers do not all build to the same stock dimensions.

When a shooter finds a gun that truly fits or modifies one so that it fits, breaking targets becomes easier. Scores go up, and the world becomes a nicer place in which to live. The purpose of shotgun fitting is to allow you and your gun to see the very same sight picture and to make this as natural as possible. You break more targets and everyone is happy, except maybe your competitors.

Master shotgun fitter Michael Murphy (www.murphyshotguns.com) says that having your shotgun properly fitted will improve your scores. Having a skilled individual help with this will get the shooter started on the right path much more quickly than if he or she tries to do it themselves. "And," Murphy says, "a better fit makes you a better shot. Surely, Butch Cassidy and the Sundance Kid would understand and approve. There is nothing soft, effeminate or old world about that!"

Tests and Results

TEST 1: Any individual with even average hand/eye coordination can pass this test. Stand on any clay target range and have a pigeon thrown. Now, smoothly and without any effort, raise your arm and track the target with a pointed finger. You do not have to consciously work the finger into position; you focus on the target with the eyes and your finger finds it every time. Were that finger "loaded" you would probably break that target practically every time, too!

Swap your finger for a shotgun, however, and the picture changes considerably. Now you are struggling with a heavy foreign object that you must place against your body with proper and consistent contact at four points – cheek, shoulder and both hands – before you can even begin to track the target. Unless that shotgun exactly fits those four spots the same way each time you bring it into position, it will not point at the same place every time. If that happens, you cannot hit the target every time.

Yet switch back to your finger and you are right on target. The purpose of fitting a shotgun is to turn it into a finger and it does not need to be difficult to be effective, although it sometimes is. Three situations can complicate proper fitting:

1) An experienced shooter who has definite opinions;

2) A shooter who may be right-hand and left-eye dominant or vice versa; or

3) An individual with a particular injury that makes good hold and fit a special challenge.

TEST 2: Make up a target approximately two feet square and place it down range, perhaps 200 yards away. Relax a few minutes and then pick up your shotgun. Snap point your shotgun at the target as if it were a grouse or a clay bird trying to get out of range. Repeat this procedure four or five times. If you had to make any adjustment whatsoever to get on that target, simply put, your shotgun stock does not fit you.

TEST 3: If the above does not work for you, then a test we

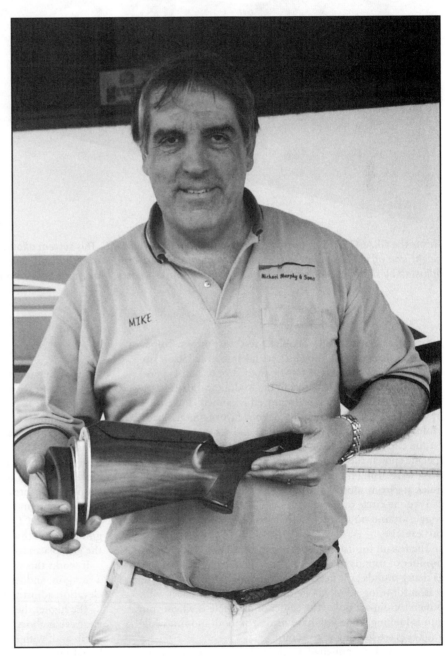

Mike Murphy of Michael Murphy & Sons, Kansas, says that fitting is not rocket science and you can certainly do it yourself. However, he cautions, there are many options that should be considered before you begin sanding and cutting a fine walnut stock. Better to spend a few extra dollars with a coach and professional fitter, he believes, than to risk ruining your shotgun stock.

This is the GRACO "CTS" adjustable comb system on an SKB 85TSS. This system allows the shooter to adjust the comb for both height and offset. Base plates fitted in the comb are etched with 1/16-inch indicating lines for offset adjustment. The comb height is adjusted by sliding 1/16-inch vinyl washers over the support posts. Maximum adjustment is one-half inch vertically and laterally.

informally refer to as the "bed sheet test" just might. To perform this test, get an old bed sheet and smoothly tack it up over a safe backstop. Use a felt-tip marker or a can of spray paint to mark a six-inch circle in the middle and then step back 25 yards. Put a Full or Improved Modified choke tube in your gun and grab a handful of your favorite target loads. Hold your gun in a low gun position and get your body set on the circle, just as if you were lining up to break a bird at a specific spot at the range.

Now, focusing on the dot, mount the gun smoothly and quickly. Fire as soon as the gun comes into position and you can see the circle over the barrel. Do not aim the gun or wiggle around on the stock. To do so defeats the purpose of this exercise.

The reason for using a bed sheet is because it will take a number of rounds to punch a clearly defined hole in it. Fire as many rounds as it takes to get one well-defined hole. The reason for using a Full choke tube at 25 yards is that it will punch a compact hole. The center of that hole is where your gun is looking when you have made a smooth mount, while your eyes are looking at the "bird."

Once you have punched a hole in the sheet, it is a simple matter to raise or lower the comb or move it a bit right or left until you and the gun are looking at the same bird. You can also use the bed sheet test to determine whether both barrels of an over/under or side-by-side are shooting to the same point of impact.

Getting Started

According to Michael Murphy, fitting usually involves reviewing your shooting mechanics before altering the dimensions of your stock. If you approach the shooting station with an awkward stance or unusual gun-hold, you definitely want to review the basics before you begin cutting walnut.

Assuming your stance and hold are acceptable, however, Murphy's approach is to train you – and the shotgun – to look at the same spot every time you throw the gun to your shoulder. His fitting sessions covers the dimensions built in to your shotgun by the manufacturer.

DROP AT COMB: Your cheek makes contact with the gun here and this measurement largely determines whether the gun places its shot charge higher or lower.

It works this way. Consider your eye to be the rear sight on a shotgun, and the height of the comb to be the means for elevation adjustment.

The higher the comb height (less drop at comb) the higher your eye is above the barrel. This leaves you looking at lots of rib and, with the gun at your cheek, actually pointing the barrel upward. The higher the comb height, the greater this effect will be and the higher the gun will shoot. On the opposite side, the lower the comb height (more drop at comb), the lower your eye is, the less rib you see, and the lower the gun will place its shot charge.

A change of about 1/8-inch in comb height will result in an

Well-attended and well-advertised shoots attract manufacturer representatives, high test shooting coaches and professional triggermen. Big events are wonderful opportunities to pick up some tips that may help you bust into the next level and perhaps to get some shooting instruction and/or gun fitting first-hand. Working with a coach, our intrepid shotgunner shoots for a pattern, makes adjustments and shoots again. Between shots, the coach re-paints the pattern board and critiques his stance and gun hold.

elevation change of an amazing eight to 10 inches at 40 yards. You can easily get that degree of change just by having a face that is fatter or thinner than "average."

The "universal" drop at comb for a flat-shooting field gun (50 percent of the pattern above and 50 percent below the bead) is 1½ inches. Trap guns, where a pattern impacting above the bead is desired, typically use a 1⅜ drop at comb, about ⅛-inch more height than a field stock. This is often referred to as a high comb.

"The point of adjusting comb height," Murphy says, "is to make the gun shoot where the eyes go and allow the shooter to adjust his mental 'bird picture' to the point of impact of the shot charge. This is a very individual thing, because different shooters may have a different subconscious bird picture ingrained over the years. Some shooters want the barrel covering the target, some want to see it just below the bird, and some may want to float the bird above it. Regardless of how much adjusting you do in the shop, this is something that must really be finished by actually shooting. That is the big advantage to an adjustable stock: the shooter can fine tune it himself."

Lateral impact of the pattern, which used to be adjusted with cast-on and cast-off of the stock, can now be more precisely adjusted with the lateral adjustment of the adjustable comb.

LENGTH OF PULL: This is the distance from the face of the trigger to the center of the recoil pad. On factory guns, length of pull is most commonly falls between 14 and 14½ inches. If your sleeve length is around 32 inches and you usually shoot in light clothing, that length is about what you want. That, of course, is a big "IF." With longer or shorter arms, you probably need a gun with a different length of pull to shoot effectively and you can either have the stock cut (for shorter arms) or have shims placed between the stock and the buttplate or recoil pad (for longer arms).

If you have a gun with a sloping comb (in contrast to a Monte Carlo-style comb that is level), a stock that is too short can cause you to shoot high. This is because your cheek (and your eye above it) seems to naturally slide farther up the comb to a higher point. It can also cause you to bang your nose with your trigger hand and that will just make life miserable in general. A stock that is too long, so that your cheek and eye slide or are positioned back toward your shoulder, can cause problems mounting the gun and makes it shoot low.

The rule of thumb for length of pull is what is most comfortable for the shooter. "Since we most often shoot a level comb," Murphy says, "length of pull has no real effect on the impact point of the shot charge, like it would with a sloping comb. I like to get the nose of the shooter no closer than one inch from the shooting hand, and not a lot farther back than that, either."

PITCH: Pitch is the angle at which the buttstock meets the shoulder. You can measure the amount of pitch by standing the shotgun against a wall with the top of the receiver contacting the wall and the buttpad flat on the floor. If the receiver and rib are in perfect contact with the wall, you have zero pitch. If the barrel is away from the wall, you have down or negative pitch. If the tip of the barrel contacts the wall before the receiver does, you have up, or positive pitch. (Sights and beads can interfere with proper measurement.)

Most shooters benefit from down pitch, and normal down pitch on a factory gun will place the barrel two to 2½ inches away from the wall. It is easy to detect if you have improper fit. When you fire the shotgun, if it flips the muzzle up or down the pitch is wrong. With proper pitch, the shotgun will recoil straight back into your shoulder.

Determining the proper pitch for the stock is not a difficult process. "All the pitch angle does is distribute the recoil forces evenly on the shoulder pocket," Murphy says. "If the pitch angle is not correct it will send most of the recoil force either to the top or the bottom of the shoulder and make the shooter uncomfortable. Pitch has no effect on point of impact with an adjustable stock, so you just make certain the angle is proper to let the pad lie evenly and comfortably on the shoulder pocket."

CAST AT TOE: The toe of the recoil pad contacts the shooter's shoulder at an angle. One of the problems in making a smooth gun mount is that shotgun recoil pads often run straight up and down, while the shoulder pocket they are supposed to fit into is at a slight angle or is curved gently. The angle increases on a shooter with a heavy chest, and this person can benefit from an angled recoil pad.

CAST-ON/OFF: Cast-off is a slight lateral bend in the buttstock that moves the comb away from the shooter's face and positions the recoil pad farther out on the shoulder. Cast-on is the reverse. The primary purpose of either measurement is to serve as a "windage adjustment" for the rear sight (your eye) and position the shooter's eye in perfect alignment with the center of the rib. If the eye is not perfectly centered on the rib, your patterns can impact to one side or the other of your aiming point.

Many English and European guns have some cast-off built in, on the theory that the shooter's eye should be moved into the comb to center the rib. American factory-made guns do not feature this.

Hands-On

Once you understand stock measurements and what information they give you, Michael Murphy says, it is time to pick up and fit your shotgun. This is not a process like the aforementioned shoe buying. No one can just look at you and tell you what is right for you, Murphy says. Fitting is a process whereby an experienced person walks you through numerous possibilities and combinations, gradually arriving – with your active participation – at the right balance of variables that put you precisely on target. It is a matter of balancing effective shooting form with comfort.

Murphy, who works with shooters who travel to his home in Kansas and makes appointments during his competitions around the U.S., says proper fitting takes a minimum of several hours. "If you think this can be done in half-an-hour, you're wrong," he says. "I can give you some tips in half an hour, but to work with your gun or guns and a try-gun can take a while, maybe all afternoon if you have a competition gun and a hunting gun or a semi-auto and an over/under. We will normally fire a lot of shells, so I recommend that students wear a light, comfortable pair of gloves to protect them from hot barrels and chafing from the checkering on the stock.

"Of course, you will also need to wear ear protection and shooting glasses, just like you would at the shooting range. I don't recommend muff-type hearing protectors though, certainly not the style with the hard plastic outer shell because your shotgun can knock against them when you're trying to make a good mount and that's pretty distracting. And of course, you have to have shooting glasses because at the distance we typically shoot the pattern plate, 16 yards, shot can come bouncing straight back at you almost as fast as it went forward.

"The problem with a quick fitting is that it can change if you change clothes, a thicker or thinner vest and shirt for example, can change your point of aim and impact. (Having two differ-

Sometimes, fitting can be accomplished with the simple addition of or change of the size, shape or density of a recoil pad. Spacers are designed to help you adjust length of pull to your best shooting needs. These pads and spacers are designed for Browning's new Cynergy Shotgun.

ent sizes of buttpads or an adjustable butt pad can help here.) It can even change if you are having a bad day and grimace rather than smile. Remember that it just takes a millimeter or two at the point of the angle to change the impact point by three or four inches at distances between 20 and 25 yards.

"I find that experienced shooters who want to reach the next level and come to me for tips and fitting have often spent a lifetime adapting themselves to their guns. You have a fitting so that you can adjust the gun so that it conforms to you."

When a shooter makes an appointment with Murphy, he gets the stock roughly adjusted and then stands in front of the muzzle while the shooter mounts the gun to make finer adjustments. "What I am doing," he says, "is watching the shooter shoulder the gun and looking right into his pupil as he looks down the rib. You get the gun very close to 'on' in this manner, but the real final test is to watch the shooter break targets and we finish the tuning from there."

Some Do-It-Yourself

Adjustable combs and recoil pads are not gimmicks. Their advantage is that they not only make it very easy for you to fit a gun yourself, but they also allow you to alter fit to meet existing conditions.

There are times when having the ability to quickly adjust a stock can be advantageous. A trap shooter, for example, shooting into a strong wind knows it will make the target rise more quickly. Increasing the comb height slightly will raise the point of impact to compensate for the wind without the shooter having to alter his hold. In short, adjustable stocks give the shotgunner the same degree of control that finely adjustable sights give riflemen and handgunners.

The range of comb movement is considerable on an adjustable stock. In fact, most shooters should be able to get all the windage and elevation adjustment they require from one, with no further stock work. Combine that with an adjustable recoil pad and you have a wide range of adjustment that will allow you to fit your gun to virtually any normal dimension or shotgunning challenge.

Stock Adjustment

One of the biggest problems with stocks made in the US today is that the comb of the stock is high and you occasionally see shooters try to scrunch down into these stocks to get on target. While at first you may think a lot of wood has to be removed to correct this, you can lightly sand this area down by hand and keep checking for fit until it is comfortable to shoot. A telltale sign that the comb is too high is when the stock smacks you on the cheekbone when you shoot.

If you feel you need to shorten your stock, never cut off more than a quarter of an inch at a time before putting everything back together and checking for fit. This may take more time to get to that perfect fit, but it is better than trying to lengthen a stock after you cut it too short.

To properly cut a stock to keep it from splintering is quite simple but requires a careful approach:
1. Make a pencil mark around the stock where you want to cut it.
2. Take a sharp utility knife and cut into the wood all the way around your stock, on your pencil mark.
3. Using a saw of fine kerf (small teeth set close together), cut the stock at the edge of where you cut with the utility knife. This method produces a clean cut with no splinters.

There is a quick and easy way however to lengthen your stock. While it does not give you the most appealing look, you can buy black and white plastic butt plate spacers and add these ahead of the butt plate or recoil pad. If you still need more length, try adding a slip-on recoil pad.

It sometimes does not take much in the way of stock adjustment to get a gun to shoot where you look. The cure is often simple. I have a Franchi Prestige 12-gauge on which I slightly lengthened the stock by simply changing the recoil pad. The Franchi is a sloping-comb field gun. Lengthening the stock moved my face down the comb a bit, which caused the gun to shoot slightly low. An adjustable and detachable cheekpiece from Meadow Industries quickly corrected that. The pad attaches with Velcro strips and it raised the comb enough to return the gun to a 50/50 shooter (half the pattern above and half below the bead). The pad comes with inserts that can be quickly installed to raise the shot pattern in about eight-inch increments at 40 yards. This pad did not add any cast, so the lateral impact of the pattern remained the same. These pads are a simple way to make minor corrections, and there are a number of different models available.

Pistol Grip Fit

Pistol grip fit is something that is not taken into consideration by manufacturers. This part of the stock should fit the shooter. If you have small hands, you will probably be better off with a narrow grip that lets you lock onto it. If you have a hand like a bear paw, you will need a thicker grip. A palm swell can also be a help. The only drawback is that if it is not in the proper position – so that it falls right into the perfect pocket of your hand – it can be a detriment.

Another easily overlooked item about a palm swell is a place for the meat of your thumb to rest comfortably. Some meticulous shooters hollow out a little spot for that, kind of 'melting' the thumb into the pistol grip.

Your pistol grip should feel good. When you slip your hand onto it, it should be like putting on a fine old glove.

Master Eye

Almost everybody has one eye that is dominant. The dominant eye often overpowers the other eye in vision decisions. If you are a right-hander and have a right dominant eye, you have a good situation. Left-handers with a left dominant eye are equally fortunate. If you happen to have a dominant eye on the opposite side of your body from your dominant hand however, you can have problems with hand-eye coordination. The eye on the other side of your body is doing the looking, while the eye you have lined up on the rib is getting short-changed. Your gun will not shoot where you are looking.

Here is a quick test to see which is your master eye. With both eyes open, point your finger at a defined spot on a wall. Now close your left eye. If the finger stays on target, your right eye is dominant. If the finger moves off target when you close your left eye, but stays on target when you close your right eye, the left eye is dominant.

Some right-handed people with a strongly left-dominant eye (or vice versa) simply cannot shoot a shotgun from their normal side. In the long run, the best solution is to learn to shoot from the same side as your dominant eye. Sometimes that does not work, though. For these shooters, the solution is a strange looking contraption called a crossover stock. It features an extreme bend in the stock that, for a right-hander, will put the left eye in exact alignment with the barrel when you shoulder the stock to the right side. These are available from a number of stockmakers.

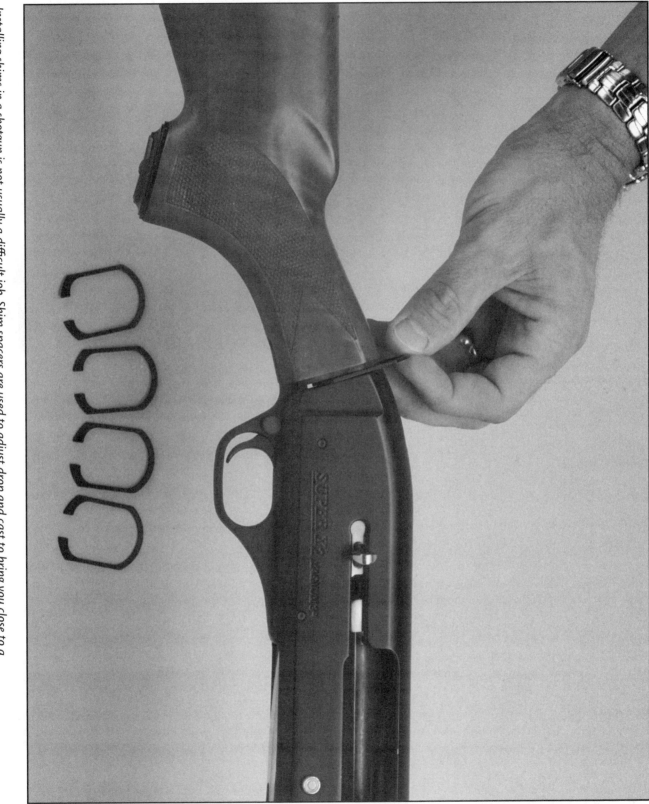

Installing shims in a shotgun is not usually a difficult job. Shim spacers are used to adjust drop and cast to bring you close to a custom fit. (Photo courtesy Winchester)

The semi-auto shotguns have a reputation for softer shooting than an over/under, but the automatic shell ejection feature can be problematic for a left-hander or if a sporting clays station is beside a tree. Pump shotguns eject below or out the side of the receiver; over/unders eject straight behind the barrels when they are opened, unless they are fitted with hand extractors – preferred by reloaders. For a left-hand shooter the typical semi-auto, built for right-handers, spits out a shell near your face. Look for a left-hand semi-auto like this Benelli Montefeltro in 12- or 20-gauge. It will shoot 2¾- or 3-inch shells comfortably.

Recoil Control

Once a gun is sighted-in, there are still a few things that can be done to fit it more comfortably to you. One area is controlling recoil.

According to Newton's Third Law, for every action there is an opposite and equal reaction. No one has yet repealed that law, but researchers have found some interesting ways to amend it.

Shotguns kick. Some kick more than others and that is not always dependent upon the gauge of the gun. I have seen some 20-gauge shotguns belt shooters harder than some 12s, and a few 28-gauges that would draw blood from the cheek.

Proper shotgun fit aids immensely in reducing felt recoil by evenly distributing the recoil forces to those areas most capable of handling them. A correctly shaped comb (especially a padded model) will further soften the blow. Too many shotguns seem to have combs designed to slice butter instead of cushion recoil. I have shot some of these and, although I did not feel pain at the time, they sliced my cheek open as effectively as a razor!

Another way to reduce recoil is to add weight to the gun, and many gunsmiths do just that. A 12-gauge competition gun in the 9- to 10-pound range has little recoil with normal target loads. Many kick less than 20-gauge guns in the 6½- to seven-pound range. Weight added to the barrel helps keep the muzzle down on recoil and prevents cheek slap. If barrel weights make the gun too muzzle-heavy, adding some weight inside the buttstock will restore the balance.

Another way to cut your punishment is to shoot a semi-auto. They can be set up with the same exact stock fit as any other shotgun and their gas systems do make them noticeably softer to shoot.

You can add a recoil reduction device to almost any gun. There are plenty of these on the market. These are essentially shock-absorbers that use a spring-loaded, air/oil or special synthetic elastic polymer (such as "sorbothane") cushion to slow the recoil impulse and turn it into a gentle push instead of a shove. They all add weight to the gun and some smiths will tell you that the additional weight is what really does the job. Others will tell you they work just as they are advertised. Regardless of the reason, they do work.

Porting your barrel(s) is supposed to help cut recoil. I have a ported gun, and it does cut muzzle jump slightly (an asset on a quick second shot), but does not seem to otherwise reduce recoil with target-level loads. I also use this gun for ducks, however, and the recoil reduction with stouter loads is noticeable.

Fit a gun properly, add whatever recoil reduction your gunsmith recommends, and you will likely find that shooting is not nearly as punishing as it used to be. If you enjoy the sport, you owe it to yourself to make it fun!

Your Trigger

It is commonly accepted that shotgun triggers are stiff, gritty, and something no rifleman would tolerate. That is okay though, because you do not "squeeze" a shotgun trigger. You "slap" the trigger on a scattergun. Therefore, it does not make any difference if they are miserable.

I do not accept that reasoning.

If you shoot an eight-pound, squishy trigger, think about having a good gunsmith tune it to a crisp 3½- to 4-pound break. Your scores will soar! A good shotgun deserves a good trigger. The first time you try a good one on a shotgun, you will agree. There have been past (and current) champions that shot "custom" triggers in the one-pound range. If they were not an asset, do you think they would have used them?

A very few shooters, especially those afflicted with "trap-shooter's flinch" or "target panic" might even need to get more radical than that!

You most commonly see flinch in trap, but it can affect any shooter (competitor or hunter). It is the inability of the shooter to pull the trigger. It is not a physical inability, but a mental one. You just cannot make your finger trigger the round.

Just what is "trapshooter's flinch?" Coaches believe it is a response by the body to the cumulative effects of recoil. The body just gets tired of taking the pounding and the subconscious says, "That's it, I'm not pulling that trigger again!" The brain short-circuits the trigger finger. Your subconscious has a lot of authority in those areas!

Once this happens to a shooter, he or she is in big trouble. One remedy is to just stop shooting for a while and let the subconscious get over its temper tantrum. Sometimes that works, just like laying off shooting in the middle of a slump will sometimes help. Other times it will not, and one item that has proven to help shooters in this situation is a "release trigger."

A release trigger works in reverse of a conventional trigger: pulling the trigger sets it, releasing the trigger fires the gun. On double guns, they can be set up to function as a "release-pull" trigger, pull to set, release to fire the first barrel, pull to fire the second. At least one Olympic trapshooter has used this in the games because he felt it was the fastest way to get off two shots.

Many gunsmiths will perform this work, but release triggers do have some controversy surrounding them. This is one of those subjects that few shooters seem to have a middle-of-the-road opinion on. You either love them or hate them.

I fall into a different group. I have played with them and personally do not like them, but if I had to use one, I am certain I could. They have extended the shooting careers of a number of competitors that would otherwise have had to quit.

I hate this to sound like whining, but "there oughta be a law" that every gun equipped with a release trigger of any configuration be so marked on the gun's buttstock in one-inch neon fluorescent letters!

Release triggers are not inherently dangerous, not as long as the shooter remembers what he has and understands how it works. These triggers can be dangerous, however, if a shooter picks up the gun without realizing it has a release trigger.

You load a round, call for the bird, pull the trigger and nothing happens. You subconsciously think, "Damn! I've got a misfire." Then you release the trigger and the gun fires! You have to hope that safe gun-handling doctrine has you pointing it down-range when you release. Nevertheless, it is most disconcerting and has the potential to be disastrous.

I am well aware that range courtesy and common sense would preclude a shooter from picking up and firing a gun that is not his. I am also aware that mistakes happen. Release trigger guns should be marked.

Other than that, release triggers are a matter of personal preference and can help some shooters. For that matter, so is shotgun fitting, on the whole, and one reason why it is worth the time and trouble. Remember to just turn your gun into your finger and smoothly point. It is not that hard to do.

It is about time shotgun manufacturers gave serious consideration to the smoothness and functioning of the trigger group. SKB says the non-detachable tournament trigger system of its 85TSS has been refined to reduce "engagement creep and over-travel." The new trigger allows the sear to disengage and drop with less pull weight so that the shooter feels a smooth and crisp trigger pull.

FINE TUNING YOUR SHOTGUN

"High-performance shotgun" is a term that can mean different things to different shooters. Some will define it in terms of how smoothly and quickly the gun gets on fast-flushing grouse. Others will consider it an indication of how well it hits with heavy steel shot loads on a distant goose or even how "hard" it smokes clay targets.

Oklahoma's Larry Nailon, president of Clearview Products, however, has a different and much more succinct definition. Although his study of recoil has now advanced far beyond the basics, he has offered these thoughts on getting to the first plateau of high performance shooting:

"When we speak about a high-performance shotgun," he ex-

With the sideplates and stock removed, the over/under is exposed as a relatively simple instrument. This cutaway from a Weatherby Athena clearly shows the sear-block safety design, the gold-plated single, selective inertia trigger find the automatic ejectors in place on the barrels. When it comes to a fine shotgun, "cleanliness is indeed next to godliness."

According to Nailon, it does not really matter how many pellets you start with in the load. "What counts is how well you take care of what you start with," Nailon says. "When we build a high-performance shotgun barrel, our goal is to get as many pellets out of the gun in as undeformed a condition as possible."

Nailon knows a thing or two about tweaking a shotgun barrel for improved performance. As the genius behind Clearview, he has earned a reputation among top-notch competitive shooters in every shotgun game for his custom barrel and choke work; yet Nailon does not consider what he does to be new or earthshaking.

Critical Areas

"There are a number of modifications one can make to a shotgun barrel," he says, "that will result in a certain degree of performance enhancement. All I do is combine these proven enhancers into a total barrel work-over. Each of these modifications complements the others and results in a much greater increase in performance than you would get if you only opted for one or two of them."

Nailon is concerned with four key areas when he begins working with a barrel: chamber, forcing cone, bore and choke. Modifications to any one of them can improve performance. However, Nailon refines all four areas to harmoniously provide maximum performance. Here is his prescription for "tweaking" a barrel.

Chamber

Modern mass-production methods work because of manufacturing tolerances. As a result, measurements need

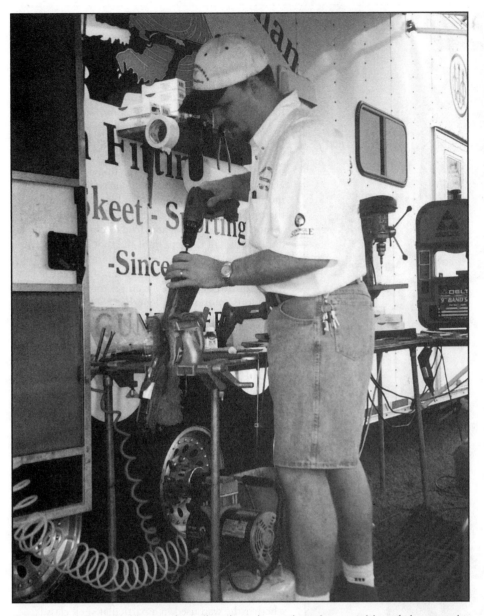

If you are handy with shims and recoil pads and resetting trigger positions (where possible), you can fit the stock to your shooting dimensions yourself. Otherwise, you may need an experienced gunsmith, because the idea of proper fit is that your dominant eye lines up with the centerline of the rib precisely, every time you bring the stock to your cheek.

plains, "what we are talking about is a gun that delivers the best down-range performance regardless of the load or distance. It is the combination of gun and load that delivers the maximum number of pellets in the load to the point of impact while simultaneously producing the largest useful pattern that has no gaps or holes a bird or clay target could slip through."

According to Larry, high performance is down-range performance. "To achieve that," he says, "you must get every pellet, or as many as is humanly possible, out of the shell, through the bore and choke, and out the gun in a perfectly smooth, round and undeformed condition. Round pellets fly true and arrive at the target together. Pellets that have been partially flattened or deformed veer off course and even lag behind the main shot charge. Sometimes, they will be far enough away from or behind the main charge to be of absolutely no use. You may as well not even have fired them for all the good they will do you on that shot."

only be "within spec." It is possible, although not common, to get a factory shotgun chamber having incorrect dimensions. Most commonly, the chamber is shorter than required. The problem with a short chamber is that it may not allow the crimp to unfold fully without protruding into the forcing cone. If this happens, the wad and shot charge are restricted in their ability to exit the shell, and that occurs at the precise moment that maximum chamber pressure is reached. This causes shot pellets to deform and increases chamber pressure and recoil.

"Checking chamber dimensions is a standard procedure for us," Nailon notes. "I also like to increase the length of the chamber to .060-inch longer than normal, especially if the shooter is a reloader. As a shell is reloaded and fired it tends to stretch just a bit, not unlike a brass cartridge case, and a slightly longer chamber becomes an asset."

Excessively long chambers, however, are not a benefit. "We

183

Forcing Cone

Directly ahead of the chamber is the forcing cone and, as its name implies, it acts as a funnel to guide the wad and shot charge from the chamber to the bore. The normal length of most factory forcing cones is between ½- and ⅝-inch. Nailon does not like that either.

"The length of a shot column is about one inch inside a light 12-gauge load and over 1½ inches in a heavy load," he explains. As the pellets at the rear of the load are rammed into the upper pellets, outward pressure is tremendous. This is highest at the moment the shot charge moves from the chamber to the forcing cone. Since the shot column is moving through a constricting area (the forcing cone) that is only about half the length of the shot column, with as much as 10,000 psi pressure behind it, it's pretty apparent that a significant number of pellets are being deformed before they even get into the barrel."

Nailon's solution is to lengthen the forcing cone.

"I feel a cone of 1½ inches is the minimum," he states. "My own patterning tests with our moving patterning board, where precise target speeds can be set and shot strings of up to 16-feet in length can be accurately measured, indicates that even a forcing cone length of over 2½ inches will help, not hurt."

Forcing cone lengthening is a custom technique that some major shotgun makers are incorporating into their better grades of guns, often those intended for trap, skeet and sporting clays shooters.

"The standard short forcing cone can be an asset if one uses the older fiber wad shells," Nailon claims, "but with modern one-piece plastic wads, this is obsolete. All a short forcing cone does here is raise pressure, increase recoil and deform shot."

Some of the biggest offenders in the short, tight forcing cone area are the low- and mid-priced Italian and Spanish imports, because many shooters in their original market area still rely on fiber wad shells. European shotshell manufacturers usually specify whether the wad used in a particular shell class is plastic or fiber (or "fibre" as Britain's Eley Hawk specifies for its shells in its printed catalog and on its Internet site at www.eleyhawkltd.com).

Bore

Larry Nailon is a big believer in back-bored barrels, the process of deliberately boring the barrel out to a larger diameter than is industry standard for that particular gauge. To understand why that is so, an understanding of choke is required.

The term "choke" is used to describe two dissimilar, but related factors: how the gun patterns and the constriction at the muzzle of the gun.

The first definition is commonly understood. A gun that patterns 70 percent is considered to have a Full choke. A 60-percent pattern is Modified, while 50 percent is Improved Cylinder. A Cylinder choke runs about 40 percent. A Skeet choke is very close to Improved Cylinder in performance. In terms of measurement, a Skeet choke is intended to throw a 30-inch pattern at 25 yards.

The second definition is much less properly understood. The actual muzzle constriction we refer to as "choke" is not

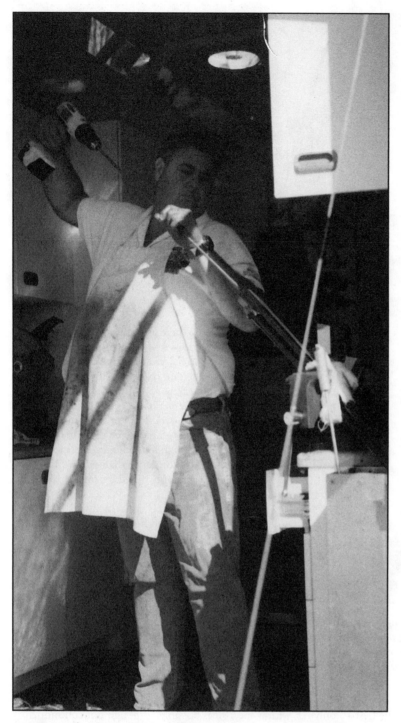

Joe Morales, president of Rhino stainless chokes, works on a barrel in his traveling shop. "The purpose of porting is to cause suction on the wad," he says, "pulling it away from the shot stream before it collides with the individual pellets to cause 'flyers' in your pattern. A byproduct of ported, extended chokes is that they further reduce recoil and muzzle jump."

have found," he explains, "that while 2¾-inch shells will function perfectly in a three-inch chamber, the down-range performance of the load can suffer. The shot column and wad have an extra ¼-inch run at its highest pressure point before it enters the forcing cone, and side pressure on the pellets at this point tends to beat up the pellets more than if they were fired in a chamber of the proper length for the shell."

Your length of pull is not right if you cannot settle on a spot for your cheek, if your trigger-arm feels cramped, or if your eye seems too close to the receiver. An aftermarket recoil pad such as the Remington R3 (pictured) can help you get the fit just right for a secure four-point hold.

completely dependent upon just the constriction at the muzzle. Actual choke achieved is the relationship between the constriction in the choke itself and the inside diameter of the barrel.

Barrel constriction is measured in thousandths of an inch. The British often refer to this as points of choke. For example, a measured constriction of .005-inch could be referred to as "five points of choke." A constriction of .019-inch would be nineteen points.

The degree of constriction required to produce different chokes varies from gauge to gauge. With the 12-gauge, for example, zero constriction gives Cylinder choke, .005-inch produces Skeet 1; .009 is Improved Cylinder; .012 equals Skeet 2; and so on. Extra-Full and Super-Full chokes run from .045- to .089-inch.

From the above it might seem that we could grab a choke tube marked Modified, screw it into our 12-gauge and get a 60-percent pattern. Maybe, maybe not.

If our 12-gauge has a bore diameter of .729-inch, and if we have a choke tube marked Modified, that has an internal diameter of .710-inch, then we do have 19 points of constriction between the two and will get a Modified pattern, assuming the load is accurate and well packed. Suppose, however, that the actual diameter of the barrel is .745-inch. If we insert our .710-inch tube, our real constriction is now .035-inch, or 35 points! Regardless of what is marked on the choke tube, we have a Full choke. Shot charges cannot read, they can only respond.

If our 12-gauge barrel has a bore diameter of .720-inch, then our modified, .710-inch tube is actually giving us only .010-inch constriction, 10 points, or about improved cylinder.

This should not sound farfetched. Every shotgunsmith I have ever talked to tells me it is common to measure factory barrels that are above or below standard bore diameter. In fact, they may vary from .710- to .750-inch in guns coming off the same factory production line.

That in itself does not explain why Nailon favors back-boring barrels. This does, however: "The degree of pattern control you exercise is dependent upon the inside diameter of both the barrel and the choke tube," he says. "If a 12-gauge barrel has an inside diameter of .725 and you put a .715-inch tube in it, you have an Improved Cylinder choke. If you have a barrel with an inside diameter of .750 and you want to install an Improved Cylinder choke, all you need to do is put in a tube with an inside diameter of .740-inch.

Most top shotgun manufacturers report that they overbore the barrels. This means that the barrel is deliberately bored to a larger diameter than industry standard specifications for that gauge. (Photo courtesy Mossberg)

"You have the same degree of constriction with either," he continues, "and you'll get the same pattern control. However, with a back-bored barrel, you get it with a bigger hole in the muzzle for the shot to go through. Once the shot pellets enter the choke constriction, they can do one of two things if they are lead: they can either reposition themselves (one pellet moving ahead of or behind another) or they can deform. With a back-bored barrel and larger choke tube in use, the pellets have more room to reposition and fewer are deformed."

With steel shot, especially the larger sizes, the situation changes. Pellets can either reposition or damage the choke! Back-boring is even more important to waterfowl hunters than to lead-shot users.

How much to over-bore depends on the individual barrel. Nailon feels most will take between .010- and .015-inch without difficulty. Going over .015-inch can produce a slight velocity loss, but often results in larger useful patterns. Nailon has one 12-gauge back-bored to .750-inch (.021-inch over industry standard) and reports that one-ounce loads lack the pellets to fill the pattern, but that the gun shoots marvelously with 1⅛-ounce loads.

An additional advantage to back-boring is that Nailon and the customer now know precisely what that barrel's inside diameter is and that it is uniform from chamber to muzzle without high spots. Back-boring will also reduce recoil to some extent.

One additional step Nailon takes on the bore is to burnish it. "If the bore isn't perfectly mirror smooth," he has found, "it tends to accumulate fouling, especially plastic fouling from the wad, at a much higher rate. This fouling acts to increase friction as successive wads

and shot charges move through the barrel, decreasing velocity and increasing recoil. In extreme cases it can actually impede the performance of the wad and cause pellet deformation."

Most manufacturers only finish a bore to "near smoothness." Complete polishing is a time-consuming job, and time is money in mass production or at a custom shop. Even if the bore is chrome-lined, that is no guarantee it is smooth. Chrome is only as smooth as the surface over which it was applied and if the bore is not polished mirror-smooth before the plating, you still have a rough bore.

Nailon polishes his bores with a set of specially designed hones running down to an ultra-fine #800 grit. If you are one of those smart shotgunners who routinely cleans his barrel with a brush wrapped in 0000 steel wool – the best way to remove plastic fouling that solvents and brushes leave behind – you are doing a little burnishing every time you clean the gun. Nailon's method is just a lot quicker.

Choke Tubes

Once Nailon has tweaked the bore this far, all that remains are the choke tubes. Once again, he disagrees with most manufacturers.

"Once the pellets enter the choke constriction they can again either reposition or deform," he explains. "My goal is to give them the maximum opportunity to reposition before they begin to deform.

"Most factory choke tubes," he continues, "are about 1½ inches long. That requires the shot to reposition within a limited amount of space. If you double the length of the choke tube, you double the time and distance they have to do that. All other factors being equal, longer choke tubes deform less shot and that is our ultimate goal with custom barrel work."

Nailon combines a three-inch tube length with an inner taper that combines a cone with parallel surfaces, instead of the more commonly seen cone style that places the maximum constriction at one extremely short point The addition of the parallel surfaces is a further aid in allowing the shot to reposition.

Making the longer, custom choke tubes is considerably more difficult than making factory-length tubes. It is more time-consuming and expensive because, as a machinist's rule of thumb, you cannot hold precise tolerances in high-speed production when boring more than twice your diameter. To make his tubes, Nailon has to make a series of precise, fine cuts instead of getting it all done in one pass.

What the customer receives is a set of custom-made choke tubes sized precisely to the diameter of the gun's barrel. Nailon normally provides these in .005-inch increments, which assures a precise degree of pattern control. In past few years, he has cut it even finer than that.

"We find that a number of competitive shooters, especially sporting clays gunners, want to go to half-step chokes to in-

If you know the precise diameter of your barrel, you should be able to develop an exact pattern with aftermarket choke tubes.

Getting the most out of your gun means performance and also emotional satisfaction. Salvatore "Sal" Echel, a New York City "beat cop" who has been shooting for a little more than a year, had his Beretta 391 semi-auto – stock and forearm – painted with a wrap-around American flag by AnglePort after 9/11/01.

crease their ability to really fine-tune their patterns for whatever conditions exist in their area," he notes. "We offer tubes in these half-step increments (i.e., .002-inch, 007-inch, etc.), and they really do make a difference. I have been shooting a .002-inch tube for close-range shots recently, and it does some amazing things. You'd be surprised the difference a simple .002-inch constriction can make over a straight cylinder bore. That small difference, in the more open chokes, makes a much bigger change in pattern control than the same .002-inch difference does in the tighter chokes."

If a shooter does not want to go to the expense of a full-blown barrel make-over, he can still benefit from custom-fitted choke tubes.

Nailon will make choke tubes in whatever reasonable incremental series a shooter requests, in any one of the various popular thread systems. This does, however, require that the shooter either have the barrel's inside diameter measurements performed by a competent local gunsmith and then supplied to Nailon, or simply send his barrel to Nailon, who would prefer to take those critical measurements himself

Aftermarket Tubes

Another alternative to improved pattern control, albeit less effective, is for a shooter to simply add aftermarket choke tubes to his existing selection. However, factory-offered choke tubes are often rather limited in scope. Generally, you can get Skeet 1, Improved Cylinder, Modified, Full and, sometimes, Extra-Full.

If you are not satisfied with the pattern control your choke

selection allows you to achieve, then adding tubes in Skeet 2, Cylinder, Improved Modified or Extra-Full may help correct the situation. If your actual barrel inside diameter is not .729-inch and, for example, your Modified tube is actually producing Improved Cylinder or Full patterns, going to some of the intermediate constrictions can help put those patterns back to where you want them.

There is, however, a pitfall with this approach if done incorrectly.

"There are a number of different choke tube systems on the market," explains Nailon. "More than one gun manufacturer may use the same system. For example, the Win-Choke system threads will fit a number of guns besides those that bear the Winchester brand. When you are talking abut different choke tube systems, you are basically talking about the thread pattern they use and the length of the choke tube itself.

"Just because a Win-Choke may screw into the barrel of your gun," he continues, "does not necessarily mean the fit is exact. If the barrel diameter is not properly matched to the choke tube, you will not get the pattern you expect. You can also have a problem with the fit at the base of the choke. A barrel will expand slightly upon firing. That expansion can range from about .002-inch to almost .010-inch. To accommodate this, there is a small step at the rear of the choke that allows for the expansion and helps guide the wad from the barrel into the choke. In effect, it acts almost like the forcing cone does at the chamber.

"If the barrel diameter varies too much from the diameter of the rear of the choke, then you get a ridge that the wad can hang up on. If that ridge is large enough, the wad can jam, the

No matter what type or brand of gun you use, you will find that it makes little difference on the shooting line. The most expensive over/unders rub elbows with semi-autos painted like racecars. The only difference that counts is how well you handle the instrument.

When you purchase aftermarket chokes tube – and there is absolutely nothing wrong with that – you will do yourself a favor if you tell the supplier precisely what the make and model of your gun is; better yet, give him the barrel's inside diameter measurements, regardless of what the "chart" says your gun will take.

If your gun is not threaded to accept interchangeable choke tubes, then the best thing you can do for it is to send the barrel off and have them fitted. This is not a complex operation in a competent custom shop. A number of aftermarket companies do an outstanding job in this area, and it is not just limited to 12-gauge guns.

You can have tubes installed in any shotgun, right down to the diminutive .410. I know, because Hastings installed the Briley tube system on one of my .410 shotguns, and the difference in performance is hard to believe. What it does for the 28-gauge is beyond words!

The point is this: If your favorite smoothbore is not fitted to accept interchangeable tubes, you are wasting over half the gun's potential, regardless of gauge.

Interchangeable tubes can greatly increase your gun's performance, and there are no real mysteries to their use.

Tube Installation

One key is in the installation of the tube. It should be fully inserted into the gun, completely bottomed out in the threads, hand-tight and not over-torqued. If a tube begins to back out from the threads even slightly, there is a risk of gun damage.

It is an excellent idea to check the snugness of your tubes before any shooting session.

Tubes should never be installed in the barrel without lubrication on the tube threads. Standard gun-grade or machine oil is not the proper lubrication because it provides no support for the threads. Far better choices are Never-Seez, Lubriplate or any of the many commercial choke tube tubes incorporating these ingredients. Improper lubrication is one of the biggest problems with interchangeable tubes. If you forget the tube, or use one that is inadequate, you may not be able to remove the tube from the barrel without the services of a gunsmith.

Barrels threaded for interchangeable tubes should never be fired without a tube in place. This is just about guaranteed to damage the threads and leave you with another costly repair bill.

It is also not a good idea to leave a choke tube in the barrel indefinitely, even with the best tube and lube. Once a year, pull out the tube, clean it, re-lube it and stick it back in. If you forget about periodic maintenance, the tube may find a permanent home in that particular barrel.

It is worth pointing out that interchangeable choke tubes, lengthened forcing cones, back-boring and long choke tubes are not new developments. Custom gunsmiths have been doing them for more than 25 years. What should be pointed out is that major gunmakers often include interchangeable tubes as standard equipment and most offer longer choke tubes, lengthened forcing cones and long chokes on their top-of-the-line competition guns.

pressure will build, and you'll blow the choke tube out the end of the barrel. That's expensive to repair. Shuffling choke tubes around just because they have the same thread system and will fit into the gun is not a good idea," Nailon feels.

In a best-case scenario, you will not get the down-range performance you expect. In a worst-case scenario, you may seriously damage the barrel.

This, of course, does not mean that aftermarket choke tubes are dangerous, just that they can be, even if the thread systems are the same and the chart says they will interchange. (For that reason, we are not going to include a chart showing the compatibility of the various systems. Though there are some systems that will truly interchange, the majority of them are just different enough that problems can arise, even if the tube seems to fit the gun perfectly.)

GIVE IT A LITTLE CHOKE

Because steel is much harder than lead, make sure that any choke you buy is certified to accept steel shot without deforming. Damage to the choke can throw your pattern into disarray and eventually cause barrel damage.

Interchangeable: Although these can be of the externally attached "screw-on" style or the internal "screw-in" recessed in the barrel, most are of the latter type. To change the degree of constriction, you simply remove and replace with a choke of a different diameter.

Adjustable: This style choke is adjustable throughout the entire range of constrictions by turning a sleeve, which collapses or expands, thus changing the exit diameter.

The internal design of choke tubes can be broken down into three main groups:

Conical Parallel: These have a cone that blends into a parallel section at the muzzle. This helps to stabilize your shot charge as it leaves the choke and the gun.

Straight Conical: This type choke has a cone only. Where the cone stops is the point where the shot exits the choke and the gun.

Wad Retarding: These chokes do not make use of constriction as either of the above designs, but instead use machined bumps or projections to alter the shot pattern.

Shotgun Patterns

George Trulock says that patterns are normally expressed as a percentage, such as 50 percent or 70 percent and so on. This is a commonly accepted method for comparing pattern density. "A 50 percent pattern means that half of the pellets in the shell will strike inside a circle 30-inches in diameter at 40 yards,"

According to George Trulock, president of Trulock Chokes (www.trulockchokes.com), a choke is "simply a tapered constriction of the gun barrel's bore at the muzzle end. The exit end of the choke is smaller by some dimension than the actual bore of the barrel. This difference is the amount of constriction. For example, if the bore of the barrel is .730 inch and the exit diameter of the choke is .710 inch, you have a constriction of .020 inch."

George and his crew have dealt with practically every shotgun made in the past half century and he says that the amount of constriction for a given type choke – Improved Cylinder or Full, for instance – varies between manufacturers. "As a general rule for standard chokes," he says, "the total range will be between .000 and .045 thousandths of an inch. The length of the choke varies also, between 1½ and four inches, and this affects your shot pattern almost as much as the type choke you are using."

Chokes are grouped in three general types:

Fixed: These are integral parts of the barrel and cannot be readily changed, except by a gunsmith. Any alteration is considered permanent.

New for 2004, Trulock's Ti (Titanium) Chokes are approximately ⅓ lighter than comparable steel chokes. They are extended, knurled and notched and each choke has a unique color, which makes them easy to identify. In addition, the heads are marked with the degree of choke and the body is marked with the exit diameter in thousandths of an inch. George Trulock, president of Trulock Chokes, says these are "perfect for long-barreled sporting clays guns." Trulock chokes come with a lifetime warranty.

Lead Shot Choke Chart

Designation	Constriction (in inches)	Percent (at 40 yards)
Cylinder	.000	40 (70 at 25 yards)
Skeet 1	.005	45 (75 at 25 yards)
Improved Cylinder	.010	50
Skeet 2 (Light Modified)	.015	55
Modified	.020	60
Improved Modified	.025	65
Full	.030	70
Extra Full	.040	73
Turkey	.045+	75

George says. "So, to find the percentage of any given load, divide the number of hits inside the circle by the total number of pellets contained in the shell. You can obtain the approximate number of pellets any given load will have from a shotshell reloading book or you can actually cut open a couple shells and count them."

Typically, pattern testing is done at 40 yards. However, Cylinder and Skeet 1 chokes in all gauges and the .410 (all chokes) are measured at 25 yards.

According to George, the purpose for patterning a shotgun is to allow you to select a choke that will throw a pattern that is as large as possible without having the pellets so far apart that the target can escape multiple hits. "For shooting both game and clay targets," he says, "you want a pattern that is perfectly even in pellet distribution over the 30-inch circle. Having said that, and after looking at thousands of patterns over a span of 25 years, I could count on my fingers the number of shots I would call perfect – and if these were measured with scientific accuracy, some of them would not have qualified. In this instance, however, "close" is good enough." (Two exceptions would be buckshot and turkey patterns, because with these you want a tight center cluster of pellets.)

George believes that the only consistency from gun to gun is that very few things are consistent. "Identical guns with the same degree of choke and using the same shell may not pattern the same," he says. "The same load between various brands of shells can pattern differently. Patterns can change when you change from hard to soft shot. Patterns can change when anything inside the shell changes: a different wad, a different powder or primer. What I am trying to get across is that when you change anything – brands, shot size or components – you need to check the pattern as it could have changed, sometimes by a surprising amount."

Once you find a choke and shell combination that gives you the pattern and results you want, it should remain reasonably consistent as long as noth-

ing is changed. For instance, if the manufacturer switches powder types, your patterns will probably change. George says that he is satisfied as long as the percentage of change is plus or minus five percent.

The associated chart shows the relationship between the degree of choke, the percentage and constriction based on lead shot. These percentages are a guide only. What you actually want is a pattern that is dense enough to insure multiple hits on your target at the distance you normally shoot.

This chart should be used as a starting point only. Select the choke and pattern it. Change chokes or loads as needed to get the pattern you want.

While there are other variables, for all practical purposes chokes will determine the density of the shot pattern. "I look at density from two different ways," George says. "The first is the pattern percentage. This is simply a figure telling you how many pellets out of the total number of pellets that were fired at the target hit inside a 30-inch circle. For example, if 250 pellets are in a shell and 200 land inside the circle, divide 200

Browning's Midas Grade Extended Tubes are designed for clay targets. Manufactured from stainless steel, they are finished with black oxide. Extended tubes feature easy installation and removal without a wrench. Browning says its "minimum gap geometry plus high-resolution 'RMS' finish reduce buildup of plastics in the shotgun bore." Available in all gauges for $49 or less each at your favorite retailer.

by 250 and you have 80 percent. Percentage is percentage and does not matter what size shot is used. The second way of looking at pattern density is 'pellet spacing.' Common sense tells us that a 1⅛ ounce load of #8 shot will have many more pellets than a 1⅛ ounce load of #4 shot. If both loads pattern at 70 percent, you have more #8 shot in the target than you will have with #4s. The #8 pellets will be as a rule, spaced closer to each other than the #4s."

How to Pattern a Gun

George likes to use paper that measures four feet square. "Paper this size may be hard to find locally," he says. "If it is not available, try taping several sheets of butcher paper or newsprint together. Bruce Buck, the 'technoid' of 'Shotgun Report,' has suggested using red resin flooring paper. This is available at any home supply store and shows the pellet holes perfectly when viewed from the back. He notes that it is available only in 36-inch wide rolls but that it cuts and tapes easily. If you use small paper and your gun does not shoot to the point of aim, part of your pattern could be off the target. You would probably confuse this with a bad pattern. If it helps, mark the target center with spray paint for use as an aiming point."

When he is patterning, George prefers to use a shooting bench. At this point, he maintains, you are not checking the gun for fit and a bench helps to remove some of the variables. From the correct distance, he shoots at the center of the target. "I recommend shooting a minimum of five times on different targets with each shell or choke you are testing," he says. "Draw a 30-inch circle around the densest portion of the pattern on each target. If you intend to do much of this get a 30-inch diameter template, like a piece of Lexan [Plexiglas]. You can easily move this around on the paper to find where to draw the circle. Count the pellets inside of the circle. Divide this number by the total number of shot in the shell and you have your percentage. Take the percentage from each target, add them and divide by the total number of shots fired for each shell or choke and this will give you the overall average for that test. Sounds like a royal pain, doesn't it? It is, but there are no short cuts if you really want to know what your shotgun is doing."

After you have finished the shooting and the math, look carefully at each pattern for holes big enough to let targets slip through. You want a dense enough pattern to ensure multiple hits.

Point of Impact

George says that he and the staff at Trulock are asked on occasion about chokes that do not center the pattern exactly on the aiming point. "Most shooters want a shotgun that centers the pattern exactly with the point of aim," he says. "In theory, most shotguns are manufactured to do this, but it is not unusu-

al to find guns shooting high or low and to the right or left … or a combination of these."

Shotguns that pattern half above and half below the point of aim have what is commonly known as a 50/50 pattern. One that shoots three-quarters of the pattern over and one-quarter under the point of aim has a 75/25 pattern and so on.

Certain guns are designed to give patterns other than 50/50. Common reasons for off-center patters are: a defective choke tube, a bent barrel, misaligned choke and barrel, a loose barrel, poor gun fit and flinch.

To check your gun for point of aim, the following procedure can be followed:

Set up with a padded rest.

Make sure to get perfect bead alignment if your gun has a center bead. If it does not the rib should be perfectly flat, with the bead visible.

Use the same load you use in the field or on the range.

Squeeze the trigger. (This is easier said than done as most shotgun trigger assemblies give anything but a good pull.)

Use targets with a center aiming point.

Shoot several targets, change chokes and repeat.

George suggests you follow this procedure with several different chokes and to test some of the factory tubes that came with the gun if you are using aftermarket chokes such as his Trulock chokes. Here are the possible results:

If all of the chokes shoot to the same spot or at least very close to the same, you do not have a problem with the chokes.

If your point of impact changes with each choke you test, you certainly have a problem, but not the chokes.

If one choke shoots to a different point of aim and the others do not, that choke is probably defective and a call to the manufacturer is in order.

One other thing you should be aware of, George notes, is "point of convergence." This problem will be found only on side-by-side or over/under shotguns. Both barrels should shoot to the same spot. Again, what works in theory seldom works in practice. Generally with over/unders the top barrel will shoot high. When testing for proper convergence you will find it easier if you use tight chokes. If the convergence is close, be happy; many are not. If you cannot live with the error, you should talk to the manufacturer.

A Note About Steel Shot

If you use your competition shotgun for hunting, you need to be aware of the effect of steel shot on choke tubes and choke fit.

Much has changed over the years with steel loadings, George Trulock says. The quality and consistency of the shells has been greatly improved. However, the fact that steel shot exerts much more stress on choke tubes has not changed. The problem is

George Trulock of Trulock Chokes says that point of convergence can be a difficulty with side-by-sides such as this $849 Italian 411 from Tristar. Ideally, both barrels should shoot to the same spot.

Charlie Boswell says there is as much variation and opportunity in choke tubes as there is in shotguns. His gold anodized slot-ported, 12-gauge Comp-N-Choke screw-in choke costs $49.95 (www.comp-n-choke.com) while his black, diagonally-ported 12-gauge choke from Kick's Industries runs $65.00 (www.kicks-ind.com).

that steel shot is much harder than lead. It transmits much more energy to the choke when it strikes the conical portion and if the tube is not of sufficient strength it will cause it to deform. This is known as "choke creep."

Over a period of time, choke creep can lock a choke in the barrel so that it is next to impossible to remove. If you buy aftermarket chokes, look for chokes rated for use with steel shot and use a good tube lube. Birchwood Casey makes a non-evaporating, metallic base Choke Tube Lube that prevents corrosion and galling due to high-pressure loads and extreme temperatures. Brownell's sells a ¾-ounce tube for $6.40.

Choke Cleaning

George recommends that you clean your chokes and the threads every time you clean your gun. Plastic fouling and powder residue build up in screw-in chokes much faster than in fixed choke guns. Powder fouling will also work between the choke and the choke counterbore in the barrel. Remove the choke and clean with a toothbrush using solvent. Trulock markets and uses a solvent called "Choke Shine" as a cleaner. Simply drop the choke into the solution for a short time and it will come out with the fouling dissolved. Clean the inside of the barrel with a cleaner/lubricant such as Clenzoil making sure the threads do not have any residue. Then, lightly wipe the choke with oil and reassemble. Remember that rust can occur in the barrel and freeze a choke in place even if the choke is made from stainless steel.

Choke Tightness

Although this seems like a "no-brainer," George believes there is a proper way to install a choke tube. When changing a choke in the field or at the range, wipe the choke with a clean rag first, he says. This keeps any abrasive from being ground

into the threaded area of the choke/barrel. Finger-tighten and then use a wrench that properly fits the tube to finish tightening using a moderate amount of pressure. This will help keep the choke from loosening when in use.

When a choke is not properly seated the possibility of the shot charge striking the edge of the choke greatly increases. If this happens, a bulged barrel and a ruined choke are almost guaranteed. Most chokes will loosen and back out to some degree if they are left finger-tight. However, a perfectly clean, dry choke installed in a clean, dry barrel and moderately tightened with a wrench should not work loose. Having said that, most shooters are better off making sure that there is a light coating of oil on the choke before installing it as this will help prevent rust in the barrel. George recommends checking chokes for tightness on a regular basis.

Frozen Chokes

"We have pulled frozen chokes of almost every brand in our shop," George Trulock says. "Normally by the time we get the barrel one or more people have attempted to remove the choke. Did you ever wonder where the saying 'Fixed Guns Repaired' came from? Frozen choke tubes is a problem that can be prevented 99 percent of the time by simply cleaning the choke and barrel on a regular basis. The number one problem is RUST in the threaded area of the choke/barrel. If you keep this from forming, amazingly you will not have any problems. The second problem is choke creep or expansion. This fortunately is much less of a problem than rust. It is caused normally by using large steel shot in tight chokes [Full or tighter]. Follow the manufacturers suggestions when using steel shot and the odds are very much in your favor that you will have no problems."

If you experience choke creep, you'll notice the choke becoming harder to remove and install and if you continue it will

If you are going to try to remove a frozen choke yourself, first unload the gun! These are the instructions from Trulock. Remove the barrel from the action and soak the muzzle in a can of penetrating oil for several days. Make sure the container has a sufficient amount of oil to completely cover the barrel as deep as the choke is recessed. Use a proper fitting wrench and try to work the choke back and forth in small increments. If this does not work, try letting it soak several more days. Heat applied to the choke area can be of help. Never get the barrel so hot that you cannot touch it with your hand for several seconds. Do not use a hammer of any kind to try and "tap" it. Soaking and low heat will get most frozen chokes out. ("Be patient when following this procedure," George says. "We have seen quite a number of barrels ruined because of apparent impatience.")

Choke Storage

Trulock suggests that you keep chokes in a padded case especially designed for them. There are a number of quality cases on the market in the under-$20.00 range. The purpose is to keep them from hitting each other or any hard object that could cause burrs or deformation. Chokes are particularly susceptible to denting in the threaded area. "We have seen this occur on numerous occasions when chokes stored in plain boxes were dropped," George says. "We also urge you to clean all of the chokes that have used when you clean your gun. Alloy steel chokes need a light coat of oil prior to storage and stainless steel keeps its rust resistant properties best when it is free from contamination."

There are almost as many ways of marking chokes with their constriction as there are chokes. These days, it hardly makes sense to require a special wrench to remove a choke when extended chokes with rough or knurled surfaces can easily be removed by hand. If you cannot remove your chokes by hand, here is a tip: Buy two (or more) wrenches. You will drop or misplace one practically every time you use it. Guaranteed. (Photo courtesy Winchester)

eventually lock in the barrel. If you find yourself with a frozen choke, George Trulock's first suggestion is to take it to a competent gunsmith. Make sure the smith has some experience in this line of work.

Remington's Express Upgrade Kit is available in 12- and 20-gauge versions. It includes Improved Cylinder and Full Rem Chokes, a Choke Tube Speed Wrench and a one-ounce bottle of Rem Oil. Comes in a rugged plastic box.

LET'S KEEP IT CLEAN, FOLKS

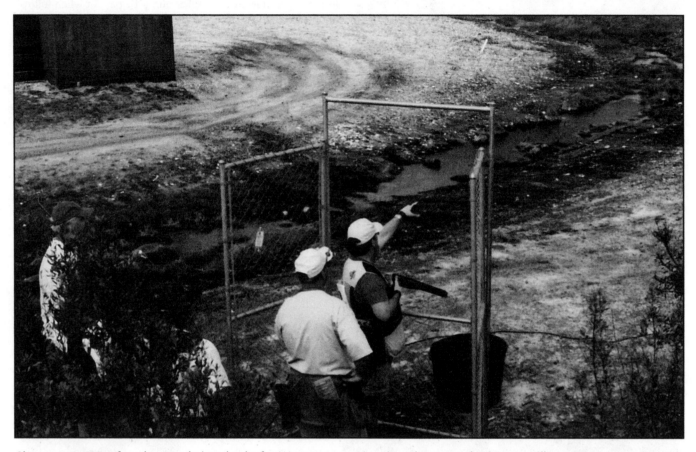

Shotgun sports are fun: they are designed to be fun. However, as you get into the games deeper, you will encounter many situations that are not ideal for the performance of your gun: blowing grit, rain, salt air and perhaps periods of inactivity. Maintaining your gun properly is necessary to stay at the top of the leader boards and to keep you from having an irritating afternoon when something goes wrong that could have been prevented with a half-hour of regular cleaning.

If you have had a chance to be involved in or even to follow the aftermath of any natural or man-made disaster that involved fire or explosion, and certainly the 9-11 tragedy is a terrible case in point, you know that the clean-up and restoration process can be an enormous amount of work. Dirty. Smelly. Time consuming.

So, imagine what happens when you pull the trigger of a loaded shotgun. A microscopic camera in the barrel would record an atomic-bomb-like flash followed by a devastating explosion, the result of combining a tiny spark and a compressed ounce or so of highly combustible gunpowder. In its own scale, the aftermath leaves as much charred debris lying about as a very nasty house fire.

There is good news however. Even though top-ranked gunners take care of their shotguns meticulously, routine or day-to-day maintenance is easy and is not at all time-consuming.

Barring a major break-down, just a couple minutes of effort performed religiously will virtually insure that your shotgun performs smoothly every time you take it out of its case or sleeve. In our experience, it does not matter whether the shotgun costs $500.00 or $5,000.00; regular attention with a swab, a brush and a cloth will maintain its efficiency and pattern. As the folks at Hoppe's say, "Be good to your gun and it will be good to you."

First Principles

You want the bore of your shotgun to be so smooth and clean that, if it were a dinner plate, you would think nothing of letting your children eat from it. More good news. The more you shoot, and the more you scrub and clean the bore, the smoother and shinier it looks.

Why clean it at all? If you do not, you are apparently run-

Perhaps the best way to learn about the care and cleaning of a shotgun is to buy a kit with a pamphlet and follow the directions. This Otis Shotgun Cleaning System kit will clean all shotguns from .410 through 10-gauge. Of course, the five ounce bottle of Bore Cleaner will not last long, but you should be able to use the rods, brushes and cable connectors for years. These small kits are the ideal size to take to the range or to the field for a quick cleaning.

ning the risk of metal corrosion from moisture build-up and of jamming due to the build-up of "gunk" in the action. This will eventually affect accuracy, cause jamming and shorten your gun's useful life. The problem for many of us is that powder residue and tiny irregularities in the barrel cannot be seen without a special bore scope. By the time you can see scratches or a marred surface finish with your "naked eye," they have already become problems.

Condensation is one of the most insidious ways that moisture attacks your gun. After a shoot in the rain, it is obvious that you must clean and dry the gun. What is not so obvious is when you are shooting outside on a cold day and then take your gun into the clubhouse. Bingo. Condensation immediately forms on all the metal surfaces, inside the gun and out. Any type of condensation or moisture (rain, fog, snow, salt water spray, etc.) will immediately start the rust-formation process. Therefore, the first rule of gun care is to wipe and dry your gun right away ... especially if you are shooting a course (or hunting) near salt water. Even miles away, salt spray can be deadly to a fine metal finish.

Storing a gun for an extended period also requires some special care. I have heard shooters complain that, knowing they would not be shooting for a while ... a "while" sometimes lasting for years ... they cleaned and oiled their gun before they put it away. Then, when they eventually got around to shooting again, they pulled the gun out and ... Ugh! It was a mess.

To store your gun for a significant period, it is important that it be kept in a clean, dry and, need we say, safe place. Even though you have cleaned it before putting it away, a gun should be stripped and cleaned periodically ... even if it is not being handled or fired. This is required because leftover oils from fingerprints and normal moisture inside the case around the gun cannot be 100 percent removed.

Patches, Brushes and Solvents

Most guns you buy from a shooting sports retailer, especially those that are still in their original box, come with a light coating of grease on all the metal parts. The idea of greasing a gun is to keep it from corroding while it sits on the retailer's rack waiting for you to buy it. (Of course, if you purchase a Perazzi and travel to Italy for a custom fitting, this will not be a problem.) The grease can slow down the action of the gun and it has to come off. Use a clean rag and a solvent such as the famous Hoppe's No. 9.

Chances are that you will religiously clean a new gun after the first few times you shoot it. Then, after a couple months a day will come when your spouse asks you to pick up bread on the way home from the shooting range and you will forget the patches and solvent. Or some every-day pressure like washing the car or taking the dog to the veterinarian will suggest that you clean the gun tomorrow. Every day you wait, the job becomes more necessary than ever.

Here is step one. Before you begin any cleaning job, you need to be sure the gun is not loaded. Although this sounds simple, almost too simple for a veteran shooter, people are killed and permanently maimed each year by guns that were not thought to be loaded. And even though a load of low base #8s may not blow your leg off, you will certainly walk with a limp for the rest of your life so why not be certain?

One of the first principles of gun cleaning and care is to always run the rods, cleaning swabs and brushes from the receiver to the muzzle, never in the opposite direction. For over/under owners, this is a simpler operation than for those with semi-automatics who must partially disassemble their gun for thorough cleaning. There is a temptation to clean semi-autos from muzzle to breech because it is quicker and easier. You have to resist this because you can cause irreparable harm to the finely machined lining of the barrel.

The first step in cleaning after an afternoon at the range is to run a patch with an all-purpose solvent – one-way only – down the barrel. To remove any tough metal residue in the barrel or in the action, a solvent such as Birchwood Casey's Bore Scrubber works well. Remember that after spraying or wiping, you want the residue to run away from the action. Let the Bore Scrubber soak for a few minutes and then run a wire brush through the barrel about 10 times again, one-way only. Next, strip your gun of all foreign oil, residue and film using a Gun Scrubber Solvent/Degreaser-style product. Spray the brush clean before you use it a second time. You can spray this into hard-to-reach spots as it dries rapidly. Do not neglect the screw-threads for choke tubes and the choke tubes themselves. (Set-up photos courtesy Otis)

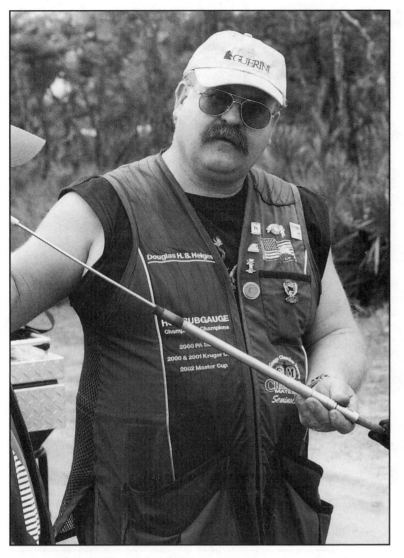

You cannot anticipate every possible problem. Sometimes things just break. They wear out. Structural flaws in the metal or the mechanism fail. These things cannot be helped. On the other hand, religious routine maintenance can prevent many ordinary problems.

As you are running patches and brushes through the bore, you should be careful to never allow the rod to scrape against the bore itself. It is said that all firearms record their history and perhaps this is the reason people look down the barrel of a firearm. An experienced eye can tell the method of cleaning, make a close guess about the number of shots put through the barrel, and understand the gun maintenance routine applied to the firearm. When people carelessly allow the tip of the rod or the rod itself to scrape along the inside of the barrel, it leaves scratches.

Your first cleaning operation is to run a patch into the receiver, past the forcing cone, through the barrel, then past the choke and out the crown or muzzle. You want to soak this patch or swab with solvent, not so much that it will form a pool, but enough that the swab will cover 360 degrees of barrel. Too much solvent and it will drip down into the trigger mechanism and cause a gummy trigger and perhaps delayed firing. Too much will drain back toward the stock and damage the finish. This action lubricates the bore and prevents sand or dirt from scratching the muzzle end of the barrel because it is picked up on the patch and carried out.

After the first swabbing, run a dry patch through the barrel until you have absorbed the solvent and then use a brush. Select something perhaps a little oversized to clean the forcing cone and the barrel—especially backbored barrels, which are honed to a diameter greater than SAAMI specifications.

Never run the bore brush down through the barrel of any gun before using a lubricated patch. This would almost certainly damage your gun. Any dirt or sand in the muzzle end would adhere to the bristles on the brush. Then, when you bring the brush into the forcing cone, the dirt will be deposited in the chamber and forcing cone, which are relatively clean even following a shot. This is the exact equivalent of cleaning in the wrong direction (from muzzle to breech).

Do not forget to spray the brush clean with a solvent like Birchwood Casey's Gun Scrubber Solvent/Degreaser after use. This Solvent/Degreaser is environmentally safe and dries rapidly leaving metal clean and free of film or grease. Solvent left on the brush is messy and can weaken the bristles. In addition, if the brush is used dirty when you are trying to clean your gun the next time, it can cause more harm than good.

After this, if you notice crud (miniscule lead or plastic fragments) inside the barrel you will almost certainly see scratches as well. These scratches may be caused when the cleaning rod – either with a patch or a brush on the end – is moved back and forth on the false assumption that this is the proper way to remove grit and lead fouling. It also means that abrasive dirt from the muzzle was brought back into the chamber and forcing cone. (Conventional cleaning equipment does not clean the wider-diameter forcing cone very well.) You are not in the kitchen scrubbing pots and pans. Run patches and brushes one way, the right way, from receiver to muzzle only.

Speaking of brushes, remember that brushes are designed to be run one way only through the barrel. Never reverse the direction while the brush is inside the bore: this will bend the bristles on the brush. This is the equivalent of bending a wire back and forth until it breaks. You will always ruin a brush if you reverse it while in the bore.

Dirt pulled backwards down the barrel causes abrasions and remember that most of these are not visible on casual inspection. Scratches allow tiny lead and plastic fragments to adhere to crevices in the bore's steel and, depending on their depth and the hardness of the eventual deposit, they become resistant to cleaning. Your pattern suffers.

So, if you clean the chamber and forcing cone by working only in the direction the shot is fired, the bore should never be scratched.

Otis makes a flexible steel cleaning rod that allows you to perform daily swabbing to your semi-auto without disassembly. Just open the action as you would to insert a shell, Otis says, and then run the flexible steel rod with lubricant-soaked patch attached down the barrel, pulling it out the muzzle end. This quick cleaning, while not complete, is very good and takes only a minute.

There is a tendency among shotgunners, especially those who have been casual about cleaning, to simply turn a patch over

Cleaning a semi-automatic without disassembling the barrel requires a flexible cable – and some care not to scratch the inside of the barrel.

or even re-use it. You may be able to get away with turning it over depending on how you fold it and how dirty the swab has become, but swabs are so cheap, why would you risk using it a second time? The abrasive material that adheres to it, the very stuff you want to remove, will certainly scratch the forcing cone and bore at the breech end. This will cause lead and plastic buildup and defeat the purpose of the cleaning.

You can use a chamber-cleaning rod with oversized bore brush to clean the chamber and the choke tube threads. It is always desirable to clean the barrel first before changing the choke tube. This will prevent dirt from getting into the threads. If you find the choke tube does not easily screw in, do not force it. Remove it and clean the threads again carefully. Force a choke tube into place and a bulged barrel could result. When you have cleaned the threads, immediately reinsert the choke tube.

After you have finished cleaning the bore, apply a small amount of lubricating or gun oil to a clean patch and run it through. Your barrel will now be clean and lightly lubricated, ready for the range or the field.

After the Barrel

The action and trigger mechanism can be cleaned with solvent and scrubbed lightly with a brush. A fast-drying spray solvent works well here unless you feel certain that you can completely disassemble the mechanics of your gun and reassemble them as good as new. Few casual shooters feel this competent,

It is a handy thing to be able to run through the barrel, and to wipe down your barrel and the outside of the receiver with a rust preventive during a long day at the range. Guns attract dust and dust attracts crud build-up. These individual five-inch by eight-inch cloths are impregnated with Sheath Rust Preventive. Use once and toss. Products like Sheath are supposed to drive out moisture from metal pores and deposit a transparent coating to protect against corrosion.

especially with a semi-auto and some parts of the action just cannot be easily cleaned or disassembled by us occasional shooters. (Always check your gun's Owner's Manual and "exploded parts list" before performing anything more than routine disassembly. Like your car engine, if there is one part left over, it just will not operate.)

After spraying and brushing using solvents and degreasers, wipe your gun as clean as possible and apply a light coating of oil. Very light, but very thorough should be the password to this operation.

The last thing to do is wipe the outer metal surfaces to remove any fingerprints or runny drips of solvent or oil. A clean cloth or even a clean patch with a light coating of Hoppe's No. 9 works fine.

If you are shooting in wet weather or perhaps near the seashore, a number of manufacturers offer specialty gun cloths and other products with ingredients that drive out moisture, lubricate and help prevent rust. It is a good thing to carry a few of these in your case to wipe down and run through the barrel right after shooting. Birchwood Casey's convenient and disposable Sheath Take-Alongs for example are small individual cloths impregnated with Sheath Rust Preventive and sealed in a foil packet for compact carrying. A 12-pack of these costs less than $6.00.

And what about the stock and forearm? Unless they are synthetic, these pieces are usually walnut and even though shooters are usually very careful of their own and other shooters' guns, it is easy to bump the metal edges of a gun rack or scratch against the tailgate of your pick up. A spot application of stock finish

It is easy to forget or ignore the choke tubes. They are as subject to fouling as the barrel, especially the threads. A good anti-seize lube will prevent tubes from sticking in the barrel from corrosion, the high stress of steel shot, and the extreme temperatures and pressures from repeated shooting.

followed by an oiling and finally a good rub-down with a clean cloth should once again bring out the gun stock's luster and original brilliance.

Barrelguard makes a super-lightweight tube (www.barrelguard.com) that should take much of the anxiety out of leaving your guns in the case for any extended period. The company's VCI (Volatile Corrosion Inhibitor) tubes slip into the barrels of your shotgun to replace more conventional treatments with cosmoline, grease, oil, preservatives, dessicants and waxed or barrier papers. Airtight packaging is not required for these tubes to work. Barrelguard says the VCI chemicals vaporize in the packaging environment and condense on all metal surfaces to form a protective molecular layer that prevents moisture, salt, dirt, oxygen and other materials from depositing on the metal and causing corrosion.

For shotguns, Barrelguard tubes are 22 inches long and 0.4 inches in diameter. They will fit any size shotgun from 10-gauge to .410. These tubes do not require a snug fit. Barrelguard tubes are sold in packs of five and cost about $5.00 each. While the automatic replenishing action of the tube's chemicals may last for years, Barrelguard recommends that for highest effectiveness, they be replaced annually.

The end of a good day shooting means you are tired and your gun needs cleaning. A minimum of 15 minutes with solvent and lubricant will make smiles possible after the next outing, too.

A HIT-OR-MISS APPROACH TO CLAYS

By Bob Knopf

Bob Knopf is a National Sporting Clays (NSCA) certified instructor and Chief Instructor for the National Wing & Clay Shooting School. He is author of the book Wing & Clay Shooting Made Easy. *Bob began shooting at age 15 and has hunted waterfowl and upland birds across the U.S. for more than 30 years.*

Bob has helped hundreds of shooters improve their shotgunning scores and hunting prowess. Bob authors numerous features on wing and clay shooting and travels to clubs, resorts, and shooting facilities teaching wing and clay shooting skills. His belief that successful wing shooting can be learned quickly and easily by anyone is reflected in his quiet, authoritative teaching style.

Bob Knopf is a National Sporting Clays Association (NSCA) Level 2 certified instructor and chief instructor for his National Wing & Clay Shooting School. His book Wing & Clay Shooting Made Easy *(www.shootinginstruction.com) is an excellent and fast-reading primer for shotgunning and for hunting.*

Second to none, the biggest concern of both beginning and experienced shooters is missing. For many, it represents some sort of shooting failure. It triggers frustration, sometimes anger, and it places our egos on our sleeves. It ruins our calm, which is what we need most when we miss.

Missing is inevitable. Viewed correctly, it can be a great teacher because, using our minds, we can learn how to shoot better when we miss. We can strive to improve our technique when we miss. We are forced to focus on hitting when we miss.

Misses are a great teacher on controlling the mental aspects of shooting because if we don't control how we think when we miss, we continue to miss, and miss, and miss again. We need to use missing to make ourselves better shooters. If we use it right, we'll excel in our shooting.

Remember this. Shotgun shooting professionals, the best of the best, easily miss more targets in one week than most clays shooters or hunters miss in a month. Why? They shoot more. They know they'll miss. They calmly work to correct their misses, to minimize them. They work to deal with them mentally. And very importantly, when they miss, they learn to leave their

The quickest, easiest and least costly way to become a proficient wing shooter is to hire a certified instructor. "The money you pay a qualified instructor will show immediate results and will save hundreds, perhaps thousands of dollars on ammunition and targets," says Bob Knopf.

learning moment should begin with, "Okay, next shot I'll give the bird more lead," or "I'll swing more smoothly to the target." Then, as you prepare for the next shot, visualize yourself on one of those days you simply couldn't miss … and call for the next bird.

Common Mistake: For most shooters, on long crossing shots, our minds will not easily accept the correct lead we must use. When missing a 35-50 yard shot, double your lead and tell yourself, "It's okay to miss in front."

As much as we will not let misses upset us, we definitely want to minimize them at every opportunity. New shooters should focus on easier-to-hit targets. Keep it easy as you develop your personal style and technique. Don't go out with an experienced shooter and shoot all the hard targets. On a sporting clays course, shoot only the easier stations. Observe the more difficult targets and shoot them with your pointer finger (no gun). Allow yourself time to develop your technique before tackling the tougher targets first-hand.

Experienced shooters, to get better, need to practice on their own personal "tough for me to hit" target list. When practicing these, and when you begin missing repeatedly, stop shooting for a minute. Determine why you aren't breaking the target. Do not focus on what you did wrong. Focus on what you need to do right. Resume practice considering some of the "miss" factors pre-

misses behind them, so that one miss doesn't breed another.

For many shooters, missing one target causes more additional misses than any other single factor. More misses than poor shooting skills, more than improper choke selection, more than poor gun fit. When we miss, our thinking mind kicks in and tries to keep us from missing again. Ironically, the opposite of what we want usually happens. Fluid gun motion becomes stiff, our timing becomes irregular, and our trigger pull becomes delayed. We think, we analyze, we miss again.

Therefore, when you miss, immediately focus on hitting the next target and shoot it with enthusiasm. Importantly, allow yourself some free misses without any thought as to why you may have missed. The target or game simply got away.

If you miss, do not focus on what you did wrong. Focus on what you need to do right to hit the target. Leave the miss behind. Quickly, get directed on hitting the next target.

It is important to learn to view missing as a learning experience. That way we will keep our calm and our misses help us learn. The

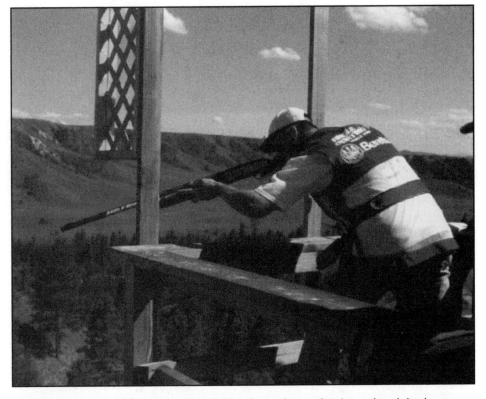

Professional shotgun shooting coach Bob Knopf says that each miss and each broken target or downed game bird must be viewed in terms of the three basic wing shooting fundamentals: moving (pointing) your gun to the target, obtaining your personal sight picture (correct lead) and pulling the trigger at the right time.

sented in this book. If you continue missing, make the target easier to hit. Move closer, reduce some of the angle. Don't force yourself into the, "I'm gonna shoot till I break it" habit unless you're calmly prepared to handle the additional misses that lie ahead. When missing regularly, be sure to change something. Alter your method, your gun hold point, or your target view point until you hit the target.

When you're missing, change something. Are you hesitating on your trigger pull? Are you being too careful? Pull the trigger as the sight picture develops or 1/10th of a second before you see the perfect sight picture.

A good way to handle misses is to keep a list of targets you commonly miss. "Long crosser right to left." Quartering away from behind on left side." An instructor can get you hitting these problem shots or spend a couple of sessions where you specifically practice them.

On tougher targets, getting a correct sight picture usually remedies the problem very quickly. When teaching, I commonly tell a shooter to miss intentionally, perhaps to "miss in front" of a target, or to "miss underneath." Many are surprised to see that when they double or triple their lead trying to miss in front, that they solidly hit the target. This is because often a miss is simply due to a wrong sight picture. But sometimes our mind won't easily let us change.

I've watched both experienced and new shooters alike hit a tiny quarter-sized spot every time in their shooting. The only problem was that it was 10 feet behind the actual target or two feet over it.

If you're missing, make the shot easier and spend some time hitting some easier targets. If you're an experienced shooter who is shooting with a novice shooter, don't let them shoot the harder shots. Very few new shooters get disgusted and give up shooting because they were overly successful.

To shoot successfully, we must learn to smile at ourselves when we miss. We must treat ourselves gently. This is not easy, and it, too, takes practice. The reward, however, is more hits than we ever imagined.

© Bob Knopf: used by permission.

HELICE: PUTTING A NEW SPIN ON THINGS

Unlike other shotgun games which are shot with clay targets (except for live pigeon shoots, of course), hélice is shot with a winged plastic flyer, the white part of which (the "witness") is knocked off when hit and reused. The standard load is 1¼ ounce.

Much to the dismay of the hundreds of sporting clay enthusiasts present, the TM Ranch east of Orlando, Florida was going out of business and its famous Seminole Cup was closing. 2004 was the last chance to see the highly-regarded shooting layout and enjoy the warm, February weather while busting ranch pigeons.

Just down the road from the headquarters and manufacturer display area, however, before competitors reached the sub-gauge and 5-Stand competitions, was an open field where Ohio's Tom Veatch had set up a hélice shooting ring.

"We're not holding a competition," Tom said. "We're just shooting for fun. We want to introduce all the clay shooters

here to the newest, hottest game sweeping through Europe."

According to Tom, who is a sales representative and distributor for Wells Hélice Equipment in the US (www.helice. us), millions of targets are shot every year in Europe and the new game is making inroads in U.S. shotgun sports as well. "Hélice isn't a side-game or some novelty," he says. "It is a prestigious, stand-alone sport. Statistics compiled over many years prove that hélice is actually more challenging than the live pigeon shooting it is designed to replace. Generally, in Europe and around the world where it has been introduced, hélice has been a highly accepted improvement over live birds. The flight of these targets is outstanding and there are no political

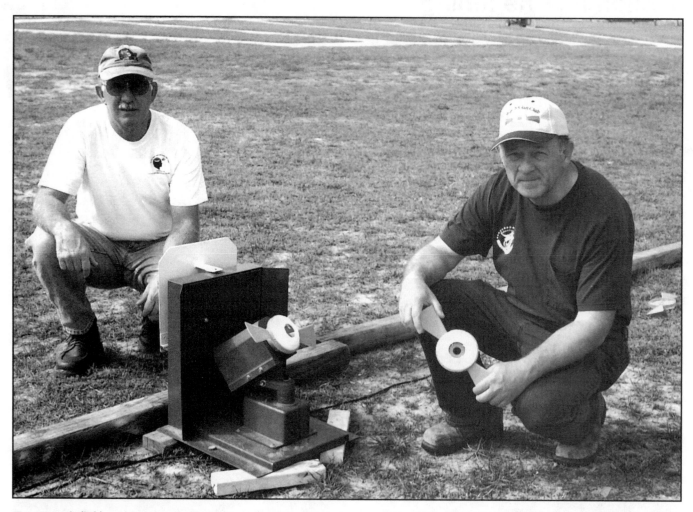

Tom Veatch (left) and Frank Mowrey go down-range to replace targets on the hélice throwing machines. These machines can spin a bird into the air from zero to 10,000 rpm, but at this time, the plastic birds must be manually replaced after all the stations have thrown a bird.

repercussions from the anti-hunting crowd. Plus, the World Cup circuit now offers some of the most exciting and difficult hélice competition available to shotgunners."

Not only did this turn out to be the author's first opportunity to shoot these dipsy-doodle plastic flyers, but also Tom handed me his Perazzi. "Try my gun," he generously offered. It was quite a moment.

Plastic, Not Clay

The US Hélice Association (USHA, www.ushelice.com) sanctions hélice shoots. It gives points and awards for shooters seeking to be Team USA members and earn expensive paid trips to the Helice World Championships each year. The USHA notes that shooting its plastic target is not intended to be a clay game. Hélice is designed to replicate and replace shooting "Box Pigeon" or live birds, where that venue is still allowed.

Hélice is shot from a single station. Depending on a shooter's earned or observed handicap, it may be as close as 24 meters or as distant as 30 meters from a semi-circle with green boxes containing hélice 110-volt throwing machines, spaced an equal distance apart. There may be five boxes (spaced 4½ to five meters), or seven (2¼ to 2½ meters between machines two and three and three and four) or even nine stations depending on the field and tournament layout.

Hélice targets are spun or thrown away from the shooter in a completely random pattern and order. This obviously differs from the highly regulated pattern of trap and skeet and to a great degree from sporting clays as well since it is impossible to guess the sequence. And no bird is thrown for general viewing before a shooter steps to the shooting stand, either.

A hélice is a two-piece target, an orange or red body with two angled wings and a white snap-on cap called the "witness." Struck by shot, the witness must separate from the spinning orange body and wings and fall within the area between the two semi-circles for the target to be scored.

Unlike a clay disk, there is no such thing as a "visible piece." The two parts of a hélice target are reusable, at least until they become visibly damaged (which happens quickly, sometimes after one shot, to the orange wings), and range operators collect the white witness and as many of the undamaged orange winged sections as possible.

The U.S. Hélice Association specifies that hélice targets are 28 cm (11 inches) from orange-red wingtip to wingtip. The raised white witness in the center is 10.4 cm wide and the lightweight target weighs a maximum of 70 grams. The wings must be built of a material fragile to impact (polystyrene) while the witness is specifically not fragile (50% polyethylene) and hence reusable. The throwing machines can be adjusted anywhere from zero rpm to 10,000 rpm.

Starting from a high gun position, the shooter calls "Ready," the range controller (inside the adjacent hut) responds with "Ready." When the shooter calls "Pull," the target is thrown instantly, triggered by a voice-activated system. Unlike trap or skeet, the birds appear in random order.

These throwing machines or "hélice traps" are not universally standardized. As long as a target or machine performs within FITASC rules, they are allowed in a sanctioned match. In international competition, you may shoot Spanish machines and Spanish targets in Spain, Italian in Italy and French in France. The best advice is to do a little research – perhaps on the internet – before heading off to a match. An hour of research may well be worth a target or two.

When they are called to shoot, participants advance to the designated shooting station with their guns empty. They load and call "Ready" when the range is declared clear. The operator must then respond with "Ready." The shooter will then call "Pull" and the target is thrown instantly by an automatic voice-activated system such as the Canterbury Voice Release (www.cvr.co.nz).

The shooter must hit the whirling hélice target before it reaches a second semi-circle marked by a fence placed 21 meters beyond the target-throw semi-circle. Another difference between hélice and more formalized clay target shooting is that any safe preliminary gun hold is allowed. Shooters may wait with their gun down or fully shouldered.

Hélice rules state that a 12 gauge is the largest gun allowed and that no credit will be given for smaller gauges. The maximum size lead shot used is 2.70 mm (a #7). The maximum shot load allowed by FITASC (which governs inter-national hélice competition) is 1¼-ounce, which is standard for Hélice.

When the shooter calls "Pull" the hélice target is thrown and the gunner has two shots to separate the witness from the wings and have the reusable witness fall between the semi-circles.

USHA gives a range operator some latitude to develop his or her shoot format, but generally 25 or 30 targets a day make up a complete competition program. Because there is not much squad rotation except on and off the stand – in a seven-machine competition, each shooter shoots five birds at a time, for instance – your entire shooting day can easily be over in an hour.

Major hélice competitions are frequently two to three day events and are often held at a range near some "destination" such as Las Vegas or Reno or Dallas or Shreveport. Although each day consists only of a 25- or 30-target main match, shorter 10- or 15-target events or "races" often follow these matches as they are called. There are typically awards for Daily Champions, Ladies, Veterans and Juniors. In addition, there are High Overall (HOA) awards for the weekend (perhaps 75 or 90 targets).

Tom Veatch says that one of the exciting things about hélice is that shooters from all major disciplines are usually present. Champions from skeet, trap, sporting clays, flyers and even the Olympics can, and will, regularly attend and are surprised

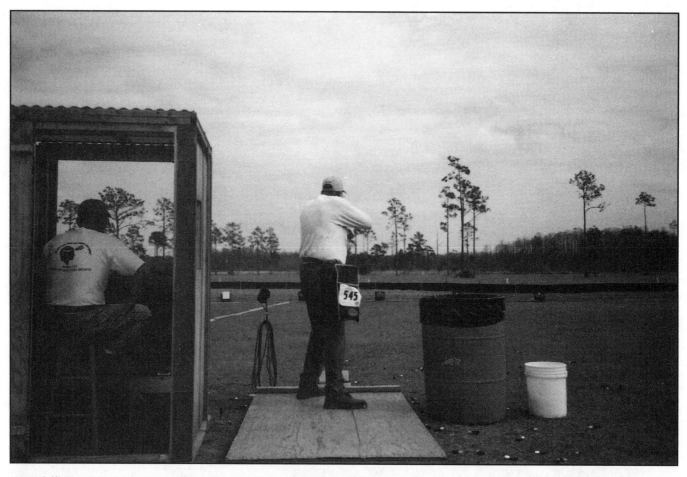

Many hélice set-ups in the US, such as the one pictured here, are still for demonstration rather than competition, because the game is new to the US. "It isn't a poor man's game," Tom Veatch says. "A cost of $13 per bird is not unusual, so a round of 30 targets may cost $390."

to learn that the HOA prize often goes to the person who breaks 86 out of 90 rather than the 100 out of 100 with a shoot-off as is common elsewhere.

The short shooting day may be fine – or not – depending on your finances. Hélice is expensive. Given the flexibility (and many would argue the necessity) of a venue to charge a little more to pay for the computerized infrastructure and all the natural variables, say $3.00 per bird, a round of 30 targets might well cost $90.00 plus options and ammo.

Why is hélice so expensive compared to shooting a clay game?

Hélice differs in numerous important ways from the clay sports and target cost is one of them. Hélice supporters say the difference is not as bad as it appears, because Hélice competitions and even practice sessions require far fewer targets to be shot. Where a full competition day at sporting clays may require 100 to 200 targets (or more), a full day of hélice may consist, as we have pointed out, of 25 to 30 birds. In addition, the base cost of the hélice target is much higher due to their more complex, non-polluting injection molded plastic

components. Clay targets cost range owners in the neighborhood of five to seven cents each. Hélice targets cost between 70 cents and $1.00 each!

"Hélice is not a poor man's sport," Tom Veatch says, stating the obvious, "but in competition the return to winners tends to be high."

Chokes and Loads

Generally, hélice is most successfully shot with comparatively tight chokes and powerful cartridges. This is because chips (the famous "visible pieces") do not count. The white "witness" must be separated from its red-orange carrier and wings. All shots will be between 32 and 47 yards, and an on-edge target presents a shallow (3.25 cm) profile. Light Modified or Modified will be the most open choke you want to use and then only for your first shot. When shooting a semi-automatic, .025 to .030 is about right and with a double barrel a Modified and or even a Full set up should be adequate. Again, the USHA specifies that the heaviest shot charge is 38 grams or 1¼ ounces.

PUTTIN' ON THE RITZ

Shotgunning is like home ownership. Once you have bought the basics, a shotgun and a few boxes of shells to try shooting skeet or trap or sporting clays, the sky is the limit on the fun you can have – and the accessories you can acquire. Of course, all these things cost money: some are not at all expensive and some can break a poor man's bank account. Then too, there are a few that you absolutely must have, such as eye and ear protection. If you are lucky, you will eventually be able to convince your spouse that the new golf car and trailer (and then the garage extension) are essential to your happiness.

Making The Case

Hard-sided cases

The trick with a hard-sided case is to buy the best you can afford. After all, this case is going to protect your shooting investment and if it fails, you may not be able to shoot. Be sure to get a case that will do the job. What do you look for in a hard sided case? Well, watch for such things as recessed hinges and locks that cannot be easily smashed by airport baggage handlers. Steel-reinforced corners help prevent a cracked or damaged case if it is dropped; and remember that a comfortable, sturdy, non-slip handle will help you avoid misery and suffering. Check the locks and the seals because you want the case to be tamper-proof and moisture-proof. If you are a traveling shooter who uses several guns, you may want a case with wheels and perhaps a canvas cover.

Fortunately, there are plenty of excellent cases to choose from. These include but certainly aren't limited to the handsome models from T.Z. Case International (www.tzcase.com), the high-performance carriers from Storm Case (www.stormcase.com), the well-known and rugged cases from Plano Molding (www.planomolding.com), and a variety profiled below.

It's a good bet that you have heard of Doskosil, a high-end hard-plastic gun case manufacturer, which also goes by the name DoskoSport (www.doskosport.com). They have a specialized case – and sometimes several – for practically every shooting (and hunting) opportunity.

The inner dimensions of their black AW Series Double Scoped Rifle/Shotgun Case are 52 x 13 x 5¼ inches, so it can conveniently carry two guns and prevent them from bumping or scratching against each other. Doskocil says that its continuous overlapping seal ensures that you will have a watertight, airtight and dustproof compartment.

To make handling this large case easy, it has two, wide wheels and swivel handles. Holes machined through the sturdy side rib allow you to fasten the case with your own padlock. The inside padding on top and bottom is thick layers of gray foam.

Winchester by Vanguard USA (www.vanguardusa.com) markets several cases for breakdown shotguns. Its 7700 and 7800 series use lightweight black PVC for the panels, dark gray eggshell foam padding and have both combination and key locks. The #7705 and #7805W have essentially the same inside dimension in inches: 31⅜ x 12⅞ x 4. Because the 13.66-pound #7805W has steel-reinforced corners, it weighs about 3¾ pounds more than the #7705.

The brushed aluminum breakdown shotgun cases from Winchester are the #WA-7048 ($160.00) and #WG-1151A. Both styles offer full eggshell foam padding, key locks and padlock receptacles. The WA case opens from both sides and weighs 16.75 pounds. The WG case only weighs 9.48 pounds,

The aluminum Winchester Breakdown Shotgun case has impact- and scratch-resistant side panels and reinforced corners. Features four heavy-duty key locks and padlock receptacles.

but it offers key-specific locks. A universal Winchester (or some other brand) key will not open these locks.

Guardforce cases built by Vanguard are similar to those marketed by Winchester. They have four portable cases for breakdown shotguns, which include those mentioned above, plus their #GDF-41000 series of molded, hard polyester cases. These lightweight cases have metal interior frames, carrying straps and handles. The #GDF-41833 weighs six pounds.

There are several specialty case manufacturers in the U.S. and Canada such as Dean Ziegel's Ziegel Engineering (www. ziegeleng.com) in California. Of particular interest is Dean's 15-pound Model 75 (6½ x 9 x 31 inches), which is designed primarily for over/under skeet or sporting clay gun sets with 28-inch barrels. This heavy-duty aluminum case has reinforced corners and will accommodate four barrel sets and two receivers in a compact format. It has four barrel compartments in the lower section, and all dividers are covered with high-density foam. A built-in inner leaf separates barrels from receivers: receivers are held in place with Velcro fastening straps. The Model 75 is lined with a black polypropylene fabric. It has one handle on each side and two catches. This case can be locked with padlocks through the stainless steel catches or with Dean's AC16 Locking Rod. The suggested retail price is around $300.

Perhaps no manufacturer has more cases specifically dedicated to carrying a shotgun than Americase (www.americase. com) of Waxahachie, Texas. Its catalog shows photos and diagrams and gives exact dimensions of dozens of cases designed for specific carrying tasks, for example: #1004 is the 17-pound Standard Skeet Tube Set (30-inch barrels) for $339 or #1012 is the Two Barrel Skeet Tube Set (32-inch barrels) for $349. Or how about mixing and matching with #1008, the 25-pound Auto or Pump and Tubed Over-and-Under case for $419? If you are strictly a pump gun or semi-auto fan, #5043, the Ameri-Lite Two Take-down Pumps or Autos, weighs 14 pounds and costs $269. Of course, for those who travel to a shoot prepared for anything there is case #2007 Two Trap Combos (Four Barrels), which weighs 26 pounds and costs $399.

Americase offers several custom accessories for its cases. Because most breakdown shotgun cases are less than 38 inches long, an adjustable shoulder strap ($35.00) with a comfortable "Gel-Pad" is available. When you order your case with this accessory, D-rings for the strap will be attached to the case or case cover at the factory. Engraved name tags can be made and riveted to the case next to the handle or on the top side panel for a minimal fee and embroidery be sewn onto any velvet interior case: game animals, initials, the name of the shotgun manufacturer and so on. Americase will also custom-build a case for you!

Soft-sided cases

Except for temporary storage and quick trips, soft-sided cases are not recommended for long-term storage. While they are excellent when you want to reduce the bulk of a large, hard-sided case, they can trap moisture and induce rust and corrosion.

The Boyt-Bob Allen connection (www.boytharness.com) has produced quite a number of good-looking, serviceable soft-sided cases. You will find these excellent on the day you are car-pooling to the range and there just is not enough room in the trunk for everyone's hard-sided case. The Boyt that will catch your eye right away is the $151 #GC36 Boundary Lakes with leather handles, saddle, tip and butt. This model has an outside choke tube/accessory pocket. A two-way brass zipper and removable, adjustable sling are included. These cases are made with 22-ounce heavy canvas siding and soft, 40-ounce cotton batting with flannel lining. The GC36 is available in green and khaki in lengths from 46 to 52 inches.

Boyt offers many specialty cases including two-gun cases such as the $114 green canvas #GS150 Two-Gun Canvas Sleeve. This model opens from the butt of the case with a strap rather than a zipper in 48-, 50- and 52-inch lengths. The #GC214 Take-Down Canvas Case is made with the same 22/40 material with a heavy-duty padded suede divider to protect your stock from the barrel lugs. This $114 green case comes with an accessory pocket, brass zipper and leather sling in three lengths: 28, 30 and 34 inches.

The great beauty in the Boyt line-up has to be its traditional leather case in lengths from 46 to 52 inches. For $433 you can own a heavy-duty, nine ounce oil-tanned, hand-cut

This Breakdown Guardforce Shotgun case by Vanguard features combination and key locks with metal-reinforced corners for the black, ABS plastic sides.

The Guardforce GDF Series has a durable polyester exterior for a semi-hard-sided case. Inside, thick padding to protect your breakdown shotgun. Weighs just six pounds!

harness leather case with double brass zipper and fleece lining. It looks good and for just a few extra dollars you can have it personalized!

Practice Traps

If you want to get in a few shots on the weekend or after work without going to the club range, Champion (www. championtarget.com) has a couple traps to consider. You can buy a lightweight hand thrower like their inexpensive Super Sport at almost any BoxMart. It tosses one bird at a time and is adjustable for all size sporting clays targets, from standard to mini.

Throw two at a time? Check out the EZ-Double Throw from MTM Case-Gard. Its adjustability allows you to throw "countless horizontal and vertical separation choices," MTM says, and you can throw with your right or left hand. In red plastic, the total assembled length is 31 inches.

When you become more serious about your practice and either do not live near a certified range or just want the convenience of shooting whenever you want to shoot, you will want to step up to a machine like Champion's High Fly string-release manual trap. The adjustable High Fly launches one or two birds with the pull of a cord and features a target clip for secure placement and consistent flight path. You can stake this one in the ground or, Champion suggests, mount it on a tire. At less than $30, it's a steal.

Champion also sells orange clays: the 108 mm standard, 90 mm midi, 60 mm mini and thick, 108 mm rabbit. For real shooting fun, Champion suggests nesting a midi underneath a standard and throwing them together for a challenging doubles presentation.

If your shooting partner wants to sit down while he or she throws your birds, Champion, Trius (www.triustraps. com) and others have practice-style traps with seats attached.

Anchored by the operator's weight, the Trius TrapMaster offers a padded orange plastic seat on one end of a string-activated trap. The trap and seat pivot so that you can surprise the shooter and the trap's large adjustment knobs allow you to change the aluminum arm's throwing angle without tools. Equipped with the Trius Trap, the TrapMaster costs $179 and weighs 36 pounds. It throws singles, doubles or piggyback (nested) doubles.

Recoil Masters

After a full day on the range and perhaps a couple hundred 1⅛ loads, your shoulder can feel like it has taken a pounding and the resulting pain or dull ache makes you resort to the Extra Strength Tylenol. A good recoil pad can soften the blow. Pachmayr (www.pachmayr.com) offers a large line-up of its Decelerator pads in skeet/sporting clays (straight to slightly convex face to prevent snagging on your clothes) or trap (concave from heel to toe to provide a positive, "hugging" grip on the shoulder) shapes. Pads are offered in black or brown, and one is available in red. Face texturing can be light to maximize mounting speed (leather, lattice or ribbed), medium for field shooting (line-checkered, screen or stippled) or heavy, which is recommended for trap or live birds (basket-weave, pigeon or grooved). The ultimate choice of face pattern depends on your personal preference for mounting ease. Thickness ranges from 0.6 to 1.1 inches and several can be purchased with a decorative white line.

The cost of a Decelerator depends on its thickness and face style, but the 1.1-inch Deluxe #S325 skeet style ribbed face is around $21. A do-it-yourself, pre-fit Decelerator pad for a Browning Citori, on the other hand, runs about $37.

Pachmayr also makes two slip-on recoil pads in small, medium and large. The $32.98 brown leather slip-on is held in place with a hidden Velcro strip and includes a soft rubber insert. Excellent for adjusting length of pull, these black or brown rubber slip-on pads cost $12.48.

100-Straight Products (www.100straight.com) advertises its $34.95 Terminator as the softest recoil pad available. A closed cell design makes this pad resistant to tearing and splitting. You can choose from black or brown with a flat or curved surface and four depths: ⅝, ¾, 1, or 1⅛-inch.

With 100-Straight's Polymer Buttstock Spacers you can easily adjust your length of pull. Available in black or white, these spacers are constructed of a plastic material that is easy to sand for a smooth, seamless fit on your gun, and the slotted holes make it easy to adjust to any butt. The cost varies from $4.50 for the ⅛-inch spacer to $8.55 for the ½-inch spacer.

Black buttstock pitch spacers are also available from 100-Straight. These are ideal for altering pitch without cutting your beautiful walnut stock. You can order positive pitch (thicker at top) or negative pitch (thicker at bottom). Quarter-inch spacers are $6.50 and ½-inch spacers are $9.00.

Point of Aim

If you do not like the mid-point steel bead and front dot sight that come on your shotgun, change them! Pachmayr (www.pachmayr.com) makes a unique Uni-Dot fiber optic front sight (#P100) that is partially encased in a black, non-reflecting tube. In either bright red or fluorescent green, you can only see this 4 mm dot when the gun is properly mounted and aligned with your aiming eye. The Uni-Dot lets you aim with both eyes open and focused on the target. Pachmayr says its Uni-Dot promotes proper gun mounting and shooting technique, because if you mount the gun improperly or lift your head, the dot disappears. The carrier is made of high impact plastic and will snap on the rib anywhere along its length. No tapping, drilling or gluing is required. Seven sizes are available to fit most shotgun ribs ($24).

Barrel Restoration

If you have an older shotgun, chances are the barrel is pitted, scratched and has some moisture-related corrosion. Several manufacturers, including Teague Precision Chokes (www.teaguechokes.co.uk), have developed a process for restoring the shooting characteristics of the gun, if not the barrel itself, to its original capabilities.

Teague virtually creates a new barrel by machining the inner barrel wall and affixing a permanent, ultra-thin wall liner from breech to muzzle. The liner restores the original bore dimensions, chamber length and gun characteristics. And yes – you can shoot the rejuvenated gun.

At the current 1.84 rate of exchange (USD to British pounds sterling) and the current L 1,100 price (1,100 pounds), the cost for a double barrel shotgun appears to be about $1,900 plus taxes (Britain has a value- added tax) and CIF (carriage, insurance and freight). Obviously, this service is intended only for very valuable and collector guns, because for this price, you could purchase new barrels for many fine quality guns and, indeed, quite a few fine-shooting over/unders – lock, stock AND barrel.

Shooting Bags and Pouches

You must have one of these. It doesn't matter which brand or color, just so you do not have to carry a box of shells in your hand or a fist-full jammed down in your pockets. That is uncomfortable and, well, it makes you look like a beginner. Who wants that? Besides, we're not talking about much money for a shooting bag or pouch.

Boyt's #SC50 Shell Pouch (www.boytharness.com) comes with a heavy-duty web belt, zippered bottom and rugged but stylish green canvas trimmed in leather. For $49, you can buy one with two interior compartments: perhaps one for "live" shells and one for "empties" in case you reload.

The $27 Bob Allen Deluxe nylon divided pouch with belt (#425T) is backed with ¼-inch foam for rigidity and comes with an adjustable, two-inch web belt. The twin compartments hold one box of shells each. It is available in navy blue, green or black.

Bob Allen also offers a very nice nylon mesh combo-pouch for just $25. You see a lot of these at shooting events. It holds a box of shells on top and 100 empties on bottom. The bottom compartment has a spring-top opening that makes it difficult to spill your reloads. This mesh pouch comes in navy, green or black.

On a big sporting clays venue, you will walk for miles and shoot for several hours. Depending on the target presentation, you may well want several types of shells, chokes, extra sunscreen and something cold to drink. Many shooter bags hold eight boxes of shells and have various pockets for miscellaneous necessary stuff. However, do you really want to carry eight boxes of shells (200 shots) on your shoulder? Just because a bag will hold eight boxes does not mean you will or even ought to carry eight boxes. Some people do though, just in case….

The $67 Bob Allen #500T Deluxe Sporting Clays Bag is made from heavy-duty nylon and has a central 14- x 8-inch inside compartment. It holds up to 12 boxes of shells and

While soft-sided cases are not recommended for long-term storage, they are excellent for trips to the range and keeping your gun from becoming dinged or scratched between rounds. The Bob Allen "Two Gun Man" detachable double gun case fastens together by a full-length zipper for use as a double or a single case.

A take-down, soft-sided shotgun case such as this one from Boyt is an excellent investment for protecting your gun. Made with a 22-ounce heavy canvas exterior, it is padded with 40-ounce cotton batting and a flannel lining. It has a leather tip and sling, plus an accessory pocket.

has a hard bottom and foam insert sides to add rigidity to your 25-pound load. The Deluxe has zippered front, back and side pockets. This bag is available in navy, green, black or, for the competitor who is also a hunter, Advantage Timber camouflage.

MTM (www.mtmcase-gard.com) makes a variation on the classic soft bag. Their hard plastic 100-Round Shotshell Case (#SW-100) holds four boxes of shells and has a removable choke tube holder that fastens to the top. MTM says you place open cartons of shells inside the case; the see-through choke-tube case holds chokes, lube and most factory wrenches. The case measures 7- x 10.6- x 6-inches and is features a swiveling plastic handle.

ShootUK Ltd. (www.shootuk.com) is importing an interesting hard-sided bag (or is it a box?) for competitors. According to ShootUK, their hard-sided Shoot Bag will "accommodate everything the serious shooter requires." The bag is black or green with an anodized aluminum lid. Inside, three compartments carry up to 200 shells plus hearing protection, and additional compartments keep miscellaneous items separate. It comes with a personalized plaque, self-balancing shoulder strap, bottle holder and clasp, fold-down rear compartment with a special box for choke tubes, side pockets for shooting glasses and personal belongings (kept safe in a "secret pocket"), a front compartment and a security lock. What else could there possibly be?

Vests and Harnesses

While most of us have, at one time or another, worn an adjustable harness to absorb some of our guns' recoil, it is my experience that most people do not find them entirely comfortable. Seems like the strap is always an irritant and that the protection offered by the padded section is minimal. Nevertheless, they are available from Boyt, Bob Allen and

others. Bob Allen's adjustable $34 khaki Absorb-a-Coil Harness has a soft, visco-elastic polymer pad enclosed in a cotton pocket. The pad is supposed to absorb up to 40 percent more recoil than the competition. It is faced with suede and available right hand or left hand.

Infinitely preferable to a harness is a full shooting vest. Your style of shooting, the place you shoot, and the climate where you shoot should help you determine what to buy. Remember that a vest is more than just a place to carry your shells. A vest is part of your shooting system, no less than your shells, that helps you achieve consistent gun mount and gun placement into the shoulder pocket. A vest is not necessary to good shooting, but in my experience, it helps.

When selecting a vest, consider the shotgun games you shoot. Vests can be had with a small gun pad, which is often favored by those who shoot trap and skeet where the gun is mounted before the bird is called. They're also available with a full front pad that is virtually mandatory in low-gun games because the gun butt can catch on an abbreviated pad. Many shooters choose the International style; perhaps most do, because it works well in any shooting situation.

Sporting clay shooters may want to consider a vest with double-divided shell pockets. This allows one to keep track of up to four different loads easily. It is not uncommon to carry several different loads to the shooting stand. Trap and skeet shooters need just one big pocket for the shells, and one for the fired hulls.

Construction of the vest is important. In the hot, humid southeast, you rarely see a full front- and back-cloth vest. They are just too hot. They quickly become sweat-soaked and wind up several pounds heavier than when they started the day. Southern and hot weather shooters favor mesh vests. Northern and cool weather shooters generally prefer fuller vests for warmth because they compete well into cold weather.

For $49 you can wear a Bob Allen #102 Series shooting vest that has a breast pocket and two extra large lower pockets for shells and empties. It is made from soft, tightly woven poly-cotton twill and features a long, lightly padded gun pad. From this price point up to $136, you can purchase a vest with a variety of side tab adjustments, choke tube pockets, interior "security" pockets with zippers, a range of colors, towel loops and a gun pad and leather trim made. The more expensive your vest, the more extras it will have and vice versa.

A Cart for the Field

Everywhere you go at a sporting clays tournament, you will see people zipping around in golf cars. Many tournaments – the final Seminole Cup held at the TM Ranch outside Orlando, Florida, in February, 2004 for instance – have dozens of golf cars on hand that you can rent for the weekend for a nominal fee. If you object to paying $50 to rent a car every time you shoot in a big sporting clays event, you should just buy a car.

Yamaha's four-stroke #G22A gas golf car has an 11.4 hp, 357 cc engine and comes in a variety of colors. You can order one of these and have it shipped free for just $4,378 (in ivory) or $4,601 (in metallic, candy apple red). For an extra $75, the folks at www.tntgolfcar.com will attach a windshield. Light kits cost $155 and three-sided curtain enclosures are $366. If you object to gas and do not feel the need for all that power and luxury, you can order the 48-volt electric #G22E for only $4,501.

Stepping down slightly to a more modest porter, many shooters enjoy the exercise of walking from station to station, while they pull a golf cart (cart, not car) that they have modified for shooting events. A basic, two-wheel folding Bag Boy #LT-450 with adjustable handle runs $70 (www.golfstockpile.com) while the deluxe Sun Mountain three-wheel Speed Cart is $179. The adjustable, folding Sun Mountain cart has pneumatic tires and a dual-tube frame and can be ordered in burgundy, blue or granite.

Out in California, Dean Ziegel has designed a fine little field cart for shooters at sporting clays events. Dean calls his cart the Jackass Field Cart (www.ziegeleng.com). In price and versatility, it falls somewhere between riding and push/pull golf carts.

According to Dean, "The Jackass uses the same kind of high quality machined aluminum materials you find on competition wheel chairs." The rear tires on a Jackass are 20 inches in diameter with 36 stainless steel spokes for stability over uneven ground. The 32-pound #J1-A model ($549) disassembles and folds into a compact unit to fit into an automobile trunk (approximately 11 x 23 x 23 inches). It will hold three to five shotguns in carpet-covered, padded foam brackets and has a large aluminum front tray for your shells and gear or perhaps to support a cooler. Gun butts rest on a one-inch polypropylene high-density block covered with carpet to absorb shock. Casters and four-inch solid urethane wheels support the front. The upright handle of a Jackass resembles a standard hand truck, but the handle of the #J1-A is offset 30 degrees for easy pulling and is 42 inches above the centerline of the rear wheels. The #J3 economy model Jackass ($150) is built on a heavy-duty 300-pound capacity industrial hand truck, so it's not very elegant. "Strong and simple," Dean says about the #J3.

If you have a place to shoot, you can easily get in a few shots at practice targets. The MTM EZ Double-Throw and a few clay targets are cheap compared to a highly qualified assistant!

Eye Protection

If you want to shoot the shotgun games of skeet, trap and sporting clays, you better protect your vision. Good, high impact shooting glasses are an absolute necessity on the line and in the field.

So, are we talking glasses or eyewear or goggles or something else? We make these distinctions because glasses differ from the new styles of shooting protection eyewear in shape, coverage, materials and versatility. Simply put, the first task of a pair of glasses is to help you see better. Glasses are generally smaller prescription lenses ground from optical quality polycarbonate – which gives them strength, clarity and light weight – specifically to correct your vision difficulties. Glasses often include multiple sections for multiple purposes (bifocals, for instance).

"Eyewear" on the other hand is designed to either look good or protect your eyes. Eyewear can be purchased from a kiosk at a shooting event, in your local mall or over the counter at a shooting sports retailer. Eyewear is not designed to correct your vision, but to protect and enhance it. On the skeet range especially, you want eyewear with lenses that will not shatter if a clay fragment hits them squarely in the center. You want a shape that will give you protection from fragments scratching your eyeball from the sides or even glancing up from the bottom. You want a comfortable, lightweight fit, especially over your nose, and perhaps polarization as well if you often shoot in bright conditions.

Several companies offer goggle-style eyewear and these are excellent for true 100 percent protection. Unlike glasses or "eyewear," goggles literally encase your eyes and on a typical summer day, they had better have anti-fog protection because they are going to feel hot, especially if their elastic strap holds them tight against your face, and you will sweat around your eyes. As a result, I generally find goggles uncomfortable and do not like the heavy-framed, confined feeling that they give my already imperfect vision.

Wiley X eyewear (www.wileyx.com) offers several styles of shatterproof eye protection. The company claims that military, law enforcement and sport shooters around the world use its eyewear. Wiley X frames are constructed from nearly indestructible "triloid nylon," while lenses are die cut from ballistic selenite polycar-

Inexpensive hand throwers and boxes of clay targets are available at most BoxMarts. They make practice cheap, easy and fun.

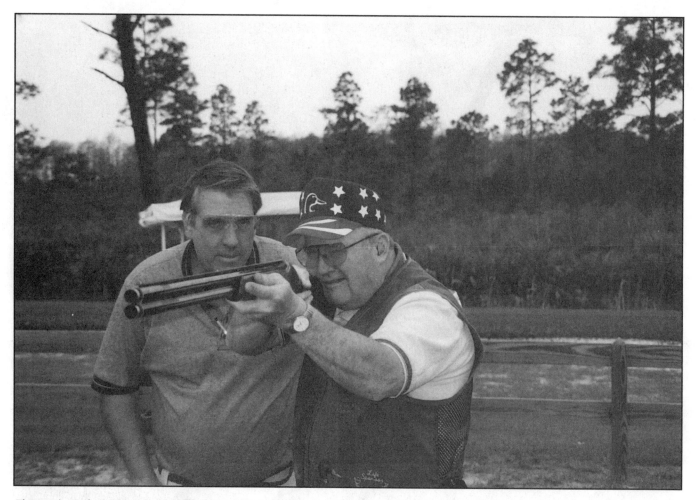

The services of a highly qualified fitting guru and shooting coach like Kansas' Michael Murphy (left) can save you countless hours, frustration, and, in the long run, probably a lot of money needed to reach your shooting goals. Instructors such as Murphy can help you make the gun comfortable and bring the rib and beads precisely in-line with your dominant eye.

bonate to eliminate distortion. Lenses provide 100 percent ultra violet protection.

Before you walk away from any sales counter with a new pair of shooting glasses, you are going to face a myriad of lens colors to choose from. The shape of the lens and frame are matters of personal choice, but most companies suggest different lens tints based on general guidelines that only you can interpret through your eyes:

Clear: allows maximum light transmission without changing the value of perceived colors.

Yellow: for use in low light. Blocks blue haze and significantly enhances clarity.

Red: improves detail and enhances depth perception in low or artificial light. Intensifies warm colors. (My personal favorite.)

Bronze/Brown: improves visual definition and glare reduction in bright light. Sharpens and enhances ground level contours.

Slate/Gray: maximum glare reduction without distorting colors.

Smoke Green: excellent general purpose use. Maximum glare reduction without distorting colors.

Mirror lenses: diminishes glare by absorbing reflection across the mirror face.

The Wiley X Internet site gives you a chance to view all eyewear and to mix and match tints. The #SG-1 ballistic eye-orbit sealing goggles, for instance, with an anti-fog coating on smoke green and clear lenses cost $100, which includes a case. The #PT-1L ballistic wrap-around one-piece lens in "Blue Ice" costs $70. Extra lenses are $20 each.

A new entry in the eyewear category is HDS or HiDef Spex Performance Optics (www.hidefspex.com). Endorsed by George Digweed, 12-time sporting clays world champion, HDS says their glasses are melanin-infused as well as tinted, and incorporate a partial blue-blocker. Why "melanin-infused" optics? Although I have not been able to test a pair of these glasses, HDS says the lens will enable you to visually acquire targets faster and there is no color distortion. Plus, the melanin blocks harmful UV and HEV rays which contribute to cataracts and "macular degeneration." If you have a favorite shooting frame, HDS will build lenses to the frames and will even build clip-on type lenses to fit your current prescription glasses.

BelOptix sunglasses (www.beloptix.com) use a photochromatic layer on the front surface of the lens that lightens and darkens according to the amount of UV light that is present. In the presence of UV rays, molecules in the layer turn inside-out. "Polarized lenses reduce glare and are standard in sunglasses,"

If you have difficulty using your front – or even your mid-point bead – sight as an aiming aid, it is easy to change. Many competitors and hunters find that they are attracted to bright non-electronic fiber optic technology.

says BelOptix President Steve Wood, "but they are often too dark for many ambient light conditions. We have combined polarization with photochromatic lens technologies to enhance vision in all outdoor daylight conditions."

Steve recommends their Target Orange lens, which darkens to Dark Brown in the most intense sunlight, for trap, skeet and sporting clays shooting.

BelOptix eyewear is available with non-corrective lenses ($169) as well as single-vision ($295) and multi-focal or progressive ($495) prescriptions. Wrap-around frames feature tinted side panels for protected peripheral vision and come in tortoise, camo and black. Each pair weighs one ounce.

Olympic Optical (www.olympicoptical.com), which markets under its own name and for Smith & Wesson (www.smith-wessonsafety.com), makes a variety of "safety glasses." Olympic even has a model with magnifying lens inserts in +1.5-, +2.0- and +2.5-power options. The S&W Ozone, Code 4 and Magnum 3G are all wrap-around styles with lenses available in many different tints.

Although it makes a variety of impact-resistant eyewear for sportsmen, Degil's #J10 Sport Spec (www.degilsafety.com) deserves special mention because the clear, all-polycarbonate lens

and frame are designed to fit over most prescription frames and glasses. Available in clear, smoke or yellow lenses and frames, the scratch-resistant Sport Spec provides almost 100 percent UV protection. The suggested retail price for the #J10 is under $5. Who said there were no "deals" available these days?

Hearing Protection

I have a love-hate relationship with earmuffs, especially the hard-shell variety. I like the way they feel and they do work for me. They are comfortable too, until the day turns warm. Then I want to take them off and switch to some other style of hearing protection, but that would be nuts. To spend time with your ear over the stock of a firing shotgun is to tempt deafness unless you use some type of decibel reducer.

When I bought my first shotgun, I bought the least expensive pair of earplugs the store had on its counter. After all, I had already paid hundreds of dollars for a gun and shells. The last thing I felt like doing was shelling out another Andrew Jackson for some stupid earmuffs. Besides, I had shot enough already to know that half the time I brought the gun up to my cheek, the stock banged on the hard cup of an earmuff or some joker would "thunk" the hard outer shell with his fingertip and send

Three different styles from the Boyt Harness and Bob Allen companies. Clockwise from upper left: the synthetic leather Classic Divided Pouch with belt has a divided compartment holding 25 shells in each with one shell each in the horizontal ready-to-be-loaded position below the belt. The water repellent, distressed synthetic leather Classic Duplex Pouch holds a full box of shells on top and has a pouch on bottom for empties. Finally, the Classic Superior Shell Pouch has two, full box compartments and a 100-hull mesh pouch behind with mesh zippered bottom.

an irritatingly loud and even painful noise through my ear and into my eyeballs and brain.

Of course, I was wrong for not buying high quality hearing protection right away, but that was some time ago and I know better today. The only hearing protection you can possibly afford is a style that protects you completely. Medical experts testify that two hours of exposure to 100 decibels of noise – think of a chain saw or a pneumatic drill – can cause permanent hearing loss. An hour at 105 decibels (dB) accomplishes the same thing, as does half an hour at 110 dB – motorcycle noise or a woodworking shop – or just 15 minutes at 115 dB.

Gunfire causes sharp flashes of noise at the highest levels. Your first .22? Figure 140 dB. Your 12 gauge? Figure 152 dB – and that astonishing noise level is immediately adjacent to your ear.

For shooters who like earmuffs, Olympic Optical has licensed the Smith & Wesson (www.smith-wessonsafety.com) name to sell their "Suppressor" earmuffs. The outer blue shells or cups are hard plastic and engraved with the S&W logo. Cups pivot on the plastic headband for a secure, comfortable fit and equal pressure distribution. According to Olympic, these earmuffs carry a noise reduction rating (NRR) of 25 dB.

Canada's Degil Safety Products (www.degilsafety.com) manufactures a variety of hearing protection products, from the most

basic to the very sophisticated. Degil's DePlug polyurethane foam is non-allergic and designed to be disposable. In three styles (tapered, cylindrical or Mul-T-Fit "beaded"), these non-allergenic earplugs weigh next to nothing. Clubs and ranges buy these by the case and often hand these out free to visitors.

The Bob Allen #255M Series Mesh Shooting Vest is made from soft, tightly woven polycotton twill base material. The International style pad is suede and it has a side tab adjustment, choke tube pocket, inside zippered pocket, side tab waist adjustment and two large front pockets. Cool, comfortable and convenient. Available for both left- and right-hand in two color styles and six sizes.

Some days a harness is just right – and on other days there is no way you can possibly squirm into one and feel comfortable. This lightly padded, adjustable harness is faced with a suede gun pad and available in right or left hand from Bob Allen.

Clyde Craddock and Brett Holcomb unlimber Clyde's golf cart for a sporting clays event. Clyde (no hat), who shoots a Krieghoff Parcours Special and owns the golf car and trailer, was a nine-year sporting clays All American. Brett has been only shooting for three years, but was the 2003 Florida 20-gauge champion with his Browning 325.

Pull carts are everywhere on a sporting clays course. Based on the push/pull golf cart, these are far less expensive, but in some ways more versatile. Custom designs built on the golf cart principle have places for several guns, boxes of ammo and chokes, snacks and drinks. Three-wheelers are more stable than two-wheelers, but in any version, these carts can go places that the powered cars cannot.

Molded from extra-soft PVC, the reusable DePlug requires no rolling or squeezing to make it fit into your ears. Its extra-long tab makes it easy to insert and remove. It is available with or without a cord and offers a NRR of 24 dB, Degil warns, "when worn properly. "

Degil divides its earmuffs into two categories, passive and electronic. The $30 Deluxe passive, foldable earmuff (#20010, NRR 25 dB) is designed to provide a comfortable and effective seal while reducing headband force. The sealing rings are ultra soft and have extra cushioning.

The $420 Supreme Pro (#75302) has an NRR of 18 dB and falls in the active or electronic category because it requires two AAA batteries for operation. Degil describes these muffs as "a foldable level dependent earmuff developed to conform to international military specifications and extreme conditions." Apparently, this high quality earmuff will limit hazardous impact noise or sound to a maximum of 82 dB. It has five am-

plification settings and provides superior stereo sound quality reception. A special socket connects to most radio handsets and dog tracking units. If the price seems a little steep, Degil's basic headband earmuff with impact protection and sound amplification (NRR 23 dB) costs only $178.

Bob Walker's original Game Ear (NRR 29 dB, www.walkersgameear.com) was developed for hunting. It weighed less than ¼-ounce and increased hearing, Bob says, up to five times by amplifying high frequency sounds with 46 dB of battery power. Even the original design from about 1989 had a safety compression circuit to protect the user from loud sounds including muzzle blast.

The Game Ear for hunters has morphed into a version for competitors called the Target Ear ($160). When the Game Ear/Target Ear II came out, it allowed users to tune their hearing device to match individual hearing needs. Consequently, you could hear range commands and still have muzzle

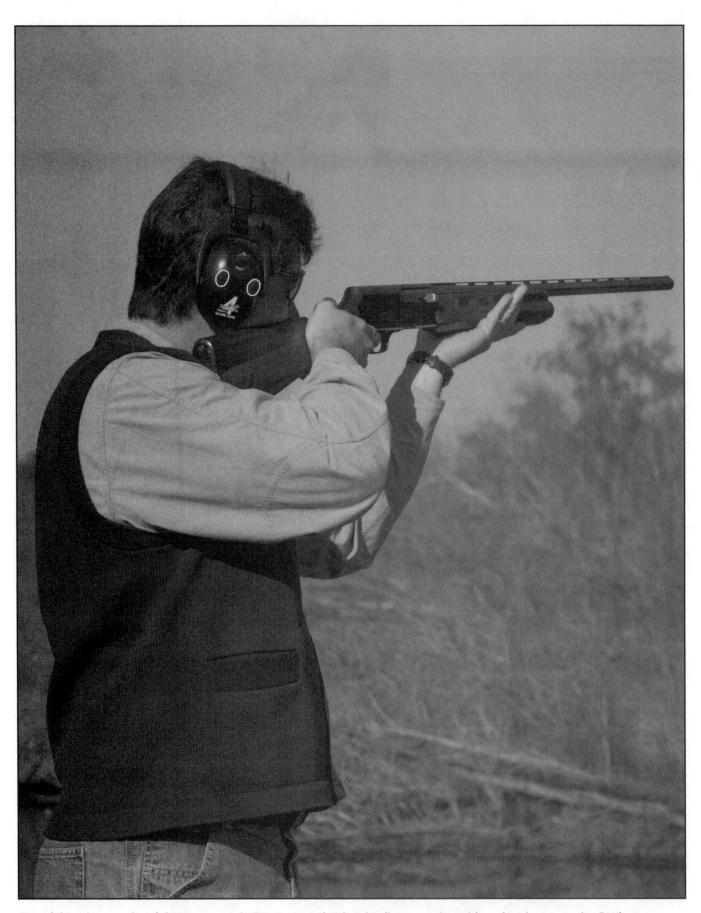

One of the primary rules of shotgun games is, "Never go to the shooting line or station without hearing protection." When you wear earmuffs with safety compression circuits like these from Bob Walker, make sure they are sculptured so that when you bring your gun to your cheek, the stock does not clatter against the hard plastic of the cups.

blast hearing protection. The Game Ear/Target Ear III allows for wireless voice communications when used with a "walkie talkie" such as a Motorola TalkAbout. Now, the new, digital version filters incoming sounds and eliminates unnecessary noise, resulting in a clear signal into your brain. Bob says it increases your hearing ability up to seven times while still incorporating the noise compression circuitry that keeps your ear from being smashed by muzzle blast.

Three sets of earmuffs are now available through Walker's Game Ear. All three sets are nicely sculptured along the bottom to prevent interference when shouldering your gun with proper shooting form. The Range Ear version has a noise reduction rating (NRR) of 24 dB. The electronic Power Muffs ($209) have two independent volume controls that allow for true stereo sound while wind-resistant high frequency microphones make it easy to identify sound and direction. The new Power Muffs Quads ($259) have 50 dB of battery power, four high-frequency directional, wind-resistant microphones and independent volume controls to decrease blast and noisesome background chatter. Bob says his Quads (NRR 24) increase the users hearing up to eight times. Both electronic models incorporate Sound Activated Compression circuits.

Chronographs

As if a simple score were not enough, everyone on the shooting line wants, no needs, to know how fast he or she is shooting. Most shotshell manufacturers freely list this data. If you are a reloader, you have tables available depending on the powder you use, the gauge, the amount and size of your shot. But for about the same price as a pair of good shooting glasses, you could own your own chronograph and then you wouldn't have to assume: you would know.

The Smith & Wesson brand earmuffs are made by Olympic Optical. When choosing hearing protection, think about comfort and always ask about the NRR or Noise Reduction Rating. S&W's earmuffs have an NRR of 25 decibels.

The Bob Allen Leather Toe Rest comes in handy when there is just nothing else to do but lean the muzzle of the EMPTY gun on your shoe!

We all know people who would never play golf without a pair of gloves but never shoot with a pair. Shooting gloves like these from GripSwell help take some of the hand stress out of shooting by absorbing shock, making it less necessary to "white knuckle" the gun and easing the discomfort of gripping a rough, checkered fore-end.

The #F-1 is the stripped-down, entry level Chrony and it only costs $88. Equip it with a monitor to bring the LCD right up to your bench and away from the bullet's path and you only add $17. It gives numbered shot velocities, and the reading stays on the display until you shoot again, reset it or turn it off. Of course, there are several upgraded features, but figure that for about $250 you could get a chronograph with absolutely all the bells and whistles.

Miscellaneous "Must Haves"

Every shooter who has been at the line for a while has tried a toe rest. A shotgun is only eight or nine pounds, but after a day on a sporting clays course or even an hour at a trap shoot, it feels like it is pulling your arm down to about your knee. A toe rest looped into your shoelaces gives you a firm surface against which to rest your unloaded gun muzzle. Bob Allen's is made from heavy leather with a tab and snap to fit over shoelaces and retails for less than $10.

At some time in your career, you will consider shooting with gloves. Some people like them and some do not. It depends on the weather and on your body's individual mechanics – sweaty or nervous hands, for instance. GripSwell ergonomic shooting gloves (www.gripswell.com) help absorb felt recoil and reduce fatigue while, GripSwell's Tosh Ono says, the padded goatskin gloves "provide a point of reference for a consistent mount" and act in the same manner as a palm swell on your shotgun's stock. Look for gloves in un-dyed natural leather that will not stain or absorb heat. Sizes available are small through XXL at $35 per pair. Unlike golf gloves, which wear out quickly due to the extreme friction of your grip, these shooting gloves could last for years.

Finally, if you carry a "wad knocker" in your pouch or tool kit, you'll eventually become everyone's

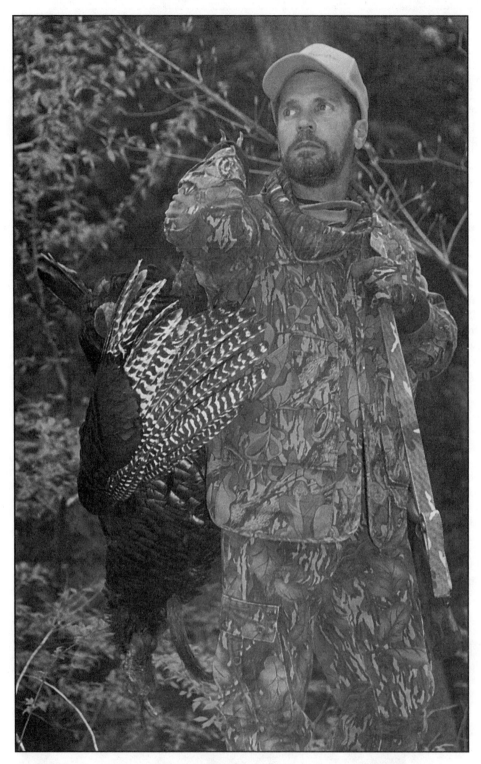

Bob Walker, the president of Bob Walker's Target Ear (and the popular Game Ear), actually began using hearing protection with safety compression circuits for turkey hunting. For hunting or clay target shooting, the theory and the circuitry are the same.

Shooting Chrony offers seven affordable portable model. Every Chrony is made of 20-gauge steel, but weighs less than 2½ pounds. They are powered by one nine-volt alkaline battery with a rated service life of 48 hours (not included) and are equipped with a large, half-inch LCD readout. All come with a three-year limited warranty but will, Shooting Chrony says, "last a lifetime."

friend. From 100 Straight Products, the $6.50 solid brass wad knocker is radiused on each end so that it will not scratch the inside of a shotgun barrel. If a wad or other debris becomes lodged in your gun's bore, just drop the wad knocker down the barrel and your problem is solved. The wad knocker weighs approximately four ounces. You'll rarely use it, but experience has shown that when you need it, you need it immediately.

ROLLING YOUR OWN

No matter how you slice it, clay target shooting is not the most inexpensive sport in the world. In addition to guns, range fees, travel and all the other associated costs, you have to factor in the cost of your shells. There are only two ways to acquire those shells: you either buy factory fodder or roll your own. At some point, every clay target shooter will have to decide whether reloading is in his or her best interest. In some cases, it may not be.

It is commonly accepted that you can save considerable sums of money reloading compared to buying factory ammo. Those mysterious savings, however, depend on how you buy the factory shells.

If you walk into your local gun shop and ask for a couple of boxes of target loads, you can expect to pay full list price. That does not mean the shop owner is gouging you. He has overhead, inventory costs and other expenses that must be recouped to stay in business. He also does not have the buying power to make big lot purchases at lower prices. The larger discount chains do, and that is why you will likely find the same shells for less there, assuming, of course, that the discount store carries the particular load you want. Often they will not stock anything other than lower-priced soft-shot field loads unless there is strong clay target interest in their area and the store manager is smart enough to realize it. Do not count on the discount stores having a steady supply of target loads on hand when you need them, though.

Sometimes, however, the chains have worthwhile buys. I remember that several years ago the local BoxMart received a large quantity of Remington's promotional loads. These normally would not excite target shooters, but in this case (for some inexplicable reason) these shells were loaded in Remington's target-grade Unibody hull, which is an excellent hull to reload. They cost only $80 a case then and local skeet shooters cleaned out the store. Not only did they get a case of shells to shoot, but also good hulls to reload, and for only slightly more money than it would have cost them to reload that same case with their own components.

If you find a bargain like that, it is worth buying as much as you can afford.

Buy by the Case

Smart clay shooters buy factory shells through their club in case lots. Most clubs will take orders for case lots from members when they restock targets. That way, they save a considerable amount on freight and can offer the shells at what amounts to wholesale.

At my club, top-grade target loads run about $100 a case for 12, 20 and .410, with the 28-gauge running about $120.

That is about $5 per box for the first three and $6 for a box of 28. It represents what I would call an average best case price. That price can vary around the country because of freight costs. Shotshells are heavy and expensive to ship. The farther you are from the manufacturer, the higher the cost.

Although $5 a box may sound cheap to someone buying retail one box at a time, you can cut that cost further by selling the empty hulls. Among skeet shooters, the going prices for once-fired brand-name hulls are: 5¢ per 12-gauge; 6¢ per 20; 8-10¢ per 100 per 28; and 10¢ for the .410. Trap shooters have no interest in anything other than the 12, and most sporting clays shooters are not especially enamored with the smaller gauges, so those prices are contingent on having a buyer.

What that means is that a full box of .410 shells costs $5 and the box of once-fired empty hulls is worth $2.50. Your cost to shoot factory .410s is around $2.50 per box. You can reload them for less than that, but not a lot less.

The 28-gauge runs a buck a box more, and you can save money there. Even selling the empty hulls, you can realize a savings of $35 or more per case if you reload this gauge. The savings on 20-gauge shells are a bit less, while the 12-gauge will be similar in cost to the 20, unless empty 12-gauge hulls are worth more than 5¢ each in your area. At a trap range, that will likely be the case.

Another way to buy ammo, and a good one for the casual shooter, is to purchase it at the range. Many ranges operate under the assumption that they are there to sell clay targets and that's where their profit is. Since it takes shells to shoot targets, they'll often sell top quality target loads for about one dollar mark-up over their costs, which can be on the low end of the scale. Buying a single box of 28-gauge shells at my club (the most expensive shell they sell) runs $7, and the empties are worth about $2.50 a box. That brings the box cost to $4.50; and while you can reload them for about $2.50 a box, if you only shoot a dozen boxes a year, there is no point in it.

No, not every shooter needs to reload. In fact, some trapshooters who belong to active clubs and can expect to be able to purchase a fresh case every month (and be assured of a market for selling their empties) have quit reloading. Why tie up their money in the equipment and components, not to mention the space it takes to set up and load or the time required to do it, when each box of factory shells costs them only about $1.50 more?

Similarly, many skeet shooters who reload the other gauges have stopped loading the .410. Why create extra work when the reward isn't worth it?

On the other hand (and it's a big hand!), circumstances may make reloading far more attractive. My situation is not unusual.

Reasons to Reload

I no longer shoot skeet on a regular competitive basis, but I still bum a lot of rounds at that game, in addition to trap. I also shoot a fair amount of Sporting Clays, primarily with the 12- and 28-gauges. In the case of the latter, reloading is mandatory if I want to realize the full potential of this gauge on the sporting clays course. That means I need a loading press, primers, shot in four sizes (#7½, 8, 8½ and 9) and a place to set up the press.

Adding the 12-gauge to that requires only a set of dies, a couple different cans of powder, some additional wads and, of course, empty 12-gauge hulls. Everything else interchanges.

If you have already made the decision to load one gauge, then there is no reason not to load the rest. After all, you have already made the most significant investment on equipment for the first gauge.

Loading all of your own shells also simplifies things. I can purchase top-quality, nickel-plated, long-range sporting clays loads in 12-gauge. But if I only need three or four boxes a year (you really don't use that many of these specialized long-range shells in an average round of sporting clays), why have a whole case sitting around? Ditto for the spreader loads; the #8½ load I like on the second shot of skeet doubles; or any of the other non-standard loads that are just not used that often. Nor do you suddenly find yourself out of a favorite load just before a match. You can always make more without having to wait for a bargain.

Yes, there are a number of shooters who do find reloading very worthwhile, both in terms of cost and shell performance. Rolling your own loads is not difficult.

Reloading Basics

As with metallic rounds, all the reloader is doing is sizing the hull back to factory specs to fit the chamber, and then replacing those components expended on firing. With a shotshell that means the primer, powder, wad and shot charge. Accomplishing this requires a loading press and a set of dies for that gauge.

Many companies offer quality shotshell loading equipment. At the moment, the big players in the game are Hornady, MEC, Ponsness/Warren and Lee Precision. They are listed in our Manufacturer's Directory at the back of this book. In years past, there have been a number of companies other than these, but they have either merged into larger companies or gone out of business. Some of their equipment is still around, and still in excellent operating condition. You can probably find some of it for sale on the used market at a gun club or gun show, but I don't recommend it. Buying a loading press that is not currently manufactured can present a major problem if a part breaks and you need service. You may not be able to replace it, and if you cannot have it custom-made, then your press is useless. Parts break on occasion or just wear out, and if you cannot fix it, there is not much point buying it, no matter how attractive the price.

Expect to pay between $100 and $500 for a quality shotshell loader set up to load one gauge. Virtually all of them will offer interchangeable die capability, meaning that once you bite the bullet for the first purchase, adding other gauges is not expensive.

Press Types

There are essentially two types of loading presses in use, single stage and progressive.

The single stage press requires that each hull be manually moved through each of the loading stations. On my no-longer-made Hornady 155, that means I move the shell to station one to de-prime and re-size it, station two to prime it, and station three to drop a powder charge, seat a wad and add the shot. At station four, I start the crimp, and station five finishes it. It sounds slow, but it is not that bad. I can load 50 to 60 rounds per hour.

The advantage of the single stage press is that every loading operation is fully monitored, and it's hard to make a mistake. The quality of the ammunition loaded on this (or other single stage presses) is high and uniform from shell to shell. I use this press when making test rounds or when I just need to run off a couple boxes of specialty rounds. Another advantage to the single stage is that they fall into the lower end of the price spectrum and changing to different gauge dies is easy. If you only shoot a couple hundred rounds a month and do not mind spending a few hours loading them, a quality single stage press will serve you well.

If you need more shells in less time, the answer is a progressive press. Feed shells into station one, and each time you cycle the handle it will automatically re-size, de-prime, move the shell, prime, drop powder and shot, and do all the other things. All you have to do is feed in an empty hull, insert a wad, and you get one reloaded shell with each pull of the handle. They can crank out several hundred rounds per hour. Some of the expensive ones do not even require you to operate the handle.

The drawback to the progressive press, other than the cost and the fact that it is not as easy to shift to other gauges, is that it requires a lot more attention on the operator's part. It is not difficult to forget to insert a wad, or drop shot or leave out the powder, or neglect something else. You will find out quickly if you messed up when you go to range and a shell fails to fire. One wag has observed that progressive press users who suffered from Attention Deficit Disorder invented shell knockers!

All the different manufacturer's presses do the same thing, just in a slightly different way. I happen to be very partial to Hornady and Ponsness/Warren equipment, but that is because their machines fit my style. All of them will work, and they come with complete instructions. In the case of the MEC equipment (whose instructions are so thorough that having an engineering degree helps), they even have an information line to call for assistance when you need it.

Heed the Data

Load data for shotshells is far more varied than for metallic rounds. With the latter there are really only a half-dozen powder, bullet and primer combinations that will produce decent results with any given cartridge. That's not the case here. Different makes and models of shotshells will have different internal volumes and shapes. These differences affect how they will react with any given wad and powder combination. For that reason, many shooters like to use just a couple of different hulls since this cuts down the number of different wads they require. Put the wrong components in the hull and you can have a lousy load, even a dangerous one!

Not all hulls are created equal, either, and a combination of components that may produce a beautifully performing load in one can be hazardous in another. This is not a knock on any particular maker's shell, because all will work very nicely with the proper components and load data.

The point here is that anyone attempting to load shotshells should have current, tested data. That data is easy to come by. Remington, Winchester, Federal, ACTIV, and other shell makers who also offer components have good loading data information, and it's yours for the asking. Companies such as Ballistic Products that sell components have plenty of data on their loads. It is available for a phone call, a letter or often on their Internet site. Do not start shotshell loading without good data. Otherwise, you are asking for trouble.

Once you have the data that gives you the proper combination of wad, powder, primer and shot charge for a given hull, it is not advisable to deviate from it. Simply changing the make of primer can raise or lower pressure enough to turn a good load into a poor performer. You can, however, fine-tune your gun's performance by choosing the right load for the conditions, and one major factor in that respect is the temperature at which you will be using the load.

Shotshell Pressures

Each shotshell recipe provided by the ammo or component makers will provide the tested working pressure for that load, expressed in psi or LUP. These are the two ways of measuring shotshell pressure and they are slightly different, but not enough to make much difference unless you are one of those who would rather pick nits than bust clays. Any pressure above 11,500 is excessive in a 12-gauge. It will not blow up your gun, probably, but it might well blow your pattern, and it will certainly increase the wear on your gun, not to mention your shoulder. Any pressure below 7500 (according to ballistic experts) will result in a shell that is not operating at full efficiency. I am not sure I fully agree with that, however. At the risk of sounding like a nitpicker myself, I have found that 12-gauge loads can function nicely down to about 6,500. The smaller gauges should run around 8,500 or above.

Within the acceptable pressure range, the higher the pressure, the more recoil and shot deformation – the lower the pressure, the less. When I am working with 12-gauge target loads, I prefer those that operate from 7,500 to 9,000 LUP. In the smaller gauges, I feel the range needs to be between 8,500 and 10,000 LUP.

On the surface, that would seem to make it a simple matter to find a good load. It is not always that simple.

It is the accepted industry standard to pressure-test loads at a uniform 70 degrees Fahrenheit (F) temperature. The reason is that for each 10-degree rise (or fall) in ambient temperature, there will be a corresponding increase or decrease of 1,000 LUP pressure.

In other words, select a load that pressure-tests at 10,500 LUP and that is what you will get at 70 degrees. Walk onto a sweltering 95-degree skeet field on a late August afternoon and you now have a load that is probably cracking 12,500 LUP! This is not good for your gun, your patterns or your shoulder. On the reverse side, select a conservative 7,500 LUP load and shoot it in 40-degree weather and some of the rounds may not even ignite! They are called "bloop" loads because that is just what they sound like when they go off. When that happens, tilt the barrel downward and pour out the shot that never left the barrel. Then, drop a shell knocker down the barrel to remove the stuck wad (fail to do this and the next round disassembles your gun for you!) and then hope all that unburned powder does not find its way into the action and bind up your gun.

This is one area where reloaders have an advantage over factory-round shooters. The factories must load to some uniform pressure, even though they have no idea at what temperature those shells will be shot. You know where and when you shoot and can load accordingly.

For cold weather 12-gauge loads, I pick one in the 10,500 LUP range. For hot weather conditions, I will go with one in the 6,000-7,000 LUP range. By the time I actually get them on the range, they are at about the temperature and pressure I want them, a fact much appreciated by my gun, my shoulder and my scorecard.

Components

Another area where the reloader has a considerable amount of control is in the shot he elects to stuff into the shell.

Generally, the harder the shot, the better the load will pattern and the shorter the shot string. The degree of pattern control a shooter can exercise by simply varying the type of shot is about 10 percent. That is about one full degree of choke.

Top-quality nickel-plated shot can tighten your patterns even more, a fact that has not been lost on world-class international trap competitors or clever sporting clays shooters.

If you want solid long-range patterns, go to hard shot. If you need to open a pattern quickly, use the cheap soft stuff. You can also open patterns by loading to higher velocity and pressure.

The type of powder you use can affect recoil and reliability. Some powders burn dirty. I do not shoot fast-burning flake powders like Red Dot because it gums up my gas guns. Sometimes you will get them in factory loads. In fact, just a week ago I was running a very good make of factory ammo through my Franchi Prestige and the gun was a bit dirty. Early in the second skeet round the gun failed to feed a round. My Prestige just does not do that. It is one of the most reliable gas guns made. The culprit? Flake powder in the action temporarily bound up the shell carrier. Racking the action vigorously a few times cleared it and I was able to continue. In sporting clays that would have been a lost bird. Even on the skeet range, where gun malfunctions are a legitimate excuse to reshoot, it was enough to interrupt my concentration.

IMR PB, Royal Scot, Hodgdon's Clays and International Clays are all clean-burning powders. They load to target velocities beautifully and will not mess up a gas gun. In the smaller gauges, you can add 800-X to that list, although it does require a hot primer like the Federal 209A to light it off well in cool weather. With the .410, I consider H-110 to be the best bet, with Winchester 296 a good second choice.

These moderate- to medium-burning powders, PB and 800-X in particular, also seem to deliver more of a shove than a jolt. They are softer shooting at the same load velocity than many other powders.

One last advantage reloaders have is the ability to create loads that do not exist in factory offerings. There is no doubt, however, that factory loads are good these days. In fact, reloaders will not be able to better the performance of many of them. That includes all established trap loads, many skeet loads and some long-range international loads. Nevertheless, you can equal them, and do it for less money. You can also create loads that are not available from the factory. As far as this shooter is concerned, those are more than enough reasons to spend time at the loading bench.

Pattern Testing

Testing what you have created requires patterning the gun and load combo. There really is no other way to be certain you're getting an effective load because each shotgun barrel, even from the same maker, is its own "musical instrument": a load that does a beautiful job in one gun can be a marginal performer in another. It is traditional to pattern the 12-, 20- and 28-gauges at 40 yards, with the .410 being shot at 30. I test them my own way.

I make up specific loads to operate with a specific choke tube within a specific range. That's where I pattern them – where I will be shooting them. It makes no sense, and provides no information, to test-pattern a 15-yard spreader load at 40 yards just because it happens to be a 12-gauge. Pattern it at 15 yards instead. The same holds true for a mid-range load or a high-performance nickel-plated long-range load. My procedure is to pattern spreader loads at 15 yards, Skeet or close-range Sporting loads at 21 yards, and 16-Yard trap loads (which are mid-range Sporting loads) at 30 yards. Handicap trap loads and other long-range loads get tested at 45 yards, although I might take a look at them at 55 yards as well. I may not be able to improve their performance, but at least I'll know what to expect of them and that may be one of the biggest reasons to reload.

Thoughts on Spreaders

Most scattergunners want their shot patterns as dense and uniform as possible. Still, there are times when a quick-opening pattern can be an asset.

This is especially true in sporting clays. Here, shooters may be faced with a number of real "in-your-face" target presentations at ranges between 10 and 15 yards. Most of these shots will be at quick crossing birds. Sometimes they will have a slight incoming or outgoing angle. It does not take a mathematical genius to see that a shooter who can only generate a 10-inch-wide pattern at that range has to be far more precise with his aim than one who uses a load that gives a 20-inch diameter pattern. In fact, the larger pattern does not give you twice as much surface area to hit the target with; it gives four times as much. When you are swinging like crazy on an orange blur, a larger diameter pattern can help your score dramatically. As a result, there has been a resurgence of interest in 12 gauge "spreader" loads.

These loads have been around for quite a while now, but they have not traditionally garnered much favor with competitive trap and skeet shooters. They were primarily hunting loads designed to open the shot charge from a modified or full choke to what might be achieved with improved cylinder choking.

Often called "brush loads," they were intended to allow a shooter with a fixed choke (which was the rule rather than the exception a decade or so ago) to have a quick and convenient way to open his patterns if he happened to wander into tight quarters. Hence the moniker "brush load."

There are a number of ways to open the pattern on a shotgun without changing the choke. Shooting softer chilled shot at high velocity will usually open a pattern one choke degree over harder shot at more moderate velocity. Wad inserts are also available to help spread the shot. These may be a simple X-divider or a post and base. They are placed into the wad prior to dropping the shot, or inserted into the shot charge after it has been dropped.

Gualandi has produced a one-piece plastic wad with an X-spreader insert molded in, and two side cup petals that instantly separate from the wad as it leaves the muzzle. These wads are available as reloading components from Ballistic Products.

The same wad is currently being loaded by ACTIV in their specially marked sporting clays loads. These use a light orange-colored hull and box instead of red. They are available in sizes #9, #8 and #7½. Will they add any birds to your sporting clays score? Maybe they will, maybe they won't.

The original intent of the spreader load was to turn a full or modified choke into an improved cylinder or cylinder choke, and the Gualandi X-Spreader wad will certainly do that whether in the ACTIV factory loads or in your own reloads.

I tested the ACTIV load with #9 shot in my Ruger Red Label with Briley long choke tubes in modified and Skeet 1. It showed that from the modified tube it would produce patterns of almost identical dimensions and density to those achieved by a standard Federal #9 skeet load from the skeet-choked tube. In short, it does just what a spreader load is intended to do. It makes the #7½ load a good item to have in your pocket in the hunting fields if you are using a more tightly choked barrel and suddenly find you need an open choke.

That makes spreader loads worthwhile additions to the contemporary factory shotshell lineup. A spreader load is not needed in the field that often, and one box is likely to last for years. Competitive shooters may not find them that valuable, however, because of their quick-change choke options.

In doing some testing to find the best close-range load for my own shooting, I tested the ACTIV load against several standard #9 skeet loads that are not only less expensive but more readily available. The results were eye-opening.

Patterning at 15 yards from the Briley Cylinder tube on my Red Label, I found that the ACTIV load produced a usable pattern of about 22 inches in diameter. The term "usable pattern" is a better reflection of the load's actual performance on targets than is a pellet count and pattern percentage figure. The usable pattern area is determined by simply using a felt marker to draw a circle around the portion of the pattern that is dense and evenly distributed enough to consistently break a target. Individual flier pellets, or small groups of two to four shot pellets outside this area might get you a target every now and then, but you cannot count on them.

A 22-inch pattern at 15 yards is nothing to sneer at! That is three to five inches larger in diameter than you can get with a Skeet 1 choke, and twice as big as what you get with a Skeet 2 (light modified) choke. It is about as much as you can open a pattern at that range and still maintain enough density with 1⅛ ounces of shot to prevent a bird from slipping through. In short, the ACTIV spreader load is probably the best bet for "in-your-face" targets.

Patterning the Federal paper-hulled 2¾-dram, 1⅛-ounce #9 skeet load from the same cylinder choke at the same range, I got a usable pattern of about 21 inches. That pattern was more evenly distributed than the ACTIV pattern, which had a couple of thin areas.

The next load I tested was the Federal plastic-hulled #9 skeet load in the three-dram size. Shotshell ballistic theory says that the heavier powder charge would tend to open the pattern a bit more quickly and it did. The three-dram, 1⅛-ounce load produced a pattern of about 23 inches. Again, it had better pellet distribution than the ACTIV load.

Cobbling up a quick reload on my Hornady press using a Victory hull, 19 grains of Clays (about a 2¾-dram charge), Federal 209 primer and a purple PC wad (a 1-ounce wad that leaves about ⅛-inch of the shot charge unprotected) I got patterns that equaled the three-dram Federal load, but with a bit less recoil. I could probably open that load a bit further by shifting to softer chilled shot, but I happened to be out of it at the time.

The results of my impromptu tests convinced me that, with my Briley cylinder choke tube in place, an expensive spreader load is simply not necessary. I am getting the same pattern diameter and slightly better density with either an easily available factory load or a quick and inexpensive reload.

Interestingly, shortly after these tests I ran into shooting champions Bill Whitehurst and Bonnie McLaurin at a local Sporting Clays range and asked them how they felt about spreaders. Their response was, "Use a cylinder choke and #9s and you get the same thing."

There is one situation where I feel I would want to have a handful of the #9 ACTIV loads in one of my pockets. That is on those rare occasions when I shoot FITASC, the international version of sporting clays. It is rare for an American-style sporting clays range to throw targets that vary more than about one choke degree in range from the same stand. As a rule, when you step into the stand to shoot, if you have made a proper choke selection, you will be okay. That is not necessarily so in FITASC competition. You may get a target that requires an improved modified or full choke on one bird only to have that followed by a bird that fairly screams improved cylinder or Skeet 1. You cannot change choke tubes once you get onto the shooting stand, so you have a dilemma. The experienced shooter here would choke for the longer bird and plug in an ACTIV spreader load (or reload if rules allow) for the closer birds.

However, that is a rare situation. For my money, when I have an "in-your-face" target, I stick with cylinder chokes and #9s. That will spread me as thin as I'm going to get.

Bigger Is Not Always Better

There is a definite and very noticeable shift among competitive 12-gauge shotgunners toward high speed one-ounce and ⅞-ounce loads for most shooting, reserving the traditional 1⅛-ounce loads for longer ranges.

That trend began in a rather unusual way. Many years back, shooters competing in the demanding game of International (bunker) trap were allowed to use full 3¼-dram, 1¼-ounce loads; many did. This was punishing to the shooter because shooting two shots at a target is the rule, not the exception. Shooting 75 targets in a day means 150 shots with a heavy load.

The UIT Rules Committee decided to spice up the game and changed the rules to allow a maximum of 1⅛ ounces of shot. That brought predictable howls from the competitors who were convinced that their scores would go down. That did not happen, though.

A few years later, they changed the rules to allow a maximum of one ounce of shot (28 grams). Again the howls, and again the same results. Scores did not go down; indeed, they went up!

How could a smaller shot charge improve scores? The answer: recoil! The less punishment a shooter absorbs, the better he or she will shoot. The experience of the UIT bunker trap shooters has proved this conclusively. In fact, when they made their most recent change to allow a maximum of 24 grams of shot (⅞-ounce) there were very few howls. The shooters had been educated.

Many of those same shooters have also realized that if an ounce of shot is enough to handle a high-speed, stoutly con-structed bunker trap target, it will certainly handle the slower standard targets.

Earlier in this chapter, I provided loading data for a mild, actually an ultra-light, 1-ounce, 12-gauge load that is an excellent American skeet load. Most one-ounce shooters favor higher velocities. An increase in velocity provides an increase in the target breaking power of the individual pellets, which means you get a good break with fewer pellet hits. I have watched one-ounce loads of #9 shot at 1,300 fps absolutely crush the sturdy international skeet targets, while an ultra-light load at 1,100 fps would merely dust them or make them wobble, but they would not produce the visible piece required to score a hit. Higher speed is one of the keys to making one-ounce loads effective beyond skeet ranges, and loading data for these high-speed loads is available. Here is the data for some of the one-ounce loads that I have found effective.

With the Remington Unibody hull, load 22 grains of Hodgdon International powder and a Federal 209 primer. Use ⅞-ounce of shot in the Federal 12S0 wad or one ounce of shot in the purple PC wad. Velocity of both is in the 1,280-1,300 fps range and recoil is very mild. Either of these is an excellent close-range load with #9 shot and my favorite for close sporting clays shots.

If you happen to prefer Green Dot powder, you get the same performance with 21.5 grains. If you use the Federal 209A primer, use 20.5 grains of Hodgdon International.

For ACTIV or Federal Gold Medal hulls, the Federal 12S0 wad with the standard Federal 209 primer puts up a lovely one-ounce load with the same powder charges listed above. It has low recoil and a velocity of about 1,250-1,280. I like this load very much with hard #8 shot as an all-round load. With a modified choke, it is eminently suitable for 16-yard and double trap. Shift to an improved cylinder choke and it does a fine job on sporting clays targets to 35 yards. Switch to #8½ shot and it is a great international skeet load, although not legal in sanctioned UIT matches. I use #7½ shot for handicap trap and bunker trap, not to mention dove, quail and woodcock. It is a very versatile load.

Every now and then, I run across a supply of Fiocchi hulls and these create some logistics problems because they do not work well with the Federal wads I normally stock. However, they are good hulls and I want to use them. I use them to make an excellent one-ounce load with the purple PC wad and 20-21 grains of Green Dot. An advantage here is that I can load these with a different shot size than my standard loads, say #7½, and use them when I want a little extra punch. Their distinctive color makes it impossible to confuse them with other loads in the heat of battle.

Note that the preceding load information is cited for reference purposes only. Neither of the authors nor the publisher accepts responsibility for any load assembled as a result of this data. Each component, each gun, and each individual is a law unto itself, and one load may be perfectly safe in one gun but unpredictable in another. For that reason, it is recommended that all reloaders stick to data provided by the reloading component manufacturers.

If you are used to shooting full 2¾ - or three-dram, 1⅛-ounce loads on a steady basis, the shift to one-ounce loads will surprise you. They will do pleasant things to your score, your cheek and shoulder as well. When it comes to busting clay targets, bigger is not always better.

TRAP RULES

SECTION I

ORGANIZATION OF THE AMATEUR TRAPSHOOTING ASSOCIATION

The following is an informative summary of the organization of the AMATEUR TRAPSHOOTING ASSOCIATION OF AMERICA (ATA). Complete, and controlling, details are as contained in the Official Rules, Articles of Incorporation and the By-Laws of the Corporation. The Official Trapshooting Rules of the ATA govern the shooting of registered targets and the conduct of shooters and the duties of shoot management The ATA has the responsibility for the formulation, regulation and enforcement of these Rules. These Rules are contained in this booklet.

The ATA reserves the right to make alterations in, or amendments to these Rules at any time, whenever it deems it to be in the best interest of the ATA.

A. PURPOSE OF THE ATA

The purpose of the ATA is to promote and govern the sport of amateur trapshooting throughout the world.

B. MEMBERSHIP

Membership is divided into two classes, life and annual, both of which have full shooting rights and privileges. The membership year runs from September 1 through August 31.

C. STATE ORGANIZATIONS AND ATA DELEGATE ELECTIONS

Shooters in the various states and provinces are organized into state and provincial associations, which under the auspices of the ATA, control shooting in their own territories and conduct state and provincial championship tournaments. Shooters are required to pay any fees and dues which may be set by these state/provincial associations in their place of residence in order to be considered members in good standing of the state/provincial association. Such associations receive assistance from the ATA in the form of trophies and cash refunds. This assistance is explained in Rule X, C.

At each annual state or provincial championship tournament sanctioned by the ATA, a business meeting will be held on a date and time specified in the program for the tournament. The meeting date must be one of the last three days of the tournament, held no earlier than 8:00 am and no later than 9:00 p.m. If however the meeting is held on the last day of the tournament, then it must commence no later than 12:00 noon. At the business meeting all members of the ATA residing in that state or province, who are present in person at the meeting and are also members of their state or provincial association, shall be entitled to vote for a state or provincial delegate and for not over two alternate delegates.

A current average card, the form of which shall be determined by the board of directors or executive committee, shall evidence ATA membership, life and annual. No membership shall be effective until after receipt of proper application at the general office of the corporation, approval, issuance of an average card, and receipt by the member. A member shall not be qualified to cast a ballot for a state or provincial delegate or alternate delegate(s) until properly qualified in accordance with this paragraph.

Any shooter who has paid his/her dues and exhibits the receipt for payment may participate in registered shoots.

The criteria for election as a state delegate or alternate delegate is:
- actual physical residence within the boundaries of the state/province of representation, and
- in receipt of life membership certificate from the ATA, and
- a member in good standing of the state/provincial association of the state/province of representation, and
- ATA member in good standing for at least five consecutive years, and
- active participation as evidenced by registration of at least 3,000 targets total (singles, handicap and doubles combined) in current and previous four years, and of at least 500 targets each year in the current and previous four years, and
- shall not have been suspended within the prior five years or for a period of one year or more.

Target registration may be waived for shooters with an extensive target history who because of documented physical problems are not currently able to participate.

Selection of the state or provincial delegate, and the alternate delegate(s) should be given the utmost consideration. Delegates (or in their absence alternate delegates), in a properly called meeting, constitute the Board of Directors of the ATA and as such have the responsibility of overseeing the operation of the Association. Only those persons who are responsible dedicated individuals should be considered.

D. ZONES

The zones are comprised of the following states and provinces:

CENTRAL: Illinois, Indiana, Michigan, Iowa, Minnesota, Nebraska, North Dakota, Ohio, South Dakota, Wisconsin, and the provinces of Manitoba and Saskatchewan, Canada.

EASTERN: Connecticut, Delaware, Maine, Maryland, Massachusetts, New Hampshire, New York, Pennsylvania, Rhode Island, Vermont, New Jersey and the provinces of Ontario and Quebec, Canada, and the provinces of Ontario, Canada and the provinces in Canada lying east thereof.

SOUTHERN: Alabama, Florida, Georgia, Kentucky, Mississippi, North Carolina, South Carolina, Tennessee, Virginia and West Virginia.

SOUTHWESTERN: Arkansas, Colorado, Kansas, Louisiana, Missouri, New Mexico, Oklahoma and Texas.

WESTERN: Alaska, Arizona, California, Hawaii, Idaho, Montana, Nevada, Oregon, Utah, Washington, Wyoming, and the provinces of Alberta and British Columbia, Canada.

E. BOARD OF DIRECTORS

The Corporate Powers of the ATA under Delaware law are vested in the Board of Directors, which consists of a Delegate from each State and Province. The Board of Directors meets annually during the Grand American World Trapshooting Championships and at other times when properly called by the Executive Committee or as provided in the By-Laws.

F. EXECUTIVE COMMITTEE AND ATA EXECUTIVE DIRECTOR

1. The Executive Committee consists of a representative from each of the five zones elected each year to the Executive Committee at the annual meeting of the Board of Directors. One member of the Executive Committee is designated President and the other four are designated Vice Presidents.

2. The Board of Directors has delegated direction of the affairs of the ATA to the Executive Committee between meetings of the Board of Directors.

3. The Executive Committee employs an Executive Director to handle the daily affairs of the ATA. The ATA Executive Director implements the policy set forth by the Board of Directors and/or the Executive Committee and follows their directions.

4. The main office and records of the ATA are located at 601 West National Road, Vandalia, Ohio 45377-1096, phone (937) 898-4638, Fax (937) 898-5472, www.shootata.com.

G. CONSTITUTION AND BYLAWS

The ATA is organized under the Corporate Laws of the State of Delaware and has a Delaware charter and corporate by-laws formulated in accordance with Delaware laws.

H. JURISDICTION

The A.T.A. has jurisdiction over all affiliated associations regardless of location.

SECTION II

INFORMATION FOR SHOOTERS

A. PROCEDURE FOR JOINING ATA

1. ANNUAL MEMBERS

Application for Annual Membership may be made at any registered shoot by filling out an application and the payment of $18.00 dues to the ATA. Sub-Junior and Junior Annual Members shall pay $9.00 dues to the ATA. A temporary receipt will be given to the shooter upon receipt of a proper application. The temporary receipt should be retained as evidence of payment and be used in lieu of an average card until the average card is received. The ATA will issue an annual average card in the usual course of business. This card will be marked to indicate the shooter's handicap yardage. Full membership rights are effective upon receipt by the member of the average card.

Annual Members have all the shooting rights and privileges of Life Members, but may hold no office in the ATA. Annual Members are entitled to vote for the state/provincial delegate and alternate(s) at the annual business meeting of the state or province.

Annual Memberships are renewable by mail or at any registered shoot. To renew by mail send your complete name, address, including zip code, and $18.00 to ATA, 601 West National Rd., Vandalia, Ohio 45377-1096.

2. LIFE MEMBERSHIPS

Life Memberships are obtained by the submission of a properly completed application and the payment of $500.00. Senior Life Memberships for those 65 years and older are $250.00. Life members pay no annual dues thereafter. Upon approval of the application, the ATA will issue a Life Membership Certificate and the Life Membership is effective upon receipt by the Member. Life Members are entitled to vote for state delegates and alternate delegates to the ATA. Only Life Members may hold office in the ATA.

PLEASE NOTE: If you pay dues at a shoot, he/she must retain his/her receipt until receipt of your average card. Unless the shooter can show evidence of membership fee payment, he/she may have to pay again. Shooters must record all scores before receipt of an ATA card and then transfer these scores to your new card.

If you do not receive an ATA card within four weeks, he/she should send a letter to the ATA, 601 West National Rd., Vandalia, Ohio 45377-1096, advising the ATA that an application was made on certain date and give ATA the name of the gun club that received the application and payment.

B. TARGET YEAR

The target year runs from September 1 thru August 31. Scores shot at any tournament ending after August 31, regardless of starting date, will be included in the following year's averages.

C. RULES OF CONDUCT OF AN ATA SHOOTER

Each member will be furnished a copy of these Official Trapshooting Rules, and it is assumed that the member will read and understand each rule. Members are strongly encouraged to know these Rules and abide by them for their own benefit and for the benefit of other shooters.

1. By entering the competition, every contestant agrees to accept all official decisions and to abide by these Rules.

2. It is the responsibility of all shooters to see that they are handicapped and classified properly in accordance with these rules and/or the official program. Any errors made by the classification committee and/or the shooter must be corrected before shooting or the shooter may be subject to disqualification and may be subject to further disciplinary action.

3. When making entry at any registered shoot, shooters should produce their plastic identification card and Average Card so that names, addresses, and membership numbers are properly noted and errors in record keeping are prevented. Shooters not having a plastic card should always list their ATA number, entire name and address on entry forms.

4. The Average Card is intended to provide classification personnel at registered shoots with current data on a member's shooting ability. Shooters not having their Average Cards up to date may be put in a higher class or otherwise penalized. Failure to accurately record scores, or the falsification of scores, can lead to disciplinary action including suspension from the ATA.

5. Any member who;
Submits false information for any reason to a participating club, ATA, or shoot management or;
Who causes false scores or other information to be recorded or;

Who commits an act of theft or;
Who commits acts which result in artificially low scores or;
Who encourages or assists others in such acts;
is subject to disciplinary action.

SECTION III

REQUIREMENTS AND RECOMMENDATIONS FOR CONDUCTING A REGISTERED SHOOT

A. APPLICATION TO CONDUCT A SHOOT

Proper blank application forms, obtained from the ATA, or local State secretaries, should be filled out and provided to the State secretary for approval prior to the scheduled shoot. If there are club dues or other obligations to the State, these must be enclosed with applications. Registered league dues of $25.00 per league must be submitted with the appropriate league application.

If the application is in order, the State secretary will approve and forward it to the ATA for the certification of registration provided that the dates of a registered event and/or tournament granted to another club or association in close proximity. The question of close proximity is left to the judgment of the officials of the State Association. State and Provincial Associations shall not unreasonably withhold approval of shoot dates from affiliated clubs. In the event the State association is unable or unwilling to decide the question of close proximity, the question will be referred to the ATA State/Provincial Delegate who has the duty to make the decision, and whose decision is final. The Delegate has no duty, responsibility or authority of the ATA to decide any shoot dates until the question of close proximity has been referred to the Delegate by the State/Province association.

Upon receipt of the approved application form, the ATA will issue the registration certificate, provided all conditions of the application have been met. A record of the issuance of the certificate of registration will be kept on file in the main office of the ATA, and prior to the holding of the registered event and/or tournament, necessary office supplies for the proper recording of scores will be sent to the club or association.

B. PREPARATION AND PROGRAMS

1. An official written program for every shoot must be published or posted. Note: the program may be handwritten or in email form. The program must, at a minimum, list all fees, events, options, trophies, penalty classification and handicap (if used) for the shoot. It is required that ATA shoot programs indicate the specific amount of fees collected on behalf of the ATA. ATA fees must be set apart from all other fees and charges made by shoot management. Programs should be made available and/or sent to an up-to-date list of shooters.

2. All shooters must be charged the same target and option fees. An exception may be made for special category shooters, i.e., charging Junior and Sub-Junior shooters half price.

3. Shoot Management should ascertain that the gun club facilities are in good condition prior to the shoot and that an adequate supply of materials and supplies needed to conduct the shoot are available.

C. CHECKLIST FOR THE SHOOT

1. Shoot management should arrange for:
   a. capable classifying and handicapping personnel who shall classify and handicap all shooters in accordance with the Official Rules, and
   b. competent cashiers who will calculate purses and options correctly and pay off as many events as possible before the close of the shoot, and
   c. squadding personnel (Note – at small shoots, all three of the above may be done by the same person or persons), and
   d. referee/scorers who know the ATA Rules, and who have been adequately trained to call all targets, or only the lost targets as directed, and to record the scores correctly on the sheets provided, and
   e. referee/scorers must be provided with an unobstructed view of shooters. It is improper at an ATA shoot for shooters to supply their own referee/scorers. (Note – one person may serve as referee/scorer. If the person or persons serving in these capacities is negligent or inefficient, the management shall remove him/her or them.), and
   f. Provide appropriate hearing and eye protection to firing line personnel. This includes all employees who perform duties on or near the trap field. Shoot management is required to enforce this provision, failure to do so may result in disciplinary action; and
   g. Any additional help needed to conduct the tournament efficiently, such as squad hustler, scoreboard recorder, score sheet runners, and enough personnel to properly operate a shooting facility.

2. Management shall confirm that all participants are ATA members in good standing who have paid their annual dues or are Life Members before accepting their entries. If shoot management accepts entry from a contestant and it is subsequently determined he/she is not an ATA member in good standing and his/her annual dues had not been paid, shoot management must make every effort to collect those dues. If shoot management, ATA or any other club is unsuccessful in collection of unpaid dues, shoot management will be assessed an amount equal to each unpaid entry. Notice of unpaid dues will be mailed to the ATA to each participant and club responsible. Failure to timely pay assessments may result in a club's shoot application being denied or held in abeyance until payment is made.

3. Shoot management of any registered event and/or tournament, at its discretion, may reject any entry, or refund any entry. In all cases except as may be otherwise provided in these Rules, the authority of the management of a registered shoot is not subject to appeal and all contestants must abide by its rulings. No entry shall be rejected on the basis of gender, race, religion, sexual orientation, or disability unless such disability renders the contestant incapable of complying with these Official Rules or results in an unsafe condition, which endangers any person or property.

4. Shoot management shall appoint a judge or judges to be called upon for ruling on official complaints when the occasion arises. If a judge has not been appointed, the president of the club, or in his absence, the secretary shall act as judge. The referee/scorer must call upon a judge to settle any controversy regarding a score or when he/she has made an error by being ahead or behind in his scoring. Officials of the ATA will not change the decisions of these judges made in accordance with these Rules, or change the report of any shoot held in accordance with these Rules.

5. No shooter will be allowed to repeat any portion of the regularly advertised program, i.e., shooting more than once in an event.

6. Additional events (not included in the official program) may be held and the scores registered provided that shooters have been notified of such events by shoot management, that the event is announced and posted, and that at least three participants shoot and complete the event.

7. The sponsors of registered events and/or tournaments are responsible for the payment of all added money, guaranteed money, purses, and/or prizes advertised or offered in their shoot programs. If the management of a registered shoot does not meet the above obligations, the ATA will not be responsible for such payments and will not be liable in any manner whatsoever. Sponsors and/or shoot management will hold harmless and indemnify the ATA for any and all disputes or causes of action arising hereunder.

8. Shoot management must make every effort to see that the Average Cards of any shooters earning yardage are punched. If for any reason an Average Card is not punched at the shoot, shoot management shall inform the ATA, the shooter, and the shooter's State ATA Delegate in writing.

D. FOLLOW UP DUTIES

Following the conclusion of a registered shoot and/or tournament shoot management is responsible or will delegate the responsibility for:
1. Completing and sending to the ATA office the following items:
   a. The ATA report form with complete names, addresses, ATA card numbers, and accurate scores of all shooters for all events.
   b. The earned yardage reports.
   c. Names and addresses of those paying ATA dues at the shoot.
   d. A check for ATA daily fees or league registration fees collected at the shoot or league.
   e. One copy of the official shoot program or league Rules. This must be done within eight calendar days following the last day of the registered shoot or league to avoid a $25.00 late shoot report fine for the first offense and a $100.00 late shoot report fine for second offense in a target year, which, if not paid, will be deducted from that state rebate. A third offense will dictate cancellation of registered shoot privileges until delinquent shoot reports and/or money are properly received by ATA. Any check(s) presented to ATA and subsequently dishonored is equal to a third offense and must be paid, including bank charges, before further registered shoots are permitted.
2. Sending State fees collected to the State Association.
3. Sending a report of the results to the Trap & Field Magazine.
4. Reporting shoot results to the local radio and TV stations and the local newspapers as practicable.

E. KEEPING SHOOT RECORDS

Shoot Management is required to keep the records from all registered shoots for at least one year.

SECTION IV

ATA TOURNAMENTS

In these Rules the words "shoot" and "tournament" are intended to include "leagues" throughout these Official Rules with exceptions only as noted.

A. REGISTERED SHOOTS

1. The ATA governs the conduct of all shoots registered with it. Only clubs affiliated with their state/provincial association will be permitted to hold registered shoots.
2. To constitute a registered shoot the following requirements must be met:
   a. all contestants must be members of ATA at the time of their entry, and
   b. each contestant must pay ATA daily registration fee of $2.00 for each day of competition at each shooting location, and such other Zone or State Association fees as may be charged, and
   c. at least 5 or more contestants must compete and complete the same event on the same day of competition. After this requirement is met, other events that follow on the same day of competition may be registered when three or more contestants compete in and complete such other events.
3. No daily fee charges shall be permitted except those assessed by the ATA, the Zone, or the State in which the tournament is being held.
4. A shooter is not required to be a member of any club or facility to participate in a duly authorized registered shoot.

B. WHO MAY PARTICIPATE

Only ATA Life or Annual Members may participate in an ATA registered trapshooting tournament event and/or tournament. Shooters must be members of the State/Provincial Association in their place of residence to compete in registered shoots in that State or Province.

C. MEMBERS OF OTHER SHOOTING ORGANIZATIONS

Targets shot and registered with any shooting organization other than ATA shall not be counted toward any published minimum target requirement, for any purpose, at any tournament where ATA trophies are awarded.

D. FIRING POSITION AND SHOOTING ORDER

1. There are five firing positions (posts), numbered 1 to 5, left to right spaced three yards apart and 16 yards from Point B.
2. The referee/scorer shall not throw a target unless all contestants are in the correct positions.
3. At any registered trapshooting competition, no person shall be permitted to "Shoot Up;" that is, enter and take part in any completed or partially completed event or events after Squad No. 1 has completed sub-event 1 of any new event. At tournaments shot "bank system" with several squads starting at the same time on several traps, the procedure shall be construed to e the same as if all squads started on the same trap.

E. SUB-EVENTS

A sub-event is any number of targets shot on any one field at one time, with one full rotation on all five posts by each shooter, such as 25 or 50 Singles or Handicap targets or 10 pairs, 15 pairs, 25 pairs or Doubles. An event is the total targets of a specific type (16 yard, Handicap, or Doubles) such as 200 16-yard targets, 100 Handicap targets, etc. for which separate entry is made. It is not necessary to change traps after each sub-event. Events of less than 50 targets may not be registered.

F. RECORDING SCORES WINS AND TIES

1. All 16 yard, Handicap and Doubles scores are required to be accurately and legibly entered on each member's Average Card in the spaces provided at the completion of each registered and/or tournament event.
2. It is the duty of each ATA member to record all wins and ties in 16 yard and Doubles events on his/her Average Card. The intent of this rule is to properly inform classification and handicap committees of prior wins and ties in 16 Yard and Doubles events.

Failure of any member to strictly comply with these rules may lead to penalty classification, disqualification and/or suspension from membership in the ATA.

G. SQUADDING, SQUAD LEADER RESPONSIBILITIES AND TARGET OBSERVATION

1. In all ATA events contestants shall shoot in squads of five except:
   a. When there are less than five contestants available for the last squad of any program.
   b. When yardage differences in Handicap events make it impractical or unsafe.
   c. When there are withdrawals from a squad after the competition has begun and squads scheduled.
   d. When in the opinion of shoot management, the harmony of the shoot may be enhanced by squadding less than five contestants.
2. In Handicap there shall be no more than two yards difference between adjacent shooters in the squad, and no more than a total difference of three yards in a squad.
3. It is illegal for more than five shooters to be in a squad.
4. The squadding of practice shooters with those shooting registered events shall not be allowed, nor shall anyone be allowed to shoot registered events on a non-registered basis. This rule shall not apply during Registered League Shooting.

5. For each squad, the shooter who has been assigned to start on post 1 is designated the "Squad Leader". If post 1 is empty, the role of the Squad Leader passes to the shooter assigned to start on post 2, and so on. The Squad Leader has the following duties:

a. After all squad members are present at their assigned positions on the trap field, the Squad Leader should ascertain that all squad members are ready to begin the sub-event. After doing so, the Squad Leader only may ask that targets be thrown for the squad's observation. For regular 16-yard Singles and Handicap sub-events, the Squad Leader may ask for one target only. For regular Doubles sub-events, the Squad Leader may ask for one pair of Doubles. For Shoot-offs in 16-yard Singles and Handicap events, the Squad Leader may ask for two targets. For Shoot-offs in Doubles events, the Squad Leader may ask for two pairs of Doubles.

b. If the targets thrown for observation are broken, irregular, or illegal, the Squad Leader may ask that another target (or pair of Doubles as applicable) be thrown. The squad has the right to see a legal target (or legal pair of Doubles as applicable) before commencing the sub-event.

c. The Squad Leader should check and initial the score sheet at the completion of each sub-event.

d. The Squad Leader shall have the responsibility to carry the score sheet, on which more than one sub-event is recorded, from trap to trap until completion of the event.

6. During a sub-event, if there is a delay due to trap or gun malfunction, the contestant in turn may ask to see a target (or pair of Doubles as applicable) thrown before he/she resumes shooting.

7. Should a trap be throwing targets that, although not necessarily illegal, appreciably vary from trap to trap, any shooter may request that management reset the trap even though prior squads have shot. The final decision as to whether or not a trap is to be reset will be made only by shoot management.

8. During a sub-event, if a contestant is subjected to 2 consecutive occurrences of "No Target" or no target is thrown on his/her call, the contestant shall have the right to see a legal target (or legal pair of Doubles as applicable) and adjust the voice release mechanism (if present) before shooting resumes.

H. SHOOT-OFFS

1. Shoot-offs shall be considered and interpreted the same as registered events and all applicable ATA Rules shall apply unless mutually agreed upon by contestants. The management of a tournament may rule that ties shall be carried over to the first (or more if needed) sub-event of the next like event. However, when there are ties in a handicap event and any tying shooter earns yardage and consequently will be shooting farther back in the subsequent handicap event, all tying shooters must agree to the carry over.

2. All ties whenever possible shall be shot off, and in such a manner as shoot management shall designate. Unless otherwise specified by the management, ties on single target events shall be shot off in 25 target events and doubles in 10 pair events.

3. Ties for High All-Around Championships shall be shot off 20 singles, 10 handicap, and 5 pair of doubles. Ties for High-Overall shall be shot off in such a manner that the shoot-off represents as closely as possible the same proportion of singles, handicap and doubles targets as the High Overall program contains but keeping the shoot off to 50 targets or less. The singles, handicap and doubles portion of the shoot off shall be shot in the order that the events occurred in the program, or as determined by shoot management.

4. When squadding shooters for shoot-offs for High-Overall and High All-Around the shooting order shall be in the order in which they shot in the last event involved except where such order would be inadvisable or dangerous because of yardage differences. The order shall remain through each portion of the shoot off.

5. The following method shall be used for rotation of shooters: Starting posts to be used shall be as follows except where handicap yardage makes it unsafe.

If one shooter - post number 2.
If two shooters - post numbers 2 and 4.
If three shooters - post numbers 2, 3 and 4.
If four shooters - post numbers 2, 3, 4 and 5.
If five shooters - post numbers 1, 2, 3, 4 and 5.

If more than five shooters are involved in the tie, they shall be divided as equally as possible into two or more squads as directed by the management.

In subsequent shoot offs, the post shall be rotated in a clockwise manner, with the shooter from post 1 advancing to post 2 and the shooter from post 5 rotating to post 1 or to the post dictated by the number of shooters remaining, but always in clockwise rotation.

6. The practice of banking targets in advance of commencement of a shot-off is not permitted unless all tying shooters are notified and are in unanimous agreement. Exception; banking of targets is permissible for telephonic shoots held in multiple locations.

7. It is recommended that shooters involved in shoot offs be given no more than three five minute calls to report for a shoot off. First call, second call and final call.

I. SAFETY

Shoot management may disqualify a contestant for violation of these Rules, and violations may also result in further disciplinary action.

1. It is the shooter's responsibility and the shoot management's responsibility to conduct a shoot in a safe manner.

2. It is the shoot management's responsibility to remove any competitor who is conducting himself/herself in an unsafe manner. (Repeat violators should be reported to the Executive Committee for further action.)

3. It is the shoot management's responsibility to instruct the trap help in the proper and safe conduct of their respective duties.

4. All trap help must have a flag or other warning device to warn of any persons exiting from the trap house.

5. Trap personnel should be thoroughly instructed of the potential danger of the trap (particularly the target throwing arm).

6. Movement and exposure on adjacent traps should be kept to the minimum.

7. The practice of tracking targets behind a shooting squad is unsafe, disconcerting to the shooter, and is not permitted.

8. Alcohol and drugs impair judgment and the ATA rules pertaining to the usage of alcohol and/or drugs must be enforced by shoot management. This rule shall be strictly complied with and shall apply to practice shooting as well as registered and tournament events.

9. A gun which for any reason fails to fire as intended, must be promptly opened without any subsequent determination by the referee/scorer of the cause of the failure to fire.

10. All guns must have the action opened and contain no live shell or empty shells at any time, except while the shooter is on the firing line. A break open gun's action may be closed when it is in a gun rack but it shall not contain a live shell or empty shell. Repeat offenders of these Rules will be given a 30 day suspension upon a second violation of these Rules; a third violation of these Rules will result in a 90 day suspension; and further violations will be reviewed by the Executive Committee for further disciplinary action.

11. As a safety precaution, test shots will not be permitted.

12. A contestant shall place a live shell in his/her gun only when on a post facing the traps. In singles and handicap shooting he/she may place only one live shell in his/her gun at a time and must remove it or the empty shells before moving from one post to another. In doubles shooting he/she may place two live shells in his/her gun at a time and must remove both live or empty shells before moving from one post to another. In changing from one post to another, the shooter shall not walk in front of the other competitors.

13. Snap caps or recall reduction devices may be excluded from the above only if colored a safety orange as to permanently identify them as not being a live or empty shell.

14. A contestant may hold his/her gun in any position when it is his/her turn to shoot. The contestant must in no manner interfere with the preceding shooter by raising his/her gun to point or otherwise create an observable distraction.

15. All guns used by contestants must be equipped, fitted and utilized so as not to eject empty shells in a manner that substantially disturbs or interferes with other contestants.

16. All persons including competitors, referee/scorers, and trap personnel must wear appropriate eye and hearing protection while on the trap field. Failure to comply may result in disqualification.

J. SPECIAL CATEGORIES

All Ladies, Juniors, Sub-Juniors, Veterans and Senior Veterans must declare their special category at the time of their entry in any registered event. Without such declaration at the time of their entry, the shooter will not be allowed to compete for the applicable special category trophy. No shooter will be allowed to declare a special category after the first shot is fired in the event by the contestant. No exceptions to this rule are allowed. Lady, Junior, Sub-Junior, Veteran and Sr. Veteran shooters who declare such eligibility shall be so designated.

1. All female shooters shall be designated as Ladies, because of age they may also be designated as Juniors, Sub-Juniors, Veterans or Sr. Veterans.

2. A shooter who has not reached his or her 15th birthday will be designated as a Sub-Junior.

3. A shooter who is 15 but has not reached his or her 18th birthday will be designated as a Junior.

4. A shooter who is 65 years or older will be designated as a Veteran.

5. A shooter who is 70 years or older will be designated as a Sr. Veteran.

6. All age-based categories are established on the first day of a Target Year and will continue as the same category through the entire target year, with the sole exception of Veterans which is effective on the Veteran's 65th birthday.

SECTION V
SINGLES AND DOUBLES EVENTS

A. 16 YARD SINGLES

This event must be shot 5 or 10 shots at each post from 16 yards (14.6m) with each shooter in order shooting at one target until all have shot 5 or 10 times, and then rotating in a clockwise manner to the next post. Should Shoot Management elect to change to 50, 16-yard targets per trap (10 per post) after a shooter has made entry, the shooter must be allowed the option to withdraw and be refunded or change his/her option entry.

B. DOUBLES

This event must be shot from 16 yards (14.6m), with each shooter in order shooting at 2 targets thrown simultaneously from the trap house until all have shot the specified number of times, then rotating in a clockwise manner to the next post. A Doubles event may be shot by having each squad shoot successive alternating 15 pair and 10 pair sub-events on the trap or traps being utilized, or Shoot Management may elect to throw Doubles in sub-events of 25 pairs.

C. CLASSIFICATION

1. For 16-yard targets and Doubles, shooters will be placed in 3 or more classes, according to their established average and/or known ability. A new shooter may be assigned to any class in 16 yards and Doubles events, at the discretion of classification personnel until the shooter establishes his/her known ability.

a. To arrive at known ability the following should be taken into consideration as far as such information is or can be made available:

(1) Official registered targets (abnormally low scores should be disregarded) Averages of all registered shooters are compiled and published annually.

(2) Non-registered scores including shoot-off scores, non-registered events, practice scores, etc.

(3) Any other information bearing on a shooter's ability to shoot and break targets.

2. For 16-yard events the following systems are suggested:

SIX CLASSES

98% and over	AAA
96.25% and under 98%	AA
94.75% and under 96.25%	A
93% and under 94.75%	B
90% and under 93%	C
under 90%	D

FIVE CLASSES

97% and over	AA
94% and under 97%	A
91% and under 94%	B
88% and under 91 %	C
Under 88%	D

FOUR CLASSES

95% and over	A
92% and under 95%	B
89% and under 92%	C
Under 89%	D

THREE CLASSES

95% and over	A
91% and under 95%	B
Under 91%	C

3. For Doubles events, the following systems are established:

SIX CLASSES

96% and over	AAA
92% and under 96%	AA
89% and under 92%	A
86% and under 89%	B
82% and under 86%	C
Under 82%	D

FIVE CLASSES

93% and over	AA
89% and under 93%	A
85% and under 89%	B
78% and under 85%	C
Under 78%	D

FOUR CLASSES

90% and over	A
85% and under 90%	B
78% and under 85%	C
Under 78%	D

THREE CLASSES

89% and over	A			
83% and under 89%	B			
Under 83%	C			

4. If shoot management desires to use different classification it may do so by printing the modified classification in the program of the shoot.

5. For better classification of shooters it is suggested that the following method be used.

a. If the shooter has less than 500 targets on current year's Average Card, use the previous year average and known ability.

b. If the shooter has between 500 and 1,000 targets (inclusive) on his/her current year's Average Card, use the current average and known ability or the previous year's average and known ability, whichever is higher.

D. PENALTY CLASSIFICATION

Shoot Management may establish penalty classification for 16-yard targets and Doubles, if target requirements are printed in the program.

SECTION VI
THE ATA HANDICAP SYSTEM

The ATA Handicap system is the method whereby shooters whose ability to win or compete at a level of accomplishment has been demonstrated and shooters whose ability is unknown are handicapped by shooting a greater distance from the trap house. The minimum handicap is 19.0 yards and the maximum is 27.0 yards. A shooter's yardage is determined by Rules governing new shooters, by yardage earned, or by his/her established handicap yardage, which is based on known ability and 1000 target reviews, thereafter. At each State or Provincial shoot, the handicapping and classifying shall be the responsibility of a State or Provincial shoot committee appointed by the State Association with the ATA delegate as chair.

A. HANDICAP EVENTS

This event must be shot 5 or 10 shots at each station as directed by shoot management from 19 to 27 yards (17.4 – 24.7m) with each shooter in order shooting at one target until all have shot 5 or 10 times as directed and then rotating in a clockwise manner to the next post. Should shoot management elect to change to 50 Handicap targets per trap (10 per post) after a shooter has made entry, the shooter must be allowed the option to withdraw and be refunded or change his/her option entry.

A contestant must stand on the highest whole yardage punched on his or her card. For example, if a card is punched at 20.5 yards, the shooter will stand on 20.0 yards. However, if one half yard is then earned, the card must be punched to 21.0 yards and the shooter must stand on the 21.0 yard line.

A shooter may not stand on a higher yardage than he/she is punched, unless assigned penalty yardage by shoot handicap personnel.

When a Handicap marathon event consisting of more than 100 targets is shot, each 100-target sub-event must not begin prior to the awarding of earned yardage based on the previous 100 targets. Shooters earning yardage must shoot subsequent sub-events from the new yardage.

It is not permitted to have more than one 50 and/or 75 target Handicap event in a registered tournament in any one day.

B. CENTRAL HANDICAP COMMITTEE (CHC)

1. The Central Handicap Committee, made up of a chair and five or more members, is appointed at the sole discretion of the Executive Committee. It is the responsibility of the Central Handicap Committee, under the direction of the Executive Committee, to oversee the handicap system and control the assigned yardage of all members of the ATA.

2. Any Central Handicap Committee member may increase a shooter's yardage at his/her discretion when applying the known ability rule. The only other ATA Officers authorized to increase a shooter's yardage are voting members of the Executive Committee.

C. HANDICAP YARDAGE ASSIGNMENT

A shooter will be handicapped between 19 and 27 yards and at the highest yardage punched on his/her Average Card, unless he/she is required to shoot penalty yardage.

1. New lady shooter – new lady shooters will be assigned a handicap of 19.0 yards.

2. New sub-junior shooter – a shooter who has not reached his or her 16th birthday will be classified as a sub-junior and will be assigned a handicap of 19.0 yards. Male shooters, on reaching their 15th birthday will be assigned a handicap of 20.0 yards unless he has previously earned or been assigned greater yardage.

3. New male shooter – a new male shooter, 16 years of age or older, will be assigned a handicap of 20.0 yards.

4. After a lapse in membership any shooter reapplying for membership in the ATA, who had been assigned a previous handicap yardage, shall resume shooting at the previously assigned yardage. The only exception is if the shooter was previously assigned a yardage based on age; because of present age the shooter may be required to shoot at a longer yardage. Failure of a shooter to shoot previously assigned yardage will result in disqualification and any and all scores and prizes, including money, forfeited thereby.

5. Rules for members of other trapshooting associations;

a. If a shooter is a member of any other trapshooting association or was a member of such association the preceding year AND shot targets in such association in the current or preceding ATA target year, he/she will shoot from the handicap yardage of whichever association shows the greater yardage.

b. A member who, at any time has previously been a member of another trapshooting association but has not shot targets in such association in the current or preceding ATA target year must shoot his/her last assigned yardage in that association (if it is greater) unless the shooter has received an ATA 1000 target review and been granted a reduction.

c. It will be the responsibility of the shooter to notify the shoot handicap committee if he/she holds or has held a card of another trapshooting association. Failure to notify the shoot handicap committee of another trapshooting association card may be cause for penalty action resulting in forfeiture of entry fees and all monies, including prizes, and possible suspension from all ATA shoots for one year.

D. KNOWN ABILITY

Handicap and 16 yard averages and/or scores in both registered and non-registered shoots may be used as the basis for determining known ability. Scores abnormally low in relation to the remainder of the scores shot may be disregarded at the discretion of the shoot committee assigned to classify and handicap shooters.

E. EARNED YARDAGE

1. Yardage will be automatically earned by shooters of high scores in all ATA registered events, according to the following table. This additional yardage is indicated by punches on the shooter's Average Card.

EARNED YARDAGE TABLE

High Scores (and all ties)

Entries	1st	2nd	3rd	4th
15-39	1/2 yd			
40-69	1 yd			
70-124	1 yd	1/2 yd		
125-249	1 yd	1 yd	1/2 yd	
250-499	1 1/2 yd	1 yd	1/2 yd	
500-1499	2 yd	1 1/2 yd	1 yd	1/2 yd
1500 and up	2 1/2 yd	2 yd	1 1/2 yd	1 yd

2. Any score of 96 will automatically earn 1/2 yard provided it does not earn at least that much under the earned yardage table. Any score of 50x50 or 75x75 in events of that length will automatically earn 1/2 yard provided it does not earn at least that much under the earned yardage table. Any score of 50x50 or 75x75 in events of that length will automatically earn ½ yard provided it does not earn at least that much under the earned yardage table.

3. The State/Provincial Handicap Champion will automatically earn 1 yard provided the score does not earn at least that much under the earned yardage table.

4. Any score of 97, 98 and 99 will automatically earn 1 yard, and a score of 100 will automatically earn 1 1/2 yards provided these scores do not earn at least that much under the earned yardage table.

5. In marathon Handicap events comprised of more than 100 targets, each 100 targets (or remaining part of 100 targets) shall constitute a separate event for earned yardage purposes and shall be reported as a separate event on the shoot report form.

6. In marathon Handicap events comprised of more than 100 handicap targets, when the total score determines winners, winning scores on the total event not earning yardage under single 100 target events shall be awarded yardage under the earned yardage table based on the largest number of entries in any singe 100 target sub-event.

7. When multiple Handicap events are shot during the same day with fewer than 15 contestants, yardage will be awarded the high scores under the earned yardage table, by combining the total number of different individual shooters in all events with fewer than 15 shooters. For example:

Event 1 – 14 shooters, Event 2 – 20 shooters, Event 3 – 12 shooters (3 of whom shot Event 1), Event 4 – 13 shooters (5 of whom shot Event 1 and/or Event 3). Event 2 stands on its own because it has more than 15 shooters. Combining Events 1, 3, 4 total of 31 different shooters (14, 9, 8). The high score among those 31 shooters will receive a yard punch based on the earned yardage table.

8. The earned yardage table applies to events of 50, 75 or 100 Handicap targets.

9. A shooter's card will be punched from the yardage actually shot (including penalty yardage if applicable). For example, if a shooter earns yardage shooting from 22 yards penalty he/she will be punched from the 22 yard line and not his/her normal yardage assignment. It is the duty of each ATA member to have is or her Average Card punched if yardage is earned. The Average Card must be punched to the correct earned yardage on the day the yardage is earned and before leaving the tournament grounds. If a member is required to leave the tournament grounds prior to the completion of a Handicap event, it is the member's duty to determine if his or her score qualified for a yardage increase and o have his or her Average Card punched o the correct yardage prior to entering any subsequent registered event and/or tournament.

10. The number of contestants starting the event will be the number used for the earned yardage table.

F. PENALTY YARDAGE

Shoot Management may establish penalty yardage based on numbers of registered targets if those target requirements are printed in the program. In no event shall any shooter be assigned a handicap of less than the minimum yardage appearing on his/her Average Card.

G. SPECIAL HANDICAP RULES

1. A shooter must continue to shoot from the last yardage assigned or earned until he/she receives a target review regardless of the length of time that has elapsed since that yardage was assigned or earned.

2. A shooter's handicap yardage may be reduced only as a result of a 1000 target review or a special review. No reduction may be made in the field. The shooter's new Average Card will be noted with the word "review".

3. A shooter's handicap yardage may be increased at any time during the year including immediately before and during the Grand American World Trapshooting Tournament:

a. because of earned yardage, or

b. as a result of a review, or

c. at the discretion of a member of the Central Handicap or voting member of the Executive Committee.

4. A shooter at all times shall have the right to appeal any Central Handicap Committee action to the Executive Committee.

5. Earned yardage of 1.5 or more yards for any single event may not be removed in part or in whole by any Central Handicap Committee action, Executive Committee action, and/or 1,000 Target Review for a minimum period of 2 years from the date the yardage is earned.

6. If a shooter earns yardage while a reduction is in process the reduction shall automatically be void.

7. When multiple 100-target Handicap events (marathons) are shot in the same day, only two 100-target events may be considered as a maximum per day towards reduction. The two events considered out of the marathon must be those two in which the highest scores are registered.

H. REVIEWS

1. 1000 TARGET REVIEW

The shooting record of each member will be automatically reviewed for possible yardage changes after each successive 1000 registered Handicap targets shot in the current and previous year if no yardage was earned.

a. A shooter with a low purified handicap average (the average with abnormally low scores deleted) accompanied by a relative 16 yard average, will receive a one yard reduction, EXCEPT:

(1) No shooter will be reduced more than two yards in any target year.

(2) No male shooter 16 years of age or older will be handicapped below 20 yards without a special review; exceptions to this policy are Veterans and Senior Veterans.

(3) The known ability rule will be used in assessing a shooter's record.

b. A shooter with a high-purified handicap average may receive a "Special Review" for possible yardage increase.

c. If a yardage change is made, the shooter will receive by mail a new Average Card with the new assigned yardage noted with the word "review".

2. SPECIAL REVIEW

a. "Special Review" is an evaluation by the Central Handicap Committee generated by a high-purified average on a 1000 Target Review or initiated by a shooter through his/her State Delegate or a member of the Central Handicap Committee. The results of a Special Review shall be agreed upon by the Central Handicap Committee and the shooter's State Delegate. If a disagreement in yardage assignment exists between the State Delegate and the Central Handicap Committee, the matter may be directed to the Executive Committee. A Special Review may be used:

(1) To determine possible yardage increases for shooters showing high-purified handicap averages on a 1000 target review.

(2) To determine possible yardage reduction for a shooter because of advancing age or physical disability. A shooter may initiate the review through his/her State Delegate.

b. Other shooting organizations' registered handicap scores may not be used in the Special Review process to determine possible yardage changes, and such scores may be used only insofar as they may indicate known ability.

3. ASSIGNED YARDAGE INCREASE

a. A member may appeal an assigned yardage increase by writing to the ATA office, to the attention of the Executive Director after having shot 500 targets at the assigned yardage. After receiving a reduction based on such an appeal for any further reduction 1000 additional registered Handicap targets must be shot.

b. There will be no yardage increase by shooter request beyond 20 yards.

c. The only persons authorized to increase a member's handicap yardage are members of the Central Handicap Committee or voting members of the Executive Committee.

SECTION VII
OFFICIAL SCORING

A. PROCEDURE

1. The official score is the record kept by the referee/scorer on a sheet furnished him/her by shoot management. The referee/scorer's decision on whether a target is dead or lost is final, subject to review only by the shoot committee or other governing body. The score sheet shall show the scores earned in the event or sub-event. It is recommended that the score sheet shall not be smaller than 12 inches by 21 inches (for four sub-event score sheets). During Handicap events the first sub-event of each score sheet shall be annotated with the yardage assignment of each contestant.

2. The referee/scorer shall keep an accurate record of each score of each contestant. If he/she rules "dead" or "lost", the referee/scorer shall promptly mark / or X for "dead" and "0" for lost on the score sheet. Any target scored other than clearly with /, X or 0, or which appears to be scored, with both an X and 0, shall be "lost", unless the word "dead" is clearly printed beside it. The scores of the competition shall be official and govern all awards and records of the competition.

3. The referee/scorer shall distinctly announce, "lost" when the target is missed and "no target" when no target is thrown or a target is thrown broken. The referee/scorer shall call the result of all targets, or only the lost targets, as directed by shoot management.

4. When the referee/scorer calls "no target" for any contestant, the next contestant shall not shoot until the first shooter has shot and the referee/scorer has ruled "dead" or "lost".

5. Should more targets be fired in a sub-event than the event calls for, then the excess targets of the sub-event will not be scored.

6. It is the duty of the referee/scorer to see that the shooters change posts at the proper time; however, any targets shot after failure to move at the proper time shall be scored.

7. Inadvertently skipped posts. A shooter is required to shoot the requisite number of targets from each post (5 or 10 as specified by shoot management). If a shooter inadvertently skips a post he/she or any member of the squad shall not be deemed to be out of turn but will be required to shoot the specified number of targets from the skipped post. While the shooter is shooting the skipped post the remainder of the squad will remain behind the trapline and will not proceed to the next trap.

8. To preserve the harmony of the competition, no member of a squad shall move toward the next post or leave the field until the squad member who is last has fired his/her final shot of the current post's specified number of targets.

9. The official score must be kept on a score sheet in plain view of the contestant. If contestant's view of the score sheet is obstructed for any reason, he/she may refuse to shoot until he/she has been provided an unobstructed view of the score sheet.

10. It is an error if the referee/scorer fails to properly mark the results of any shot in the section of the score sheet where the results should be recorded. In such cases it is the duty of that contestant to have any error corrected before he/she has fired the first shot at the next post before leaving the trap. If the shooter fails to have the score corrected, the recorded scores shall remain unchanged and no valid protest will be entertained.

11. Every contestant in a squad shall be permitted to examine his/her score before the sheet is sent to the bulletin board or to the cashier's office. The score sheet should be checked, confirmed and initialed by the squad leader. After the completion of the last sub-event the score sheet will be handled as directed by shoot management.

12. Errors in the recorded details of the official score can only be corrected in strict accordance with the aforementioned rules, but an error made in totaling or compilation of targets shall be corrected whenever the error is discovered. Shoot management must correct scores recorded in error by field personnel as a result of misapplication of the rules.

13. Any protest concerning a score or scores must be made before or immediately after the close of the competition to which such scores relate. A valid protest may only be made by a contestant who competed in the event.

B. BROKEN OR DEAD TARGET

A target (called "dead") is one that is fired upon and has a visible broken piece from it, or one that is completely reduced to dust. The referee/scorer shall record a target dead when it is broken in the air.

C. LOST TARGET

The referee shall rule "LOST":

1. When the contestant fires and fails to break the target whether missed completely or when ONLY DUST falls from it. A "Dusted Target" is a target from which there is a puff of dust, but no perceptible piece is seen; it is not a dead target; or

2. When a whole target appears promptly after a contestant's recognizable command and is within the legal limits of flight and the contestant voluntarily does not fire; or

3. When an illegal target, a freak target, or a target of a markedly different color is fired at and missed. A contestant may refuse illegal, freak or off-colored targets, but if he/she fires at them the result must be scored; or

4. When a contestant voluntarily withdraws from, or is otherwise disqualified, and takes no further part in a sub-event after having fired at 1 or more targets of a sub-event and does not fire at all the targets in the sub-event, the referee/scorer shall rule all targets not fired upon "LOST" targets and they shall be scored and reported accordingly. When the shooter is prevented by reasons beyond his/her control from completing a sub-event, the scores for that partial sub-event shall not be recorded or reported. Example: shooters have 61 targets of a 100-target event when a storm permanently stops shooting. The management should report the scores for the first 50 targets only; or

5. When a score sheet is delivered to the office with one or more targets that are not properly scored either "DEAD" or "LOST", they shall be scored as "LOST" targets by shoot management; or

6. When a contestant deliberately fires at the same target twice in Doubles Events. This rule is not applicable to a gun "doubling" or "machine-gunning", see Rule VII, D., 3.; or

7. When a commonly called "soft load" occurs, and the shot is fired but no part of the over powder wad or shot remains in the barrel and the target is missed. A soft load where the over powder wad or shot remain in the barrel shall be deemed a "Failure to Fire" and the "Failure to Fire" Rules apply.

D. FAILURE TO FIRE

1. A contestant shall be allowed one 2 failures to fire in Singles and Handicap events, for any reason

other than stated in Paragraph C.,2. above, during each sub-event regardless of the length of the sub-event. When the first or second allowable Failure to Fire in any sub-event occurs, the contestant shall be allowed to call for and fire at another target, and the result of the shot will be scored in accordance with these Official Rules. During shoot-offs for All Around and High Overall events shooters will be allowed 1 Failure to Fire in each of the 3 disciplines (Singles, Handicap, Doubles).

2. A contestant shall be allowed 2 failures to fire, for any reason other than stated in Paragraph C.2, above, during each Doubles sub-events if the Failure to Fire occurs when the contestant attempts to shoot the first target of a Doubles pair, or when the contestant attempts to shoot the second target of a Doubles pair after the first target has been fired at and broken and would have been scored "DEAD". When the first target of a Doubles pair is fired at and missed and that target would be scored "LOST", there shall be no allowable Failure to Fire at the second target. (See exception in VII. E., 11., f.) When a pair is ruled lost there shall be no "Failure to Fire" charged. When the first or second allowable Failure to Fire occurs in any Doubles sub-event, the contestant shall be allowed to call for and fire at another pair of targets and results of the shots at the new pair will be scored in accordance with these Official Rules.

3. Machine-gunning or doubling only occurs when in Doubles Events both shotshells fire simultaneously in a break open gun, or two shots are fired with a single operation of the trigger in an autoloading gun, rendering the competitor incapable of firing at the second target because both shotshells have fired. When a defective gun malfunctions and doubles or machine guns, whether or not the first target would have been scored "DEAD" or "LOST" and whether or not either target is legal or illegal, the referee/scorer shall rule this occurrence a Failure to Fire and score it accordingly.

4. Whenever an allowable Failure to Fire as provided in this Rule occurs, the referee/scorer shall mark a large legible F1 on the score sheet in the space where the target is scored along with the score for that target, and also place the same mark beside the total sub-event score. After one F1 and F2 is in the place where individual targets are scored, any subsequent Failure to Fire in the same sub-event and for any reason, when a target is called and the target appears promptly and within the legal limits of flight, shall be ruled "LOST" and shall be scored accordingly. Cumulative application of the rule is prohibited (failures to fire do not accumulate from sub-event to sub-event) and "sub-event" shall be as defined by Official Rule IV, E.

5. Shoot management is required to examine each score sheet before the score is posted, and any target scored which contains an F1 and F2 in the scoring space, other than for an allowable Failure to Fire as set forth above, shall be scored "LOST" whether originally scored as "LOST" by the referee/scorer or not.

E. NO TARGET

The referee/scorer shall rule "NO TARGET" and allow another target in the following instances:

1. When an allowable "Failure to Fire" as described above occurs.

2. In single target events when the target is thrown broken, regardless of the result of any shot fired.

3. When a whole target appears on the call of the shooter along with target debris.

4. When a contestant shoots out of turn. All contestants must shoot in regular order or sequence according to his or her position in the squad. A contestant who does not shoot in regular order is "out of turn" and the results are not scored.

5. When two contestants fire at the same target.

6. When the trap is sprung without any call of pull, or when it is sprung at any material interval of time before or after the call of the contestant, provided the contestant does not fire. If the contestant fires, the result must be scored.

7. When two targets are thrown at the same time in single target events, regardless of whether the contestant fires.

8. When an "illegal" target is thrown, which is a target that is not within the prescribed angle or height limits for single target shooting, or what is known as a "flipper" or "freak" target is thrown, which is a target that may have slipped out of the carrier of the trap or one not properly placed on the trap, provided the contestant does not fire at it. If the contestant fires, the result must be scored.

9. When a target whose color is markedly different from that of the others is thrown, and the contestant does not fire. If the contestant fires, the result must be scored.

10. When firing, the contestant's feet must be behind the firing mark at sixteen (16) yards, or behind the mark for the Handicap yardage assigned to him/her, depending upon the event being participated in. The contestant must stand with at least one foot on an imaginary line drawn through the center of the trap and continuing through the center of the post, or have one foot on each side of the line. Exceptions to the rule contained in the second sentence of this paragraph may be granted by the referee/scorer due to inequalities in the shooting platform, and shall be granted for wheelchair contestants. Wheelchair contestants shall position their chair so that the center of mass of their body is near the place where they would stand as required by this rule if no chair were used. If a contestant fails to follow this rule in its entirety, the referee/scorer shall rule any target fired at and broken a "NO TARGET", but if fired at and missed, the referee/scorer shall rule the target "LOST". For example, targets shot at and broken from the wrong yardage marker must be shot over, targets shot at from the wrong yardage marker and missed will be scored "LOST".

11. In addition, in DOUBLES EVENTS, the referee/scorer shall rule "NO TARGET" and allow another pair of targets in the following instances ONLY:

a. When only one target is thrown.

b. When more than two targets are thrown.

c. When both targets are broken by one shot.

d. When one or both targets are thrown broken even though the contestant fires at one or both targets.

e. When one or both targets are not within the prescribed angle or height limits and the contestant does not fire at either target.

f. If the contestant fires at an illegal first target and the second target is legal, he/she must also fire at the second target, and if he/she fails to do so, the legal second target shall be ruled "LOST". After a contestant has fired at either a legal or illegal first target, he/she is not required to fire at an illegal second target, but if he/she does fire, the result must be scored.

SECTION VIII
PURSES AND OPTIONS

A. COMPULSORY PURSES

No compulsory purse and/or option of any type shall be permitted in any tournament in which ATA trophies or ATA added monies are provided.

B. OPTIONS AND MONEY DIVISIONS

Failure to comply with these Rules shall result in disciplinary action by the State or Provincial Association and/or the Executive Committee.

1. Added Money. No tournament promoter or other person responsible therefore shall in any advertisement or program mention any purse or money in excess of the money actually added or guaranteed. Examples of money divisions may be included provided it is clearly stated that the amounts listed are only examples and not guaranteed amounts. The word "example" must be included. Failure to observe the above provisions shall be grounds for disciplinary action by the State or Provincial Association and/or by the Executive Committee. The ATA does not guarantee and it assumes no responsibility whatsoever for actual payment and receipt of added money, guaranteed money and prizes

advertised or offered at any shoot except the money, prizes and trophies directly supplied by and/or authorized by ATA.

2. At every registered tournament the cashier, or other official in charge, is required to post on a bulletin board available to the participants the names of all contestants who have entered any purse, options or any other monies, with each type of entry and contestant noted in an orderly and discernable fashion. Purses, options, etc., may be entered by and for contestants only. Any club or cashier may deduct up to one-half (1/2) of one percent of the gross amount of purse and options to help defray costs of computations. Breakage accumulated by rounding off is to be considered part of the one-half (1/2) of one percent. The one-half (1/2) of one percent may be deducted from the gross amount of monies collected from purses, options, Lewis Class purses, guaranteed purses, or otherwise, but in no event shall Hall of Fame contribution awards be included in the computation or deduction. The deductions mentioned above shall be made in such manner that no individual purse, option, Lewis class purse, guaranteed purse or otherwise shall be reduced in any amount greater than the percentage that particular item bears to the whole amount of monies collected. All monies collected shall be returned to the shooters in the same event in which collected unless otherwise noted in the program. In such cases the program must state clearly the circumstance under which the money will be paid. This rule shall not apply to any monies collected above the actual costs of any merchandise or other such prizes, for which a separate fee is charged. Any excess monies of that type shall not be required to be returned to the shooters provided specific notification of non-return of such monies has been conspicuously inserted into each program indicating where and under what circumstances such monies are to be collected.

3. The cashier shall post on the bulletin board the amount to be paid each purse or option winner. In the event payment is made by check after the shoot is over and the contestants have left the ground, a payoff sheet for unposted events must accompany each check indicating the amount paid for each individual purse and option included in the payment.

4. Any reasonable request to inspect the cashier sheets must be honored by the shoot management. Any shooter or gun club must file a written complaint to validly contest any payoff or trophy award within 60 days after the competition of the registered shoot or forfeit the right to do so without right of appeal.

C. CALCUTTAS

The ATA does not encourage Calcuttas or similar events at any registered ATA Tournament. ATA Rules concerning payment or non-payment of monies shall not be applicable in any manner to any dispute involving Calcuttas or similar events.

SECTION IX
REGISTERED LEAGUE SHOOTING

The following Rules shall apply to League Shooting only:

A. Registered League Shooting shall apply only to 16 yard single targets and Doubles targets.

B. Registered League Shooting shall be subject to and governed by Official ATA Rules. In the event of any conflict between any Registered League's Rules and any official ATA Rule, official ATA Rules shall take precedence and shall govern in all aspects. The Official ATA Rules shall govern all complaints of ATA Rules violation or any Registered League's Rules violation, as a result of which any contestant or league is subject to possible disqualification, suspension or expulsion.

C. The ATA will maintain and publish Registered League Targets history, and all Registered League Targets shall be counted for purses of target attainment accomplishments.

D. All Registered League Targets shall be counted toward target requirements for the Grand American World Trapshooting Championships and for all other ATA Registered Tournaments.

E. Registered League Target Averages shall be reported in the annual Average Book, separate from ATA Target Averages, and shall be maintained on a separate column on the ATA Average Card.

F. The following conditions are required to be met before any league targets will be registered:

1. A League must elect to become a Registered League.

2. Any member of a Registered League electing to register scores must be a Life or Annual Member of the ATA.

3. Applications for Registered League Shooting must be made on application forms approved and supplied by the ATA, and each form must be fully completed before submission to the ATA. An application fee of $25.00 for each Registered League must be paid at the time of submission of the application to the ATA office. The application must be approved in writing by the State or Provincial Association Secretary before the form is submitted to the ATA.

4. Each Registered League's total score will be registered upon payment of a fee equal to the standard ATA Daily Fee charged for registered tournaments. Registration will be made when the designated league representative provides shoot reports to the ATA office containing the total number of targets thrown and broken for the League, and the total number of targets broken by each individual League participant, along with the required fee.

5. League shoot reports are required to be sent to the ATA office within 8 calendar days after the date of the last shoot of the League. Failure to comply with this deadline shall result in a penalty of $25.00 assessed against the defaulting League. In the event the penalty is not timely paid, the $25.00 penalty shall be deducted from the State Association's annual rebate. (see section X., C.)

6. In the event any League fails to comply with the requirements set forth in this Rule, League scores for the League and for individual participants in the League will not be registered.

SECTION X
STATE AND ZONE SHOOTS

A. RESIDENCE

No person may compete for ATA trophies or titles in State, Provincial or Zone tournaments, unless he/she, for the immediately preceding 6 months, has been a bona fide resident of said Province, State or Zone, and a member in good standing of the State or Provincial Association and the ATA. No person may compete for any such ATA Trophies or Titles in more than 1 State, Province or Zone each target year. However, nothing shall preclude a shooter from returning to the former State, Province or Zone residence and competing for trophies in the event he/she has not been a bona fide resident of another State, Province or Zone for the immediately preceding 6 month period prior to such competition. In case there is a dispute with respect to the residence of a shooter attending a State, Provincial or Zone tournament, it shall be the duty of the State or Provincial Association (for a State/Provincial Shoot) or the Zone Officials (for a Zone Shoot) in which the shoot is being held to rule as to said shooter's right to compete as a resident shooter. The ruling of the State, Provincial Association or Zone Officials shall be final.

B. LINE REFEREE/SCORERS

At all shoots where ATA trophies are furnished shoot management is encouraged to provide a line referee.

C. ATA SUPPORT FOR STATES

The ATA in its commitment to build strong state and provincial associations aids them financially. From the $18.00 annual membership, $3.00 is returned to the state or provincial organization. No portion of the $9.00 annual membership for Junior and Sub Junior members is included in the state rebate. From the $500 life membership, $250.00 is returned to the state or provincial organization over a 10-year

period and part is retained in a special ATA emergency fund. From the $2.00 daily fee, 20% is returned to the state organization. These refunds are made to the State/Provincial Association ten days prior to the State/Provincial Shoot, provided such shoot is held and provided the State or Province turns into the ATA at least $200.00 from annual membership dues and registration fees. From this refund, there is deducted an amount equal to any fines due because of late shoot reports. On or before January 1 of each year the ATA shall inform the Secretary of each State/Province of the approximate amount of refund to be paid to that State/Province. This information must be printed in the program for that annual State Shoot.

D. ATA TROPHIES

Only one ATA trophy shall be awarded to any person in any separate event. A contestant cannot win both an ATA special category trophy and any other ATA championship trophy in the same event. Special awards that are not specific ATA trophies enumerated above may be exempt from this Rule. When a contestant's score qualifies for more than 1 ATA trophy in the same event, the burden is on the contestant to choose from ATA trophy he/she will take or Shoot-off for. The contestant's failure to notify shoot management within 15 minutes after posting of the last event scores, gives shoot management the right, and imposes upon them the duty, to make the determination and the choice of trophy for that contestant. Shoot management's determination shall be final. Shoot management, when making this determination shall be final. Shoot management, when making this determination, is required to consider special category championship trophies superior to class championship trophies. This rule shall not be interpreted to affect the right of all contestants whose score qualifies them to do so from shooting off for the championship trophy in any event. Championship trophy, for purposes of this Rule, means the trophy awarded to the highest scoring event winner, and any runner-up or place trophies, but does not mean class champions, special category champions, or any other than the event high score winner and runner-up or place trophies. A special category shooter shooting off for Championship trophies only may "fall back" to the special category or class trophy.

When there are both Junior and Sub-Junior ATA trophies, the Junior must take the Junior trophy, and the Sub-junior must take the Sub-junior trophy regardless of the high score between the 2 of them. Likewise, this Rule also applies to Veterans and Senior Veterans.

E. STATE ATA TROPHIES

The ATA will also donate the following trophies to each State and Provincial association holding a State or Provincial Shoot:

Singles	Handicap
Singles Champion	Handicap Champion
Singles Runner-up	Handicap Runner-up
Lady Singles Champion	Handicap Third
Veteran Singles Champion	Handicap Fourth
Senior Veteran Singles Champion	Handicap Fifth
Junior Singles Champion	Handicap Sixth
Sub-junior Singles Champion	

Class Champions, which may be utilized in the Singles or Class Singles Championship (AA, A, B, C, D) awarded in Class or Singles Championship.

Doubles	All Around Championship
Doubles Champion	All Around Champion
Doubles Runner Up	
Doubles Class Championships	
(AA, A, B, C, D)	

in Class or Doubles Championship

F. CHAMPIONSHIP EVENTS AT STATE TOURNAMENTS

The 4 State championships shall be determined on the following:

Singles - 200 targets
Doubles - 50 pair
Handicap - 100 targets
High All-Around - the sum of the above, 400 targets

Ladies, Junior, Veterans, Sub-Junior, Senior Veterans and any other championships not listed above may be determined on a lesser number of targets at the discretion of the State shoot management.

G. ATA SUPPORT FOR ZONES

The A.TA. donates $3,000.00 in added money to be awarded at each Zone tournament. Zone Officials may determine the division of the ATA added money for Zone tournaments in the Singles and Doubles class championships and in the championship events of Singles, Handicap, and Doubles. It shall be made available to all ATA registered shooters regardless of location unless the money is specifically restricted to Zone residents at the discretion of the various ATA Zones and it must be so stated in the Zone programs.

H. ZONE ATA TROPHIES

The ATA will donate the following trophies to each Zone for its Zone Tournament:

Singles	Doubles
Singles Champion	Doubles Champion
Singles Runner-up	Doubles Runner-up
Singles Championship	Doubles Championship
Veteran Singles Champion	Doubles Champion
AAA, AA, A, B, C, D	AAA, AA, A, B, C, D
Junior Singles Champion	Junior Doubles Champion
Sub-Junior Singles Champion	Sub-Junior Doubles Champion
Senior Veteran Singles Champion	Veteran Doubles Champion
Senior Veteran Singles	Senior Veteran Doubles
Class Singles	Class Doubles
Singles Class Championship	Doubles Class Championship
AAA, AA, A, B, C, D	AAA, AA, A, B, C, D
Handicap	All-Around
Handicap Champion	All-Around Champion
Handicap Runner-up	
Handicap Third	
Handicap Fourth	
Handicap Fifth	
Handicap Sixth	
Lady Handicap Champion	
Junior Handicap Champion	
Sub-Junior Handicap Champion	
Veteran Handicap Champion	
Senior Veteran Handicap Champion	

I. CHAMPIONSHIP EVENTS AT ZONE TOURNAMENTS

Zone championships shall be determined on the following:

Singles – 200 targets
Doubles – 50 pair
Handicap – 100 targets
All-Around, the sum of the above, 400 targets
Class Singles and Class Doubles – a minimum of 100 targets (not to be shot concurrently with the Singles and Doubles Championships). Zone tournament programs shall call for a minimum of 600 registered targets.

J. CONCURRENT STATE AND ZONE SHOOTS

When a State or Provincial Shoot is held concurrently with a Zone telephonic shoot a shooter may win both an ATA state trophy and an ATA zone trophy.

SECTION XI
GRAND AND ALL AMERICAN QUALIFICATION

A. GRAND AMERICAN QUALIFICATION

No participant shall be classified to shoot Handicap events at less than 25.0 yards handicap unless he/she has a minimum of 2000 registered ATA Handicap targets combined for the current and previous 2 years. Of those 2000 targets 1000 Handicap targets must have been registered since September 1 of the previous year and not later than the Sunday preceding the first regular day of the Grand American World Trapshooting Championships of the current year. However, participants who fail to meet Grand American Handicap qualification as described above shall have the choice of shooting penalty yardage as described above, or shooting targets only from their assigned yardage provided they waive and forfeit all rights to trophies, options, purses, added money or any other prize. Handicap target requirements are waived for Sr. Veterans, making them eligible for trophies and monies. Handicap target requirements are waived for Junior and Sub Junior shooters who do not participate in options.

No shooter shall shoot 16 yard events at the Grand American World Trapshooting Championships in less than Class A unless he/she has a minimum of 2000 registered 16 yard targets combined for the current year and/or the previous 2 years. Of those 2000, 1000 must have been registered since September 1 of the previous year and not later than the Sunday preceding the first regular day of the Grand American World Trapshooting Championships of the current year. Sixteen-yard target requirements are waived for Junior and Sub Junior shooters who do not participate in options.

No shooter shall shoot doubles events at the Grand American World Trapshooting Championships in less than Class A unless he/she has a minimum of 1500 registered doubles targets combined for the current year and/or the previous 2 years. Of those 1500 targets, 700 must have been registered since September 1 of the previous year and not later than the Sunday preceding the first regular day of the Grand American World Trapshooting Championships of the current year. Doubles target requirements are waived for Junior and Sub Junior shooters who do not participate in options.

B. ALL-AMERICAN TEAM REQUIREMENTS

	16s	Hdcp	Dbls	
Men	3000	2500	1500	
Women, Juniors, Veterans	3000	2000	1000	
Sub-Juniors, Sr. Veterans	2000	1000	500	

1. Qualified competitions are the Grand American, Satellite Grand Americans, Annual Resident Zone Tournaments, Annual State or Provincial Tournaments or any other ATA Registered Tournament where total entries in the Singles Championship Event, Doubles Championship Event, and Handicap Championship Event, individually or in any combination, total at least 600 entries.

2. Shooters must have competed in qualified tournaments in at least three states. (State of residence may be included.)

SECTION XII
DISCIPLINARY ACTION, DISQUALIFICATION AND REINSTATEMENT

A. PAYMENTS AND OVERPAYMENTS

Any club, which conducts a registered event and/or tournament, should make payment of all added money, purses, options, and other monies to the shooters as promptly as possible. Failure to do so within 15 days may result in the cancellation of registration privileges of that club for the remainder of the year, and no further registration shall be granted to that club until all monies due to shooters, the ATA and State organizations have been paid in full. The persons responsible and/or officers of such delinquent clubs, shall be barred from shooting registered targets until such payments have been made. Any ATA member who is due payment of money from a gun club and refuses to provide his/her Social Security Number or Tax ID Number is not protected by this 15 day Rule.

Any competitor at a registered shoot who, through error, has been overpaid on any purse, added money, option, or other awards, and who is notified of the overpayment by certified mail, must return the overpayment within 15 days. Failure to do so shall result in disqualification from participation in any ATA registered event and/or tournament until payment is made in full.

B. DISQUALIFICATION

1. A shooter may be disqualified for an event or for a whole tournament at any time by shoot management, or at any time by the Executive Committee or such person as they shall designate for that purpose, or disciplined by the Executive Committee, whenever the following prohibited conduct is brought to their attention:

a. if in the opinion of management or the Executive Committee the shooter disrupts the harmony of the shoot, or

b. Contestants not timely reporting for competition, including shoot-offs; or

c. if the shooter shoots at any place other than the regular firing line; or

d. if the shooter fails to shoot at his/her correct yardage; or

e. if the shooter has failed to have his/her Average Card punched for earned yardage at a prior shoot, and fails to report earned yardage at the time of any subsequent registration; or

f. if the shooter behaves in other than a sportsman-like manner such as physical abuse, verbal abuse or threats of any type directed to shoot personnel, other competitors, or any other person, whether on or off the shooting line, if such conduct occurs on gun club grounds and during any day when ATA registered trapshooting takes place; or

g. if the shooter interferes with the management's procedures in conducting the shoot; or

h if the shooter does not respond and report to the firing line in a timely manner when his/her squad is called to shoot; or

i. if the shooter does not abide by the Rules of the ATA, by the Rules set out by management, and/or in the official program.

2. It is the responsibility and the required duty of shoot management to immediately remove and disqualify any contestant at any time during an ATA sanctioned tournament:

a. who is under the obvious influence of alcoholic beverages or drugs before starting or during any event, sub-event, shoot-off or practice, or who consumes any alcoholic beverage or drugs during participation in any event, sub-event or between events or sub events held on the same day including shoot-offs and practice. For purposes of this rule, "drugs" shall mean any illegal drug, and shall also mean any prescription medication if that prescription medication affects the judgment or conduct of the contestant to a degree that renders the contestant incapable of safely participating in the sport of trapshooting, whether during a registered event and/or tournament or practice.

b. who handles a gun dangerously on or off the firing line, or

c. who deliberately or carelessly violates gun safety precautions, Official Rules regarding safety, or in any manner endangers contestants, spectators, or gun club personnel.

3. Disqualification for a single event does not prevent a contestant from participating in other events in the same tournament and scores shot in other events are not affected. However, any disqualification pursuant to Rule 2., a. above, shall include all events or practice on the same day after the time of disqualification.

4. If the infraction is severe, the management may disqualify the contestant for the entire tournament and require him/her to leave the grounds.

5. Disqualification for a tournament does not prevent a shooter from participating in other tournaments.

6. All entrance monies in events not competed in as a result of disqualification are to be returned in full. Events, which have been started, do not qualify for refunds due to disqualification.

7. Scores shot in a registered event and/or tournament for which a shooter is disqualified will not be registered, and any trophies or monies, which the contestant has received for an event for which he/she is disqualified MUST be returned. Any shooter who is disqualified from any registered event or tournament and fails to return any trophies or monies which the shooter received in that event or tournament will remain disqualified and will be barred from shooting ATA targets or otherwise participating in ATA activities until all trophies and monies have been returned and written certification from the gun club involved is received at the ATA Main Offices.

C. SUSPENSIONS, EXPULSIONS, AND REINSTATEMENT

1. The Executive Committee may at any time at its discretion suspend any member or discipline shoot management for any conduct specified in Rule XII, B., 1., and/or anyone who:

a. presents a check at any shoot for fees and targets, or has or allows his/her fees and targets to be paid by such check, that is returned or dishonored for insufficient funds or any other reason. Further, any person who presents such a check 2 times shall be automatically suspended for a period of 1 year. The Executive Committee may designate authority to the Executive Director to suspend any member for presentation of dishonored checks, on first and second offenses, until the gun club where the check(s) was written has been reimbursed and the reinstatement fee has been paid. Clubs receiving such a check shall report the name and address of the shooter or individual issuing the check to the ATA along with a copy and a statement that the check was for registered targets and/or fees. After having been reimbursed the club MUST immediately inform the ATA so that reinstatement proceedings may be initiated. Any ATA member who has been suspended for presenting a check that is returned for insufficient funds or other causes and becomes eligible for reinstatement shall be required to pay the sum of $25.00 to the ATA as a reinstatement fee. This fee must be paid before reinstatement will be considered, or

b. falsifies his/her scores; or

c. fails to have his/her Average Card properly punched for earned yardage or fails to report earned yardage at the time of registration for any subsequent tournament; or

d. fails to return any overpayment after proper notification; or

e. is convicted of any gun or firearms violation; or

f. willfully, deliberately, or repeatedly violates the rules of the ATA as contained in the Official Rules; or

g. encourages, participates in or allows a willful role violation by any minor of which he/she is parent or for whom he/she is acting as legal or actual guardian, either temporary or permanent. For purposes of these Rules only, a "minor" shall mean a person who has not attained his or her 18th birthday, and "guardian" shall mean a person who has actual physical custody or control of a minor, either temporarily or permanently and custody or control for the purpose of attending a single registered trapshooting tournament shall satisfy that definition of "guardian" for the purpose of enforcement of this rule only; or

h. engages in conduct or behavior which constitutes cause for suspension in the opinion of the Executive Committee.

2. A member who is suspended for any reason is barred from shooting ATA targets or otherwise participating in ATA activities for the period of his/her suspension.

3. If the Executive Committee feels the violations warrant suspension for longer than 3 years, or expulsion, the member shall have the right of appeal if he/she complies with the terms and provisions of the By-Laws of the Amateur Trapshooting Association of America.

4. Investigating Complaints

The procedure for investigations of complaints of any Rules violation, including those that may result in suspension or disciplinary action, is as follows:

a. All complaints of ATA rules violations shall meet the following requirements:

(1) Shall be in writing and shall be signed by the complainants. Verbal or anonymous written complaints will not be accepted or considered.

(2) Shall be dated with the effective date that the complaint is made, and shall contain the exact dates of the alleged Rules violations in the statement of facts upon which the complaint is based.

(3) Specific Official Rules alleged to have been violated shall be stated if known by the complainant.

(4) Full details of the incidents upon which the complaint is based must be made, and must include a statement of facts sufficient to describe the incident upon which the complaint is based, and sufficient to establish that violation of Official Rules occurred.

(5) The location and name and address of the gun club where the alleged violation occurred must be stated, and if a violation of Rule XII, B., I.e. is alleged then the exact location of the violations must be described.

(6) Names and addresses of any witnesses to the alleged violations must be stated.

(7) A complaint may only be made by an ATA life or annual member in good standing on the date the alleged violations occurred, or by a gun club in good standing where the alleged violations occurred and signed by an unauthorized officer or director of the gun club.

b. All complaints of violations of ATA Official Rules must be made within 60 days after the date on which the alleged violations occurred. In the event a claim is made, or a defense is raised that a complaint was not timely made, the earliest of the following dates shall control:

(1) The date of receipt by the ATA Executive Director; or

(2) The date of postmark of the envelope in which the complaint was transmitted; or

(3) The date of transmittal to the ATA Executive Director by any electronic media, provided, that a hard copy showing date of transmittal can be printed, and provided further that the original signed complaint and hard copy of proof of electronic transmittal are mailed or delivered to the ATA Executive Director on the same date transmitted.

c. All complaints shall be sent or delivered to the ATA Executive Director at the ATA Main office, and any statement of procedure in any previous Rule stating otherwise is void and of no effect. Upon receipt of a written complaint the ATA Executive Director shall:

(1) Cause each complaint to be assigned a number, consecutive of the last complaint received in order of receipt, and consisting of the year of receipt and consecutive number of receipt, e.g. 99-01, 99-02, etc.

(2) Examine the complaint to determine it substantially complies with the requirements set forth herein.

(3) If the Executive Director determines that the complaint alleges a serious breach of safety he/she shall immediately notify the ATA President of the alleged violation. The President, after consideration of the allegation, may direct the Executive Director to issue an administrative suspension of the member pending inquiry and action by the Executive Committee as set forth herein. While under administrative suspension a member may not participate as a contestant in any ATA registered events and/or tournaments. Notification of administrative suspension shall be by certified mail, return receipt requested.

(4) If the Executive Director determines that the complaint substantially complies with the requirements herein, he/she shall mail the complaint to the ATA State or Provincial Delegate representing the State or Province in which the alleged violation occurred, with instructions to proceed as required in accordance with ATA Official Rules.

(5) If the Executive Director determines that any of the following conditions exits:

(a) The complaint is directed against the ATA State or Provincial Delegate representing the State or Province in which the alleged violation occurred; or

(b) The Delegate has an obvious conflict of interest; or

(c) The Delegate recuses himself/herself,

He/She shall assign the investigation to the Alternate Delegates in succession. If one of the conditions described in (5.), (a), (b.), or (c.) exist as to all available Alternate Delegates, then the Executive Director shall notify the ATA President. Within 5 days after the receipt of such notification, the ATA President shall contact each voting member of the Executive Committee and, based on the majority vote of the Executive Committee, shall instruct the Executive Director who shall be assigned to conduct the investigation. In the event the person so assigned shall be unable or unwilling to conduct the investigation the ATA President shall repeat this procedure until an individual has been selected to conduct the investigation.

(6) If the Executive Director determines the complaint does not substantially comply with the requirements set forth herein, he/she shall return the complaint to the complainant with a letter informing the complainant of the reasons why the complaint does not comply with these Official Rules. Any deficient complaint may be resubmitted at the option of the complainant, however, the time limit specified in Paragraph 4.b., above, is not extended and the time limitation is not tolled by this procedure.

d. Within 10 days after receipt of the complaint from the ATA Executive Director, the Delegate or individual appointed to conduct the investigation shall serve written notice of the complaint and a copy of the complaint on the alleged violator, by certified mail, return receipt requested. The written notice shall state the date and location of the alleged violations, the acts alleged to have occurred, the Official ATA Rules alleged to have been violated, and shall inform the alleged violator that a written response is required within 10 days of receipt of the notice. A copy of the notice and a copy of the complaint, along with copies of any other documentation that is in the possession of the Delegate or individual appointed to conduct the investigation at that time, shall be sent to the Vice-President of the one in which the alleged violation occurred. The Delegate or individual appointed to conduct the investigation shall thoroughly investigate the allegations of the complaint and shall obtain witness statements in writing, signed by the witnesses, whenever reasonable, possible, or practicable.

e. Upon receipt of any answer from the alleged violator, or if no such answer is received within 10 days after his/her receipt of the notice, or immediately upon receipt of notice of non-acceptance if the alleged violator refuses to accept the certified mail, the Delegate or individual appointed to conduct the investigation shall confer with such State officers as deemed necessary, and then within 7 days shall, in writing, recommend appropriate action to the Zone Vice-President. The entire file, including the return receipt or notice of refusal, and any responses, answers, statements or other documents relating to the complaint or investigation not previously sent or provided shall be delivered to the one Vice-President at the time the Delegate or individual appointed to conduct the investigation makes his/her recommendation. Action recommended shall be specific, and shall not be general or left to the discretion of the Zone Vice-President or Executive Committee.

f. The Zone Vice-President, upon receipt of the recommendations, shall review the entire file, and within 10 days after receipt shall write his/her own recommendations, with supporting facts, to all members of the Executive Committee. Each member of the Executive Committee will be provided a complete copy of the file and all recommendations.

g. All members of the Executive Committee shall, within 7 days after their receipt of the Zone Vice-President's recommendations, advise the ATA President of their agreement or disagreement with the recommendations of the Zone Vice-President, or any modification thereof.

h. After receipt of notice of agreement or disagreement from each member of the Executive Committee, or modifications approved by a majority of the Executive Committee, the ATA President shall immediately cause appropriate action to be taken in accordance with the majority vote of the Executive Committee. Suspensions and/or expulsions made under this section shall conform to the applicable provisions pertaining thereto as fully set forth in the Articles of Incorporation and By-Laws of the Amateur Trapshooting Association of America.

i. Any time requirement set forth in this Rules may, for good cause, and after written request of a Zone Vice-President, be extended by the President or his/her designate.

5. REINSTATEMENT

Any ATA member who has been suspended for any reason must pay a $25.00 reinstatement fee to the ATA when his/her period of suspension is completed or when, in the case of returned checks, he/she has reimbursed the club where the check was written. This fee must be paid before reinstatement.

SECTION XIII

STANDARDS FOR TRAPHOUSES, TARGETS, TARGET SETTING, GUNS AND AMMUNITION

A. TRAP MACHINE

A trap machine, which throws targets at an unknown angle, shall be used. All trap machines used to throw ATA registered targets shall be so manufactured, modified, or equipped as to interrupt irregularly the oscillation of the trap or otherwise assure the unpredictability of the flight of substantially all targets thrown.

Each gun club that throws ATA registered targets must have on file in the ATA main offices a signed Affidavit that the trap machines used to throw registered targets meet the requirements of this rule. The State/Provincial ATA Delegate is responsible for the enforcement of this Rule.

B. TRAPHOUSES

Traphouses must adequately protect the trap loaders and shall not be higher than necessary for the purpose. Traphouses constructed after September 1, 2003 shall conform to the following specifications:

Length not less than 7 feet, 6 inches (2.3m), nor more than 9 feet, 6 inches (2.89m).

Width not less than 7 feet, 6 inches (2.3m), nor more than 9 feet, 6 inches (2.89m).

Height not less than 2 feet, 2 inches (.7m), nor more than 3 feet, 0 inches (.91m), the height to be measured from the plane of the number 3 shooting position and the target height pad known as the target height setting distance in Diagram 2.

It is recommended that the throwing surface (throwing arm or plate) of the trap machine be on the same level as that of Post 3 and the target height setting pad, plus or minus 1.5 inches (38.1 mm). All new trap fields built after September 1, 2003 shall conform to these specifications. It is recommended that all trap fields conform to these specifications to give uniformity to all fields.

C. POSTS

The posts shall be 3 yards (2.7m) apart on the circumference of a circle whose radius is 16 yards (14.6m). Handicap posts, when used, shall be prolongations of the lines given in Diagram II, commonly known as fan shaped. The distance between posts at 16 yards (14.6m) shall then be 3 yards (2.7m).

D. TARGETS

No target shall measure more than four and five-sixteenths (4 5/16, 4.300) inches (10.94cm) in diameter, not more than one and one-eighth (1 1/8, 1.125) inches (28.58mm) in height, and with an allowable variation of not more than five (5) percent from these specifications. A target shall not weigh less than 95 grams or more than 105 grams with a variation of not more than plus or minus 5 grams per Target Lot. A Target Lot is defined as all targets with the same production lot number.

E. FLIGHTS AND ANGLES

Singles targets shall be thrown not less than 49 yards nor more than 51 yards. Distance measurements are on level ground in still air. Targets shall be between 8 feet (2.4m) and 10 feet (3.07m) high, when 10 yards from Point B. Point B is defined as the intersection of a line measured 2 feet 6 inches (.76m) from the outside vertical surface of the traphouse the farthest away from the shooting point and the centerline of the trap (see Diagram I) from which the trap field layout radius is determined. The recommended height is 9 feet. The height at a point 10 yards (9m) from Point B is to be understood to mean height above an imaginary horizontal straight line drawn through the post and Point B. (See Diagram II)

In Singles shooting the trap shall be so adjusted that within the normal distribution of angles as thrown by the trap, the right angle shall not be less than 17.14 degrees measured to the right of center (3BF), and not less than 17.14 degrees measured to the left of center (3BF), with a total angle between outside target limits of not less than 34.28 degrees. (see Diagram II) Under no circumstances shall a Standard Model 1524 trap be set in less than the #2 hole. Any other trap machine shall be adjusted so as to throw not less than equivalent angles. Where terrain allows a visible stake must be placed on the centerline of the trap on the arc of a circle that has a radius of 50 yards (46m) and its center is Point B (Point F, Diagram II). To help in determining legal angles, stakes may be placed on the arc of a circle that has a radius of 50 yards (46m) and its center is Point B. One stake should be placed where a line drawn through Point A and Point B intersects this arc and another stake placed where a line drawn through Point C and Point B intersects the arc. These lines and stakes will assist in determining the required angles, but it is to be understood that the angle specifications apply when the target is from 15 yards to 20 yards (14-18m) from the trap rather than where the target strikes the ground. However, no target is to be declared illegal unless it is more than 25 degrees outside the angles prescribed.

In doubles shooting, targets shall be thrown not less than 44 yards (40m) nor more than 52 yards (47m). Distance measurements are on level ground in still air. Targets shall be between 8 feet (2.4m) and 12 feet (3.7m) high, when 10 yards from Point B. The recommended height is 9 feet. The height at a point 10 yards (9m) from Point B is to be understood to mean height above an imaginary horizontal straight line drawn through the post and Point B. The trap shall be adjusted so the angle of target spread is not less than 34.28 degrees, and under no circumstances less than an angle of target spread thrown by a Standard Model 1524 trap set in the #2 hole. Any other trap machine shall be adjusted so as to throw not less than equivalent angles.

F. GUNS AND AMMUNITION

Any shooter violating any of these Rules shall be disqualified from competition in accordance with these Rules. Any such violator shall be referred to the Executive Committee for possible further disciplinary action.

A contestant cannot use:

1. A gun with a chamber larger than 12 gauge. Guns of smaller gauges are permissible in registered and tournament shooting, but no competitive consideration shall be given in recognition of that fact for handicap and classification purposes. Only ammunition provided by the ATA and purchased at the time of entry may be used at, or during, the Grand American Tournament. A contestant may not use a gun capable of chambering more than one gauge of shells at the same time. For example, chambering 12 gauge and 20 gauge shells in the same gun at the same time is prohibited.

2. Loads that contain nickel or copper coated shot or tracer loads. However, the use of lead, steel, bismuth, or other composite non-toxic shot materials shall be allowed. Any gun club allowing shot materials described in this Rule, other than lead, shall be required to cover or shield all hard surfaces on trap fields which are known, or reasonably believed, to cause pellet ricochet with material which will prevent the shot pellets from rebounding and/or ricocheting.

3. Any load with a velocity greater than 1290 FPS (Feet Per Second) with maximum shot charge of 1 1/8 ounces (31.89 grams), or 1325 FPS with a maximum shot charge of 1 ounce (28.30 grams), or 1350 FPS with a maximum shot charge of 7/8 ounces (24.80 grams), as measured in any individual shotshell. These velocities are maximum and no individual shotshell shall exceed these limits for the designated shot charge. In addition, no load containing more than 1 1/8 ounces (31.89 grams) or any shot larger than Number 7 ½ can be used. Shot charges are maximum and no charge may exceed the charge amount by more than 3%.

4. Any shell loaded with black powder.

5. Shot Management, ATA officials or any contestant may challenge the load of any other contestant. Any challenge shall be initiated so as to not disrupt the harmony of the shoot or interfere with other contestants not involved with the challenge. On receipt of a challenge management or ATA officials shall obtain a shell or shells from the challenged party, and if after examination, management or ATA officials find the contestant violated the ATA rule, he/she may be disqualified. Any such initiated challenges, determined to be abusive in nature, will be referred to the ATA Executive Committee for disciplinary action.

SKEET RULES

SKEET WELCOMES YOU

The great sport of skeet shooting, designed in 1920 by a group of Andover, Massachusetts upland game hunters to improve their wing shooting, has rapidly caught the fancy of people in all age groups and both sexes. It is now a major sport, with its own international and state organizations. A dedicated group is guiding it carefully to even greater popularity and prestige.

Skeet has developed into much more than just an aid to better wing shooting or a substitute for hunting. It is now a competitive sport equaled by few in universal appeal. Matches are conducted for all gun gauges, and under skeet's universal classification system all shooters compete against others of like ability. Note classification rules, Section V. Competition is held for four gauges of shotguns, 12, 20, 28 and .410, though many people never use more than one.

Guns must be capable of firing two shots since four sets of doubles are included in the regulation 25-shot round. In addition, competitive Doubles Events are offered at many tournaments. The gun may be a double barrel (side-by-side or over-and-under), a pump gun or an automatic, depending on the shooter's preference. Major manufacturers offer specially made skeet guns, and you should consult them or a good gunsmith before buying a shotgun for skeet. Details such as weight, choke, drop and pitch and fit of the gun vary with shooters. It is actually better to try out several guns, all types if possible, before buying.

The National Skeet Shooting Association (NSSA) is a nonprofit organization owned and operated by and for its members, sportsmen who are dedicated to the development among its members of those qualities of patriotism and good sportsmanship which are the basic ingredients of good citizenship, and in general to promote and advance the interests, welfare and development of skeet shooting and related sports.

In addition to the present regulation skeet most commonly shot, the NSSA has an international division for those who wish to shoot under the rules used in international competition with low gun position and variable timing.

We believe that in skeet you will find the finest fellowship of sportsmen in the world. This is a rewarding recreational adventure where the best of sportsmanship prevails. You are welcome to this unique fraternity.

SECTION I – EQUIPMENT

A. TARGETS

Standard targets of good quality measuring no more than four and five-sixteenth (4-5/16) inches in diameter nor more than one and one-eighth (1-1/8) inches in height shall be used.

B. AMMUNITION

1. Gauge Specifications - Lead Shot.
    a. Shells commercially manufactured by reputable companies, which are clearly labeled and guaranteed as to lead shot sizes and weight are recommended for use in registered skeet shoots. However, NSSA will accept results of shoots and register scores where reloads have been used. NSSA assumes no responsibility in connection with the use of reloads.
    b. Gun Clubs are allowed to use alternate shot (other than lead) for registered shoots by written request to NSSA Headquarters: alternate loads must meet industry standards for "target load" ammunition.
2. Reloads
    a. The maximum load permissible is described below. This table makes ample allowance for manufacturing purposes, but the use of a proper shot bar is cautioned (a 12 gauge bar designed for 7-1/2 shot will weigh approximately 11 grains heavy when No. 9 shot is used).

Gauge	Ounces Lead	Grains Standard	Grains Maximum
12	1-1/8	492.2	507
20	7/8	382.8	394
28	3/4	328.1	338
.410	1/2	218.8	229

    b. Any shooter may elect to have his/her shells weighed by management before entering an event. The shooter must submit all shells to be used in said event. After one shell is selected, weighed and approved by these standards, the balance of the shells shall be stamped, approved and sealed by some suitable method and not be opened until on the field where the event is to be shot in the presence of the field referee. Failure to have the field referee witness the breaking of the sealed boxes or containers on their respective fields shall necessitate the shooter using factory ammunition or risk having his/her score disqualified. Any shooter using approved and sealed ammunition shall be immune from further checking.
    c. Challenge Rule: At shoots where shells have not been checked, any contestant may, upon formal challenge presented to shoot management, have the chief referee, who shall use timely discretion, select a shell from an-other contestant and have said shell checked against the standards listed in Rule I-B-2-a. To prevent abuse of a shooter with this rule, shoot management shall make known the challenger and the individual challenged. Entire groups or squads shall not be challenged for purposes of anonymity.
3. Checking Factory Loads

Any shooter found to be using commercial loads heavier than the maximum grains permissible as listed in I-B-2-a shall have his/her score disqualified for that event.

C. FIELD LAYOUT

It is recommended and desirable for all NSSA registered targets to be shot on fields constructed according to the following specifications and the diagram shown on the centerfold of this book. Field Layout deviation will not affect NSSA's consideration of scores. Under no circumstances will protests based on alleged irregularity of field layout be considered.

1. A skeet field shall consist of eight shooting stations arranged on a segment of a circle of twenty-one (21) yards radius, with a base cord exactly one hundred twenty (120) feet, nine (9) inches long, drawn six (6) yards from the center of the circle. The center of the circle is known as the target-crossing point and is marked by a stake. Station 1 is located at the left end of the base while standing on the periphery of the segment. Stations 2 to 6, inclusive, are located on the periphery at points equidistant from each other. The exact distance between Stations 1 and 2, 2 and 3, etc., is twenty-six (26) feet, eight and three-eighths (8-3/8) inches. Station 8 is located at the center of the base chord.
    a. Shooting Stations 1 and 7, each a square area three feet on a side, shall have two sides parallel to the base chord.
    b. Shooting Stations 2 to 6, inclusive, each a square area, three feet on a side, shall have two sides parallel to a radius of the circle drawn through the station marker.
    c. Shooting Station 8 is a rectangular area 3 feet wide by 6 feet long, with the long sides parallel to the base chord.
2. The location of each shooting station shall be accurately designated.
    a. The marker for shooting Stations 1-7, inclusive, is on the center of the side nearest the target crossing point.
    b. The marker for shooting Station 8 is on the center point of the base chord.
3. One target should emerge from a skeet house (called high house) at a point three (3) feet in back of Station Marker 1 (measured along the base chord extended), and ten (10) feet above the ground level. The other should emerge from a skeet house (called low house) at a point three (3) feet in back of Station Marker 7 (measure along the base chord extended), and two and one-half (2-1/2) feet from the base chord extended (measure on side of target-crossing point), and three and one-half (3-1/2) feet above the ground.
4. Mandatory markers (where geographically possible) shall be placed at points 44 yards and 60 yards from both the high house and the low house to indicate the shooting boundary limit of 44 yards. These distances shall be measured along a line and the flight of a regular target 60 yards from the opening (where target emerges) in skeet house through the target-crossing point. The 60-yard distance markers must be suitably marked to indicate Station 8 ground level where geographically possible.
5. The target-crossing point must be marked in a visible manner where geographically possible.
6. It is recommended to remove posts or box stands tangent to the front of the stations interfering with the shooter.
7. It is recommended and desirable that the side of the skeethouse, from the bottom of the chute to the top of the house, be very light color or painted white where feasible.
8. It is recommended if more than one field is inline that a fence be constructed between fields.
9. Unusual or undesirable field variations must be corrected before contract negotiations are completed.
10. The pull cord will be a minimum length to allow the referee to reach all mandatory referee positions and will have high house, low house and doubles release buttons.

D. MANDATORY POSITIONS FOR REFEREES

1. For shooting Station 1 (1R), stand six feet to the right and three feet back of the front of Station 1 where possible.
2. For shooting Station 2 (2R), stand six feet back and three feet to the right of Station 2.
3. For shooting Stations 3, 4, 5 and 6 (3-4-5-6R), stand six feet back and three feet to the left of the respective station.
4. For shooting Station 7 (7R), stand six feet to the left and three feet back of the front of Station 7 where possible.
5. For shooting Station 8 (8R), stand on center line of the field, not less than 6 feet from shooter (and not more than 10 feet).
6. During Doubles shooting, as shooters are coming back around the circle, referees should stand six feet back and three feet to the right of Stations 5, 4 and 3. (See diagram on pages 32-33)

Exception: A shooter may request the referee to move behind the station at Station 3 or 5.

E. RECOMMENDED POSITIONS FOR SHOOTERS

It is recommended for courtesy to team members that shooters do not advance more than one-third of the way to the next shooting station until all shooters on the squad have completed the station. Furthermore, shooters should stand a minimum of six feet behind the shooter while waiting to shoot.

F. RECOMMENDED PROCEDURE FOR SETTING DISTANCE ON TARGETS

It is recommended to adjust the skeet machine spring to a tension that will just reach the 60 yard stake, passing near dead center on the target setting hoop, under a "no wind" condition. This distance setting has a plus/or minus two yard allowance, but should be as close to 60 yards as possible. Once this setting is made, it is unnecessary to change the spring tension during a tournament unless the spring becomes defective. The prevailing wind during a shoot may cause the targets to fall far short or long, but they are legal targets providing they pass through the setting hoop.

G. USE OF A RADAR GUN

The use of a radar gun for setting targets is permitted so long as the height and distance requirements specified under Rule III-A-4, Definition of a Regular Target, are complied with.

SECTION II - REGISTERED SHOOTS

A. GENERAL

1. Identification of Eligible Shooters

Members shall receive a new classification card as soon as possible after October 31.

a. This card will be of high quality paper and is to be used throughout the shooting year. Classification cards will be a different color each year for ease of identification. Replacement cards can be obtained from NSSA home office if lost or accidentally destroyed.

b. Presentation of a classification card, indicating a member's shooting record and paid membership status, and a plastic NSSA membership card is required for entry in a registered shoot.

c. Classification for the beginning of the year shall be indicated in the appropriate place on each classification shoot record card.

d. These cards also shall contain columns in which the holders are to keep their up-to-date averages posted for each gun.

2. Open Shoot Registration

The term open, as it may appear in any application for registration or sanction, or in the shoot program, if any, shall be deemed to mean open to NSSA members without regard to residence.

3. Night Shooting

Registered shooting at night is permissible. All scores recorded for night registered shoots will receive the same treatment as any other registered shoot. Participants in night registered shoots must accept the conditions at the club where the shoot is held and no protest concerning shooting conditions; e.g., light conditions, natural or artificial, etcetera, will be allowed. At night registered shoots, white targets will be used unless otherwise published in the program.

4. Shooting Order

The management shall determine the shooting order of the individuals in each squad at the beginning of the round, and the shooters shall adhere to this order. If the order is changed during any succeeding round of the same event, each squad member shall be responsible that his/her name be in the proper order on the respective score sheet, and that the change be plainly indicated for the attention of the final recorder. Each squad shall report to the field at its appointed time. Upon failure of a shooter to appear at the appointed time, where a regular schedule has been posted in advance, or after proper call, the squad shall proceed without the absent shooter and the offender be dropped to the first vacancy in the schedule, or if there is no vacancy, to the bottom of the list. Weather conditions shall not be deemed sufficient excuse for delay in taking the field or proceeding with the round, unless all shooting has been officially suspended at the discretion of the management.

5. Squadding Restrictions

The squadding of practice shooting in a registered event shall not be allowed. It is permissible to squad Event 6 registered with regular registered events. Violations of this rule shall be sufficient cause for non-registration of all scores in the squad. Exception: IF THERE SHOULD BE A SINGLE ENTRY IN THE LAST SQUAD OF ANY EVENT, SHOOT MANAGEMENT MAY ALLOW NO MORE THAN TWO ADDITIONAL SHOOTERS TO SHOOT FOR PRACTICE, BUT ONLY IF RE-QUESTED TO DO SO BY THE LONE ENTRY ON SAID LAST SQUAD. Pacer for lone participant on a field in shootoff shall not be permitted.

6. Checks - Payments, Over-Payment

Anyone who presents a check at any shoot that is returned for insufficient funds or other causes, may not compete in any registered shoot until full payment has been made to the individual or club to which it was presented. Any club receiving such a check shall report name and address of the shooter issuing the check to the NSSA and to its own state, territorial or district association. Upon notification by NSSA, the shooter has 15 days to make the check good, or he/she will be suspended for six months. A second offense will result in indefinite suspension, and the shooter must petition the Executive Committee for reinstatement. The Executive Committee will determine penalties and suspensions as each case merits. Any competitor at a registered shoot who, through error, has been overpaid on any purse, added money, optional or other prize money and who is notified of the overpayment by registered mail, must return the over-payment within fifteen days. Failure to do so shall result in disbarment from all registered shoots until repayment is made.

7. Club Qualifications and Responsibilities

a. Only clubs affiliated with NSSA with affiliation fees currently paid up for the year concerned shall be eligible to conduct registered shoots. Evidence of club's status in this regard must be displayed in the form of official NSSA membership certificate for the appropriate year. Only clubs also affiliated and in good standing with their state or territorial association will be permitted to hold registered shoots in areas where such associations are active. No registered shoot may be held at a facility which has been suspended or is in violation of NSSA rules.

b. Where state or territorial associations exist, application for a registered shoot must be made through those bodies, which, in turn after giving approval, will submit application to NSSA. NSSA will then issue proper certification and supplies on which to report scores, winners and make financial reports. When an area association does not exist, clubs will make application directly to NSSA.

1) The application form furnished by NSSA shall include the scheduled shooting dates and may not be altered without 10 days notice. Shoot applications, properly sanctioned, must be postmarked or received by NSSA at least 10 days prior to the shoot date.

2) Applications for night registered shoots must designate on the face of application that it will be a night shoot and all promotion by club shall clearly indicate that it is a night shoot.

c. Open shoots should be advertised to a majority of local contestants, and closed club shoots posted a minimum of seven days prior to the shoot date. Failure to so advertise may result in a disqualification of shoot scores. Exception may, however, be granted by the Executive Director on merit.

d. It shall be the responsibility of the management of the club, association or other organization granted a certificate of registration, to see that each shoot is conducted in accordance with the official rules of the NSSA.

e. The group or club sponsoring the shoot shall check the NSSA membership of each shooter before accepting his/her entry and shall be responsible for the annual dues if they allow a participant to shoot when said participant's membership in NSSA has expired.

1) All individual shooters in all registered shoots must be members in good standing of the NSSA. IT SHALL BE THE RESPONSIBILITY OF THE CLUB HOLDING A REGISTERED SHOOT TO CHECK CARDS OF ALL PARTICIPANTS AND ENFORCE THIS RULE RIGIDLY.

2) Management will be billed by NSSA in all cases where expired members are allowed to shoot. Management may seek reimbursement from said shooters.

f. Management shall check the shooter's classification card to ascertain the proper classifications in which he/she should compete and enter on the shooter's classification card the classification in which it is entering him/her in each gun.

g. Class winners must be reported if they are to be reported in the magazine.

h. Scores in shoots on which complete records are not made by shoot management will not be recorded and the national association shall not be liable to refund fees received in such cases.

i. It is the shoot management's responsibility to appoint a chief referee.

j. In the interest of safety, interference and time, only the club management's personnel shall be permitted to pick up empty shells from the grounds during a registered shoot, and extreme care must be exercised to prevent interference with other squads shooting.

k. Shoot management shall determine the number of targets to be shot on a field. When shooting background is fairly uniform, it saves time to shoot 50 or 100 targets on the same field.

l. Shoot management has the right to determine the rotation and shooting sequence of events in their program, as well as shooting mixed guns in squads, unless their state association rules otherwise. When a participant is allowed to shoot an additional increment of targets (50 or 100 targets) above those shot in a program event, the first increment shot shall be the targets registered for the program event.

m. All two-man and five-man team events must be limited to club teams unless management exercises their prerogative of holding open or state team events duly announced in the program, or posted prior to acceptance of the first entry.

8. Individual Qualifications and Responsibilities

a. Residents of a state or territory must be members in good standing of their own state or territorial association before they can register targets shot in that state.

b. It shall be the sole responsibility of the shooters to see that they are entered into all the events desired. The official cashier sheet/entry form or equivalent must be used. Once entered, clerical errors are the responsibility of shoot management.

c. Each shooter must verify his/her score and initial the official score sheet before leaving each field or accept it as the record. It shall be the responsibility of every shooter to enter in his/her proper class or classes at each shoot, including advancing himself in class when required by the rules based on averages at the completion of the regular string.

d. A shooter who fails to keep all of his/her correct scores posted on his/her card and shoots in a lower class than the one in which his/her record places him/her shall forfeit any winnings earned while shooting in the wrong class for the first offense, and for the second offense shall forfeit all winnings and also be disbarred from registered competition for one year.

1) A shooter winning trophies or money by shooting in a lower class or wrong class, including concurrent age groups than the one in which he/she was entitled to shoot return his/her winnings within 15 days after notification by NSSA headquarters that said winnings must be returned. Failure to comply within this 15 day period shall subject the shooter to suspension as an NSSA member and permanent disbarment from registered competition.

2) A shooter who enters, or allows himself to be entered in an event in a class lower than the class in which he/she was entitled to shoot forfeits all rights to any trophies or purses he/she would have earned shooting in his/her proper class unless the mistake is corrected prior to the distribution of such trophies or purse money.

e. It is the responsibility of the shooter to see that his/her safety is off and his/her gun is properly loaded with unfired shells of proper size and loaded before calling for a target (for safety purposes).

B. STANDARD EVENT SPECIFICATION

For the purpose of uniformity in records, averages, etcetera, the following provisions shall apply to all shoots registered or sanctioned by NSSA.

1. Gauge Specifications

a. Twelve gauge events shall be open to all guns of 12 gauge or smaller, using shot loads not exceeding one and one-eighth (1-1/8) ounces.

b. Twenty gauge events shall be open to all guns of 20 gauge or smaller, using shot loads not exceeding seven-eighths (7/8) of an ounce.

c. Twenty-eight gauge events shall be open to all guns of 28 gauge or smaller, using shot loads not exceeding three-quarters (3/4) of an ounce.

d. Four-ten events shall be open to all guns of .410 bore or smaller using shot not exceeding one-half (1/2) ounce.

e. A gun of larger gauge, which has been converted to take a smaller gauge shell may be used in an event for which it has been converted providing that the shell itself complies with the rule requirements for that event.

f. No shot smaller than No. 9 (2mm) or larger than 7-1/2 shall be used in any load.

2. Awards Eligibility

Anyone that participates in an event for a reduced entry fee (i.e. an N/C shooter or any shooter that shoots for targets only) shall not be eligible for tangible (i.e. purses, trophies) or intangible awards (i.e. event champion, sub-senior champion). Such shooter may not enter any concurrent events. This rule does not prohibit, junior, sub-junior or collegiate shooter from participating in an event without paying that portion of an entry fee to be returned in the form of money, as outlined in II-C-4-b. Junior, sub-junior, and collegiate shooters who elect not to pay into any purse, or who elect not to pay that portion of the entry fee to be returned in the form of money, are still eligible to win intangible awards (listed above) and tangible awards, except money.

3. Concurrent Events

a. Events designated for senior-veterans, veterans, seniors, sub-seniors, sub-sub-seniors, women, triple sub, juniors, sub-juniors, military service, retired military, two-man team or five-man team may be shot concurrently with the corresponding event on the regular program, or separately, at the discretion of the management.

b. NO JUNIOR, SUB-JUNIOR OR COLLEGIATE SHALL BE REQUIRED TO PAY ANY PART OF ENTRY FEE THAT IS TO BE RETURNED TO THE SHOOTERS IN THE FORM OF MONEY, INCLUDING OPEN PURSES AND CONCURRENT PURSES, BUT NOT TO INCLUDE TEAM EVENTS IF THE INVOLVED JUNIOR, SUB-JUNIOR OR COLLEGIATE IS SHOOTING AS PART OF AN OPEN TEAM.

4. Concurrent Event Awards

Any shooter charged an entry fee for a regular event and an additional entry fee for a concurrent event shall be eligible to win in both events unless clearly stipulated in the written program.

5. All-Around Titles

All-around titles must be an aggregate of all gauges offered in that registered tournament (preliminary events, Champion of Champions, not to be included) and will officially be recognized by the NSSA only when they include champion-ships or title events in at least three of the four standard gauges and load divisions defined in paragraph No. 1 above and a total of at least 200 targets. Provided that the foregoing shall not be deemed to forbid local awards of special prizes for events of combination not recognized.

6. Minimum Number of Targets

No event of less than fifty (50) targets shall be designated as a championship or title event.

7. High Gun System

In explanation of the high gun system: If, for example, in a class, three should tie for high score and two tie for a second high score, the top three scores would divide evenly the monies for first, second and third places, and the two tying for second high score would divide evenly the monies for fourth and fifth places.

8. Method of Breaking Ties

In all registered NSSA tournaments, ties shall be decided in a uniform manner as prescribed in the following paragraph unless the shoot management gives due notice of any deviation in its published shoot programs. In the absence of a shoot program, notice of deviation must be posted conspicuously at the place of registration, thus informing all shooters of deviation before accepting entry fees.

    a.   Shoot management may elect to use regular skeet or a doubles event and shall follow NSSA rules for whichever event elected.

    b.   All ties for championship titles, such as event champion, two-man and five-man teams, veterans, seniors, sub-seniors, women, triple sub, juniors, sub-juniors, junior women, military or any other concurrent title designated by the management, must be shot off by miss-and-out (sudden death).WHEN THE SAME INDIVIDUALS ARE TIED FOR CONCURRENT TITLES, SUCH AS EVENT CHAMPION AND SENIOR CHAMPION, ONLY ONE SHOOTOFF WILL BE HELD TO DETERMINE BOTH TITLES UNLESS THE SHOOT MANAGEMENT ANNOUNCED IN ADVANCE OF THE FIRST SHOOTOFF THAT SEPARATE SHOOTOFFS WILL BE HELD. Management may combine other shootoffs only by approval of all the individuals involved in same.

    c.   After determining the position of all persons involved in shootoffs, all other awards shall be decided on the basis of the longest run in the event.

    d.   Long runs in an event shall be determined by using the shooter's FRONT or BACK Long Run (WHICHEVER IS LONGEST). If longest runs are tied, the Long Run from the opposite end shall be used to break the tie. If Long Runs are still tied, miss-and-out shootoffs must decide.

1)   A shooters FRONT LONG RUN is figured by counting all targets shot in the event before the first miss.

2)   To determine the BACK LONG RUN, count all targets broken after the shooter's last miss in the event. The optional shot must be counted in the proper sequence where it was fired.

    e.   Long runs for team scores shall be the total of targets broken by the members of the team combined up to the first miss by any member of the team; or the total number of targets broken by all members of the team after the last miss by any member of the team, which-ever run is longest.

    f.   All ties for all-around championship must be decided by a miss-and-out shootoff using the smallest gauge gun of which the all-around score is comprised.

    g.   All other tied scores for all-around awards shall be decided on the basis of the longest run from front or rear (whichever is longest) in that all-around event. If this also results in a tie, a shoot-off using the smallest gauge in the all-around event shall determine the winner of all places.

    h.   Shootoffs take precedence over long runs, so all persons competing in a shootoff must continue to shoot off for all places beneath the event championship for which they may be tied.

9.   NSSA Procedures for Shootoffs
NSSA rules shall apply subject to the following:

    a.   In employing doubles for shootoffs a 50 target event is not required.

    b.   Doubles shootoffs shall be conducted doubles stations 3-4-5, miss-and-out by station. This means that a shooter must break both targets on a station in order to beat a shooter who only broke one target (i.e. if one shooter breaks the first target and another shooter breaks the second target, they are still tied).

    c.   If shoot management has elected to conduct shootoff using total score of a complete round, the shooter with the highest score shall be determined the winner. Tied high scores must continue to shoot complete rounds until the tie is broken and the winners determined. Lesser place winners shall be decided by the highest scores and if a tie exists, long run from the front shall determine these winners; if still tied, continue to shoot until the tie is broken.

    d.   In regular skeet miss-and-out shootoffs, long run from the front shall determine the winners. Ties shall continue to shoot the round until the tie is broken.

    e.   For Team Shootoffs management may combine or separate teams for shootoffs. Not all team members have to be present for the shootoff. However, any team member not present will be moved to the last position(s) on the team shootoff, and their targets will be scored as lost. Methods for different types of shootoffs are as follows and should be noted in the shoot program. If not noted in the program, "miss and out by station" will be used.

            1)   If "miss-and-out" team winners shall be determined by the full team shooting until the first miss and com-paring this long run with other teams involved. Any teams tied with long runs shall continue to shoot their rounds until the tie is broken.

            2)   If "miss-and-out by station", team winners shall be determined by counting a team's total score on a station and comparing it with that of the other teams involved. Any teams still tied shall continue until the tie is broken.

            3)   If "total score", the total of the team scores shall determine the winner.

    f.   Shoot management shall post notice of time of shootoff as soon as possible during each event and shall also announce same by the public address system if possible.

    g.   Contestants involved in shootoffs forfeit all rights to the shootoff if absent or if they do not report within five minutes of the time the shootoff is called. However, any such person shall be entitled to any award he/she would have won by finishing last in the shootoff. It shall be the shooter's sole responsibility to determine the time of the shootoff before leaving the grounds. Shootoffs may not be held prior to the completion of an event (registration for the event has closed and no possible ties or winners left on the field) or of events of that day UNLESS ALL PARTIES INVOLVED AGREE.

    h.   If completion of shootoff is prevented by darkness, as defined in rule IV-C-4, the management and the contestants concerned shall determine the champion by a mutually agreeable method, but if no mutually agreeable method can be decided upon, then the shoot management shall determine in what manner ties shall be decided. Management should make every effort to schedule the last squad of the day early enough to permit normal shootoffs.

    i.   If shooters involved in a shootoff offer management a mutually agreed upon method of determining the places, management may accept. If management does not accept, shootoffs must continue and any shooter or shooters who refuse to continue forfeits as in paragraph "g" above.
            Declaring of event co-champions at the world championship shall not be permitted. Contestants must continue to shoot or forfeit.

    j.   The shooting order for shootoffs shall be the sequence of finishing the event, where possible. In team shootoffs, team members shall line up adjacent to each other (i.e. shoulder to shoulder). Each leadoff person, or team, shall be dropped to the last position on subsequent rounds.

    k.   Where shootoffs are held under lights, all white targets will be used unless otherwise published in the shoot program.

    l.   A shooter involved in a shootoff with a broken gun shall be allowed a ten minute time limit to repair or replace a broken gun, and then must continue in the shootoff.

C.   ELIGIBILITY OF INDIVIDUALS

1.   Membership

    a.   All competitors must be members of NSSA in good standing, with current dues paid.

    b.   Neither state champions nor provincial champions will be recognized by NSSA unless sanctioned by state organization, provincial organization, recognized with proper bylaws on record at NSSA.

2.   Amateurs
Before participating in any event, NSSA shooters who might want to maintain their amateur status in any sport shall be familiar with associations they are involved with as to the definition of an amateur to maintain their eligibility. It is the shooter's responsibility to know those rules before entering any event where prizes consist of money or prizes over a certain limit.

3.   Residency Requirements

    a.   An individual must be a bona fide resident (permanent abode) of a state to be eligible for state championships or to shoot as a state team member and must be a bona fide resident of a state within the zone to be eligible for closed zone championships or to shoot as a zone team member. Persons with residence in more than one state must declare their eligibility by writing their state and club affiliation on the face of the current year membership card. Servicemen, by the same act, may choose their home state or the place in which they are permanently assigned for duty. Persons who change their official abode shall become immediately eligible to shoot as an individual in the state or zone shoot. They should contact NSSA for new member-ship cards reflecting change of address and present same before entering shoot. An exception to the residency requirements may be allowed to the individual residency requirements, providing all the following conditions are met:

1)   The individual resides in a state without an association.

2)   The individual joins the association of an adjacent state.

3)   The state association agrees to accept non-bona fide residents into its association.

4)   The state association notifies NSSA of these exceptions.

    b.   No person shall be eligible for more than one closed state or zone competition during the NSSA shooting year.

4.   Concurrent Events

    a.   A shooter's eligibility for concurrent events shall be determined by his/her age or status on 1 November.

    b.   No junior, sub-junior or collegiate shall be required to pay any part of any entry fee that is to be returned to the shooter in the form of money.

    c.   Where shoot programs offer special concurrent events based upon age, shooter entering such special events must shoot in the one for which they are qualified by age, if such a class is available. Example: Seniors cannot enter as sub-seniors if a senior event is offered. However, sub-juniors can enter a juniors event if a sub-junior event is not available.

    d.   In parent and child events, unless specifically stated otherwise in the shoot program, the child must be of junior or sub-junior eligibility age.

    e.   A sub-junior is any person who has not reached their fourteenth birthday.

    f.   A junior is any person who has not reached their eighteenth birthday.

    g.   A collegiate shooter shall be defined as a full-time undergraduate student in an accredited degree oriented learning institution up to a maximum of five (5) years of eligibility. For one time only, a shooter is eligible to compete as a collegiate shooter prior to his/her freshman year as long as he/she produces a letter of acceptance from a degree oriented learning institution. At shoot entry eligible individuals must provide a valid student I.D. card. The card must be valid on November 1.

    h.   A triple sub is any person 18-39 years of age.

    i.   A sub-sub-senior is any person who has reached their fortieth birthday.

    j.   A sub-senior is any person who has reached their fiftieth birthday.

    k.   A senior is any person who has reached their sixtieth birthday.

    l.   A veteran is any person who has reached their seventieth birthday.

    m.   A senior-veteran is any person who has reached their eightieth birthday.

    n.   A military shooter is any ACTIVE DUTY member of the Air Force, Army, Coast Guard, Marine Corps, Navy, Reserves or National Guard/Air National Guard.

    o.   A retired military shooter is any retired member of the Air Force, Army, Coast Guard, Marine Corps, Navy or National Guard/Air National Guard.

    p.   Where shoot programs offer special concurrent events for military shooters, retired military shooters are only eligible to compete in a retired military event, and are NOT eligible to compete in a military event, even if a retired military concurrent is not offered.

D.   TEAM ELIGIBILITY
The spirit and intent of these rules shall be interpreted to include all bona fide teams properly organized in pursuance of club and/or domicile requirements, and to exclude all teams of makeshift or pick-up character, organized on the grounds and seeking to take advantage of technicalities either herein or in program stipulations or omissions.

1.   Team Representation

    a.   The members of a team must be designated before the team begins the event.

    b.   Team members shall be accredited by NSSA to the state in which they reside, but irrespective of residence, team members must not have represented any other club in a team event in any NSSA registered shoot at any time during the current year. A shooter who shoots on one club team, either two-man or five-man, shall by that act elect that club as the only club he/she shall represent in club team events during the current year. Exception: Service personnel who have, within this period, shot on teams sponsored by military organizations, such as division teams or teams representing specific departments of the same branch of the service, and have been required to do so as a duty assignment, may immediately shoot on teams representing individual military clubs, providing that said former teams have been definitely disbanded and also providing that they have been members in good standing of the clubs they are about to represent for a period of at least 90 days prior to the shoot.

    c.   No individual may shoot on more than one team in any one event, even though both teams represent the same club, except in re-entry events where the program states that it is permissible.

    d.   Team members shall not be eligible to shoot for any state championships except in the state in which they reside.

2.   State Teams

    a.   A state five-man team shall consist of five (5) individuals; a state two-man team, two (2) individuals.

    b.   Each member of a state team must have resided in the same state for at least ninety (90) days prior to the date of the shoot.

    c.   State teams may shoot in national competition, or in state shoots if approved by the state organization.

    d.   State Championship Team Events. Any out-of-state team whose membership complies with state residency requirements and Rule II-D-3-b and II-D-3-d, may enter club team events but may be subject to a surcharge at the discretion of the state association.

3.   Club Teams

    a.   A club five-man team shall consist of five (5) individuals; a club two-man team, two (2) individuals.

b. Team members must have been fully paid members of the club they represent for a period of at least 90 days prior to the date of the shoot (honorary, inactive, non-resident members, or members whose dues or assessments are in arrears are not eligible).

c. No person shall reside more than 100 miles from the club he/she represents unless he/she resides in the same state in which the club he/she represents is located.

d. The club represented must be affiliated and in good standing with the NSSA with dues currently paid.

4. Exceptions to Domicile and Club Membership Requirements
The provisions of domicile and club membership of individuals on club teams do not apply to:

a. Shooters who have affected a bona fide change in place of domicile with resultant change in club membership affiliation.

b. Clubs organized within less than 90 days prior to the date of the shoot, provided that members representing such clubs comply with II-D-1-b.

c. New members of any club who have never previously fired in a team event in an NSSA registered shoot.

d. Privately operated clubs, which require no paid membership, may with the approval of NSSA be represented by either two-man or five-man teams if the members of such teams meet all of the other requirements except those applying to club dues and club membership. Such team members must be certified by management of such club as having been active shooters of the club for a minimum of 90 days before they are eligible to shoot for that club.

e. Former members of college teams and school teams who have become members of senior clubs after their graduation.

5. Open Teams (Definition)
An open team is one which is composed of members with no restriction as to club or domicile. Records established by open teams shall not be accepted to establish official records.

6. Five-Man Teams

a. Five-man club teams and five-man state teams must shoot shoulder-to-shoulder, unless management publishes otherwise in their program or same is posted prior to accepting the first entry. To be eligible for tying or establishing world records, any five-man team MUST shoot shoulder-to-shoulder.

b. Each five-man club team and state team shall designate a team captain who shall be the team representative.

c. At the completion of each round, the shooters shall view their respective scores and initial them. However, in the case of team shooting, the captain of the team may assume the responsibility for the shooters and sign for his/her entire squad.

7. Two-Man Teams
Two-man teams may shoot in separate squads.

8. Armed Forces Team Representation
For team representation, the domicile of members on active duty with the Army, Navy, Air Force and other military establishments shall be defined as the place at which they are permanently assigned for duty. Retired, reserve or National Guard personnel are not eligible for service team membership unless on active duty for a period in excess of 90 days.

9. NSSA World Championship Five-Man Teams

a. In the NSSA World Championships all members of a five-man team will shoot in the same squad through that particular event. If any team member fails to finish with his/her proper squad for any reason whatsoever, the team shall be disqualified as such but not the members as individual contestants.

b. Under no circumstances, however, will the provisions on broken gun and shooting up affect the requirement of shooting shoulder-to-shoulder throughout the five-man team competition at the NSSA World Champion-ships.

c. MANAGEMENT MAY DEVIATE FROM THIS RULE IS THEY DEEM IT TO BE ADVISABLE TO CONDUCT FIVE-MAN TEAMS IN MORE THAN ONE SQUAD. FOR CONVENIENCE IN TABULATING TEAM SCORES, IT IS MORE DESIRABLE TO KEEP A FIVE-MAN TEAM IN ONE SQUAD.

E. PROTESTS

1. A Shooter May Protest:

a. If in his/her opinion the rules as herein stated have been improperly applied.

b. The conditions under which another shooter has been permitted to shoot.

c. Where he/she feels an error has been made in the compilation of a score.

2. How To Protest
A protest shall be initiated immediately when it is possible to do so upon the occurrence of the protested incident. No protest may be initiated by the shooter involved after thirty (30) minutes have elapsed after the occurrence of the incident for which a protest is desired to be made. Failure to comply with the following procedure will automatically
void the protest. A protest involving the scoring of a target, if filed immediately on the station, a second shot, or shots will be fired and the results recorded and noted as a protest. The protest shall proceed in the prescribed manner.

a. State the complaint verbally to the chief referee. If not satisfied with his/her decision, then:

b. File with the shoot management a protest in writing, stating all the facts in the case. Such protest must be filed within 12 hours after the occurrence of the pro-tested incident. If not satisfied with the decision of the shoot management, then:

c. File with the NSSA a written appeal, stating all the facts. Such appeal must be filed within 48 hours after the decision of the shoot management has been made known to the shooter. Protests in team events must be made by the team captain. Team members who believe they have reason to protest will state the facts to their team captain, who will make the protest if he/she feels such action justified by the facts. The shoot management may appoint a shoot judge to handle protests referred to it which have been handled in the manner stated above.

F. DISQUALIFICATION AND EXPULSION

The shoot management shall upon proper evidence:

1. Disqualify any shooter for the remainder of the shoot program for willful or repeated violation of gun safety precautions which endanger the safety of shooters, field personnel and/or spectators.

2. Elect to refuse the entry or cause the withdrawal of any contestant whose conduct in the opinion of the shoot management is unsportsmanlike or whose participation is in any way detrimental to the best interests of the shoot.

3. Any shooter may be disqualified from a shoot for misrepresentation of his/her status under the eligibility rules.

4. Expel any shooter physically assaulting a referee or any shooter using extreme, abusive language to a referee upon adequate evidence presented by the chief referee.

5. The shoot management shall report to the NSSA all cases of disqualification and expulsion and the reasons for same. Subsequent action by the Executive Committee could result in being expelled and barred from further membership in the NSSA, after the shooter has had the opportunity to appear before the Executive Committee and present his/her case.

G. OFFICIAL SCORES

1. All scores or records, to be recognized as official, must be shot under the official NSSA rules.

2. a. All scores shall be recorded as having been shot with the gun in which event they shot (e.g. scores shot with a 20 gauge gun in a 12 gauge event must be recorded as 12 gauge scores.) Such scores may not be included as part of a 20 gauge long run or average.

b. When a shooter has started an event and realizes during or after the event the incorrect ammunition was used (e.g., 1 oz. 20 gauge shells in the 20 gauge event, etc.), that shooter must immediately notify the field referee or shoot management of the error. If possible, the competitor will be allowed to re-shoot the targets incorrectly fired upon and continue with the proper ammunition or re-shoot the entire event. If not possible, the shooter is disqualified from that event and the targets will not be registered. All targets incorrectly fired upon will not be reported to or recorded with NSSA.

3. Only the scores shot on scheduled dates, approved by NSSA, shall be registered. Scores made in shootoffs shall not be registered, however, all NSSA rules shall apply in shootoffs.

4. No shooter will be permitted to enter the same event more than once, even though his/her score has been disqualified. EXCEPT as noted and allowed in II-G-2.b. When a participant is allowed to shoot an additional increment of targets (50 or 100 targets) above those shot in a program event, the first increment shot shall be the targets for the program event.

5. The scores of any shooter who takes part in a registered shoot shall be considered official, and shall be registered with the NSSA even though the shooter had given notice that it was not his/her intention to have his/her score recorded.

6. While the management may refund the entry fees and permit withdrawal of shooters who would be required to compete under drastically changed and clearly intolerable weather conditions or darkness not confronted by a majority of participants in an event, scores of any shooters who do participate must be recorded. In the event of extreme weather conditions, power failure, trap failure, or unusually early darkness, the shoot management may elect to continue the event some other time (e.g. the next morning or the following weekend) but must immediately notify NSSA, with a full explanation, who will sanction the change, provided it is deemed in the best interest of skeet.

7. When a contestant stops or withdraws without finishing an event in which he/she has started, his/her partial scores shall be reported to the NSSA along with the other scores of the event.

8. If a contestant stops or withdraws voluntarily, or after disqualification by the management, his/her partial score for the round in which he/she is shooting shall be entered as his/her score of targets broken for that full round of twenty-five targets. He/she shall not be penalized, however, for any of the remaining full rounds of that particular event. Where such withdrawal is the result of sickness, injury, or unrepairable gun, the shooter withdrawing shall be charged only with the targets actually fired upon in compiling and reporting his/her score. It shall be the shooter's responsibility to verify that the reason for this withdrawal is recorded on the scoresheet.

9. The shoot management is responsible to see that each squad's scores are posted on the scoreboards within thirty minutes of the time the squad finishes shooting.

H. REGISTERED SHOOT REPORTS

1. Reporting Requirements
It is the duty of each club or association holding a registered shoot to fulfill the following obligations. Payments and re-ports must be postmarked no more than 15 days after the last day of the shoot.

a. Make payments of all money, purses and options to the shooters.

b. Submit fees and reports due to state association.

c. Two reports (Financial and Registered Target Official Re-port) must be made to NSSA on all registered shoots. Standard forms available from NSSA headquarters, or equivalent approved by NSSA Headquarters, must be used. Rules II-H-3 and 4 outline required method of completing these reports.

2. Penalties Failure to fulfill the reporting requirements shall carry the following penalties:

a. All shoot reports and wrap-ups MUST be postmarked within 15 days of the last day of the shoot. A $25.00 DELINQUENT FEE will be charged to all clubs that have not submitted a registered shoot report and financial report (including all payments due) within the postmarked date. For the second and all subsequent late shoot reports, a $100.00 fine will be imposed. Shoot reports received past November 15 will have the fine, plus additional fees imposed depending on the lateness of the report. Also, after the second offense, suspension by NSSA from further sanctioned registered shoots is possible at the discretion of NSSA.

b. Cancellation of all subsequent shoot dates for the offending club or association.

c. Denial of right to apply or reapply for any further registered shoot dates for a period of thirty (30) days in case of first offense, or ninety (90) days in case of second or subsequent offense or until obligations have been met.

d. Officers of any delinquent club or association shall be barred from shooting registered targets until all required obligations of said club association are met to the shooters, to the state association and to NSSA.

3. Financial Report

a. Daily Fees: List number of targets shot each day of shoot and remit to NSSA the required daily registration fee (in U.S. funds).

b. NSSA Dues Collected: Remittance (in U.S. funds) and duplicate copies of receipts for all types of NSSA memberships sold at your shoot must be attached. Membership applications must be completely and legibly filled out, including complete and accurate mailing address of purchaser. (Shooter buying membership receives original receipt.)

4. Registered Target Official Report
An individual entry form/cashier sheet must be submitted on every shooter. These individual reports must include:

a. NSSA membership number

b. Full name or initials, corresponding to NSSA membership records

c. Member's complete address
Note: All of the above information is included on the plastic membership card. If an imprinter is not used, all information must be legibly written on individual shoot report form.

d. For each gauge in which the member participates (and HOA if appropriate) you must enter:

1) number of targets shot
2) number of targets broken
3) class in which member was entered (if member declares into a higher class at your shoot this information must be noted on shoot report form)
4) awards won. Regardless of what method was used in making awards, winners must be determined and reported under NSSA classification system. This applies even if no awards are made. Do not list winners above class champions unless such awards were made.

5. Clubs are NOT REQUIRED to deliver or mail a copy of official shoot reports to the shooter. They are, however, required to retain copies of scoreboard and/or field score sheet on file for 90 days

after the end of the applicable shooting year.

I.   RECOGNITION AND AWARDS

1.   High Average Leaders
a.   For the purpose of determining yearly champions and High Overall Leaders on the basis of average alone, leaders will be recognized if they have shot the following standard requirements of registered targets.

		12	20	28	.410
Open Team	1200	1000	1000	1000	
All Concurrent		1000	800	800	800
Sub-Jr/Sr-Veteran		700	500	400	400

b.   High Average Leaders in the Doubles Event and High Overall Leaders will be recognized if they shot 500 registered doubles targets. For Sub-Junior and Senior-Veteran, the requirements are 300 registered doubles targets.

2.   All-American Team
Candidates for All-American selection must have shot standard target requirements as defined for High Average selection in II-I-1 in the .410, 28, 20, 12 and Doubles events.

3.   Long Run Records
a.   Only scores shot in registered events shall be included in official long runs. Scores shot with a smaller gun than the one for which the event is scheduled shall not be accredited as part of a long run with the smaller gun.
b.   Shootoff targets and other non-registered targets shall not be counted as part of a long run.
c.   All long runs shall be compiled in the order in which the scoring appears on the official score sheets except the optional shot shall be counted in the proper sequence where it was fired. The sequence in which the official score sheets are posted must coincide with the sequence in which the scores were broken.

4.   High Overall Averages
For purposes of determining yearly all-around averages, divide by 4 the total of a shooter's year end averages in all four gauges.

5.   World Records
Current World Records are listed in the NSSA Record Annual each year. Any shooter, or team, who feels they have tied or broken an established World Record must follow the procedure outlined below for official recognition of a World Record score.
a.   Establish that the event in which the record was tied or broken was a part of the shoot program and available to all eligible competitors.
b.   Establish that the shooter or team properly entered the event prior to firing the record score.
c.   Submit application for recognition to NSSA headquarters on the standard form which is available at NSSA member clubs. The form is also available from headquarters, upon request.
d.   In the event that more than one shooter or team should break a world record score on the same calendar day, and provided they have correctly followed the outlined procedures, they shall become co-holders of that record.

6.   Determination of Age Groups
Age or Concurrent event status based on status as of November 1.

7.   Rookie is an individual who shoots NSSA standards and has never received an initial classification in any gauge.

8.   Honor Squad is comprised of those individuals who have shot NSSA standards in the current and previous years who show the most improvement in their HOA averages.

SECTION III - SHOOTING PROCEDURE

A.   DEFINITIONS

1.   Shooting Positions
a.   Shooter must stand with any part of both feet within the boundaries of the designated shooting station.
b.   Station 8 the designated shooting station is the half of the rectangular pad most distant from the respective high or low house.
c.   Any shooter with one or both feet definitely off the shooting station should first be made to shoot over and, if he/she persists in standing off the station, he/she shall be penalized by loss of the target for each subsequent violation in that event. However, if the shooter missed the target while committing the first violation of shooting position, the result shall be scored "lost".

2.   Gun Position
Any safe position which is comfortable to the shooter.

3.   No Bird
Any target thrown for which no score is recorded, or failure of a target to be thrown within the prescribed time limit of one second. This permits the throwing of instant targets, but gives a short time period in order to prevent a contestant from refusing a target which does not appear immediately after his/her call. If a shooter fires upon a target which appears after one second has elapsed between his/her call and the emergence of the target, and also before the referee calls no bird, the result of his/her shot shall be scored. If he/she withholds his/her shot after such an alleged slow pull, the referee may declare the target no bird provided he/she, in his/her sole judgment, decides that the delay exceeded the one second time allowance. The pull is not required to be instantaneous.

4.   Regular Target
A regular target is one that appears after the shooter's call and within a period not to exceed one (1) second, and which passes within a three-foot circle centered at a point fifteen (15) feet above the target-crossing point. The target-crossing point shall be measured from the level of Station 8. The target, in still air, must carry to a distance equivalent, on level ground, to 60 yards from the skeet house when passing through the center of the hoop, with an allowance tolerance of plus or minus two yards.

5.   Irregular Target
a.   An unbroken target that has not conformed to the definition of a regular target.
b.   Two targets thrown simultaneously in singles. However, if by error or for mechanical reasons doubles are thrown, and the shooter shoots and breaks or misses the correct target, it shall be scored as in singles. It shall be the shooter's prerogative to elect to shoot or withhold his/her shot when doubles are thrown in the calling of singles.
c.   Target thrown broken. Under no circumstances shall the result of firing upon a broken target be scored.

6.   Regular Double
A regular target thrown from each skeet house simultaneously.

7.   Irregular Double

8.   Proof Double
A repeat of a double.

9.   Shooting Bounds
For Stations 1 to 7, inclusive, an area forty-four (44) yards in front of the skeet house from which the target is thrown. For Station 8, the distance from the skeet house to a point directly over a line with Station 4, 8 and the target crossing point.

10.   Balk
Failure to shoot at a regular target or double due to the fault of the shooter.

11.   Malfunction of Gun
Failure of gun to operate or function through no fault of the shooter.

12.   Defective Ammunition
a.   Defective Ammunition will be defined as:
1)   Failure to fire, provided firing pin indentation is clearly noticeable.
2)   When a target is missed in the case of an odd-sounding shell, which in the sole judgment of the field referee does not deliver the shot the distance to the target, and therefore does not give the shooter a fair opportunity to break the target. NOTE: If a target is broken with an odd-sounding shell, it shall be scored dead regardless and will not be considered defective ammo. Odd-sounding shells where the shot does travel the distance to the bird and provide the shooter a fair chance to break the target will not be considered defective ammo and the results of those shots will be scored.
3)   Brass pulling off hull between shots on doubles.
4)   Separation of brass from casing when gun is fired (usually accompanied by a whistling sound as the plastic sleeve leaves the barrel).
b.   Wrong sized shells or empty shells shall not be considered defective ammunition.
c.   Repeated Targets - A target shall be repeated for each allowable instance of defective ammunition.
d.   Number allowed - A shooter will be allowed only 2 instances of defective ammunition from the first box of shells used in that round. After 2 instances of defective ammunition in a round or a shoot off round, a shooter may obtain a FACTORY box of ammunition and is then allowed 2 additional instances per box of FACTORY shells in that round. If shells are not changed in a round after 2 ammo malfunctions have been ruled, the third and all subsequent occurrences in that round will be excessive. EXCEPTION: If a shooter is provided a proof shell by the referee and defective ammunition is ruled on that proof shot, that instance will not count against the shooter as defective ammunition.

13.   Dead Target
A target from which, in the sole judgment of the referee, a visible piece is observed before the target hits the ground as a result of having been legally fired upon.

14.   Lost Target
A target from which in the sole judgment of the referee no visible piece is broken as a result of having been fired upon.

15.   Optional Shot
The shot fired after the first 24 targets have been scored dead in any one round (Station 8 low house only); or fired following the shooter's first lost target. In the latter in-stance it must be fired from same station and at the same house as the one first missed.

16.   Skeet Squad
a.   A normal skeet squad is composed of five shooters.
b.   Any five (5) shooters may designate themselves as a squad. All shooters shall be formed into squads of five (5) shooters each, as nearly as possible. Less than five (5) is permissible for expedience, but more than six (6) should not be squadded for safety reasons.

17.   Round of Skeet
A round of skeet for one person consists of twenty-five (25) shots, the object being to score the greatest number of dead targets. Twenty-four shots are fired as described in III-B-1. The first shot scored lost in any round shall be repeated immediately and the result scored as the twenty-fifth shot. Should the first shot lost occur in a double, the lost target shall be repeated as a single with the result of this shot scored as the twenty-fifth shot. If the first shot lost should be the first target of an irregular double, then a proof regular double shall be fired upon to determine the result of the second shot, and then the first target scored lost shall be repeated as a single and scored as the twenty-fifth shot. Should the first twenty-four (24) targets of a round be scored dead, the shooter shall take his/her optional shot at low house eight only.

18.   Shooting Up
The procedure of a late shooter shooting out of turn to catch up with his/her squad (III-B-6).

B.   GENERAL

1.   Squad Shooting Procedure For A Round Of Skeet
a.   A squad shall start shooting at Station 1 in the order in which the names appear on the score sheet. The first shot scored lost in the round shall be repeated immediately as the optional shot.
b.   The first shooter shall start shooting singles at Station 1, shooting the high house target first and the low house target second. Then, loading two shells, he/she shall proceed to shoot doubles (shooting the first shot at the target from the nearest skeet house and the second shot at the target from the farthest skeet house) before leaving the station. The second shooter shall then proceed likewise followed by the other members of the squad in their turn.
c.   Then the squad shall proceed to Station 2 and repeat the same sequence as on Station 1.
d.   The squad shall proceed to Station 3 where each shooter will shoot at a high house single target first and a low house single target second before leaving the shooting station.
e.   The same procedure shall be followed at Stations 4 and 5.
f.   Upon advancing to Station 6 the leadoff shooter will shoot singles in the same sequence as at the previous stations. Then, loading two shells, he/she shall shoot doubles by shooting at the low house target first and the high house target second before leaving the station. The other shooters will follow in their turn.
g.   The same procedure will be followed on Station 7.
h.   The squad will then advance to Station 8 where each shooter shall shoot at a target from the high house be-fore any member of the squad shoots at a target from the low house.
i.   The squad shall then turn to Station 8 low house and the leadoff shooter will shoot at the low house target.
j.   The shooter shall repeat the low house target for his/her optional shot before leaving the station, provided he/she is still straight (no lost targets in the round). The other shooters will follow in turn.
k.   At this time the shooter should verify his/her own score.

2.   Rules and Procedures for Doubles Events
a.   No less than a fifty (50) target event.
b.   Shooting commences at Station 1 and continues through 7 and backwards from 6 through 5, 4, 3 and 2. Rounds 2 and 4 will end with doubles on Station 1 using the 25th shell from

rounds 1 and 3. That is, rounds 1 and 3 will consist of 24 shots ending with doubles at Station 2, and rounds 2 and 4 will consist of 26 shots ending with doubles at Station 1.

   c. When shooting doubles at Stations 1, 2, 3, 5, 6 and 7, shoot the first shot at the target from the nearest skeet house and the second shot at the target from the farthest skeet house. When shooting doubles at Station 4 the shooter must shoot first at the high house target going around the stations from 1 through 7 and shoot at the low house 4 target first when coming back around the stations from 7 through 2 (or 1).

   d. The rules for doubles in a Doubles event are the same as the rules for doubles in a regular round of skeet.

   e. All other NSSA rules apply.

3. Shooter's Right To Observe Targets

   a. At the beginning of each round the squad shall be entitled to observe two (2) regular targets from each skeet house and shall have the option of observing one regular target after each irregular target.

   b. Shoot management, State Association, State Chief Referee and/or Zone Chief Referee shall have the right, where topographically possible, to make it mandatory to use a hoop or other suitable device whenever a target adjustment is necessary.

4. Progress From Station To Station

   a. No member of the squad shall advance to the shooting station until it is his/her turn to shoot, and until the previous shooter has left the station. No shooter shall order any target or shoot at any target except when it is his/her turn. Targets fired upon while shooting out of turn, without permission of the referee, shall be declared "no bird."

   b. No member of a squad, having shot from one station, shall proceed toward the next station in such a way as to interfere with another shooter. The penalty for willful interference in this manner shall be disqualification from the event.

   c. No shooter shall unduly delay a squad without good and sufficient reason in the judgment of the referee in charge of his/her squad. A shooter who persists in deliberately causing inexcusable delays after receiving a first warning from the referee shall be subject to disqualification from the event.

5. Broken Gun

When a gun breaks in such a manner so as to render it unusable, the shooter has the option of using another gun if such gun can be secured without delay, or dropping out of the squad until the gun is repaired and finishing the event at a later time when a vacancy occurs or after all other contestants have finished the event. Nothing shall prohibit the shooter from missing one round because of a broken gun, having the gun repaired and then rejoining the squad for all later rounds that the squad has not started. In that case the shooter will finish any or all rounds, starting with the shot where the breakdown occurred, that were not shot because of a broken gun, on the proper fields and in the first vacancy that may occur, or after the event has been finished by all other contestants.

6. Shooting Up

   a. Where a shooter has registered in but does not show up to start an event with his/her squad, he/she will not be permitted to shoot up after the first man in the squad has fired a shot at Station 2.

   b. He/she may join the squad for all later rounds, but the round missed because of lateness must be shot on the proper field in the first vacancy, or after all other contestants have finished.

   c. In the interest of conserving time the shoot management may modify this rule to meet special conditions, if it so desires.

7. Slow Squads

It is suggested that shoot management use substitute fields when breakdowns or unusually slow shooting squads are disrupting the normal sequence of squads. Under normal conditions, a squad should complete a round in 20 minutes, including breaks between rounds. Squads using more time cannot object to being transferred to a substitute field.

C.   SCORING

1. The score in any one round shall be the total number of dead targets.

2. Targets declared no bird shall not be scored.

3. One lost target shall be scored on:

   a. A balk or failure of gun to fire due to fault of shooter. Should this include both targets of a regular double, it shall be scored as first target lost, and a proof double shall be thrown to determine the result of the second shot only. If a balk should occur, or his/her gun fail to fire because of the shooter's fault, when a proof double is thrown and the result of the first shot has already been scored, the second target shall be scored as lost.

   b. Each excessive instance of defective ammunition, or excessive malfunction or malfunctions of gun.

   c. Doubles fired upon in reverse order.

   d. Target fired upon after it is outside the shooting bounds.

   e. Each target fired upon and allegedly missed because the shooter's gun had a bent barrel, or a bent compensator, or any other bent tube or accessory.

   f. Each successive foot position violation.

   g. Each successive time balk. It shall be considered a time balk if a shooter deliberately delays more than 15 seconds for each shot on a station and the referee shall warn him/her once each round without penalty.

4. If a shell having once misfired is used again, and fails to fire, the results shall be considered a fault on the part of the shooter and scored lost.

5. No claim of irregularity shall be allowed, either on singles or doubles, where the target or targets were actually fired upon and alleged irregularity consists of deviation from the prescribed line of flight, or because of an alleged quick pull or slow pull, unless the referee has distinctly called no bird prior to the firing of the shot. Otherwise, if the shooter fires, the result shall be scored. The referee shall have final say as to whether he/she called no bird before the shooter fired.

6. If the brass pulls off a hull between shots on doubles, score as defective ammunition but do not score it as a gun mal-function.

7. During a regular round or a doubles event, if the brass pulls off a hull, or if a defective ammunition occurs between shots on doubles, the referee shall rule that if the first target was a dead bird, nothing is established, and a proof double shall be fired upon to determine the result of both birds. However, if the first target was lost, it shall be so established, and a proof double shot to establish the second shot result.

D.   GUN MALFUNCTIONS

The shooter must not be considered at fault if he/she has complied with the manufacturer's operating instructions for loading the gun, and the gun does not fire. In the case of a gun going into battery (locking closed) for the first shot on doubles or any shot on singles, if the shooter has closed the action in accordance with the manufacturer's instructions, and if the bolt appears visually to be closed, the failure of a gun to fire shall be scored as malfunction.

1. Semi-Automatics

   a. On a semi-automatic the shooter is not required to push forward or strike the breech bolt retraction lever to insure locking the gun. This is a normal gun function.

   b. The shooter must load the shell or shells into the gun and see that the action appears closed. If he/she loads 2 shells on singles or doubles, and if the second shell fails to go into the chamber or is thrown out of the gun, it shall be scored a malfunction.

2. Pump Guns

   a. The shooter is required to pump the gun, as recommended by the manufacturer, on doubles and to close the action completely forward (visually) on singles.

   b. If the shooter short-shucks the gun, the hammer will not be cocked, a fault of the shooter.

   c. If the lifter throws the second shell out of the gun it shall be a malfunction.

   d. It shall be a malfunction if between shots on singles or doubles the gun returns the empty shell to the chamber provided the hammer is cocked.

   e. The referee shall check for a malfunction as instructed under that title and shall then apply forward pressure on the forearm to see if the shell is lodged (a malfunction). However, if the gun closes smoothly, without jiggling, it is not a malfunction.

3. Double-Barreled Guns

   a. The shooter is responsible for loading a shell in the proper barrel, or two shells for doubles.

   b. The shooter must close the action in accordance with manufacturer's recommendations.

4. Shell Catching Devices

Where any device is attached to a shotgun which must be adjusted or removed to permit shooting doubles, it shall be the shooter's responsibility to perform such adjustment or removal. Failure to fire a second shot on doubles, due to such device, shall not be an allowable malfunction, and the bird shall be scored lost.

5. Repeated Targets

A target shall be repeated for each allowable malfunction and/or each allowable defective ammunition.

6. Number Allowed

Only two malfunctions of any one gun in the same round or shootoff round shall be allowable. The third and all subsequent malfunctions of the same gun shall be excessive.

However, when more than one person is using the same gun in the same round, this rule shall apply to each person separately.

7. Loading Two Shells

During the shooting of single targets, a shooter may load two shells except at Station 8 high house, or for the last single target on any station, or unless forbidden by club rules, and if the gun jams or malfunctions between shots, it shall be scored as a malfunction and the shooter permitted to shoot the target over. However, the shooter is still restricted to two allowable malfunctions with one gun in one round.

8. Malfunction on Singles or First Shot Doubles

To establish that a malfunction has occurred the shooter must not open the gun or touch the safety before the referee's inspection.

   a. If the shooter is holding the trigger pulled, the referee, after seeing that the gun is pointed in a safe direction, will place his/her finger over the shooter's and apply normal pressure.

   b. If the shooter has released the trigger, the referee, after seeing that the gun is pointed in a safe direction, will exercise extreme caution not to jiggle or attempt to further close the action and will apply normal pressure to the trigger.

   c. The target shall be scored lost if the gun fires or is opened before the referee's inspection. A malfunction will be ruled if it does not fire and the referee's examination for ammunition, safety, barrel selection, etcetera, establishes that the shooter had fulfilled required responsibilities.

9. Malfunction Between Shots on Doubles

If an apparent malfunction occurs between the first and second shot on doubles:

a. The referee shall apply the same procedures as listed under malfunction on singles to determine if an allowable malfunction has occurred.

b. During a regular round or a doubles event, if an allowable malfunction has occurred, the referee shall rule if the first target was a dead bird, nothing is established, and a proof double shall be fired upon to determine the result of both birds. However, if the first target was lost, it shall be so established and a proof double shot to establish the second shot result.

c. If such malfunction is excessive (not allowable) and the first shot is a dead bird, it shall be scored first bird dead, second bird lost, but, if the first bird is lost then both birds shall be scored lost.

10. Fan-Fire

If a gun doubles or fan-fires while shooting singles or doubles the referee shall rule a malfunction, and during a regular round or a doubles event, if the first target was a dead bird, nothing established, and a proof single or double shall be fired upon to determine the results. However, if the first target was lost, it shall be so established and a proof double shot to establish the second shot result.

E.   DOUBLES OR PROOF DOUBLES

1. If first target emerges broken, the doubles shall, in all cases, be declared no bird and a proof double shall be thrown to determine the result of both shots.

2. If a double is thrown but the targets collide, before the result of the first bird is determined, it shall be declared no bird, and the result of a proof double shall determine the score of both shots.

3. If the first target of a double is thrown irregular as to deviate from the prescribed line of flight and is not shot at, a proof double shall determine the score for both shots, whether the second target is fired upon or not. The referee shall be the sole judge of irregularity.

4. If the first target of a double is thrown irregular as to deviation from the prescribed line of flight, and is shot at, the result shall be scored for the first shot in accordance with III-C-5 and if the shooter is deprived of a normal second shot for any of the reasons in III-E-5 the second target only shall be declared no bird and a proof double shall be fired to determine the result of the second shot.

5. If the shooter is deprived of a normal second shot for any of the following reasons, the result of the first shot shall be scored, and the second target only shall be declared no bird and a proof double shall be fired to determine the result of the second shot.

   a. The second target is thrown broken.

   b. The second target is thrown irregular as to deviation from the prescribed line of flight and is not shot at.

   c. The second target is not thrown at all.

   d. The second target is not thrown simultaneously.

   e. Both targets are broken with the first shot.

   f. The wrong target is broken with the first shot. (For proof double ruling see paragraph 8 below.)

   g. The first shot is lost and a collision occurs before the result of the second shot is determined.

   h. The second target collides with fragments of the first target properly broken, before the result of the second target is determined.

   i. The result of the first shot is determined, and interference occurs before the second shot is fired.

6. There shall be no penalty for withholding the first shot when either target of a double is irregular.

A proof double shall determine the score of both shots thereafter.

7. If a double is thrown and an allowable gun malfunction or defective ammunition occurs on the first shot, it shall be declared no bird, and the result of a proof double shall determine the score of both shots. If such malfunction is excessive, (not allowable), the proof double shall be thrown to determine the result of the second shot only.

8. In shooting a proof double after the first target (of a double) is lost, if the shooter fires at, or breaks the wrong target first, said proof double shall be scored as both targets lost. If, in such a proof double after the first target (of a double) is dead, the shooter fires at, or breaks, the wrong target first, it shall be scored as first target dead and second target lost.

F.   INTERFERENCE

1. Any circumstance beyond the shooter's control which unduly affects his/her opportunity to break any particular tar-get is interference.
   a. If a shooter fires his/her shot, the appearance of a target, or a piece of target, from an adjoining field shall not be ruled as interference, unless such target, or piece of target strikes or threatens to strike the shooter or his/her gun. It shall be the final judgment of the referee to consider the evidence and determine whether a target or piece of target strikes or threatens to strike shooter or his/her gun.
   b. If a shooter withholds his/her shot due to what he/she considers to be an interference, and if the cause is ob-served and ruled interference by the referee, the interference may be allowed.
   c. If a shooter withholds a shot for safety purposes, the referee may give the shooter the benefit of the doubt and rule interference, providing he/she agrees safety was involved.
   d. Activities on other fields shall not be ruled as interference under any circumstances if safety to any person is not in question.

2. If the shooter shoots at a target, he/she accepts it. He/she must abide by the result unless the referee considers that there was legal interference. Following are a few illustrations of what may be considered legal interference.
   a. A target box being thrown out the door in the shooter's line of vision between the time of the shooter's call and the firing of his/her shot.
   b. Opening the skeet house door unexpectedly or suddenly under the same circumstances.
   c. Any sudden disturbance or exceptionally loud noise, except an announcement over the loud speaker.
   d. A bird flying directly across the target's line of flight just before it is fired upon.
   e. A child or any other person or animal running out on the field suddenly in the shooter's line of vision.
   f. A thrown object, or wind blown object, blown through the air so as to cause a conflict (a piece of paper being merely blown along the ground shall not qualify in this category).
   g. The sun shall not be considered as interference. It must be accepted as a normal hazard.

G.   SAFETY PRECAUTIONS

The safety of competitors, field personnel and spectators is of primary importance and requires continuous attention and self-discipline. On any part of club grounds, as well as on the shooting field, particular attention must be given to the safety procedures outlined in the following paragraphs and to other safe gun handling techniques. Caution must also be used in moving about the field and club grounds. Where self-discipline and attention to safety procedures is lacking, it is the duty of the field personnel to enforce them and the duty of competitors to assist in such enforcement.

1. Eye and Ear Protection - All persons (including shooters, referees and trap personnel) must wear some form of eye and ear protection on a skeet range at a shoot sanctioned by NSSA.
2. No gun shall be loaded until the shooter is on the shooting station. Loading is considered as putting any part of a loaded shell in any part of the gun.
3. As a safety precaution, test shots will not be permitted without permission of the Field Referee. Such permission shall not unreasonably be withheld.
4. The loaded gun shall be kept pointed in a direction that will not endanger the lives of shooters, field personnel or spectators.
5. When not on the shooting station, the gun shall be carried with breech open and empty. Pumps and automatics will have the bolt open. Fixed breech (double barrels including over and unders and side-by-sides) will be broken open.
6. When the shooter is on the shooting station and ready to shoot and a delay occurs, such as equipment breakdown, the gun shall be opened and all shells extracted.
7. During the shooting of single targets, management may permit the loading of two shells. However, no one will be allowed to load two shells to shoot their last singles target on any station. Management cannot compel the loading of two shells in the shooting of singles.
8. The loading of more than two shells in the gun shall not be allowed at any time.
9. A gun may not be used that will accept more than one (1) gauge of shells at the same time.
10. A shooter will not be permitted to use a gun with a release-type trigger unless the referee and the other members of the squad are notified. Extra caution must be exercised if the gun is given to a referee who is unfamiliar with its operation. Guns with release type triggers must be clearly marked. Safety stickers designating. Release trigger with instruction on placement are available from Headquarters. Please send your request in writing.
11. Any shooter whose gun accidentally discharges twice within one round for mechanical reasons shall be required to change guns or, if time permits, have his/her gun repaired, before continuing to shoot the round or subsequent rounds.
12. When a shooter intentionally fires a second time at the same target, he/she shall be warned by the referee. The second time the shooter intentionally fires a second shot at the same target in any event, the penalty shall be automatic disqualification from the event.
13. The placement of markers other than those specified in NSSA Rule Book shall be deemed illegal. 14. In the interest of safety, interference and time, only the club management's personnel shall be permitted to pick up empty shells from the grounds during a registered shoot, and extreme care must be exercised to prevent interference with other squads shooting.
15. No spectator shall be allowed on the skeet fields, and the referee shall be responsible for the enforcement of this rule.
16. The use of any drug, legal or illegal and including alcohol, prior to or during an NSSA sanctioned event by a registered competitor or referee is prohibited, with the exception of prescription or non-prescription over-the-counter medications that do not impair a shooter's or referee's ability to perform safely.

SECTION IV – REFEREES

A.   LICENSED REFEREE

1. NSSA official referees shall pass prescribed written examinations (with the aid of a rule book) and also eye tests, using glasses if necessary. For the eye test, a visual card system will suffice and save cost of a professional eye examination.
   a. These examinations will be given by their state associations or NSSA affiliated clubs.
   b. Applications for official NSSA referee cards and emblems shall be approved by the applicant's state association, where one exists, or by an NSSA affiliated club where there is

   c. no state or district association.
   c. It is recommended that all state organizations adopt the policy of using only NSSA official referees as chief referees.
   d. All applicants for referee licenses must be paid up regular members of the NSSA.
2. Referees for NSSA World Championship Shoots
   a. All applicants must be licensed NSSA referees for current year.
   b. Each applicant must be recommended in writing by two current officers of his/her state association or by one NSSA director from his/her state or zone.

B.   ASSOCIATE REFEREE

1. NSSA Associate Referees must meet all eligibility requirements specified for NSSA licensed referees (IV-A-1), with the exception of paid up membership in the NSSA.
2. An Associate Referee is eligible for an Associate Referee patch.
3. Application for Associate Referee status must be approved by applicant's state and/or zone Chief Referee.
4. An Associate Referee is not eligible to referee the World Championships.

C.   CHIEF REFEREE

When shoot management designates a chief referee, he/she shall have general supervision over all other referees and shall be present throughout the shooting.

1. It shall be his/her responsibility to appoint the necessary assistant chief referees and all other referees shall meet with his/her approval.
2. The chief referee shall designate and assign the referees to the fields and shall be held responsible for their conduct at all times during the shoot.
3. It is recommended that the chief referee also have the responsibility of instructing all other referees and being certain they are acquainted with the rules and approved interpretations.
4. It shall be the chief referee and/or shoot management's responsibility to stop a shoot or shootoff when darkness or other conditions prevent a fair chance to shoot. This action must be carried out simultaneously on all fields. Example: Use of public address system or the shutting off of power; or a suitable signal, the significance of which is known to all referees. Use of the referee's eye test card - 5/16" dot at 21 yards - is MANDATORY.
5. Where practical, each state association should appoint a Chief Referee for its state. It is suggested that this chief referee be placed in charge of all referees in the state and that he/she conduct training courses to develop better referees.

D.   FIELD REFEREE

The field referee is responsible for the conduct of shooting on the field to which he/she has been assigned. On this field, he/she shall have jurisdiction over the area in rear of the field (that used by other shooters and spectators) as well as over the actual shooting area.

1. He/she shall be completely familiar with the shoot program and the NSSA rules.
2. He/she must be constantly alert, impartial and courteous (though firm) in the handling of shooters.
3. Upon protest, the referee shall rule upon the occurrence, and then without delay, proceed with the round as if nothing had happened. At the completion of the round, he/she shall notify the Chief Referee.
4. The referee shall distinctly announce all lost targets and all no bird targets.
5. The referee shall see that each shooter has a fair opportunity to shoot in his/her turn, and if a shooter has been unduly interfered with while shooting, he/she shall declare no bird and allow the shooter another shot.
6. The referee shall declare no bird as soon as possible when:
   a. The shooter's position is not according to the rules. The shooter shall be warned by the referee of his/her illegal shooter's position, but if he/she continues to violate the position, he/she shall be penalized by the loss of one target for each subsequent violation in that event.
   b. Target does not emerge within the allowed time after the shooter's call.
   c. Target emerges before shooter's call.
   d. An irregular target is thrown in singles, doubles or proof doubles.
7. It shall be the referee's first duty to declare "no bird" as quickly as possible when he/she determines that an irregular target has been thrown.
   a. If the shooter fires before the no bird call, the result of the shot shall be scored.
   b. In the case of doubles or proof doubles, if the referee's call of no bird occurs after the firing of the first shot the result of the first shot shall be scored and a proof double shall be thrown to determine the result of the second shot only.
   c. NO RESULT OF FIRING ON A BROKEN TARGET SHALL BE SCORED.
8. The result of shooting at a target after it has been declared no bird shall not be scored and the shot will be repeated in all instances.
9. Dusted targets or perforated targets that are retrieved after landing shall be declared lost.
10. When the targets thrown from any machine are repeatedly irregular, the referee shall suspend shooting and order the machine adjusted or repaired. At shooter's request, after such repair or adjustment, the referee should allow shooter to observe a target, if such request is reasonable and not excessive.
11. The referee shall grant a shooter permission to shoot out of his/her regular turn where it is justified.
12. The referee shall disqualify, for the event:
   a. A shooter who in his/her opinion has willfully interfered with another shooter while the latter is shooting.
   b. Any shooter who repeatedly violates any of the safety precautions listed in Section III or for any act that in the referee's opinion endangers the safety of shooters, field personnel or spectators.
13. It shall also be the field referee's responsibility to supervise the keeping of correct scores and to see that all scores are verified by the respective shooters before the score sheet is taken from the field.
   a. Every regular target fired upon shall be shown on the score pad and it is recommended that the mark / or X be used to signify dead and O to signify lost.
   b. If an error in scorekeeping is discovered on the field, the field referee shall remedy it promptly at the time of discovery.
   c. In the event there is any question as to the correctness of a score after the score sheet leaves the field, shoot management shall check with the field referee and order the score corrected if it is determined that an error has been made.
   d. The referee's responsibility in seeing that shooters verify their scores is to announce after each round, Please check your scores.
14. The referee shall be the SOLE judge of decision of fact. For example, his/her decision as to whether a target is dead or lost shall be irrevocable, regardless of the opinion of spectators or other members of the squad.
15. It is better for a referee to continue to officiate at the same field.
   a. Relief referees shall not take over the fields until the shooters have completed the round,

except in cases of emergency, such as illness, etcetera.

    b.   No NSSA official referee may be disqualified in the middle of a round but he/she may choose to disqualify himself.

16.   Only assigned field referees, as designated by shoot management or the chief referee, may pull, score, or referee registered targets. A voice release system may be used.

17.   Whenever possible, have assigned field referees at registered shoots. However, in an effort to offer reduced shoot entry fees, shoot management may elect to have squads self-referee IF it is published in the shoot program and/or at the shoot registration desk. In such cases, the squad leadoff shooter shall be responsible for carrying the score sheet to and from the field, and having each shooter initial his/her final score at the end of the final round. In cases of any dispute or protest situation, these should be taken to shoot management immediately upon completion of the last round. Any protest to be filed must follow existing procedures as published in Section II.E in this Rule Book.

SECTION V - NSSA CLASSIFICATION

A.   DEFINITIONS

1.   NSSA Shooting Year
The NSSA shooting year shall be any twelve month period running from November 1 through the following October 31.

2.   Current Year
The twelve month period November 1 through October 31 of the year for which classification is being determined.

3.   Previous Year
The twelve month period immediately preceding the current shooting year, (i.e. November 1 - October 31).

4.   Gauge
The term gauge used in this Classification Section includes International skeet and doubles as well as 12 gauge, 20 gauge, 28 gauge and .410.

5.   Initial String
The required minimum number of registered targets necessary for an initial Classification is 200 for each gauge independent of each other gauge.

6.   Regular String
The required minimum number of registered targets necessary for RECLASSIFICATION of a classified shooter is 300 for each gauge independent of each other gauge.

7.   Initial Classification
The first classification of a newly classified shooter based on his/her INITIAL STRING of registered targets shot during the CURRENT year, or during the PREVIOUS year and the CURRENT year combined.

8.   Regular Classification
    a.   The classification of a classified shooter at the beginning of the CURRENT year in each gauge will be based on all registered targets shot during the previous year, providing at least two hundred targets were shot.
    b.   The reclassification of a classified shooter based on his/her average for totals of all registered targets shot during the CURRENT YEAR.

9.   Class Assigned
The class to which a shooter is assigned and would be required to shoot were he/she to compete in a subsequent shoot, whether or not he/she ever shot in that class.

10.   Classification/Shoot Record Cards
    a.   As soon as possible after October 31 of each year, each PAID member will receive from NSSA a classification/shoot record card.
    b.   This classification/shoot record card shall include provisions for club designation, targets shot and targets broken in each gauge, and shall be imprinted with:
1)   Member's name, address, membership expiration date and membership number.
2)   Shooter's class for the start of the current year in each gauge in which he/she is a classified shooter, or NC if he/she shot less than 200 targets during previous year.
3)   The number of targets shot at and broken in each gauge during previous year, if any.
4)   The highest class in which shooter shot or was assigned during the previous year.
    c.   Any errors on shooter's new classification card, including those caused by failure of shoot reports to be received at NSSA headquarters in time to be included on new card, should be promptly reported to NSSA by the shooter so that a corrected card can be supplied and to insure proper inclusion in permanent record.

11.   Classified Shooter
    a.   One who has fired at least the required INITIAL STRING of registered targets, or more, during the PREVIOUS year, or
    b.   One who has fired at least the required INITIAL STRING of registered targets, or more, during the CURRENT year, or
    c.   One who has fired at least the required INITIAL STRING of registered targets, or more, during the PREVIOUS year and the CURRENT year combined.

12.   Previously Classified Shooter (PC)
One who attained a classification during any of the three years prior to the current year but in the year immediately prior to the current year shot less than the 200 targets required for regular classification.
    a.   A PC shooter shall be solely responsible for his/her own record and, if requested by shoot management at the time of registration, be required to sign an affidavit attesting to his/her highest classification in the three years prior to current year. Falsification subjects shooter to action on II-A-8-d.
    b.   For classification procedures see V-B-4-c. For classifying PC shooters in concurrent events see V-D-2-a.

13.   Non-Classified Shooter (NC)
A new shooter, or one whose record does not conform with any of the preceding requirements for Classified or Previously Classified shooters.
a.   For classification procedures see V-B-4.
b.   For classifying NC shooters in concurrent events see V-D-2-b.

B.   PROCEDURES

1.   Maintaining Shoot Record Card
    a.   Each shooter shall bear the responsibility of promptly and accurately entering his/her own score with the date, etcetera, in the proper gauge division at the conclusion of each registered EVENT in which he/she participates. Where a single EVENT extends more than one day, he/she should enter the total, not the day-to-day scores.
    b.   Shooter shall PROMPTLY have his/her classification changed in reclassification spaces on his/her classification/shoot record card whenever they have changed by averages on a regular string or cumulative regular stings, or because of class assigned.

    c.   The shooter is required to carry his/her card to each registered shoot and present it at registration.
1)   A shooter failing to present his/her classification card, for any reason, MAY BE ASSIGNED CLASS AA AT THE DISCRETION OF SHOOT MANAGEMENT.
2)   In the case of a lost card, or accidentally forgetting a card, the shooter may sign an affidavit attesting to his/her classification, subject to specified penalties. Such affidavit MUST be attached to the shoot report when it is forwarded to NSSA for tabulation. NOTE: REPLACE-MENT FOR A LOST CARD (INCLUDING REPORTED SCORES TO DATE) MAY BE OBTAINED FROM NSSA UPON REQUEST. IF THE ORIGINAL CARD IS LATER FOUND, THE SHOOTER SHOULD CAREFULLY CON-SOLIDATE THE RECORD, THEN DESTROY THE EXTRA CARD.
    d.   In the space provided for club on his/her classification/shoot record card, each member shall designate, not later than his/her first competition in such events, the club he/she has elected to represent in club two-man and five-man team competition.
    e.   A shooter falsifying any entries or improperly using more than one card shall be disqualified and reported to NSSA for action according to section II-A-8-d.

2.   Classification Review
A state association, director, club or shooter has the right to request a review of a shooter's record if it appears that he/she is unfairly competing in a class below his/her true level of ability. Upon review by a duly authorized national committee the shooter may be assigned a higher class and may be required to disregard certain abnormally low scores for the purpose of classification and reclassification only.

3.   Classification/Reclassification of Classified Shooter
Also see Reclassification Limitations.
    a.   Using the Universal Classification Tables, a classified shooter's class for the start of the current year shall be figured on the basis of his/her average on the total number of registered targets shot during the previous year, however, such class shall be no lower than:
1)   One class below the HIGHEST class in which he/she shot during the PREVIOUS year, or
2)   The class he/she was assigned if, because of a classification review, he/she was required to move to a higher class than that required by average.
    b.   A shooter shall maintain throughout each shoot his/her classes and running averages as they were at the time of entry. A classified shooter shall not be subject to changes in classification during a shoot for any reason nor have his/her classification changed for a consolation event held after the regular shoot.
1)   EXCEPTION: A non-classified or previously classified shooter who completes an INITIAL STRING of targets at the end of a preliminary event be-comes classified for all remaining events of that gauge.
2)   The total number of targets scheduled for an EVENT ARE TO BE USED IN DETERMINING STRINGS FOR CLASSIFICATION AND RECLASSIFI-CATION.
    Example 1: A non-classified or previously classified shooter has shot 150 registered 12 gauge targets and enters a 100 target 12 gauge event. He/she shall be classified on the total of 250 targets and NOT after shooting the first 50 targets of the event, which would total 200 targets.
    Example 2: A classified shooter has shot 550 registered 20 gauge targets and enters a 100 target 20 gauge event. He/she shall be reclassified on the total 650 targets and NOT after shooting the first 50 targets of the event, which would total 600.
    c.   A shooter who is classified at the beginning of the year on a class assigned or totals of targets shot during previous year will RECLASSIFY (UP-WARD ONLY) at the end of his/her first REGULAR STRING and at the end of all succeeding regular strings shot during the CURRENT YEAR.

Example (12 ga):	SHOT	BROKE/AVERAGE		CLASS	
CURRENT YEAR	100	93		C	
		100	98		C
		100	97		C
Reclassify on	300	288	.9600	A	
		100	95		A
		100	98		A
		100	96		A
Reclassify on and again on	600 900, etc.	577	.9617	A	

    d.   Shooters must, however, always reclassify at the end of each regular string even though the correct number of targets for reclassification comes between the preliminary and the main event. Reclassification is not effective until AFTER the shoot, but must be accomplished on the correct number of targets.

Example (12 ga):	SHOT	BROKE	AVERAGE	CLASS
CURRENT YEAR	100	96		C
		100	99	C
*Preliminary	100*	97		C
Reclassify on	300	292	.9733	A
*Main Event of above shoot	100*	95		C*
		100	98	A
		200	197	A
Reclassify on	700	682	.9743	A

Example (12 ga):	SHOT	BROKE	AVERAGE	CLASS
		100	100	A
		100	98	A
		100	99	A
Reclassify on	1000**	979	.9790	AA

• Note that shooter must reclassify at end of regular string EVEN THOUGH he/she does not CHANGE CLASS until AFTER the shoot:
** and that reclassification is at end of each regular string; not necessarily on multiples of 300.

    e.   A shooter who becomes a CLASSIFIED SHOOTER on combination of targets shot during the PREVIOUS year and CURRENT year shall be RECLASSIFIED on each succeeding REGULAR STRING of registered targets shot during the current year.

Example (12 ga):	SHOT	BROKE	AVERAGE		
CLASS					
PREVIOUS YEAR	100	87		NC	
CURRENT YEAR	100	92		C	
CLASSIFY ON	200	179	.8950	D	
		100	96		D
		100	93		D

243

	100	94		D
Reclassify on 400 shot in current year	400	375	.9375	B
	100	91		B
	100	95		B
	100	94		B
Reclassify on 700 shot in current year	700	655	.9357	B

NOTE: After Initial Classification, targets shot in PREVIOUS YEAR are not used in calculating averages.

    f.   A classified shooter who wishes to voluntarily declare himself/ herself up in class may do so, including AAA. Any shooter voluntarily declaring into AAA must remain in AAA for the remainder of the year. When he/she so elects, he/she must (at a registered shoot) have his/her card marked before competing in the event in the class for which he/she is declaring himself. His/her card shall be marked with the new classification by self-declaration in the class where he/she declared himself, and be entered on the Official Entry Form with notation self-declared.

4.   Classification of Previously Classified and Non-Classified Shooters

    a.   A shooter who has not attained a classification during the previous year will compete in a class deter-mined by the score he/she shot for that day until he/she has shot an Initial String of 200 targets in that gauge. For a 50 target event, the score would be doubled to determine the class.

    b.   Management may reserve the right to restrict PC and NC shooters from entering purses and/or class options but MAY NOT REQUIRE PC and/or NC shooters to pay any part of the entry fee that is to be returned to the shooters in the form of cash or other tangible awards. NC or PC shooters will not be eligible for cash or tangible awards for which they have not paid the required entry fee prior to shooting the event.

    c.   Upon completing an Initial String in each individual gauge, the shooter will be given a classification based on average; however, a previously classified shooter may not be classed more than one class below the highest class he/she held in any of the 3 years immediately prior to the current year.

    d.   A PC or NC shooter who completes an INITIAL STRING of targets at the end of a preliminary event becomes classified for all remaining events of that gauge.

    e.   After this INITIAL CLASSIFICATION, a shooter will reclassify after each succeeding REGULAR STRING, using the total number of targets shot during the current year and will follow procedures as outlined in items b through f of this Classification/ Reclassification of Classified Shooters.

    f.   A previously classified or a non-classified shooter who voluntarily wishes to declare himself classified may do so provided he/she declares himself in Class AA. When he/she so elects, he/she must have his/her card marked (at a registered shoot) in AA before competing in the event for which he/she is declaring himself and Class AA must be entered on the Official Entry Form with notation self-declared.

C.   UNIVERSAL CLASSIFICATION TABLES

1.   Use of the Universal Classification Tables shall be required for all registered shoots and shall be in accordance with the tables of averages shown below. Standard rounding procedures will be used to calculate an individual's average. Calculate the average to 5 digits and rounding to the 4th digit, and if the 5th digit is greater than or equal to 5, then the 4th digit will be rounding up.

    a.   Shooter's correct class and average shall be posted on his/her shoot entry form.

    b.   Classification in each gauge gun is independent and shall be treated without regard to classification in any other gauge.

2.   Individual Classification

CLASSIFICATION TABLES FOR OPEN INDIVIDUAL CLASSES

12 GAUGE	20 GAUGE	28 GAUGE
Class/Average	Class/Average	Class/Average
AAA/98.50 and over	AAA/98.00 and over	AAA/97.50 and over
AA/97.50 to 98.49	AA/97.00 to 97.99	AA/96.50 to 97.49
A/96.00 to 97.49	A/94.50 to 96.99	A/94.00 to 96.49
B/93.50 to 95.99	B/91.00 to 94.49	B/90.50 to 93.99
C/90.00 to 93.49	C/85.50 to 90.99	C/85.50 to 90.49
D/85.50 to 89.99	D/Under 85.50	D/Under 85.50
E Under 85.50		

.410 BORE	DOUBLES
Class/Average	Class/Average/Doubles
AAA/96.00 and over	AAA 97.00 and over
AA/94.70 to 95.99	AA/95.00 to 96.99
A/91.00 to 94.69	A/91.00 to 94.99
B/86.00 to 90.99	B/85.00 to 90.99
C/80.00 to 85.99	C/80.00 to 84.99
D/Under 80.00	D/Under 80.00

3.   Compulsory Classes

Only Classes AA, A, B, C and D (and E in 12 Gauge) shall be compulsory.

    a.   Class AAA shall be optional and when AAA is not offered Class AA shall include all shooters who would be in Class AAA if it were offered.

    b.   Class AAA is optional, however, it should be considered for use in any event where the number of entries exceeds 100, or where the number of entries eligible for AAA justifies doing so.

    c.   It shall be the sole responsibility of shoot management to determine whether Class AAA shall be offered and its decision shall be published in the shoot program or posted before the shoot.

4.   High Overall /High All Around

Unless otherwise published in the program or posted at the shoot, a shooter's HOA /HAA class will be based on his/her 4 or 5-gun average using the NSSA HOA /HAA Classification Tables. In no case will shooters HOA /HAA class be any lower than his/her lowest gun class. For classified shooters who have voluntarily declared upward in class or on any gun, or all guns, to calculate a HOA /HAA class, use the bottom percentage of the class in each respective self-declared gun. For a non-classified shooter, not wanting to voluntarily declare AA, who wishes to shoot HOA HAA

event, use the highest percentage in B Class for any non-classified gun in calculating the shooter's HOA HAA, but in no case will the shooter's HOA/HAA be more than one class below his/her highest class in any one gun.

D.   TEAM AND OTHER CONCURRENT EVENT CLASSIFICATIONS

1.   Division of two-man team, five-man team, women, junior and other concurrent events into classes is NOT MANDATORY. In cases where shoot management should desire to establish classes in these events, they may do so. When such classes are established, they should be designated by NUMBER rather than by letter, i.e., Class 1 (or I) XX –and over, Class 2 (or II) under XX -.

2.   Classification for team events shall be combined average of team members' scores, carried to the fourth decimal place at their initial or last reclassification (i.e. - .9525). Standard rounding procedures will be used to calculate an individual's average. Calculate the average to 5 digits and rounding to the 4th digit, and if the 5th digit is greater than or equal to 5, then the 4th digit will be rounding up.

    a.   The average for a PREVIOUSLY CLASSIFIED shooter competing in a team or other concurrent event that has been divided into classes shall be his/her highest published average in the three years prior to the current year for the gauge entered.

    b.   The average for a NON-CLASSIFIED shooter competing in a team or other concurrent event shall be considered the highest percentage in B class of the gauge entered.

E.   RECLASSIFICATION LIMITATIONS

1.   DURING THE CURRENT YEAR A SHOOTER IS SUBJECT TO RECLASSIFICATION UPWARD ONLY WITH THE EXCEPTION OF AAA.

    a.   Reclassification DOWN will only be accomplished by NSSA headquarters at the beginning of the next skeet year; however,

    b.   Any shooter who believes he/she is entitled to compete in a lower class due to illness, accident, age, may appeal to the Classification Review Committee of NSSA after prior approval of his/her request by his/her state association. In the absence of a state association in the shooter's state, his/her appeal may be made directly to the Classification Review Committee.

2.   Each shooter classified at the beginning of the skeet year will shoot in that class or a higher class as deter-mined by average or as assigned by the Classification Review Committee.

3.   Reclassification in all cases shall be subject to the restriction and qualifications set out in this section and in the sections headed Classification , unless he/she voluntarily declared AAA, then downward classification into AA is not permitted.

4.   NSSA HOA/HAA CLASSIFICATION TABLES

4 Gun HOA	5 Gun HAA
AAA/97.50 & over	97.40 & over
AA/96.43 - 97.49	96.14 - 97.39
A/93.88 - 96.42	93.30 - 96.13
B/90.25 - 93.87	89.20 - 93.29
C/85.25 - 90.24	84.20 - 89.19
D/84.12 - 85.24	83.30 - 84.19
E/84.11 & under	83.30 & under

Shoot Management has the discretion to offer Class E HOA/HAA if necessary.

Use of these tables is not mandatory, however, if no other method for determining HOA/HAA is listed in the shoot program of prominently posted prior to beginning registration, the tables listed above will be used to determine HOA/HAA classification. It is important for clubs to remember that the method for determining HOA/HAA classification must be posted or published in the shoot program.

F.   ALTERNATE AWARD SYSTEM

Recommended for Small Shoots

This proposal represents an alternative method for small shoots to award tangible prizes (e.g. awards, trophies or added money). By cutting down the quantity, a club could increase the quality of awards and hopefully attract more shooters. Use of this system will not affect an individual's NSSA classification and shoot management MUST report the shooter's score as per NSSA rules and classification. Use of this system is only for that shoot and clubs who choose to use this system MUST print it in the shoot program and also post it at the registration table. The Alternate Award System may be used for any of the four guns or doubles. The shooter's average used to determine his/her group for that day is based on reclassification at the last regular string.

Example:

Upper Third	Group 1 - .9500 and over
Middle Third	Group 2 - .9000 to .9499
Lower Third	Group 3 - Under .9000

Other equal breakdowns are also permissible depending on the gauge being shot and size of the field. This system is for awards purpose only, used only for that day of shooting, and will not affect any part of a shooters regular classification.

SECTION VI – INTERNATIONAL SHOOTING

USA Shooting and the National Skeet Shooting Association (NSSA) have common goals concerning the support and growth of International Skeet. The major goal, after joint compliance with UIT rules and procedures, is one of congruent classification rules procedures. Unfortunately, the two organizations have not yet totally achieved that goal; Therefore, NSSA members will use the following rules for classification and record keeping in NSSA registered international skeet events.

A.   ELIGIBLE SHOOTERS

All competitors in NSSA registered International events must have a current NSSA membership.

B.   CLASSIFICATION PROCEDURES

The classification rules and procedures for participation in NSSA registered International events are exactly the same as those set out in Section V of this rule book.

C.   CLASSIFICATION TABLE FOR INTERNATIONAL EVENTS

Class	Averages
AA	92 and above
A	86 to 91.99
B	80 to 85.99
C	74 to 79.99
D	68 to 73.99
E	67.99 and below

D.   RECORDING SCORES

1.   Only those scores shot in NSSA registered International events are to be used for determination of a shooter's NSSA International classification.

    a.   These are the only scores that will be included in NSSA records and publications.

b. These scores will NOT be included in USA shooting records unless the tournament has also been registered with USA shooting.

2. It is the responsibility of all shooters entering NSSA/USA shooting registered events to determine their correct classification according to NSSA/USA shooting rules.

E. REPORTING SCORES

Clubs registering International events with NSSA are subject to all requirements of Rule II-H, including payment of the required Daily Fees (in U.S. funds) for each target shot in the tournament.

F. RECOGNITION AND AWARDS

1. Scores shot and awards won by NSSA members in USA shooting and other UIT approved competitions will be recognized by NSSA for the purpose of All American team selection, if in addition, the shooter has shot the NSSA standards of 1200 NSSA registered targets, provided such scores and awards can be substantiated by official records or published re-ports.
2. Candidates for All-American team selection must:
   a. Shoot at least 1200 International NSSA registered targets during the NSSA shooting year.
   b Concurrent categories in International shooting will follow the 12 gauge NSSA standard registered tar-gets subject to Rule II-I-1(a) page 24.

G. MODIFIED INTERNATIONAL - SEE "EVENT 6" SECTION VIII-E-2

SECTION VII - RULES OF CONDUCT

A. EACH MEMBER AND MEMBER CLUB WILL BE FURNISHED A COPY OF THE OFFICIAL NSSA RULES, WITH THE UNDERSTANDING THAT THE MEMBER AND MEMBER CLUB WILL READ AND UNDERSTAND EACH RULE. ALL MEMBERS AND MEMBER CLUBS ARE RESPONSIBLE TO KNOW THESE RULES AND ABIDE BY THEM, FOR THEIR OWN BENEFIT AND SAFETY AS WELL AS THAT OF OTHER SHOOTERS.
B. BY PAYING THE MEMBERSHIP FEE, ENTERING A COMPETITION OR HOLDING A COMPETITION, EVERY MEMBER AND MEMBER CLUB AGREES TO ABIDE BY THESE RULES AND TO ACCEPT ALL OFFICIAL DECISIONS OF THE NSSA INTERPRETING AND/OR APPLYING THESE RULES.
C. IT SHALL BE A VIOLATION OF THESE RULES TO:
   1. Exhibit unsportsmanlike conduct of any kind, including but not limited to: falsifying scores or classification, cheating, verbal abuse, physical abuse of any shooter, scorer, field judge, shoot official, or protest committee.
   2. Disobey the order of any scorer, field judge or shoot official.
   3. Violate any safety rules as set forth in Section III of these rules and regulations, or engage in any activity that is considered unsafe by the NSSA Executive Committee.
   4. Shoot at any place other than the designated station.
   5. Interfere with the shoot management's procedures in conducting the shoot.
   6. Violate any rule or regulation of a club or range.
   7. Exhibit any conduct that is deemed by the Executive Committee to be harmful to the NSSA, its membership, or the sport as a whole.
   8. Failure of shoot management to submit a written report to NSSA of written complaints received along with a report of action taken.
   9. Violate any other rule or regulation of the NSSA as set forth in any other section or paragraph of the NSSA's rules and regulations.

D. SUSPENSIONS, EXPULSIONS AND REINSTATEMENT
   1. The Executive Committee may at any time at its discretion suspend or expel any member or member club or discipline any member or member club for the violation of any NSSA rule or regulation.
   2. The procedure for suspension, expulsion or other disciplinary action is as follows:
   a. Any member, shooter, scorer, field judge, shoot official or owner or member of management of a club or range who witnesses a violation of any NSSA rule shall if warranted submit to the NSSA Director or Executive Director a written complaint within thirty (30) days of the alleged violation which shall include:
      1) the name of the alleged violator;
      2) the date and location of the alleged violation;
      3) a reasonably detailed description of the alleged violation;
      4) the names and addresses, if known, of any wit-nesses;
      5) the name, address, phone number and signature of the complainants(s).
   b. Upon receipt, the NSSA Director or Executive Director shall assign each complaint a complaint number consisting of the year of receipt and consecutive number of receipt, i.e. 01-01, 01-02, etc.
   c. The NSSA Director or Executive Director shall review the complaint within ten (10) days of receipt and determine if it meets the requirements set forth above. The NSSA Director or Executive Director has the discretion to consider and investigate or dismiss any complaint that does not meet the foregoing requirements. Any complaint may be resubmitted to the Executive Committee within ten (10) days of receipt of rejection.
   d. Within ten (10) days of receipt of a complaint the NSSA Director or Executive Director, or anyone acting pursuant to direction from the Director or Executive Director, shall serve written notice of the complaint and a copy of the complaint on the alleged violator, by certified mail, return receipt requested. The written notice shall instruct the alleged violator of his right to submit a written statement, which must be signed and should include the names, addresses and phone numbers of any witnesses not named in the complaint. Such written statement must be received by the NSSA Director or Executive Director within ten (10) days of the alleged violator's receipt of the notice and complaint. All statements received after such date shall not be considered.
   e. The NSSA Director or Executive Director, or someone acting pursuant to direction from the Director or Executive Director, shall thoroughly investigate the allegations of the complaint by attempting to obtain written statements from all known witnesses. All witness statements must be in writing and signed by the witness.
   f. After time for the alleged violator to respond expires, the NSSA Director or Executive Director shall review the complaint, the statement of the alleged violator, witness statements and any other relevant evidence. Upon such review, the NSSA Director or Executive Director shall recommend to the NSSA Executive Committee a specific disciplinary action. The recommendation shall include:
      1) all evidence that was considered, including the names of any witnesses who submitted statements;
      2) a determination of whether the alleged violation occurred; and
      3) the disciplinary action, if any, the NSSA Director or Executive Director recommends that the NSSA Executive Committee impose.
   g. The NSSA Director or Executive Director shall provide each member of the NSSA Executive Committee with a copy of the complaint, the statement of the alleged violator, copies of any witness statements and a copy of the recommendation.
   h. The NSSA Director or Executive Director shall schedule a conference call between the members of the NSSA Executive Committee wherein the NSSA Executive Committee shall review all information provided by the NSSA Director or Executive Director and issue a ruling on the matter

by majority vote. The NSSA Executive Committee's ruling shall include:
      1) the date of issuance;
      2) all evidence that was considered, including the names of any witnesses who submitted statements;
      3) a determination of whether the alleged violation occurred; and
      4) the disciplinary action, if any, imposed by the NSSA Executive Committee.

E. THE NSSA EXECUTIVE COMMITTEE SHALL HAVE THE DISCRETION TO SUSPEND OR EXPEL A MEMBER OR TO IMPOSE ANY OTHER DISCIPLINARY ACTION IT DEEMS APPROPRIATE. UPON ISSUANCE OF A RULING, THE NSSA DIRECTOR OR EXECUTIVE DIRECTOR SHALL SERVE THE RULING ON THE VIOLATOR BY CERTIFIED MAIL, RETURN RECEIPT REQUESTED. THE RULING SHALL BECOME EFFECTIVE ON THE DATE OF ISSUANCE AND CONTINUE UNTIL A HEARING, IF ANY, IS HELD.
F. THE VIOLATOR SHALL HAVE THE RIGHT TO APPEAL THE NSSA EXECUTIVE COMMITTEE'S RULING BY NOTIFYING THE NSSA EXECUTIVE COMMITTEE. SUCH NOTIFICATION OF APPEAL MUST BE IN WRITING AND MUST BE POST-MARKED NO LATER THAN THIRTY (30) DAYS FROM THE DATE THE RULING WAS ISSUED.
   1. Upon receipt of the notification of appeal the NSSA Executive Committee shall hold a hearing on the matter, which will take place at the next regularly scheduled quarterly meeting of the NSSA Executive Committee.
   2. At the hearing, the violator shall have the right to be present, the right to bring counsel, the right to testify and the right to present any evidence he so chooses. No record or transcript of the hearing will be made or allowed.
   3. The NSSA Executive Committee shall review the complaint, the written statement of the violator, and any other evidence it deems appropriate. The NSSA Executive Committee may allow any and all witnesses to testify by telephone or in person. The Executive Committee may make inquiries of the witnesses but no other persons may do so.
   4. At the conclusion of such hearing, the NSSA Executive Committee shall have the authority to affirm, reverse or modify the disciplinary action imposed previously by majority vote.

G. BY PAYING THE MEMBERSHIP FEE, ENTERING A COMPETITION OR HOLDING A COMPETITION, EVERY MEMBER AND MEMBER CLUB AGREES TO ABIDE BY ANY DECISION OF THE NSSA EXECUTIVE COMMITTEE AND FURTHER AGREES AND RECOGNIZES THAT AS A VOLUNTARY AMATEUR ASSOCIATION, THE NSSA HAS THE RIGHT TO IMPOSE, INTERPRET AND ENFORCE ITS RULES AND REGULATIONS AND THAT ALL DECISION BY THE NSSA EXECUTIVE COMMITTEE FOLLOWING A HEARING ARE FINAL.

SECTION VIII - EVENT 6

In an effort to promote and introduce shooters to skeet shooting without causing additional expense to gun clubs "Event 6" can be used to host a variety of different skeet shooting matches. These matches can be tailored to members and non-members wants and desires. Event 6 is designed to put the fun back in local skeet shoots. Anyone can shoot and be eligible for all awards. You don't have to be a member of the NSSA to shoot, and the awards are based on a class system similar to Lewis Class, so anyone can win. Awards are provided to clubs by NSSA on a cost basis. The targets are registered for NSSA members and count toward lifetime targets only. Results of Event 6 shoots will be published in the Skeet Shooting Review.

A. RULES:
1. Any gun or gauge may be used.
2. Pulling/Scoring/Refereeing and following NSSA rules can be the responsibility of the squad.
3. All targets will be registered separately and will only be counted towards lifetime-registered targets.
4. Anyone and everyone can shoot and be eligible for all awards.
5. All NSSA Safety Rules apply.
6. It is permissible to squad Event 6 registered with regular registered shooters.

B. SHOOT APPLICATIONS:
1. Handle the same as in Rule II-A-7a through b2). Designate shoot as an Event 6 shoot. This will provide for standardization and effective management of shoot and financial reports.
2. When application is received and a shoot number is assigned applicable shoot, financial report forms and award order forms will be forwarded to clubs.

C. FEES:
Standard NSSA and State fees apply for both NSSA members and non-members. Fees for non-members go for daily membership to be eligible for prizes.

D. SHOOT REPORT:
1. Report all NSSA member scores by name and NSSA member number this will insure targets are added to lifetime target totals.
2. Report winners list. This list includes NSSA members and non-members as applicable. This list will be published in the Skeet Shooting Review.

E. TYPES OF "EVENT – 6" MATCHES:
1. Regular Skeet and Doubles: It is permissible to squad Event 6 registered with regular registered shooters.
2. NSSA Modified International: The same format used by the UIT, USA Shooting and NSSA will apply with the following exceptions:
   a. Targets can be thrown at standard NSSA distances requiring no modification of equipment.
   b. Ammunition used is of standard NSSA specifications and any gauge can be used.
   c. No automatic timers are required. The puller can control target release time.
   d. Target requirements can be standard NSSA specified. International targets are not required.
3. NSSA Vintage Skeet: The same format used in standard NSSA skeet with the following possible exceptions:
   a. Only pump/slide action or side-by-side guns are to be used.
   b. After mounting the gun the stock can be dropped slightly before calling for the target.

F. DETERMINING AWARDS: BOTH NSSA AND DAILY MEMBERS ARE ELIGIBLE TO WIN.
1. Your program (or poster) has promised 1 award every 6 entries. You have 22 entries divided by 6 = 3.66 or 4 awards.
2. Example of scores:
   98   Winner
   97
   95

95
94*
94*   *Tied for Winner
94*
93
92
92
92
91**   **Tied for Winner
91*
91*
90
90
89
88*** ***Tied for Winner
88***
88***
88***
82

Score below line is winner; however, if more than one score exists either above or below the line there is a tie. Ties may be divided by shoot-off or combined total of either long runs (forward and backward) or coin flip/draw card or any other method you may choose. Club must decide how to determine winners when ties exist and post this information before shoot starts!

SECTION IX - GUIDELINES FOR PROTESTS

In order that protests may be more uniformly and fairly handled, the protesting shooter and the protest committee* should observe the following guidelines.

A.   RECORD THE EXACT TIME THAT:
1.   The incident occurred.
2.   A verbal protest was made to the field referee (if at all).
3.   A verbal protest was made to the chief referee (if at all).
4.   The chief referee ruled on the protest (if at all).
5.   The Protest Committee's decision was made known to the protesting shooter.

B.   DETERMINE AND RECORD:
1.   If there was a chief referee, was the complaint brought to his/her attention by the protesting shooter?
2.   Was the written protest tendered to Shoot Management within 12 hours of the protested incident?
3.   Is the shooter not protesting a referee's decision of fact?
4.   Is the shooter protesting: Improper application of the NSSA rules, or the conditions under which another shooter has been allowed to shoot or an error in scorekeeping?

C.   IF B-1 THROUGH B-4 ABOVE CAN ALL BE ANSWERED YES, THE PROTEST COMMITTEE SHOULD THEN DECIDE WHETHER TO GRANT OR DENY THE PROTEST. IF THE ANSWER TO ANY OF THE QUESTIONS B-1 THROUGH B-4 ABOVE IS NO THE PROTEST IS INVALID.

D.   ANY APPEAL TO THE NSSA OF THE PROTEST COMMITTEE'S DECISION SHOULD INCLUDE:
1.   The facts outlined above.
2.   A copy of the written protest.
3.   A copy of the Protest Committee's decision.

E.   SHOOT MANAGEMENT SHOULD BE PREPARED TO PROVIDE THE INFORMATION IN D-1 THROUGH D-3 ABOVE TO THE NSSA UPON REQUEST.

*"PROTEST COMMITTEE" SHALL BE DEFINED AS: SHOOT MANAGEMENT, OR A JUDGE APPOINTED BY SHOOT MANAGEMENT, OR A PANEL OF JUDGES APPOINTED BY SHOOT MANAGEMENT.

CLAY RULES

ORGANIZATION OF THE NATIONAL SPORTING CLAYS ASSOCIATION

The National Sporting Clays Association (NSCA) was formed in April of 1989, as a division of the National Skeet Shooting Association (NSSA), to promote sporting clays in the United States and other countries. The following is an informative summary of the organization of the NSCA, important official policies and rules that govern the NSCA, the shooting of registered targets, the conduct of shooters and the duties of shoot management. The NSCA has the responsibility for the formulation, regulation and enforcement of these rules. For any rules or policies not contained in this book, or in the official minutes of the NSCA Advisory Council meetings, refer to the bylaws of the NSSA. The NSCA reserves the right to make alterations in, or amendments to, these rules and policies at any time, when it deems it to be in the best interest of the National Sporting Clays Association and it's members.

I. GENERAL INFORMATION

A. PURPOSE OF NSCA

The purpose of the National Sporting Clays Association is to promote and govern the sport of sporting clays throughout the United States and other countries, in a way which is beneficial to all who enjoy and participate in the game. The NSCA is dedicated to the development of the sport at all levels of participation. NSCA vows to create an atmosphere of healthy and safe competition and meaningful fellowship within its membership.

B. MEMBERSHIP

1. Individual

a. Annual membership dues for an individual are $40 and include a copy of the official magazine, Sporting Clays Magazine, beginning with the first issue available for mailing after dues received at headquarters. A $30 Associate membership is available to dependents of members but does not include magazine.

b. Six Year membership dues for an individual are $200 and include a copy of the official magazine, Sporting Clays Magazine, beginning with the first issue available for mailing after dues are received at headquarters. A Six Year Associate Membership is available to dependents of members for $150 but does not include the magazine.

c. Life membership for an individual is $500.00 and a Husband & Wife Life membership is $750.00.

d. The membership and shooting year begins on October 1 and ends on September 30 of the following year.

e. Annual membership may be applied for by filling out an application provided at an NSCA club/range or by contacting NSCA Headquarters for an application.

2. Clubs and Ranges

a. Annual membership dues for a club or range are $100.00 a year.

b. The membership and shooting year begins on October 1 and ends September 30 of the following year.

c. Annual Club/Range membership may be applied for by filling out an application provided by the NSCA.

3. Rules of Conduct

a. Each member and club will be furnished a copy of the Official NSCA rules, with the understanding that the member / member club will read and understand each rule. All members and member clubs are responsible to know these rules and abide by them, for their own benefit and safety as well as that of other shooters.

b. By paying the membership fee, entering a competition or holding a competition, every member and member club agrees to abide by these rules and to accept all official decisions of the NSCA in interpreting and/or applying these rules.

c. It shall be a violation of these rules to:

1. Exhibit unsportsmanlike conduct of any kind, including but not limited to, falsifying scores or classification, cheating, swearing, verbal or physical abuse of any shooter, scorer, field judge, shoot official, or protest committee.

2. Disobey the order of any scorer, field judge or shoot official.

3. Violate any safety rules as set forth in Section II of these rules and regulations, or engage in any activity that is considered unsafe by the NSCA Executive Council.

4. Shoot at any place other than the designated station.

5. Interfere with the shoot management's procedures in conducting the shoot.

6. Violate any rule or regulation of a club or range.

7. Exhibit any conduct that is harmful to the NSCA, its membership, or the sport as a whole.

8. Failure to submit a written complaint to shoot management after witnessing the violation of one of the NSCA's rules or regulations.

9. Failure of shoot management to submit a written report to NSCA of written complaints received along with a report of action taken.

10. Violate any other rule or regulation of the NSCA as set forth in any other section or paragraph of the NSCA's rules and regulations.

4. Suspensions, Expulsions and Reinstatement

a. The Executive Council may, at any time at its discretion, suspend , expel, or discipline any member or member club for the violation of any NSCA rule or regulation.

b. The procedure for suspension, expulsion or other disciplinary action is as follows:

1. Any member, shooter, scorer, field judge, shoot official or owner or member of management of a club or range who witnesses a violation of any NSCA rule shall submit to the NSCA Director or Executive Director a written complaint within thirty (30) days of the alleged violation which shall include:

    i. the name of the alleged violator;

    ii. the date and location of the alleged violation;

    iii. a reasonably detailed description of the alleged violation;

    iv. the names and addresses, if known, of all witnesses;

    v. the name, address, phone number and signature of the complainant(s).

2. Upon receipt, the NSCA Director or Executive Director shall assign each complaint a complaint number consisting of the year of the receipt and consecutive number of receipt, i.e. 01-01, 01-02, etc.

3. The NSCA Director or Executive Director shall review the complaint and determine if it meets the requirements set forth above. Any complaint may be resubmitted so long as it is received within the requisite time period, described above. The NSCA Director or Executive Director has the discretion to consider and investigate or dismiss any complaint that does not meet the foregoing requirements.

4. Within ten (10) days of receipt of a complaint the NSCA Director or Executive Director, or anyone acting pursuant to direction from the Director or Executive Director, shall serve written notice of the complaint and a copy of the complaint on the alleged violator, by certified mail, return receipt requested. The written notice shall instruct the alleged violator of his right to submit a written statement, which must be signed and should include the names, addresses and phone numbers of any witnesses not named in the complaint. Such written statement must be received by the NSCA Director or Executive Director within ten (10) days of the alleged violator's receipt of the notice and complaint. All statements received after such date shall not be considered.

5. The NSCA Director or Executive Director, or some-one acting pursuant to direction from the Director or Executive Director, shall thoroughly investigate the allegations of the complaint by attempting to obtain written statements from all known witnesses. All witness statements must be in writing and signed by the witness.

6. After time for the alleged violator to respond expires, the NSCA Director or Executive Director shall review the complaint, the statement of the alleged violator, witness statements and any other relevant evidence. Upon such review, the NSCA Director or Executive Director shall recommend to the NSCA Executive Council a specific disciplinary action. The recommendation shall include:

    i. all evidence that was considered, including the names of any witnesses who submitted statements;

    ii. a determination of whether the alleged violation occurred; and

    iii. the disciplinary action, if any, the NSCA Director or Executive Director recommends that the NSCA Executive Council impose.

7. The NSCA Director or Executive Director shall provide each member of the NSCA Executive Council with a copy of the complaint, the statement of the alleged violator, copies of any witness statements and a copy of the recommendation.

8. The NSCA Director or Executive Director shall schedule a conference call between the members of the NSCA Executive Council wherein the NSCA Executive Council shall review all information provided by the NSCA Director or Executive Director and issue a ruling on the matter by majority vote. The NSCA Executive Council's ruling shall include:

    i. the date of issuance;

    ii. all evidence that was considered, including the names of any witnesses who submitted statements;

    iii. a determination of whether the alleged violation occurred; and

    iv. the disciplinary action, if any, imposed by the NSCA Executive Council. The NSCA Executive Council shall have the discretion to suspend or expel a member or to impose any other disciplinary action it deems appropriate.

9. Upon issuance of a ruling, the NSCA Director or Executive Director shall serve the ruling on the violator by certified mail, return receipt requested. The ruling shall become effective on the date of issuance and continue until a hearing, if any, is held.

c. The violator shall have the right to appeal the NSCA Executive Council's ruling by notifying the NSCA Executive Council. Such notification of appeal must be in writing and must be post-marked no later than twenty (20) days from the date the ruling was issued.

1. Upon receipt of the notification of appeal, the NSCA Executive Council shall hold a hearing on the matter, which will take place at the next regularly scheduled quarterly meeting of the NSCA Executive Council.

2. At the hearing, the violator shall have the right to be present, the right to bring counsel, the right to testify and the right to present any evidence he so chooses. The violator does not have the right to cross-examine witnesses. The violator does not have the right to make a record and no transcript of the hearing will be made or allowed.

3. The NSCA Executive Council shall review the complaint, the written statement of the violator, and any other evidence it deems appropriate. The NSCA Executive Council may allow any and all witnesses to testify by telephone or in person.

4. At the conclusion of such hearing, the NSCA Executive Council shall have the authority to affirm, reverse or modify the disciplinary action imposed previously by majority vote. By paying the membership fee, entering a competition or holding a competition, every member and member club agrees to abide by any decision of the NSCA Executive Council and further agrees and recognizes that as a voluntary amateur association, the NSCA has the right to impose, interpret and enforce its rules and regulations and that all decisions by the NSCA Executive Council following a hearing are final.

C. STRUCTURE

1. Advisory Council

The Advisory Council is comprised of NSCA members exhibiting the highest devotion to the sport, the members, and the Association. There are 45 available positions, divided equally between representatives of Industry, Range Owners, and Shooters. The primary function of the Advisory Council is to promote and guide the Association.

    a. Elections are held at the Annual Advisory Council meeting for terms to begin at the end of the meeting. Candidates must be present at this meeting in order to be considered for a council position and must receive a majority of votes in order to be elected.

    b. Their term the first time elected is one year. For second and subsequent elections the term is two years. Term of office is from Annual Meeting to Annual Meeting.

    c. An Advisory Council member must attend the annual meeting (date determined by Executive Council) each year and either the U.S. Open or the National Championship
meeting or lose his/her position on the Advisory Council.

    d. Advisory Council members are required to shoot the following minimums each year: Range Owners–500, Shooters–1,000. The Advisory Council will continue their present duties and responsibilities until such time as a new form of electing the Association management has been decided on. The NSCA Advisory Council will form a committee made up of Advisory Council members from all three categories, National Delegates and State Associations to make recommendations on how the NSCA can go forward
with electing members to manage our Association.

2. Executive Council

The Executive Council is elected from and comprised of 6 members of the Advisory Council, 2 representing Industry, 2 representing Range Owners, and 2 representing Shooters for a two year term. These 6 members elected to the Executive Council must have served a minimum of three (3) cumulative years on the Advisory Council. The Executive Council election will always follow the annual meeting's Advisory Council election. The primary function of the Executive Council is to promote and guide the Advisory Council and act on behalf of the Advisory Council on matters needing immediate action.

3. National Delegate

National Delegates shall consist of members in good standing to hold office as follows: National Delegates shall be bona fide residents of and be elected from the various states of the United States and from the provinces, territories or similar political subdivisions recognized by the Association in ratio of one National Delegate for a member population of 25 to 150; two National Delegates for a member population of 151 to 300; three National Delegates for a member population of 301 to 500; four National Delegates for a member population of 501 to 750; and five National Delegates for a member population over 750.

    a. National Delegates must be nominated by five (5) current NSCA members in their state and receive a minimum of five (5) votes from the state membership in order for the election to be valid. Write-in candidates are allowed but must receive five votes to be elected.

    b. The term of office for all National Delegates shall be two (2) years and shall begin October 1 of the year elected and end September 30 two (2) years later.

    c. All changes made in rules, regulations, classification and other issues will be decided by the National Delegates. If no state association exists, their responsibilities would also include the approval of NSCA registered shoot dates and the location of the state shoot within that state; however, their primary duties will be on a national level governing our sport and the Association.

    d. In the event that a National Delegate position is vacated before the end of the Delegate's term, the State Association (if one exists) will appoint a person to fill that position for the remainder of the current term. If no State Association exists, the Zone Delegate will make the appointment.

4. State Association

An association, recognized by the NSCA, comprised of NSCA members and NSCA member clubs within each individual state. The primary function of the State Association is to work with the National Delegate(s) and support the NSCA member clubs and NSCA members of their state through individual state bylaws, within the rules and parameters of the NSCA. Recognized NSCA State Associations will be responsible for the approval of shoot dates within the state.

5. Zones / Zone Delegates

Zones are groupings of states in a particular geographic area. There are seven zones. The Zone Map is located on [a later page].

    a. One Zone Delegate is elected from each of the seven zones by vote of the National Delegates in that Zone. Candidates for Zone Delegate must be currently elected National Delegates.

    b. The Zone Delegate's duties and responsibilities are set forth in the NSCA Delegates Manual. The primary responsibility of the Zone Delegate is to organize and oversee the selection of the Zone Shoot host range.

II. SAFETY

A. SAFETY IS EVERYONE'S RESPONSIBILITY

1. It is everyone's responsibility to report any unsafe shooting condition or action immediately to Shoot Officials.

2. Mandatory Eye and Ear Protection—All persons, spectators, shooters, field judges, and trap personnel, must wear eye and ear protection on the course at a tournament sanctioned by NSCA.

3. Trap Personnel Protection—All trap personnel in front of the line of fire must be out of sight with screen protection able to withstand the charge of shot at the given distance.

4. All shooting stations must require the shooter (except wheelchair shooters) to engage all targets from the standing position.

5. Shooters must have the permission of a Field Judge to test fire any gun. Guns will be discharged only in attempt at competition targets.

6. The first person on every squad shall be allowed to view a good presentation of targets from within the shoot station. This person is the only person permitted to mount their unloaded gun and track the targets being viewed.

7. It is the sole responsibility of the shooter to begin any event, station, and/or field with sufficient equipment, including safety equipment and ammunition. Failure to do so, which, in the opinion of the Field Judge will delay the shoot, will result in the loss of all targets as required to keep the shoot moving. Make-up targets will be provided only at the discretion of the Shoot Officials.

8. The shooting stations must be positioned in such a way that all shooters, trappers, and spectators are protected from shot/target fall. Additionally, the shooting stations must be
designed to restrict dangerous gun hold/movement.

9. Target Drop Zones must be clear of ALL shooters and spectators.

10. Course Design Safety is the sole responsibility of the Range Owner/Shoot Officials.

11. The shooter must fire with his/her gun shouldered for all targets.

12. The use of any drug, legal or illegal and including alcohol, prior to or during an NSCA event by a registered competitor is prohibited with the exception of prescription
medicine which does not impair a shooters ability to perform safely.

13. Failure to comply with the NSCA Safety Rules may subject the Range Owner/Shoot Officials / Competitor to possible suspension.

14. Shotgun shooting safety is everyone's responsibility.

III. CLASSIFICATION

A. CLASSIFICATION SYSTEM

A shooter's classification carries over from one shooting year to the next. All new shooters will be assigned a class. During the current year, a shooter is subject to reclassify UPWARDS ONLY (with the exception of appeals). A classification card will be provided to all shooters. To maintain the integrity of the classification system, all NSCA members shooting on the course where a NSCA Registered Event is taking place must register their targets.

1. Determining Class

    a. There are seven (7) classes a shooter can classify into: Master-AA-A-B-C-D-E. All registered events using the NSCA Classification system will offer all classes (including Master).

    b. Non-Classified and New Members

      1. A shooter who has never shot any registered clay targets will be assigned Class "D".

      2. A shooter who has shot registered targets with any clay target organization other than a Sporting Clays Association (i.e., NSSA, ATA, NRA, International skeet or trap) will be assigned into Class "B" or one class lower than his/her highest class attained in that clay target organization, whichever is greater. Shooters, who are classed higher than "B", may use the "KNOWN ABILITY" appeal process should they think their classification is incorrect. (See III-A-6 Appeals.)

      3. A shooter from another sporting clays organization, (i.e., USSCA/SCA, CPSA, F.I.T.A.S.C., Non-Registered Sporting Clay Events) will shoot their earned class or higher.

      4. A shooter may be classified based on his/her "known ability". (See III-A-3 Reclassification/Known Ability.)

2. Moving up in Class

    a. Shooters earn their way out of class by shooting the high score(s) or tying for the high score(s) in class.

      1. NSCA Nationals and U.S. Open (main event only):
The top 5 scores and all ties in each class receive 4 punches; the sixth and seventh highest scores and all ties in each class receive 3 punches; the eighth and ninth highest scores and all ties in each class receive 2 punches; the tenth highest score and all ties in each class receive 1 punch.

      2. In all events using the NSCA classification system, except the NSCA Nationals and U.S. Open main events, shooters will earn punches based on the number of entries in their respective class. Punches are awarded as follows:

Number of entries in class	Punches earned
0–4	No punch
5–9	One (1) punch for high score and all ties
10–14	Two (2) punches for high score and all ties
15-29	Four (4) punches for high score and all ties.
	Two (2) punches for second Highest score in all ties.
	One (1) punch for third Highest score and all ties.
30-44	Four (4) punches for high score and all ties.
	Four (4) punches for second highest score and ties.
	Two (2) punches for third highest score and ties.
	One (1) punch for fourth highest score and all ties.
45+	Four (4) punches to first, second, and third highest scores and all ties.
	Three (3) punches fourth highest score and all ties.
	Two (2) punches for fifth highest score and all ties.
	One (1) punch for sixth highest score and all ties.

    b. It is the shooter's responsibility to determine these punches and move up one class after reaching the following number of punches:

      E Class to D Class 4 punches
      D Class to C Class 4 punches
      C Class to B Class 6 punches
      B Class to A Class 8 punches
      A Class to AA Class 10 punches
      AA Class to Master Class 16 punches

Note: Punches must be earned in Shooter's current class in order for them to be used in moving up in class. A person earning more than the necessary punches to move up in class enters the new class with no punches.

    c. In events of 100+ entries, it is the responsibility of shoot management to notify all shooters of their move up in class or punches received. The shooter is also equally responsible to shoot in his/her proper class and to inquire and inform shoot management of any move up at the next tournament entered.

    d. Upon entering a shoot with multiple events, a person will remain in the class he/she started in for all events held, and any punches he/she accrues will be awarded at the conclusion of all of the events at that shoot. A shooter cannot be moved up more than one class at the conclusion of the registered events based on punches; however, a shooter can be moved up more than one class based on "KNOWN ABILITY."

    e. All punches, except Lewis Class, earned in a shooter's current class in 2003 will carry over into 2004. Carry over punches are for the target year just ended and the current year. Punches from prior target years (2002 and before) will not carry over.

    f. Registered Lewis Class events—All NSCA members must register their targets. No shooter will be moved out of class for having the high score at a registered Lewis Class event.

    g. All registered events of 50 targets or more, except Lewis Class Events (see III-A-2-g above), are subject to receive punches based on the number of participants and the
number of shooters in class if the NSCA classification system is used. Note: This will include sub-gauge events where the NSCA classification system is used. (See III-A-2 Moving Up In Class)

    h. The NSCA National Championship, U.S. Open, Zone Shoot, and State Shoot must use the NSCA Classification system. NSCA strongly suggests that major shoots utilize the NSCA Classification system. (See IV-B-2 Major Shoot.)

3. Reclassification / Known Ability

    a. A shooter may be reclassified based on their "KNOWN ABILITY."

    b. An NSCA club, State Association, National Delegate, member (shooter) or member of the Advisory Council has the right to request a "known ability" review of a shooter's record if it appears that he/she is competing in a class other than his/her true level of ability. This request must be in writing. Upon review by the appropriate NSCA Committee, the shooter may be assigned a different class.

    c. A shooter reclassified by NSCA will receive a new class card with the notice of the change from NSCA. The different class will become effective with the receipt of the class card. Should the shooter wish to appeal this different class they must do so within 30 days from receipt of the NSCA notice. (See III-A-6 Appeals.)

    d. A shooter may voluntarily declare into a class higher than assigned; however, the shooter must stay in that class or higher for the entire year. This applies to all classes except for Master, which must be earned and not declared.

When the shooter so elects, they must (at a registered shoot) have their classification card marked before competing in the event in the class for which they are declaring. Their card shall be marked with the new classification by self-declaration in the class where they declared, and be entered on the Official Entry Form with notation "self-declared".

e. A shooter may also be reclassified to a higher class by Shoot Officials based on their "known ability". This reclassification will be for that event only and shooter will return to his/her original class, with one exception. If the shooter wins in the class they are placed in based on "known ability", depending on the shoot size (See III-A-2 Moving up in Class), they would then receive punches or be moved to the next higher class (one above

the "known ability" class) for the remainder of the year.

f. Any person who has experienced a permanent medical impairment may request a review on their classification during the shooting year.

4. Classification Review

a. A shooter's classification may be reviewed after each 1,000 registered targets. Shooters must request such a review in writing. The 1,000 target review may be used

to move a shooter down in class. An annual review will be done on each NSCA member with a minimum of 300 registered competition targets shot in their current class in the current shooting year.

b. A shooter who is assigned to a lower class may reject the class if the shooter wishes to remain in a higher class. To reject the assigned class, the shooter must sign the "refusal form" which will be at the bottom of the classification card and return it to NSCA Headquarters.

5. Shooter's Responsibility

a. The shooter is responsible for presenting his/her classification card and/or additional documentation upon entry at any registered shoot and entering into the proper class. The classification card is intended for the purpose of providing Shoot Officials with up-to-date information regarding classification of each shooter entering a registered event.

b. The shooter is responsible for entering their scores with the date and score shot on the back of their classification card or, if more space is needed, on a supplemental record form, and to make certain that all placements and punches are properly recorded on their classification card at the conclusion of each NSCA registered tournament. Failure to accurately record scores and punches may lead to suspension from the NSCA.

c. A shooter who enters or allows themselves to be entered into a class lower than the one in which their record places them, unless the error is corrected prior to a specific time posted by shoot management, a time announced in the shoot program, completion of shoot-offs, and/or the awarding of trophies and/or monies, shall be subject to the following:

1. Forfeit all rights to all winnings he/she would have earned shooting in his/her proper class.

2. For the first offense, be disqualified and forfeit all winnings earned while shooting in the wrong class. (see also IV-S-3) The shooter must return all winnings within 15 days after notification by the host club, National Delegates, State Association or NSCA Head-quarters requesting the winnings be returned. Failure to return the winnings within the 15 day period shall subject the shooter to suspension and being PERMANENTLY barred from registered competition.

3. In the case of a second or subsequent offense of shooting in a lower class, the shooter will forfeit all winnings and also be barred from registered competition for a minimum of one year and / or suspended from NSCA.

6. Appeals

a. The shooter's appeal must be in writing and state specific reasons why they think they should not be moved up in class. Pending a determination of the appeal all shoots entered by the shooter must be entered at the new higher class.

b. The NSCA Classification Committee has 30 days from the receipt of the appeal to respond. At the Committee's option, additional information may be requested from the Zone Coordinator, National Delegate(s), and/or State Association (if one exists) for additional input.

IV. RULES & REGULATIONS FOR REGISTERED TOURNAMENTS

A. PARTICIPATION

1. Club

a. Eligibility and Responsibility

1. Only clubs affiliated with NSCA with current fees paid and in good standing with NSCA as well as their State Association (if one exists) shall be eligible to conduct registered shoots. Evidence of club's status in this regard must be displayed in the form of an official NSCA membership certificate for the appropriate year.

2. In applying for and holding a registered shoot it shall be deemed the responsibility of club owners, management, and Shoot Officials to ensure that the shoot is conducted within NSCA official rules and safety regulations.

3. The club sponsoring a registered shoot shall check the NSCA membership card and classification card of each shooter before accepting his/her entry, and shall be responsible for the annual dues if they allow a participant to shoot when said participant's membership in NSCA has expired.

4. Shoot management may be billed by NSCA in all cases where expired members are allowed to shoot. Management may seek reimbursement from said shooters, but must first abide by IV-A-1-a-3 above.

5. Any club sponsoring a registered shoot accepts the responsibility for any clerical errors made through-out the shoot and shall correct those errors.

b. Applying for a Registered Shoot Date

1. The club should complete an NSCA registered shoot application and forward to the State Association (if one exists) or the National Delegate(s) for signature of approval at the state level.

2. The signed application should be forwarded immediately to the NSCA office for final approval. Shoot applications must be postmarked or received by NSCA at least 10 days

prior to the shoot date.

3. A notice of the approval will be forwarded by NSCA to the club at the address on file.

4. Shoot dates may not be altered without prior approval at the state level and notification to headquarters.

2. Individual

a. Only members who have paid their annual dues and are in good standing with NSCA as well as their State Association (if one exists) may participate in registered NSCA shoots. It is the shooter's responsibility to provide their current year classification card to Shoot Officials when entering a registered shoot. This ensures that name, address, and membership number are properly recorded so that errors in records and scores can be prevented.

b. It shall be the sole responsibility of the shooter, upon entering the shoot, to see that they are entered into all the events desired on the official NSCA cashier sheet/entry form. Once entered, clerical errors are the responsibility of shoot management.

c. Residency Requirements

1. An individual must be a bona fide resident (permanent abode) of a state to be eligible for state championships or to shoot as a state team member, and must be a bona fide resident of a state within the zone to be eligible for zone championships or to shoot as a zone team member.

a. Persons with residence in more than one state must declare their eligibility by writing their home state on the face of the current year membership card. Servicemen, by the same act, may choose their home state or place in which they are permanently assigned

for duty, and declare the state on the current year membership card.

b. Persons who change their official abode shall become immediately eligible to shoot as an individual in the state or zone shoot of their new permanent address. They should contact NSCA for a new membership card reflecting change of address and present same before entering shoot.

c. No person shall be eligible for more than one closed state or zone competition during the NSCA shooting year.

B. TYPES OF TOURNAMENTS

Registered Shoot

A SHOOT WHERE TARGETS SHOT BY NSCA MEMBERS MUST BE REGISTERED. Non-members may participate, but in a separate category. Any non-member participating in a registered event in a separate category shall not be eligible for any NSCA awards or monies. If offered by shoot management, the separate category may have its own separate awards and/or monies. Shoot date(s) must be submitted to the appropriate State Association (if one exists) or the National Delegate for signature of approval at state level, who will then submit to NSCA Headquarters for final approval.

1. Registered Small Gauge Events

Small Gauge Events may be registered, punches will be awarded, and combined with punches earned in 12 gauge events for classification purposes. Small Gauges are .410, 28 and 20. The member's 12 Gauge classification will be used for all Small Gauge Event classes.

2. Major Shoot

A registered shoot, where by projection or past experience, 100 or more shooters are expected to attend. NSCA strongly suggests that these shoots utilize the NSCA Classification system.

3. State Shoot

An annual shoot held within each state, the location and dates of which are decided by the following process: Interested clubs (within the state) who are in good standing with the NSCA and the State Association (if one exists), or the National Delegate(s).

a. The State Association and/or National Delegate(s) should then take a vote of (1) State Association members (if one exists) or (2) All NSCA clubs in good standing for a decision.

b. If the second method is used and the vote results in a tie, the National Delegate(s) shall cast a vote for the club they think should be awarded the tournament. This vote should break the tie; however, if there is still a tie, the Zone Delegate will be contacted. The Zone Delegate will in turn consult with the National Delegates Committee Chairman and, after discussing the situation, the Zone Delegate will cast a tie-breaking vote for the club they feel should host the state tournament

c. All State Shoots must utilize the NSCA Classification system and it is strongly recommended that the shoot be held before July 31 of each year.

d. To be eligible for class prizes, monies, and/or awards at State Shoots, a shooter must have shot a minimum of 300 registered targets in the current year, prior to the shoot. If a shooter does not have a minimum of 300 targets, he/she may shoot the event and win prizes, monies, and/or awards in a penalty class, one class above his/her current class.

e. Following the State Shoot all shooters who were placed in a penalty class as a result of their failure to meet the 300 registered target requirement, will return to their original class, with one exception. If the shooter wins the penalty class, depending on the shoot size (See III-A-2 Moving up in Class), they would then receive punches or be moved to the next higher class (one above the penalty class) for the remainder of the year.

4. Zone Shoot

One annual shoot held within each zone, the location and dates of which are decided as follows: NSCA clubs in good standing send a bid to either their State Association (if one exits) or National Delegate who will then submit the bid to the Zone Delegate. Zone Delegates then send a ballot to all National Delegates within the zone for a vote.

a. Zone Shoots must be conducted utilizing the NSCA Classification system and it is strongly suggested that the shoot be held before August 31 of each year. The date and location for each Zone Championship is to be established before the end of the preceding Zone Championship.

b. To be eligible for class prizes, monies, and/or awards at Zone Shoots, a shooter must have shot a minimum of 300 registered targets in the current year, prior to the shoot. If a shooter does not have a minimum of 300 targets, he/she may shoot the event and win prizes, monies, and/or awards in a penalty class, one class above his/her current class.

c. Following the Zone Shoot all shooters who were placed in a penalty class as a result of their failure to meet the 300 registered target requirement, will return to their original class, with one exception. If the shooter wins the penalty class, depending on the shoot size (See III-A-2 Moving up in Class), they would then receive punches or be moved to the next higher class (one above the penalty class) for the remainder of the year.

5. U.S. Open

An annual shoot awarded by the NSCA Advisory Council according to the criteria set for the upcoming year.

a. To be eligible for class prizes, monies, and/or awards a shooter must have shot a minimum of 500 registered targets in the current shoot year prior to the U.S. Open. If a shooter does not have a minimum of 500 targets, he/she may shoot events and win prizes, monies, and /or awards in a penalty class, one class above his/her current class.

b. Following the U.S. Open all shooters who were placed in a penalty class as a result of their failure to meet the 500 registered target requirement, will return to their original class, with one exception. If the shooter wins the penalty class, depending on the shoot size (See III-A-2 Moving up in Class), they would then receive punches or be moved to the next higher class (one above the penalty class) for the remainder of the year.

6. National Championship

An annual shoot held by the National Sporting Clays Association on its Home Grounds.

a. To be eligible for open and/or concurrent prizes, monies, and awards at the National Championship, a shooter must have shot a minimum of 500 registered targets in the current year, prior to the shoot. If a shooter does not have a minimum of 500 targets, he/she may shoot at the event and win prizes, monies, and/or awards in a penalty class, one class above his/her current class.

b. Following the National Championship all shooters who were placed in a penalty class as a result of their failure to meet the 500 registered target requirement, will return to their original class, with one exception. If the shooter wins the penalty class, depending on the shoot size (See III-A-2 Moving up in Class), they would then receive punches or be moved to the next higher class (one above the penalty class) for the remainder of the year.

c. A program will be published each year giving all details of the current year's tournament.

7. Any NSCA registered target may be used to meet target minimums.

C. GAUGE SPECIFICATIONS

1. Twelve gauge events shall be open to all guns of 12 gauge or smaller, using shot loads not exceeding one and one-eighth (1 1/8) ounces.

2. Twenty gauge events shall be open to all guns of 20 gauge or smaller, using shot loads not exceeding seven-eights (7/8) of an ounce.

3. Twenty-eight gauge events shall be open to all guns of 28 gauge or smaller, using shot loads not exceeding three-quarters (3/4) of an ounce.

4. Four-ten events shall be open to all guns of .410 bore or smaller, using shot loads not exceeding one-half (1/2) of an ounce.

D. CONCURRENT EVENTS

These are events which are offered in concurrence with the seven (7) classes of shooters (Master, AA, A, B, C, D, E) that allow the participating shooters to compete and receive prizes or awards in these separate events in addition to their class. These events are based on age (Sub-Junior, Junior, Veteran, and Super Veteran) or sex (Lady). Where shoot programs offer special concurrent events based upon age, a shooter entering such special events must be allowed to shoot in the one for which they are qualified for by age along with any other concurrent class for which they are eligible if such a concurrent class is available (i.e. Lady could also be a Veteran, Super Veteran, Junior, or Sub-Junior).

1. A shooter's eligibility for concurrent events which are based on age is determined by the age of the shooter on the 1st day of the target year and shall determine their eligibility for the entire upcoming shooting year. No contestant shall be eligible for more than one individual concurrent event based on age.

Sub-Junior—Any person who has not reached their 14th birthday.

Junior—Any person who has not reached their 18th birthday.

Veteran—Any person 55 years of age or over who has not yet reached their 65th birthday.

Super Veteran—Any person 65 years of age and over.

For concurrent eligibility for F.I.T.A.S.C. (See Section VII-D.)

Lady—A female shooter of any age.

2. NSCA Nationals, U.S. Open, Zone, State, and Major shoots must offer all Concurrent Events and provide some type of award.

3. Shooters are eligible to compete for both concurrent and class awards. Shoot Official(s) may specify in tournament program that a reduced fee is offered for concurrent events. At time of entry the shooter has the option to pay the full entry fee and compete for both concurrent and class (open) titles, or pay a reduced fee and compete for

concurrent titles only. If the shooter elects to pay a reduced fee and compete for concurrent titles only they are still subject to earning punches according to Rule III-A-2 Moving Up In Class.

4. No Junior or Sub-Junior shall be required to pay any part of

entry fee that is to be returned to the shooter in the form

of money.

5. Youth Teams

This is a concurrent category that can be offered at the host club's discretion. If offered, this team event will be shot simultaneously with an already established tournament event.

a. Teams will consist of four or five members and are required to shoot as a group.

b. All team members must be in the Junior or Sub-Junior age group.

c. Each team must have a designated coach nearby.

d. For team competition, the lowest individual score will be dropped from a five-member team score even though there may be no four-member teams participating.

e. Even though the scores of all team members may not count toward the team's event score, all team members will be counted as participants in the shoot, and in their respective classes, and all individual scores will be registered.

E. EQUIPMENT

1. Targets

Targets thrown in any event may include any or all of the following:

a. Regulation SKEET or TRAP targets as specified by ATA, NSSA or NSCA.

b. Specialty targets—Mini, midi, battue, rocket, or rabbit targets as specified by NSCA.

c. Any sporting clays target approved by NSCA.

d. Poison Bird—Not Allowed.

e. Pairs

    1. Report Pair—Two sequential targets where the second target is launched at the sound of the gun firing at the first target. Targets may be launched from one or more traps.

    2. Following Pair—Two sequential targets where the second target is launched at the official's discretion after the first target. Targets may be launched from one or more traps.

    3. Simultaneous Pair—Two targets launched simultaneously. Targets may be launched from one or more traps.

f. Target number, selection, and order of presentation for any competition shall be at the discretion of the Shoot Officials, but must be the same for all shooters. It is recommended that 30% to 40% of targets for tournaments be specialty targets.

g. No less than 80% of all targets in a shoot shall be presented with a reasonably consistent trajectory, distance, and velocity to all shooters (See IV-E-2-b).

2. Traps

a. Targets will be propelled by, and launched from, any of a number of commercially produced, modified, or handmade devices which will propel an approved target in a manner to approach the characteristics (in the opinion of the Shoot Officials) of a game bird or animal typically taken by a sporting shotgun.

b. Launching devices which provide for targets traveling at varying angles and distances to the competitors are acceptable (i.e. wobble traps). No more than 20% of the targets shall be presented from such devices.

c. Devices which provide for propelling multiple targets are permitted.

d. Devices propelling targets of more than one type, and devices capable of providing targets at varying angles and distances, shall be employed only as the varying aspects

of these devices will be the same for all shooters and will be free of all human element of selection.

3. Shotguns

a. Shotguns of 12 gauge or smaller, in safe working order, and capable of firing two shots are to be used in attempting all targets. No more than two (2) shells may be loaded in the gun at one time.

b. Shotguns fitted for multiple barrels (of various chokes and/or lengths) are permitted. The shooter is allowed to change barrels only between stations. Failure to comply will result in all targets on that station attempted after the infraction being scored as "lost" or "missed".

c. Shotguns with interchangeable or adjustable chokes are permitted at the shooter's discretion. Chokes may be changed or adjusted only between stations. Failure to comply will result in all targets on that station attempted after the infraction being scored as "lost" or "missed".

d. Competitors may enter a shoot with various guns and attempt targets at various stations with different guns, or the gun of another competitor. Guns may be changed only between stations except in the case of a malfunction (IV-L-1-b). Failure to comply will result in all targets on that station attempted after the infraction being scored as "lost" or "missed".

e. Guns with release type triggers are allowed and must be clearly marked and Shoot Officials notified of their presence. Safety stickers designating "release trigger", with instructions on placement, are available at no charge from NSCA Headquarters. Please send your request in writing.

4. Ammunition

a. All shot shell ammunition including reloads may be used. Shoot Officials may limit the ammunition to commercially manufactured shot shells. The National Sporting Clays Association assumes no responsibility in connection with the use of reloads.

b. Maximum loads for any gauge EVENT may not exceed:

Gauge	Ounce Lead
12	1 1/8
20	7/8
28	3/4
.410 (2 1/2" Max.)	1/2

c. No shot smaller than U. S. No. 9 (diameter 0.08) or larger than U.S. No. 7-1/2 (diameter 0.095) shall be used in any load. No steel shot smaller than U.S. No. 9 (a nominal diameter 0.080") or larger than U.S. No. 6 (a nominal diameter 0.110) shall be used in any load.

d. Shot shall be normal production spherical shot. Plated shot is permitted.

F. COURSE SETUP AND REQUIREMENTS

1. Station

A shooting position from which one or more targets are attempted.

2. Field

A station or group of stations from which targets are attempted sequentially. Once a squad or individual checks into a field, all stations and/or all targets on the field are attempted before moving to another field. NSCA 5-STAND is a group of stations considered to be one (1) field. The Shoot Officials will provide direction for execution of shooting at each field.

3. Registered events are required to throw a minimum of 25 targets. The course will provide for a predetermined number of shooting fields from which each competitor will attempt various targets.

4. The number of Stations and the number and characteristics of targets from each station, on each field, will be determined by the Shoot Officials, and will be the same for all shooters. Changes in target trajectory, distance, and/or velocity due to wind, rain, time of day, or any other natural cause does not constitute a violation of this rule.

G. SHOOT OFFICIALS AND PERSONNEL

1. Shoot Promoter

Individual(s) or entity which provides for the facilities and organization of the competition. Shoot Promoters may also act as Shoot Officials.

2. Shoot Official

Individual(s) appointed by the Shoot Promoter and responsible for course layout, target selection, and appointment of Field Judges. Shoot Officials shall be responsible for both layout and testing of the course for safety. Shoot Officials are responsible for ensuring that competitors are not allowed to shoot the course prior to the competition.

a. Anyone who shoots the course prior to the competition is ineligible to compete in the tournament but may shoot for registered targets only.

b. Any person who sets or designs a course shall be allowed to shoot that course for registered targets only but will not be eligible for awards.

3. Field Judge (Referee)

An individual, who has integrity and a knowledge of NSCA Rules, assigned by the Shoot Officials to enforce the rules and score targets at any NSCA event. This individual can be the chief referee, a certified referee or any individual appointed by the Shoot Official(s).

a. Field Judges will be required at each station in sufficient number to competently enforce all rules for the shooter, as well as to score the attempts accurately.

b. Numbers and positions for Field Judges shall be determined by the Shoot Officials.

4. Chief Referee

A person may be appointed by shoot management who is responsible for the general supervision over all other referees at a tournament, and who shall be present throughout the shooting.

5. Certified Referee

A person who has completed and passed an NSCA Certified Referee Examination. Examination forms may be requested from NSCA Headquarters by recognized State Associations, National Delegate(s) and NSCA club owners/managers: all of whom may administer the test to an applicant in their presence. The completed examination should then be forwarded to NSCA Headquarters, with a fee of $20.00 for processing. Certification will be for a period of 3 years, ending September 30 of the 3rd year. The applicant may refer to the NSCA Rule Book to complete the examination, however, ALL questions on the examination must be answered correctly in order to pass. NSCA will issue Certified Referee credentials (patch and card) to applicants who pass the examination. This is a voluntary program. All Certified Instructor courses will automatically include this examination.

H. SHOOTING ORDER / ROTATIONS

1. Format

Contestants shall proceed through the course and competition in one of the following formats:

a. European Rotation—Individual competitors or groups of 2 through 6 competitors will proceed to the various stations at random. Groups may shoot in any order of rotation selected by the shooters and may change the rotation from field to field. In European Rotation, a shoot start and shoot end time will be established. It will be the responsibility of each shooter to complete the entire event between these times.

b. Squadding—At the discretion of the Shoot Officials, groups of 3 to 6 shooters will be formed to proceed from field to field in a fixed sequence. Unless specified by Shoot Officials, squads may shoot in any order of rotation selected by the shooters and may change the rotation from field to field.

    1. In squadding sequence, squads will be assigned a start time and it is the responsibility of each shooter to be ready on time, or within no more than 5 minutes of that time.

    2. Time—Shots not attempted by the "shoot end time" (European Rotation), or shots not attempted by the shooter joining his squad after they have begun (squadding), will be scored as "lost". The Shoot Officials shall have the right to provide for make up targets if sufficient justification can be presented. Make up targets are provided solely at the discretion of the Shoot Officials.

I. ATTEMPTING TARGETS

1. It will be the responsibility of each shooter to be familiar with these rules. Ignorance of the rules will not be a cause to "re-attempt" targets lost because of rule violations.

2. It is the sole responsibility of the shooter to begin any event, station, and/or field with sufficient equipment, including safety equipment, and ammunition. Failure to do so, which in the opinion of the Field Judges will delay the shoot, will result in the loss of all targets as required to keep the shoot moving. Make-up targets will be provided only at the discretion of the Shoot Officials.

3. Call for Target—The target may be launched immediately or with a delay of up to 3 seconds.

4. Shotgun Mount and Position—The shooter may start with a low gun or a pre-mounted gun when calling for the target.

J. TARGET PRESENTATION AND SCORING

1. Targets will be presented for attempt by the shooter and scored at each station in one or more of the following formats.

a. Single Target

Two shots are allowed and the target will be scored "dead" if broken by either shot.

b. Pairs

Only two shots are allowed. Pairs may be presented as report, following or simultaneous.

1. In simultaneous pairs the shooter has the right to shoot either of the targets first. If the shooter has missed the first target he may fire the second cartridge at the same target.

2. When shooting report or following pairs, the shooter will have the right, if missing the first target, to fire the second cartridge at the same target (the result being scored on the first target and the second target being scored as "lost").

c. Scoring Pairs

1. Should the shooter break both targets with either the first or second shot then the result will be scored as two hits.

2. In the event of a "no Bird" on a simultaneous or following pair, nothing can be established. Two good targets must be present to record the score. This will also apply for gun/ammunition malfunctions while shooting pairs. See IV-L-Malfunctions.

3. In the event of a "no bird" on the second target of a report pair, the first bird will be established as "dead" or "lost" and the shooter will repeat the pair to establish the result of the second target. When repeating the pair, the shooter must make a legitimate attempt at the first target.

4. In the event of a "shooter malfunction" on the first bird of a report pair, the first bird will be established as "lost" and the shooter will repeat the pair to establish the result of the second target. When repeating the pair the shooter must make a legitimate attempt at the first target. The first target has already been established as "lost" and the result of the second target will be recorded. (See IV-L-2 "Shooter Malfunctions".)

d. Multiple Targets

Only 2 shots are allowed; 2 "hits" or "dead birds" maximum.

2. Time Reloads

Targets presented with set time periods for shooter to reload prior to the presentation of the subsequent targets are permitted. Five seconds is the normal reload time, but other intervals may be used at the discretion of the Shoot Official(s).

3. Shooters Viewing Targets

The first person on every squad shall be allowed to view a good presentation of targets from within the shooting station. This person is the only person permitted to mount their unloaded gun and track the targets being viewed.

K. SCORING PROCEDURE

1. Each shooter will be assigned a score card to be presented to the Field Judges at the various stations or fields. Field Judges will score each shooter's attempts on the individuals score card. The total shall be tallied and the scores written in ink and initialed by the Field Judge.

2. Each shooter is responsible for his score card from assignment, at the start of the shoot, until the card is filed with the Shoot Officials at the end of each day's shooting.

3. Scores made on re-entry shall not qualify for prizes.

4. Shooters are responsible for checking the Field Judge's totals of "hits and misses" at each station and/or field.

5. Field Judges may be assisted by markers to record scores on the shooter's score cards.

6. Targets shall be scored as "hit" or "dead" and designated on score cards by an (X) when in the opinion of the Field Judge, a visible piece has been broken from the target.

Targets not struck and broken by the shooters shot shall be called "lost" or "missed" and designated on score cards by an (O).

7. The call of "lost" or "dead", "hit" or "miss" shall be announced by the Field Judge prior to recording the score on every target.

8. If the shooter disagrees with the Field Judge's call, he/she must protest before firing at another set of targets or before leaving that station. The Field Judge may poll the spectators and may reverse his/her original call. In all cases the final decision of the Field Judge will stand.

9. During a registered event, each shooter must verify his/her score before leaving the station. Once the shooter has left the station, his/her score is final.

L. MALFUNCTIONS

The shooter shall be allowed a combined total of three (3) malfunctions per day, per event attributed to either the shooter's gun or ammunition. Targets not attempted on the

three (3) allowed malfunctions shall be treated as "no birds". Targets not attempted due to the fourth or latter malfunctions shall be scored as "lost".

1. Gun Malfunctions

a. In the case of a gun malfunction, the shooter must remain in place, the gun pointed safely down range and must not open the gun or tamper with trigger, safety or barrel selector, until the field judge has determined the cause and made his/her ruling.

b. In the case of an inoperable gun, the shooter has the option to use another gun, if one is available, or he/she may drop out of competition until the gun is repaired. The shooter must, however, finish the event during the allotted scheduled shooting time.

2. Shooter Malfunctions

Targets shall be scored as "lost" if the shooter is unable to fire because of the following. Examples include but are not limited to:

a. Shooter has left the safety on.

b. Shooter has forgotten to load, load unfired shells, or properly cock the gun.

c. Shooter has forgotten to disengage the locking device from the magazine of a semi-automatic shotgun.

d. Shooter has not sufficiently released the trigger of a single trigger gun having fired the first shot.

e. Shooter not seeing the target.

f . If the shooter fails to comply with item IV-L-1-a, the target or targets will be scored as "lost" or "missed".

3. Ammunition Malfunctions

In the case of an ammunition malfunction, the shooter must remain in place, the gun pointing safely down range and must not open the gun or tamper with the trigger, safety or barrel selector, until the Field Judge has deter-mined the cause and made his/her ruling. Examples include but are not limited to:

a. Failure to fire, providing firing pin indentation is clearly noticeable.

b. One in which the primer fires, but through failure of the shell or lack of components, and which, consequently, leaves part of or all of the charge of shot or wad in the gun. A soft load in which the shot and wad leave the barrel, is not a misfire and shall be scored as "lost" or "missed".

c. Brass pulling off hull between shots on pairs.

d. Separation of brass from casing when gun is fired (usually accompanied by a "whistling" sound as the plastic sleeve leaves the barrel).

e. If the shooter fails to comply with item IV-L-3, the target or targets will be scored as "lost" or

"missed".

4. Trap/Target Malfunctions

a. A target which breaks at launching shall be called a "no bird" and shooter will be provided a new target.

b. A target which is launched in an obviously different trajectory shall be called a "no bird" and the shooter will be provided a new target.

c. If a bad target or "no bird" is thrown during a timed reload sequence, the shooter will repeat the sequence beginning with the last target established. The shooter must make an attempt at the last established target before proceeding with the remaining sequence. If the last established target occurred before the timed reload, the shooter shall begin the sequence accordingly and proceed through the reloading again. The Field Judge shall enforce his/her judgment (either by implementing a suitable penalty, or allowing a repeat of the reloading sequence) to prevent a "no bird" or "bad target" thrown after either a successful or an unsuccessful reloading attempt from changing the results of the initial sequence.

d. At a station of multiple targets (two or more – simultaneously launched), at least two good targets must be presented simultaneously or a "no bird" will be called and the multiple targets will be attempted again. Multiple targets shall be shot as "fair pair in the air", two new shots will be attempted and scored, no scores from previous "no bird" attempts will stand.

M. WEATHER / MITIGATING CIRCUMSTANCES

In the event of extreme weather conditions, power failure, trap failure, or unusually early darkness, the shoot management may elect to continue the event some other time (i.e., the next morning or the following weekend) but must immediately notify NSCA, with a full explanation, who will sanction the change, provided it is deemed in the best interest of sporting clays.

N. SHOOTOFFS

In all registered NSCA tournaments, all ties shall be shot off unless otherwise specified by shoot management and published in the program or posted at the registration table. Procedures for shootoffs and squads shall be posted prior to beginning of shoot. If shootoffs are held, the shootoffs must be held on targets or positions not previously shot by any participating competitor.

O. PROTESTS

1. A shooter may protest, if in his/her opinion, the rules as stated herein are improperly applied.

2. Any protest concerning calls or scoring of hits or misses must be made on the shooting station prior to leaving the station. The Field Judge's final decision will stand and no further protest allowed.

3. Protests shall be made immediately upon completion of the shooting at a given field with the Field Judge and with Shoot Official(s).

4. The Shoot Official(s) shall convene a predetermined "jury" of 3 to 5 Field Judges or competitors who are known to be representative of the shooters present and knowledgeable about these rules. The jury will decide on the validity of the protest and the resolution of the case. They will prescribe penalties or award bonuses as they determine to be fair and in the spirit of the competition.

P. CHECKS / PAYMENTS / OVERPAYMENTS

1. Anyone who presents a check at any shoot that is returned for insufficient funds, or other causes, must be notified by registered mail by the club to which it was presented and has fifteen (15) days to make full payment, plus penalty, to the club. Any club receiving such a check shall report name and address of the shooter issuing the check to the NSCA.

2. Any competitor at a registered shoot who, through error, has been overpaid on any purse, added money, optional or other prize money and who is notified of the overpayment by registered mail, must return the overpayment within fifteen days of notification. Failure to do so shall result in disbarment from all registered shoots until repayment is made.

3. See Section I-B-4 Suspension and Reinstatement.

Q. OFFICIAL SCORES

1. All scores or records, to be recognized as official, must be shot under all of the official NSCA rules.

2. Only the scores shot on scheduled dates, approved by NSCA, shall be registered. Scores made in shootoffs shall not be registered, however, all NSCA rules shall apply in shootoffs.

3. The scores of any NSCA member shooting on a course where a registered shoot is taking place shall be considered official, and shall be registered with the NSCA even though the shooter had given notice that it was not his/her intention to have their score recorded.

4. The score of a contestant who voluntarily stops or withdraws (without just cause) or who is disqualified by shoot management from an event which the contestant has started will be reported to NSCA along with the other scores of the event. This contestant's partial score for the station in which he/she is shooting shall be entered as the score for that station even though the contestant may not have actually fired on all targets. However, the total score for this contestant will not include targets from any station where he/she did not actually fire on at least one target.

5. Scores for contestants who withdraw because of sickness or injury shall be based on and reported only on number of targets actually fired upon.

6. In the event that a station/stations must be eliminated from the competition and results must be determined on less than the original number of targets intended for the competition shoot officials must give all competitors (whether they shot the station/stations or not) credit for all targets planned for the eliminated station/stations and must report the total number of targets shot at as originally intended (i.e. 100, 150, 200, etc.) to NSCA Headquarters.

7. Scores in shoots on which complete records are not made by shoot management will not be recorded and the national association shall not be liable to refund fees received in such cases.

R. REGISTERED SHOOT REPORTS

1. Reporting Requirements

It is the duty of each club holding a registered shoot to fulfill the following obligations:

a. Make payments of all money, purses and options to the shooters. (See Section IX Nonpayment Penalties.)

b. All money collected for optional purses must be paid out 100% to the eligible shooter(s).

c. Range Owners are required to fulfill all registered shoot reporting requirements within 15 days of their event or a $25.00 delinquent fine will be imposed for all shoot reports, financial statements and fees not received at NSCA Headquarters within that period. NSCA Headquarters will also have 15 days from the date the registered shoot report is received to have all scores input or be faced with the same $25.00 fine to be returned to the club hosting the tournament. (See IX Nonpayment Penalties.)

d. Shoot report and financial form must be sent to NSCA on all registered shoots. Standard forms available from NSCA Headquarters must be used or any NSCA approved spreadsheet which includes all information in rules IV-R-2 and 3.

e. If an approved State Association exists, clubs within the state must submit all required documents to their State Association within 15 days.

2. Financial Report

a.   Daily Fees

List number of targets shot each day of shoot and remit to NSCA the required daily registration fee (in U.S. Funds). Daily fees are $.03 per target.

b.   NSCA dues collected—Remittance (in U.S. Funds) and original copies of receipts for all NSCA memberships sold at your shoot must be attached. Membership applications must be completely and legibly filled out with name and address.

3. Shoot Report

An individual entry form/cashier sheet must be submitted on every shooter unless the club is using an NSCA approved spreadsheet. For every event (except Lewis events are not required to provide items "f" and "g") these reports must include:

a. NSCA membership number
b. Member's full name
c. Member's complete address
d. Number of targets shot
e. Number of targets broken
f . Class in which member was entered (not required for Lewis Class shoots)
g. Awards won. Except for Lewis Class events, winners must be determined and reported under NSCA Classification system. This applies even if no awards are made. Do not list winners above class champions unless such awards were made.
h. Clubs are required to retain copies of scoreboard and/or field score sheet on file for 90 days after the end of the applicable shooting year. And for shooter's reference keep an accurate record of the number of entries at each and every registered event.
i. It shall be the range owner's responsibility to keep on hand throughout the shoot year, a detailed list of shooters, scores and all monies paid out to shooters. If requested in writing by any participant in any event, it shall be the range owners responsibility to provide the participants with a detailed list of all participants, their scores and all money and prizes paid out and presented to shooters no sooner than within fifteen (15) days of the shoot report due date. All requests for such information shall be in writing accompanied by a stamped, self-addressed envelope. Clubs are required to retain this information on file for 90 days after the end of the applicable shooting year.

S. DISQUALIFICATION AND EXPULSION

The shoot management shall upon proper evidence:

1. Disqualify any shooter for the remainder of the shoot program for willful or repeated violation of gun safety precautions which endanger the safety of shooters, field personnel and/or spectators.
2. Elect to refuse the entry or cause the withdrawal of any contestant whose conduct, in the sole opinion of shoot management, is unsportsmanlike or whose participation is in any way detrimental to the best interests of the shoot.
3. Disqualify any shooter from a shoot for misrepresentation of his/her status under the eligibility rules (SANDBAGGING).
4. Expel or disqualify any shooter physically assaulting a Field Judge or any shooter using abusive language to a Field Judge upon sufficient evidence presented.
5. The shoot management shall report to NSCA all cases of disqualification and expulsion and the reasons for same. The circumstances under which any shooter is expelled from or disqualified from any NSCA function, event, or club will be reviewed by the Executive Director after giving the shooter involved an opportunity to be heard. The Executive Council will direct the Executive Director to notify the shooter, in writing, of his/her membership status: A) No action taken B) Expulsion/loss of membership for a term to be determined by the Executive Council C) Probation for one (1) year and if any other mishaps, immediate expulsion and loss of membership for one (1) year. The Executive Council can amend the length of expulsion or probation. Members may be suspended for failing to pay for goods or services ordered from NSCA/NSCA Member Club or who give to NSCA/NSCA Member Club a check that is returned for insufficient funds or other cause. Members MAY BE reinstated upon receipt in full of the outstanding balance and any fees incurred, such as bank charges, as a result of the incident. The Executive Council can determine any penalties and/or suspensions as each case merits. (See I-B-3 Rules of Conduct.)

V. NSCA 5-STAND SPORTING™

NSCA 5-STAND Sporting events consist of targets shot in 25 bird increments from five shooting stands with each shooter rotating from station to station. The game offers several different skill levels and utilizes six or eight automatic traps to simulate game birds. Targets are released in a predetermined set sequence marked on a menu card in front of each shooting cage. Targets are registered separately under a special set of rules, however utilize the NSCA Classification system, and all targets are included for total targets shot for the year. NSCA 5-STAND SPORTING rules must be followed at all times while conducting this event.

A. LAND

1. Minimum area 50 yards wide along Shooting Stand line.
2. Minimum 300 yards deep left and right of the center of Shooting Stand line creating an 80 degree arc for safe shot fall. (Game can be overlaid on a Skeet and or Trap field.)

B. EQUIPMENT

1. Six or eight automatic traps required.
2. Machines must include a rabbit trap and a vertical trap (minimum 60%).
3. Five Shooting Stands not less than seven feet tall and not more than 54 inches across the front opening.
4. One tower not less than 12 feet in height.
5. Controller (any NSCA approved).
6. Target sequence menu cards.
7. Trap location numbers.
8. Shooting Stand numbers.
9. Safety rules sign.

C. LAYOUT

1. Shooting Stands must be in a STRAIGHT LINE (for safety) not less than four yards apart or more than six yards apart (recommended five yards) center to center.
2. Trap placement and target flight paths must be arranged to include the following:
  a. Left to right crossing and/or quartering away target.
  b. Right to left crossing and/or quartering away target.
  c. Vertical target (Springing Teal).
  d. Rabbit target.
  e. Tower target going away.
  f. Incoming target.
3. For safety reasons, traps must be placed to prevent broken targets hitting the competitors or causing competitor's gun to be pointed in an unsafe direction. Traps placed parallel or too close to the Shooting Stand line can create a serious hazard. Recommended five yard minimum for any traps placed in front of Shooting Stands. Tower placement must be a sufficient distance back or to the side of the Shooting Stand line to prevent broken targets from falling on the competitors. Traps placed to the side of the Shooting Stand line should be a sufficient distance forward or behind the Shooting Stands to prevent competitors from selecting a hold point too close to the Shooting Stand line when calling for the target.

D. RULES

1. Gun must be open and empty while changing stands.
2. Shooters may not leave their station until instructed to do so by the referee or until the last shooter has fir d his last shot.
3. Only load gun while Shooting Stand in ready position.
4. Shooter's feet must be behind the front opening of the Shooting Stand except when changing

stands. Shooters will be warned, a "No-Bird" will be called, continued disregard will result in losing a target or being disqualified.

5. No chokes may be changed after the round has begun. Failure to comply will result in loss of all targets attempted (in that round) after choke changed.
6. Target sequence menu cards must be posted.

VI. F.I.T.A.S.C.

F.I.T.A.S.C. (Federation Internationale de Tir aux Armes Sportives de Chasse), headquartered in Paris, France, has recognized the National Sporting Clays Association as the sole, exclusive association to govern Parcours de Chasse Sporting and Compak Sporting in the United States. F.I.T.A.S.C. targets will be registered separately and shot under F.I.T.A.S.C. rules. The F.I.T.A.S.C. gun mount rule applies in all F.I.T.A.S.C. events. The NSCA Classification system used and all targets will be included in the shooters total targets shot for the year. In case of controversial interpretation of the present regulation, the text written in French will make faith. NOTE: Chapters and numbers in parentheses correspond with official Federation rules.

A. GENERAL (Chapter 1)

1. (1..01) Shooting Stand—Taking into considerations the terrain, a sporting course must be equipped with a sufficient amount of traps so that the competitors will shoot under conditions as close as possible to game shooting: partridges, pheasants, ducks, rabbits, etc. In front, low and high, crossing and quartering in fields or in woods, hidden or not by trees and bushes.
2. (1..02) The course must have been approved by the National Federations, for the organization of national competitions and by the International Federation for the organization of international competitions.
3. (1.03) Traps—A minimum of 4 traps are required for each old system layout. And a minimum of 3 traps for each new system shooting stand, that is 12 traps for each layout machines may be either manual, automatic or mixed, 5 1 MARKED by alphabetical letters (A, B, C, D) from left to right of the shooting stand.
4. (1.04) Clays—The clays to be used are the standard targets and rabbit clays, as well as thinner clays and clays with a smaller diameter. They may also include midi, mini, battue, bourdon, flash and zz targets. The targets must be black or orange according to the layout background.
5. (1.05) Shooting Position—The shooter will adopt the ready position, i.e. standing with both feet within the limits of the shooting stand, WITH THE HEEL OF THE GUN TOUCHING THE BODY UNDER A HORIZONTAL LINE MARKED ON THE SHOOTER'S JACKET. THIS LINE WILL BE INDICATED BY A TAPE OF CONTRASTING COLOR FIXED TO THE JACKET BY SOME PERMANENT MEANS. THE HORIZONTAL LINE SHALL BE LOCATED 25 cm (9.85") BELOW AN IMAGINARY LINE DRAWN OVER THE TOP OF THE SHOULDERS ALONG THEIR AXIS. The shooter will maintain this position with the gun not premounted until the target(s) are in sight.
6. (1.06) In a double on report simultaneous or rafale, the position of the gun is optional for the second target only.
7. (1.07) If the shooter is in a position NOT IN ACCORDANCE with (1.05) or if he aims his gun before the target appears, he will receive an initial WARNING.
8. (1.08) After *the first such occurrence* on the same layout the target(s) will be declared:
  a. Zero for a single target
  b. Zero and no bird for a double on report
  c. Zero & Zero for a simultaneous double
  d. Zero & Zero for a rafale double
9. (1.09) The shooter does not have the right to refuse a target unless he has not called for it. The referee alone shall decide on the regularity of a trajectory or on a NO BIRD.
10. (1..10) The shooting stands will be marked by a 1 meter square or by a circle of 1 meter in diameter.
11. (1.11) The shooter must fire with his gun shouldered for all targets.
12. (1.12) Under no circumstances, once the referee has clearly declared a target NO BIRD, may it be fired at. After the *first* warning, the shooter will be penalized:
  a. Zero for a single target
  b. Zero & no bird for a double on report
  c. Zero & Zero for a simultaneous double
  d. Zero & Zero for a rafale double.

B. ORGANIZATION OF COMPETITION (Chapter 2)

JURY

1. (2.01) International events will be supervised by a jury consisting of a representative of each country participating *with a seniors team* with the representative of the organizing country as chairman.
2. (2.02) The jury shall make decisions by majority vote of members present. In the case of equal votes, the chairman's casting vote is final.
3. (2.03) The jury can only make valid decisions in the presence of its chairman or his representative accompanied by a quarter of the members of the jury.
4. (2.04) In urgent cases (example: the risk of cessation of shooting) two members of the jury, nominated by the chairman, may make a decision with the consent of the referee, provided that this decision is endorsed by the jury.
  THE ROLE OF THE JURY IS:
5. (2.05) To verify, before the shooting begins, that the course conforms to regulations and that the preparatory arrangements are suitable and correct.
6. (2.06) To appoint a technical committee whose responsibility shall be to set, on the day before the competition, the various trajectories, the location of the shooting stands, the choice and speed of the targets which will be shot during the event.
7. (2.07)No practice will be permitted before the start of events over the layouts set by the technical committee.
8. (2.08) Before the beginning of the championships the director of shooting will publish a list of the trajectories for each of the traps. Should these trajectories, established and calculated in calm conditions, be disturbed by the wind, they will still be considered regular.
9. (2.09) To require that, during the shooting, the rules are adhered to and to check the weapons, ammunition and targets by means of technical tests.
10. (2.10) To make the necessary decisions in cases of technical defects *if* these are not resolved by the referee.
11. (2.11) To deal with protests.
12. (2.12) To make decisions regarding penalties to be imposed on a shooter who does not adhere to the rules or behaves in an unsporting manner.
13. (2.13) To ensure that there are always at least two members of the jury present at the shooting ground.
  APPEAL JURY
14. (2.14) An appeal jury will be set up for each international competition.
15. (2.15) In the case of a dispute concerning the decision of the jury by the shooters or by F.I.T.A.S.C., an appeal jury may be referred to. This appeal jury will consist of: the President of F.I.T.A.S.C. or his representative, the President of the Technical Committee or his representative, and the *President of the Organizing Federation*. This appeal jury will be formed at the same time as the jury. *If*

there is no Appeal Jury, the Jury's decision is definitive. All the disciplinary problems will be submitted to the F.I.T.A.S.C. Disciplinary Commission.

16. (2.16) During international competitions, representatives of the same country shall be dispersed over the various squads. The organizing committee will announce the time and arrangements for a draw for the composition of the squads. Delegates from participating nations may be present.

17. (2.17) Shooting shall take place in squads of 6 shooters VI-B-8 (2.08) as drawn, with rotation of shooters not only at each stand but also for shooting doubles. At each stand all 6 shooters of a squad will first fire at the single targets before any shoot at the doubles.

18. (2.18) All target trajectories will be presented at each stand to the first shooter of each group. This shooter must observe them from within the shooting stand.

19. (2.19) At the time of the presentation of the target, no shooting, aiming or pretense of firing is permitted (for penalty see article 1.07).

20. (2.20) "Report" pairs will not be shown, only targets of SIMULTANEOUS and RAFALE doubles will be shown to the first shooter of each group.

21. (2.21) Only targets having already been fired at as singles may be shot at as "report" pairs.

22. (2.22) In international competitions, shooting will be conducted in stages of 25 targets. However, exception-ally, the technical committee may change this if it is judged necessary.

23. (2.23) Shooters must take all precautions in order to be at the shooting stand on time. If a shooter is not present when his name is called, the referee must call the name and number of the shooter loudly 3 times during the period of one minute. If he has not missed his turn to shoot the singles on the first stand, he may rejoin the squad. If he has failed to join the squad before his turn, those targets not fired at, singles or doubles will be scored zero. If the shooter presents himself at one of the following stands, ALL THE CLAYS NOT SHOT AT THE PREVIOUS STAND WILL BE SCORED ZERO. In no circumstances may the shooter shoot that layout in another squad. (See VI-B-24.)

24. (2.24) If the shooter feels that he has a valid excuse for his lateness, he MUST
   a. Not join his squad if it is in the process of shooting on that layout.
   b. Put his case to the jury in writing.
   c. Abide by the jury's decision.
   d. Only the jury may authorize him to repeat the shoot of that layout in another squad.
   e. If the jury decides that the reason put forward by the shooter is unacceptable, the latter will be scored 25 zeros corresponding to the 25 clays not shot at.

25. (2.25) In the case of malfunction of a trap during the shoot, the referee will decide if the stage should be continued or interrupted because of mechanical troubles. After the trouble has been rectified the shooter has the right to have the regular target(s) shown before continuing the shoot.

26. (2.26) During international competitions the scores will be recorded by the referee or his delegate who may be a shooter. The results of each stage will then be posted on a central notice board.

27. (2.27) On leaving each stand the shooter must check that his correct score is recorded on the score card. If the shooter CONTESTS the result, HE MUST INFORM THE REFEREE IMMEDIATELY, BUT THE FINAL DECISION RESTS WITH THE REFEREE. However, the referee may seek information and advice before making his final decision. NO OBJECTION WILL BE ALLOWED AFTER THIS CHECK.

C. FIREARMS AND AMMUNITION (Chapter 3)

1. (3.01) All firearms, including semi- automatics, are permitted providing their caliber does not exceed 12 bore, with a barrel length of 66 cms minimum.

2. (3.02) All firearms, even unloaded, must be handled with the greatest care at all times.

3. (3.03) Guns must be carried open; semi-automatic guns must be carried WITH THE BREECH OPEN, and the muzzle pointing straight upwards or downwards.

4. (3.04) Straps or slings on guns are forbidden.

5. (3.05) When the shooter is not using a gun, it must be placed vertically in a gun rack or in a similar place as designated.

6. (3.06) It is forbidden to handle another shooter's gun without his specific permission.

7. (3.07) It is forbidden, during a competition or official championship, for two shooters of the same squad to use the same gun. (See 3.08.)

8. (3.08) In exceptional cases, owing to a malfunction of his gun, a shooter may be permitted to borrow the gun of another shooter with his permission.

9. (3.09) Complete or partial CHANGING OF A FIREARM, MOBILE CHOKE OR BARREL is allowed during the same round, between two stands or between single or double targets. However, no delay will be permitted for any of these reasons.

10. (3.10) Once the shooter is on the shooting stand he will not be allowed to carry out any changes which are permitted in 3.09.

11. (3.11) A shooter is permitted a maximum time to ready himself between targets, whether singles or doubles, of 20 seconds. In a case where the shooter exceeds this time the referee may, after two warnings to the shooter, apply article 1.08.

12. (3.12) In the case of a gun malfunction, verified by the referee, the shooter will twice only have the right to a new target in the course of the same round. The third and subsequent malfunction will be considered ZERO. Following the decision of the referee, the shooter will have the right to continue with his squad on condition that he obtains another weapon without delay (3.08). If this is not possible he must leave his place in the squad and shoot his remaining birds when there is a free place in another squad and when the jury has given permission. If the gun is repaired before the sequence on that stand is finished by his squad, the shooter may retake his place in the squad with the referee's permission.

13. (3.13) Should both barrels fire simultaneously (double discharge) due to a gun malfunction and not the shooters error, the target, whether a single or the first of a double will be declared NO BIRD with nothing established and Rule 3.12 will apply.

14. (3.14) The cartridge shot load must not exceed 36 grams. The shot will be SPHERICAL and of diameter between 2.0 and 2.5 mm.

15. (3.15) The use of dispersers or any other unusual loading device is strictly forbidden (spreader or duplex loads are not allowed). Reloaded cartridges are not permitted.

16. (3.16) The mixing of various qualities and diameters of shots is strictly forbidden.

17. (3.17) The use of black powder and tracers is forbidden.

18. (3.18) Two cartridges may be used on each single target, but the shooter will only be allowed two cartridges for each double.

19. (3.19) In a double if the two targets are broken by one shot they will be scored KILL AND KILL.

20 (3.20) The referee may, at any time, remove unused cartridges from a shooter's gun for inspection.

D. DRESS AND RULES OF CONDUCT (Chapter 4)

1. (4.01) Participants in competitions must be correctly dressed. Diminutive shorts are not allowed, only long shorts (Bermuda style ending no higher than a maximum of 5 cm above the knee) are acceptable. Shirts must be worn and should have at least short sleeves and a collar (round neck tee-shirt style is permitted). The wearing of sandals is not allowed for reasons of safety. The shooter's number must be worn in its entirety and the whole of the number must be visible. Any failure to comply with these rules of conduct will be penalized by A REFEREE'S FIRST WARNING which may be followed by penalties up to exclusion from the competition, following the jury's decision.

2. (4.02) A shooter may only fire on his proper turn and only when a target has been thrown, except when permitted by the referee (test firing).

3. (4.03) It is forbidden to aim or shoot at other shooters' target.

4. (4.04) It is also forbidden to aim or shoot intentionally at living animals.

5. (4.05) No pretense of shooting is permitted on the shooting stand or outside it.

6. (4.06) If a shooter, on the shooting stand, before saying READY makes a pretense of shooting, or

involuntarily fires a shot, the referee is obliged to issue a WARNING to the shooter. After two warnings, any further occurrence will be scored ZERO for the next target hit.

7. (4.07) When his name is called, the shooter must be ready to shoot immediately and he must have with him sufficient ammunition and equipment for that stand.

8. (4.08) In no case must a shooter move to a stand before the preceding shooter has left it and it is his turn to shoot.

9. (4.09) The shooter is allowed to load his gun only when on the stand where he has taken his place, his gun always pointing down the range and only when the referee has authorized him to start shooting.

10. (4.10) Semi-automatic guns must only be loaded with a maximum of two cartridges.

11. (4.11) The shooter must not turn around or leave the stand before he has broken his gun and removed the cartridges from the chambers, whether they have been fired or not.

12. (4.12) During the presentation of targets or when shooting is temporarily interrupted, the shooter must open and unload his gun. It shall only be closed when authorized by the referee.

13. (4.13) In the case of a misfire or any other malfunction of the gun or ammunition, the shooter must remain in his place, the gun pointing safely down the range, not broken, and without touching the safety catch until the referee has examined the gun.

14. (4.14) Shooting must proceed without interruption, shooters being allowed to pronounce only the necessary words of command READY, PULL, GO or another command and to answer the referee's questions.

15. (4.15) If a member of the jury observes anything which is not according to the rules, he must inform the referee. If the referee is unable to take the immediate necessary action, he must inform the jury.

E. REFEREE (Chapter 5)

1. (5.01) The referees must have been approved by the jury before the competition. In the case of a large number of referees not being fully qualified or experienced, they must be supervised by international referees.

2. (5.02) A referee must have a wide experience of clay shooting and must possess a valid F.I.T.A.S.C. Referee's Certificate and his National Association's License. If this is not the case, the jury must agree to accept assistant referees.

3. (5.03) The referees must ensure order and proper conduct on the shooting stand and during shoot-offs.

4. (5.04) The referee alone shall make decisions. If a shooter disagrees with the referee, the objection must be made immediately on the shooting stand by raising the arm and
saying PROTEST or APPEAL. The referee must then interrupt the shooting and pronounce his final decision.

5. (5.05) The shooter may appeal against the referee's decision. The objection must be made in writing to the jury, accompanied by a deposit of a certain sum in operation on the day of the competition and which will be returned only if the objection is upheld. If the jury finds the objection justified, it may give instructions to the referee concerning future judgments or name a new referee or, finally, alter the referee's decision. No dispute shall be concerned with whether a clay was hit or missed, nor whether the thrown clay was defective - in these cases, no appeal may be made against the referee's decision.

6. (5.06) When the competitor is ready to shoot, he shall say READY to the referee and the target must be thrown during a period which may vary between 0 and 3 seconds after the referee has passed on the shooter's command to the pullers.

7. (5.07) The referee must pass on the shooter's command to the pullers in the shortest time possible.

8. (5.08) In exceptional circumstances, the referee may suspend the shooting if there is sudden heavy rain or a violent storm which appears to be a short duration. However,
he must inform the jury if it looks likely that this interruption will last any length of time.

9. (5.09) In no circumstances is it permitted to pick up a target to see if it has been hit or not.

F. SINGLE BIRDS – HIT OR MISSED (Chapter 6)

THE TARGET IS DECLARED "KILLED" WHEN:

1. (6.01) It has been launched and the shooter has fired according to the rules and when at least one visible piece of it is broken off or is totally or partially destroyed. This applies equally to FLASH clays.

THE TARGET IS DECLARED "ZERO" (missed):

2. (6.02) If it is not hit and no piece is broken off or if only dust is raised (dusted bird).

3. (6.03) If the shooter has left the safety catch on, has forgotten to load or cock it, if the gun has not been sufficiently broken or closed or if he has forgotten to take the necessary measures to load the cartridge into the chamber when he is using a semi-automatic gun.

4. (6.04) If there is a third malfunction of the gun during the same round: Article 3.12 will apply.

5. (6.05) If the shooter is unable to fire his SECOND shot because he has not loaded the second cartridge or he has not canceled the locking device of the loading chamber in a6 1
semiautomatic weapon or for any other reason.

6. (6.06) If the second shot cannot be fired because the shooter, using a single trigger gun, has not released it sufficiently after firing the first shot.

7. (6.07) If the shooter, in the case of malfunction of his gun, opens it himself or touches the safety catch before the referee has examined the gun.

8. (6.08) If the shooter adopts a ready position which is not according to Articles 1.05, 1.07 and 1.11 and if he has already been warned once during the same round.

G. SINGLE CLAYS

NO BIRD (Chapter 7)

1. (7.01) The target will be declared NO BIRD and a new target will be launched, whether the shooter has fired or not:
   a. If the bird is thrown broken.
   b. If the bird is thrown from the wrong trap.
   c. If for a single bird two clays are launched from traps on the same shooting stand.
   d. On a rabbit, if the clay breaks after being launched and missed by the first shot, but before the second shot has been fired, the rabbit will be declared "NO BIRD". A new target will be launched, the shooter must miss with his first shot, and the result of the second shot scored. Although "rabbit" is specifically mentioned, this rule in some instances, may apply to other targets that are prematurely terminated.

2. (7.02) If the target is definitely of another color from that of the other targets used on the same trajectory of the same stand.

3. (7.03) If the target is thrown before the shooter has called READY.

4. (7.04) If the target is thrown after a delay of more than 3 seconds after the referee's command.

5. (7.05) If the trajectory is judged irregular by the referee.

6. (7.06) If, when a semi-automatic gun is being used, the ejection of the first cartridge impedes the loading of the second cartridge (in this case when the target is thrown again the first shot shall be directed near the target but must not hit it and the result of second shot only shall be scored).

7. (7.07) If there is a fault on the first shot as a result of failure of the cartridge or malfunction of the gun not attributable to the shooter and if the shooter does not fire his second shot IF THE SHOOTER FIRES THE SECOND SHOT, THE RESULT WILL BE SCORED.

8. (7.08) The referee may also declare NO BIRD when the shooter has clearly been disturbed.

9. (7.09) When another competitor shoots at the same target. 10.   (7.10) When the referee, for any reason, cannot decide if a target has been hit or missed.

253

11. (7.11) All targets NOT declared NO BIRD by the referee, must be shot at. However, the referee may declare NO BIRD after the target(s) have been shot at (as in the case of a fast or slow pull or irregular trajectory).

12. (7.12) In the case of a cartridge misfire or malfunction of the gun not attributable to the shooter, a target will be declared NO BIRD and a new clay will be thrown. After two misfires or two malfunctions of the weapon in the same stage (whether the shooter has changed his gun or not) further incident or incidents will be declared ZERO.

(See article 3.12)

H. DOUBLE ON REPORT (Chapter 8)

DEFINITION OF DOUBLES "ON THE GUN" (Report Pairs)

1. (8.01) Two targets from one or two different traps, the second clay being launched within a period of 0 to 3 seconds after the first clay has been shot at.

NO BIRD SHALL BE DECLARED:

2. (8.02) If two targets are launched simultaneously.

3. (8.03) When a shooter does not fire, without legitimate reason, at his first target. The second target cannot be thrown (because there is no first shot), the double will be declared ZERO/NO BIRD and a second double will be thrown to determine the result of the second shot only.

4. (8.04) If the clay is not thrown by the correct trap.

5. (8.05) If the first target is regular and the second irregular, (however, the result of the first target shall be scored KILL OR ZERO as the case may be).

6. (8.06) The double will be declared NO BIRD and the shooter will be asked to fire a second double to determine the scores of both shots:

a. Violation of article 1.05, ready position for the first target (1.07 & 1.08).

b. If during a double, the two shots are fired simultaneously due to a gun malfunction, even if the first bird was broken (See articles 3.12 & 3.13).

c. If the shooter fires his gun involuntarily on the shooting stand, whether whilst loading or because of a mishap before saying READY.

7. (8.07) In a double when the second target is irregular a NO BIRD shall be declared and the double must be attempted again, but the result of the first target will be recorded. The shooter will not have the chance to repeat the first target if it was declared ZERO but must still shoot at it.

a. If the shooter misses his first clay, and this clay hits the second one, before the second shot.

b. If pieces from the first clay hit and break the second one before the second shot.

c. If during a double, the second shot cannot be fired because of the malfunction of gun or ammunition, article 3.12 & 3.13.

8. (8.08) A malfunction of the gun or cartridge prevents the shooter from shooting his first bird articles 3.12 & 3.13 will apply.

9. (8.09) If the shooter does not shoot in his proper turn he will receive a WARNING, at the third incident on the same layout, the target will be declared ZERO FOR A SINGLE CLAY or ZERO NO BIRD IF IT IS A DOUBLE ON REPORT or ZERO/ZERO IF IT IS A SIMULTANEOUS DOUBLE OR RAFALE DOUBLE.

10. (8.10) The rules of articles 6.01 to 7.12 ARE APPLICABLE TO THE FIRING OF DOUBLES ON REPORT.

I. DOUBLE ON REPORT -DECLARED KILL (Chapter 9)

ZERO AND ZERO/KILL OR ZERO/ZERO

1. (9.01) If the shooter, without legitimate reason, does not shoot at the second target of a regular double, the result of the first target shall be recorded and the second declared ZERO.

2. (9.02) The target will be declared ZERO on the third malfunction of the gun or cartridge in the same round articles 3.12 & 3.13.

3. (9.03) When a shooter in a double fires both shots at the same target. The result shall be scored, and the second target of the double be declared ZERO.

4. (9.04) The rules of articles 6.01 to 7.12 are applicable to the shooting of doubles.

J. SIMULTANEOUS DOUBLE (Chapter 10)

1. (10.01) There are two targets thrown at the same time by one or two traps.

2. (10.02) In a simultaneous double NO SCORE shall be recorded if either target has been declared NO BIRD.

3. (10.03) May be broken by a single shot and scored KILL/KILL.

4. (10.04) The targets may be shot in any order.

5. (10.05) Without any legitimate reason, the shooter does not shoot a regular double, both clays will be ZERO (VI-H-3).

SIMULTANEOUS DOUBLE NO BIRD

6. (10.06) The double will be declared NO BIRD and the shooter will be asked to shoot a second double to determine the results of both shots:

a. If the target(s) break on being thrown;

b. If the target(s) are not thrown by the correct trap;

c. If the target(s) are of clearly a different color from those used for the same double;

d. If the target(s) are thrown before the shooter has called ready;

e. If the double is thrown more than 3 seconds after the referee's command;

f. If one of the trajectories of the doubles is judged irregular by the referee;

g. If the shooter misses his first target and it collides with the second before the shooter has fired his 2nd shot;

h. If the fragments of the first target breaks the second before the shooter has fired his second shot;

i. Violation of articles 1.05 & 1.06, ready position for the first target (1.07 & 1.08);

j. A malfunction of the gun or cartridge prevents the shooter from shooting his first target(s) (see also 3.12 & 3.13);

k. If in a double the second shot cannot be fired simultaneously due to gun malfunction, the double is NO BIRD and must be repeated (see also 3.12 & 3.13);

l. If, during a double, the two shots are fired simultaneously due to gun malfunction, the double is NO BIRD and must be repeated (see also 3.12 & 3.13);

m. If the shooter involuntarily fires his gun on the shooting stand, whether while loading or because of a mishap before calling READY.

7. (10.07) The rules of articles 6.02 to 6.08 ARE APPLICABLE TO THE SHOOTING OF SIMULTANEOUS DOUBLES.

K. RAFALE DOUBLES (Chapter 11)

DEFINITION OF A RAFALE DOUBLE (following pair)

1. (11.01) Two targets are thrown from the same trap on the same trajectory.

2. (11.02) Two cartridges may be fired at the same target.

3. (11.03) They may be fired at in any order by the shooter.

4. (11.04) In a rafale double NO SCORE IS OBTAINED in the case of a NO BIRD of one of the targets.

5. (11.05) All the rules relating to a simultaneous double are applicable to a rafale double, that is

articles 10.04 to 10.06.

6. (11.06) Also rules of articles 6.02 to 6.08 ARE APPLICABLE TO THE SHOOTING OF RAFALE DOUBLES.

L. PENALTIES (Chapter 12)

1. (12.01) All shooters are required to acquaint themselves with the current regulations which apply to shooting under PARCOURS DE CHASSE rules. By taking part in competitions, they accept the penalties and other consequences resulting from violation of the rules and referees' orders.

2. (12.02) Deliberate violation of the rules will, in the first place, incur a warning from the referee or jury. In the case of further or more serious offenses, the jury may penalize the shooter with a lost bird and, in more serious cases exclude him from the round and or competition.

3. (12.03) In the case of a jury being aware that the competitor has intentionally delayed the shooting or that he has acted in a dishonorable manner, it may give him a warning or penalize him one bird or disqualify him from the competition.

M. SHOOT-OFF (Chapter 13)

1. (13.01) In case of a shoot-off, if the time allows, a new layout may be set up by the jury.

2. (13.02) Shoot-offs for the first three places (Individual or National teams) will take place in a round of 25 targets, if a result has not been established, the shooters will shoot a second "zero eliminator" (sudden death) round, i.e. the first target on which scores differ, the shooter with a ZERO will be eliminated, until only the winner remains. Other shooters with the same score will show as "drawn".

3. (13.03) Shooting will be carried out in accordance with the preceding rules, the empty places in the squad will not be filled.

4. (13.04) When the shoot-off is not carried out at a previously announced time, the shooters concerned must remain in contact with the committee in order to be ready to shoot within 15 MINUTES after being called.

5. (13.05) Shooters not present at the start of the shoot-off will be declared "scratched".

6. (13.06) The jury may, in exceptional circumstances, decide that the shoot-off should be carried over to the following day. Shooters not present in this case shall be considered "scratched".

N. SCORE SHEET (Chapter 14)

1. (14.01) The score sheet will be held by the referee or under his responsibility to someone selected by himself. Every referee will use a different color pen on the same layout or on the same shooting line.

2. (14.02) Only clays ZERO will be notified on the score sheet. Every clay ZERO will be written down in order from left to right on the score sheet. Clays will be numbered in shooting order.

Example = station n°1

Clay n°1, n°2, n°3, n°4, Double n°5 and n°6.

Example = station n°2

Clay n°1, n°2, n°3, Double n°4 and n°5, Double n°6 and n°7.

To allow a further control, the number of the clay ZERO will be written in the corresponding space of the score sheet.

O. GLOSSARY

1. SQUAD: Group of 6 competitors shooting at the same time on the same layout.

2. ROUND: A round consists of 25 clays thrown from the same layout.

3. TRAP: Machine or device for throwing the clay.

4. SHOT: Firing of a cartridge.

5. CLAY: Clay pigeon or target.

6. TRAJECTORY: The line of flight of the clay through the air.

RULES APPROVED BY THE TECHNICAL COMMISSION SPORTING 2ND NOVEMBER 1996.

VII. AWARDS AND RECOGNITION

A. ALL-AMERICAN

1. NSCA annually recognizes up to three All-American teams in each of the six categories, depending upon the number of members who qualify based on the following criteria:

Open Team—Minimum 1,200 registered targets.

Lady, Veteran and Super Veteran Teams—Mini-mum 1,000 registered targets.

Junior and Sub-Junior Teams—Minimum 800 registered targets.

2. Mandatory attendance is a requirement at the National Sporting Clays Championship (participating in the Main Event) for all categories.

3. Performance in U.S. Open, Zone, State, and Major shoots will be applied as additional criteria for All-American qualification.

4. To be eligible for the All-American team you must be a citizen of the United States and be eligible for a U.S. passport.

B. NSCA ALL-STATE TEAM

NSCA will annually select an NSCA All-State Team for each state in order to recognize more shooters for their shooting ability. Selection is based on the following criteria:

1. Team consists of 17 All -State members as follows:

Five from Open = 5

One person from each class = 7

One person from each concurrent = 5

2. Persons who have been selected for an All-American Team would be ineligible in order to recognize an entire new category of shooters.

3. A minimum number of 500 registered targets must be shot annually within the home state by each individual.

4. Mandatory participation is required at the State Championship for all categories. If there was not a state championship, no team will be selected for that state.

5. NSCA All- State Teams may be in addition to any team that may have been selected by the State Association.

6. Team selection priority: Open, concurrent, then class.

7. Selection is based on wins, state shoot score and total shoot performance.

8. Team selection for each class is based on a shooter's beginning year class.

9. To be eligible for the Open team, shooters must have attained "AA" classification by year end.

10. End of year residence determines state status.

C. TARGET PARTICIPATION PIN

An annual target participation pin provided to recognize shooters who have shot 1000 or more targets during the year.

D. TEAM USA (F.I.T.A.S.C.)

Four teams will be selected for Team USA (F.I.T.A.S.C.) – Senior (Open), Lady, Junior*, and Veteran*.

MINIMUM CRITERIA FOR ANNUAL TEAM USA SELECTION:

1. Must be a U.S. citizen. A U.S. citizen is defined as anyone who is eligible for a U.S. passport.

2. Must shoot a minimum of 500 registered F.I.T.A.S.C. targets.

3. Qualification tournaments, of which a shooter must attend five(5), will be printed in *Sporting Clays Magazine* in "Headlines From Headquarters".

4. F.I.T.A.S.C. experience and performance will be the deciding criteria.

5. Consideration will be given to international performance not captured by the NSCA system

provided that the results are submitted to NSCA Headquarters along with the appropriate daily fees.

*Concurrent Eligibility for Team USA (F.I.T.A.S.C.): The NSCA International Committee will select individuals to Team USA (F.I.T.A.S.C.) using international concurrent rules.

Junior—a shooter who is less than 21 years of age, and who will not have their 21st birthday during the year of the competition.

Veteran—a shooter who had their 55th birthday the year before the competition and who is less than 66 years of age the year of the competition.

Super Veteran—a shooter who had their 65th birthday the year before the competition.

E. MASTERS PIN

A pin sent to those shooters who have "earned" their way into "Master Class" honoring their accomplishment.

VIII. CERTIFIED INSTRUCTORS PROGRAM

Members who have participated in and passed an NSCA Instructor Certification Course. There are *four* levels of Instructor Certification available: Youth Coach, Level I, II, and III. Levels I-III must be taken in sequence. Youth Coach - teaching beginner and novice in organized youth programs. Level I—teaching beginner to novice, Level II—teaching intermediates, and Level III—for advanced teachers. It takes a minimum of four (4) years and over 1700 hours of teaching to complete the certification program.

IX. NONPAYMENT PENALTIES

A. CLUBS

1. Failure to fulfill the reporting and payment requirements shall carry the following penalties:

a. Cancellation of all subsequent shoot dates for the offending club.

b. Denial of right to apply or reapply for any further registered shoot dates for a period of thirty (30) days in case of first offense, or ninety (90) days in case of second or subsequent offense or until obligations have been met.

c. Owners, officers, and managers of any delinquent club may be barred from shooting registered targets and from all functions of the NSCA either certified, elected, or appointed (for example but not limited to: Advisory Council positions, National Delegate positions, Zone Delegate, Certified Instructor) until which time as written verification is provided that all required obligations of said club are met to the shooters and NSCA.

2. Club membership may be suspended for any member club who fails to pay for goods or services ordered from NSCA or who gives to NSCA a check that is returned for insufficient funds or other cause. Membership may be reinstated upon receipt in full of the outstanding balance and any penalties incurred, such as bank charges, as a result of the incident.

3. Nothing in this section shall affect, modify or overrule the provisions in Section I-B-4 or the rights and powers of the NSCA as set forth therein.

B. INDIVIDUALS

1. Members may be suspended for failing to pay for goods or services ordered from NSCA or who give to NSCA a check that is returned for insufficient funds or other cause. Members may be reinstated upon receipt in full of the outstanding balance and any fees incurred, such as bank charges, as a result of the incident.

2. Nothing in this section shall affect, modify or overrule the provisions in Section I-B-4 or the rights and powers of the NSCA as set forth therein.

DIRECTORY OF TRAP/SKEET/ SPORTING CLAYS-RELATED MANUFACTURERS AND AFFILIATES

AcuSport Corporation
1 Hunter Place, Bellefontaine, OH 43311-3001
513-593-7010; FAX: 513-592-5625

ADCO Sales, Inc.
4 Draper St. #A, Woburn, MA 01801
781-935-1799; FAX: 781-935-1011

All American Lead Shot Corp.
P.O. Box 224566, Dallas, TX 75062

Americase
P.O. Box 271, 1610 E. Main, Waxahachie, TX 75165

Armas Garbi, S.A.
12-14 20.600 Urki, 12, Eibar (Guipuzcoa), SPAIN
SPAIN
943203873; FAX: 943203873

Kemen S. A. (See U.S. Importers)

Armi Perazzi S.P.A.
Via Fontanelle 1/3, 1-25080, Botticino Mattina, ITALY
ITALY
030-2692591; FAX: 030 2692594

AYA
New England Custom Gun Service
438 Willow Brook Rd., Plainfield, NH 03781
603-469-3450; FAX: 603-469-3471

Benelli Armi S.P.A.
Via della Stazione, 61029, Urbino, ITALY
ITALY
39-722-307-1; FAX: 39-722-327427

Benelli USA Corp
17603 Indian Head Hwy, Accokeek, MD 20607
301-283-6981; FAX: 301-283-6988

Beretta S.P.A., Pietro
Via Beretta, 18, 25063, Gardone Vae Trompia, ITALY
ITALY
39-30-8341-1

Beretta U.S.A. Corp.
17601 Beretta Drive, Accokeek, MD 20607
301-283-2191; FAX: 301-283-0435

Bismuth Cartridge Co.
3500 Maple Ave., Suite 1650, Dallas, TX 75219
214-521-5880; FAX: 214-521-9035

Bob Allen Co.
P.O. Box 477, 214 SW Jackson, Des Moines, IA 50315
800-685-7020; FAX: 515-283-0779

Bob Allen Sportswear
220 S. Main St., Osceola, IA 50213
210-344-8531; FAX: 210-342-2703

Browning Arms Co.
One Browning Place, Morgan, UT 84050
801-876-2711; FAX: 801-876-3331

Browning Arms Co. (Parts & Service)
3005 Arnold Tenbrook Rd., Arnold, MO 63010
617-287-6800; FAX: 617-287-9751

Briley Mfg. Inc.
1230 Lumpkin, Houston, TX 77043
800-331-5718; or 713-932-6995; FAX: 713-932-1043

British Sporting Arms
RR1, Box 130, Millbrook, NY 12545
914-677-8303

Cabela's
One Cabela Drive, Sidney, NE 69160
308-254-5505; FAX: 308-254-8420

Claybuster Wads & Harvester Bullets
309 Sequoya Dr., Hopkinsville, KY 42240
800-922-6287; or 800-284-1746; FAX: 502-885-8088

DBI Books Division of Krause Publications
700 E. State St., Iola, WI 54990-0001
715-445-2214

Doskocil Mfg. Co.,Inc.
P.O. Box 1246, 4209 Barnett, Arlington, TX 76017
817-467-5116; FAX: 817-472-9810

E.A.A. Corp.
P.O. Box 1299, Sharpes, FL 32959
407-639-4842; or 800-536-4442; FAX: 407-639-7006

Electronic Shooters Protection, Inc.
15290 Gadsden Ct., Brighton, CO 80603
800-797-7791; FAX: 303-659-8668

Eley Ltd.
P.O. Box 705, Witton, Birmingham, B6 7UT ENGLAND
ENGLAND
021-356-8899; FAX: 021-331-4173

F.A.I.R.
Via Gitti, 41, 25060 Marcheno Bresc, ITALY
ITALY
030/861162-8610344; FAX: 030/8610179

Fiocchi Munizioni S.P.A
Fiocchi of America, Inc.

5030 Fremont Rd., Ozark, MO 65721
417-725-4118; or 800-721-2666; FAX: 417-725-1039

Federal Cartridge Co
900 Ehlen Dr., Anoka, MN 55303
612-323-2300; FAX: 612-323-2506
918-652-3314; FAX: 918-652-3400

Gamebore Division, Polywad, Inc.
P.O. Box 7916, Macon, GA 31209
478-477-0669; or 800-998-0669

Hodgdon Powder Co.
6231 Robinson, Shawnee Mission, KS 66202
913-362-9455; FAX: 913-362-1307

Hoppe's Div. Penguin Industries, Inc.
P.O. Box 1690, Oregon City, OR 97045-0690
610-384-6000

Ithaca Gun Company LLC
901 Rt. 34 B, King Ferry, NY 13081

Kemen America
2550 Hwy. 23, Wrenshall, MN 55797
218-384-3670

Kent Cartridge America, Inc.
PO Box 849, 1000 Zigor Rd., Kearneysville, WV 25430

Krause Publications, Inc.
700 E. State St., Iola, WI 54990
715-445-2214; FAX: 715-445-4087

Krieghoff Gun Co., H.
Boschstrasse 22, D-89079 Elm,GERMANY
GERMANY
731-4018270

Krieghoff International,Inc.
7528 Easton Rd., Ottsville, PA 18942
610-847-5173; FAX: 610-847-8691

Laurona Armas Eibar, S.A.L.
Avenida de Otaola 25, P.O. Box 260, Eibar 20600,
SPAIN
34-43-700600; FAX: 34-43-700616

Lee Precision, Inc.
4275 Hwy. U, Hartford, WI 53027
262-673-3075; FAX: 262-673-9273

Ljutic Industries, Inc.
732 N. 16th Ave., Suite 22, Yakima, WA 98902
509-248-0476; FAX: 509-576-8233

New SKB Arms Co.
C.P.O. Box 1401, Tokyo, JAPAN
JAPAN
81-3-3943-9550; FAX: 81-3-3943-0695

Oehler Research, Inc.
P.O. Box 9135, Austin, TX 78766
615-794-1556; FAX: 615-790-8005

O.F. Mossberg & Sons, Inc.
7 Grasso Ave., North Haven, CT 06473
203-230-5300; FAX: 203-230-5420

Pachmayr Div. Lyman Products
475 Smith St., Middletown, CT 06457
860-632-2020; or 800-225-9626; FAX: 860-632-1699

Pattern Control
114 N. Third St., P.O. Box 462105, Garland, TX 75046
214-494-3551; FAX: 214-272-8447

Perazzi U.S.A. Inc.
1010 West Tenth, Azusa, CA 91702
626-334-1234; FAX: 626-334-0344

PMC/Eldorado Cartridge Corp.
P.O. Box 62508, 12801 U.S. Hwy. 95 S., Boulder City,
NV 89005
702-294-0025; FAX: 702-294-0121

Ponsness/Warren
768 Ohio St., Rathdrum, ID 83858
800-732-0706; FAX: 208-687-2233

Precision Reloading, Inc.
P.O. Box 122, Stafford Springs, CT 06076
860-684-7979; FAX: 860-684-6788

Reloaders Equipment Co.
4680 High Street
Ecorse, MI 48229

Reloading Specialties, Inc.
Box 1130, Pine Island, MN 55463
507-356-8500; FAX: 507-356-8800

Remington Arms Co., Inc.
870 Remington Drive, P.O. Box 700, Madison, NC
27025-0700
800-243-9700; FAX: 910-548-8700

Shotgun Sports
P.O. Box 6810, Auburn, CA 95604
530-889-2220; FAX: 530-889-9106

Shotgun Sports Magazine
P.O. Box 6810, Auburn, CA 95604
530-889-2220

Shotguns Unlimited
2307 Fon Du Lac Rd., Richmond, VA 23229
804-752-7115

Sporting Clays Of America
9257 Buckeye Rd, Rockbridge, OH 43149-9632
740-746-8334; FAX: 740-746-8605

Stoeger Industries
17603 Indian Head Hwy., Suite 200, Accokeek, MD
20607-2501
301-283-6300; FAX: 301-283-6986

Sturm Ruger & Co. Inc.
200 Ruger Rd., Prescott, AZ 86301
928-541-8820; FAX: 520-541-8850

Tristar Sporting Arms, Ltd.
1814 Linn St. #16, N. Kansas City, MO 64116-3627
816-421-1400; FAX: 816-421-4182

Trius Traps, Inc.
P.O. Box 25, 221 S. Miami Ave., Cleves, OH 45002
513-941-5682; FAX: 513-941-7970

U.S. Repeating Arms Co., Inc.
275 Winchester Ave., Morgan, UT 84050-9333
801-876-3440; FAX: 801-876-3737

Truglo, Inc.
P.O. Box 1612, McKinna, TX 75070
972-774-0300; FAX: 972-774-0323

Vihtavuori Oy/Kaltron-Pettibone
1241 Ellis St., Bensenville, IL 60106
708-350-1116; FAX: 708-350-1606

Weatherby, Inc.
3100 El Camino Real, Atascadero, CA 93422
805-466-1767; FAX: 805-466-2527

Widener's Reloading & Shooting Supply, Inc.
P.O. Box 3009 CRS, Johnson City, TN 37602
615-282-6786; FAX: 615-282-6651